APPLIED MULTIVARIATE STATISTICS FOR THE SOCIAL SCIENCES

Fifth Edition

James P. Stevens
University of Cincinnati

Routledge
Taylor & Francis Group
New York   London

Routledge
Taylor & Francis Group
270 Madison Avenue
New York, NY 10016

Routledge
Taylor & Francis Group
27 Church Road
Hove, East Sussex BN3 2FA

© 2009 by Taylor & Francis Group, LLC
Routledge is an imprint of Taylor & Francis Group, an Informa business

Printed in the United States of America on acid-free paper
10 9 8 7 6 5 4 3 2 1

International Standard Book Number-13: 978-0-8058-5903-4 (0)

Library of Congress Cataloging-in-Publication Data

Stevens, James (James Paul)
    Applied multivariate statistics for the social sciences / James P. Stevens. -- 5th ed.
    p. cm.
  Includes bibliographical references.
  ISBN 978-0-8058-5901-0 (hardback) -- ISBN 978-0-8058-5903-4 (pbk.)
  1. Multivariate analysis. 2. Social sciences--Statistical methods. I. Title.

QA278.S74 2009
519.5'350243--dc22
                                                    2008036730

Visit the Taylor & Francis Web site at
http://www.taylorandfrancis.com

and the Routledge Web site at
http://www.routledge.com

To My Grandsons:

Henry and Killian

Contents

Preface

The first four editions of this text have been received very warmly, and I am grateful for that.

This text is written for those who use, rather than develop, advanced statistical methods. The focus is on conceptual understanding of the material rather than proving results. The narrative and many examples are there to promote understanding, and I have included a chapter on matrix algebra to serve as a review for those who need the extra help. Throughout the book you will find many printouts from SPSS and SAS with annotations. These annotations are intended to demonstrate what the numbers mean and to encourage you to interpret the results. In addition to demonstrating how to use the packages effectively, my goal is to show you the importance of checking the data, assessing the assumptions, and ensuring adequate sample size (by providing guidelines) so that the results can be generalized.

To further promote understanding of the material I have included numerous conceptual, numerical, and computer-related exercises with answers to half of them in the back of the book.

This edition has several major changes, and I would like to mention those first.

There are two new chapters (15 and 16) on two very important topics. Chapter 15 on the Hierarchical Linear Model was written by Dr. Natasha Beretvas of the University of Texas at Austin. This model deals with correlated observations, which occur very frequently in social science research. The general linear model assumes the observations are INDEPENDENT, and even a small violation causes the actual alpha level to be several times the nominal level. The other major topic, Structural Equation Modeling (Chapter 16), was written by Dr. Leandre Fabrigar of Queen's University and Dr. Duane Wegener of Purdue (both were former students of Dr. MacCallum). Among the strengths of this technique, as they note, are the ability to account for measurement error and the ability to simultaneously assess relations among many variables. It has been called by some the most important advance in statistical methodology in 30 years. Although I have a concern with equivalent models, SEM is an important technique one should be aware of.

This edition features new exercises to demonstrate the actual use of some statistical topics in key journals. For the past 15 years I have had students of mine select an article from one of the better journals in their content area within the last 5 years for each quarter of my three-quarter multivariate sequence. They select an article on the main statistical topic for that quarter. For the fall quarter that topic is multiple regression, for the winter topic it is MANOVA, and for the spring quarter it is repeated measures. I tell them to select from one of the better journals so that can't argue the article is mediocre because it is an inferior journal, and I tell them to select an article from within the last 5 years so that they can't argue that things have changed. This edition features exercises in Chapters 3 (multiple regression), 5 (MANOVA), and 13 (repeated measures) that deal with the above. These exercises are an eye opener for most students.

The answers to all odd numbered exercises are in the back of the text. The answers to all even numbered exercises will be made available to adopters of the text.

Updated versions of SPSS (15.0) and SAS (8.0) have been used.

A book website www.psypress.com/applied-multivariate-statistics-for-the-social-sciences now contains the data sets and the answers to the even numbered exercises (available only to adopters of the text).

Chapter 1 has seen several changes. Section 1.7 emphasizes that the quality of the research design is crucial. Section 1.8 deals with conflict of interest, and indicates that financial conflict of interest can be a real problem. Chapter 3 (on multiple regression) has a new Table 3.8, which indicates that the amount of shrinkage depends very strongly on the magnitude of the squared multiple correlation AND on whether the selection of predictors is from a much larger set. Chapter 6 has a new appendix on the analysis of correlated observations, which occur frequently in social science research. Chapter 13 (on repeated measures) has an expanded section on obtaining nonorthogonal comparisons with SPSS. I have found that the material in Appendix B was not sufficient for most students in obtaining nonorthogonal contrasts. Chapter 14 (Categorical Data Analysis) now has the levels for each factor labeled. This makes identifying the cells easier, especially for four- or five-way designs.

As the reader will see, many of the multivariate procedures in this text are MATHEMATICAL MAXIMIZATION procedures and hence there is great opportunity for capitalization on chance, seizing on the properties of the sample. This has severe implications for external validity, i.e., generalizing results. In this regard, we paraphrase a comment by Efron and Tibshrani in their text *An Introduction to the Bootstrap*: Investigators find nonexistent patterns that they want to find.

As in previous editions, this book is intended for courses on multivariate statistics found in psychology, social science, education, and business departments, but the book also appeals to practicing researchers with little or no training in multivariate methods.

A word on the prerequisites students should have before using this book. They should have a minimum of two quarter courses in statistics (should have covered factorial ANOVA and covariance). A two-semester sequence of courses in statistics would be preferable. Many of my students have had more than two quarter courses in statistics. The book does not assume a working knowledge of matrix algebra.

Acknowledgments

I wish to thank Dr. Natasha Beretvas of the University of Texas at Austin, Dr. Leandre Fabrigar of Queen's University (Kingston, Ontario), and Dr. Duane Wegener of Purdue University (Lafayette, Indiana) for their valuable contributions to this edition.

The reviewers for this edition provided me with many helpful suggestions. My thanks go to Dale R. Fuqua (Oklahoma State University), Philip Schatz (Saint Joseph's University), Louis M. Kyriakoudes (University of Southern Mississippi), Suzanne Nasco (Southern Illinois University), Mark Rosenbaum (University of Hawaii at Honolulu), and Denna Wheeler (Connors State College) for their valuable insights.

I wish to thank Debra Riegert for encouraging me to do this new edition. In addition, a special thanks to Rick Beardsley, who was very instrumental in getting my intermediate text out and assisted me in many ways with this text. Finally, I would like to thank Christopher Myron for his help in getting the manuscript ready for production, and Sylvia Wood, the project editor.

In closing, I encourage readers to send me an email regarding the text at Mstatistics@ Hotmail.Com

James Stevens

1

Introduction

1.1 Introduction

Studies in the social sciences comparing two or more groups very often measure their subjects on several criterion variables. The following are some examples:

1. A researcher is comparing two methods of teaching second grade reading. On a posttest the researcher measures the subjects on the following basic elements related to reading: syllabication, blending, sound discrimination, reading rate, and comprehension.

2. A social psychologist is testing the relative efficacy of three treatments on self-concept, and measures the subjects on the academic, emotional, and social aspects of self-concept. Two different approaches to stress management are being compared.

3. The investigator employs a couple of paper-and-pencil measures of anxiety (say, the State-Trait Scale and the Subjective Stress Scale) and some physiological measures.

4. Another example would be comparing two types of counseling (Rogerian and Adlerian) on client satisfaction and client self acceptance.

A major part of this book involves the statistical analysis of several groups on a set of criterion measures simultaneously, that is, multivariate analysis of variance, the multivariate referring to the multiple dependent variables.

Cronbach and Snow (1977), writing on aptitude–treatment interaction research, echoed the need for multiple criterion measures:

> Learning is multivariate, however. Within any one task a person's performance at a point in time can be represented by a set of scores describing aspects of the performance ... even in laboratory research on rote learning, performance can be assessed by multiple indices: errors, latencies and resistance to extinction, for example. These are only moderately correlated, and do not necessarily develop at the same rate. In the paired associates task, subskills have to be acquired: discriminating among and becoming familiar with the stimulus terms, being able to produce the response terms, and tying response to stimulus. If these attainments were separately measured, each would generate a learning curve, and there is no reason to think that the curves would echo each other. (p. 116)

There are three good reasons that the use of multiple criterion measures in a study comparing treatments (such as teaching methods, counseling methods, types of reinforcement, diets, etc.) is very sensible:

1. Any worthwhile treatment will affect the subjects in more than one way. Hence, the problem for the investigator is to determine in which specific ways the subjects will be affected, and then find sensitive measurement techniques for those variables.

2. Through the use of multiple criterion measures we can obtain a more complete and detailed description of the phenomenon under investigation, whether it is teacher method effectiveness, counselor effectiveness, diet effectiveness, stress management technique effectiveness, and so on.

3. Treatments can be expensive to implement, while the cost of obtaining data on several dependent variables is relatively small and maximizes information gain.

Because we define a multivariate study as one with several dependent variables, multiple regression (where there is only one dependent variable) and principal components analysis would not be considered multivariate techniques. However, our distinction is more semantic than substantive. Therefore, because regression and component analysis are so important and frequently used in social science research, we include them in this text.

We have four major objectives for the remainder of this chapter:

1. To review some basic concepts (e.g., type I error and power) and some issues associated with univariate analysis that are equally important in multivariate analysis.

2. To discuss the importance of identifying outliers, that is, points that split off from the rest of the data, and deciding what to do about them. We give some examples to show the considerable impact outliers can have on the results in univariate analysis.

3. To give research examples of some of the multivariate analyses to be covered later in the text, and to indicate how these analyses involve generalizations of what the student has previously learned.

4. To introduce the Statistical Analysis System (SAS) and the Statistical Package for the Social Sciences (SPSS), whose outputs are discussed throughout the text.

1.2 Type I Error, Type II Error, and Power

Suppose we have randomly assigned 15 subjects to a treatment group and 15 subjects to a control group, and are comparing them on a single measure of task performance (a univariate study, because there is a single dependent variable). The reader may recall that the t test for independent samples is appropriate here. We wish to determine whether the difference in the sample means are large enough, given sampling error, to suggest that the underlying population means are different. Because the sample means estimate the population means, they will generally be in error (i.e., they will not hit the population values right "on the nose"), and this is called *sampling error*. We wish to test the null hypothesis (H_0) that the population means are equal:

$$H_0 : \mu_1 = \mu_2$$

It is called the null hypothesis because saying the population means are equal is equivalent to saying that the difference in the means is 0, that is, $\mu_1 - \mu_2 = 0$, or that the difference is null.

Now, statisticians have determined that if we had populations with equal means and drew samples of size 15 repeatedly and computed a t statistic each time, then 95% of the time we would obtain t values in the range −2.048 to 2.048. The so-called sampling distribution of t under H_0 would look like:

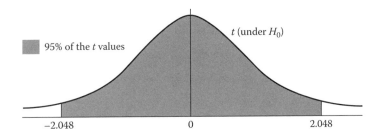

This sampling distribution is extremely important, for it gives us a frame of reference for judging what is a large value of t. Thus, if our t value was 2.56, it would be very plausible to reject the H_0, since obtaining such a large t value is *very unlikely* when H_0 is true. Note, however, that if we do so there is a chance we have made an error, because it is possible (although very improbable) to obtain such a large value for t, even when the population means are equal. In practice, one must decide how much of a risk of making this type of error (called a type I error) one wishes to take. Of course, one would want that risk to be small, and many have decided a 5% risk is small. This is formalized in hypothesis testing by saying that we set our level of significance (α) at the .05 level. That is, we are willing to take a 5% chance of making a type I error. In other words, *type I error (level of significance) is the probability of rejecting the null hypothesis when it is true.*

Recall that the formula for degrees of freedom for the t test is $(n_1 + n_2 - 2)$; hence, for this problem $df = 28$. If we had set $\alpha = .05$, then reference to Appendix B of this book shows that the critical values are −2.048 and 2.048. They are called critical values because they are critical to the decision we will make on H_0. These critical values define critical regions in the sampling distribution. If the value of t falls in the critical region we reject H_0; otherwise we fail to reject:

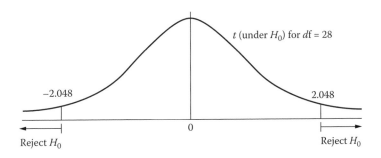

Type I error is equivalent to saying the groups differ when in fact they do not. The α level set by the experimenter is a subjective decision, but is usually set at .05 or .01 by most researchers. There are situations, however, when it makes sense to use α levels other than .05 or .01. For example, if making a type I error will not have serious substantive consequences, or if sample size is small, setting α = .10 or .15 is quite reasonable. Why this is reasonable for small sample size will be made clear shortly. On the other hand, suppose we are in a medical situation where the null hypothesis is equivalent to saying a drug is unsafe, and the alternative is that the drug is safe. Here, making a type I error could be quite serious, for we would be declaring the drug safe when it is not safe. This could cause some people to be permanently damaged or perhaps even killed. In this case it would make sense to take α very small, perhaps .001.

Another type of error that can be made in conducting a statistical test is called a type II error. Type II error, denoted by β, is the probability of accepting H_0 when it is false, that is, saying the groups don't differ when they do. Now, not only can either type of error occur, but in addition, they are inversely related. Thus, as we control on type I error, type II error increases. This is illustrated here for a two-group problem with 15 subjects per group:

α	β	$1 - \beta$
.10	.37	.63
.05	.52	.48
.01	.78	.22

Notice that as we control on α more severely (from .10 to .01), type II error increases fairly sharply (from .37 to .78). Therefore, the problem for the experimental planner is achieving an appropriate balance between the two types of errors. While we do not intend to minimize the seriousness of making a type I error, we hope to convince the reader throughout the course of this text that much more attention should be paid to type II error. Now, the quantity in the last column of the preceding table $(1 - \beta)$ is the *power of a statistical test, which is the probability of rejecting the null hypothesis when it is false.* Thus, power is the probability of making a correct decision, or saying the groups differ when in fact they do. Notice from the table that as the α level decreases, power also decreases. The diagram in Figure 1.1 should help to make clear why this happens.

The power of a statistical test is dependent on three factors:

1. The α level set by the experimenter
2. Sample size
3. Effect size—How much of a difference the treatments make, or the extent to which the groups differ in the population on the dependent variable(s)

Figure 1.1 has already demonstrated that power is directly dependent on the α level. Power is *heavily* dependent on sample size. Consider a two-tailed test at the .05 level for the t test for independent samples. Estimated effect size for the t test, as defined by Cohen (1977), is simply $\hat{d} = (x_1 - x_2)/s$, where s is the standard deviation. That is, effect size expresses the difference between the means in standard deviation units. Thus, if $x_1 = 6$ and $x_2 = 3$ and $s = 6$, then $\hat{d} = (6 - 3)/6 = .5$, or the means differ by $\frac{1}{2}$ standard deviation. Suppose for the preceding problem we have an effect size of .5 standard deviations. Power changes dramatically as sample size increases (power values from Cohen, 1977):

n (subjects per group)	power
10	.18
20	.33
50	.70
100	.94

As the table suggests, when sample size is large (say, 100 or more subjects per group), power is not an issue. It is an issue when one is conducting a study where the group sizes will be small ($n \le 20$), or when one is evaluating a completed study that had small group size, then, it is imperative to be very sensitive to the possibility of poor power (or equivalently, a type II error). Thus, in studies with small group size, it can make sense to test at a more liberal level (.10 or .15) to improve power, because (as mentioned earlier) power is directly related to the α level. We explore the power issue in considerably more detail in Chapter 4.

1.3 Multiple Statistical Tests and the Probability of Spurious Results

If a researcher sets $\alpha = .05$ in conducting a single statistical test (say, a t test), then the probability of rejecting falsely (a spurious result) is under control. Now consider a five-group problem in which the researcher wishes to determine whether the groups differ

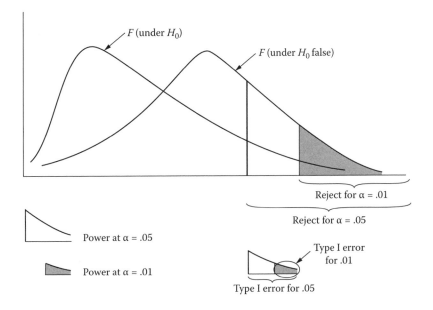

FIGURE 1.1

Graph of F distribution under H_0 and under H_0 false showing the direct relationship between type I error and power. Since type I error is the probability of rejecting H_0 when true, it is the area underneath the F distribution in critical region for H_0 true. Power is the probability of rejecting H_0 when false; therefore it is the area underneath the F distribution in critical region when H_0 is false.

significantly on some dependent variable. The reader may recall from a previous statistics course that a one-way analysis of variance (ANOVA) is appropriate here. But suppose our researcher is unaware of ANOVA and decides to do 10 tests, each at the .05 level, comparing each pair of groups. The probability of a false rejection is no longer under control for the *set* of 10 t tests. We define the *overall α for a set of tests as the probability of at least one false rejection when the null hypothesis is true.* There is an important inequality called the *Bonferroni Inequality,* which gives an upper bound on overall α:

$$\text{Overall } \alpha \le .05 + .05 + \cdots + .05 = .50$$

Thus, the probability of a few false rejections here could easily be 30 or 35%, that is, much too high.

In general then, if we are testing k hypotheses at the $\alpha_1, \alpha_2, \ldots, \alpha_k$ levels, the Bonferroni inequality guarantees that

$$\text{Overall } \alpha \le \alpha_1 + \alpha_2 + \cdots + \alpha_k$$

If the hypotheses are each tested at the same alpha level, say α', then the Bonferroni upper bound becomes

$$\text{Overall } \alpha \le k\alpha'$$

This Bonferroni upper bound is conservative, and how to obtain a sharper (tighter) upper bound is discussed later.

If the tests are independent, then an *exact* calculation for overall α is available.

First, $(1 - \alpha_1)$ is the probability of no type I error for the first comparison. Similarly, $(1 - \alpha_2)$ is the probability of no type I error for the second, $(1 - \alpha_3)$ the probability of no type I error for the third, and so on. If the tests are independent, then we can multiply probabilities. Therefore, $(1 - \alpha_1)(1 - \alpha_2) \cdots (1 - \alpha_k)$ is the probability of *no* type I errors for all k tests. Thus,

$$\text{Overall } \alpha = 1 - (1 - \alpha_1)(1 - \alpha_2) \cdots (1 - \alpha_k)$$

is the probability of at least one type I error. If the tests are not independent, then overall α will still be *less* than given here, although it is very difficult to calculate. If we set the alpha levels equal, say to α' for each test, then the above expression becomes

$$\text{Overall } \alpha = 1 - (1 - \alpha')(1 - \alpha') \cdots (1 - \alpha') = 1 - (1 - \alpha')^k$$

This expression, that is, $1 - (1 - \alpha')^k$, is approximately equal to $k\alpha'$ for small α'. The next table compares the two for $\alpha' = .05, .01,$ and $.001$ for number of tests ranging from 5 to 100.

No. of Tests	$\alpha' = .05$		$\alpha' = .01$		$\alpha' = .001$	
	$1-(1-\alpha')^k$	$k\alpha'$	$1-(1-\alpha')^k$	$k\alpha'$	$1-(1-\alpha')^k$	$k\alpha'$
5	.226	.25	.049	.05	.00499	.005
10	.401	.50	.096	.10	.00990	.010
15	.537	.75	.140	.15	.0149	.015
30	.785	1.50	.260	.30	.0296	.030
50	.923	2.50	.395	.50	.0488	.050
100	.994	5.00	.634	1.00	.0952	.100

First, the numbers greater than 1 in the table don't represent probabilities, because a probability can't be greater than 1. Second, note that if we are testing each of a large number of hypotheses at the .001 level, the difference between $1 - (1 - \alpha')^k$ and the Bonferroni upper bound of $k\alpha'$ is very small and of no practical consequence. Also, the differences between $1 - (1 - \alpha')^k$ and $k\alpha'$ when testing at $\alpha' = .01$ are also small for up to about 30 tests. For more than about 30 tests $1 - (1 - \alpha')^k$ provides a tighter bound and should be used. When testing at the $\alpha' = .05$ level, $k\alpha'$ is okay for up to about 10 tests, but beyond that $1 - (1 - \alpha')^k$ is much tighter and should be used.

The reader may have been alert to the possibility of spurious results in the preceding example with multiple *t* tests, because this problem is pointed out in texts on intermediate statistical methods. Another frequently occurring example of multiple *t* tests where overall α gets completely out of control is in comparing two groups on *each* item of a scale (test); for example, comparing males and females on each of 30 items, doing 30 *t* tests, each at the .05 level.

Multiple statistical tests also arise in various other contexts in which the reader may not readily recognize that the same problem of spurious results exists. In addition, the fact that the researcher may be using a more sophisticated design or more complex statistical tests doesn't mitigate the problem.

As our first illustration, consider a researcher who runs a four-way ANOVA ($A \times B \times C \times D$). Then 15 statistical tests are being done, one for each effect in the design: *A*, *B*, *C*, and *D* main effects, and *AB*, *AC*, *AD*, *BC*, *BD*, *CD*, *ABC*, *ABD*, *ACD*, *BCD*, and *ABCD* interactions. If each of these effects is tested at the .05 level, then all we know from the Bonferroni inequality is that overall $\alpha \leq 15\ (.05) = .75$, which is not very reassuring. Hence, two or three significant results from such a study (if they were *not* predicted ahead of time) could very well be type I errors, that is, spurious results.

Let us take another common example. Suppose an investigator has a two-way ANOVA design ($A \times B$) with seven dependent variables. Then, there are three effects being tested for significance: *A* main effect, *B* main effect and the $A \times B$ interaction. The investigator does separate two-way ANOVAs for each dependent variable. Therefore, the investigator has done a total of 21 statistical tests, and if each of them was conducted at the .05 level, then the overall α has gotten completely out of control. This type of thing is done *very frequently* in the literature, and the reader should be aware of it in interpreting the results of such studies. Little faith should be placed in scattered significant results from these studies.

A third example comes from survey research, where investigators are often interested in relating demographic characteristics of the subjects (sex, age, religion, SES, etc.) to responses to items on a questionnaire. The statistical test for relating each demographic characteristic to response on each item is a two-way χ^2. Often in such studies 20 or 30 (or many more) two-way χ^2's are run (and it is so easy to get them run on SPSS). The investigators often seem to be able to explain the frequent small number of significant results perfectly, although seldom have the significant results been predicted a priori.

A fourth fairly common example of multiple statistical tests is in examining the elements of a correlation matrix for significance. Suppose there were 10 variables in one set being related to 15 variables in another set. In this case, there are 150 between correlations, and if each of these is tested for significance at the .05 level, then 150(.05) = 7.5, or about 8 significant results could be expected by chance. Thus, if 10 or 12 of the between correlations are significant, most of them could be chance results, and it is very difficult to separate out the chance effects from the real associations. A way of circumventing this problem is to simply test each correlation for significance at a much more stringent level, say $\alpha = .001$.

Then, by the Bonferroni inequality, overall $\alpha \le 150\ (.001) = .15$. Naturally, this will cause a power problem (unless n is large), and only those associations that are quite strong will be declared significant. Of course, one could argue that it is only such strong associations that may be of practical significance anyway.

A fifth case of multiple statistical tests occurs when comparing the results of many studies in a given content area. Suppose, for example, that 20 studies have been reviewed in the area of programmed instruction and its effect on math achievement in the elementary grades, and that only 5 studies show significance. Since at least 20 statistical tests were done (there would be more if there were more than a single criterion variable in some of the studies), most of these significant results could be spurious, that is, type I errors.

A sixth case of multiple statistical tests occurs when an investigator(s) selects a small set of dependent variables from a much larger set (the reader doesn't know this has been done—this is an example of selection bias). The much smaller set is chosen because all of the significance occurs here. This is particularily insidious. Let me illustrate. Suppose the investigator has a three-way design and originally 15 dependent variables. Then $105 = 15 \times 7$ tests have been done. If each test is done at the .05 level, then the Bonferroni inequality guarantees that overall alpha is less than $105(.05) = 5.25$. So, if 7 significant results are found, the Bonferroni procedure suggests that most (or all) of the results could be spurious. If all the significance is confined to 3 of the variables, and those are the variables selected (without the reader's knowing this), then overall alpha $= 21(.05) = 1.05$, and this conveys a very different impression. Now, the conclusion is that perhaps a few of the significant results are spurious.

1.4 Statistical Significance versus Practical Significance

The reader probably was exposed to the statistical significance versus practical significance issue in a previous course in statistics, but it is sufficiently important to have us review it here. Recall from our earlier discussion of power (probability of rejecting the null hypothesis when it is false) that power is heavily dependent on sample size. Thus, given very large sample size (say, group sizes > 200), most effects will be declared statistically significant at the .05 level. If significance is found, then we must decide whether the difference in means is large enough to be of practical significance. There are several ways of getting at practical significance; among them are

1. Confidence intervals
2. Effect size measures
3. Measures of association (variance accounted for)

Suppose you are comparing two teaching methods and decide ahead of time that the achievement for one method must be *at least* 5 points higher on average for practical significance. The results are significant, but the 95% confidence interval for the difference in the population means is (1.61, 9.45). You do not have practical significance, because, although the difference could be as large as 9 or slightly more, it could also be less than 2.

You can calculate an effect size measure, and see if the effect is large relative to what others have found in the same area of research. As a simple example, recall that the Cohen effect size measure for two groups is $\hat{d} = (\bar{x}_1 - \bar{x}_2)/s$, that is, it indicates how many standard deviations the groups differ by. Suppose your t test was significant and the estimated effect size measure was $\hat{d} = .63$ (in the medium range according to Cohen's rough characterization). If this is large relative to what others have found, then it probably is practically significant. As Light, Singer, and Willett indicated in their excellent text *By Design* (1990), "Because practical significance depends upon the research context, only *you* can judge if an effect is large enough to be important" (p. 195).

Measures of association or strength of relationship, such as Hay's $\hat{\omega}^2$, can also be used to assess practical significance because they are essentially independent of sample size. However, there are limitations associated with these measures, as O'Grady (1982) pointed out in an excellent review on measures of explained variance. He discussed three basic reasons that such measures should be interpreted with caution: measurement, methodological, and theoretical. We limit ourselves here to a theoretical point O'Grady mentioned that should be kept in mind before casting aspersions on a "low" amount of variance accounted. The point is that most behaviors have *multiple causes,* and hence it will be difficult in these cases to account for a large amount of variance with just a single cause such as treatments. We give an example in chapter 4 to show that treatments accounting for only 10% of the variance on the dependent variable can indeed be practically significant.

Sometimes practical significance can be judged by simply looking at the means and thinking about the range of possible values. Consider the following example.

1.4.1 Example

A survey researcher compares four religious groups on their attitude toward education. The survey is sent out to 1,200 subjects, of which 823 eventually respond. Ten items, Likert scaled from 1 to 5, are used to assess attitude. There are only 800 usable responses. The Protestants are split into two groups for analysis purposes. The group sizes, along with the means and standard deviations, are given here:

	Protestant1	Catholic	Jewish	Protestant2
n_i	238	182	130	250
$\bar{x}$	32.0	33.1	34.0	31.0
s_i	7.09	7.62	7.80	7.49

An analysis of variance on these groups yields $F = 5.61$, which is significant at the .001 level. The results are "highly significant," but do we have practical significance? Very probably not. Look at the size of the mean differences for a scale that has a range from 10 to 50. The mean differences for all pairs of groups, except for Jewish and Protestant2, are about 2 or less. These are trivial differences on a scale with a range of 40.

Now recall from our earlier discussion of power the problem of finding statistical significance with small sample size. That is, *results in the literature that are not significant may be simply due to poor or inadequate power, whereas results that are significant, but have been obtained with huge sample sizes, may not be practically significant.* We illustrate this statement with two examples.

First, consider a two-group study with eight subjects per group and an effect size of .8 standard deviations. This is a large effect size (Cohen, 1977) and most researchers would consider this result to be practically significant. However, if testing for significance at the .05 level (two-tailed test), then the chances of finding significance are only about 1 in 3 (.31 from Cohen's power tables). The danger of not being sensitive to the power problem in such a study is that a researcher may abort a promising line of research, perhaps an effective diet or type of psychotherapy, because significance is not found. And it may also discourage other researchers.

On the other hand, now consider a two-group study with 300 subjects per group and an effect size of .20 standard deviations. In this case, when testing at the .05 level, the researcher is likely to find significance (power = .70 from Cohen's tables). To use a domestic analogy, this is like using a sledgehammer to "pound out" significance. Yet the effect size here would probably not be considered practically significant in most cases. Based on these results, for example, a school system may decide to implement an expensive program that may yield only very small gains in achievement.

For further perspective on the practical significance issue, there is a nice article by Haase, Ellis, and Ladany (1989). Although that article is in the *Journal of Counseling Psychology*, the implications are much broader. They suggest five different ways of assessing the practical or clinical significance of findings:

1. Reference to previous research—the importance of *context* in determining whether a result is practically important.
2. Conventional definitions of magnitude of effect—Cohen's (1977) definitions of small, medium, and large effect sizes.
3. Normative definitions of clinical significance—here they reference a special issue of *Behavioral Assessment* (Jacobson, 1988) that should be of considerable interest to clinicians.
4. Cost-benefit analysis.
5. The good enough principle—here the idea is to posit a form of the null hypothesis that is more difficult to reject: for example, rather than testing whether two population means are equal, testing whether the difference between them is at least 3.

Finally, although in a somewhat different vein, with various multivariate procedures we consider in this text (such as discriminant analysis and canonical correlation), unless sample size is large relative to the number of variables, the results will not be reliable—that is, they will not generalize. A major point of the discussion in this section is that *it is critically important to take sample size into account in interpreting results in the literature.*

1.5 Outliers

Outliers are data points that split off or are very different from the rest of the data. Specific examples of outliers would be an IQ of 160, or a weight of 350 lb in a group for which the median weight is 180 lb. Outliers can occur for two fundamental reasons: (a) a data recording or entry error was made, or (b) the subjects are simply different from the rest. The first type of outlier can be identified by always listing the data and checking to make sure the data has been read in accurately.

The importance of listing the data was brought home to me many years ago as a graduate student. A regression problem with five predictors, one of which was a set of random scores, was run without checking the data. This was a textbook problem to show the student that the random number predictor would not be related to the dependent variable. However, the random number predictor was significant, and accounted for a fairly large part of the variance on y. This all resulted simply because one of the scores for the random number predictor was mispunched as a 300 rather than as a 3. In this case it was obvious that something was wrong. But with large data sets the situation will not be so transparent, and the results of an analysis could be completely thrown off by one or two errant points. The amount of time it takes to list and check the data for accuracy (even if there are 1,000 or 2,000 subjects) is well worth the effort, and the computer cost is minimal.

Statistical procedures in general can be quite sensitive to outliers. This is particularly true for the multivariate procedures that will be considered in this text. *It is very important to be able to identify such outliers and then decide what to do about them.* Why? Because we want the results of our statistical analysis to reflect most of the data, and not to be highly influenced by just one or two errant data points.

In small data sets with just one or two variables, such outliers can be relatively easy to spot. We now consider some examples.

Example 1.1

Consider the following small data set with two variables:

Case Number	x_1	x_2
1	111	68
2	92	46
3	90	50
4	107	59
5	98	50
6	150	66
7	118	54
8	110	51
9	117	59
10	94	97

Cases 6 and 10 are both outliers, but for different reasons. Case 6 is an outlier because the score for Case 6 on x_1 (150) is deviant, while Case 10 is an outlier because the score for that subject on x_2 (97) splits off from the other scores on x_2. The graphical split-off of cases 6 and 10 is quite vivid and is given in Figure 1.2.

In large data sets involving many variables, however, some outliers are not so easy to spot and could go easily undetected. Now, we give an example of a somewhat more subtle outlier.

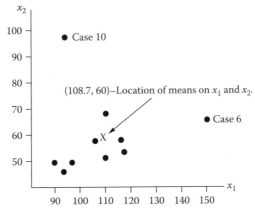

FIGURE 1.2
Plot of outliers for two-variable example.

Example 1.2

Consider the following data set on four variables:

Case	x_1	x_2	x_3	x_4
1	111	68	17	81
2	92	46	28	67
3	90	50	19	83
4	107	59	25	71
5	98	50	13	92
6	150	66	20	90
7	118	54	11	101
8	110	51	26	82
9	117	59	18	87
10	94	67	12	69
11	130	57	16	97
12	118	51	19	78
13	155	40	9	58
14	118	61	20	103
15	109	66	13	88

The somewhat subtle outlier here is Case 13. Notice that the scores for Case 13 on none of the x's really split off dramatically from the other subjects scores. Yet the scores tend to be low on x_2, x_3, and x_4 and high on x_1, and the cumulative effect of all this is to isolate Case 13 from the rest of the cases. We indicate shortly a statistic that is quite useful in detecting multivariate outliers and pursue outliers in more detail in chapter 3.

Now let us consider three more examples, involving material learned in previous statistics courses, to show the effect outliers can have on some simple statistics.

Example 1.3

Consider the following small set of data: 2, 3, 5, 6, 44. The last number, 44, is an obvious outlier; that is, it splits off sharply from the rest of the data. If we were to use the mean of 12 as the measure of central tendency for this data, it would be quite misleading, as there are no scores around 12. That is why you were told to use the median as the measure of central tendency when there are extreme values (outliers in our terminology), because the median is unaffected by outliers. That is, it is a robust measure of central tendency.

Example 1.4

To show the dramatic effect an outlier can have on a correlation, consider the two scatterplots in Figure 1.3. Notice how the inclusion of the outlier in each case *drastically* changes the interpretation of the results. For Case A there is no relationship without the outlier but there is a strong relationship with the outlier, whereas for Case B the relationship changes from strong (without the outlier) to weak when the outlier is included.

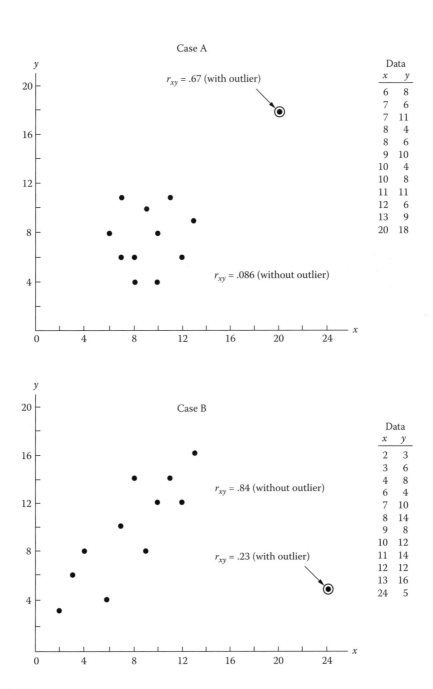

FIGURE 1.3
The effect of an outlier on a correlation coefficient.

Example 1.5

As our final example, consider the following data:

Group 1		Group 2		Group 3	
15	21	17	36	6	26
18	27	22	41	9	31
12	32	15	31	12	38
12	29	12	28	11	24
9	18	20	47	11	35
10	34	14	29	8	29
12	18	15	33	13	30
20	36	20	38	30	16
		21	25	7	23

For now, ignore the second column of numbers in each group. Then we have a one-way ANOVA for the first variable.

The score of 30 in Group 3 is an outlier. With that case in the ANOVA we do not find significance ($F = 2.61$, $p < .095$) at the .05 level, while with the case deleted we do find significance well beyond the .01 level ($F = 11.18$, $p < .0004$). Deleting the case has the effect of producing greater separation among the three means, because the means with the case included are 13.5, 17.33, and 11.89, but with the case deleted the means are 13.5, 17.33, and 9.63. It also has the effect of reducing the within variability in Group 3 substantially, and hence the pooled within variability (error term for ANOVA) will be much smaller.

1.5.1 Detecting Outliers

If the variable is approximately normally distributed, then z scores around 3 in absolute value should be considered as potential outliers. Why? Because, in an approximate normal distribution, about 99% of the scores should lie within three standard deviations of the mean. Therefore, any z value > 3 indicates a value very unlikely to occur. Of course, if n is large, (say > 100), then simply by chance we might expect a few subjects to have z scores > 3 and this should be kept in mind. However, even for *any type of distribution* the above rule is reasonable, although we might consider extending the rule to $z > 4$. It was shown many years ago that regardless of how the data is distributed, the percentage of observations contained within k standard deviations of the mean must be *at least* $(1 - 1/k^2)100\%$. This holds only for $k > 1$ and yields the following percentages for $k = 2$ through 5:

Number of standard deviations	Percentage of observations
2	at least 75%
3	at least 88.89%
4	at least 93.75%
5	at least 96%

Shiffler (1988) showed that the largest possible z value in a data set of size n is bounded by $(n - 1)/\sqrt{n}$. This means for $n = 10$ the largest possible z is 2.846 and for $n = 11$ the largest possible z is 3.015. Thus, for small sample size, any data point with a z around 2.5 should be seriously considered as a possible outlier.

After the outliers are identified, what should be done with them? The action to be taken is not to automatically drop the outlier(s) from the analysis. If one finds after further investigation of the outlying points that an outlier was due to a recording or entry error, then of course one would correct the data value and redo the analysis. Or, if it is found that the errant data value is due to an instrumentation error or that the process that generated the data for that subject was different, then it is legitimate to drop the outlier. If, however, none of these appears to be the case, then one should *not* drop the outlier, but perhaps report two analyses (one including the outlier and the other excluding it). Outliers should not necessarily be regarded as "bad." In fact, it has been argued that outliers can provide some of the most interesting cases for further study.

1.6 Research Examples for Some Analyses Considered in This Text

To give the reader something of a feel for several of the statistical analyses considered in succeeding chapters, we present the objectives in doing a multiple regression analysis, a multivariate analysis of variance and covariance, and a canonical correlation analysis, along with illustrative studies from the literature that used each of these analyses.

1.6.1 Multiple Regression

In a previous course, simple linear regression was covered, where a dependent variable (say chemistry achievement) is predicted from just one predictor, such as IQ. It is certainly reasonable that other factors would also be related to chemistry achievement and that we could obtain better prediction by making use of these other factors, such as previous average grade in science courses, attitude toward education, and math ability. Thus, the objective in multiple regression (called multiple because we have multiple predictors) is:

Objective: Predict a dependent variable from a set of independent variables.

Example

Feshbach, Adelman, and Fuller (1977) conducted a longitudinal study on 850 middle-class kindergarten children. The children were administered a psychometric battery that included the Wechsler Preschool and Primary Scale of Intelligence, the deHirsch–Jansky Predictive Index (assessing various linguistic and perceptual motor skills), and the Bender Motor Gestalt test. The students were also assessed on a Student Rating Scale (SRS) developed by the authors, which measured various cognitive and affective behaviors and skills. These various predictors were used to predict reading achievement in grades 1, 2, and 3. Reading achievement was measured with the Cooperative Reading Test. The major thrust of the study in the authors' words was:

> The present investigation evaluates and contrasts one major psychometric predictive index, that developed by deHirsch … with an alternative strategy based on a systematic behavioral analysis and ratings made by the kindergarten teacher of academically relevant cognitive and affective behaviors and skills (assessed by the SRS) …. This approach, in addition to being easier to implement and less costly than psychometric testing, yields assessment data which are more closely linked to intervention and remedial procedures. (p. 300)

The SRS scale proved equal to the deHirsch in predicting reading achievement, and because of the described rationale might well be preferred.

1.6.2 One-Way Multivariate Analysis of Variance

In univariate analysis of variance, several groups of subjects were compared to determine whether they differed on the average on a single dependent variable. But, as was mentioned earlier in this chapter, any good treatment(s) generally affects the subjects in several ways. Hence, it makes sense to measure the subjects on those variables and then test whether they differ on the average on the set of variables. This gives a more accurate assessment of the true efficacy of the treatments. Thus, the objective in multivariate analysis of variance is:

Objective: Determine whether several groups differ on the average on a set of dependent variables.

Example

Stevens (1972) conducted a study on National Merit scholars. The classification variable was the educational level of both parents of the scholars. Four groups were formed:

1. Students for whom at least one parent had an eighth-grade education or less
2. Students whose both parents were high school graduates
3. Students with both parents having gone to college, with at most one graduating
4. Students with both parents having at least one college degree

The dependent variables were a subset of the Vocational Personality Inventory: realistic, intellectual, social, conventional, enterprising, artistic, status, and aggression. Stevens found that the parents' educational level was related to their children's personality characteristics, with conventional and enterprising being the key variables. Specifically, scholars whose parents had gone to college tended to be more enterprising and less conventional than scholars whose parents had not gone to college. This example is considered in detail in the chapter on discriminant analysis.

1.6.3 Multivariate Analysis of Covariance

Objective: Determine whether several groups differ on a set of dependent variables after the posttest means have been adjusted for any initial differences on the covariates (which are often pretests).

Example

Friedman, Lehrer, and Stevens (1983) examined the effect of two stress management strategies, directed lecture discussion and self-directed, and the locus of control of teachers on their scores on the State-Trait Anxiety Inventory and on the Subjective Stress Scale. Eighty-five teachers were pretested and posttested on these measures, with the treatment extending 5 weeks. Those subjects who received the stress management programs reduced their stress and anxiety more than those in a control group. However, subjects who were in a stress management program compatible with their locus of control (i.e., externals with lectures and internals with the self-directed) did not reduce stress significantly more than those subjects in the unmatched stress management groups.

1.6.4 Canonical Correlation

With a simple correlation we analyzed the nature of the association between two variables, such as anxiety and performance. However, in many situations one may want to examine the nature of the association between two *sets* of variables. For example, we may wish to relate a set of interest variables to a set of academic achievement variables, or a set of biological variables to a set of behavioral variables, or a set of stimulus variables to a set of response variables. Canonical correlation is a procedure for breaking down the complex association present in such situations into additive pieces. Thus, the objective in canonical correlation is:

Objective: Determine the number and nature of independent relationships existing between two sets of variables.

Example

Tetenbaum (1975), in a study of the validity of student ratings of teachers, hypothesized that specified student needs would be related to ratings of specific teacher orientations congruent with those needs. Student needs were assessed by the Personality Research Form, and fell into four broad categories: need for control, need for intellectual striving, need for gregariousness, and need for ascendancy. There were 12 need variables. There were also 12 teacher-rating variables. These two sets of variables were analyzed using canonical correlation. The first canonical dimension revealed quite cleanly the intellectual striving–rating correspondence and the ascendancy need–rating correspondence. The second canonical dimension revealed the control need–rating correspondence, and the third the gregariousness need–rating correspondence. This example is considered in detail in the chapter on canonical correlation.

1.7 The SAS and SPSS Statistical Packages

The SAS and the SPSS were selected for use in this text for several reasons:

1. They are very widely distributed.
2. They are easy to use.
3. They do a very wide range of analyses—from simple descriptive statistics to various analyses of variance designs to all kinds of complex multivariate analyses (factor analysis, multivariate analysis of variance, discriminant analysis, multiple regression, etc.).
4. They are well documented, having been in development for over two decades.

The control language that is used by both packages is quite natural, and you will see that with a little practice complex analyses are run quite easily, and with a small set of control line instructions. Getting output is relatively easy; however, this can be a mixed blessing. Because it is so easy to get output, it is also easy to get "garbage." Hence, although we illustrate the complete control lines in this text for running various analyses, several other facets are much more important, such as interpretation of printout (in particular, knowing what to focus on in the printout), careful selection of variables, adequate sample size for reliable results, checking for outliers, and knowing what assumptions are important to check for a given analysis.

It is assumed that the reader will be accessing the packages through use of a terminal (on a system such as the VAX) or a microcomputer. Also, we limit our attention to examples where the data is part of the control lines (inline data, as SPSS refers to it). It is true that data will be accessed from disk or tape fairly often in practice. However, accessing data from tape or disk, along with data management (e.g., interleaving or matching files), is a whole other arena we do not wish to enter. For those who are interested, however, SAS is very nicely set up for ease of file manipulation.

Structurally, a SAS program is composed of three fundamental blocks:

1. Statements setting up the data
2. The data lines
3. Procedure (PROC) statements—Procedures are SAS computer programs that read the data and do various statistical analyses

To illustrate how to set up the control lines, suppose we wish to compute the correlations between locus of control, achievement motivation, and achievement in language for a hypothetical set of nine subjects. First we create a data set and give it a name. The name *must* begin with a letter and be eight or fewer characters. Let us call the data set LOCUS. Now, each SAS statement *must* end with a semicolon. So our first SAS line looks like this

```
DATA LOCUS;
```

The next statement needed is called an INPUT statement. This is where we give names for our variables and indicate the format of the data (i.e., how the data is arranged on each line). We use what is called free format. With this format the scores for each variable do not have to be in specific columns. However, at least one blank column must separate the score for each variable from the next variable. Furthermore, we will put in our INPUT statement the following symbols @@. In SAS this set of symbols allows you to put the data for more than one subject on the same line.

In SAS, as with the other packages, there are certain rules for variable names. Each variable name must begin with a letter and be eight or fewer characters. The variable name can contain numbers, but *not* special characters or an embedded blank(s). For example, IQ, $x1 + x2$, and also SOC CLAS, are not valid variable names. We have special characters in the first two names (periods in I.Q. and the + in $x1 + x2$) and there is an embedded blank in the abbreviation for social class.

Our INPUT statement is as follows:

```
INPUT LOCUS ACHMOT ACHLANG @@;
```

Following the INPUT statement there is a LINES statement, which tells SAS that the data is to follow. Thus, the first three statements here setting up the data look like this:

```
DATA LOCUS;
INPUT LOCUS ACHMOT ACHLANG @@;
LINES;
```

Recall that the next structural part of a SAS program is the set of data lines. Remember there are three variables, so we have three scores for each subject. We will put the scores for three subjects on each data line. Adding the data lines to the above three statements, we now have the following part of the SAS program:

```
DATA LOCUS;
INPUT LOCUS ACHMOT ACHLANG @@;
LINES;

11  23  31  13  25  38  21  28  29
21  34  28  14  36  37  29  20  37
17  24  39  19  30  39  23  28  41
```

The first three scores (11, 23, and 31) are the scores on locus of control, achievement motivation, and achievement in language for the first subject, the next three numbers (13, 25, and 38) are the scores on these variables for Subject 2, and so on.

Now we come to the last structural part of a SAS program, calling up some SAS procedure(s) to do whatever statistical analysis(es) we desire. In this case, we want correlations, and the SAS procedure for that is called CORR. Also, as mentioned earlier, we should always print the data. For this we use PROC PRINT. Adding these lines we get our complete SAS program:

```
DATA LOCUS;
INPUT LOCUS ACHMOT ACHLANG @@;
LINES;

11  23  31  13  25  38  21  28  29
21  34  28  14  36  37  29  20  37
17  24  39  19  30  39  23  28  41

PROC CORR;
PROC PRINT;
```

Note there is a semicolon at the end of each statement, but *not* for the data lines.

In Table 1.1 we present some of the basic rules of the control language for SAS, and in Table 1.2 give the complete SAS control lines for obtaining a set of correlations (this is the example we just went over in detail), a *t* test, a one-way ANOVA, and a simple regression. Although the rules are basic, they are important. For example, failing to end a statement in SAS with a semicolon, or using a variable name longer than eight characters, will cause the program to terminate. The four sets of control lines in Table 1.2 show the structural similarity of the control line flow for different types of analyses. Notice in each case we start with the DATA statement, then an INPUT statement (naming the variables being read in and describing the format of the data), and then the CARDS statement preceding the data. Then, after the data, one or more PROC statements are used to perform the wanted statistical analysis, or to print the data (PROC PRINT).

These four sets of control lines serve as useful models for running analyses of the same type, where only the variable names change or the names and number of variables change. For example, suppose you want all correlations on five attitudinal variables (call them X1, X2, X3, X4, and X5). Then the control lines are:

```
DATA ATTITUDE;
INPUT X1 X2 X3 X4 X5 @@;
LINES;
DATA LINES
PROC CORR;
PROC PRINT;
```

TABLE 1.1

Some Basic Elements of the SAS Control Language

Non-column oriented. Columns relevant only when using column input.

SAS statements give instructions. Each statement *must* end with a semicolon.

Structurally, an SAS program is composed of three fundamental blocks:

> (1) statements setting up the data (2) the data lines and (3) procedure (PROC) statements—procedures are SAS computer programs that read the data and do various statistical analyses.

DATA SETUP—First there is the DATA statement where you are creating a data set. The name for the data set must begin with a letter and be eight or fewer characters.

VARIABLE NAMES—must be eight or fewer characters, must begin with a letter, and cannot have special characters or blanks.

COLUMN INPUT—scores for the variables go in specific columns.
If the variable is nonnumeric then we need to put a $ after the variable name.

EXAMPLE—Suppose we have a group of subjects measured on IQ, attitude toward education, and grade point average (GPA), and will label them as M for male and F for female.

SEX $ 1 IQ 3–5 ATTITUDE 7–8 GPA 10–12.2

This tells SAS that sex (M or F) is in column 1, IQ in columns 3 to 5, ATTITUDE in columns 7 and 8, and GPA in columns 10 to 12.
The .2 is to insert a decimal point *before* the last two digits.

FREE FORMAT—the scores for the variables do not have to be in specific columns, they simply need to be separated from each other by at least one blank.

The lines statement follows the DATA and INPUT statements and precedes the data lines.

ANALYSIS ON SUBSET OF VARIABLES—analysis on a subset of variables from the INPUT statement is done through the VAR (abbreviation for VARIABLE) statement. For example, if we had six variables (X1 X2 X3 X4 X5 X6) on the INPUT statement and only wished correlations for the first three, then we would insert VAR X1 X2 X3 after the PROC CORR statement.

STATISTICS FOR SUBGROUPS—obtained through use of BY statement. Suppose we want the correlations for males and females on variables X, Y, and Z. If the subjects have not been sorted on sex, then we sort them first using PROC SORT, and the control lines are

```
PROC CORR;
PROC SORT;
BY SEX;
```

MISSING VALUES—these are represented with either periods or blanks. If you are using FIXED format (i.e., data for variables in specific columns), then use blanks for missing data. If you are using FREE format, then you must use periods to represent missing data.

CREATING NEW VARIABLES—put the name for the new variable on the left and insert the statement after the INPUT statement. For example, to create a subtest score for the first three items on a test, use TOTAL=ITEMl+ITEM2+ITEM3. Or, to create a difference score from pretest and posttest data, use

```
DIFF=POSTTEST-PRETEST
```

TABLE 1.2

SAS Control Lines for Set of Correlations, *t* Test, One-Way ANOVA, and a Simple Regression

	CORRELATIONS		*T* TEST
①	DATA LOCUS;		DATA ATTITUDE;
②	INPUT LOCUS ACHMOT;	⑤	INPUT TREAT $ ATT @@;
	ACHLANG @@;		LINES;
③	LINES;		C 82 C 95 C 89 C 99 C 87
	11 23 31 13 25 38 21 28 29		C 79 C 98 C 86
	21 34 28 14 36 37 29 20 27		T 94 T 97 T 98 T 93 T 96
	17 24 39 19 30 39 23 28 41		T 99 T 88 T 92 T 94 T 90
④	PROC CORR;	⑥	PROC TTEST;
	PROC PRINT;		CLASS TREAT;
	ONE WAY ANOVA		SIMPLE REGRESSION
	DATA ONEWAY;		DATA REGRESS;
	INPUT GPID Y @@;		INPUT Y X @@;
	LINES;		LINES;
⑦	1 2 1 3 1 5 1 6		34 8 23 11 26 12
	2 7 2 9 2 11		31 9 27 14 37 15
	3 4 3 5 3 8 3 11 3 12		19 6 25 13 33 18
⑧	PROC MEANS;		PROC REG SIMPLE CORR;
	BY GPID;		MODEL Y=X;
⑨	PROC ANOVA;		SELECTION=STEPWISE;
	CLASS GPID;		
	MEANS GPID/TUKEY;		

① Here we are giving a name to the data set. Remember it must be eight or fewer letters and must begin with a letter. Note that there is a semicolon at the end of the line, and at the end of *every* line for all four examples (except for the data lines).

② Note that the names for the variables all begin with a letter and are less than or equal to 8 characters. The double @@ is needed in order to put the data for more than one subject on the same data line; here we have data for 3 subjects on each line.

③ When the data is part of the control lines, as here, then this lines command always precedes the data.

④ PROC (short for procedure) CORR yields the correlations, and PROC PRINT gives a listing of the data.

⑤ The $ after TREAT is used to denote a nonnumeric variable; note in the data lines that TREAT is either *C*(control) or *T*(treatment).

⑥ We call up the *t*-test procedure and tell it that TREAT is the grouping variable.

⑦ The first number of each pair is the group identification of the subject and the second number is the score on the dependent variable.

⑧ This PROC MEANS is necessary to obtain the means on the dependent variable in each group.

⑨ The ANOVA procedure is called and GPID is identified as the grouping (independent) variable through this CLASS statement.

Some basic elements of the SPSS control language are given in Table 1.3, and the *complete* control lines for obtaining a set of correlations, a *t* test, a one-way ANOVA, and a simple regression analysis with this package are presented in Table 1.4.

TABLE 1.3

Some Basic Elements of the SPSS Control Language

SPSS operates on commands and subcommands.

It is column oriented to the extent that each command begins in column 1 and continues for as many lines as needed. All continuation lines are indented at least one column.

Examples of Commands: TITLE, DATA LIST, BEGIN DATA, COMPUTE.

The title may be put in apostrophes, and may be up to 60 characters.

All subcommands begin with a keyword followed by an equal sign, then the specifications, and are terminated with a slash.

Each subcommand is indented at least one column.

Subcommands are further specifications for the commands.

For example, if the command is DATA LIST, then DATA LIST FREE involves the subcommand FREE, which indicates the data will be in free format.

FIXED FORMAT—this is the default format for data.

EXAMPLE—We have a group of subjects measured on IQ, attitude toward education, and grade point average (GPA), and will label them as M for male and F for female.

DATA LIST FIXED/SEX 1(A) IQ 3–5 ATTITUDE 7–8 GPA 10–12(2)

A nonnumeric variable is indicated in SPSS by specifying (A) after the variable name and location.

The rest of the statement indicates IQ is in columns 3 through 5, attitude is in columns 7 and 8, and GPA in columns 10 through 12.

An *implied* decimal point is indicated by specifying the implied number of decimal places in parentheses; here that is two.

FREE FORMAT—the variables must be in the same order for each case but do not have to be in the same location. Also, multiple cases can go on the same line, with the values for the variables separated by blanks or commas.

When that data is part of the command file, then the BEGIN DATA command precedes the data and the END DATA follows the last line of data.

We can use the keyword TO in specifying a set of consecutive variables, rather than listing all the variables. For example, if we had the six variables X1, X2, X3, X4, X5, X6, the following subcommands are equivalent:

VARIABLES=X1, X2, X3, X4, X5, X6/ or VARIABLES=X1 TO X6/

MISSING VALUES—The missing values command consists of a variables name(s) with value for each variable in parentheses:

Examples: MISSING VALUES X (8) Y (9)

Here 8 is used to denote missing for variable X and 9 to denote missing for variable Y.

If you want the same missing value designation for all variables, then use the keyword ALL, followed by the missing value designation, e.g., MISSING VALUES ALL (0)

If you are using FREE format, do *not* use a blank to indicate a missing value, but rather assign some number to indicate missing.

CREATING NEW VARIABLES—THE COMPUTE COMMAND

The COMPUTE command is used to create a new variable, or to transform an existing variable.

Examples: COMPUTE TOTAL=ITEM1+ ITEM2+ITEM3+ITEM4 COMPUTE NEWTIME=SORT(TIME)

SELECTING A SAMPLE OF CASES—

To obtain a *random* sample of cases, select an approximate percentage of cases desired (say 10%) and use SAMPLE .10

If you want an exact 10% sample, say exactly 100 cases from 1000, then use SAMPLE 100 FROM 1000

You can also select a sample(s) based on logical criteria.

For example, suppose you only want to use females from a data set, and they are coded as 2's. You can accomplish this with SELECT IF (SEX EQ 2)

TABLE 1.4

SPSS Control Lines for Set of Correlations, *t* Test, One-Way ANOVA, and Simple Regression

CORRELATIONS		T TEST
	TITLE 'CORRELATIONS FOR 3 VARS'.	TITLE 'T TEST'.
		DATA LIST FREE/TREAT ATT.
①	DATA LIST FREE/LOCUS ACMOT ACHLANG.	BEGIN DATA.
②	BEGIN DATA.	⑥ 1 82 1 95 1 89 1 99
	11 23 31 13 25 38 21 28 29	1 87 1 79 1 98 1 86
	11 34 28 14 36 37 29 20 37	2 94 2 97 2 98 2 93
	17 24 39 19 30 39 23 28 41	2 96 2 99 2 88 2 92
	END DATA.	2 94 2 90
③	CORRELATIONS	END DATA.
	VARIABLES=LOCUS	⑦ T-TEST GROUPS=TREAT(1,2)/
	ACHMOT ACHLANG/	VARIABLES=ATT/.
	PRINT=TWOTAIL/	
④	STATISTICS=DESCRIPTIVES/	
		SIMPLE REGRESSION
		TITLE 'ONE PREDICTOR'.
	ONE WAY	DATA LIST FREE/Y X.
	TITLE 'ONE WAY ANOVA'.	⑤ LIST.
	DATA LIST FREE/GPID Y.	BEGIN DATA.
	BEGIN DATA.	34 8 23 11 26 12
	1 2 1 3 1 5 1 6	31 9 27 14 37 15
	2 7 2 9 2 11	19 6 25 13 33 18
	3 4 3 5 3 8 3 11 3 12	END DATA.
	END DATA.	REGRESSION DESCRIPTIVES=
⑧	ONEWAY Y BY GPID(1,3)/	DEFAULT/
	RANGES=TUKEY/.	VARIABLES=Y X/
⑨	STATISTICS ALL.	DEPENDENT=Y/STEPWISE/.

① The FREE on this DATA LIST command is a further specification, indicating that the data will be in free format.

② When the data is part of the command file, it is preceded by BEGIN DATA and terminated by END DATA.

③ This VARIABLES subcommand specifies the variables to be analyzed.

④ This yields the means and standard deviations for all variables.

⑤ This LIST command gives a listing of the data.

⑥ The first number for each pair is the group identification and the second is the score for the dependent variable. Thus, 82 is the score for the first subject in Group 1 and 97 is the score for the second subject in Group 2.

⑦ The *t*-test procedure is called and the number of levels for the grouping variables is put in parentheses.

⑧ ONEWAY is the code name for the one-way analysis of variance procedure in SPSS. The numbers in parentheses indicate the levels of the groups being compared, in this case levels 1 through 3. If there were six groups, this would become GPID(1,6).

⑨ This yields the means, standard deviations, and the homogeneity of variance tests.

1.7.1 A More Complex Example Using SPSS

Often in data analysis things are not as neat or clean as in the previous examples. There may be missing data, we may need to do some recoding, we may need to create new variables, and we may wish to obtain some reliability information on the variables that will be used in the analysis. We now consider an example in which we deal with three of these four issues. I do not deal with recoding in this example; interested readers can refer to the second edition of this text for the details.

Before we get to the example, it is important for the reader to understand that there are different types of reliability, and they will not necessarily be of similar order of magnitude. First, there is test–retest (or parallel or alternate forms) reliability where the same subjects are measured at two different points in time. There is also interrater reliability, where you examine the consistency of judges or raters. And there is internal consistency reliability, where you are measuring the subjects at a single point in time as to how their responses on different items correlate or "hang together." The following comments from *By Design* (Light, Singer, and Willett, 1990) are important to keep in mind:

> Because different reliability estimators are sensitive to different sources of error, they will not necessarily agree. An instrument can have high internal consistency, for example, but low test-retest reliability …. This means you must examine several different reliability estimates before deciding whether your instrument is really reliable. Each separate estimate presents an incomplete picture. (p. 167)

Now, let us consider the example. A survey researcher is conducting a pilot study on a 12-item scale to check out possible ambiguous working, whether any items are sensitive, whether they discriminate, and so on. The researcher administers the scale to 16 subjects. The items are scaled from 1 to 5, with 1 representing strongly agree and 5 representing strongly disagree. There are some missing data, which are coded as 0. The data are presented here:

ID	1	2	3	4	5	6	7	8	9	10	11	12	SEX
1	1	2	2	3	3	1	1	2	2	1	2	2	1
2	1	2	2	3	3	3	1	2	2	1	1	1	1
3	1	2	1	3	3	2	3	3	2	1	2	3	1
4	2	2	4	2	3	3	2	2	3	3	2	3	1
5	2	3	2	4	2	1	2	3	0	3	4	0	1
6	2	3	2	3	3	2	3	4	3	2	4	2	1
7	3	4	4	3	5	2	2	1	2	3	3	4	1
8	3	2	3	4	4	3	4	3	3	3	4	2	1
9	3	3	4	2	4	3	3	4	5	3	5	3	2
10	4	4	5	5	3	3	5	4	4	4	5	3	2
11	4	4	0	5	5	5	4	3	0	5	4	4	2
12	4	4	4	5	5	4	3	3	5	4	4	5	2
13	4	4	0	4	3	2	5	1	3	3	0	4	2
14	5	5	3	4	4	4	4	5	3	5	5	3	2
15	5	5	4	5	3	5	5	4	4	5	3	5	2
16	5	4	3	4	3	5	4	4	3	2	2	3	2

Again, the 0 indicates missing data. Thus, we see that Subject 5 did not respond to items 9 and 12, Subject 11 didn't respond to items 3 and 9, and finally Subject 13 didn't respond to items 3 and 11. If data is missing on any variable for a subject, it is dropped from the analysis by SPSS.

Suppose the first eight subjects in this file are male and the last eight are female. The researcher wishes to compare males and females on three subtests of this scale obtained as follows:

```
SUBTEST1=I1+I2+I3+I4+I5
SUBTEST2=I6+I7+I8+I9
SUBTEST3=I10+I11+I12
```

To create these new variables we make use of three COMPUTE statements (cf. Table 1.1). For example, for SUBTEST3, we have

```
COMPUTE SUBTEST3=I10+I11+I12.
```

To determine the internal consistency of these three subscales, we access the RELIABILITY program and tell it to compute Cronbach's alpha for each of the three subscales with three subcommands. Finally, suppose the researcher uses three *t* tests for independent samples to compare males and females on these three subtests. The complete control lines for doing all of this are:

```
TITLE 'MISSING DATA SURVEY'.
DATA LIST FREE/ID I1 I2 I3 I4 I5 I6 I7 I8 I9 I10 I11 I12 SEX.
BEGIN DATA.
1 1 2 2 3 3 1 1 2 2 1 2 2 1
  DATA LINES CONTINUE
16 5 4 3 4 3 5 4 4 3 2 2 3 2
END DATA.
LIST.
MISSING VALUES ALL (0).
COMPUTE SUBTEST1=I1+I2+I3+I4.
COMPUTE SUBTEST2=I6+I7+I8+I9.
COMPUTE SUBTEST3=I10+I11+I12.
RELIABILITY VARIABLES=I1 TO I12/
  SCALE(SUBTEST1)=I1 TO I5/
  SCALE(SUBTEST2)=I6 TO I9/
  SCALE(SUBTEST3)=I10 I11 I12/
  STATISTICS=CORR/.
T-TEST GROUPS=SEX(1,2)/
  VARIABLES=SUBTEST1 SUBTEST2 SUBTEST3/.
```

Before leaving this example, we wish to note that missing data (attrition) is a fairly common occurrence in certain areas of research (e.g., repeated measures analysis). Significant attrition has been found in various areas, e.g., smoking cessation, psychotherapy, early childhood education.

There is no simple solution for this problem. If it can be assumed that the data are missing *at random*, then there is a sophisticated procedure available for obtaining good estimates (Johnson & Wichern, 1988, pp. 197–202). On the other hand, if the random missing data assumption is not tenable (usually the case), there is no consensus as to what should be done. There are various suggestions, like using the mean of the scores on the variable as an estimate, or using regression analysis (Frane, 1976), or more recently, imputation or multiple imputation. Attrition is usually systematically biased, not random. This means that even if a study got off to a good start with random assignment, it is NOT safe to assume (after attrition) that the groups are still equivalent. One can check, with a multivariate test, whether the groups are still equivalent (but don't count on it). If they are, then one can proceed with confidence. If they are not, then the analyses are always questionable.

Regarding the randomness assumption, no less a statistician than Rao (1983) argued that maximum likelihood estimation methods for estimating missing values should not be used …. He asserted that in practical problems missing values usually occur in a nonrandom way. Also, see Shadish et al. (2002, p. 337).

Probably the best solution to attrition is to cut down on the amount. Eliminating all attrition is unrealistic, but minimizing the amount is important. Attrition can occur for a variety of reasons. In psychotherapy or counseling, individuals may come to the first couple of sessions and not after that. In medicine, compliance with taking some type of medication is a problem. Shadish et al. (2002, p. 325) note:

> Other times attrition is caused by the research process. The demands of research exceed those normally expected by treatment recipients. An example is the tradeoff between the researcher's desire to measure many relevant constructs as accurately as possible and the respondent's desire to minimize the time spent in answering questionnaires. Shadish et al. (324–340) discuss attrition at length.

The statistical packages SAS and SPSS have various ways of handling missing data. The default option for both, however, is to delete the case if there is missing data on any variable for the subject.

Examining the *pattern* of missing values is important. If, for example, there is at least a moderate amount of missing data, and most of it is concentrated on just a few variables, it might be wise to drop those variables from the analysis. Otherwise, you will suffer too large a loss of subjects.

1.7.2 SAS and SPSS Statistical Manuals

Some of the more recent manuals from SAS are contained in a three-volume set (1999). The major statistical procedures contained in Volume 1 are clustering techniques, structural equation modeling (a very extensive program called CALIS), categorical data analysis (another very extensive program called CATMOD), discriminant analysis, and factor analysis. One of the major statistical procedures that is included in Volume 2 is the GLM (General Linear Models) program, which is quite comprehensive and handles equal and unequal factorial ANOVA designs and does analysis of covariance, multivariate analysis of variance, and repeated-measures analysis. Contained in Volume 3 are several fundamental regression procedures, including REG and RSREG.

Since the introduction of SPSS for Windows in 1993 (Release 6.0), there have been a series of manuals. To use SPSS effectively, the manuals one should have, in my opinion, are *SPSS BASE 16.0 User's Guide*, *SPSS ADVANCED Models 16.0*, and *SPSS BASE 16.0 Applications Guide*.

1.8 SPSS for Windows—Releases 15.0 and 16.0

The SAS and SPSS statistical packages were developed in the 1960s, and they were in widespread use during the 1970s on mainframe computers.

The emergence of microcomputers in the late 1970s had implications for the way in which data is processed today. Vastly increased memory capacity and more sophisticated microprocessors made it possible for the packages to become available on microcomputers by the mid 1980s.

I made the statement in the first edition of this text (1986) that "The days of dependence on the mainframe computer, even for the powerful statistical packages, will probably diminish considerably within the next 5 to 10 years. We are truly entering a new era in data processing." In the second edition (1992) I noted that this had certainly come true in at least two ways. Individuals were either running SAS or SPSS on their personal computers, or were accessing the packages via minicomputers such as the VAX.

Rapid changes in computer technology have brought us to the point now where "Windows" versions of the packages are available, and sophisticated analyses can be run by simply clicking a series of buttons.

Since the introduction of SPSS for Windows in 1993, data analysis has changed considerably. As noted in the *SPSS for Windows Base Guide (Release 6)*, "SPSS for Windows Release 6 brings the full power of the mainframe version of SPSS to the personal computer environment .... *SPSS for Windows provides a user interface that makes statistical analysis more accessible for the casual user and more convenient for the experienced user.* Simple menus and dialog box selections make it possible to perform complex analyses without typing a single line of command syntax. The Data Editor offers a simple and efficient spreadsheet-like facility for entering data and browsing the working data file."

The introduction of SPSS for Windows (Release 7.0) in 1996 brought further enhancements. One of the very nice ones was the introduction of the Output Navigator. This divides the output into two panes: the left pane, having the analysis(es) that was run in outline (icon) form, and the statistical content in the right pane. One can do all kinds of things with the output, including printing all or just some of the output. We discuss this feature in more detail shortly.

A fantastic bargain, in my opinion, is the SPSS Graduate Pack for Windows 15.0 or the SPSS Graduate Pack for Windows 16.0, both of which come on a compact disk and sell at a university for students for only $190. It is important to note that you are getting the full package here, not a student version.

Statistical analysis is done on data, so getting data into SPSS for Windows is crucial.

One change in SPSS for Windows versus running SPSS on the mainframe or a minicomputer such as the VAX is that each command *must* end with a period.

Also, if you wish to do structural equation modeling, you will need LISREL. An excellent book here is *LISREL 8: The Simplis Command Language* by Joreskog and Sorbom (1993). Readers who have struggled with earlier versions of LISREL may find it difficult to believe, but the SIMPLIS language in LISREL 8 makes running analyses very easy. This text has several nice examples to illustrate this fact.

1.9 Data Files

As noted in the *SPSS Base 15.0 User's Guide* (2006, p. 21), Data files come in a wide variety of formats, and this software is designed to handle many of them, including:

- Spreadsheets created with EXCEL and LOTUS
- Database files created with dBASE and various SQL formats
- Tab-delimited and other types of ASCII text files
- SAS data files
- SYSTAT data files

It is easy to import files of different types into SPSS. One simply needs to tell SPSS *where* (LOOK IN) the file is located and what *type* of file it is. For example, if it is an EXCEL file (stored in MY DOCUMENTS), then one would select MY DOCUMENTS and EXCEL for file type.

The TEXT IMPORT WIZARD (described on pp. 43–53) of the above SPSS guide is very nice for reading in-text files. We describe two data situations and how one would use the TEXT WIZARD to read the data. The two situations are:

1. There are spaces between the variables (free format), but each line represents a case.

2. There are spaces between the variables, but there are several cases on each line.

1.9.1 Situation 1: Free Format—Each Line Represents a Case

To illustrate this situation we use the Ambrose data (Exercise 12 from chapter 4). Two of the steps in the Text Wizard are illustrated in Table 1.5. To go from step 1 to step 2, step 2 to step 3, etc., simply click on NEXT. Notice in Step 3 that each line represents a case, and that we are importing all the cases. In Step 4 we indicate which delimiter(s) appears between the variables. Since in this case there is a space between each variable, this is checked.

Step 4 shows how the data will look. In Step 5 we can give names to the variables. This is done by clicking on V1. The column will darken, and then one inserts the variable name for V1 within the VARIABLE NAME box. To insert a name for V2, click on it and insert the variable name, etc.

1.9.2 Situation 2: Free Format—A Specific Number of Variables Represents a Case

To illustrate this situation we use the milk data from chapter 6. There are three cases on each line and four variables for each case. In Table 1.6 we show steps 1 and 3 of the Text Wizard. Notice in step 3 that since a specific number of variables represents a case we have changed the 1 to a 4. Step 4 shows how the data look and will be read.

1.10 Data Editing

As noted in the *SPSS Base 15.0 User's Guide* (2006, p. 103): The data editor provides a convenient, spreadsheet-like method for creating and editing data files. The DATA EDITOR window, shown here, opens automatically when you start an SPSS session:

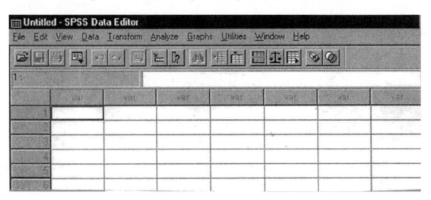

TABLE 1.5

Using the Text Import Wizard: Free Format[a]

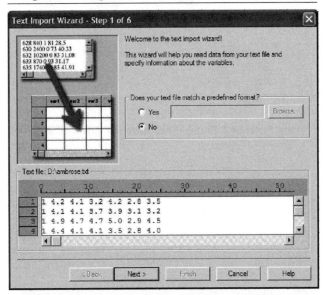

As they indicate, rows are cases and columns are variables. For illustrative purposes, let us reconsider the data set on 10 subjects for three variables (QUALITY, NFACULTY, NGRADS) that was saved previously in SPSS 15.0 as FREFIELD.SAV.

TABLE 1.6

Using the Text Import Wizard: Free Format[a]

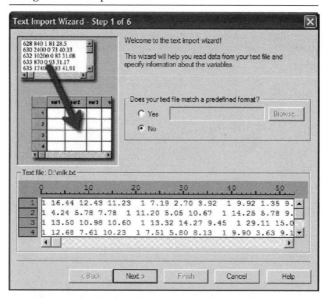

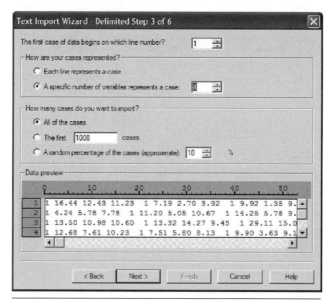

[a] specific number of variables represents a case.

1.10.1 Opening a Data File

Click on FILE ⇒ OPEN ⇒ DATA. Scroll over to FREFIELD and double click on it. That SPSS data set in the editor looks like this:

	quality	nfaculty	ngrads
1	12.00	13.00	19.00
2	23.00	29.00	72.00
3	29.00	38.00	111.00
4	36.00	⑯.00	28.00
5	44.00	40.00	104.00
6	21.00	14.00	28.00
7	40.00	44.00	16.00
8	42.00	60.00	57.00
9	24.00	16.00	18.00
10	30.00	37.00	41.00
11			

1.10.2 Changing a Cell Value

Suppose we wished to change the circled value to 23. Move to that cell. Enter the 23 and press ENTER. The new value appears in the cell. It is as simple as that.

1.10.3 Inserting a Case

Suppose we wished to insert a case after the seventh subject. How would we do it? As they point out:

1. Select any cell in the case (row) *below* the position where you want to insert the new case.

2. From the menus choose:

```
DATA
INSERT CASE
```

A new row is inserted for the case and all variables receive the system-missing value. It would look as follows:

	quality	nfaculty	ngrads
1	12.00	13.00	19.00
2	23.00	29.00	72.00
3	29.00	38.00	111.00
4	36.00	16.00	28.00
5	44.00	40.00	104.00
6	21.00	14.00	28.00
7	40.00	44.00	16.00
8			
9	42.00	60.00	57.00
10	24.00	16.00	18.00
11	30.00	37.00	41.00

Suppose the new case we typed in was 35 17 63.

1.10.4 Inserting a Variable

Now we wish to add a variable after NFACULTY. How would we do it?

1. Select any cell in the variable (column) to the *right* of the position where you want to insert the new variable.
2. From the menus choose:

```
DATA
INSERT A VARIABLE
```

When this is done, the data file in the editor looks as follows:

	quality	nfaculty	var00001	ngrads
1	12.00	13.00		19.00
2	23.00	29.00		72.00
3	29.00	38.00		111.00
4	36.00	16.00		28.00
5	44.00	40.00		104.00
6	21.00	14.00		28.00
7	40.00	44.00		16.00
8	35.00	17.00		63.00
9	42.00	60.00		57.00
10	24.00	16.00		18.00
11	30.00	37.00		41.00
12				

1.10.5 Deleting a Case

To delete a case is also simple. Click on the row (case) you wish to delete. The entire row is highlighted. From the menus choose:

```
EDIT
CLEAR
```

The selected row (case) is deleted and the cases below it move it up. To illustrate, suppose for the above data set we wished to delete Case 4 (Row 4). Click on 4 and choose EDIT and CLEAR. The case is deleted, and we are back to 10 cases, as shown next:

	quality	nfaculty	var00001	ngrads
1	12.00	13.00		19.00
2	23.00	29.00		72.00
3	29.00	38.00		111.00
4	44.00	40.00		104.00
5	21.00	14.00		28.00
6	40.00	44.00		16.00
7	35.00	17.00		63.00
8	42.00	60.00		57.00
9	24.00	16.00		18.00
10	30.00	37.00		41.00
11				

1.10.6 Deleting a Variable

Deleting a variable is also simple. Click on the variable you wish to delete. The entire column is highlighted (blackened):

From the menus choose:

```
EDIT
CLEAR
```

The variable is deleted. To illustrate, if we choose VAR00001 to delete, the blank column will be gone.

1.10.7 Splitting and Merging Files

Split-file analysis (*SPSS BASE 15.0 User's Guide* p. 234) splits the data file into separate groups for analysis, based on the values of the grouping variable (there can be more than one). We find this useful in chapter 6 on assumptions when we wish to obtain the z scores *within* each group. To obtain a split-file analysis, click on DATA and then on SPLIT FILE from the dropdown menu. Select the variable on which you wish to divide the groups and then select ORGANIZE OUTPUT BY GROUPS.

Merging data files can be done in two different ways: (a) merging files with the same variables and different cases, and (b) merging files with the same cases and different variables (*SPSS BASE 15.0 User's Guide*, pp. 221–224). SPSS gives the following marketing example for the first case. For example, you might record the same information for customers in two different sales regions and maintain the data for each region in separate files. We give an example to illustrate how one would merge files with the same variables and different cases. As they note, open one of the data files. Then, from the menus choose:

```
DATA
MERGE FILES
ADD CASES
```

Then select the data file to merge with the open data file.

Example

To illustrate the process of merging files, we consider two small artificial data sets. We denote these data sets by MERGE1 and MERGE2, respectively, and they are shown here:

caseid	y1	y2	y3
1.00	23.00	45.00	56.00
2.00	26.00	38.00	63.00
3.00	32.00	48.00	59.00
4.00	41.00	31.00	51.00

caseid	y1	y2	y3
1.00	23.00	34.00	67.00
2.00	34.00	45.00	76.00
3.00	21.00	42.00	63.00
4.00	27.00	41.00	65.00
5.00	31.00	48.00	72.00
6.00	34.00	49.00	68.00

As indicated, we open MERGE1 and then select DATA and MERGE FILES and ADD CASES from the dropdown menus. When we open MERGE2 the ADD CASES window appears:

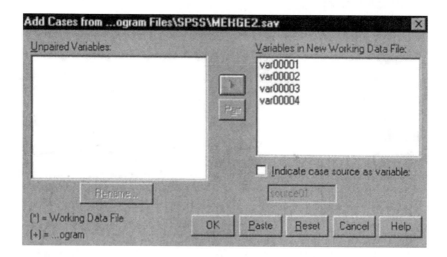

When you click on OK the merged file appears, as given here:

	caseid	y1	y2	y3
1	1.00	23.00	45.00	56.00
2	2.00	26.00	38.00	63.00
3	3.00	32.00	48.00	59.00
4	4.00	41.00	31.00	51.00
5	1.00	23.00	34.00	67.00
6	2.00	34.00	45.00	76.00
7	3.00	21.00	42.00	63.00
8	4.00	27.00	41.00	65.00
9	5.00	31.00	48.00	72.00
10	6.00	34.00	49.00	68.00

1.11 SPSS Output Navigator

The output navigator was introduced in SPSS for Windows (7.0) in 1996. It is very useful. You can browse (scroll) through the output, or go directly to a part of the output, and do all kinds of things to format only that part of the output you want. We illustrate only *some* of the things that can be done with output for the missing data example. First, the entire command syntax for running the analysis is presented here:

```
TITLE 'SURVEY RESEARCH WITH MISSING DATA'.
DATA LIST FREE/ID I1 I2 I3 I4 I5 I6 I7 I8 I9 I10 I11 I12 SEX.
BEGIN DATA.
1 1 2 2 3 3 1 1 2 2 1 2 2 1
2 1 2 2 3 3 3 1 2 2 1 1 1 1
3 1 2 1 3 3 2 3 3 2 1 2 3 1
4 2 2 4 2 3 3 2 2 3 3 2 3 1
5 2 3 2 4 2 1 2 3 0 3 4 0 1
6 2 3 2 3 3 2 3 4 3 2 4 2 1
7 3 4 4 3 5 2 2 1 2 3 3 4 1
8 3 2 3 4 4 3 4 3 3 3 4 2 1
9 3 3 4 2 4 3 3 4 5 3 5 3 2
10 4 4 5 5 3 3 5 4 4 4 5 3 2
11 4 4 0 5 5 5 4 3 0 5 4 4 2
12 4 4 4 5 5 4 3 3 5 4 4 5 2
13 4 4 0 4 3 2 5 1 3 3 0 4 2
14 5 5 3 4 4 4 4 5 3 5 5 3 2
15 5 5 4 5 3 5 5 4 4 5 3 5 2
16 5 4 3 4 3 5 4 4 3 2 2 3 2
END DATA.
LIST.
MISSING VALUES ALL (0).
COMPUTE SUBTEST1=I1+I2+I3+I4+I5.
COMPUTE SUBTEST2=I6+I7+I8+I9.
COMPUTE SUBTEST3=I10+I11+I12.
RELIABILITY VARIABLES=I1 TO I12/
  SCALE(SUBTEST 1)=I1 TO I5/
  SCALE(SUBTEST 2)=I6 TO I9/
  SCALE(SUBTEST 3)=I10 I11 I12/
  STATISTICS=CORR/.
T-TEST GROUPS=SEX(1,2)/
```

This is run from the command syntax window by clicking on RUN and then on ALL. The first thing you want to do is save the output. To do that click on FILE and then click on SAVE AS from the dropdown menu. Type in a name for the output (we will use MISSING), and then click on OK.

The output is divided into two panes. The left pane gives in outline form the analysis(es) that has been run, and the right pane has the statistical contents. To print the entire output simply click on FILE and then click on PRINT from the dropdown menu. Select how many copies you want and click on OK. It is also possible to print only part of the output. To illustrate: Suppose we wished to print only the reliability part of the output. Click on that in the left part of the pane; it is highlighted (as shown in the figure given next). Click on FILE and PRINT from the dropdown menu. Now, when the print window appears click on SELECTION and then OK. Only the reliability part of the output will be printed.

```
R E L I A B I L T Y      A N A L Y S I S    -    S C A L E    ( S U B T E S T  1 )
```

Correlation Matrix

	I1	I2	I3	I4	I5
I1	1.0000				
I2	.8992	1.0000			
I3	.6202	.5338	1.0000		
I4	.6754	.6389	.3417	1.0000	
I5	.2811	.3117	.3683	.1258	1.0000

N of Cases =   13.0

Reliability Coefficients   5 items

Alpha =   .8331   Standardized item alpha =   .8211

It is also easy to move and delete output in the output navigator. Suppose for the missing data example we wished to move the corresponding to LIST to just above the *t* test. We simply click on the LIST in the outline pane and drag it (holding the mouse down) to just above the *t* test and then release.

To delete output is also easy. Suppose we wish to delete the LIST output. Click on LIST. To delete the output one can either hit DEL (delete) key on the keyboard, or click on EDIT and then click on DELETE from the dropdown menu.

As mentioned at the beginning of this section, there are many, many other things one can do with output.

1.12 Data Sets on the Internet

There are 15 SPSS data sets and 20 ASCII data sets on the Internet (www/psypress.com/applied-multivariate-statistics-for-the-social-sciences). All of the SPSS data sets involve real data, and most of the ASCII data sets have real data. You must be in SPSS to access all the data sets. So double click on the SPSS icon, and then use FILE—OPEN—DATA to get to the OPEN FILE dialog box. Change LOOK IN to the Interneticon and FILE TYPE to SPSS*(SAV) and the 15 SPSS data files will appear. When you double click on an SPSS file, it will appear in the spreadsheet-like editor, ready for analysis. To access the ASCII (text) files leave LOOK IN as the Interneticon, but change FILE TYPE to TEXT. When you double click on an ASCII file the TEXT WIZARD will appear. For these data sets just click NEXT several times. In the final step (step 6) press FINISH and the data file will appear in the spreadsheet-like editor, ready for analysis.

1.13 Importing a Data Set into the Syntax Window of SPSS

Highlight all the data, starting at the BOTTOM, so it is blackened. Then, click on EDIT and select COPY. Next, click on FILE and go to NEW and then across to SYNTAX. A blank screen will appear. Click on EDIT and select PASTE, and the data will appear in the syntax window. Sandwich the control lines around the data, and run the file by using RUN and then ALL.

1.14 Some Issues Unique to Multivariate Analysis

Many of the techniques discussed in this text are *mathematical maximization procedures,* and hence there is great opportunity for capitalization on chance. Often, as the reader can see as we move along in the text, the results "look great" on a given sample, but do not generalize to other samples. Thus, the results are sample specific and of limited scientific utility. Reliability of results is a real concern.

The notion of a *linear combination* of variables is fundamental to all the types of analysis we discuss. A general linear combination for p variables is given by:

$$y = a_1 x_1 + a_2 x_2 + a_3 x_3 + \cdots + a_p x_p$$

where $a_1, a_2, a_3, \ldots, a_p$ are the coefficients for the variables. This definition is abstract; however, we give some simple examples of linear combinations that the reader will be familiar with.

Suppose we have a treatment versus control group design with the subjects pretested and posttested on some variable. Then sometimes analysis is done on the difference scores (gain scores), that is, posttest–pretest. If we denote the pretest variable by x_1 and the posttest variable by x_2, then the difference variable $y = x_2 - x_1$ is a simple linear combination where $a_1 = -1$ and $a_2 = 1$.

As another example of a simple linear combination, suppose we wished to sum three subtest scores on a test (x_1, x_2, and x_3). Then the newly created sum variable $y = x_1 + x_2 + x_3$ is a linear combination where $a_1 = a_2 = a_3 = 1$.

Still another example of linear combinations that the reader has encountered in an intermediate statistics course is that of contrasts among means, as in the Scheffé *post hoc* procedure or in planned comparisons. Consider the following four-group ANOVA, where T_3 is a combination treatment, and T_4 is a control group.

$$\frac{T_1 \, T_2 \, T_3 \, T_4}{\mu_1 \, \mu_2 \, \mu_3 \, \mu_4}$$

Then the following meaningful contrast

$$L_1 = \frac{\mu_1 + \mu_2}{2} - \mu_3$$

is a linear combination, where $a_1 = a_2 = \frac{1}{2}$ and $a_3 = -1$, while the following contrast among means

$$L_1 = \frac{\mu_1 + \mu_2 + \mu_3}{3} - \mu_4$$

is also a linear combination, where $a_1 = a_2 = a_3 = \frac{1}{3}$ and $a_4 = -1$. The notions of mathematical maximization and linear combinations are combined in many of the multivariate procedures. For example, in multiple regression we talk about the linear combination of the predictors that is maximally correlated with the dependent variable, and in principal components analysis the linear combinations of the variables that account for maximum portions of the total variance are considered.

1.15 Data Collection and Integrity

Although in this text we finesse the issues of data collection and measurement of variables, the reader should be forewarned that these are critical issues. No analysis, no matter how sophisticated, can compensate for poor data collection and measurement problems. Iverson and Gergen (1997) in chapter 14 of their text on statistics hit on some key issues. First, they discussed the issue of obtaining a random sample, so that one can generalize to some population of interest. They noted:

> We believe that researchers are aware of the need for randomness, but achieving it is another matter. In many studies, the condition of randomness is almost never truly satisfied. A majority of psychological studies, for example, rely on college students for their research results. (Critics have suggested that modern psychology should be called the psychology of the college sophomore.) Are college students a random sample of the adult population or even the adolescent population? Not likely. (p. 627)

Then they turned their attention to problems in survey research, and noted:

> In interview studies, for example, differences in responses have been found depending on whether the interviewer seems to be similar or different from the respondent in such aspects as gender, ethnicity, and personal preferences…. The place of the interview is also important…. Contextual effects cannot be overcome totally and must be accepted as a facet of the data collection process. (pp. 628–629)

Another point they mentioned, which I have been telling my students for years, is that what people say and what they do often do not correspond. They noted, "A study that asked about toothbrushing habits found that on the basis of what people said they did, the toothpaste consumption in this country should have been three times larger than the amount that is actually sold" (pp. 630–631).

Another problem, endemic in psychology, is using college freshmen or sophomores. This raises real problems, in my mind, in terms of data integrity. I had a student who came to me recently, expecting that I would recommend some fancy multivariate analysis(es) to data he had collected from college freshmen. I raised some serious concerns about the integrity of the data. For most 18- or 19-year-olds, the concentration lapses after 5 or 10 minutes, and I am not sure what the remaining data mean. Many of them are thinking about the next party or social event, and filling out the questionnaire is far from the most important thing in their minds.

In ending this section I wish to point out that, in my opinion, most mail questionnaires and telephone interviews are much too long. Mail questionnaires, for the most part, should be limited to two pages, and telephone interviews to 5 to 10 minutes. If one thinks about it, most if not all relevant questions can be asked within 5 minutes. I have seen too many

6- to 10-page questionnaires and heard about (and experienced) long telephone interviews. People have too many other things going in their lives to spend the time filling out a 10-page questionnaire, or to spend 20 minutes on the telephone.

1.16 Nonresponse in Survey Research

A major problem in doing either mail or telephone surveys is the nonresponse problem. Studies have shown that nonrespondents differ from respondents, yet researchers very often ignore this fact. The nonresponse problem has been known for more than 50 years, and one would think that substantial progress has been made. A recent text on survey nonresponse indicates that there is still reason for considerable concern. The text *Survey Nonresponse* (Groves et al., 2001) was written, according to the preface, "to provide a review of the current state of the field in survey nonresponse." Chapter 2, written by Tom Smith of the University of Chicago, presents a sobering view on the reporting of *response rates*. He notes that of 14 university-based organizations only 5 routinely report response rates.

To illustrate how misleading results can be if there is substantial nonresponse, we give an example. Suppose 1000 questionnaires are sent out and only 200 are returned (a definite possibility). Of the 200 returned, 130 are in favor and 70 are opposed. It appears that most of the people favor the issue. But 800 were not returned, and respondents tend to differ from nonrespondents. Suppose that 55% of the nonrespondents are opposed and 45% are in favor. Then 440 of the nonrespondents are opposed and 360 are in favor. But now we have 510 opposed and 490 in favor. What looked like an overwhelming majority in favor is now about evenly split for all subjects.

The study may get off to a good start by perhaps randomly sampling 1000 subjects from some population of interest. Then only 250 of the questionnaires are returned and a few follow-ups increase this to 300 respondents. Although the 1,000 would be representative of the population, one can't assume the 300 are representative. I had a student recently who sent out a random sample of questionnaires to high school teachers and obtained a response rate of 15%. The sad thing was, when I pointed out the severe bias, he replied that his response rate was better than 10%.

It is sometimes suggested that, if one anticipates a low response rate and wants a certain number of questionnaires returned, to simply increase sample size. For example, if one wishes 400 returned and a response rate of 20% is anticipated, send out 2000. *This is a dangerous and misleading practice.* Let me illustrate. Suppose 2,000 are sent out and 400 are returned. Of these, 300 are in favor and 100 are opposed. It appears there is an overwhelming majority in favor, and this is true for the respondents. But 1,600 did NOT respond. Suppose that 60% of the nonrespondents (a distinct possibility) are opposed and 40% are in favor. Then, 960 of the nonrespondents are opposed and 640 are in favor. Again, what appeared to be an overwhelming majority in favor is stacked against (1060 vs. 940) for ALL subjects.

1.17 Internal and External Validity

Although this is a book on statistics, the design one sets up is crucial. In a course on research methods, one learns of internal and external validity, and of the threats to each.

If one is comparing groups, then internal validity refers to the confidence we have that the treatment(s) made the difference. There are various threats to internal validity (e.g., history, maturation, selection, regression toward the mean). In setting up a design, one wants to be confident that the treatment made the difference, and not one of the threats. Random assignment of subjects to groups controls most of the threats to internal validity, and for this reason is often referred to as the "gold standard." Is the best way of assuring, within sampling error, that the groups are "equal" on all variables. However, if there is a variable (we will use gender and two groups to illustrate) that is related to the dependent variable, then one should stratify on that variable and then randomly assign within each stratum. For example, if there were 36 females and 24 males, we would randomly assign 18 females and 12 males to each group. That is, we ensure an equal number of each gender in each group, rather than leaving this to chance. It is extremely important to understand that a good design is essential. Light, Singer, and Willet (1990), in the preface of their book, summed it up best by stating bluntly, "You can't fix by analysis what you bungled by design."

Treatment, as stated above, is generic and could refer to teaching methods, counseling methods, drugs, diets, etc. It is dangerous to assume that the treatment(s) will be implemented as you planned, and hence it is very important to monitor the treatment.

Now let us turn our attention to external validity. External validity refers to the generalizability of results. That is, to what population(s) of subjects we can generalize our results. Also, to what settings or conditions do our results generalize? A recent very good book on external validity is by Shadish, Cook, and Campbell (2002).

Two excellent books on research design are the aforementioned *By Design* by Light, Singer, and Willet (which I used for 10 years) and a book by Alan Kazdin entitled *Research Design in Clinical Psychology* (2003). Both of these books require, in my opinion, that the students have at least two courses in statistics and a course on research methods.

Before leaving this section a word of warning on ratings as the dependent variable. Often one will hear of training the raters so that they agree. This is fine, however, it does not go far enough. There is still the issue of bias with the raters, and this can be very problematic if the rater has a vested interest in the outcome. I have seen too many dissertations where the person writing it is one of the raters.

1.18 Conflict of Interest

Kazdin notes that conflict of interest can occur in many different ways (2003, p. 537). One way is through a conflict between the scientific responsibility of the investigator(s) and a vested financial interest. We illustrate this with a medical example. In the book *Overdosed America* (2004), Abramson in the introduction gives the following medical conflict:

> The second part, "The Commercialization of American Medicine," presents a brief history of the commercial takeover of medical knowledge and the techniques used to manipulate doctors' and the public's understanding of new developments in medical science and health care. One example of the depth of the problem was presented in a 2002 article in the *Journal of the American Medical Association*, which showed that 59% of the experts who write the clinical guidelines that define good medical care have direct financial ties to the companies whose products are being evaluated.

Kazdin (2003, p. 539) gives examples that hit closer to home, i.e., from psychology and education:

> In psychological research and perhaps specifically in clinical, counseling and educational psychology, it is easy to envision conflict of interest. Researchers may own stock in companies that in some way are relevant to their research and their findings. Also, a researcher may serve as a consultant to a company (e.g., that develops software or psychological tests or that publishes books) and receive generous consultation fees for serving as a resource for the company. Serving as someone who gains financially from a company and who conducts research with products that the company may sell could be a conflict of interest or perceived as a conflict.

The example I gave earlier of someone serving as a rater for their dissertation is a potential conflict of interest. That individual has a vested interest in the results, and for him or her to remain objective in doing the ratings is definitely questionable.

1.19 Summary

This chapter reviewed type I error, type II error, and power. It indicated that power is dependent on the alpha level, sample size, and effect size. The problem of multiple statistical tests appearing in various situations was discussed. The important issue of statistical versus practical significance was discussed, and some ways of assessing practical significance (confidence intervals, effect sizes, and measures of association) were mentioned. The importance of identifying outliers (subjects who are three or more standard deviations from the mean) was emphasized. The SAS and SPSS statistical packages, whose printouts are discussed throughout much of the text, are detailed. Regarding data integrity, what people say and what they do often don't correspond. The nonresponse problem in survey research (especially mail surveys) and the danger it represents in generalizing results is detailed. The critical importance of a good design is emphasized. Finally, conflict of interest can undermine the integrity of results.

1.20 Exercises

1. Consider a two-group independent-samples *t* test with a treatment group (treatment is generic and could be intervention, diet, drug, counseling method, etc.) and a control group. The null hypothesis is that the population means are equal. What are the consequences of making a type I error? What are the consequences of making a type II error?

2. This question is concerned with power.

   (a) Suppose a clinical study (10 subjects in each of 2 groups) does not find significance at the .05 level, but there is a medium effect size (which is judged to be of practical significance). What should the investigator do in a future replication study?

(b) It has been mentioned that there can be "too much power" in some studies. What is meant by this? Relate this to the "sledgehammer effect" that I mentioned in the chapter.

3. This question is concerned with multiple statistical tests.

(a) Consider a two-way ANOVA (A × B) with six dependent variables. If a univariate analysis is done at $\alpha = .05$ on each dependent variable, then how many tests have been done? What is the Bonferroni upper bound on overall alpha? Compute the tighter bound.

(b) Now consider a three-way ANOVA (A × B × C) with four dependent variables. If a univariate analysis is done at $\alpha = .05$ on each dependent variable, then how many tests have been done? What is the Bonferroni upper bound on overall alpha? Compute the tighter upper bound.

4. This question is concerned with statistical versus practical significance: A survey researcher compares four religious groups on their attitude toward education. The survey is sent out to 1,200 subjects, of which 823 eventually respond. Ten items, Likert scaled from 1 to 5, are used to assess attitude. A higher positive score indicates a more positive attitude. There are only 800 usable responses. The Protestants are split into two groups for analysis purposes. The group sizes, along with the means are given below.

	Protestant1	Catholic	Jewish	Protestant2
n	238	182	130	250
$\bar{x}$	32.0	33.1	34.0	31.0

An analysis of variance on these four groups yielded $F = 5.61$, which is significant at the .001 level. Discuss the practical significance issue.

5. This question concerns outliers: Suppose 150 subjects are measured on 4 variables. Why could a subject not be an outlier on any of the 4 variables and yet be an outlier when the 4 variables are considered jointly?

Suppose a Mahalanobis distance is computed for each subject (checking for multivariate outliers). Why might it be advisable to do each test at the .001 level?

6. What threats to internal validity does random assignment NOT control on?

7. Kazdin has indicated that there are various reasons for conflict of interest to occur. One reason mentioned in this chapter was a financial conflict of interest. What are some other conflicts?

2

Matrix Algebra

2.1 Introduction

A matrix is simply a rectangular array of elements. The following are examples of matrices:

$$\begin{bmatrix} 1 & 2 & 3 & 4 \\ 4 & 5 & 6 & 9 \end{bmatrix} \qquad \begin{bmatrix} 1 & 2 & 1 \\ 2 & 3 & 5 \\ 5 & 6 & 8 \\ 1 & 4 & 10 \end{bmatrix} \qquad \begin{bmatrix} 1 & 2 \\ 2 & 4 \end{bmatrix}$$

$$2 \times 4 \qquad\qquad 4 \times 3 \qquad\qquad 2 \times 2$$

The numbers underneath each matrix are the dimensions of the matrix, and indicate the size of the matrix. The first number is the number of rows and the second number the number of columns. Thus, the first matrix is a 2×4 since it has 2 rows and 4 columns.

A familiar matrix in educational research is the score matrix. For example, suppose we had measured six subjects on three variables. We could represent all the scores as a matrix:

Variables

$$\begin{array}{c} \\ \\ \text{Subjects} \end{array} \begin{array}{c} 1 \\ 2 \\ 3 \\ 4 \\ 5 \\ 6 \end{array} \begin{bmatrix} 10 & 4 & 18 \\ 12 & 6 & 21 \\ 13 & 2 & 20 \\ 16 & 8 & 16 \\ 12 & 3 & 14 \\ 15 & 9 & 13 \end{bmatrix}$$

$$\begin{array}{ccc} 1 & 2 & 3 \end{array}$$

This is a 6×3 matrix. More generally, we can represent the scores of N subjects on p variables in a $N \times p$ matrix as follows:

Variables

	1	2	3		p

$$
\text{Subjects} \quad \begin{array}{c} 1 \\ 2 \\ \vdots \\ N \end{array} \begin{bmatrix} x_{11} & x_{12} & x_{13} & \cdots & x_{1p} \\ x_{21} & x_{22} & x_{23} & \cdots & x_{2p} \\ \vdots & \vdots & \vdots & & \vdots \\ x_{N1} & x_{N2} & x_{N3} & \cdots & x_{Np} \end{bmatrix}
$$

The first subscript indicates the row and the second subscript the column. Thus, x_{12} represents the score of subject 1 on variable 2 and x_{2p} represents the score of subject 2 on variable p.

The *transpose* $\mathbf{A}'$ of a matrix $\mathbf{A}$ is simply the matrix obtained by interchanging rows and columns.

Example 2.1

$$
\mathbf{A} = \begin{bmatrix} 2 & 3 & 6 \\ 5 & 4 & 8 \end{bmatrix} \Rightarrow \mathbf{A}' = \begin{bmatrix} 2 & 5 \\ 3 & 4 \\ 6 & 8 \end{bmatrix}
$$

The first row of $\mathbf{A}$ has become the first column of $\mathbf{A}'$ and the second row of $\mathbf{A}$ has become the second column of $\mathbf{A}'$.

$$
\mathbf{B} = \begin{bmatrix} 3 & 4 & 2 \\ 5 & 6 & 5 \\ 1 & 3 & 8 \end{bmatrix} \rightarrow \mathbf{B}' = \begin{bmatrix} 3 & 5 & 1 \\ 4 & 6 & 3 \\ 2 & 5 & 8 \end{bmatrix}
$$

In general, if a matrix $\mathbf{A}$ has dimensions $r \times s$, then the dimensions of the transpose are $s \times r$.

A matrix with a single row is called a row vector, and a matrix with a single column is called a column vector. Vectors are always indicated by small letters and a row vector by a transpose, for example, $\mathbf{x}'$, $\mathbf{y}'$, and so on. Throughout this text a matrix or vector is denoted by a boldface letter.

Example 2.2

$$
\mathbf{x}' = (1,2,3) \qquad \mathbf{y} = \begin{bmatrix} 4 \\ 6 \\ 8 \\ 7 \end{bmatrix} 4 \times 1 \text{ column vector}
$$

1×3 row vector

A row vector that is of particular interest to us later is the vector of means for a group of subjects on several variables. For example, suppose we have measured 100 subjects on the

California Psychological Inventory and have obtained their average scores on five of the subscales. We could represent their five means as a column vector, and the transpose of this column vector is a row vector **x'**.

$$\mathbf{x} = \begin{bmatrix} 24 \\ 31 \\ 22 \\ 27 \\ 30 \end{bmatrix} \rightarrow \quad \mathbf{x'} = (24, 31, 22, 27, 30)$$

The elements on the diagonal running from upper left to lower right are said to be on the main diagonal of a matrix. A matrix **A** is said to be *symmetric* if the elements below the main diagonal are a mirror reflection of the corresponding elements above the main diagonal. This is saying $a_{12} = a_{21}$, $a_{13} = a_{31}$, and $a_{23} = a_{32}$ for a 3×3 matrix, since these are the corresponding pairs. This is illustrated by:

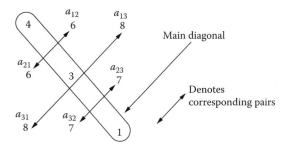

In general, a matrix **A** is symmetric if $a_{ij} = a_{ji}$, $i \neq j$, i.e., if all corresponding pairs of elements above and below the main diagonal are equal.

An example of a symmetric matrix that is frequently encountered in statistical work is that of a correlation matrix. For example, here is the matrix of intercorrelations for four subtests of the Differential Aptitude Test for boys:

	VR	NA	Cler.	Mech.
Verbal Reas.	1.00	.70	.19	.55
Numerical Abil.	.70	1.00	.36	.50
Clerical Speed	.19	.36	1.00	.16
Mechan. Reas.	.55	.50	.16	1.00

This matrix is obviously symmetric because, for example, the correlation between VR and NA is the same as the correlation between NA and VR.

Two matrices **A** and **B** are equal if and only if all corresponding elements are equal. That is to say, two matrices are equal only if they are identical.

2.2 Addition, Subtraction, and Multiplication of a Matrix by a Scalar

Two matrices **A** and **B** are added by adding corresponding elements.

Example 2.3

$$\mathbf{A} = \begin{bmatrix} 2 & 3 \\ 3 & 4 \end{bmatrix} \quad \mathbf{B} = \begin{bmatrix} 6 & 2 \\ 2 & 5 \end{bmatrix}$$

$$\mathbf{A} + \mathbf{B} = \begin{bmatrix} 2+6 & 3+2 \\ 3+2 & 4+5 \end{bmatrix} = \begin{bmatrix} 8 & 5 \\ 5 & 9 \end{bmatrix}$$

Notice the elements in the (1, 1) positions, that is, 2 and 6, have been added, and so on.

Only matrices of the same dimensions can be added. Thus addition would not be defined for these matrices:

$$\begin{bmatrix} 2 & 3 & 1 \\ 1 & 4 & 6 \end{bmatrix} + \begin{bmatrix} 1 & 4 \\ 5 & 6 \end{bmatrix} \text{ not defined}$$

Two matrices of the same dimensions are subtracted by subtracting corresponding elements.

$$\overset{\mathbf{A}}{\begin{bmatrix} 2 & 1 & 5 \\ 3 & 2 & 6 \end{bmatrix}} - \overset{\mathbf{B}}{\begin{bmatrix} 1 & 4 & 2 \\ 1 & 2 & 5 \end{bmatrix}} = \overset{\mathbf{A}-\mathbf{B}}{\begin{bmatrix} 1 & -3 & 3 \\ 2 & 0 & 1 \end{bmatrix}}$$

Multiplication of a matrix or a vector by a scalar (number) is accomplished by multiplying each element of the matrix or vector by the scalar.

Example 2.4

$$2(3,1,4) = (6,2,8) \quad \tfrac{1}{3}\begin{bmatrix} 4 \\ 3 \end{bmatrix} = \begin{bmatrix} 4/3 \\ 1 \end{bmatrix}$$

$$4\begin{bmatrix} 2 & 1 \\ 1 & 5 \end{bmatrix} = \begin{bmatrix} 8 & 4 \\ 4 & 20 \end{bmatrix}$$

2.2.1 Multiplication of Matrices

There is a restriction as to when two matrices can be multiplied. Consider the product **AB**. Then *the number of columns in* **A** *must equal the number of rows in* **B**. For example, if **A** is 2 × 3, then **B** must have 3 rows, although **B** could have any number of columns. If two matrices can be multiplied they are said to be *conformable*. The dimensions of the product matrix, call it **C**, are simply the number of rows of **A** by number of columns of **B**. In the above example, if **B** were 3 × 4, then **C** would be a 2 × 4 matrix. In general then, if **A** is an $r \times s$ matrix and **B** is an $s \times t$ matrix, then the dimensions of the product **AB** are $r \times t$.

Example 2.5

$$
\begin{array}{ccc}
\mathbf{A} & \mathbf{B} & \mathbf{C} \\
\begin{bmatrix} 2 & 1 & 3 \\ 4 & 5 & 6 \end{bmatrix} & \begin{bmatrix} 1 & 0 \\ 2 & 4 \\ -1 & 5 \end{bmatrix} = & \begin{bmatrix} c_{11} & c_{12} \\ c_{21} & c_{22} \end{bmatrix} \\
2 \times 3 & 3 \times 2 & 2 \times 2
\end{array}
$$

Notice first that **A** and **B** can be multiplied because the number of columns in **A** is 3, which is equal to the number of rows in **B**. The product matrix **C** is a 2 × 2, that is, the outer dimensions of **A** and **B**. To obtain the element c_{11} (in the first row and first column), we multiply corresponding elements of the first row of **A** by the elements of the first column of **B**. Then, we simply add the sum of these products. To obtain c_{12} we take the sum of products of the corresponding elements of the first row of **A** by the second column of **B**. This procedure is presented next for all four elements of **C**:

Element

$$c_{11} \quad (2,1,3) \begin{pmatrix} 1 \\ 2 \\ -1 \end{pmatrix} = 2(1) + 1(2) + 3(-1) = 1$$

$$c_{12} \quad (2,1,3) \begin{pmatrix} 0 \\ 4 \\ 5 \end{pmatrix} = 2(0) + 1(4) + 3(5) = 19$$

$$c_{21} \quad (4,5,6) \begin{pmatrix} 1 \\ 2 \\ -1 \end{pmatrix} = 4(1) + 5(2) + 6(-1) = 8$$

$$c_{22} \quad (4,5,6) \begin{pmatrix} 0 \\ 4 \\ 5 \end{pmatrix} = 4(0) + 5(4) + 6(5) = 50$$

Therefore, the product matrix **C** is:

$$\mathbf{C} = \begin{bmatrix} 1 & 19 \\ 8 & 50 \end{bmatrix}$$

Now we multiply two more matrices to illustrate an important property concerning matrix multiplication

Example 2.6

$$
\begin{matrix}
\mathbf{A} & \mathbf{B} & & \mathbf{AB}
\end{matrix}
$$

$$
\begin{bmatrix} 2 & 1 \\ 1 & 4 \end{bmatrix}\begin{bmatrix} 3 & 5 \\ 5 & 6 \end{bmatrix} = \begin{bmatrix} 2\cdot3+1\cdot5 & 2\cdot5+1\cdot6 \\ 1\cdot3+4\cdot5 & 1\cdot5+4.6 \end{bmatrix} = \begin{bmatrix} 11 & 16 \\ 23 & 29 \end{bmatrix}
$$

$$
\begin{matrix}
\mathbf{B} & \mathbf{A} & & \mathbf{BA}
\end{matrix}
$$

$$
\begin{bmatrix} 3 & 5 \\ 5 & 6 \end{bmatrix}\begin{bmatrix} 2 & 1 \\ 1 & 4 \end{bmatrix} = \begin{bmatrix} 3\cdot2+5\cdot1 & 3\cdot1+5\cdot4 \\ 5\cdot2+6\cdot1 & 5\cdot1+6\cdot4 \end{bmatrix} = \begin{bmatrix} 11 & 23 \\ 16 & 29 \end{bmatrix}
$$

Notice that **AB** ≠ **BA**; that is, the *order* in which matrices are multiplied makes a difference. The mathematical statement of this is to say that multiplication of matrices is not commutative. Multiplying matrices in two different orders (assuming they are conformable both ways) in general yields different results.

Example 2.7

$$
\begin{matrix}
\mathbf{A} & \mathbf{x} & \mathbf{Ax}
\end{matrix}
$$

$$
\begin{bmatrix} 3 & 1 & 2 \\ 1 & 4 & 5 \\ 2 & 5 & 2 \end{bmatrix}\begin{bmatrix} 2 \\ 6 \\ 3 \end{bmatrix} = \begin{bmatrix} 18 \\ 41 \\ 40 \end{bmatrix}
$$

$$
(3\times3)\quad (3\times1)\ (3\times1)
$$

Notice that multiplying a matrix on the right by a column vector takes the matrix into a column vector.

$$
(2,5)\begin{bmatrix} 3 & 1 \\ 1 & 4 \end{bmatrix} = (11,22)
$$

Multiplying a matrix on the left by a row vector results in a row vector. If we are multiplying more than two matrices, then we may *group at will*. The mathematical statement of this is that multiplication of matrices is associative. Thus, if we are considering the matrix product **ABC**, we get the same result if we multiply **A** and **B** first (and then the result of that by **C**) as if we multiply **B** and **C** first (and then the result of that by **A**), i.e.,

$$\mathbf{A}\ \mathbf{B}\ \mathbf{C} = (\mathbf{A}\ \mathbf{B})\ \mathbf{C} = \mathbf{A}\ (\mathbf{B}\ \mathbf{C})$$

A matrix product that is of particular interest to us in Chapter 4 is of the following form:

$$
\begin{matrix}
\mathbf{x'} & \mathbf{S} & \mathbf{x} \\
1\times p & p\times p & p\times 1
\end{matrix}
$$

Note that this product yields a number, i.e., the product matrix is 1×1 or a number. The multivariate test statistic for two groups is of this form (except for a scalar constant in front).

Example 2.8

$$(4,2)\begin{bmatrix} 10 & 3 \\ 3 & 4 \end{bmatrix}\begin{bmatrix} 4 \\ 2 \end{bmatrix} = (46,20)\begin{bmatrix} 4 \\ 2 \end{bmatrix} = 184 + 40 = 224$$

2.3 Obtaining the Matrix of Variances and Covariances

Now, we show how various matrix operations introduced thus far can be used to obtain a very important quantity in statistical work, i.e., the matrix of variances and covariances for a set of variables. Consider the following set of data

x_1	x_2
1	1
3	4
2	7
$\bar{x}_1 = 2$	$\bar{x}_2 = 4$

First, we form the matrix $\mathbf{X}_d$ of deviation scores, that is, how much each score deviates from the mean on that variable:

$$\mathbf{X}_d = \begin{bmatrix} 1 & 1 \\ 3 & 4 \\ 2 & 7 \end{bmatrix} - \begin{bmatrix} 2 & 4 \\ 2 & 4 \\ 2 & 4 \end{bmatrix} = \begin{bmatrix} -1 & -3 \\ 1 & 0 \\ 0 & 3 \end{bmatrix}$$

Next we take the transpose of $\mathbf{X}_d$:

$$\mathbf{X}_d' = \begin{bmatrix} -1 & 1 & 0 \\ -3 & 0 & 3 \end{bmatrix}$$

Now we can obtain the so-called matrix of sums of squares and cross products **(SSCP)** as the product of $\mathbf{X}_d'$ and $\mathbf{X}_d$:

Deviation scores for x_1 $\mathbf{X}_d'$ $\mathbf{X}_d$ Deviation scores for x_2

$$\mathbf{SSCP} = \begin{bmatrix} -1 & 1 & 0 \\ -3 & 0 & 3 \end{bmatrix}\begin{bmatrix} -1 & -3 \\ 1 & 0 \\ 0 & 3 \end{bmatrix} = \begin{bmatrix} ss_1 & ss_{12} \\ ss_{21} & ss_2 \end{bmatrix}$$

The diagonal elements are just sums of squares:

$$ss_1 = (-1)^2 + 1^2 + 0^2 = 2$$

$$ss_2 = (-3)^2 + 0^2 + 3^2 = 18$$

Notice that these deviation sums of squares are the numerators of the variances for the variables, because the variance for a variable is

$$s^2 = \sum_i (x_{ii} - \bar{x})^2 / (n-1).$$

The sum of deviation cross products (ss_{12}) for the two variables is

$$ss_{12} = ss_{21} = (-1)(-3) + 1(0) + (0)(3) = 3$$

This is just the numerator for the covariance for the two variables, because the definitional formula for covariance is given by:

$$S_{12} = \frac{\sum_{i=1}^{n}(x_{i1} - \bar{x}_1)(x_{i2} - \bar{x}_2)}{n-1},$$

where $(x_{i1} - \bar{x}_1)$ is the deviation score for the ith subject on x_1 and $(x_{i2} - \bar{x}_2)$ is the deviation score for the ith subject on x_2.

Finally, the matrix of variances and covariances **S** is obtained from **SSCP** matrix by multiplying by a constant, namely, $1/(n-1)$:

$$S = \frac{SSCP}{n-1} \qquad \text{Variance for variable 1}$$

$$S = \frac{1}{2} \begin{bmatrix} 2 & 3 \\ 3 & 18 \end{bmatrix} = \begin{bmatrix} 1 & 1.5 \\ 1.5 & 9 \end{bmatrix} \longrightarrow \text{Variance for variable 2}$$

$$\text{Covariance}$$

Thus, in obtaining **S** we have:

1. Represented the scores on several variables as a matrix.
2. Illustrated subtraction of matrices—to get X_d.
3. Illustrated the transpose of a matrix—to get X'_d.
4. Illustrated multiplication of matrices, i.e., $X'_d X_d$, to get **SSCP**.
5. Illustrated multiplication of a matrix by a scalar, i.e., by $1/(n-1)$, to finally obtain **S**.

2.4 Determinant of a Matrix

The determinant of a matrix **A**, denoted by $|A|$, is a unique number associated with each *square* matrix. There are two interrelated reasons that consideration of determinants is quite important for multivariate statistical analysis. First, the determinant of a covariance matrix represents the *generalized* variance for several variables. That is, it characterizes in a single number how much variability is present on a set of variables. Second, because the determinant represents variance for a set of variables, it is intimately involved in several multivariate test statistics. For example, in Chapter 3 on regression analysis, we use a test statistic called Wilks' Λ that involves a ratio of two determinants. Also, in k group, multivariate analysis of variance the following form of Wilks' Λ ($\Lambda = |\mathbf{W}|/|\mathbf{T}|$) is the most widely used test statistic for determining whether several groups differ on a set of variables. The $\mathbf{W}$ and $\mathbf{T}$ matrices are multivariate generalizations of SS_w (sum of squares within) and SS_t (sum of squares total) from univariate ANOVA, and are defined and described in detail in Chapters 4 and 5.

There is a formal definition for finding the determinant of a matrix, but it is complicated and we do not present it. There are other ways of finding the determinant, and a convenient method for smaller matrices (4×4 or less) is the method of cofactors. For a 2×2 matrix, the determinant could be evaluated by the method of cofactors; however, it is evaluated more quickly as simply the difference in the products of the diagonal elements.

Example 2.9

$$\mathbf{A} = \begin{bmatrix} 4 & 1 \\ 1 & 2 \end{bmatrix} \Rightarrow |\mathbf{A}| = 4 \cdot (2) - 1 \cdot (1) = 7$$

In general, for a 2×2 matrix $\mathbf{A} = \begin{bmatrix} a & b \\ c & d \end{bmatrix}$, then $|\mathbf{A}| = ad - bc$.

To evaluate the determinant of a 3×3 matrix we need the method of cofactors and the following definition.

Definition: The *minor* of an element a_{ij} is the determinant of the matrix formed by deleting the ith row and the jth column.

Example 2.10

Consider the following matrix

$$\begin{array}{cc} & a_{12} \quad a_{13} \\ & \downarrow \quad \downarrow \\ \mathbf{A} = \begin{bmatrix} 1 & 2 & 3 \\ 2 & 2 & 1 \\ 3 & 1 & 4 \end{bmatrix} \end{array}$$

The minor of $a_{12} = 2$ is the determinant of the matrix $\begin{bmatrix} 2 & 1 \\ 3 & 4 \end{bmatrix}$ obtained by deleting the first row

and the second column. Therefore, the minor of 2 is $\begin{vmatrix} 2 & 1 \\ 3 & 4 \end{vmatrix} = 8 - 3 = 5.$

The minor of $a_{13} = 3$ is the determinant of the matrix $\begin{bmatrix} 2 & 2 \\ 3 & 1 \end{bmatrix}$ obtained by deleting the first row

and the third column. Thus, the minor of 3 is $\begin{vmatrix} 2 & 2 \\ 3 & 1 \end{vmatrix} = 2 - 6 = -4.$

Definition: The cofactor of $a_{ij} = (-1)^{i+j} \times$ minor

Thus, the cofactor of an element will differ at most from its minor by sign. We now evaluate $(-1)^{i+j}$ for the first three elements of the **A** matrix given:

$$a_{11} : (-1)^{1+1} = 1$$

$$a_{12} : (-1)^{1+2} = -1$$

$$a_{13} : (-1)^{1+3} = 1$$

Notice that the signs for the elements in the first row alternate, and this pattern continues for all the elements in a 3×3 matrix. Thus, when evaluating the determinant for a 3×3 matrix it will be convenient to write down the pattern of signs and use it, rather than figuring out what $(-1)^{i+j}$ is for each element. That pattern of signs is:

$$\begin{bmatrix} + & - & + \\ - & + & - \\ + & - & + \end{bmatrix}$$

We denote the matrix of cofactors **C** as follows:

$$\mathbf{C} = \begin{bmatrix} c_{11} & c_{12} & c_{13} \\ c_{21} & c_{22} & c_{23} \\ c_{31} & c_{32} & c_{33} \end{bmatrix}$$

Now, *the determinant is obtained by expanding along any row or column of the matrix of cofactors.* Thus, for example, the determinant of **A** would be given by

$$|\mathbf{A}| = a_{11}c_{11} + a_{12}c_{12} + a_{13}c_{13}$$
(expanding along the first row)

or by

$$|\mathbf{A}| = a_{12}c_{12} + a_{22}c_{22} + a_{32}c_{32}$$
(expanding along the second column)

We now find the determinant of **A** by expanding along the first row:

Element	Minor	Cofactor	Element × Cofactor
$a_{11} = 1$	$\begin{vmatrix} 2 & 1 \\ 1 & 4 \end{vmatrix} = 7$	7	7
$a_{12} = 2$	$\begin{vmatrix} 2 & 1 \\ 3 & 4 \end{vmatrix} = 5$	-5	-10
$a_{13} = 3$	$\begin{vmatrix} 2 & 2 \\ 3 & 1 \end{vmatrix} = -4$	-4	-12

Therefore, $|\mathbf{A}| = 7 + (-10) + (-12) = -15$.

For a 4×4 matrix the pattern of signs is given by:

$$
\begin{array}{cccc}
+ & - & + & - \\
- & + & - & + \\
+ & - & + & - \\
- & + & - & +
\end{array}
$$

and the determinant is again evaluated by expanding along any row or column. However, in this case the minors are determinants of 3×3 matrices, and the procedure becomes quite tedious. Thus, we do not pursue it any further here.

In the example in 2.3 we obtained the following covariance matrix:

$$\mathbf{S} = \begin{bmatrix} 1.0 & 1.5 \\ 1.5 & 9.0 \end{bmatrix}$$

We also indicated at the beginning of this section that the determinant of **S** can be interpreted as the generalized variance for a set of variables.

Now, the generalized variance for the above two variable example is just $|\mathbf{S}| = 1 \times (9) - (1.5 \times 1.5) = 6.75$. Because for this example there is a covariance, the generalized variance is reduced by this. That is, some of the variance in variable 2 is accounted for by variance in variable 1. On the other hand, if the variables were uncorrelated (covariance = 0), then we would expect the generalized variance to be larger (because none of the variance in variable 2 can be accounted for by variance in variable 1), and this is indeed the case:

$$|\mathbf{S}| = \begin{vmatrix} 1 & 0 \\ 0 & 9 \end{vmatrix} = 9$$

variables, each of which has a variance. In addition, each pair of variables has a covariance. Thus, to represent variance in the multivariate case, we must take into account all the variances and covariances. This gives rise to a matrix of these quantities. Consider the simplest case of two dependent variables. The population covariance matrix Σ looks like this:

$$\Sigma = \begin{bmatrix} \sigma_1^2 & \sigma_{12} \\ \sigma_{21} & \sigma_2^2 \end{bmatrix}$$

where σ_1^2 is the population variance for variable 1 and σ_{12} is the population covariance for the two variables.

2.5 Inverse of a Matrix

The inverse of a square matrix **A** is a matrix $\mathbf{A}^{-1}$ that satisfies the following equation:

$$\mathbf{A}\,\mathbf{A}^{-1} = \mathbf{A}^{-1}\mathbf{A} = \mathbf{I}_n$$

where $\mathbf{I}_n$ is the identity matrix of order n. The identity matrix is simply a matrix with 1's on the main diagonal and 0's elsewhere.

$$\mathbf{I}_2 = \begin{bmatrix} 1 & 0 \\ 0 & 1 \end{bmatrix} \quad \mathbf{I}_3 = \begin{bmatrix} 1 & 0 & 0 \\ 0 & 1 & 0 \\ 0 & 0 & 1 \end{bmatrix}$$

Why is finding inverses important in statistical work? Because we do not literally have division with matrices, *inversion for matrices is the analogue of division for numbers.* This is why finding inverses is so important. An analogy with univariate ANOVA may be helpful here. In univariate ANOVA, recall that the test statistic $F = MS_b/MS_w = MS_b\,(MS_w)^{-1}$, that is, a ratio of between to within variability. The analogue of this test statistic in multivariate analysis of variance is $\mathbf{BW}^{-1}$, where **B** is a matrix that is the multivariate generalization of SS_b (sum of squares between); that is, it is a measure of how differential the effects of treatments have been on the set of dependent variables. In the multivariate case, we also want to "divide" the between-variability by the within-variability, but we don't have division per se. However, multiplying the **B** matrix by $\mathbf{W}^{-1}$ accomplishes this for us, because inversion is the analogue of division. Also, as shown in the next chapter, to obtain the regression coefficients for a multiple regression analysis, it is necessary to find the inverse of a matrix product involving the predictors.

2.5.1 Procedure for Finding the Inverse of a Matrix

1. Replace each element of the matrix **A** by its minor.
2. Form the matrix of cofactors, attaching the appropriate signs from the pattern of signs.
3. Take the transpose of the matrix of cofactors, forming what is called the adjoint.
4. Divide each element of the adjoint by the determinant of **A**.

For symmetric matrices (with which this text deals almost exclusively), taking the transpose is *not* necessary, and hence, when finding the inverse of a symmetric matrix, Step 3 is omitted.

We apply this procedure first to the simplest case, finding the inverse of a 2×2 matrix.

Example 2.11

$$\mathbf{D} = \begin{bmatrix} 4 & 2 \\ 2 & 6 \end{bmatrix}$$

The minor of 4 is the determinant of the matrix obtained by deleting the first row and the first column. What is left is simply the number 6, and the determinant of a number is that number. Thus we obtain the following matrix of minors:

$$\begin{bmatrix} 6 & 2 \\ 2 & 4 \end{bmatrix}$$

Now the pattern of signs for any 2×2 matrix is

$$\begin{bmatrix} + & - \\ - & + \end{bmatrix}$$

Therefore, the matrix of cofactors is

$$\begin{bmatrix} 6 & -2 \\ -2 & 4 \end{bmatrix}$$

The determinant of $\mathbf{D} = 6(4) - 2(2) = 20$.

Finally then, the inverse of $\mathbf{D}$ is obtained by dividing the matrix of cofactors by the determinant, obtaining

$$\mathbf{D}^{-1} = \begin{bmatrix} \dfrac{6}{20} & \dfrac{-2}{20} \\ \dfrac{-2}{20} & \dfrac{4}{20} \end{bmatrix}$$

To check that $\mathbf{D}^{-1}$ is indeed the inverse of $\mathbf{D}$, note that

$$\overset{\mathbf{D}}{\begin{bmatrix} 4 & 2 \\ 2 & 6 \end{bmatrix}} \overset{\mathbf{D}^{-1}}{\begin{bmatrix} \dfrac{6}{20} & \dfrac{-2}{20} \\ \dfrac{-2}{20} & \dfrac{4}{20} \end{bmatrix}} = \overset{\mathbf{D}^{-1}}{\begin{bmatrix} \dfrac{6}{20} & \dfrac{-2}{20} \\ \dfrac{-2}{20} & \dfrac{4}{20} \end{bmatrix}} \overset{\mathbf{D}}{\begin{bmatrix} 4 & 2 \\ 2 & 6 \end{bmatrix}} = \overset{\mathbf{I}_2}{\begin{bmatrix} 1 & 0 \\ 0 & 1 \end{bmatrix}}$$

Example 2.12

Let us find the inverse for the 3×3 **A** matrix that we found the determinant for in the previous section. Because **A** is a symmetric matrix, it is not necessary to find nine minors, but only six, since the inverse of a symmetric matrix is symmetric. Thus we just find the minors for the elements on and above the main diagonal.

$$\mathbf{A} = \begin{bmatrix} 1 & 2 & 3 \\ 2 & 2 & 1 \\ 3 & 1 & 4 \end{bmatrix}$$ Recall again that the minor of an element is the determinant of the matrix obtained by deleting the row and column that the element is in.

Element	Matrix	Minor
$a_{11} = 1$	$\begin{bmatrix} 2 & 1 \\ 1 & 4 \end{bmatrix}$	$2 \times 4 - 1 \times 1 = 7$
$a_{12} = 2$	$\begin{bmatrix} 2 & 1 \\ 3 & 4 \end{bmatrix}$	$2 \times 4 - 1 \times 3 = 5$
$a_{13} = 3$	$\begin{bmatrix} 2 & 2 \\ 3 & 1 \end{bmatrix}$	$2 \times 1 - 2 \times 3 = -4$
$a_{22} = 2$	$\begin{bmatrix} 1 & 3 \\ 3 & 4 \end{bmatrix}$	$1 \times 4 - 3 \times 3 = -5$
$a_{23} = 1$	$\begin{bmatrix} 1 & 2 \\ 3 & 1 \end{bmatrix}$	$1 \times 1 - 2 \times 3 = -5$
$a_{33} = 4$	$\begin{bmatrix} 1 & 2 \\ 2 & 2 \end{bmatrix}$	$1 \times 2 - 2 \times 2 = -2$

Therefore, the matrix of minors for **A** is

$$\begin{bmatrix} 7 & 5 & -4 \\ 5 & -5 & -5 \\ -4 & -5 & -2 \end{bmatrix}$$

Recall that the pattern of signs is

$$\begin{matrix} + & - & + \\ - & + & - \\ + & - & + \end{matrix}$$

Thus, attaching the appropriate sign to each element in the matrix of minors and completing Step 2 of finding the inverse we obtain:

$$\begin{bmatrix} 7 & -5 & -4 \\ -5 & -5 & 5 \\ -4 & 5 & -2 \end{bmatrix}$$

Now the determinant of **A** was found to be −15. Therefore, to complete the final step in finding the inverse we simply divide the preceding matrix by −15, and the inverse of **A** is

$$\mathbf{A}^{-1} = \begin{bmatrix} \dfrac{-7}{15} & \dfrac{1}{3} & \dfrac{4}{15} \\ \dfrac{1}{3} & \dfrac{1}{3} & \dfrac{-1}{3} \\ \dfrac{4}{15} & \dfrac{-1}{3} & \dfrac{2}{15} \end{bmatrix}$$

Again, we can check that this is indeed the inverse by multiplying it by **A** to see if the result is the identity matrix.

Note that for the inverse of a matrix to exist the determinant of the matrix must *not* be equal to 0. This is because in obtaining the inverse each element is divided by the determinant, and division by 0 is not defined. If the determinant of a matrix **B** = 0, we say **B** is *singular*. If |**B**| ≠ 0, we say **B** is nonsingular, and its inverse does exist.

2.6 SPSS Matrix Procedure

The SPSS matrix procedure was developed at the University of Wisconsin at Madison. It is described in some detail in *SPSS Advanced Statistics 7.5* (1997, pp. 469–512). Various matrix operations can be performed using the procedure, including multiplying matrices, finding the determinant of a matrix, finding the inverse of a matrix, etc. To indicate a matrix you must: (a) enclose the matrix in braces, (b) separate the elements of each row by commas, and (c) separate the rows by semicolons.

The matrix procedure *must* be run from the syntax window. To get to the syntax window, recall that you first click on FILE, then click on NEW, and finally click on SYNTAX. Every matrix program must begin with MATRIX. and end with END MATRIX. The periods are crucial, as each command *must* end with a period. To create a matrix A, use the following COMPUTE A = {2,4,1; 3,−2,5}.

Note that this is a 2 × 3 matrix. I do not like the use of COMPUTE to create a matrix, as this is definitely not intuitive. However, at present, that is the way the procedure is set up. In the program below I have created the matrices A, B and E, multiplied A and B, found the determinant and inverse for E, and printed out everything.

```
MATRIX.
COMPUTE A= { 2, 4, 1; 3,-2, 5} .
COMPUTE B= { 1, 2; 2, 1; 3, 4} .
COMPUTE C= A*B.
COMPUTE E= { 1,-1, 2;-1, 3, 1;2, 1, 10} .
COMPUTE DETE= DET(E).
COMPUTE EINV= INV(E).
PRINT A.
PRINT B.
PRINT C.
PRINT E.
PRINT DETE.
PRINT EINV.
END MATRIX.
```

The A, B, and E matrices are taken from the exercises. Notice in the preceding program that we have all commands, and in SPSS for Windows each command must end with a period. Also, note that each matrix is enclosed in braces, and rows are separated by semi-colons. Finally, a separate PRINT command is required to print out each matrix.

To run (or EXECUTE) the above program, click on RUN and then click on ALL from the dropdown menu. When you do, the following output will appear:

```
Matrix

Run Matrix procedure:

A
    2    4    1
    3   -2    5

B
    1    2
    2    1
    3    4

C
   13   12
   14   24

E
    1   -1    2
   -1    3    1
    2    1   10

DETE
    3

EINV
     9.666666667      4.000000000     -2.333333333
     4.000000000      2.000000000     -1.000000000
    -2.333333333     -1.000000000       .666666667

----End Matrix----
```

2.7 SAS IML Procedure

The SAS IML procedure replaced the older PROC MATRIX procedure that was used in version 5 of SAS. SAS IML is documented thoroughly in *SAS/IML: Usage and Reference, Version 6* (1990). There are several features that are very nice about SAS IML, and these are spelled out on pages 2 and 3 of the manual. We mention just three features:

1. SAS/IML is a programming language.
2. SAS/IML software uses operators that apply to entire matrices.
3. SAS/IML software is interactive.

IML is an acronym for Interactive Matrix Language. You can execute a command as soon as you enter it. We do not illustrate this feature, as we wish to compare it with the SPSS Matrix procedure. So we collect the SAS IML commands in a file (or module as they call it) and run it that way.

To indicate a matrix, you (a) enclose the matrix in braces, (b) separate the elements of each row by a blank(s), and (c) separate the columns by commas.

To illustrate use of the SAS IML procedure, we create the same matrices as we did with the SPSS matrix procedure and do the same operations and print out everything. Here is the file and the printout:

```
proc iml;
a= { 2 4 1, 3 -2 5} ;
b= { 1 2, 2 1, 3 4} ;
c= a*b;
e= { 1 -1 2, -1 3 1, 2 1 10} ;
dete= det(e);
einv= inv(e);
print a b c e dete einv;
```

A			B		C	
2	4	1	1	2	13	12
3	-2	5	2	1	14	24
			3	4		
E			DETE	EINV		
1	-1	2	3	9.6666667	4	-2.333333
-1	3	1		4	2	-1
2	1	10		-2.333333	-1	0.6666667

2.8 Summary

Matrix algebra is important in multivariate analysis because the data come in the form of a matrix when N subjects are measured on p variables. Although addition and subtraction of matrices is easy, multiplication of matrices is much more difficult and non-intuitive. Finding the determinant and inverse for 3 x 3 or larger square matrices is quite tedious. Finding the determinant is important because the determinant of a covariance matrix represents the generalized variance for a set of variables. Finding the inverse of a matrix is important since inversion for matrices is the analogue of division for numbers. Fortunately, SPSS MATRIX and SAS IML will do various matrix operations, including finding the determinant and inverse.

2.9 Exercises

1. Given:

$$\mathbf{A} = \begin{bmatrix} 2 & 4 & 1 \\ 3 & -2 & 5 \end{bmatrix} \quad \mathbf{B} = \begin{bmatrix} 1 & 2 \\ 2 & 1 \\ 3 & 4 \end{bmatrix} \quad \mathbf{C} = \begin{bmatrix} 1 & 3 & 5 \\ 6 & 2 & 1 \end{bmatrix}$$

$$\mathbf{D} = \begin{bmatrix} 4 & 2 \\ 2 & 6 \end{bmatrix} \quad \mathbf{E} = \begin{bmatrix} 1 & -1 & 2 \\ -1 & 3 & 1 \\ 2 & 1 & 10 \end{bmatrix} \quad \mathbf{X} = \begin{bmatrix} 1 & 2 \\ 3 & 1 \\ 4 & 6 \\ 5 & 7 \end{bmatrix}$$

$$\mathbf{u}' = (1,3), \mathbf{v} = \begin{bmatrix} 2 \\ 7 \end{bmatrix}$$

Find, where meaningful, each of the following:

(a) $\mathbf{A} + \mathbf{C}$

(b) $\mathbf{A} + \mathbf{B}$

(c) $\mathbf{AB}$

(d) $\mathbf{AC}$

(e) $\mathbf{u}'\mathbf{D}\,\mathbf{u}$

(f) $\mathbf{u}'\mathbf{v}$

(g) $(\mathbf{A} + \mathbf{C})'$

(h) $3\,\mathbf{C}$

(i) $|\mathbf{D}|$

(j) $\mathbf{D}^{-1}$

(k) $|\mathbf{E}|$

(l) $\mathbf{E}^{-1}$

(m) $\mathbf{u}'\mathbf{D}^{-1}\mathbf{u}$

(n) $\mathbf{BA}$ (compare this result with [c])

(o) $\mathbf{X}'\mathbf{X}$

2. In Chapter 3, we are interested in predicting each person's score on a dependent variable y from a linear combination of their scores on several predictors (x_i's). If there were three predictors, then the prediction equations for N subjects would look like this:

$$y_1 = e_1 + b_0 + b_1 x_{11} + b_2 x_{12} + b_3 x_{13}$$

$$y_2 = e_2 + b_0 + b_1 x_{21} + b_2 x_{22} + b_3 x_{23}$$

$$y_3 = e_3 + b_0 + b_1 x_{31} + b_2 x_{32} + b_3 x_{33}$$

$$\vdots \qquad \vdots \qquad \vdots$$

$$y_N = e_N + b_0 + b_1 x_{N1} + b_2 x_{N2} + b_3 x_{N3}$$

Note: The e_i's are the portion of y not predicted by the x's, and the b's are the regression coefficient. Express this set of prediction equations as a single matrix equation. Hint: The right hand portion of the equation will be of the form:

vector + matrix times vector

3. Using the approach detailed in section 2.3, find the matrix of variances and covariances for the following data:

x_1	x_2	x_3
4	3	10
5	2	11
8	6	15
9	6	9
10	8	5

4. Consider the following two situations:

(a) $s_1 = 10, s_2 = 7, r_{12} = .80$

(b) $s_1 = 9, s_2 = 6, r_{12} = .20$

For which situation is the generalized variance larger? Does this surprise you?

5. Calculate the determinant for

$$\mathbf{A} = \begin{bmatrix} 9 & 2 & 1 \\ 2 & 4 & 5 \\ 1 & 5 & 3 \end{bmatrix}$$

Could $\mathbf{A}$ be a covariance matrix for a set of variables? Explain.

6. Using SPSS MATRIX or SAS IML, find the inverse for the following 4 × 4 symmetric matrix:

$$
\begin{matrix}
6 & 8 & 7 & 6 \\
8 & 9 & 2 & 3 \\
7 & 2 & 5 & 2 \\
6 & 3 & 2 & 1
\end{matrix}
$$

7. Run the following SPSS MATRIX program and show that the output yields the matrix, determinant and inverse.

```
MATRIX.
COMPUTE A={6,2,4;2,3,1;4,1,5}.
COMPUTE DETA=DET(A).
COMPUTE AINV=INV(A).
PRINT A.
PRINT DETA.
PRINT AINV.
END MATRIX.
```

8. Consider the following two matrices:

$$
A = \begin{bmatrix} 2 & 3 \\ 3 & 6 \end{bmatrix} \quad B = \begin{bmatrix} 1 & 0 \\ 0 & 1 \end{bmatrix}
$$

Calculate the following products: AB and BA

What do you get in each case? Do you see now why B is called the identity matrix?

3

Multiple Regression

3.1 Introduction

In multiple regression we are interested in predicting a dependent variable from a set of predictors. In a previous course in statistics the reader probably studied simple regression, predicting a dependent variable from a single predictor. An example would be predicting college GPA from high school GPA. Because human behavior is complex and influenced by many factors, such single-predictor studies are necessarily limited in their predictive power. For example, in a college GPA study, we are able to predict college GPA better by considering other predictors such as scores on standardized tests (verbal, quantitative), and some noncognitive variables, such as study habits and attitude toward education. That is, we look to other predictors (often test scores) that tap other aspects of criterion behavior.

Consider two other examples of multiple regression studies:

1. Feshbach, Adelman, and Fuller (1977) conducted a study of 850 middle-class children. The children were measured in kindergarten on a battery of variables: WPPSI, deHirsch-Jansky Index (assessing various linguistic and perceptual motor skills), the Bender Motor Gestalt, and a Student Rating Scale developed by the authors that measures various cognitive and affective behaviors and skills. These measures were used to predict reading achievement for these same children in grades 1, 2, and 3.

2. Crystal (1988) attempted to predict chief executive officer (CEO) pay for the top 100 of last year's Fortune 500 and the 100 top entries from last year's Service 500. He used the following predictors: company size, company performance, company risk, government regulation, tenure, location, directors, ownership, and age. He found that only about 39% of the variance in CEO pay can be accounted for by these factors.

In modeling the relationship between y and the x's, we are assuming that a *linear* model is appropriate. Of course, it is possible that a more complex model (curvilinear) may be necessary to predict y accurately. Polynomial regression may be appropriate, or if there is nonlinearity in the parameters, then either the SPSS NONLINEAR program or the SAS nonlinear program (*SAS/STAT User's Guide*, vol. 2, 1990, chap. 29) can be used to fit a model.

This is a long chapter with many sections, not all of which are equally important. The three most fundamental sections are on model selection (3.8), checking assumptions underlying the linear regression model (3.10), and model validation (3.11). The other sections should be thought of as supportive of these. We discuss several ways of selecting a "good" set of predictors, and illustrate these with two computer examples.

An important theme throughout this entire book is determining whether the assumptions underlying a given analysis are tenable. This chapter initiates that theme, and we can see that there are various graphical plots available for assessing assumptions underlying the regression model. Another very important theme throughout this book is the mathematical maximization nature of many advanced statistical procedures, and the concomitant possibility of results' looking very good on the sample on which they were derived (because of capitalization on chance), but not generalizing to a population. Thus, it becomes extremely important to validate the results on an independent sample(s) of data, or at least obtain an estimate of the generalizability of the results. Section 3.11 illustrates both of the aforementioned ways of checking the validity of a given regression model.

A final pedagogical point on reading this chapter: Section 3.14 deals with outliers and influential data points. We already indicated in Chapter 1, with several examples, the dramatic effect an outlier(s) can have on the results of any statistical analysis. Section 3.14 is rather lengthy, however, and the applied researcher may not want to "plow" through all the details. Recognizing this, I begin that section with a brief overview discussion of statistics for assessing outliers and influential data points, with prescriptive advice on how to flag such cases from computer printout.

We wish to emphasize that our focus in this chapter is on the use of multiple regression for prediction. Another broad related area is the use of regression for explanation. Cohen and Cohen (1983) and Pedhazur (1982) have excellent, extended discussions of the use of regression for explanation (e.g., causal modeling).

There have been innumerable books written on regression analysis. In my opinion, the books by Cohen and Cohen (1983), Pedhazur (1982), Myers (1990), Weisberg (1985), Belsley, Kuh, and Welsch (1980) and Draper and Smith (1981) are worthy of special attention. The first two books are written for individuals in the social sciences and have very good narrative discussions. The Myers and Weisberg books are excellent in terms of the modern approach to regression analysis, and have especially good treatments of regression diagnostics. The Draper and Smith book is one of the classic texts, generally used for a more mathematical treatment, with most of its examples slanted toward the physical sciences.

We start this chapter with a brief discussion of simple regression, which most readers probably encountered in a previous statistics course.

3.2 Simple Regression

For one predictor the mathematical model is

$$y_i = \beta_0 + \beta_1 x_i + e_i \quad i = 1, 2, \ldots, n$$

where b_0 and b_1 are parameters to be estimated. The e_i's are the errors of prediction, and are assumed to be independent, with constant variance and normally distributed with a mean of 0. If these assumptions are valid for a given set of data, then the estimated errors ($\hat{e}_i$) should have similar properties. For example, the $\hat{e}_i$ should be normally distributed, or at least approximately normally distributed. This is considered further in section 3.9. The $\hat{e}_i$ are called the residuals. How do we estimate the parameters? The *least squares* criterion is used; that is, the sum of the squared estimated errors of prediction is minimized:

$$\hat{e}_1^2 + \hat{e}_2^2 + \cdots + \hat{e}_n^2 = \sum_{i=1}^{n} \hat{e}_i^2 = \min$$

Now, $\hat{e}_i = y_i - \hat{y}_i$, where y_i is the actual score on the dependent variable and $\hat{y}_i$ is the estimated score for the ith subject.

The scores for each subject (x_i, y_i) define a point in the plane. What the least squares criterion does is find the line that best fits the points. Geometrically, this corresponds to minimizing the sum of the squared vertical distances ($\hat{e}_i^2$) of each subject's score from their estimated y score. This is illustrated in Figure 3.1.

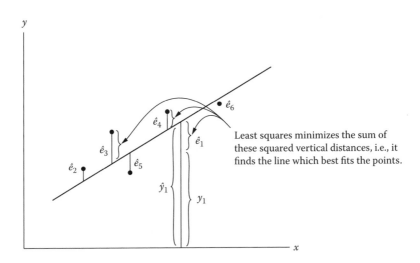

FIGURE 3.1
Geometrical representation of least squares criterion.

TABLE 3.1

Control Lines for Simple Regression
on SPSS Regression

	TITLE 'SIMPLE REGRESSION ON SESAME DATA'.
	DATA LIST FREE/PREBODY POSTBODY.
	BEGIN DATA.
	DATA LINES
	END DATA.
	LIST.
	REGRESSION DESCRIPTIVES = DEFAULT/
	VARIABLES = PREBODY POSTBODY/
	DEPENDENT = POSTBODY/
①	METHOD = ENTER/
②	SCATTERPLOT (POSTBODY, PREBODY)/
③	RESIDUALS = HISTOGRAM(ZRESID)/.

① DESCRIPTIVES = DEFAULT subcommand yields the means, standard deviations and the correlation matrix for the variables.

② This SCATTERPLOT subcommand yields the scatterplot for the variables. Note that the variables have been standardized (z scores) and then plotted.

③ This RESIDUALS subcommand yields the histogram of the standardized residuals.

Example 3.1

To illustrate simple regression we consider a small part of a Sesame Street database from Glasnapp and Poggio (1985), who present data on many variables, including 12 background variables and 8 achievement variables, for 240 subjects. Sesame Street was developed as a television series aimed mainly at teaching preschool skills to 3- to 5-year-old children. Data were collected on many achievement variables both before (pretest) and after (posttest) viewing of the series. We consider here only one of the achievement variables, knowledge of body parts. In particular, we consider pretest and posttest data on body parts for a sample of 80 children.

The control lines for running the simple regression on SPSSX REGRESSION are given in Table 3.1, along with annotation on how to obtain the scatterplot and plot of the residuals in the same run. Figure 3.2 presents the scatterplot, along with some selected printout. The scatterplot shows a fair amount of clustering, reflecting the moderate correlation of .583, about the regression line. Table 3.2 has the histogram of the standardized residuals, which indicates a fair approximation to a normal distribution.

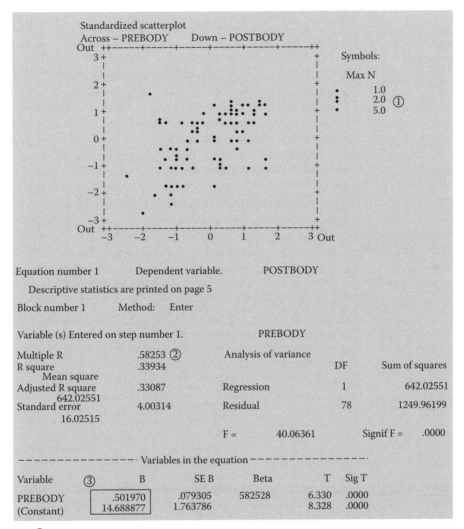

Equation number 1   Dependent variable.   POSTBODY

Descriptive statistics are printed on page 5

Block number 1   Method: Enter

Variable (s) Entered on step number 1.   PREBODY

		Analysis of variance		
Multiple R	.58253 ②			
R square	.33934		DF	Sum of squares
Mean square				
Adjusted R square	.33087	Regression	1	642.02551
642.02551				
Standard error	4.00314	Residual	78	1249.96199
16.02515				
		F = 40.06361	Signif F =	.0000

— — — — — — — — — — — — — — Variables in the equation — — — — — — — — — — — — — —

Variable ③	B	SE B	Beta	T	Sig T
PREBODY	.501970	.079305	582528	6.330	.0000
(Constant)	14.688877	1.763786		8.328	.0000

① This legend means there is one observation whenever a single dot appears, two observations whenever a : appears, and 5 observations where there is an asterisk (*).

② The multiple correlation here is in fact the simple correlation between postbody and prebody, since there is just one predictor.

③ These are the raw coefficients which define the prediction equation: POSTBODY = .50197 PREBODY + 14.6888.

FIGURE 3.2
Scatterplot and selected printout for simple regression.

TABLE 3.2

Histogram of Standardized Residuals

NExp	N	(* = 1 Cases, . : = Normal Curve)
0	.09	Out
0	.04	3.00
0	.06	2.88
0	.09	2.75
0	.13	2.63
0	.18	2.50
0	.24	2.38
0	.32	2.25
0	.42	2.13
1	.54	2.00 :
1	.69	1.88 :
1	.86	1.75 :
1	1.07	1.63 :
2	1.30	1.50 :*
0	1.55	1.38 .
3	1.83	1.25 *:*
1	2.12	1.13 *.
4	2.42	1.00 *:**
2	2.72	.88 **.
6	3.01	.75 **:***
6	3.28	.63 **:***
4	3.52	.50 ***:
5	3.72	.38 ***:*
4	3.86	.25 ***:
4	3.96	.13 ***:
2	3.99	.00 **.
7	3.96	−.13 ***:***
1	3.86	−.25 * .
1	3.72	−.38 * .
3	3.52	−.50 ***.
3	3.28	−.63 **:
1	3.01	−.75 * .
2	2.72	−.88 **.
2	2.42	−1.00 *:
2	2.12	−1.13 *:
3	1.83	−1.25 *:*
1	1.55	−1.38 *.
0	1.30	−1.50 .
1	1.07	−1.63 :
2	.86	−1.75 :*
1	.69	−1.88 :
1	.54	−2.00 :
1	.42	−2.13 *
1	.32	−2.25 *
0	.24	−2.38
0	.18	−2.50
0	.13	−2.63
0	.09	−2.75
0	.06	−2.88
0	.04	−3.00
0	.09	Out

3.3 Multiple Regression for Two Predictors: Matrix Formulation

The linear model for two predictors is a simple extension of what we had for one predictor:

$$y_i = \beta_0 + \beta_1 x_1 + \beta_2 x_2 + e_i$$

where β_0 (regression constant), β_1 and β_2 are the parameters to be estimated, and e is error of prediction. We consider a small data set to illustrate the estimation process.

y	x_1	x_2
3	2	1
2	3	5
4	5	3
5	7	6
8	8	7

We model each subject's y score as a linear function of the β's:

$$y_1 = 3 = \boxed{1 \times \beta_0 + 2 \times \beta_1 + 1 \times \beta_2} + e_1$$

$$y_2 = 2 = \boxed{1 \times \beta_0 + 3 \times \beta_1 + 5 \times \beta_2} + e_2$$

$$y_3 = 4 = \boxed{1 \times \beta_0 + 5 \times \beta_1 + 3 \times \beta_2} + e_3$$

$$y_4 = 5 = \boxed{1 \times \beta_0 + 7 \times \beta_1 + 6 \times \beta_2} + e_4$$

$$y_5 = 8 = \boxed{1 \times \beta_0 + 8 \times \beta_1 + 7 \times \beta_2} + e_5$$

This series of equations can be expressed as a single matrix equation:

$$\mathbf{y} = \begin{bmatrix} 3 \\ 2 \\ 4 \\ 5 \\ 8 \end{bmatrix} = \overset{\mathbf{X}}{\begin{bmatrix} 1 & 2 & 1 \\ 1 & 3 & 5 \\ 1 & 5 & 3 \\ 1 & 7 & 6 \\ 1 & 8 & 7 \end{bmatrix}} \overset{\boldsymbol{\beta}}{\begin{bmatrix} \beta_0 \\ \beta_1 \\ \beta_2 \end{bmatrix}} + \overset{\mathbf{e}}{\begin{bmatrix} e_1 \\ e_2 \\ e_3 \\ e_4 \\ e_5 \end{bmatrix}}$$

It is pretty clear that the y scores and the $\mathbf{e}$ define column vectors, while not so clear is how the boxed-in area can be represented as the product of two matrices, $\mathbf{X}\boldsymbol{\beta}$.

The first column of 1's is used to obtain the regression constant. The remaining two columns contain the scores for the subjects on the two predictors. Thus, the classic matrix equation for multiple regression is:

$$\mathbf{y} = \mathbf{X}\boldsymbol{\beta} + \mathbf{e} \tag{1}$$

Now, it can be shown using the calculus that the least square estimates of the β's are given by:

$$\hat{\beta} = (X'X)^{-1}X'y \tag{2}$$

Thus, for our data the estimated regression coefficients would be:

$$\hat{\beta} \left\{ \begin{array}{ccccc} & X' & & & \\ \begin{bmatrix} 1 & 1 & 1 & 1 & 1 \\ 2 & 3 & 5 & 7 & 8 \\ 1 & 5 & 3 & 6 & 7 \end{bmatrix} & \overset{X}{\begin{bmatrix} 1 & 2 & 1 \\ 1 & 3 & 5 \\ 1 & 5 & 3 \\ 1 & 7 & 6 \\ 1 & 8 & 7 \end{bmatrix}} \end{array} \right\}^{-1} \overset{X'}{\begin{bmatrix} 1 & 1 & 1 & 1 & 1 \\ 2 & 3 & 5 & 7 & 8 \\ 1 & 5 & 3 & 6 & 7 \end{bmatrix}} \overset{y}{\begin{bmatrix} 3 \\ 2 \\ 4 \\ 5 \\ 8 \end{bmatrix}}$$

Let us do this in pieces. First

$$X'X = \begin{bmatrix} 5 & 25 & 22 \\ 25 & 151 & 130 \\ 22 & 130 & 120 \end{bmatrix} \text{ and } X'y = \begin{bmatrix} 22 \\ 131 \\ 111 \end{bmatrix}$$

Furthermore, the reader should show that

$$(X'X)^{-1} = \frac{1}{1016} \begin{bmatrix} 1220 & -140 & -72 \\ -140 & 116 & -100 \\ -72 & -100 & 130 \end{bmatrix}$$

where 1016 is the determinant of $X'X$. Thus, the estimated regression coefficients are given by

$$\hat{\beta} = \frac{1}{1016} \begin{bmatrix} 1220 & -140 & -72 \\ -140 & 116 & -100 \\ -72 & -100 & 130 \end{bmatrix} \begin{bmatrix} 22 \\ 131 \\ 111 \end{bmatrix} = \begin{bmatrix} .50 \\ 1 \\ -.25 \end{bmatrix}$$

Therefore, the regression (prediction) equation is

$$\hat{y}_i = .50 + x_1 - .25x_2$$

To illustrate the use of this equation, we find the predicted score for Subject 3 and the residual for that subject:

$$\hat{y}_3 = .5 + 5 - .25(3) = 4.75$$

$$\hat{e}_3 = y_3 - \hat{y}_3 = 4 - 4.75 = -.75$$

3.4 Mathematical Maximization Nature of Least Squares Regression

In general then, in multiple regression the *linear combination* of the x's that is maximally correlated with y is sought. Minimizing the sum of squared errors of prediction is equivalent to *maximizing* the correlation between the observed and predicted y scores. This maximized Pearson correlation is called the multiple correlation, shown as $R = r_{y_i\hat{y}_i}$. Nunnally (1978, p. 164) characterized the procedure as "wringing out the last ounce of predictive power" (obtained from the linear combination of x's, that is, from regression equation). Because the correlation is maximum for the sample from which it is derived, when the regression equation is applied to an independent sample from the same population (i.e., cross-validated), the predictive power drops off. If the predictive power drops off sharply, then the equation is of limited utility. That is, it has no generalizability, and hence is of limited scientific value. After all, we derive the prediction equation for the purpose of predicting with it on future (other) samples. If the equation does not predict well on other samples, then it is not fulfilling the purpose for which it was designed.

Sample size (n) and the number of predictors (k) are two crucial factors that determine how well a given equation will cross-validate (i.e., generalize). In particular, the n/k ratio is crucial. For small ratios (5:1 or less) the shrinkage in predictive power can be substantial. A study by Guttman (1941) illustrates this point. He had 136 subjects and 84 predictors, and found the multiple correlation on the original sample to be .73. However, when the prediction equation was applied to an independent sample, the new correlation was only .04. In other words, the good predictive power on the original sample was due to capitalization on chance, and the prediction equation had no generalizability.

We return to the cross-validation issue in more detail later in this chapter, where we show that *for social science research, about 15 subjects per predictor are needed for a reliable equation*, that is, for an equation that will cross-validate with little loss in predictive power.

3.5 Breakdown of Sum of Squares and *F* Test for Multiple Correlation

In analysis of variance we broke down variability about the grand mean into between- and within-variability. In regression analysis, variability about the mean is broken down into variability due to regression and variability about the regression. To get at the breakdown, we start with the following identity:

$$y_i - \hat{y}_i = (y_i - \bar{y}) - (\hat{y}_i - \bar{y})$$

Now we square both sides, obtaining

$$(y_i - \hat{y}_i)^2 = [(y_i - \bar{y}) - (\hat{y}_i - \bar{y})]^2$$

Then we sum over the subjects, from 1 to n:

$$\sum_{i=1}^{n}(y_i - \hat{y}_i)^2 = \sum_{i=1}^{n}[(y_i - \bar{y}) - (\hat{y}_i - \bar{y})]^2$$

By algebraic manipulation (see Draper & Smith, 1981, pp. 17–18), this can be rewritten as:

$$\sum(y_i - \bar{y})^2 = \sum(y_i - \hat{y}_i)^2 + \sum(\hat{y}_i - \bar{y})^2 \quad (3)$$

| sum of squares about mean | = | sum of squares about regression (SS_{res}) | + | sum of squares due to regression (SS_{reg}) |

| $df{:}\, n-1$ | = | $(n-k-1)$ | + | k(df = degrees of freedom) |

This results in the following analysis of variance table and the F test for determining whether the population multiple correlation is different from 0.

Analysis of Variance Table for Regression

Source	SS	df	MS	F
Regression	SS_{reg}	k	S_{reg}/k	$\dfrac{MS_{reg}}{MS_{res}}$
Residual (error)	SS_{res}	$n-k-1$	$SS_{res}/(n-k-1)$	

Recall that since the residual for each subject is $\hat{e}_i = y_i - \hat{y}_i$, the mean square error term can be written as $MS_{res} = \Sigma\hat{e}_i^2/(n-k-1)$. Now, R^2 (squared multiple correlation) is given by:

$$R^2 = \frac{\text{sum of squares due to regression}}{\text{sum of squares about the mean}} = \frac{\Sigma(\hat{y}_i - \bar{y})^2}{\Sigma(y_i - \bar{y})^2} = \frac{SS_{reg}}{SS_{tot}}$$

Thus, R^2 measures the proportion of total variance on y that is accounted for by the set of predictors. By simple algebra then we can rewrite the F test in terms of R^2 as follows:

$$F = \frac{R^2/k}{(1-R^2)/(n-k-1)} \text{ with } k \text{ and } (n-k-1)df \quad (4)$$

We feel this test is of limited utility, because it does *not necessarily* imply that the equation will cross-validate well, and this is the crucial issue in regression analysis.

Example 3.2

An investigator obtains $R^2 = .50$ on a sample of 50 subjects with 10 predictors. Do we reject the null hypothesis that the population multiple correlation = 0?

$$F = \frac{.50/10}{(1-.50)/(50-10-1)} = 3.9 \text{ with } 10 \text{ and } 39\, df$$

This is significant at .01 level, since the critical value is 2.8.

However, because the *n/k* ratio is only 5/1, the prediction equation will probably not predict well on other samples and is therefore of questionable utility.

Myers' (1990) response to the question of what constitutes an acceptable value for R^2 is illuminating:

> This is a difficult question to answer, and, in truth, what is acceptable depends on the scientific field from which the data were taken. A chemist, charged with doing a linear calibration on a high precision piece of equipment, certainly expects to experience a very high R^2 value (perhaps exceeding .99), while a behavioral scientist, dealing in data reflecting human behavior, may feel fortunate to observe an R^2 as high as .70. An experienced model fitter senses when the value of R^2 is large enough, given the situation confronted. Clearly, some scientific phenomena lend themselves to modeling with considerably more accuracy then others. (p. 37)

His point is that how well one can predict depends on *context*. In the physical sciences, generally quite accurate prediction is possible. In the social sciences, where we are attempting to predict human behavior (which can be influenced by many systematic and some idiosyncratic factors), prediction is much more difficult.

3.6 Relationship of Simple Correlations to Multiple Correlation

The ideal situation, in terms of obtaining a high R, would be to have each of the predictors significantly correlated with the dependent variable and for the predictors to be uncorrelated with each other, so that they measure different constructs and are able to predict different parts of the variance on *y*. Of course, in practice we will not find this because almost all variables are correlated to some degree. A good situation in practice then would be one in which most of our predictors correlate significantly with *y* and the predictors have relatively low correlations among themselves. To illustrate these points further, consider the following three patterns of intercorrelations for three predictors.

		X_1	X_2	X_3			X_1	X_2	X_3			X_1	X_2	X_3
(1)	Y	.20	.10	.30	(2)	Y	.60	.50	.70	(3)	Y	.60	.70	.70
	X_1		.50	.40		X_1		.20	.30		X_1		.70	.60
	X_2			.60		X_2			.20		X_2			.80

In which of these cases would you expect the multiple correlation to be the largest and the smallest respectively? Here it is quite clear that R will be the smallest for 1 because the highest correlation of any of the predictors with *y* is .30, whereas for the other two patterns at least one of the predictors has a correlation of .70 with *y*. Thus, we know that R will be at least .70 for Cases 2 and 3, whereas for Case 1 we know only that R will be at least .30. Furthermore, there is no chance that R for Case 1 might become larger than that for cases 2 and 3, because the intercorrelations among the predictors for 1 are approximately as large or larger than those for the other two cases.

We would expect R to be largest for Case 2 because each of the predictors is moderately to strongly tied to *y* and there are low intercorrelations (i.e., little redundancy) among the predictors, exactly the kind of situation we would hope to find in practice. We would expect R to be greater in Case 2 than in Case 3, because in Case 3 there is considerable redundancy among the predictors. Although the correlations of the predictors with *y* are slightly higher in Case 3 (.60, .70, .70) than in Case 2 (.60, .50, .70), the much higher inter-correlations among the predictors for Case 3 will severely limit the ability of X_2 and X_3 to predict additional variance beyond that of X_1 (and hence significantly increase R), whereas this will not be true for Case 2.

3.7 Multicollinearity

When there are moderate to high intercorrelations among the predictors, as is the case when several cognitive measures are used as predictors, the problem is referred to as *multicollinearity*. Multicollinearity poses a real problem for the researcher using multiple regression for three reasons:

1. It severely limits the size of R, because the predictors are going after much of the same variance on y. A study by Dizney and Gromen (1967) illustrates very nicely how multicollinearity among the predictors limits the size of R. They studied how well reading proficiency (x_1) and writing proficiency (x_2) would predict course grades in college German. The following correlation matrix resulted:

	x_1	x_2	y
x_1	1.00	.58	.33
x_2		1.00	.45
y			1.00

   Note the multicollinearity for x_1 and x_2 ($r_{x_1 x_2} = .58$), and also that x_2 has a simple correlation of .45 with y. The multiple correlation R was only .46. Thus, the rela-tively high correlation between reading and writing severely limited the ability of reading to add hardly anything (only .01) to the prediction of German grade above and beyond that of writing.

2. Multicollinearity makes determining the importance of a given predictor difficult because the effects of the predictors are confounded due to the correlations among them.

3. Multicollinearity increases the variances of the regression coefficients. The greater these variances, the more unstable the prediction equation will be.

The following are two methods for diagnosing multicollinearity:

1. Examine the simple correlations among the predictors from the correlation matrix. These should be observed, and are easy to understand, but the researcher needs to be warned that they do not always indicate the extent of multicollinearity. More subtle forms of multicollinearity may exist. One such more subtle form is dis-cussed next.

2. Examine the variance inflation factors for the predictors.

The quantity $1/(1 - R_j^2)$ is called the *j*th *variance inflation factor*, where R_j^2 is the squared multiple correlation for predicting the *j*th predictor from all other predictors.

The variance inflation factor for a predictor indicates whether there is a strong linear association between it and all the remaining predictors. It is distinctly possible for a predictor to have only moderate or relatively weak associations with the other predictors in terms of simple correlations, and yet to have a quite high R when regressed on all the other predictors. When is the value for a variance inflation factor large enough to cause concern? Myers (1990) offered the following suggestion: "Though no rule of thumb on numerical values is foolproof, it is generally believed that if any VIF exceeds 10, there is reason for at least some concern; then one should consider variable deletion or an alternative to least squares estimation to combat the problem" (p. 369). The variance inflation factors are easily obtained from SAS REG (Table 3.6).

There are at least three ways of combating multicollinearity. One way is to combine predictors that are highly correlated. For example, if there are three measures relating to a single construct that have intercorrelations of about .80 or larger, then add them to form a single measure.

A second way, if one has initially a fairly large set of predictors, is to consider doing a principal components analysis (a type of factor analysis) to reduce to a much smaller set of predictors. For example, if there are 30 predictors, we are undoubtedly not measuring 30 different constructs. A factor analysis will tell us how many main constructs we are actually measuring. The factors become the new predictors, and because the factors are uncorrelated by construction, we eliminate the multicollinearity problem. Principal components analysis is discussed in some detail in Chapter 11. In that chapter we show how to use SAS and SPSS to do a components analysis on a set of predictors and then pass the factor scores to a regression program.

A third way of combating multicollinearity is to use a technique called ridge regression. This approach is beyond the scope of this text, although Myers (1990) has a nice discussion for those who are interested.

3.8 Model Selection

Various methods are available for selecting a good set of predictors:

1. *Substantive Knowledge.* As Weisberg (1985) noted, "The single most important tool in selecting a subset of variables for use in a model is the analyst's knowledge of the substantive area under study" (p. 210). It is important for the investigator to be judicious in his or her selection of predictors. Far too many investigators have abused multiple regression by throwing everything in the hopper, often merely because the variables are available. Cohen (1990), among others, commented on the indiscriminate use of variables: I have encountered too many studies with prodigious numbers of dependent variables, or with what seemed to me far too many independent variables, or (heaven help us) both.

There are several good reasons for generally preferring to work with a small number of predictors: (a) principle of scientific parsimony, (b) reducing the number of predictors improves the n/k ratio, and this helps cross validation prospects, and (c) note the following from Lord and Novick (1968):

> Experience in psychology and in many other fields of application has shown that it is seldom worthwhile to include very many predictor variables in a regression equation, for the incremental validity of new variables, after a certain point, is usually very low.

This is true because tests tend to overlap in content and consequently the addition of a fifth or sixth test may add little that is new to the battery and still relevant to the criterion. (p. 274)

Or consider the following from Ramsey and Schafer (p. 325):

There are two good reasons for paring down a large number of exploratory variables to a smaller set. The first reason is somewhat philosophical: simplicity is preferable to complexity. Thus, redundant and unnecessary variables should be excluded on principle. The second reason is more concrete: unnecessary terms in the model yield less precise inferences.

2. *Sequential Methods.* These are the forward, stepwise, and backward selection procedures that are very popular with many researchers. All these procedures involve a partialing-out process; i.e., they look at the contribution of a predictor with the effects of the other predictors partialed out, or held constant. Many readers may have been exposed in a previous statistics course to the notion of a partial correlation, but a review is nevertheless in order.

The partial correlation between variables 1 and 2 with variable 3 partialed from both 1 and 2 is the correlation with variable 3 held constant, as the reader may recall. The formula for the partial correlation is given by:

$$R_{12.3} = \frac{r_{12} - r_{13}\, r_{23}}{\sqrt{1 - r_{13}^2}\,\sqrt{1 - r_{23}^2}} \tag{5}$$

Let us put this in the context of multiple regression. Suppose we wish to know what the partial of y (dependent variable) is with predictor 2 with predictor 1 partialed out. The formula would be, following what we have above:

$$R_{y2.1} = \frac{r_{y2} - r_{y1}\, r_{21}}{\sqrt{1 - r_{y1}^2}\,\sqrt{1 - r_{21}^2}} \tag{6}$$

We apply this formula to show how SPSS obtains the partial correlation of .528 for INTEREST in Table 3.4 under EXCLUDED VARIABLES in the first upcoming computer example. In this example CLARITY (abbreviated as clr) entered first, having a correlation of .862 with dependent variable INSTEVAL (abbreviated as inst). The correlations below are taken from the correlation matrix, given near the beginning of Table 3.4.

$$R_{\text{inst int.clr}} = \frac{.435 - (.862)\,(.20)}{\sqrt{1 - .862^2}\,\sqrt{1 - .20^2}}$$

The correlation between the two predictors is .20, as shown.

We now give a brief description of the forward, stepwise, and backward selection procedures.

FORWARD—The first predictor that has an opportunity to enter the equation is the one with the largest simple correlation with y. If this predictor is significant, then the predictor with the largest partial correlation with y is considered, etc. At some stage a given predictor will not make a significant contribution and the procedure terminates. It is important to remember that with this procedure, once a predictor gets into the equation, it stays.

STEPWISE—This is basically a variation on the forward selection procedure. However, at each stage of the procedure, a test is made of the least useful predictor. The importance of each predictor is constantly reassessed. Thus, a predictor that may have been the best entry candidate earlier may now be superfluous.

BACKWARD—The steps are as follows: (a) An equation is computed with ALL the predictors. (b) The partial F is calculated for every predictor, treated as though it were the last predictor to enter the equation. (c) The smallest partial F value, say F_1, is compared with a preselected significance, say F_0. If $F_1 < F_0$, remove that predictor and recomputed the equation with the remaining variables. Reenter stage B.

3. *Mallows' C_p.* Before we introduce Mallows' C_p, it is important to consider the consequences of underfitting (important variables are left out of the model) and overfitting (having variables in the model that make essentially no contribution or are marginal). Myers (1990, pp. 178–180) has an excellent discussion on the impact of underfitting and overfitting, and notes that, "A model that is too simple may suffer from biased coefficients and biased prediction, while an overly complicated model can result in large variances, both in the coefficients and in the prediction."

This measure was introduced by C. L. Mallows (1973) as a criterion for selecting a model. It measures total squared error, and it was recommended by Mallows to choose the model(s) where $C_p \approx p$. For these models, the amount of underfitting or overfitting is minimized. Mallows' criterion may be written as

$$C_p = p + \frac{(s^2 - \hat{\sigma}^2)(N - p)}{\hat{\sigma}^2}(p = k + 1) \tag{7}$$

where s^2 is the residual variance for the model being evaluated and $\hat{\sigma}^2$ is an estimate of the residual variance that is usually based on the full model.

4. *Use of MAXR Procedure From SAS.* There are *nine* methods of model selection in the SAS REG program (*SAS/STAT User's Guide*, Vol. 2, 1990), MAXR being one of them. This procedure produces several models; the best one-variable model, the best two-variable model, and so on. Here is the description of the procedure from the *SAS/STAT* manual:

> The MAXR method begins by finding the one variable model producing the highest R^2. Then another variable, the one that yields the greatest increase in R^2, is added. Once the two variable model is obtained, each of the variables in the model is compared to each variable not in the model. For each comparison, MAXR determines if removing one variable and replacing it with the other variable increases R^2. After comparing all possible switches, MAXR makes the switch that produces the largest increase in R^2. Comparisons begin again, and the process continues until MAXR finds that no switch could increase R^2.... Another variable is then added to the model, and the comparing and switching process is repeated to find the best three variable model. (p. 1398)

5. *All Possible Regressions.* If you wish to follow this route, then the SAS REG program should be considered. The number of regressions increases quite sharply as k increases, however, the program will efficiently identify good subsets. Good subsets are those which have the smallest Mallows' C value. I have illustrated this in Table 3.6. This pool of candidate models can then be examined further using regression diagnostics and cross-validity criteria to be mentioned later.

Use of one or more of the above methods will often yield a number of models of roughly equal efficacy. As Myers (1990) noted, "The successful model builder will eventually understand that with many data sets, several models can be fit that would be of nearly equal effectiveness. Thus the problem that one deals with is the selection of *one model* from a pool of *candidate models*" (p. 164). One of the problems with the stepwise methods, which are very frequently used, is that they have led many investigators to conclude that they have found *the* best model, when in fact there may be some better models or several other models that are about as good. As Huberty noted (1989), "And one or more of these subsets may be more interesting or relevant in a substantive sense" (p. 46).

3.8.1 Semipartial Correlations

We consider a procedure that, for a *given ordering* of the predictors, will enable us to determine the unique contribution each predictor is making in accounting for variance on y. This procedure, which uses semipartial correlations, will disentangle the correlations among the predictors.

The partial correlation between variables 1 and 2 with Variable 3 partialed from both 1 and 2 is the correlation with Variable 3 held constant, as the reader may recall. The formula for the partial correlation is given by

$$r_{12.3} = \frac{r_{12} - r_{13}r_{23}}{\sqrt{1 - r_{13}^2}\sqrt{1 - r_{23}^2}}$$

We have introduced the partial correlation first for two reasons: (1) the semipartial correlation is a variant of the partial correlation and (2) the partial correlation will be involved in computing more complicated semipartial correlations.

For breaking down R^2 we will want to work with the semipartial, sometimes called part, correlation. The formula for the semipartial correlation is:

$$r_{12.3(s)} = \frac{r_{12} - r_{13}r_{23}}{\sqrt{1 - r_{23}^2}}$$

The only difference between this equation and the previous one is that the denominator here doesn't contain the standard deviation of the partialed scores for Variable 1.

In multiple correlation we wish to partial the independent variables (the predictors) from one another, but not from the dependent variable. We wish to leave the dependent variable intact, and not partial any variance attributable to the predictors. Let $R^2_{y12 \ldots k}$ denote the squared multiple correlation for the k predictors, where the predictors appear after the dot. Consider the case of one dependent variable and three predictors. It can be shown that:

$$R^2_{y.123} = r_{y1}^2 + r_{y2.1(s)}^2 + r_{y3.12(s)}^2 \tag{8}$$

where

$$r_{y2.1(s)} = \frac{r_{y2} - r_{y1}r_{21}}{\sqrt{1 - r_{21}^2}} \qquad (9)$$

is the semipartial correlation between y and Variable 2, with Variable 1 partialed only from Variable 2, and $r_{y3.12(s)}$ is the semipartial correlation between y and Variable 3 with variables 1 and 2 partialed only from Variable 3:

$$r_{y3.12(s)} = \frac{r_{y3.1(s)} - r_{y2.1(s)}r_{23.1}}{\sqrt{1 - r_{23.1}^2}} \qquad (10)$$

Thus, through the use of semipartial correlations, we disentangle the correlations among the predictors and determine how much *unique* variance on each predictor is related to variance on y.

Use of one or more of the above methods will often yield a number of models of roughly equal efficacy. As Myers (1990) noted, "The successful model builder will eventually understand that with many data sets, several models can be fit that would be of nearly equal effectiveness. Thus the problem that one deals with is the selection of *one model* from a pool of *candidate models*" (p. 164). One of the problems with the stepwise methods, which are very frequently used, is that they have led many investigators to conclude that they have found *the* best model, when in fact there may be some better models and/or several other models that are about as good. As Huberty noted (1989), "And one or more of these subsets may be more interesting or relevant in a substantive sense" (p. 46).

As mentioned earlier, Mallows' criterion is useful in guarding against both underfitting and overfitting. Three other very important criteria that can be used to select from the candidate pool all relate to the generalizability of the prediction equation, that is, how well will the equation predict on an independent sample(s) of data. The three methods of model validation, which are discussed in detail in section 3.11, are:

1. Data splitting—Randomly split the data, obtain a prediction equation on one half of the random split and then check its predictive power (cross-validate) on the other sample.

2. Use of the PRESS statistic.

3. Obtain an *estimate* of the average predictive power of the equation on many other samples from the same population, using a formula due to Stein (Herzberg, 1969).

The SPSS application guides comment on overfitting and the use of several models. There is no one test to determine the dimensionality of the best submodel. Some researchers find it tempting to include too many variables in the model, which is called overfitting. Such a model will perform badly when applied to a new sample from the same population (cross validation). Automatic stepwise procedures cannot do all the work for you. Use them as a tool to determine roughly the number of predictors needed (for example, you might find 3 to 5 variables). If you try several methods of selection, you may identify candidate predictors that are not included by any method. Ignore them, and fit models with, say, 3 to 5 variables, selecting alternative subsets from among the better candidates. You may find several subsets that perform equally as well. Then knowledge of the subject matter, how accurately individual variables are measured, and what a variable "communicates" may guide selection of the model to report.

I don't disagree with the above comments, however, I would favor the model that cross validates best. If two models cross validate about the same, then I would favor the model that makes most substantive sense.

3.9 Two Computer Examples

To illustrate the use of several of the aforementioned model selection methods, we consider two computer examples. The first example illustrates the SPSS REGRESSION program, and uses data from Morrison (1983) on 32 students enrolled in an MBA course. We predict instructor course evaluation from 5 predictors. The second example illustrates SAS REG on quality ratings of 46 research doctorate programs in psychology, where we are attempting to predict quality ratings from factors such as number of program graduates, percentage of graduates who received fellowships or grant support, etc. (Singer & Willett, 1988).

Example 3.3: SPSS Regression on Morrison MBA Data

The data for this problem are from Morrison (1983). The dependent variable is instructor course evaluation in an MBA course, with the five predictors being clarity, stimulation, knowledge, interest, and course evaluation. We illustrate two of the sequential procedures, stepwise and backward selection, using the SPSSX REGRESSION program. The control lines for running the analyses, along with the correlation matrix, are given in Table 3.3.

SPSSX REGRESSION has "*p* values," denoted by PIN and POUT, which govern whether a predictor will enter the equation and whether it will be deleted. The default values are PIN = .05 and POUT = .10. In other words, a predictor must be "significant" at the .05 level to enter, or must not be significant at the .10 level to be deleted.

First, we discuss the stepwise procedure results. Examination of the correlation matrix in Table 3.3 reveals that three of the predictors (CLARITY, STIMUL, and COUEVAL) are strongly related to INSTEVAL (simple correlations of .862, .739, and .738, respectively). Because clarity has the highest correlation, it will enter the equation first. Superficially, it might appear that STIMUL or COUEVAL would enter next; however, we must take into account how these predictors are correlated with CLARITY, and indeed both have fairly high correlations with CLARITY (.617 and .651 respectively). Thus, they will not account for as much unique variance on INSTEVAL, above and beyond that of CLARITY, as first appeared. On the other hand, INTEREST, which has a considerably lower correlation with INSTEVAL (.44), is correlated only .20 with CLARITY. Thus, the variance on INSTEVAL it accounts for is relatively independent of the variance CLARITY accounted for. And, as seen in Table 3.4, it is INTEREST that enters the regression equation second.

STIMUL is the third and final predictor to enter, because its *p* value (.0086) is less than the default value of .05. Finally, the other predictors (KNOWLEDGE and COUEVAL) don't enter because their *p* values (.0989 and .1288) are greater than .05.

Selected printout from the backward selection procedure appears in Table 3.5. First, all of the predictors are put into the equation. Then, the procedure determines which of the predictors makes the *least* contribution when entered last in the equation. That predictor is INTEREST, and since its *p* value is .9097, it is deleted from the equation. None of the other predictors can be further deleted because their *p* values are much less than .10.

TABLE 3.3

SPSS Control Lines for Stepwise and Backward Selection Runs on the Morrison MBA Data and the Correlation Matrix

```
TITLE 'MORRISON MBA DATA'.
DATA LIST FREE/INSTEVAL CLARITY STIMUL KNOWLEDG INTEREST COUEVAL.
BEGIN DATA.
1 1 2 1 1 2   1 2 2 1 1 1   1 1 1 1 1 2   1 1 2 1 1 2
2 1 3 2 2 2   2 2 4 1 1 2   2 3 3 1 1 2   2 3 4 1 2 3
2 2 3 1 3 3   2 2 2 2 2 2   2 2 3 2 1 2   2 2 2 3 3 2
2 2 2 1 1 2   2 2 4 2 2 2   2 3 3 1 1 3   2 3 4 1 1 2
2 3 2 1 1 2   3 4 4 3 2 2   3 4 3 1 1 4   3 4 3 1 2 3
3 4 3 2 2 3   3 3 4 2 3 3   3 3 4 2 3 3   3 4 3 1 1 2
3 4 5 1 1 3   3 3 5 1 2 3   3 4 4 1 2 3   3 4 4 1 1 3
3 3 3 2 1 3   3 3 5 1 1 2   4 5 5 2 3 4   4 4 5 2 3 4
END DATA.
① REGRESSION DESCRIPTIVES = DEFAULT/
    VARIABLES = INSTEVAL TO COUEVAL/
  ②STATISTICS = DEFAULTS TOL SELECTION/
    DEPENDENT = INSTEVAL/
  ③METHOD = STEPWISE/
  ④CASEWISE = ALL PRED RESID ZRESID LEVER COOK/
  ⑤SCATTERPLOT(*RES, *PRE)/.
```

CORRELATION MATRIX

	INSTEVAL	CLARITY	STIMUL	KNOWLEDGE	INTEREST	COUEVAL
INSTEVAL	1.000	.862	.739	.282	.435	.738
CLARITY	.862	1.000	.617	.057	.200	.651
STIMUL	.739	.617	1.000	.078	.317	.523
KNOWLEDGE	.282	.057	.078	1.000	.583	.041
INTEREST	.435	.200	.317	.583	1.000	.448
COUEVAL	.738	.651	.523	.041	.448	1.000

① The DESCRIPTIVES = DEFAULT subcommand yields the means, standard deviations, and the correlation matrix for the variables.

② The DEFAULTS part of the STATISTICS subcommand yields, among other things, the ANOVA table for each step, R, R^2, and adjusted R^2. The HISTORY part is needed to obtain a summary table, which is very helpful to have.

③ To obtain the backward selection procedure, we would simply put METHOD = BACKWARD/

④ This CASEWISE subcommand yields important regression diagnostics: ZRESID (standardized residuals—for identifying outliers on y), LEVER (hat elements—for identifying outliers on predictors), and COOK (Cook's distance—for identifying influential data points).

⑤ This SCATTERPLOT subcommand yields the plot of the residuals vs. the predicted values, which is very useful for determining whether any of the assumptions underlying the linear regression model may be violated.

Interestingly, note that two *different* sets of predictors emerge from the two sequential selection procedures. The stepwise procedure yields the set (CLARITY, INTEREST, and STIMUL), where the backward procedure yields (COUEVAL, KNOWLEDGE, STIMUL, and CLARITY). However, CLARITY and STIMUL are common to both sets. On the grounds of parsimony, we might prefer the set (CLARITY, INTEREST, and STIMUL), especially because the adjusted R^2's for the two sets are quite close (.84 and .87).

Three other things should be checked out before settling on this as our chosen model:

1. We need to determine if the assumptions of the linear regression model are tenable.
2. We need an estimate of the cross validity power of the equation.
3. We need to check for the existence of outliers and/or influential data points.

TABLE 3.4

Regression

Descriptive Statistics

	Mean	Std. Deviation	N
INSTEVAL	2.4063	.7976	32
CLARITY	2.8438	1.0809	32
STIMUL	3.3125	1.0906	32
KNOWLEDG	1.4375	.6189	32
INTEREST	1.6563	.7874	32
COUEVAL	2.5313	.7177	32

Correlations

		INSTEVAL	CLARITY	STIMUL	KNOWLEDG	INTEREST	COUEVAL
Pearson Correlation	INSTEVAL	1.000	.862	.739	.282	.435	.738
	CLARITY	.862	1.000	.617	.057	.200	.651
	STIMUL	.739	.617	1.000	.078	.317	.523
	KNOWLEDG	.282	.057	.078	1.000	.583	.041
	INTEREST	.435	.200	.317	.583	1.000	.448
	COUEVAL	.738	.651	.523	.041	.448	1.000

Variables Entered/Removed[a]

Model	Variables Entered	Variables Removed	Method	
1	CLARITY		Stepwise (Criteria: Probability-of-F-to-enter <= .050, Probability-of-F-to-remove >= .100).	This predictor enters the equation first, since it has the highest simple correlation (.862) with the dependent variable INSTEVAL.
2	INTEREST		Stepwise (Criteria: Probability-of-F-to-enter <= .050, Probability-of-F-to-remove >= .100).	INTEREST has the opportunity to enter the equation next since it has the largest partial correlation of .528 (see the box with EXCLUDED VARIABLES), and does enter since its p value (.002) is less than the default entry value of .05.
3	STIMUL		Stepwise (Criteria: Probability-of-F-to-enter <= .050, Probability-of-F-to-Remove >= .100).	Since STIMULUS has the strongest tie to INSTEVAL, after the effects of CLARITY and INTEREST are partialed out, it gets the opportunity to enter next. STIMULUS does enter, since its p value (.009) is less than .05.

[a] Dependent Variable: INSTEVAL

Selected Printout From SPSS Syntax Editor Stepwise Regression Run on the Morrison MBA Data

TABLE 3.4 (*Continued*)

					Selection Criteria			
Model	R	R Square	Adjusted R Square	Std. Error of the Estimate	Akaike Information Criterion	Amemiya Prediction Criterion	Mallows' Prediction Criterion	Schwarz Bayesian Criterion
1	.862[a]	.743	.734	.4112	−54.936	.292	35.297	−52.004
2	.903[b]	.815	.802	.3551	−63.405	.224	19.635	−59.008
3	.925[c]	.856	.840	.3189	−69.426	.186	11.517	−63.563

Model Summary[d]

[a] Predictors: (Constant), CLARITY
[b] Predictors: (Constant), CLARITY, INTEREST
[c] Predictors: (Constant), CLARITY, INTEREST, STIMUL
[d] Dependent Variable: INSTEVAL

With just CLARITY in the equation we account for 74.3% of the variance; adding INTEREST increases the variance accounted for to 81.5%, and finally with 3 predictors (STIMUL added) we account for 85.6% of the variance in this sample.

ANOVA[d]

Model		Sum of Squares	df	Mean Square	F	Sig.
1	Regression	14.645	1	14.645	86.602	.000[a]
	Residual	5.073	30	.169		
	Total	19.719	31			
2	Regression	16.061	2	8.031	63.670	.000[b]
	Residual	3.658	29	.126		
	Total	19.719	31			
3	Regression	16.872	3	5.624	55.316	.000[c]
	Residual	2.847	28	.102		
	Total	19.719	31			

[a] Predictors: (Constant), CLARITY
[b] Predictors: (Constant), CLARITY, INTEREST
[c] Predictors: (Constant), CLARITY, INTEREST, STIMUL
[d] Dependent Variable: INSTEVAL

TABLE 3.4 (*Continued*)

Coefficients[a]

Model		Unstandardized Coefficients		Standardized Coefficients	t	Sig.	Collinearity Statistics	
		B	Std. Error	Beta			Tolerance	VIF
1	(Constant)	.598	.207		2.882	.007		
	CLARITY	.636	.068	.862	9.306	.000	1.000	1.000
2	(Constant)	.254	.207		1.230	.229		
	CLARITY	.596	.060	.807	9.887	.000	.960	1.042
	INTEREST	.277	.083	.273	3.350	.002	.960	1.042
3	(Constant)	2.137E-02	.203		.105	.917		
	CLARITY	.482	.067	.653	7.158	.000	.619	1.616
	INTEREST	.223	.077	.220	2.904	.007	.900	1.112
	STIMUL	.195	.069	.266	2.824	.009	.580	1.724

[a] Dependent Variable: INSTEVAL

These are the raw regression coefficients that define the prediction equation, i.e., INSTEVAL = .482 CLARITY + .223 INTEREST + .195 STIMUL + .021. The coefficient of .482 for CLARITY means that for every unit change on CLARITY there is a change of .482 units on INSTEVAL. The coefficient of .223 for INTEREST means that for every unit change on INTEREST there is a change of .223 units on INSTEVAL.

Excluded Variables[d]

Model		Beta In	t	Sig.	Partial Correlation	Collinearity Statistics		Minimum Tolerance
						Tolerance	VIF	
1	STIMUL	.335[a]	3.274	.003	.520	.619	1.616	.619
	KNOWLEDG	.233[a]	2.783	.009	.459	.997	1.003	.997
	INTEREST	.273[a]	3.350	.002	.528	.960	1.042	.960
	COUEVAL	.307[a]	2.784	.009	.459	.576	1.736	.576
2	STIMUL	.266[b]	2.824	.009	.471	.580	1.724	.580
	KNOWLEDG	.116[b]	1.183	.247	.218	.656	1.524	.632
	COUEVAL	.191[b]	1.692	.102	.305	.471	2.122	.471
3	KNOWLEDG	.148[c]	1.709	.099	.312	.647	1.546	.572
	COUEVAL	.161[c]	1.567	.129	.289	.466	2.148	.451

[a] Predictors in the Model: (Constant), CLARITY
[b] Predictors in the Model: (Constant), CLARITY, INTEREST
[c] Predictors in the Model: (Constant), CLARITY, INTEREST, STIMUL
[d] Dependent Variable: INSTEVAL

Since neither of these *p* values is less than .05, no other predictors can enter, and the procedure terminates.

TABLE 3.5

Selected Printout from SPSS Regression for Backward Selection on the Morrison MBA Data

Model Summary[c]

Model	R	R Square	Adjusted R Square	Std. Error of the Estimate	Selection Criteria			
					Akaike Information Criterion	Amemiya Prediction Criterion	Mallows' Prediction Criterion	Schwarz Bayesian Criterion
1	.946[a]	.894	.874	.2831	−75.407	.154	6.000	−66.613
2	.946[b]	.894	.879	.2779	−77.391	.145	4.013	−70.062

[a] Predictors: (Constant), COUEVAL, KNOWLEDG, STIMUL, INTEREST, CLARITY
[b] Predictors: (Constant), COUEVAL, KNOWLEDG, STIMUL, CLARITY
[c] Dependent Variable: INSTEVAL

Coefficients[a]

Model	Unstandardized Coefficients		Standardized Coefficients	t	Sig.	Collinearity Statistics	
	B	Std. Error	Beta			Tolerance	VIF
1 (Constant)	−.443	.235		−1.886	.070		
CLARITY	.386	.071	.523	5.415	.000	.436	2.293
STIMUL	.197	.062	.269	3.186	.004	.569	1.759
KNOWLEDG	.277	.108	.215	2.561	.017	.579	1.728
INTEREST	1.114E-02	.097	.011	.115	.910	.441	2.266
COUEVAL	.270	.110	.243	2.459	.021	.416	2.401
2 (Constant)	−.450	.222		−2.027	.053		
CLARITY	.384	.067	.520	5.698	.000	.471	2.125
STIMUL	.198	.059	.271	3.335	.002	.592	1.690
KNOWLEDG	.285	.081	.221	3.518	.002	.994	1.006
COUEVAL	.276	.094	.249	2.953	.006	.553	1.810

[a] Dependent Variable: INSTEVAL

Figure 3.4 shows the plot of the residuals versus the predicted values from SPSSX. This plot shows essentially random variation of the points about the horizontal line of 0, indicating no violations of assumptions.

The issues of cross-validity power and outliers are considered later in this chapter, and are applied to this problem in section 3.15, after both topics have been covered.

Applied Multivariate Statistics for the Social Sciences

Example 3.4: SAS REG on Doctoral Programs in Psychology

The data for this example come from a National Academy of Sciences report (1982) that, among other things, provided ratings on the quality of 46 research doctoral programs in psychology. The six variables used to predict quality are:

NFACULTY—number of faculty members in the program as of December 1980

NGRADS—number of program graduates from 1975 through 1980

PCTSUPP—percentage of program graduates from 1975–1979 who received fellowships or training grant support during their graduate education

PCTGRANT—percentage of faculty members holding research grants from the Alcohol, Drug Abuse, and Mental Health Administration, the National Institutes of Health, or the National Science Foundation at any time during 1978–1980

NARTICLE—number of published articles attributed to program faculty members from 1978–1980

PCTPUB—percentage of faculty with one or more published articles from 1978–1980

Both the stepwise procedure and the MAXR procedure were used on this data to generate several regression models. The control lines for doing this, along with the correlation matrix, are given in Table 3.6.

One very nice feature of SAS REG, is that Mallows' C_p is given for each model. The stepwise procedure terminated after 4 predictors entered. Here is the summary table, exactly as it appears on the printout:

Summary of Stepwise Procedure for Dependent Variable QUALITY

Step	Variable Entered	Variable Removed	Partial $R**2$	Model $R**2$	$C(p)$	F	Prob > F
1	NARTIC		0.5809	0.5809	55.1185	60.9861	0.0001
2	PCTGRT		0.1668	0.7477	18.4760	28.4156	0.0001
3	PCTSUPP		0.0569	0.8045	7.2970	12.2197	0.0011
4	NFACUL		0.0176	0.8221	5.2161	4.0595	0.0505

This four predictor model appears to be a reasonably good one. First, Mallows' C_p is very close to p (recall $p = k + 1$), that is, $5.216 \approx 5$, indicating that there is not much bias in the model. Second, $R^2 = .8221$, indicating that we can predict quality quite well from the four predictors. Although this R^2 is *not* adjusted, the adjusted value will not differ much because we have not selected from a large pool of predictors.

Selected printout from the MAXR procedure run appears in Table 3.7. From Table 3.7 we can construct the following results:

BEST MODEL	VARIABLE(S)	MALLOWS C_p
for 1 variable	NARTIC	55.118
for 2 variables	PCTGRT, NFACUL	16.859
for 3 variables	PCTPUB, PCTGRT, NFACUL	9.147
for 4 variables	NFACUL, PCTSUPP, PCTGRT, NARTIC	5.216

In this case, the *same* four-predictor model is selected by the MAXR procedure that was selected by the stepwise procedure.

TABLE 3.6

SAS Reg Control Lines for Stepwise and MAXR Runs on the National Academy of Sciences Data and the Correlation Matrix

---

DATA SINGER;
INPUT QUALITY NFACUL NGRADS PCTSUPP PCTGRT NARTIC PCTPUB;
CARDS;

    DATA LINES

① PROC REG SIMPLE CORR;

② MODEL QUALITY = NFACUL NGRADS PCTSUPP PCTGRT NARTIC PCTPUB/
SELECTION = STEPWISE VIF R INFLUENCE;
MODEL QUALITY = NFACUL NGRADS PCTSUPP PCTGRT NARTIC PCTPUB/
SELECTION = MAXR VIF R INFLUENCE;

① SIMPLE is needed to obtain descriptive statistics (means, variances, etc) for all variables. CORR is needed to obtain the correlation matrix for the variables.

② In this MODEL statement, the dependent variable goes on the left and all predictors to the right of the equals. SELECTION is where we indicate which of the 9 procedures we wish to use. There is a wide variety of other information we can get printed out. Here we have selected VIF (variance inflation factors), R (analysis of residuals—standard residuals, hat elements, Cooks D), and INFLUENCE (influence diagnostics).

Note that there are two separate MODEL statements for the two regression procedures being requested. Although multiple procedures can be obtained in one run, you *must* have separate MODEL statement for each procedure.

CORRELATION MATRIX

		NFACUL	NGRADS	PCTSUPP	PCTGRT	NARTIC	PCTPUB	QUALITY
		2	3	4	5	6	7	1
NFACUL	2	1.000						
NGRADS	3	0.692	1.000					
PCTSUPP	4	0.395	0.337	1.000				
PCTGRT	5	0.162	0.071	0.351	1.000			
NARTIC	6	0.755	0.646	0.366	0.436	1.000		
PCTPUB	7	0.205	0.171	0.347	0.490	0.593	1.000	
QUALITY	1	0.622	0.418	0.582	0.700	0.762	0.585	1.000

N = 23   Regression Models for Dependent Variable: QUALITY

C(p)	R-square	In	Variables in Model			
1.32366	0.88491102	3	PCTSUPP	PCTGRT	NARTIC	
3.11858	0.88635690	4	NGRADS	PCTSUPP	PCTGRT	NARTIC
3.15124	0.88612665	4	PCTSUPP	PCTGRT	NARTIC	PCTPUB

TABLE 3.6 (Continued)

The SAS System
Correlation

CORR	NFACUL	NGRADS	PCTSUPP	PCTGRT
NFACUL	1.0000	0.8835	0.4275	0.2582
NGRADS	0.8835	1.0000	0.3764	0.2861
PCTSUPP	0.4275	0.3764	1.0000	0.4027
PCTGRT	0.2582	0.2861	0.4027	1.0000
NARTIC	0.8416	0.8470	0.4430	0.5020
PCTPUB	0.2673	0.2950	0.3336	0.5017
QUALITY	0.7052	0.6892	0.6288	0.6705

CORR	NARTIC	PCTPUB	QUALITY
NFACUL	0.8416	0.2673	0.7052
NGRADS	0.8470	0.2950	0.6892
PCTSUPP	0.4430	0.3336	0.6288
PCTGRT	0.5020	0.5017	0.6705
NARTIC	1.0000	0.5872	0.8770
PCTPUB	0.5872	1.0000	0.6114
QUALITY	0.8770	0.6114	1.0000

TABLE 3.7
Selected Printout from the MAXR Run on the National Academy of Sciences Data

Maximum R-Square Improvement of Dependent Variable QUALITY

Step 1   Variable NARTIC Entered   R-square = 0.58089673   C(p) = 55.11853652

The above model is the best 1-variable model found.

Step 2   Variable PGTGRT Entered   R-square = 0.74765405   C(p) = 18.47596774

Step 3   Variable NARTIC Removed   R-square = 0.75462892   C(p) = 16.85968570
          Variable NFACUL Entered

The above model is the best 2-variable model found.

Step 4 Variable PCTPUB Entered   R-square = 0.79654184   C(p) = 9.14723035

The above model is the best 3-variable model found.

Step 5 Variable PCTSUPP Entered   R-square = 0.81908649   C(p) = 5.92297432

Step 6 Variable PCTPUB Removed   R-square = 0.82213698   C(p) = 5.21608457
          Variable NARTIC Entered

	DF	Sum of Squares	Mean Square	F	Prob > f
Regression	4	3752.82298869	938.20574717	47.38	0.0001
Error	41	811.89440261	19.80230250		
Total	45	4564.71739130			

Variable	Parameter Estimate	Standard Error	Type II Sum of Squares	F	Prob > F
INTERCEP	9.06132974	1.64472577	601.05272060	30.35	0.0001
NFACUL	0.13329934	0.06615919	80.38802096	4.06	0.0505
PCTSUPP	0.09452909	0.03236602	168.91497705	8.53	0.0057
PCTGRT	0.24644511	0.04414314	617.20528404	31.17	0.0001
NARTIC	0.05455483	0.01954712	154.24691982	7.79	0.0079

3.9.1 Caveat on *p* Values for the "Significance" of Predictors

The *p* values that are given by SPSS and SAS for the "significance" of each predictor at each step for stepwise or the forward selection procedures should be treated tenuously, especially if your initial pool of predictors is moderate (15) or large (30). The reason is that the ordinary *F* distribution is *not* appropriate here, because the largest *F* is being selected out of all *F*'s available. Thus, the appropriate critical value will be larger (and can be considerably larger) than would be obtained from the ordinary null *F* distribution. Draper and Smith (1981) noted, "Studies have shown, for example, that in some cases where an entry *F* test was made at the *a* level, the appropriate probability was *qa*, where there were *q* entry candidates at that stage" (p. 311). This is saying, for example, that an experimenter may think his or her probability of erroneously including a predictor is .05, when in fact the *actual* probability of erroneously including the predictor is .50 (if there were 10 entry candidates at that point).

Thus, the F tests are positively biased, and the greater the number of predictors, the larger the bias. Hence, these *F* tests should be used only as rough guides to the usefulness of the predictors chosen. The acid test is how well the predictors do under cross validation. It can be unwise to use *any* of the stepwise procedures with 20 or 30 predictors and only 100 subjects, because capitalization on chance is great, and the results may well not cross-validate. To find an equation that probably will have generalizability, it is best to carefully select (using substantive knowledge or any previous related literature) a small or relatively small set of predictors.

Ramsey and Schafer (1997, p. 93) comment on this issue:

> The cutoff value of 4 for the *F*-statistic (or 2 for the magnitude of the *t*-statistic) corresponds roughly to a two-sided *p*-value of less than .05. The notion of "significance" cannot be taken seriously, however, because sequential variable selection is a form of data snooping.
>
> At step 1 of a forward selection, the cutoff of *F* = 4 corresponds to a hypothesis test for a single coefficient. But the actual statistic considered is the largest of several *F*-statistics, whose sampling distribution under the null hypothesis differs sharply from an *F*-distribution.
>
> To demonstrate this, suppose that a model contained ten explanatory variables and a single response, with a sample size of *n* = 100. The *F*-statistic for a single variable at step 1 would be compared to an *F*-distribution with 1 and 98 degrees of freedom, where only 4.8% of the *F*-ratios exceed 4. But suppose further that all eleven variables were generated completely at random (and independently of each other), from a standard normal distribution. What should be expected of the largest *F*-to-enter?
>
> This random generation process was simulated 500 times on a computer. The following display shows a histogram of the largest among ten *F*-to-enter values, along with the theoretical *F*-distribution. The two distributions are very different. At least one *F*-to-enter was larger than 4 in 38% of the simulated trials, even though none of the explanatory variables was associated with the response.

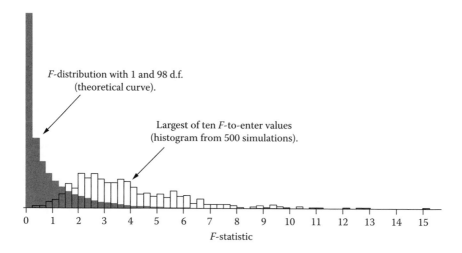

F-distribution with 1 and 98 d.f.
(theoretical curve).

Largest of ten F-to-enter values
(histogram from 500 simulations).

F-statistic

Simulated distribution of the largest of 10 F-statistics.

3.10 Checking Assumptions for the Regression Model

Recall that in the linear regression model it is assumed that the errors are independent and follow a normal distribution with constant variance. The normality assumption can be checked through use of the histogram of the standardized or studentized residuals, as we did in Table 3.2 for the simple regression example. The independence assumption implies that the subjects are responding independently of one another. This is an important assumption. We show in Chapter 6, in the context of analysis of variance, that if independence is violated only mildly, then the probability of a type I error will be *several* times greater than the level the experimenter thinks he or she is working at. Thus, instead of rejecting falsely 5% of the time, the experimenter may be rejecting falsely 25 or 30% of the time.

We now consider an example where this assumption was violated. Nold and Freedman (1977) had each of 22 college freshmen write four in-class essays in two 1-hour sessions, separated by a span of several months. In doing a subsequent regression analysis to predict quality of essay response, they used an n of 88. However, the responses for each subject on the four essays are obviously going to be correlated, so that there are not 88 independent observations, but only 22.

3.10.1 Residual Plots

Various types of plots are available for assessing potential problems with the regression model (Draper & Smith, 1981; Weisberg, 1985). One of the most useful graphs the standardized residuals (r_i) versus the predicted values ($\hat{y}_i$). If the assumptions of the linear regression model are tenable, then the standardized residuals should scatter randomly about a horizontal line defined by $r_i = 0$, as shown in Figure 3.3a. *Any systematic pattern or clustering of the residuals suggests a model violation(s).* Three such systematic patterns are indicated in Figure 3.3. Figure 3.3b shows a systematic quadratic (second-degree equation) clustering of the residuals. For Figure 3.3c, the variability of the residuals increases systematically as the predicted values increase, suggesting a violation of the constant variance assumption.

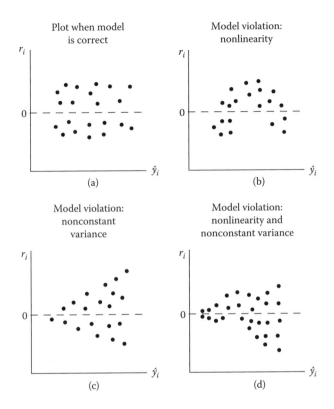

FIGURE 3.3
Residual plots of studentized residuals vs. predicted values.

It is important to note that the plots in Figure 3.3 are somewhat idealized, constructed to be clear violations. As Weisberg (1985) stated, "Unfortunately, these idealized plots cover up one very important point; in real data sets, the true state of affairs is rarely this clear" (p. 131).

In Figure 3.4 we present residual plots for three real data sets. The first plot is for the Morrison data (the first computer example), and shows essentially random scatter of the residuals, suggesting no violations of assumptions. The remaining two plots are from a study by a statistician who analyzed the salaries of over 260 major league hitters, using predictors such as career batting average, career home runs per time at bat, years in the major leagues, and so on. These plots are from Moore and McCabe (1989), and are used with permission. Figure 3.4b, which plots the residuals versus predicted salaries, shows a clear violation of the constant variance assumption. For lower predicted salaries there is little variability about 0, but for the high salaries there is considerable variability of the residuals. The implication of this is that the model will predict lower salaries quite accurately, but not so for the higher salaries.

Figure 3.4c plots the residuals versus number of years in the major leagues. This plot shows a clear curvilinear clustering, that is, quadratic. The implication of this curvilinear trend is that the regression model will tend to overestimate the salaries of players who have been in the majors only a few years or over 15 years, and it will underestimate the salaries of players who have been in the majors about 5 to 9 years.

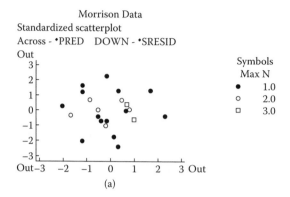

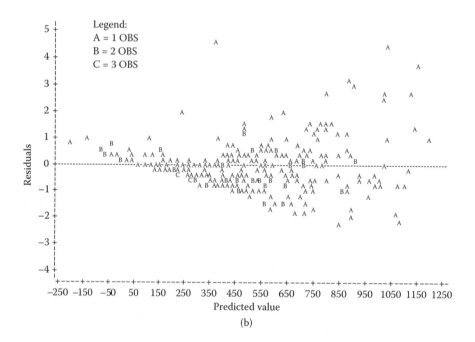

FIGURE 3.4
Residual plots for three real data sets showing no violations, heterogeneous variance, and curvilinearity.

In concluding this section, note that if nonlinearity or nonconstant variance is found, there are various remedies. For nonlinearity, perhaps a polynomial model is needed. Or sometimes a transformation of the data will enable a nonlinear model to be approximated by a linear one. For nonconstant variance, weighted least squares is one possibility, or more commonly, a variance-stabilizing transformation (such as square root or log) may be used. I refer the reader to Weisberg (1985, chapter 6) for an excellent discussion of remedies for regression model violations.

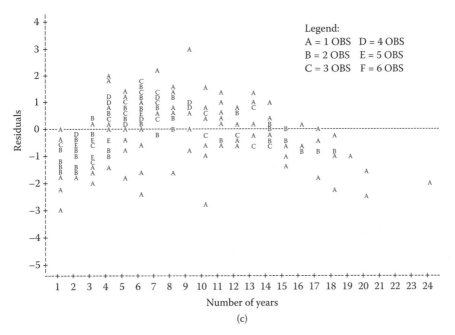

FIGURE 3.4 (*Continued*)

3.11 Model Validation

We indicated earlier that it was crucial for the researcher to obtain some measure of how well the regression equation will predict on an independent sample(s) of data. That is, it was important to determine whether the equation had generalizability. We discuss here three forms of model validation, two being empirical and the other involving an *estimate* of average predictive power on other samples. First, I give a brief description of each form, and then elaborate on each form of validation.

1. *Data splitting.* Here the sample is randomly split in half. It does not have to be split evenly, but we use this for illustration. The regression equation is found on the so-called derivation sample (also called the screening sample, or the sample that "gave birth" to the prediction equation by Tukey). This prediction equation is then applied to the other sample (called validation or calibration) to see how well it predicts the y scores there.

2. *Compute an adjusted R^2.* There are various adjusted R^2 measures, or measures of shrinkage in predictive power, but they do not all estimate the same thing. The one most commonly used, and that which is printed out by both major statistical packages, is due to Wherry (1931). It is very important to note here that the Wherry formula estimates how much variance on y would be accounted for if we had derived the prediction equation in the population from which the sample was drawn. The Wherry formula does *not* indicate how well the derived equation will predict on other samples from the same population. A formula due to Stein (1960) does estimate average cross-validation predictive power. As of this writing it is not printed out by any of the three major packages. The formulas due to Wherry and Stein are presented shortly.

3. *Use the PRESS statistic.* As pointed out by several authors, in many instances one does not have enough data to be randomly splitting it. One can obtain a good measure of *external* predictive power by use of the PRESS statistic. In this approach the y value for *each* subject is set aside and a prediction equation derived on the remaining data. Thus, n prediction equations are derived and n true prediction errors are found. To be very specific, the prediction error for subject 1 is computed from the equation derived on the remaining $(n - 1)$ data points, the prediction error for subject 2 is computed from the equation derived on the other $(n - 1)$ data points, and so on. As Myers (1990) put it, "PRESS is important in that one has information in the form of n validations in which the fitting sample for each is of size $n - 1$" (p. 171).

3.11.1 Data Splitting

Recall that the sample is randomly split. The regression equation is found on the derivation sample and then is applied to the other sample (validation) to determine how well it will predict y there. Next, we give a hypothetical example, randomly splitting 100 subjects.

Derivation Sample	*Validation Sample*		
$n = 50$	$n = 50$		
Prediction Equation $\hat{y}_i = 4 + .3x_1 + .7x_2$	y	x_1	x_2
	6	1	.5
	4.5	2	.3
		...	
	7	5	.2

Now, using this prediction equation, we predict the y scores in the validation sample:

$$\hat{y}_1 = 4 + .3\,(1) + .7\,(.5) = 4.65$$

$$\hat{y}_2 = 4 + .3\,(2) + .7\,(.3) = 4.81$$

$$\dots$$

$$\hat{y}_{50} = 4 + .3\,(5) + .7\,(.2) = 5.64$$

The cross-validated R then is the correlation for the following set of scores:

y	$\hat{y}_i$
6	4.65
4.5	4.81
...	
7	5.64

Random splitting and cross validation can be easily done using SPSS and the filter case function.

3.11.2 Cross Validation with SPSS

To illustrate cross validation with SPSS for Windows 15.0, we use the Agresti data on the web site (www/psypress.com/applied-multivariate-statistics-for-the-social-sciences). Recall that the sample size here was 93. First, we randomly select a sample and do a stepwise regression on this random sample. We have selected an approximate random sample of 60%. It turns out there is an n = 60 in our sample. This is done by clicking on DATA, choosing SELECT CASES from the dropdown menu, then choosing RANDOM SAMPLE and finally selecting a random sample of approximately 60%. When this is done a FILTER_$ variable is created, with value = 1 for those cases included in the sample and value = 0 for those cases *not* included in the sample. When the stepwise regression was done, the variables SIZE, NOBATH and NEW were included as predictors and the coefficients, etc., are given below for that run:

		Unstandardized Coefficients		Standardized Coefficients		
Model		**B**	**Std. Error**	**Beta**	**t**	**Sig.**
1	(Constant)	−28.948	8.209		−3.526	.001
	SIZE	78.353	4.692	.910	16.700	.000
2	(Constant)	−62.848	10.939		−5.745	.000
	SIZE	62.156	5.701	.722	10.902	.000
	NOBATH	30.334	7.322	.274	4.143	.000
3	(Constant)	−62.519	9.976		−6.267	.000
	SIZE	59.931	5.237	.696	11.444	.000
	NOBATH	29.436	6.682	.266	4.405	.000
	NEW	17.146	4.842	.159	3.541	.001

Coefficients[a]

[a] Dependent Variable: PRICE

The next step in the cross validation is to use the COMPUTE statement to compute the predicted values for the dependent variable. This COMPUTE statement is obtained by clicking on TRANSFORM and then selecting COMPUTE from the dropdown menu. When this is done the following screen appears:

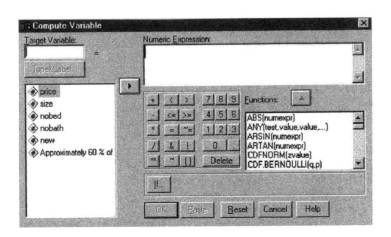

Using the coefficients obtained from the above regression we have:

$$PRED = \ -62.519 + 59.931*SIZE + 29.436*NOBATH + 17.146*NEW$$

We wish to correlate the predicted values in the other part of the sample with the y values there to obtain the cross validated value. We click on DATA again, and use SELECT IF FILTER_$ = 0. That is, we select those cases in the *other* part of the sample. There are 33 cases in the other part of the random sample. When this is done all the cases with FILTER_$ = 1 are selected, and a partial listing of the data appears as follows:

	price	size	nobed	nobath	new	filter_$	pred
1	48.50	1.10	3.00	1.00	.00	0	32.84
2	55.00	1.01	3.00	2.00	.00	0	56.88
3	68.00	1.45	3.00	2.00	.00	1	83.25
4	137.00	2.40	3.00	3.00	.00	0	169.62
5	309.40	3.30	4.00	3.00	1.00	0	240.71
6	17.50	.40	1.00	1.00	.00	1	−9.11
7	19.60	1.28	3.00	1.00	.00	0	43.63
8	24.50	.74	3.00	1.00	.00	0	11.27

Finally, we use the CORRELATION program to obtain the bivariate correlation between PRED and PRICE (the dependent variable) in this sample of 33. That correlation is .878, which is a drop from the maximized correlation of .944 in the derivation sample.

3.11.3 Adjusted R^2

Herzberg (1969) presented a discussion of various formulas that have been used to estimate the amount of shrinkage found in R^2. As mentioned earlier, the one most commonly used, and due to Wherry, is given by

$$\hat{\rho}^2 = 1 - \frac{(n-1)}{(n-k-1)}(1-R^2) \tag{11}$$

where $\hat{\rho}$ is the estimate of ρ, the population multiple correlation coefficient. This is the adjusted R^2 printed out by SAS and SPSS. Draper and Smith (1981) commented on Equation 11:

> A related statistic … is the so called adjusted $r(R_a^2)$, the idea being that the statistic R_a^2 can be used to compare equations fitted not only to a specific set of data but also to two or more entirely different sets of data. The value of this statistic for the latter purpose is, in our opinion, not high. (p. 92)

Herzberg noted:

> In applications, the population regression function can never be known and one is more interested in how effective the *sample* regression function is in *other* samples. A measure of this effectiveness is r_c, the sample cross-validity. For any given regression function r_c will vary from validation sample to validation sample. The average value of r_c will be

approximately equal to the correlation, in the *population*, of the sample regression function with the criterion. This correlation is the population cross-validity, ρ_c. Wherry's formula estimates ρ rather than ρ_c. (p. 4)

There are two possible models for the predictors: (a) regression—the values of the predictors are fixed, that is, we study y only for certain values of x, and (b) correlation—the predictors are random variables—this is a much more reasonable model for social science research. Herzberg presented the following formula for estimating ρ_c^2 under the correlation model:

$$\hat{\rho}_c^2 = 1 - \frac{(n-1)}{(n-k-1)}\left(\frac{n-2}{n-k-2}\right)\left(\frac{n+1}{n}\right)(1-R^2) \tag{12}$$

where n is sample size and k is the number of predictors. It can be shown that $\rho_c < \rho$.

If you are interested in cross validity predictive power, then the Stein formula (Equation 12) should be used. As an example, suppose $n = 50$, $k = 10$ and $R^2 = .50$. If you used the Wherry formula (Equation 11), then your estimate is

$$\hat{\rho}^2 = 1 - 49/39\,(.50) = .372$$

whereas with the proper Stein formula you would obtain

$$\hat{\rho}_c^2 = 1 - (49/39)(48/38)(51/50)(.50) = .191$$

In other words, use of the Wherry formula would give a misleadingly positive impression of the cross validity predictive power of the equation.

Table 3.8 shows how the estimated predictive power drops off using the Stein formula (Equation 12) for small to fairly large subject/variable ratios when $R^2 = .50$, .75, and .85.

TABLE 3.8

Estimated Cross Validity Predictive Power for Stein Formula[a]

	Subject/Variable Ratio	Stein Estimate
Small (5:1)	$N = 50$, $k = 10$, $R^2 = .50$	.191[b]
	$N = 50$, $k = 10$, $R^2 = .75$	.595
	$N = 50$, $k = 10$, $R^2 = .85$	.757
Moderate (10:1)	$N = 100$, $k = 10$, $R^2 = .50$	.374
	$N = 100$, $k = 10$, $R^2 = .75$	.690
Fairly Large (15:1)	$N = 150$, $k = 10$, $R^2 = .50$	.421

[a] If there is selection of predictors from a larger set, then the *median* should be used as the k. For example, if 4 predictors were selected from 30 by say stepwise regression, then the median between 4 and 30 (i.e., 17) should be the k used in the Stein formula.

[b] If we were to apply the prediction equation to many other samples from the same population, then on the *average* we would account for 19.1% of the variance on y.

3.11.4 PRESS Statistic

The PRESS approach is important in that one has n validations, each based on $(n - 1)$ observations. Thus, each validation is based on essentially the entire sample. This is very important when one does not have large n, for in this situation data splitting is really not practical. For example, if $n = 60$ and we have 6 predictors, randomly splitting the sample involves obtaining a prediction equation on only 30 subjects.

Recall that in deriving the prediction (via the least squares approach), the sum of the squared errors is *minimized*. The PRESS residuals, on the other hand, are true prediction errors, because the y value for each subject was not simultaneously used for fit and model assessment. Let us denote the predicted value for subject i, where that subject was *not* used in developing the prediction equation, by $\hat{y}_{(-i)}$. Then the PRESS residual for each subject is given by

$$\hat{e}_{(-i)} = y_t - \hat{y}_{(-i)}$$

and the PRESS sum of squared residuals is given by

$$\text{PRESS} = \Sigma \hat{e}_{(-i)}{}^2 \tag{13}$$

Therefore, one might prefer the model with the smallest PRESS value. The preceding PRESS value can be used to calculate an R^2-like statistic that more accurately reflects the generalizability of the model. It is given by

$$R^2_{\text{Press}} = 1 - (PRESS) / \Sigma (y_i - \overline{y})^2 \tag{14}$$

Importantly, the SAS REG program does routinely print out PRESS, although it is called PREDICTED RESID SS (PRESS). Given this value, it is a simple matter to calculate the R^2 PRESS statistic, because $s_y^2 = \Sigma(y_i - \overline{y})^2 / (n - 1)$.

3.12 Importance of the Order of the Predictors

The order in which the predictors enter a regression equation can make a great deal of difference with respect to how much variance on y they account for, especially for moderate or highly correlated predictors. Only for uncorrelated predictors (which would rarely occur in practice) does the order not make a difference. We give two examples to illustrate.

Example 3.5

A dissertation by Crowder (1975) attempted to predict ratings of trainably mentally (TMs) retarded individuals using IQ (x_2) and scores from a Test of Social Inference (TSI). He was especially interested in showing that the TSI had incremental predictive validity. The criterion was the average ratings by two individuals in charge of the TMs. The intercorrelations among the variables were:

$$r_{x_1 x_2} = .59, r_{yx_2} = .54, r_{yx_1} = .566$$

Now, consider two orderings for the predictors, one where TSI is entered first, and the other ordering where IQ is entered first.

	First Ordering % of variance		*Second Ordering* % of variance
TSI	32.04	IQ	29.16
IQ	6.52	TSI	9.40

The first ordering conveys an overly optimistic view of the utility of the TSI scale. Because we know that IQ will predict ratings, it should be entered first in the equation (as a control variable), and then TSI to see what its incremental validity is—that is, how much it adds to predicting ratings above and beyond what IQ does. Because of the moderate correlation between IQ and TSI, the amount of variance accounted for by TSI differs considerably when entered first versus second (32.04 vs. 9.4).

The 9.4% of variance accounted for by TSI when entered second is obtained through the use of the semipartial correlation previously introduced:

$$r_{y1.2(s)} = \frac{.566 - .54(.59)}{\sqrt{1 - .59^2}} = .306 \Rightarrow r^2_{y1.2(s)} = .0$$

Example 3.6

Consider the following matrix of correlations for a three-predictor problem:

	x_1	x_2	x_3
y	.60	.70	.70
x_1		.70	.60
x_2			.80

Notice that the predictors are strongly intercorrelated.

How much variance in y will x_3 account for if entered first? if entered last?

If x_3 is entered first, then it will account for $(.7)^2 \times 100$ or 49% of variance on y, a sizable amount.

To determine how much variance x_3 will account for if entered last, we need to compute the following second-order semipartial correlation:

$$r_{y3.12(s)} = \frac{r_{y3.1(s)} - r_{y2.1(s)}r_{23.1}}{\sqrt{1 - r^2_{23.1}}}$$

We show the details next for obtaining $r_{y3.12(s)}$.

$$r_{y2.1(s)} = \frac{r_{y2} - r_{y1}r_{21}}{\sqrt{1-r_{21}^2}} = \frac{.70 - (.6)(.7)}{\sqrt{1-.49}}$$

$$r_{y2.1(s)} = \frac{.28}{.714} = .392$$

$$r_{y3.1(s)} = \frac{r_{y3} - r_{y1}r_{31}}{\sqrt{1-r_{31}^2}} = \frac{.7 - .6(6)}{\sqrt{1-.6^2}} = .425$$

$$r_{23.1} = \frac{r_{23} - r_{21}r_{31}}{\sqrt{1-r_{21}^2}\sqrt{1-r_{31}^2}} = \frac{.80 - (.7)(.6)}{\sqrt{1-.49}\sqrt{1-.36}} = .665$$

$$r_{y3.1(s)} = \frac{.425 - .392(.665)}{\sqrt{1-.665^2}} = \frac{.164}{.746} = .22$$

$$r_{y3.12(s)}^2 = (.22)^2 = .048$$

Thus, when x_3 enters last it accounts for only 4.8% of the variance on y. This is a tremendous drop from the 49% it accounted for when entered first. Because the three predictors are so highly correlated, most of the variance on y that x_3 could have accounted for has already been accounted for by x_1 and x_2.

3.12.1 Controlling the Order of Predictors in the Equation

With the forward and stepwise selection procedures, the order of entry of predictors into the regression equation is determined via a mathematical maximization procedure. That is, the first predictor to enter is the one with the largest (maximized) correlation with y, the second to enter is the predictor with the largest partial correlation, and so on. However, there are situations where one may not want the mathematics to determine the order of entry of predictors. For example, suppose we have a five-predictor problem, with two proven predictors from previous research. The other three predictors are included to see if they have any incremental validity. In this case we would want to enter the two proven predictors in the equation first (as control variables), and then let the remaining three predictors "fight it out" to determine whether any of them add anything significant to predicting y above and beyond the proven predictors.

With SPSS REGRESSION or SAS REG we can control the order of predictors, and in particular, we can *force* predictors into the equation. In Table 3.9 we illustrate how this is done for SPSS and SAS for the above five-predictor situation.

3.13 Other Important Issues

3.13.1 Preselection of Predictors

An industrial psychologist hears about the predictive power of multiple regression and is excited. He wants to predict success on the job, and gathers data for 20 potential predictors on 70 subjects. He obtains the correlation matrix for the variables, and then picks

TABLE 3.9

Controlling the Order of Predictors and Forcing Predictors into the Equation with SPSS Regression and SAS Reg

SPSS REGRESSION

TITLE 'FORCING X3 AND X4 & USING STEPWISE SELECTION FOR OTHERS'.
DATA LIST FREE/Y X1 X2 X3 X4 X5.
BEGIN DATA.

      DATA LINES

END DATA.
LIST.
REGRESSION VARIABLES = Y X1 X2 X3 X4 X5/
    DEPENDENT = Y/
①   ENTER X3/ENTER X4/STEPWISE/.

SAS REG

DATA FORCEPR;
INPUT Y X1 X2 X3 X4 X5;
CARDS;

      DATA LINES

PROC REG SIMPLE CORR;
②   MODEL Y = X3 X4 X1 X2 X5/INCLUDE = 2 SELECTION = STEPWISE;

① These two ENTER subcommands will force the predictors in the specific order indicated. Then the STEPWISE subcommand will determine whether any of the remaining predictors (X1, X2 or X5) have semipartial correlations large enough to be "significant." If we wished to force in predictors X1, X3, and X4 and then use STEPWISE, the subcommand is ENTER X1 X3 X4/STEPWISE/

② The INCLUDE = 2 forces the first 2 predictors listed in the MODEL statement into the prediction equation. Thus, if we wish to force X3 and X4 we must list them first on the = statement.

out 6 predictors that correlate significantly with success on the job and that have low intercorrelations among themselves. The analysis is run, and the R^2 is highly significant. Furthermore, he is able to explain 52% of the variance on y (more than other investigators have been able to do). Are these results generalizable? Probably not, since what he did involves a *double* capitalization on chance:

1. In preselecting the predictors from a larger set, he is capitalizing on chance. Some of these variables would have high correlations with y because of sampling error, and consequently their correlations would tend to be lower in another sample.

2. The mathematical maximization involved in obtaining the multiple correlation involves capitalizing on chance.

Preselection of predictors is common among many researchers who are unaware of the fact that this tends to make their results sample specific. Nunnally (1978) had a nice discussion of the preselection problem, and Wilkinson (1979) showed the considerable positive bias preselection can have on the test of significance of R^2 in forward selection. The following example from his tables illustrates. The critical value for a four-predictor problem ($n = 35$) at .05 level is .26, and the appropriate critical value for the *same n* and α level, when preselecting 4 predictors from a set of 20 predictors is .51. Unawareness of the positive bias has led to many results in the literature that are not replicable, for as Wilkinson noted, "A computer assisted search for articles in psychology using stepwise regression from 1969 to 1977 located 71 articles. Out of these articles, 66 forward selections analyses reported as significant by the usual F tests were found. Of these 66 analyses, 19 were *not* significant by [his] Table 1."

It is important to note that both the Wherry and Herzberg formulas do *not* take into account preselection. Hence, the following from Cohen and Cohen (1983) should be seriously considered: "A more realistic estimate of the shrinkage is obtained by substituting for k the *total* number of predictors from which the selection was made." (p. 107) In other words, they are saying if 4 predictors were selected out of 15, use $k = 15$ in the Herzberg formula. While this may be conservative, using 4 will certainly lead to a positive bias. Probably a median value between 4 and 15 would be closer to the mark, although this needs further investigation.

3.13.2 Positive Bias of R^2

A study by Schutz (1977) on California principals and superintendents illustrates how capitalization on chance in multiple regression (if the researcher is unaware of it) can lead to misleading conclusions. Schutz was interested in validating a contingency theory of leadership, that is, that success in administering schools calls for different personality styles depending on the social setting of the school. The theory seems plausible, and in what follows we are not criticizing the theory per se, but the empirical validation of it. Schutz's procedure for validating the theory involved establishing a relationship between various personality attributes (24 predictors) and several measures of administrative success in heterogeneous samples with respect to social setting using multiple regression, that is, find the multiple R for each measure of success on 24 predictors. Then he showed that the magnitude of the relationships was greater for subsamples homogeneous with respect to social setting. The problem was that he had nowhere near adequate sample size for a reliable prediction equation. Here we present the total sample sizes and the subsamples homogeneous with respect to social setting:

	Superintendents	Principals
Total	$n = 77$	$n = 147$
Subsample(s)	$n = 29$	$n_1 = 35, n_2 = 61, n_2 = 36$

Indeed, Schutz did find that the R's in the homogeneous subsamples were on the average .34 greater than in the total samples; however, this was an artifact of the multiple regression procedure in this case. As Schutz went from total to his subsamples the number of predictors (k) approached sample size (n). For this situation the multiple correlation increases to 1 *regardless* of whether there is any relationship between y and the set of predictors. And in three of four of Schutz's subsamples the n/k ratios became dangerously close to 1. In particular, it is the case that $E(R^2) = k/(n - 1)$, when the population multiple correlation = 0 (Morrison, 1976).

To dramatize this, consider Subsample 1 for the principals. Then $E(R^2) = 24/34 = .706$, even when there is *no* relationship between y and the set of predictors. The critical value required just for statistical significance of R at .05 is 2.74, which implies $R^2 = .868$, just to be confident that the population multiple correlation is different from 0.

3.13.3 Suppressor Variables

Lord and Novick (1968) stated the following two rules of thumb for the selection of predictor variables:

1. Choose variables that correlate highly with the criterion but that have low intercorrelations.
2. To these variables add other variables that have low correlations with the criterion but that have high correlations with the other predictors. (p. 271)

   At first blush, the second rule of thumb may not seem to make sense, but what they are talking about is suppressor variables. To illustrate specifically why a suppressor variable can help in prediction, we consider a hypothetical example.

Example 3.7

Consider a two-predictor problem with the following correlations among the variables:

$$r_{yx_1} = .60, r_{yx_2} = 0, \text{ and } r_{x_1x_2} = .50.$$

Note that x_1 by itself accounts for $(.6)^2 = 100$, or 36% of the variance on y. Now consider entering x_2 into the regression equation first. It will of course account for no variance on y, and it may seem like we have gained nothing. But, if we now enter x_1 into the equation (after x_2), its predictive power is enhanced. This is because there is irrelevant variance on x_1 (i.e., variance that does not relate to y), which is related to x_2. In this case that irrelevant variance is $(.5)^2 = 100$ or 25%. When this irrelevant variance is partialed out (or suppressed), the remaining variance on x_1 is more strongly tied to y. Calculation of the semipartial correlation shows this:

$$r_{y1.2(s)} = \frac{r_{yx_1} - r_{yx_2}r_{x_1x_2}}{\sqrt{1 - r_{x_1x_2}^2}} = \frac{.60 - 0}{\sqrt{1 - .5^2}} = .693$$

Thus, $r_{y1.2(s)}^2 = .48$, and the predictive power of x_1 has increased from accounting for 36% to accounting for 48% of the variance on y.

3.14 Outliers and Influential Data Points

Because multiple regression is a mathematical maximization procedure, it can be very sensitive to data points that "split off" or are different from the rest of the points, that is, to outliers. Just one or two such points can affect the interpretation of results, and it is certainly moot as to whether one or two points should be permitted to have such a profound influence. Therefore, it is important to be able to detect outliers and influential points. There is a distinction between the two because a point that is an outlier (either on y or for the predictors) will *not necessarily* be influential in affecting the regression equation.

The fact that a simple examination of summary statistics can result in misleading interpretations was illustrated by Anscombe (1973). He presented three data sets that yielded the same summary statistics (i.e., regression coefficients and same $r^2 = .667$). In one case, linear regression was perfectly appropriate. In the second case, however, a scatterplot showed that curvilinear regression was appropriate. In the third case, linear regression was appropriate for 10 of 11 points, but the other point was an outlier and possibly should have been excluded from the analysis.

Two basic approaches can be used in dealing with outliers and influential points. We consider the approach of having an arsenal of tools for isolating these important points for further study, with the possibility of deleting some or all of the points from the analysis. The other approach is to develop procedures that are relatively insensitive to wild points (i.e., robust regression techniques). (Some pertinent references for robust regression are Hogg, 1979; Huber, 1977; Mosteller & Tukey, 1977). It is important to note that even robust regression may be ineffective when there are outliers in the space of the predictors (Huber, 1977). Thus, even in robust regression there is a need for case analysis. Also, a modification of robust regression, called bounded-influence regression, has been developed by Krasker and Welsch (1979).

3.14.1 Data Editing

Outliers and influential cases can occur because of recording errors. Consequently, researchers should give more consideration to the data editing phase of the data analysis process (i.e., *always* listing the data and examining the list for possible errors). There are many possible sources of error from the initial data collection to the final keypunching. First, some of the data may have been recorded incorrectly. Second, even if recorded correctly, when all of the data are transferred to a single sheet or a few sheets in preparation for keypunching, errors may be made. Finally, even if no errors are made in these first two steps, an error(s) could be made in entering the data into the terminal.

There are various statistics for identifying outliers on y and on the set of predictors, as well as for identifying influential data points. We discuss first, in brief form, a statistic for each, with advice on how to interpret that statistic. Equations for the statistics are given later in the section, along with a more extensive and somewhat technical discussion for those who are interested.

3.14.2 Measuring Outliers on y

For finding subjects whose predicted scores are quite different from their actual y scores (i.e., they do not fit the model well), the *standardized residuals* (r_i) can be used. If the model is correct, then they have a normal distribution with a mean of 0 and a standard deviation of 1. Thus, about 95% of the r_i should lie within two standard deviations of the mean and about 99% within three standard deviations. Therefore, any standardized residual greater than about 3 in absolute value is unusual and should be carefully examined.

3.14.3 Measuring Outliers on Set of Predictors

The *hat elements* (h_{ii}) can be used here. It can be shown that the hat elements lie between 0 and 1, and that the average hat element is p/n, where $p = k + 1$. Because of this, Hoaglin and Welsch (1978) suggested that $2p/n$ may be considered large. However, this can lead to more points than we really would want to examine, and the reader should consider using

$3p/n$. For example, with 6 predictors and 100 subjects, any hat element (also called leverage) greater than $3(7)/100 = .21$ should be carefully examined. This is a very simple and useful rule of thumb for quickly identifying subjects who are very different from the rest of the sample on the set of predictors.

3.14.4 Measuring Influential Data Points

An influential data point is one that when deleted produces a substantial change in at least one of the regression coefficients. That is, the prediction equations with and without the influential point are quite different. *Cook's distance* (Cook, 1977) is very useful for identifying influential points. It measures the *combined* influence of the case's being an outlier on y and on the set of predictors. Cook and Weisberg (1982) indicated that a Cook's distance = *1 would generally be considered large*. This provides a "red flag," when examining computer printout for identifying influential points.

All of the above diagnostic measures are easily obtained from SPSS REGRESSION (see Table 3.3) or SAS REG (see Table 3.6).

3.14.5 Measuring Outliers on y

The raw residuals, $\hat{e}_i = y_i - \hat{y}_i$, in linear regression are assumed to be independent, to have a mean of 0, to have constant variance, and to follow a normal distribution. However, because the n residuals have only $n - k$ degrees of freedom (k degrees of freedom were lost in estimating the regression parameters), they can't be independent. If n is large relative to k, however, then the $\hat{e}_i$ are essentially independent. Also, the residuals have different variances. It can be shown (Draper & Smith, 1981, p. 144) that the variance for the ith residual is given by:

$$s_{e_i}^2 = \hat{\sigma}^2(1 - h_{ii})$$ (15)

where $\hat{\sigma}^2$ is the estimate of variance not predictable from the regression (MS_{res}), and h_{ii} is the ith diagonal element of the hat matrix $X(X'X)^{-1}X'$. Recall that X is the score matrix for the predictors. The h_{ii} play a key role in determining the predicted values for the subjects. Recall that

$$\hat{\beta} = (X'X)^{-1}X'y \text{ and } \hat{y} = X\hat{\beta}$$

Therefore, $\hat{y} = X(X'X)^{-1}X'y$, by simple substitution. Thus, the predicted values for y are obtained by postmultiplying the hat matrix by the column vector of observed scores on y.

Because the predicted values ($\hat{y}_i$) and the residuals are related by $\hat{e}_i = y_i - \hat{y}_i$ it should not be surprising in view of the above that the variability of the $\hat{e}_i$ would be affected by the h_{ii}.

Because the residuals have different variances, we need to standardize to meaningfully compare them. This is completely analogous to what is done in comparing raw scores from distributions with different variances and different means. There, one means of standardizing was to convert to z scores, using $z_i = (x_i - x)/s$. Here we also subtract off the mean (which is 0 and hence has no effect) and then divide by the standard deviation. The standard deviation is the square root of Equation 12. Therefore,

$$r_i = \frac{\hat{e}_i - 0}{\hat{\sigma}\sqrt{1 - h_{ii}}} = \frac{\hat{e}_i}{\hat{\sigma}\sqrt{1 - h_{ii}}} \qquad (16)$$

Because the r_i are assumed to have a normal distribution with a mean of 0 (if the model is correct), then about 99% of the r_i should lie within 3 standard deviations of the mean.

3.14.6 Measuring Outliers on the Predictors

The h_{ii}'s are one measure of the extent to which the ith observation is an outlier for the predictors. The h_{ii}'s are important because they can play a key role in determining the predicted values for the subjects. Recall that

$$\hat{\beta} = (\mathbf{X'X})^{-1}\mathbf{X'y} \text{ and } \hat{\mathbf{y}} = \mathbf{X}\hat{\beta}$$

Therefore, $\mathbf{y} = \mathbf{X}(\mathbf{X'X})^{-1}\mathbf{X'y}$ by simple substitution.

Thus, the predicted values for y are obtained by postmultiplying the hat matrix by the column vector of observed scores on y. It can be shown that the h_{ii}'s lie between 0 and 1, and that the average value for $h_{ii} = k/n$. From Equation 12 it can be seen that when h_{ii} is large (i.e., near 1), then the variance for the ith residual is near 0. This means that $y_i \approx \hat{y}_i$. In other words, an observation may fit the linear model well and yet be an influential data point. This second diagnostic, then, is "flagging" observations that need to be examined carefully because they may have an unusually large influence on the regression coefficients.

What is a significant value for the h_{ii}? Hoaglin and Welsch (1978) suggested that $2p/n$ may be considered large. Belsey et al. (1980, pp. 67–68) showed that when the set of predictors is multivariate normal, then $(n - p) [h_{ii} - 1/n]/(1 - h_{ii})(p - 1)$ is distributed as F with $(p - 1)$ and $(n - p)$ degrees of freedom.

Rather than computing the above F and comparing against a critical value, Hoaglin and Welsch suggested $2p/n$ as rough guide for a large h_{ii}.

An important point to remember concerning the hat elements is that the points they identify will not necessarily be influential in affecting the regression coefficients.

Mahalanobis's (1936) distance for case $i(D_i^2)$ indicates how far the case is from the centroid of all cases for the predictor variables. A large distance indicates an observation that is an outlier for the predictors. The Mahalanobis distance can be written in terms of the covariance matrix $\mathbf{S}$ as

$$D_i^2 = (\mathbf{x}_i - \bar{\mathbf{x}})'\mathbf{S}^{-1}(\mathbf{x}_i - \bar{\mathbf{x}}), \qquad (17)$$

where $\mathbf{x}_i$ is the vector of the data for case i and $\bar{\mathbf{x}}$ is the vector of means (centroid) for the predictors.

For a better understanding of D_i^2, consider two small data sets. The first set has two predictors. In Table 3.10, the data is presented, as well as the D_i^2 and the descriptive statistics (including $\mathbf{S}$). The D_i^2 for cases 6 and 10 are large because the score for Case 6 on x_i (150) was deviant, whereas for Case 10 the score on x_2 (97) was very deviant. The graphical split-off of Cases 6 and 10 is quite vivid and was displayed in Figure 1.2 in Chapter 1.

TABLE 3.10

Raw Data and Mahalanobis Distances for Two Small Data Sets

Case	Y	X_1	X_2	X_3	X_4		D_i^2
1	476	111	68	17	81		0.30
2	457	92	46	28	67		1.55
3	540	90	50	19	83		1.47
4	551	107	59	25	71		0.01
5	575	98	50	13	92		0.76
6	698	150	66	20	90	①	5.48
7	545	118	54	11	101		0.47
8	574	110	51	26	82		0.38
9	645	117	59	18	87		0.23
10	556	94	97	12	69		7.24
11	634	130	57	16	97		
12	637	118	51	19	78		
13	390	91	44	14	64		
14	562	118	61	20	103		
15	560	109	66	13	88		
Summary Statistics							
M	561.70000	108.70000	60.00000				
SD	70.74846	17.73289	14.84737				

$$S = \begin{bmatrix} 314.455 & 19.483 \\ 19.483 & 220.444 \end{bmatrix}$$

Note: Boxed-in entries are the first data set and corresponding D_i^2. The 10 case numbers having the largest D_i^2 for a four-predictor data set are: 10, 10.859; 13, 7.977; 6, 7.223; 2, 5.048; 14, 4.874; 7, 3.514; 5, 3.177; 3, 2.616; 8, 2.561; 4, 2.404.
① Calculation of D_i^2 for Case 6:

$$D_6^2 = (41.3, 6) \begin{bmatrix} 314.455 & 19.483 \\ 19.483 & 220.444 \end{bmatrix}^{-1} \begin{pmatrix} 41.3 \\ 6 \end{pmatrix}$$

$$S^{-1} = \begin{bmatrix} .00320 & -.00029 \\ -.00029 & .00456 \end{bmatrix} \rightarrow D_6^2 = 5.484$$

In the previous example, because the numbers of predictors and subjects were few, it would have been fairly easy to spot the outliers even without the Mahalanobis distance. However, in practical problems with 200 or 300 subjects and 10 predictors, outliers are not always easy to spot and can occur in more subtle ways. For example, a case may have a large distance because there are moderate to fairly large differences on many of the predictors. The second small data set with 4 predictors and $N = 15$ in Table 3.10 illustrates this latter point. The D_i^2 for case 13 is quite large (7.97) even though the scores for that subject do not split off in a striking fashion for any of the predictors. Rather, it is a cumulative effect that produces the separation.

TABLE 3.11

Critical Values for an Outlier on the Predictors as Judged by Mahalanobis D^2

	Number of Predictors							
	K = 2		K = 3		K = 4		K = 5	
n	5%	1%	5%	1%	5%	1%	5%	1%
5	3.17	3.19						
6	4.00	4.11	4.14	4.16				
7	4.71	4.95	5.01	5.10	5.12	5.14		
8	5.32	5.70	5.77	5.97	6.01	6.09	6.11	6.12
9	5.85	6.37	6.43	6.76	6.80	6.97	7.01	7.08
10	6.32	6.97	7.01	7.47	7.50	7.79	7.82	7.98
12	7.10	8.00	7.99	8.70	8.67	9.20	9.19	9.57
14	7.74	8.84	8.78	9.71	9.61	10.37	10.29	10.90
16	8.27	9.54	9.44	10.56	10.39	11.36	11.20	12.02
18	8.73	10.15	10.00	11.28	11.06	12.20	11.96	12.98
20	9.13	10.67	10.49	11.91	11.63	12.93	12.62	13.81
25	9.94	11.73	11.48	13.18	12.78	14.40	13.94	15.47
30	10.58	12.54	12.24	14.14	13.67	15.51	14.95	16.73
35	11.10	13.20	12.85	14.92	14.37	16.40	15.75	17.73
40	11.53	13.74	13.36	15.56	14.96	17.13	16.41	18.55
45	11.90	14.20	13.80	16.10	15.46	17.74	16.97	19.24
50	12.23	14.60	14.18	16.56	15.89	18.27	17.45	19.83
100	14.22	16.95	16.45	19.26	18.43	21.30	20.26	23.17
200	15.99	18.94	18.42	21.47	20.59	23.72	22.59	25.82
500	18.12	21.22	20.75	23.95	23.06	26.37	25.21	28.62

How large must D_i^2 be before one can say that case i is significantly separated from the rest of the data at the .05 level of significance? If it is tenable that the predictors came from a multivariate normal population, then the critical values (Barnett & Lewis, 1978) are given in Table 3.11 for 2 through 5 predictors. An easily implemented graphical test for multivariate normality is available (Johnson & Wichern, 1982). The test involves plotting ordered Mahalanobis distances against chi-square percentile points.

Referring back to the example with 2 predictors and $n = 10$, if we assume multivariate normality, then Case 6 ($D_i^2 = 5.48$) is not significantly separated from the rest of the data at .05 level because the critical value equals 6.32. In contrast, Case 10 is significantly separated.

Weisberg (1980, p. 104) showed that if n is even moderately large (50 or more), then D_i^2 is approximately proportional to h_{ii}:

$$D_i^2 \approx (n-1)h_{ii} \tag{18}$$

Thus, with large n, either measure may be used. Also, because we have previously indicated what would correspond roughly to a significant h_{ii} value, from Equation 16 we can immediately determine the corresponding significant D_i^2 value. For example, if $k = 7$ and $n = 50$, then a large $h_{ii} = .42$ and the corresponding large $D_i^2 = 20.58$. If $k = 20$ and $n = 200$, then a large $h_{ii} = 2k/n = .20$ and the corresponding large $D_i^2 = 39.90$.

3.14.7 Measures for Influential Data Points

3.14.7.1 Cook's Distance

Cook's distance (CD) is a measure of the change in the regression coefficients that would occur if this case were omitted, thus revealing which cases are most influential in affecting the regression equation. It is affected by the case's being an outlier both on y and on the set of predictors. Cook's distance is given by

$$CD_i = (\hat{\boldsymbol{\beta}} - \hat{\boldsymbol{\beta}}_{(-i)})' \mathbf{X}' \mathbf{X} (\hat{\boldsymbol{\beta}} - \hat{\boldsymbol{\beta}}_{(-i)}) / (k+1) MS_{\text{res}} \qquad (19)$$

where $\hat{\boldsymbol{\beta}}_{(-i)}$ is the vector of estimated regression coefficients with the ith data point deleted, k is the number of predictors, and MS_{res} is the residual (error) variance for the full data set.

Removing the ith data point should keep $\hat{\boldsymbol{\beta}}_{(-i)}$ close to $\hat{\boldsymbol{\beta}}$ unless the ith observation is an outlier. Cook and Weisberg (1982, p. 118) indicated that *a $CD_i > 1$ would generally be considered large*. Cook's distance can be written in an alternative revealing form:

$$CD_i = \frac{1}{(k+1)} r_i^2 \frac{h_{ii}}{1 - h_{ii}}, \qquad (20)$$

where r_i is the standardized residual and h_{ii} is the hat element. Thus, *Cook's distance measures the joint (combined) influence of the case being an outlier on y and on the set of predictors.* A case may be influential because it is a significant outlier only on y, for example,

$$k = 5, n = 40, r_i = 4, h_{ii} = .3 : CD_i > 1$$

or because it is a significant outlier only on the set of predictors, for example,

$$k = 5, n = 40, r_i = 2, h_{ii} = .7 : CD_i > 1$$

Note, however, that a case may not be a significant outlier on either y or on the set of predictors, but may still be influential, as in the following:

$$k = 3, n = 20, h_{ii} = .4, r = 2.5 : CD_i > 1$$

3.14.7.2 DFFITS

This statistic (Belsley, Kuh, & Welsch, 1980) indicates how much the ith fitted value will change if the ith observation is deleted. It is given by

$$(\text{DFFITS})_i \frac{\hat{y}_i - \hat{y}_{i-1}}{s_{-i} h_{ii}} \qquad (21)$$

The numerator simply expresses the difference between the fitted values, with the ith point in and with it deleted. The denominator provides a measure of variability since $s_y^2 = \sigma^2 h_{ii}$. Therefore, *DFFITS indicates the number of estimated standard errors that the fitted value changes when the ith point is deleted.*

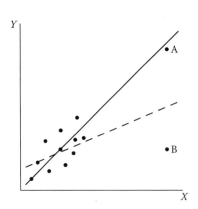

FIGURE 3.5
Examples of two outliers on the predictors: one influential and the other not influential.

3.14.7.3 DFBETAS

These are very useful in dictating how much *each* regression coefficient will change if the ith observation is deleted. They are given by

$$(\text{DFBETAS})_i \frac{b_j - b_{j,-i}}{s_{-i}\bar{c}_{jj}} \tag{20}$$

Each of the DFBETAS *therefore indicates the number of standard errors the coefficient changes when the ith point is deleted*. The DFBETAS are available on both SAS and SPSS. Any DFBETA with a value > |2| indicates a sizable change and should be investigated. Thus, although Cook's D is a *composite* measure of influence, the DFBETAS indicates which specific coefficients are being most affected.

It was mentioned earlier that a data point that is an outlier either on y or on the set of predictors will not *necessarily* be an influential point. Figure 3.5 illustrates how this can happen. In this simplified example with just one predictor, both points A and B are outliers on x. Point B is influential, and to accommodate it, the least squares regression line will be pulled downward toward the point. However, Point A is not influential because this point closely follows the trend of the rest of the data.

3.14.8 Summary

In summarizing then, use of the Weisberg test (with standardized residuals) will detect y outliers, and the hat elements or the Mahalanobis distances will detect outliers on the predictors. Such outliers will not necessarily be influential points. To determine which outliers are influential, find those whose Cook's distances are >1. Those points that are flagged as influential by Cook's distance need to be examined carefully to determine whether they should be deleted from the analysis. If there is a reason to believe that these cases arise from a process different from that for the rest of the data, then the cases should be deleted. For example, the failure of a measuring instrument, a power failure, or the occurrence of an unusual event (perhaps inexplicable) would be instances of a different process.

If a point is a significant outlier on y, but its Cook distance is < 1, there is no real need to delete the point because it does not have a large effect on the regression analysis. However, one should still be interested in studying such points further to understand why they did not fit the model. After all, the purpose of any study is to understand the data. In particular, one wants to ascertain if there are any communalities among the S's corresponding to such outliers, suggesting that perhaps these subjects come from a different population. For an excellent, readable, and extended discussion of outliers, influential points, identification of and remedies for, see Weisberg (1980, chapters 5 and 6).

In concluding this summary, the following from Belsley, Kuh, and Welsch (1980) is appropriate:

> A word of warning is in order here, for it is obvious that there is room for misuse of the above procedures. High-influence data points could conceivably be removed solely to effect a desired change in a particular estimated coefficient, its *t* value, or some other regression output. While this danger exists, it is an unavoidable consequence of a procedure that successfully highlights such points … the benefits obtained from information on influential points far outweigh any potential danger. (pp. 15–16)

Example 3.8

We now consider the data in Table 3.10 with four predictors ($n = 15$). This data was run on SPSS REGRESSION, which compactly and conveniently presents all the outlier information on a single page. The regression with all four predictors is significant at the .05 level ($F = 3.94$, $p < .0358$). However, we wish to focus our attention on the outlier analysis, a summary of which is given in Table 3.12. Examination of the studentized residuals shows no significant outliers on y. To determine whether there are any significant outliers on the set of predictors, we examine the Mahalanobis distances. Case 10 is an outlier on the x's since the critical value from Table 3.12 is 10, whereas Case 13 is not significant. Cook's distances reveal that both cases 10 and 13 are influential data points, since the distances are >1. Note that Case 13 is an influential point even though it is *not* a significant outlier on either y or on the set of predictors. We indicated that this is possible, and indeed it has occurred here. This is the more subtle type of influential points which Cook's distance brings to our attention.

In Table 3.13 we present the regression coefficients that resulted when cases 10 and 13 were deleted. There is a fairly dramatic shift in the coefficients in each case. For Case 10 the dramatic shift occurs for x_2, where the coefficient changes from 1.27 (for all data points) to –1.48 (with case 10 deleted). This is a shift of just over two standard errors (standard error for x_2 on printout is 1.34). For Case 13 the coefficients change in sign for three of the four predictors (x_4, x_2, and x_3).

TABLE 3.12

Selected Output for Sample Problem on Outliers and Influential Points

Outlier Statistics[a]		Case Number	Statistic	Sig. F
Std. Residual	1	1	−1.602	
	2	12	1.235	
	3	9	1.049	
	4	13	−1.048	
	5	5	1.003	
	6	14	−.969	
	7	3	.807	
	8	7	−.743	
	9	2	−.545	
	10	10	.460	
Std. Residual	1	13	−1.739	
	2	1	−1.696	
	3	12	1.391	
	4	14	−1.267	
	5	5	1.193	
	6	10	1.160	
	7	9	1.093	
	8	3	.934	
	9	7	−.899	
	10	2	−.721	
Cook's Distance	1	10	1.436	.292
	2	13	1.059	.437
	3	14	.228	.942
	4	5	.118	.985
	5	12	.104	.989
	6	2	.078	.994
	7	7	.075	.995
	8	1	.069	.996
	9	3	.059	.997
	10	9	.021	1.000
Centered Leverage Value	1	10	.776	
	2	13	.570	
	3	6	.516	
	4	2	.361	
	5	14	.348	
	6	7	.251	
	7	5	.227	
	8	3	.187	
	9	8	.183	
	10	4	.172	

[a] Dependent Variable: Y

TABLE 3.13

Selected Output for Sample Problem on Outliers and Influential Points

BEGINNING BLOCK NUMBER 1. METHOD: ENTER

VARIABLES(S) ENTERED ON STEP NUMBER		1..	X4
		2..	X2
		3..	X3
		4..	X1

MULTIPLE R	.78212	ANALYSIS OF VARIANCE			
				SUM OF	
R SQUARE	.61171		DF	SQUARES	MEAN SQUARE
ADJUSTED R SQUARE					
STANDARD ERROR	57.57994	RESIDUAL	10	33154.49775	3315.44977
		F = 3.93849		SIGNIF F = .0358	

VARIABLES IN THE EQUATION

VARIABLE	B	SE B	BETA	T	SIG T
X4	1.48832	1.78548	.23194	.834	.4240
X2	1.27014	1.34394	.21016	.945	.3669
X3	2.01747	3.55943	.13440	.567	.5833
X1	2.80343	1.26554	.58644	2.215	.0511
(CONSTANT)	15.85866	180.29777		.088	.9316

FOR BLOCK NUMBER 1 ALL REQUESTED VARIABLES ENTERED

REGRESSION COEFFICIENTS WITH CASE 10 DELETED		REGRESSION COEFFICIENTS WITH CASE 13 DELETED	
VARIABLE	B	VARIABLE	B
X4	2.07788	X4	−1.33883
X2	−1.48076	X2	−.70800
X3	2.75130	X1	3.41539
X1	3.52924	X3	−3.45596
(CONSTANT)	23.36214	(CONSTANT)	410.45740

3.15 Further Discussion of the Two Computer Examples

3.15.1 Morrison Data

Recall that for the Morrison data the stepwise procedure yielded the more parsimonious model involving three predictors: CLARITY, INTEREST, and STIMUL. If we were interested in an estimate of the predictive power in the population, then the Wherry estimate given by Equation 8 is appropriate. This is given under STEP NUMBER 3 on the SPSS printout in Table 3.6 as ADJUSTED R SQUARE .84016. Here the estimate is used in a descriptive sense: to describe the relationship in the population. However, if we are interested in the cross-validity predictive power, then the Stein estimate (Equation 9) should be used. The Stein adjusted R^2 in this case is

$$\rho_c^2 = 1 - (31/28)(30/27)(33/32)(1 - .856) = .82$$

This estimates that if we were to cross-validate the prediction equation on many other samples from the same population, then *on the average* we would account for about 82% of the variance on the dependent variable. In this instance the estimated dropoff in predictive power is very little from the maximized value of 85.56%. The reason is that the association between the dependent variable and the set of predictors is *very* strong. Thus, we can have confidence in the future predictive power of the equation.

It is also important to examine the regression diagnostics to check for any outliers or influential data points. Table 3.14 presents the appropriate statistics, as discussed in section 3.16, for identifying outliers on the dependent variable (standardized residuals), outliers on the set of predictors (hat elements), and influential data points (Cook's distance).

First, we would expect only about 5% of the standardized residuals to be > |2| if the linear model is appropriate. From Table 3.14 we see that two of the ZRESID are > |2|, and we would expect about 32(.05) = 1.6, so nothing seems to be awry here. Next, we check for outliers on the set of predictors. The rough "critical value" here is $3p/n = 3(4)/32 = .375$. Because there are no values under LEVER in Table 3.14 exceeding this value, we have no outliers on the set of predictors. Finally, and perhaps most importantly, we check for the existence of influential data points using Cook's D. Recall that Cook and Weisberg (1982) suggested if $D > 1$, then the point is influential. All the Cook D's in Table 3.15 are far less than 1, so we have no influential data points.

In summary then, the linear regression model is quite appropriate for the Morrison data. The estimated cross-validity power is excellent, and there are no outliers or influential data points.

3.15.2 National Academy of Sciences Data

Recall that both the stepwise procedure and the MAXR procedure yielded the same "best" four-predictor set: NFACUL, PCTSUPP, PCTGRT, AND NARTIC. The maximized R^2 = .8221, indicating that 82.21% of the variance in quality can be accounted for by these four predictors in *this* sample. Now we obtain two measures of the cross-validity power of the equation. First, from the SAS REG printout, we have PREDICTED RESID SS (PRESS) = 1350.33. Furthermore, the variance for QUALITY is 101.438, so that $\Sigma(Y_i - Y)^2 = 4564.71$. From these numbers we can compute

$$R^2_{Press} = 1 - (1350.33)/4564.71 = .7042$$

This is a good measure of the external predictive power of the equation, where we have n validations, each based on $(n - 1)$ observations.

The Stein *estimate* of how much variance on the average we would account for if the equation were applied to many other samples is

$$\rho_c^2 = 1 - (45/41)(44/40)(1 - .822) = .7804$$

Now we turn to the regression diagnostics from SAS REG, which are presented in Table 3.15. In terms of the standardized residuals for y, two stand out (−3.0154 and 2.5276 for observations 25 and 44). These are for the University of Michigan and Virginia Polytech. In

TABLE 3.14

Regression Diagnostics (Standardized Residuals, Hat Elements, and Cook's Distance) for Morrison MBA Data

Casewise Plot of Standardized Residual
*: Selected   M: Missing

Case #	-3.0 0.0 3.0 O:..........................:O	① *PRED	② *RESID	③ *ZRESID	④ *LEVER	⑤ *COOK D
1	. * .	1.1156	-.1156	-.3627	.1021	.0058
2	. * .	1.5977	-.5977	-1.8746	.0541	.0896
3	. *	.9209	.0791	.2481	.1541	.0043
4	. * .	1.1156	-.1156	-.3627	.1021	.0058
5	. *	1.5330	.4670	1.4645	.1349	.1281
6	. * .	1.9872	.0128	.0401	.1218	.0001
7	. * .	2.2746	-.2746	-.8612	.0279	.0124
8	. * .	2.6920	-.6920	-2.1703	.0180	.0641
9	. * .	2.2378	-.2378	-.7459	.1381	.0341
10	. *	1.8204	.1796	.5632	.0708	.0100
11	. *	1.7925	.2075	.6508	.0412	.0089
12	. * .	2.0431	-.0431	-.1351	.2032	.0018
13	. *	1.5977	.4023	1.2616	.0541	.0406
14	. * .	2.2099	-.2099	-.6583	.0863	.0164
15	. * .	2.2746	-.2746	-.8612	.0279	.0124
16	. * .	2.4693	-.4693	-1.4719	.0541	.0553
17	. * .	2.0799	-.0799	-.2504	.0953	.0026
18	. * .	3.1741	-.1741	-.5461	.0389	.0060
19	. *	2.7567	.2433	.7630	.1039	.0263
20	. * .	2.9794	.0206	.0647	.0933	.0002
21	. * .	2.9794	.0206	.0647	.0933	.0002
22	. .* .	2.9147	.0853	.2676	.0976	.0030
23	. .* .	2.9147	.0853	.2676	.0976	.0030
24	. *	2.7567	.2433	.7630	.1039	.0263
25	. * .	3.1462	-.1462	-.4585	.1408	.0132
26	. *	2.8868	.1132	.3552	.1116	.0061
27	. * .	3.1741	-.1741	-.5461	.0389	.0060
28	. .* .	2.9514	.0486	.1523	.0756	.0008
29	. *	2.2746	.7254	2.2750	.0279	.0865
30	. *	2.6641	.3359	1.0535	.1738	.0900
31	. *. .	4.0736	-.0736	-.2310	.1860	.0047
32	. *	3.5915	.4085	1.2810	.1309	.0948
Case #	O:..........................:O -3.0 0.0 3.0	*PRED	*RESID	*ZRESID	*LEVER	*COOK D

① These are the predicted values.
② These are the raw residuals, that is, $\hat{e}_i = y_i - \hat{y}_i$. Thus, for the first subject we have $\hat{e}_i = 1 - 1.1156 = -.1156$.
③ These are the standardized residuals.
④ The hat elements—they have been called leverage elements elsewhere; hence the abbreviation LEVER.
⑤ Cook's distance—useful for identifying influential data points. Cook suggests if $D > 1$, then the point generally would be considered influential.

TABLE 3.15

Regression Diagnostics (Standardized Residuals, Hat Elements, and Cook's Distance) for National Academy of Science Data

Obs	Student Residual	-2-1-0 1 2	Cook's D	Rstudent	Hat Diag H
1	-0.708	*	0.007	-0.7039	0.0684
2	-0.078		0.000	-0.0769	0.1064
3	0.403		0.003	0.3992	0.0807
4	0.424		0.009	0.4193	0.1951
5	0.800	*	0.012	0.7968	0.0870
6	-1.447	**	0.034	-1.4677	0.0742
7	1.085	**	0.038	1.0874	0.1386
8	-0.300		0.002	-0.2968	0.1057
9	-0.460		0.010	-0.4556	0.18765
10	1.694	****	0.48	1.7346	0.0765
11	-0.694	*	0.004	-0.6892	0.0433
12	-0.870	*	0.016	-0.8670	0.0956
13	-0.732		0.007	-0.7276	0.0652
14	0.359	*	0.003	0.3556	0.0885
15	-0.942	**	0.054	-0.9403	0.2328
16	1.282		0.063	1.2927	0.1613
17	0.424		0.001	0.4200	0.0297
18	0.227		0.001	0.2241	0.1196
19	0.877	*	0.007	0.8747	0.0464
20	0.643	*	0.004	0.6382	0.0456
21	-0.417		0.002	-0.4127	0.0429
22	0.193		0.001	0.1907	0.0696
23	0.490		0.002	0.4856	0.0460
24	0.357		0.001	0.3533	0.0503
25	-2.756	*****	2.292	-3.0154	0.6014
26	-1.370	**	0.068	-1.3855	0.1533
27	-0.799	*	0.017	-0.7958	0.1186
28	0.165		0.000	0.1629	0.0573
29	0.995	*	0.018	0.9954	0.0844
30	-1.786	***	0.241	-1.8374	0.2737
31	-1.171	**	0.018	-1.1762	0.0613
32	-0.994	*	0.017	-0.9938	0.0796
33	1.394	**	0.037	1.4105	0.0859
34	1.568	***	0.051	1.5978	0.0937
35	-0.622	*	0.006	-0.6169	0.0714
36	0.282		0.002	0.2791	0.1066
37	-0.831	*	0.009	-0.8277	0.0643
38	1.516	***	0.039	1.5411	0.0789
39	1.492	**	0.081	1.5151	0.1539
40	0.314		0.001	0.3108	0.0638
41	-0.977	*	0.016	-0.9766	0.0793
42	-0.581	*	0.006	-0.5766	0.0847
43	0.059		0.000	0.0584	0.0877
44	2.376	****	0.164	2.5276	0.1265
45	-0.508	*	0.003	-0.5031	0.0592
46	-1.505	***	0.085	-1.5292	0.1583

terms of outliers on the set of predictors, using $2p/n = 2(5)/46 = .217$, there are outliers for observation 15 (University of Georgia), observation 25 (University of Michigan again), and observation 30 (Northeastern).

Using the criterion of Cook $D > 1$, there is one influential data point, observation 25 (University of Michigan). Recall that whether a point will be influential is a *joint* function of being an outlier on y and on the set of predictors. In this case, the University of Michigan definitely doesn't fit the model and it differs dramatically from the other psychology departments on the set of predictors. A check of the DFBETAS reveals that it is very different in terms of number of faculty (DFBETA = −2.7653), and a scan of the raw data shows the number of faculty at 111, whereas the average number of faculty members for all the departments is only 29.5. The question needs to be raised as to whether the University of Michigan is "counting" faculty members in a different way from the rest of the schools. For example, are they including part-time and adjunct faculty, and if so, is the number of these quite large?

For comparison purposes, the analysis was also run with the University of Michigan deleted. Interestingly, the same four predictors emerge from the stepwise procedure, although the results are better in some ways. For example, Mallows' C_k is now 4.5248, whereas for the full data set it was 5.216. Also, the PRESS residual sum of squares is now only 899.92, whereas for the full data set it was 1350.33.

3.16 Sample Size Determination for a Reliable Prediction Equation

The reader may recall that in power analysis one is interested in determining a priori how many subjects are needed per group to have, say, power = .80 at the .05 level. Thus, planning is done ahead of time to ensure that one has a good chance of detecting an effect of a given magnitude. Now, in multiple regression, the focus is different and the concern, or at least one very important concern, is development of a prediction equation that has generalizability. A study by Park and Dudycha (1974) provided several tables that, given certain input parameters, enable one to determine how many subjects will be needed for a reliable prediction equation. They considered from 3 to 25 random variable predictors, and found that with about 15 subjects per predictor the amount of shrinkage is small (< .05) with high probability (.90), if the squared population multiple correlation (ρ^2) is .50. In Table 3.16 we present selected results from the Park and Dudycha study for 3, 4, 8, and 15 predictors.

To use Table 3.16 we need an estimate of ρ^2, that is, the squared *population* multiple correlation. Unless an investigator has a good estimate from a previous study that used similar subjects and predictors, we feel taking $\rho^2 = .50$ is a reasonable guess for social science research. In the physical sciences, estimates > .75 are quite reasonable. If we set $\rho^2 = .50$ and want the loss in predictive power to be less than .05 with probability = .90, then the required sample sizes are as follows:

	Number of Predictors			
$\rho^2 = .50$ $\varepsilon = .05$	3	4	8	15
n	50	66	124	214
n/k ratio	16.7	16.7	15.5	14.3

The n/k ratios in all 4 cases are around 15/1.

TABLE 3.16

Sample Size Such That the Difference Between the Squared Multiple Correlation and Squared Cross-Validated Correlation Is Arbitrarily Small With Given Probability

| | | Three Predictors | | | | | | | | Four Predictors | | | | | |
| | | γ | | | | | | | | γ | | | | | |
ρ^2	ε	.99	.95	.90	.80	.60	.40	ρ^{22}	ε	.99	.95	.90	.80	.60	.40
.05	.01	858	554	421	290	158	81	.05	.01	1041	707	559	406	245	144
	.03	269	166	123	79	39	18		.03	312	201	152	103	54	27
	.01	825	535	410	285	160	88		.01	1006	691	550	405	253	155
.10	.03	271	174	133	91	50	27	.10	.03	326	220	173	125	74	43
	.05	159	100	75	51	27	14		.05	186	123	95	67	38	22
	.01	693	451	347	243	139	79		.01	853	587	470	348	221	140
	.03	232	151	117	81	48	27		.03	283	195	156	116	73	46
.25	.05	140	91	71	50	29	17	.25	.05	168	117	93	69	43	28
	.10	70	46	36	25	15	7		.10	84	58	46	34	20	14
	.20	34	22	17	12	8	6		.20	38	26	20	15	10	7
	.01	464	304	234	165	96	55		.01	573	396	317	236	152	97
	.03	157	104	80	57	34	21		.03	193	134	108	81	53	35
.50	.05	96	64	50	36	22	14	.50	.05	117	82	66	50	33	23
	.10	50	34	27	20	13	9		.10	60	43	35	27	19	13
	.20	27	19	15	12	9	7		.20	32	23	19	15	11	9
	.01	235	155	120	85	50	30		.01	290	201	162	121	78	52
	.03	85	55	43	31	20	13		.03	100	70	57	44	30	21
.75	.05	51	35	28	21	14	10	.75	.05	62	44	37	28	20	15
	.10	28	20	16	13	9	7		.10	34	25	21	17	13	11
	.20	16	12	10	9	7	6		.20	19	15	13	11	9	7
	.01	23	17	14	11	9	7		.01	29	22	19	15	12	10
	.03	11	9	8	7	6	6		.03	14	11	10	9	8	7
.98	.05	9	7	7	6	6	5	.98	.05	10	9	8	8	8	7
	.10	7	6	6	6	5	5		.10	8	8	7	7	7	7
	.20	6	6	5	5	5	5		.20	7	7	7	6	6	6

| | | Eight Predictors | | | | | | | | Fifteen Predictors | | | | | |
| | | γ | | | | | | | | γ | | | | | |
ρ^2	ε	.99	.95	.90	.80	.60	.40	ρ^{22}	ε	.99	.95	.90	.80	.60	.40
.05	.01	1640	1226	1031	821	585	418	.05	.01	2523	2007	1760	1486	1161	918
	.03	447	313	251	187	116	71		.03	640	474	398	316	222	156
.10	.01	1616	1220	1036	837	611	450	.10	.01	2519	2029	1794	1532	1220	987
	.03	503	373	311	246	172	121		.03	762	600	524	438	337	263
	.05	281	202	166	128	85	55		.05	403	309	265	216	159	119
.25	.01	1376	1047	893	727	538	404	.25	.01	2163	1754	1557	1339	1079	884
	.03	453	344	292	237	174	129		.03	705	569	504	431	345	280
	.05	267	202	171	138	101	74		.05	413	331	292	249	198	159
	.10	128	95	80	63	45	33		.10	191	151	132	111	87	69
	.20	52	37	30	24	17	12		.20	76	58	49	40	30	24
.50	.01	927	707	605	494	368	279	.50	.01	1461	1188	1057	911	738	608
	.03	312	238	204	167	125	96		.03	489	399	355	306	249	205
	.05	188	144	124	103	77	59		.05	295	261	214	185	151	125
	.10	96	74	64	53	40	31		.10	149	122	109	94	77	64
	.20	49	38	33	28	22	18		.20	75	62	55	48	40	34
.75	.01	470	360	308	253	190	150	.75	.01	741	605	539	466	380	315
	.03	162	125	108	90	69	54		.03	255	210	188	164	135	113
	.05	100	78	68	57	44	35		.05	158	131	118	103	86	73
	.10	54	43	38	32	26	22		.10	85	72	65	58	49	43
	.20	31	25	23	20	17	15		.20	49	42	39	35	31	28
.98	.01	47	38	34	29	24	21	.98	.01	75	64	59	53	46	41
	.03	22	19	18	16	15	14		.03	36	33	31	29	27	25
	.05	17	16	15	14	13	12		.05	28	26	25	24	23	22
	.10	14	13	12	12	11	11		.10	23	21	21	20	20	19
	.20	12	11	11	11	11	10		.20	20	19	19	18	18	18

Note: Entries in the body of the table are the sample size such that $P(\rho^2 - \rho_c^2 < \varepsilon) = \gamma$ where ρ is population multiple correlation, ε is some tolerance, and γ is the probability.

We had indicated earlier that *generally* about 15 subjects per predictor are needed for a reliable regression equation in the social sciences, that is, an equation that will cross-validate well. Three converging lines of evidence support this conclusion:

1. The Stein formula for estimated shrinkage (Table 3.8).
2. My own experience.
3. The results just presented from the Park and Dudycha study.

However, the Park and Dudycha study (see Table 3.16) clearly shows that *the magnitude of* ρ (population multiple correlation) strongly affects how many subjects will be needed for a reliable regression equation. For example, if $\rho^2 = .75$, then for three predictors only 28 subjects are needed, whereas 50 subjects were needed for the same case when $\rho^2 = .50$.

Also, from the Stein formula (Table 3.8), you will see if you plug in .40 for R^2 that more than 15 subjects per predictor will be needed to keep the shrinkage fairly small, whereas if you insert .70 for R^2, significantly fewer than 15 will be needed.

3.17 Logistic Regression

We now consider the case where the dependent variable we wish to predict is dichotomous. Let us look at several instances where this would be true:

1. In epidemiology we are interested in whether someone has a disease or does not. If it is heart disease, then predictors such as age, weight, systolic blood pressure, number of cigarettes smoked, and cholesterol level all are relevant.
2. In marketing we may wish to know whether someone will or will not buy a new car in the upcoming year. Here predictors such as annual income, number of dependents, amount of home mortgage, and so on are all relevant as predictors.
3. In education, suppose we wish to know only if someone passes a test or does not.
4. In psychology we may wish to know only whether someone has or has not completed a task.

In each of these cases the dependent variable is dichotomous: that is, it has only two values. These could be, and often are, coded as 0 and 1. As Neter, Wasserman, and Kutner (1989) pointed out, special problems arise when the dependent variable is dichotomous (binary):

1. There are nonnormal error terms.
2. We have nonconstant error variance.
3. There are constraints on the response function.

They further noted, "The difficulties created by the third problem are the most serious. One could use weighted least squares to handle the problem of unequal error variances. In addition, with large sample sizes the method of least squares provides estimators that are asymptotically normal under quite general conditions" (pp. 580–581).

In logistic regression we directly estimate the probability of an event's occurring (because there are only two possible outcomes for the dependent variable). For one predictor (X), the probability of an event can be written as

$$\text{Prob(event)} = \frac{1}{1 + e^{-(B_0 + B_1 X)}}$$

where B_0 and B_1 are the estimated regression coefficients and e is the base of the natural logarithms.

For several predictors ($X_1, \ldots X_p$), the probability of an event can be written as

$$\text{Prob(event)} = \frac{1}{1 + e^{-Z}}$$

where Z is the linear combination

$$Z = B_0 + B_1 X_1 + B_2 X_2 + \cdots + B_p X_p$$

The probability of the event's not occurring is

$$\text{Prob (no event)} = 1 - \text{Prob (event)}$$

There are two important things to note regarding logistic regression:

1. The relationship between the predictor(s) and the dependent variable is *nonlinear*.
2. The regression coefficients are estimated using *maximum likelihood*.

Here is a plot of the nonlinear relationship (*SPSS Professional Statistics 7.5*, 1997, p. 39):

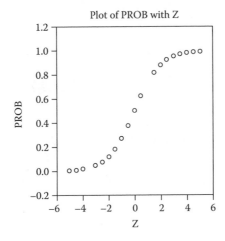

The various predictor selection schemes we talked about earlier in this chapter are still relevant here (forward, stepwise, etc.), and we illustrate these with two examples.

Example 3.9

For our first example we use data from Neter et al. (1989, p. 619). A marketing research firm is conducting a pilot study to ascertain whether a family will buy a new car during the next year. A random sample of 33 suburban families is selected, and data are obtained on family income (in thousands of dollars) and current age of the oldest family auto. A follow-up interview is conducted 12 months later to determine whether the family bought a new car.

Working within SPSS for Windows 10.0, we first bring the car data into the spreadsheet data editor. Then we click on ANALYZE and scroll down to REGRESSION from the dropdown menu. At this point, the screen looks as follows:

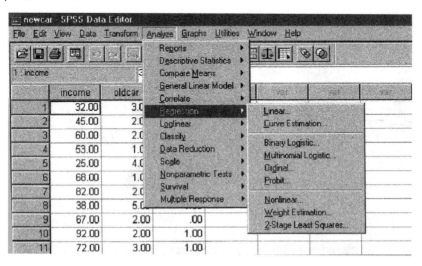

When we click on LOGISTIC, the LOGISTIC REGRESSION screen appears. Make NEWCAR the dependent variable and INCOME and OLDCAR the covariates (predictors). When this is done the screen appears as follows:

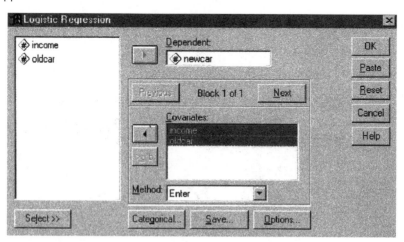

Note that ENTER is the default method. This will *force* both predictors into the equation. When you click on OK the logistic regression will be run and the following selected output will appear. Concerning the output, first note that only INCOME is significant at the .05 level ($p = .023$). Second, from the classification table, note that the two predictors are pretty good at predicting who will not buy a car (16 out of 20), whereas they are not so good at predicting who will buy a car (8 of 13).

Example 3.10

For our second example we consider data from Brown (1980) for 53 men with prostate cancer. We wish to predict whether the cancer (Table 3.17) has spread to the lymph nodes. For each patient, Brown reports the age, serum acid phosphatase (a value that is evaluated if the tumor has spread to other areas), the stage of the disease, the grade of the tumor (an indication of aggressiveness), and x-ray results. We wish to predict whether the nodes are positive for cancer from these predictors that can be measured without surgery. We ran the FORWARD STEPWISE procedure on this data, using again the LOGISTIC REGRESSION procedure within SPSS for WINDOWS (10.0). Selected printout, along with the raw data, is given next.

LOGISTIC 3.1

Logistic Regression Output For Car Data—SPSS For Windows (10.0)

```
Dependent Variable..  NEWCAR
Beginning Block Number   0.   Initial Log Likelihood Function
– 2 Log Likelihood      44.251525
*Constant is included in the model.

Beginning Block Number   1.   Method: Enter
Variable(s) Entered on Step Number
1...  INCOME
      OLDCAR
```

Estimation terminated at iteration number 3 because Log Likelihood decreased by less than .01 percent.

– 2 Log Likelihood	37.360
Goodness of Fit	33.946
Cox & Snell –R^2	.188
Nagelkerke –R^2	.255

	Chi-Square	df	Significance
Model	6.892	2	.0319
Block	6.892	2	.0319
Step	6.892	2	.0319

Classification Table for NEWCAR

The Cut Value is .50

		Predicted		
		.00	1.00	Percent Correct
Observed		0	1	
.00	0	16	4	80.00%
1.00	1	5	8	61.54%
			Overall	72.73%

Variables in the Equation

Variable	B	S.E.	Wald	df	Sig	R	Exp (B)
INCOME:	.0595	.0262	5.1442	1	.0233	.2666	1.0613
OLDCAR	.6243	.3894	2.5703	1	.1089	.1135	1.8670
Constant	–4.6595	2.0635	5.0989	1	.0239		

LOGISTIC 3.2

Logistic Regression Output For Cancer Data—SPSS for Windows (10.0)

Beginning Block Number   1.   Method: Forward Stepwise (LR)

Variables not in the Equation

Residual Chi Square		19.451 with			5 df	Sig = .0016
Variable	Score	df	Sig	R		
ACID	3.1168	1	.0775	.1261		
AGE	1.0945	1	.2955	.0000		
GRADE	4.0745	1	.0435	.1718		
STAGE	7.4381	1	.0064	.2782		
XRAY	11.2829	1	.0008	.3635		

Variable(s) Entered on Step Number
1..   XRAY

Estimation terminated at iteration number 3 because Log Likelihood decreased by less than .01 percent.

– 2 Log Likelihood	59.001
Goodness of Fit	53.000
Cox & Snell – R^2	.191
Nagelkerke – R^2	.260

	Chi-Square	df	Significance
Model	11.251	1	.0008
Block	11.251	1	.0008
Step	11.251	1	.0008

Classification Table for NODES

The Cut Value is .50

		Predicted		Percent Correct
		.00	1.00	
Observed		0	1	
.00	0	29	4	87.88%
1.00	1	9	11	55.00%
			Overall	75.47%

Variables in the Equation

Variable	B	S.E.	Wald	df	Sig	R	Exp(B)
XRAY	2.1817	.6975	9.7835	1	.0018	.3329	8.8611
Constant	–1.1701	.3816	9.4033	1	.0022		

Model if Term Removed

Term Removed	Log Likelihood	–2 Log LR	df	Significance of Log LR
XRAY	–35.126	11.251	1	.0008

Variables not in the Equation					
Residual Chi Square		*10.360 with*		*4 df*	*Sig = .0348*
Variable	*Score*	*df*	*Sig*	*R*	
ACID	2.0732	1	.1499	.0323	
AGE	1.3524	1	.2449	.0000	
GRADE	2.3710	1	.1236	.0727	
STAGE	5.6393	1	.0176	.2276	

Variable(s) Entered on Step Number
2.. STAGE

Estimation terminated at iteration number 4 because Log Likelihood decreased by less than .01 percent.

−2 Log Likelihood	53.353
Goodness of Fit	54.018
Cox & Snell −R^2	.273
Nagelkerke −R^2	.372

	Chi-Square	df	Significance
Model	16.899	2	.0002
Block	16.899	2	.0002
Step	5.647	1	.0175

Classification Table for NODES

The Cut Value is .50

		Predicted			
		.00	1.00	Percent Correct	
Observed		0	1		
.00	0	29	4	87.88%	
1.00	1	9	11	55.00%	
			Overall	75.47%	

Variables in the Equation							
Variable	*B*	*S.E.*	*Wald*	*df*	*Sig*	*R*	*Exp(B)*
STAGE	1.5883	.7000	5.1479	1	.0233	.2117	4.8953
XRAY	2.1194	.7468	8.0537	1	.0045	.2935	8.3265
Constant	−2.0446	.6100	11.2360	1	.0008		

Model if Term Removed				
Term Removed	*Log Likelihood*	*−2 Log LR*	*df*	*Significance of Log LR*
STAGE	−29.500	5.647	1	.0175
XRAY	−31.276	9.199	1	.0024

Variables not in the Equation					
Residual Chi Square		*5.422 with*		*3 df*	*Sig = .1434*
Variable	*Score*	*df*	*Sig*	*R*	
ACID	3.0917	1	.0787	.1247	
AGE	1.2678	1	.2602	.0000	
GRADE	.5839	1	.4448	.0000	

No more variables can be deleted or added.

TABLE 3.17

Brown Data

	X-ray	Stage	Grade	Age	Acid	Nodes
1	.00	.00	.00	66.00	48.00	.00
2	.00	.00	.00	68.00	56.00	.00
3	.00	.00	.00	66.00	50.00	.00
4	.00	.00	.00	56.00	52.00	.00
5	.00	.00	.00	58.00	50.00	.00
6	.00	.00	.00	60.00	49.00	.00
7	1.00	.00	.00	65.00	46.00	.00
8	1.00	.00	.00	60.00	62.00	.00
9	.00	.00	1.00	50.00	56.00	1.00
10	1.00	.00	.00	49.00	55.00	.00
11	.00	.00	.00	61.00	62.00	.00
12	.00	.00	.00	58.00	71.00	.00
13	.00	.00	.00	51.00	65.00	.00
14	1.00	.00	1.00	67.00	67.00	1.00
15	.00	.00	1.00	67.00	47.00	.00
16	.00	.00	.00	51.00	49.00	.00
17	.00	.00	1.00	56.00	50.00	.00
18	.00	.00	.00	60.00	78.00	.00
19	.00	.00	.00	52.00	83.00	.00
20	.00	.00	.00	56.00	98.00	.00
21	.00	.00	.00	67.00	52.00	.00
22	.00	.00	.00	63.00	75.00	.00
23	.00	.00	1.00	59.00	99.00	1.00
24	.00	.00	.00	64.00	187.00	.00
25	1.00	.00	.00	61.00	136.00	1.00
26	.00	.00	.00	56.00	82.00	1.00
27	.00	1.00	1.00	64.00	40.00	.00
28	.00	1.00	.00	61.00	50.00	.00
29	.00	1.00	1.00	64.00	50.00	.00
30	.00	1.00	.00	63.00	40.00	.00
31	.00	1.00	1.00	52.00	55.00	.00
32	.00	1.00	1.00	66.00	59.00	.00
33	1.00	1.00	.00	58.00	48.00	1.00
34	1.00	1.00	1.00	57.00	51.00	1.00
35	.00	1.00	.00	65.00	49.00	1.00
36	.00	1.00	1.00	65.00	48.00	.00
37	1.00	1.00	1.00	59.00	63.00	.00
38	.00	1.00	.00	61.00	102.00	.00
39	.00	1.00	.00	53.00	76.00	.00
40	.00	1.00	.00	67.00	95.00	.00
41	.00	1.00	1.00	53.00	66.00	.00
42	1.00	1.00	1.00	65.00	84.00	1.00
43	1.00	1.00	1.00	50.00	81.00	1.00
44	1.00	1.00	1.00	60.00	76.00	1.00
45	.00	1.00	1.00	45.00	70.00	1.00
46	1.00	1.00	1.00	56.00	78.00	1.00
47	.00	1.00	.00	46.00	70.00	1.00
48	.00	1.00	.00	67.00	67.00	1.00
49	.00	1.00	.00	63.00	82.00	1.00
50	.00	1.00	1.00	57.00	67.00	1.00
51	1.00	1.00	.00	51.00	72.00	1.00
52	1.00	1.00	.00	64.00	89.00	1.00
53	1.00	1.00	1.00	68.00	126.00	1.00

Note that from the CLASSIFICATION TABLE, after two predictors have entered, that the equation is quite good at predicting correctly those patients who will not have cancerous nodes (29 of 33), but is not so good at predicting accurately those who will have cancerous nodes (11 of 20). Let us calculate the probability of having cancerous nodes for a few patients. First, consider Patient 2:

$$\text{Prediction equation} = -2.0446 + 1.5883 \text{ STAGE} + 2.1194 \text{ XRAY}$$

$$z = -2.0446 + 1.5883(0) + 2.1194(0) = -2.0446 \qquad \text{(for Patient 2)}$$

$$\text{Prob(node is cancerous)} = 1/(1 + e^{2.0446}) = 1/(1 + 7.726) = .1146$$

Therefore, the probability of nodal involvement is only about 11% and indeed the nodes were not cancerous.

Now consider Patient 14, for which XRAY = 1 (one of the significant predictors).

$$z = -2.0446 + 1.5883(1) + 2.1194(0) = -.4563$$

$$\text{Prob(node is cancerous)} = 1/(1 + e^{.4563}) = 1/(1 + 1.578) = .388$$

Because the probability is < .50 we would predict the nodes will *not* be involved, but in fact the nodes are involved for this patient (node = 1). This is just one of several misclassifications.

3.18 Other Types of Regression Analysis

Least squares regression is only one (although the most prevalent) way of conducting a regression analysis. The least squares estimator has two desirable statistical properties; that is, it is an unbiased, minimum variance estimator. Mathematically, unbiased means that $E(\hat{\boldsymbol{\beta}}) = \boldsymbol{\beta}$, the expected value of the vector of estimated regression coefficients, is the vector of population regression coefficients. To elaborate on this a bit, unbiased means that the estimate of the population coefficients will not be consistently high or low, but will "bounce around" the population values. And, if we were to average the estimates from many repeated samplings, the averages would be very close to the population values.

The minimum variance notion can be misleading. It does not mean that the variance of the coefficients for the least squares estimator is small per se, but that *among the class* of unbiased estimators $\boldsymbol{\beta}$ has the minimum variance. The fact that the variance of $\boldsymbol{\beta}$ can be quite large led Hoerl and Kenard (1970a, 1970b) to consider a biased estimator of $\boldsymbol{\beta}$, which has considerably less variance, and the development of their ridge regression technique. Although ridge regression has been strongly endorsed by some, it has also been criticized (Draper & Smith, 1981; Morris, 1982; Smith & Campbell, 1980). Morris, for example, found that ridge regression never cross-validated better than other types of regression (least squares, equal weighting of predictors, reduced rank) for a set of data situations.

Another class of estimators are the James-Stein (1961) estimators. Regarding the utility of these, the following from Weisberg (1980) is relevant: "The improvement over least squares will be very small whenever the parameter $\boldsymbol{\beta}$ is well estimated, i.e., collinearity is not a problem and $\boldsymbol{\beta}$ is not too close to $\mathbf{O}$."

Since, as we have indicated earlier, least square regression can be quite sensitive to outliers, some researchers prefer regression techniques that are relatively insensitive to outliers, i.e., robust regression techniques. Since the early 1970s, the literature on these techniques has grown considerably (Hogg, 1979; Huber, 1977; Mosteller and Tukey, 1977). Although these techniques have merit, we believe that use of least squares, along with the appropriate identification of outliers and influential points, is a quite adequate procedure.

3.19 Multivariate Regression

In multivariate regression we are interested in predicting several dependent variables from a set of predictors. The dependent variables might be differentiated aspects of some variable. For example, Finn (1974) broke grade point average (GPA) up into GPA required and GPA elective, and considered predicting these two dependent variables from high school GPA, a general knowledge test score, and attitude toward education. Or, one might measure "success as a professor" by considering various aspects of success such as: rank (assistant, associate, full), rating of institution working at, salary, rating by experts in the field, and number of articles published. These would constitute the multiple dependent variables.

3.19.1 Mathematical Model

In multiple regression (one dependent variable), the model was

$$\mathbf{y} = \mathbf{X}\boldsymbol{\beta} + \mathbf{e},$$

where $\mathbf{y}$ was the vector of scores for the subjects on the dependent variable, $\mathbf{X}$ was the matrix with the scores for the subjects on the predictors, and $\mathbf{e}$ was the vectors of errors and $\boldsymbol{\beta}$ was vector of regression coefficients.

In multivariate regression the $\mathbf{y}$, $\boldsymbol{\beta}$, and $\mathbf{e}$ vectors become matrices, which we denote by $\mathbf{Y}$, $\mathbf{B}$, and $\mathbf{E}$:

$$\mathbf{Y} = \mathbf{X}\mathbf{B} + \mathbf{E}$$

$$
\underset{\mathbf{Y}}{\begin{bmatrix} y_{11} & y_{12} \cdots y_{1p} \\ y_{21} & y_{22} \cdots y_{2p} \\ \cdots\cdots \\ y_{n1} & y_{n2} & y_{np} \end{bmatrix}}
=
\underset{\mathbf{X}}{\begin{bmatrix} 1 & x_{12} \cdots x_{1k} \\ 1 & x_{22} \cdots y_{2k} \\ \cdots\cdots \\ 1 & x_{n2} & x_{nk} \end{bmatrix}}
$$

$$
\underset{\mathbf{B}}{\begin{bmatrix} b_{01} & b_{02} \cdots b_{1p} \\ b_{11} & b_{12} \cdots b_{1p} \\ \cdots\cdots \\ b_{k1} & b_{k2} & b_{kp} \end{bmatrix}}
+
\underset{\mathbf{E}}{\begin{bmatrix} e_{11} & e_{12} \cdots e_{1p} \\ e_{21} & e_{22} \cdots e_{2p} \\ \cdots\cdots \\ e_{n1} & e_{n2} \cdots e_{np} \end{bmatrix}}
$$

The first column of **Y** gives the scores for the subjects on the first dependent variable, the second column the scores on the second dependent variable, etc. The first column of **B** gives the set of regression coefficients for the first dependent variable, the second column the regression coefficients for the second dependent variable, and so on.

Example 3.11

As an example of multivariate regression, we consider part of a data set from Timm (1975). The dependent variables are Peabody Picture Vocabulary Test score and score on the Ravin Progressive Matrices Test. The predictors were scores from different types of paired associate learning tasks, called "named still (ns)," "named action (na)," and "sentence still (ss)." The control lines for running the analysis on SPSS MANOVA are given in Table 3.18, along with annotation. In understanding the annotation the reader should refer back to Table 1.4, where we indicated some of the basic elements of the SPSS control language.

TABLE 3.18

Control Lines for Multivariate Regression Analysis of Timm Data—Two Dependent Variables and Three Predictors

TITLE 'MULT. REGRESS. – 2 DEP. VARS AND 3 PREDS'.									
① DATA LIST FREE/PEVOCAB RAVIN NS NA SS.									
③ BEGIN DATA.									
48	8	6	12	16	76	13	14	30	27
40	13	21	16	16	52	9	5	17	8
63	15	11	26	17	82	14	21	34	25
71	21	20	23	18	68	8	10	19	14
74	11	7	16	13	70	15	21	26	25
70	15	15	35	24	61	11	7	15	14
54	12	13	27	21	55	13	12	20	17
54	10	20	26	22	40	14	5	14	8
66	13	21	35	27	54	10	6	14	16
64	14	19	27	26	47	16	15	18	10
48	16	9	14	18	52	14	20	26	26
74	19	14	23	23	57	12	4	11	8
57	10	16	15	17	80	11	18	28	21
78	13	19	34	23	70	16	9	23	11
47	14	7	12	8	94	19	28	32	32
63	11	5	25	14	76	16	18	29	21
59	11	10	23	24	55	8	14	19	12
74	14	10	18	18	71	17	23	31	26
54	14	6	15	14					
END DATA.									
② LIST.									
④ MANOVA PEVOCAB RAVIN WITH NS NA SS/									
PRINT = CELLINFO(MEANS,COR)/.									

① The variables are separated by blanks; they could also have been separated by commas.
② This LIST command is to get a listing of the data.
③ The data is preceded by the BEGIN DATA command and followed by the END DATA command.
④ The predictors follow the keyword WITH in the MANOVA command.

TABLE 3.19

Multivariate and Univariate Tests of Significance and Regression Coefficients for Timm Data

EFFECT.. WITHIN CELLS REGRESSION

MULTIVARIATE TESTS OF SIGNIFICANCE (S = 2, M = 0, N = 15)

TEST NAME	VALUE	APPROX. F	HYPOTH. DF	ERROR DF	SIG. OF F
PILLAIS	.57254	4.41203	6.00	66.00	.001
HOTELLINGS	1.00976	5.21709	6.00	62.00	.000
WILKS	.47428	4.82197	6.00	64.00	.000
ROYS	.47371				

This test indicates there is a significant (at α = .05) regression of the set of 2 dependent variables on the three predictors.

UNIVARIATE F-TESTS WITH (3.33) D.F.

VARIABLE	SQ. MUL. R.	MUL. R	ADJ. R-SQ	F	SIG. OF F
PEVOCAB	.46345	.68077	.41467	① 9.50121	.000
RAVIN	.19429	.44078	.12104	2.65250	.085

These results show there is a significant regression for PEVOCAB, but RAVIN is not significantly related to the three predictors at .05, since .065 > .05.

DEPENDENT VARIABLE.. PEVOCAB

COVARIATE	B	BETA	STD. ERR.	T-VALUE	SIG. OF T.
NS	−.2056372599	−.1043054487	.40797	−.50405	.618
NA	② 1.01272293634	.5856100072	.37685	2.68737	.011
SS	.3977340740	.2022598804	.47010	.84606	.404

DEPENDENT VARIABLE.. RAVIN

COVARIATE	B	BETA	STD. ERR.	T-VALUE	SIG. OF T.
NS	.2026184278	.4159658338	.12352	1.64038	.110
NA	.0302663367	.0708355423	.11410	.26527	.792
SS	−.0174928333	−.0360039904	.14233	−.12290	.903

① Using Equation 4, $F = \dfrac{R^2/k}{(1-R^2)/(n-k-1)} = \dfrac{.46345/3}{.53655/(37-3-1)} = 9.501$

② These are the raw regression coefficients for predicting PEVOCAB from the three predictors, excluding the regression constant.

Selected output from the multivariate regression analysis run is given in Table 3.19. The multivariate test determines whether there is a significant relationship between the two *sets* of variables, that is, the two dependent variables and the three predictors. At this point, the reader should focus on Wilks' Λ, the most commonly used multivariate test statistic. We have more to say about the other multivariate tests in chapter 5. Wilks' Λ here is given by:

$$\Lambda = \frac{|SS_{resid}|}{|SS_{tot}|} = \frac{|SS_{resid}|}{|SS_{reg} + SS_{resid}|}, 0 \le \Lambda \le 1$$

Recall from the matrix algebra chapter that the determinant of a matrix served as a multivariate generalization for the variance of a set of variables. Thus, $|SS_{resid}|$ indicates the amount of variability for the set of two dependent variables that is not accounted for by regression, and $|SS_{tot}|$ gives the total variability for the two dependent variables about their means. The sampling distribution of Wilks' Λ is quite complicated; however, there is an excellent F approximation (due to Rao), which is what appears in Table 3.19. Note that the multivariate $F = 4.82$, $p < .000$, which indicates a significant relationship between the dependent variables and the three predictors beyond the .01 level.

The univariate F's are the tests for the significance of the regression of each dependent variable separately. They indicate that PEVOCAB is significantly related to the set of predictors at the .05 level ($F = 9.501$, $p < .000$), while RAVIN is not significantly related at the .05 level ($F = 2.652$, $p < .065$). Thus, the overall multivariate significance is primarily attributable to PEVO-CAB's relationship with the three predictors.

It is important for the reader to realize that, although the multivariate tests take into account the correlations among the dependent variables, the regression equations that appear in Table 3.19 are those that would be obtained if each dependent variable were regressed *separately* on the set of predictors. That is, in deriving the prediction equations, the correlations among the dependent variables are ignored, or not taken into account.

We indicated earlier in this chapter that an R^2 value around .50 occurs quite often with educational and psychological data, and this is precisely what has occurred here with the PEVOCAB variable ($R^2 = .463$). Also, we can be fairly confident that the prediction equation for PEVOCAB will cross-validate, since the n/k ratio is $= 12.33$, which is close to the ratio we indicated is necessary.

3.20 Summary

1. A particularly good situation for multiple regression is where each of the predictors is correlated with y and the predictors have low intercorrelations, for then each of the predictors is accounting for a relatively distinct part of the variance on y.

2. Moderate to high correlation among the predictors (multicollinearity) creates three problems: it (a) severely limits the size of R, (b) makes determining the importance of given predictor difficult, and (c) increases the variance of regression coefficients, making for an unstable prediction equation. There are at least three ways of combating this problem. One way is to combine into a single measure a set of predictors that are highly correlated. A second way is to consider the use of principal components analysis (a type of "factor analysis") to reduce the number of predictors. Because the components are uncorrelated, we have eliminated multicollinearity. A third way is through the use of ridge regression. This technique is beyond the scope of this book.

3. Preselecting a small set of predictors by examining a correlation matrix from a large initial set, or by using one of the stepwise procedures (forward, stepwise, backward) to select a small set, is likely to produce an equation that is sample specific. If one insists on doing this, and I do not recommend it, then the onus is on the investigator to demonstrate that the equation has adequate predictive power beyond the derivation sample.

4. Mallows' C_p was presented as a measure that minimizes the effect of underfitting (important predictors left out of the model) and overfitting (having predictors in the model that make essentially no contribution or are marginal). This will be the case if one chooses models for which $C_p \approx p$.

5. With many data sets, more than one model will provide a good fit to the data. Thus, one deals with selecting a model from a *pool* of candidate models.

6. There are various graphical plots for assessing how well the model fits the assumptions underlying linear regression. One of the most useful graphs the standardized residuals (y axis) versus the predicted values (x axis). If the assumptions are tenable, then one should observe roughly a random scattering. Any *systematic clustering* of the residuals indicates a model violation(s).

7. It is crucial to validate the model(s) by either randomly splitting the sample and cross-validating, or using the PRESS statistic, or by obtaining the Stein estimate of the *average* predictive power of the equation on other samples from the same population. Studies in the literature that have not cross-validated should be checked with the Stein estimate to assess the generalizability of the prediction equation(s) presented.

8. Results from the Park and Dudycha study indicate that the magnitude of the *population* multiple correlation strongly affects how many subjects will be needed for a reliable prediction equation. If your estimate of the squared population value is .50, then about 15 subjects per predictor are needed. On the other hand, if your estimate of the squared population value is substantially *larger* than .50, then far fewer than 15 subjects per predictor will be needed.

9. Influential data points, that is, points that strongly affect the prediction equation, can be identified by seeing which cases have Cook distances > 1. These points need to be examined very carefully. If such a point is due to a recording error, then one would simply correct it and redo the analysis. Or if it is found that the influential point is due to an instrumentation error or that the process that generated the data for that subject was different, then it is legitimate to drop the case from the analysis. If, however, none of these appears to be the case, then one should *not* drop the case, but perhaps report the results of several analyses: one analysis with all the data and an additional analysis(ses) with the influential point(s) deleted.

3.21   Exercises

1. Consider this set of data:

x	y
2	3
3	6
4	8
6	4
7	10
8	14
9	8
10	12
11	14
12	12
13	16

(a) Run these data on SPSS, obtaining the case analysis.

(b) Do you see any pattern in the plot of the standardized residuals? What does this suggest?

(c) Plot the points, sketch in the regression equation, and indicate the raw residuals by vertical lines.

2. Consider the following small set of data:

PREDX	DEP
0	1
1	4
2	6
3	8
4	9
5	10
6	10
7	8
8	7
9	6
10	5

(a) Run these data set on SPSS, forcing the predictor in the equation and obtaining the casewise analysis.

(b) Do you see any pattern in the plot of the standardized residuals? What does this suggest?

(c) Plot the points. What type of relationship exists between PREDX and DEP?

3. Consider the following correlation matrix:

	y	x_1	x_2
y	1.00	.60	.50
x_1	.60	1.00	.80
x_2	.50	.80	1.00

(a) How much variance on y will x_1 account for if entered first?

(b) How much variance on y will x_1 account for if entered second?

(c) What, if anything, do these results have to do with the multicollinearity problem?

4. A medical school admissions official has two proven predictors (x_1 and x_2) of success in medical school. He has two other predictors under consideration (x_3 and x_4), from which he wishes to choose just one that will add the most (beyond what x_1 and x_2 already predict) to predicting success. Here is the matrix of intercorrelations he has gathered on a sample of 100 medical students:

	x_1	x_2	x_3	x_4
y	.60	.55	.60	.46
x_1		.70	.60	.20
x_2			.80	.30
x_3				.60

(a) What procedure would he use to determine which predictor has the greater incremental validity? Do *not* go into any numerical details, just indicate the general procedure. Also, what is your educated guess as to which predictor (x_3 or x_4) will probably have the greater incremental validity?

(b) Suppose the investigator has found his third predictor, runs the regression, and finds $R = .76$. Apply the Herzberg formula (use $k = 3$), and tell exactly what the resulting number represents.

5. In a study from a major journal (Bradley, Caldwell, and Elardo, 1977) the investigators were interested in predicting the IQ's of 3-year-old children from four measures of socioeconomic status and six environmental process variables (as assessed by a HOME inventory instrument). Their total sample size was 105. They were also interested in determining whether the prediction varied depending on sex and on race. The following is from their PROCEDURE section:

> To examine the relations among SES, environmental process, and IQ data, three multiple correlation analyses were performed on each of five samples: total group, males, females, whites, and blacks. First, four SES variables (maternal education, paternal education, occupation of head of household, and father absence) plus six environmental process variables (the six HOME inventory subscales) were used as a set of predictor variables with IQ as the criterion variable. Third, the six environmental process variables were used as the predictor set with IQ as the criterion variable.

Here is the table they present with the 15 multiple correlations:

Multiple Correlations Between Measures of Environmental Quality and IQ

Measure	Males (n = 57)	Females (n = 48)	Whites (n = 37)	Black (n = 68)	Total (N = 105)
Status variables (A)	.555	.636	.582	.346	.556
HOME inventory (B)	.647	.790	.622	.576	.742
A and B	.682	.825	.683	.614	.765

(a) The authors state that all of the multiple correlations are statistically significant (.05 level) except for .346 obtained for Blacks with Status variables. Show that .346 is not significant at .05 level.

(b) For Males, does the addition of the Home inventory variables to the prediction equation significantly increase (use .05 level) predictive power beyond that of the Status variables?

The following F statistic is appropriate for determining whether a set B significantly adds to the prediction beyond what set A contributes:

$$F = \frac{(R^2_{y.AB} - R^2_{y.A})/k_b}{(1 - R^2_{y.AB})(n - k_A - k_{B1} - 1)}, k_B \text{ and } (n - k_A - k_B - 1)df$$

where k_A and k_B represent the number of predictors in sets A and B, respectively.

6. Consider the following RESULTS section from a study by Sharp (1981):

   The regression was performed to determine the extent to which a linear combination of two or more of the five predictor variables could account for the variance in the dependent variable (posttest). Three steps in the multiple regression were completed before the contributions of additional predictor variables were deemed insignificant ($p > .05$). In Step #1, the pretest variable was selected as the predictor variable that explained the greatest amount of variance in posttest scores. The R^2 value using this single variable was .25. The next predictor variable chosen (Step #2) in conjunction with pretest, was interest in participating in the CTP. The R^2 value using these two variables was .36. The final variable (Step #3), which significantly improved the prediction of posttest scores, was the treatment—viewing the model videotape (Tape). The multiple regression equation, with all three significant predictor variables entered, yielded an R^2 of .44. The other two predictor variables, interest and relevance, were not entered into the regression equation as both failed to meet the statistical significance criterion.

   Correlations Among Criterion and Predictor Variables

	Posttest	Pretest	Tape	Campus Teaching Program	Interest	Relevance
Posttest	1.0					
Pretest	.50*	1.0				
Tape	.27	−.02	1.0			
Campus Teaching Program	.35*	.06	−.07	1.0		
Interest	−.02	.14	.07	−.06	1.0	
Relevance	−.06	−.02	.07	.05	.31	10

   Note: $N = 37$, *$p < .05$.

(a) Which specific predictor selection procedure were the authors using?

(b) They give the R^2 for the first predictor as .25. How did they arrive at this figure?

(c) The R^2 for the first two predictors was .36, an increase of .11 over the R^2 for just the first predictor. Using the appropriate correlations in the Table show how the value of .11 is obtained.

(d) Is there evidence of multicollinearity among the predictors? Explain.

(e) Do you think the author's regression equation would cross-validate well? Explain.

7. Plante and Goldfarb (1984) predicted social adjustment from Cattell's 16 personality factors. There were 114 subjects, consisting of students and employees from two large manufacturing companies. They stated in their RESULTS section:

   > Stepwise multiple regression was performed... . The index of social adjustment significantly correlated with 6 of the primary factors of the 16 PF... . Multiple regression analysis resulted in a multiple correlation of $R - .41$ accounting for 17% of the variance with these 6 factors. The multiple R obtained while utilizing all 16 factors was $R = .57$, thus accounting for 32% of the variance.

   (a) Would you have much faith in the reliability of either of these regression equations?

   (b) Apply the Stein formula for random predictors (Equation 9) to the 16-variable equation to estimate how much variance on the average we could expect to account for if the equation were cross validated on many other random samples.

8. Consider the following data for 15 subjects with two predictors. The dependent variable, MARK, is the total score for a subject on an examination. The first predictor, COMP, is the score for the subject on a so called compulsory paper. The other predictor, CERTIF, is the score for the subject on a previous exam.

Candidate	MARK	COMP	CERTIF	Candidate	MARK	COMP	CERTIF
1	476	111	68	9	645	117	59
2	457	92	46	10	556	94	97
3	540	90	50	11	634	130	57
4	551	107	59	12	637	118	51
5	575	98	50	13	390	91	44
6	698	150	66	14	562	118	61
7	545	118	54	15	560	109	66
8	574	110	51				

   (a) Run stepwise regression on this data.

   (b) Does CERTIF add anything to predicting MARK, above and beyond that of COMP?

   (c) Write out the prediction equation.

9. An investigator has 15 variables on a file. Denote them by X1, X2, X3, ..., X15. Assume that there are spaces between all variables, so that free format can be used to read the data. The investigator wishes to predict X4. First, however, he obtains the correlation matrix among the predictors. He finds that variables 7 and 8 are very highly correlated and decides to combine those as a single predictor. He also finds that the correlations among variables 2, 5, and 10 are quite high, so he will combine those and use as a single predictor. He will also use variables 1, 3, 11, 12, 13, and 14 as individual predictors. Show the single set of control lines for doing both a stepwise and backward selection, obtaining the casewise statistics and scatterplot of residuals versus predicted values for both analyses.

10. A different investigator has eight variables on a data file, with no spaces between the variables, so that fixed format will be needed to read the data. The data looks as follows:

2534674823178659

3645738234267583

etc.

The first two variables are single-digit integers, the next three variables are two-digit integers, the sixth variable is GPA (where you will need to deal with an implied decimal point), the seventh variable is a three-digit integer and the eighth variable is a two-digit integer. The eighth variable is the dependent variable. She wishes to force in variables 1 and 2, and then determine whether variables 3 through 5 (as a block) have any incremental validity. Show the complete SPSS REGRESSION control lines.

11. A statistician wishes to know the sample size he will need in a multiple regression study. He has four predictors and can tolerate at most a .10 dropoff in predictive power. But he wants this to be the case with .95 probability. From previous related research he estimates that the squared population multiple correlation will be .62. How many subjects will he need?

12. Recall that the Nold and Freedman (1977) study had each of 22 college freshmen write four essays, and used a stepwise regression analysis to predict quality of essay response. It has already been mentioned that the n of 88 used in the study is incorrect, since there are only 22 independent responses. Now let us concentrate on a different aspect of the study. They had 17 predictors, and found 5 of them to be "significant," accounting for 42.3% of the variance in quality. Using a median value between 5 and 17 and the proper sample size of 22, apply the Stein formula to estimate the cross-validity predictive power of the equation. What do you conclude?

13. It was mentioned earlier that $E(R^2) = k/(n-1)$ when there is no relationship between the dependent variable and set of predictors in the population. It is very important to be aware of the extreme positive bias in the sample multiple correlation when the number of predictors is close or fairly close to sample size in interpreting results from the literature. Comment on the following situation:

(a) A team of medical researchers had 32 subjects measured on 28 predictors, which were used to predict three criterion variables. If they obtain squared multiple correlations of .83, .91, and .72, respectively, should we be impressed? What value for squared multiple correlation would be expected, even if there is no relationship? Suppose they used a stepwise procedure for one of the criterion measures and found six significant predictors that accounted for 74% of the variance. Apply the Stein formula, using a median value between 6 and 28, to estimate how much variance we would expect to account for on other samples. This example, only slightly modified, is taken from a paper (for which I was one of the reviewers) that was submitted for publication by researchers at a major university.

14. A regression analysis was run on the Sesame Street (n = 240) data set, predicting postbody from the following five pretest measures: prebody, prelet, preform, prenumb, and prerelat. The control lines for doing a stepwise regression, obtaining a histogram of the residuals, obtaining 10 largest values for the standardized residuals, the hat elements, and Cook's distance, and for obtaining a plot of the standardized residuals versus the predicted y values are given below:

```
title 'mult reg for sesame data'.
data list free/id site sex age viewcat setting viewenc
  prebody prelet preform prenumb prerelat preclasf postbody
  postlet postform postnumb postrel postclas peabody.
begin data.
data lines
end data.
regression descriptives=default/
  variables = prebody to prerelat postbody/
  statistics = defaults history/
  dependent = postbody/
  method = stepwise/
  residuals = histogram(zresid) outliers(zresid, sresid, lever, cook)/
  scatterplot (*res, *pre)/.
```

The SPSS printout follows. Answer the following questions:

(a) Why did PREBODY enter the prediction equation first?

(b) Why did PREFORM enter the prediction equation second?

(c) Write the prediction equation, rounding off to three decimals.

(d) Is multicollinearity present? Explain.

(e) Compute the Stein estimate and indicate in words exactly what it represents.

(f) Show by using the appropriate correlations from the correlation matrix how the RSQCH = .0219 is obtained.

(g) Refer to the standardized residuals. Is the number of these greater than 121 about what you would expect if the model is appropriate? Why, or why not?

(h) Are there any outliers on the set of predictors?

(i) Are there any influential data points? Explain.

(j) From examination of the residual plot, does it appear there may be some model violation(s)? Why, or why not?

(k) From the histogram of standardized residuals, does it appear that the normality assumption is reasonable?

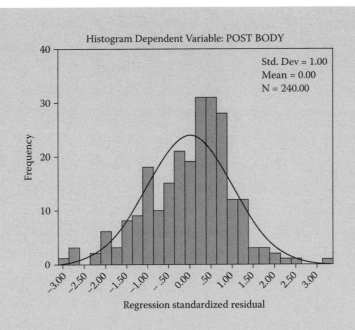

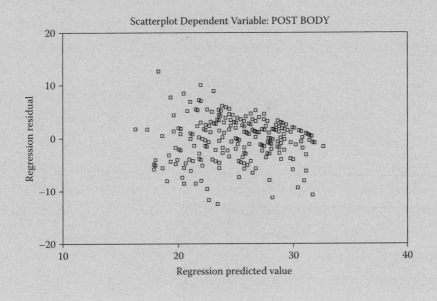

Regression

Descriptive Statistics

	Mean	Std. Deviation	N
PREBODY	21.4000	6.3909	240
PRELET	15.9375	8.5364	240
PREFORM	9.9208	3.7369	240
PRENUMB	20.8958	10.6854	240
PRERELAT	9.9375	3.0738	240
POSTBODY	25.2625	5.4121	240

Correlations

	PREBODY	PRELET	PREFORM	PRENUMB	PRERELAT	POSTBODY
PREBODY	1.000	.453	.680	.698	.623	.650
PRELET	.453	1.000	.506	.717	.471	.371
PREFORM	.680	.506	1.000	.673	.596	.551
PRENUMB	.698	.717	.673	1.000	.718	.527
PRERELAT	.623	.471	.596	.718	1.000	.449
POSTBODY	.650	.371	.551	.527	.449	1.000

Variables Entered/Removed[a]

Model	Variables Entered	Variables Removed	Method
1	PREBODY		Stepwise (Criteria: Probability-of-F-to-enter < = .050, Probability-of-F-to-remove > = .100).
2	PREFORM		Stepwise (Criteria: Probability-of-F-to-enter < = .050, Probability-of-F-to-remove > = .100).

a. Dependent Variable: POSTBODY

Model Summary[c]

Model	R	R Square	Adjusted R Square	Std. Error of the Estimate
1	.650[a]	.423	.421	4.1195
2	.667[b]	.445	.440	4.0491

Model Summary[c]

Model	Selection Criteria			
	Akaike Information Criterion	Amemiya Prediction Criterion	Mallows' Prediction Criterion	Schwarz Bayesian Criterion
1	681.539	.587	8.487	688.500
2	674.253	.569	1.208	684.695

ANOVA[c]

Model		Sum of Squares	df	Mean Square	F	Sig.
1	Regression	2961.602	1	2961.602	174.520	.000[a]
	Residual	4038.860	238	16.970		
	Total	7000.462	239			
2	Regression	3114.883	2	1557.441	94.996	.000[b]
	Residual	3885.580	237	16.395		
	Total	7000.462	239			

[a] Predictors: (Constant), PREBODY
[b] Predictors: (Constant), PREBODY, PREFORM
[c] Dependent Variable: POSTBODY

Coefficients[a]

Model		Unstandardized Coefficients		Standardized Coefficients			Collinearity Statistics	
		B	Std. Error	Beta	t	Sig.	Tolerance	VIF
1	(Constant)	13.475	.931		14.473	.000		
	PREBODY	.551	.042	.650	13.211	.000	1.000	1.000
2	(Constant)	13.062	.925		14.120	.000		
	PREBODY	.435	.056	.513	7.777	.000	.538	1.860
	PREFORM	.292	.096	.202	3.058	.002	.538	1.860

[a] Dependent Variable: POSTBODY

Excluded Variables[c]

Model		Beta In	t	Sig.	Partial Correlation
1	PRELET	.096[a]	1.742	.083	.112
	PREFORM	.202[a]	3.058	.002	.195
	PRENUMB	.143[a]	2.091	.038	.135
	PRERELAT	.072[a]	1.152	.250	.075
2	PRELET	.050[b]	.881	.379	.057
	PRENUMB	.075[b]	1.031	.304	.067
	PRERELAT	.017[b]	.264	.792	.017

Excluded Variables[c]

Model		Collinearity Statistics		
		Tolerance	VIF	Minimum Tolerance
1	PRELET	.795	1.258	.795
	PREFORM	.538	1.860	.538
	PRENUMB	.513	1.950	.513
	PRERELAT	.612	1.634	.612
2	PRELET	.722	1.385	.489
	PRENUMB	.439	2.277	.432
	PRERELAT	.557	1.796	.464

[a] Predictors in the Model: (Constant), PREBODY
[b] Predictors in the Model: (Constant), PREBODY, PREFORM
[c] Dependent Variable: POSTBODY

Outlier Statistics[a]

		Case Number	Statistic	Sig. F
Std. Residual	1	219	3.138	
	2	139	−3.056	
	3	125	−2.873	
	4	155	−2.757	
	5	39	−2.629	
	6	147	2.491	
	7	210	−2.345	
	8	40	−2.305	
	9	135	2.203	
	10	36	2.108	
Cook's Distance	1	219	.081	.970
	2	125	.078	.972
	3	39	.042	.988
	4	38	.032	.992
	5	40	.025	.995
	6	139	.025	.995
	7	147	.025	.995
	8	177	.023	.995
	9	140	.022	.996
	10	13	.020	.996
Centered Leverage Value	1	140	.047	
	2	32	.036	
	3	23	.030	
	4	114	.028	
	5	167	.026	
	6	52	.026	
	7	233	.025	
	8	8	.025	
	9	236	.023	
	10	161	.023	

[a] Dependent Variable: POSTBODY

15. A study was done in which data was gathered from 60 metropolitan areas in the United States. Age-adjusted mortality from all causes, in deaths per 100,000 population, is the response (dependent) variable. The predictors are annual mean precipitation (in inches), median number of school years completed (education) percentage of the population that is nonwhite, relative pollution potential of oxides of nitrogen (NO_X) and relative pollution potential of sulfur dioxide (SO_2). Controlling on precipitation, education, and nonwhite, is there evidence that mortality is associated with either of the pollution variables? (The data is on pp. 322–323 in *The Statistical Sleuth*; Ramsey and Shafer, 1997).

(a) Show the complete SPSS lines for forcing in precip, education, and nonwhite, and then determining whether either NO_X or SO_2 is significant. Obtain the casewise statistics and the scatterplot of the residuals vs the predicted values. Put DATA LINES for the data.

16. For the 23 space shuttle flights that occurred before the Challenger mission disaster in 1986, the table below shows the temperature (°F) at the time of the flight and whether at least one primary O-ring suffered thermal distress.

Ft	Temp	TD	Ft	Temp	TD	Ft	Temp	TD
1	66	0	9	57	1	17	70	0
2	70	1	10	63	1	18	81	0
3	69	0	11	70	1	19	76	0
4	68	0	12	78	0	20	79	0
5	67	0	13	67	0	21	75	1
6	72	0	14	53	1	22	76	0
7	73	0	15	67	0	23	58	1
8	70	0	16	75	0			

Note: Ft = flight no., Temp = temperature, TD = thermal distress (1 = yes, 0 = no).
Source: Data based on Table 1 in S. R. Dalal, E. B. Fowlkes, and B. Hoadley. *J. Amer. Statist. Assoc,* *84:* 945–957 (1989). Reprinted with permission of the American Statistical Association.

(a) Use logistic regression to determine the effect of temperature on the probability of thermal distress.

(b) Calculate the predicted probability of thermal distress at 31°, the temperature at the time of the Challenger flight.

17. From one of the better journals in your content area within the last 5 years find an article that used multiple regression. Answer the following questions:

(a) Did the authors talk about checking the assumptions for regression?

(b) Did the authors report an adjusted squared multiple correlation?

(c) Did the authors talk about checking for outliers and/or influential points?

(d) Did the authors say anything about validating their equation?

18. Consider the following data:

X_1	X_2
14	21
17	23
36	10
32	18
25	12

Find the Mahalanobis distance for subject 4.

19. Using SPSS, run backward selection on the National Academy of Sciences data. What model is selected?

4

Two-Group Multivariate Analysis of Variance

4.1 Introduction

In this chapter we consider the statistical analysis of two groups of subjects on several dependent variables simultaneously; focusing on cases where the variables are correlated and share a common conceptual meaning. That is, the dependent variables considered together make sense as a group. For example, they may be different dimensions of self-concept (physical, social, emotional, academic), teacher effectiveness, speaker credibility, or reading (blending, syllabication, comprehension, etc.). We consider the multivariate tests along with their univariate counterparts and show that the multivariate two-group test (Hotelling's T^2) is a natural generalization of the univariate t test. We initially present the traditional analysis of variance approach for the two-group multivariate problem, and then later present and compare a regression analysis of the same data. In the next chapter, studies with more than two groups are considered, where multivariate tests are employed that are generalizations of Fisher's F found in a univariate one-way ANOVA. The last part of the chapter (sections 4.9–4.12) presents a fairly extensive discussion of power, including introduction of a multivariate effect size measure and the use of SPSS MANOVA for estimating power.

There are two reasons one should be interested in using more than one dependent variable when comparing two treatments:

1. Any treatment "worth its salt" will affect the subjects in more than one way—hence the need for several criterion measures.

2. Through the use of several criterion measures we can obtain a more complete and detailed description of the phenomenon under investigation, whether it is reading achievement, math achievement, self-concept, physiological stress, or teacher effectiveness or counselor effectiveness.

If we were comparing two methods of teaching second-grade reading, we would obtain a more detailed and informative breakdown of the differential effects of the methods if reading achievement were split into its subcomponents: syllabication, blending, sound discrimination, vocabulary, comprehension, and reading rate. Comparing the two methods only on total reading achievement might yield no significant difference; however, the methods may be making a difference. The differences may be confined to only the more basic elements of blending and syllabication. Similarly, if two methods of teaching sixth-grade mathematics were being compared, it would be more informative to compare them on various levels of mathematics achievement (computations, concepts, and applications).

4.2 Four Statistical Reasons for Preferring a Multivariate Analysis

1. The use of fragmented univariate tests leads to a greatly inflated overall type I error rate, that is, the probability of at least one false rejection. Consider a two-group problem with 10 dependent variables. What is the probability of one or more spurious results if we do 10 t tests, each at the .05 level of significance? If we assume the tests are independent as an approximation (because the tests are not independent), then the probability of *no* type I errors is:

$$\underbrace{(.95)(.95)\cdots(.95)}_{10\,\text{times}} \approx .60$$

   because the probability of not making a type I error for each test is .95, and with the independence assumption we can multiply probabilities. Therefore, the probability of at least one false rejection is $1 - .60 = .40$, which is unacceptably high. Thus, with the univariate approach, not only does overall α become too high, but we can't even accurately estimate it.

2. The univariate tests ignore important information, namely, the correlations among the variables. The multivariate test incorporates the correlations (via the covariance matrix) right into the test statistic, as is shown in the next section.

3. Although the groups may not be significantly different on any of the variables individually, *jointly* the set of variables may reliably differentiate the groups. That is, small differences on several of the variables may combine to produce a reliable overall difference. Thus, the multivariate test will be more powerful in this case.

4. It is sometimes argued that the groups should be compared on total test score first to see if there is a difference. If so, then compare the groups further on sub-test scores to locate the sources responsible for the global difference. On the other hand, if there is no total test score difference, then stop. This procedure could definitely be misleading. Suppose, for example, that the total test scores were not significantly different, but that on subtest 1 Group 1 was quite superior, on subtest 2 Group 1 was somewhat superior, on subtest 3 there was no difference, and on subtest 4 Group 2 was quite superior. Then it would be clear why the univariate analysis of total test score found nothing—because of a canceling out effect. But the two groups do differ substantially on two of the four subsets, and to some extent on a third. A multivariate analysis of the subtests would reflect these differences and would show a significant difference.

Many investigators, especially when they first hear about multivariate analysis of variance (MANOVA), will lump all the dependent variables in a single analysis. This is not necessarily a good idea. If several of the variables have been included without any strong rationale (empirical or theoretical), then small or negligible differences on these variables may obscure a real difference(s) on some of the other variables. That is, the multivariate test statistic detects mainly error in the system (i.e., in the set of variables), and therefore declares no reliable overall difference. In a situation such as this what is called for are two separate multivariate analyses, one for the variables for which there is solid support, and a separate one for the variables that are being tested on a heuristic basis.

4.3 The Multivariate Test Statistic as a Generalization of Univariate *t*

For the univariate *t* test the null hypothesis is:

$$H_0: \mu_1 = \mu_2 \text{ (population means are equal)}$$

In the multivariate case the null hypothesis is:

$$H_0: \begin{pmatrix} \mu_{11} \\ \mu_{21} \\ \vdots \\ \mu_{p1} \end{pmatrix} = \begin{pmatrix} \mu_{12} \\ \mu_{22} \\ \vdots \\ \mu_{p2} \end{pmatrix} \text{ (population mean vectors are equal)}$$

Saying that the vectors are equal implies that the groups are equal on all *p* dependent variables. The first part of the subscript refers to the variable and the second part to the group. Thus, μ_{21} refers to the population mean for variable 2 in group 1.

Now, for the univariate *t* test, the reader should recall that there are three assumptions involved: (1) independence of the observations, (2) normality, and (3) equality of the population variances (homogeneity of variance). In testing the multivariate null hypothesis the corresponding assumptions are: (a) independence of the observations, (b) multivariate normality on the dependent variables in each population, and (c) equality of the covariance matrices. The latter two multivariate assumptions are much more stringent than the corresponding univariate assumptions. For example, saying that two covariance matrices are equal for four variables implies that the variances are equal for each of the variables *and* that the six covariances for each of the groups are equal. Consequences of violating the multivariate assumptions are discussed in detail in Chapter 6.

We now show how the multivariate test statistic arises naturally from the univariate *t* by replacing scalars (numbers) by vectors and matrices. The univariate *t* is given by:

$$t = \frac{\bar{y}_1 - \bar{y}_2}{\sqrt{\frac{(n_1 - 1)s_1^2 + (n_2 - 1)s_2^2}{n_1 + n_2 - 2}\left(\frac{1}{n_1} + \frac{1}{n_2}\right)}} \tag{1}$$

where s_1^2 and s_2^2 are the sample variances for groups 1 and 2, respectively. The quantity under the radical, excluding the sum of the reciprocals, is the pooled estimate of the assumed common within population variance, call it s^2. Now, replacing that quantity by s^2 and squaring both sides, we obtain:

$$t^2 = \frac{(\bar{y}_1 - \bar{y}_2)^2}{s^2\left(\frac{1}{n_1} + \frac{1}{n_2}\right)}$$

$$= (\bar{y}_1 - \bar{y}_2)\left[s^2\left(\frac{1}{n_1} + \frac{1}{n_2}\right)\right]^{-1}(\bar{y}_1 - \bar{y}_2)$$

$$= (\bar{y}_1 - \bar{y}_2)\left[s^2\left(\frac{n_1 + n_2}{n_1 n_2}\right)\right]^{-1}(\bar{y}_1 - \bar{y}_2)$$

$$t^2 = \frac{n_1 n_2}{n_1 + n_2}(\bar{y}_1 - \bar{y}_2)(s^2)^{-1}(\bar{y}_1 - \bar{y}_2)$$

Hotelling's T^2 is obtained by replacing the means on each variable by the vectors of means in each group, and by replacing the univariate measure of within variability s^2 by its multivariate generalization $\mathbf{S}$ (the estimate of the assumed common population covariance matrix). Thus we obtain:

$$T^2 = \frac{n_1 n_2}{n_1 + n_2} \cdot (\bar{y}_1 - \bar{y}_2)' \mathbf{S}^{-1} (\bar{y}_1 - \bar{y}_2) \tag{2}$$

Recall that the matrix analogue of division is inversion; thus $(s^2)^{-1}$ is replaced by the inverse of $\mathbf{S}$.

Hotelling (1931) showed that the following transformation of T^2 yields an exact F distribution:

$$F = \frac{n_1 + n_2 - p - 1}{(n_1 + n_2 - 2)p} \cdot T^2 \tag{3}$$

with p and $(N - p - 1)$ degrees of freedom, where p is the number of dependent variables and $N = n_1 + n_2$, that is, the total number of subjects.

We can rewrite T^2 as:

$$T^2 = k d' \mathbf{S}^{-1} d$$

where k is a constant involving the group sizes, d is the vector of mean differences, and $\mathbf{S}$ is the covariance matrix. Thus, what we have reflected in T^2 is a comparison of between-variability (given by the d vectors) to within-variability (given by $\mathbf{S}$). This is perhaps not obvious, because we are not literally dividing between by within as in the univariate case (i.e., $F = MS_h / MS_w$). However, recall again that inversion is the matrix analogue of division, so that multiplying by $\mathbf{S}^{-1}$ is in effect "dividing" by the multivariate measure of within variability.

4.4 Numerical Calculations for a Two-Group Problem

We now consider a small example to illustrate the calculations associated with Hotelling's T^2. The fictitious data shown next represent scores on two measures of counselor effectiveness, client satisfaction (SA) and client self-acceptance (CSA). Six subjects were originally randomly assigned to counselors who used either Rogerian or Adlerian methods; however, three in the Rogerian group were unable to continue for reasons unrelated to the treatment.

Rogerian		Adlerian	
SA	CSA	SA	CSA
1	3	4	6
3	7	6	8
2	2	6	8
$\bar{y}_{11} = 2$	$\bar{y}_{21} = 4$	5	10
		5	10
		4	6
		$\bar{y}_{12} = 5$	$\bar{y}_{22} = 8$

Recall again that the first part of the subscript denotes the variable and the second part the group, that is, y_{12} is the mean for variable 1 in group 2.

In words, our multivariate null hypothesis is, "There is no difference between the Rogerian and Adlerian groups when they are compared simultaneously on client satisfaction and client self-acceptance." Let client satisfaction be Variable 1 and client self-acceptance be Variable 2. Then the multivariate null hypothesis in symbols is:

$$H_0 : \begin{pmatrix} \mu_{11} \\ \mu_{21} \end{pmatrix} = \begin{pmatrix} \mu_{12} \\ \mu_{22} \end{pmatrix}$$

That is, we wish to determine whether it is tenable that the population means are equal for Variable 1 ($\mu_{11} = \mu_{12}$) and that the population means for Variable 2 are equal ($\mu_{21} = \mu_{22}$). To test the multivariate null hypothesis we need to calculate F in Equation 3. But to obtain this we first need T^2, and the tedious part of calculating T^2 is in obtaining S, which is our pooled estimate of within-group variability on the set of two variables, that is, our estimate of error. Before we begin calculating S it will be helpful to go back to the univariate t test (Equation 1) and recall how the estimate of error variance was obtained there. The estimate of the assumed common within-population variance (σ^2) (i.e., error variance) is given by

$$s^2 = \frac{(n_1 - 1)s_1^2 + (n_2 - 1)s_2^2}{n_1 + n_2 - 2} = \frac{ss_{g1} + ss_{g2}}{n_1 + n_2 - 2} \qquad (4)$$

$$\downarrow \qquad\qquad\qquad \downarrow$$

(cf. Equation 1)   (from the definition of variance)

where ss_{g1} and ss_{g2} are the within sums of squares for groups 1 and 2. In the multivariate case (i.e., in obtaining S) we replace the univariate measures of within-group variability (ss_{g1} and ss_{g2}) by their matrix multivariate generalizations, which we call W_1 and W_2.

W_1 will be our estimate of within variability on the two dependent variables in Group 1. Because we have two variables, there is variability on each, which we denote by ss_1 and ss_2, and covariability, which we denote by ss_{12}. Thus, the matrix W_1 will look as follows:

$$W_1 = \begin{bmatrix} ss_1 & ss_{12} \\ ss_{21} & ss_2 \end{bmatrix}$$

Similarly, W_2 will be our estimate of within variability (error) on variables in Group 2. After W_1 and W_2 have been calculated, we will pool them (i.e., add them) and divide by the degrees of freedom, as was done in the univariate case (see Equation 4), to obtain our multivariate error term, the covariance matrix S. Table 4.1 shows schematically the procedure for obtaining the pooled error terms for both the univariate t test and for Hotelling's T^2.

4.4.1 Calculation of the Multivariate Error Term S

First we calculate W_1, the estimate of within variability for group 1.

Now, ss_1 and ss_2 are just the sum of the squared deviations about the means for variables 1 and 2, respectively. Thus,

TABLE 4.1

Estimation of Error Term for t Test and Hotelling's T^2

	t test (univariate)	T^2 (multivariate)
Assumption	Within-group population variances are equal, i.e., $\sigma_1^2 = \sigma_2^2$ Call the common value σ^2	Within-group population covariance matrices are equal, $\Sigma_1 = \Sigma_2$ Call the common value Σ
	To estimate these assumed common population values we employ the three steps indicated below:	
Calculate the within-group measures of variability.	ss_{g1} and ss_{g2}	$\mathbf{W}_1$ and $\mathbf{W}_2$
Pool these estimates.	$ss_{g1} + ss_{g2}$	$\mathbf{W}_1 + \mathbf{W}_2$
Divide by the degrees of freedom	$\dfrac{SS_{g1} + SS_{g2}}{n_1 + n_2 - 2} = \hat{\sigma}^2$	$\dfrac{\mathbf{W}_1 + \mathbf{W}_2}{n_1 + n_2 - 2} = \hat{\Sigma} = \mathbf{S}$

Note: The rationale for pooling is that if we are measuring the same variability in each group (which is the assumption), then we obtain a better estimate of this variability by combining our estimates.

$$ss_1 = \sum_{i=1}^{3}(y_{1(i)} - \bar{y}_{11})^2 = (1-2)^2 + (3-2)^2 + (2-2)^2 = 2$$

($y_{1(i)}$ denotes the score for the ith subject on variable 1)

and

$$ss_2 = \sum_{i=1}^{3}(y_{2(i)} - \bar{y}_{21})^2 = (3-4)^2 + (7-4)^2 + (2-4)^2 = 14$$

Finally, ss_{12} is just the sum of deviation cross products:

$$ss_{12} = \sum_{i=1}^{3}(y_{1(i)} - 2)(y_{2(i)} - 4)$$

$$= (1-2)(3-4) + (3-2)(7-4) + (2-2)(2-4) = 4$$

Therefore, the within SSCP matrix for Group 1 is

$$\mathbf{W}_1 = \begin{bmatrix} 2 & 4 \\ 4 & 14 \end{bmatrix}$$

Similarly, as we leave for the reader to show, the within matrix for Group 2 is

$$\mathbf{W}_2 = \begin{bmatrix} 4 & 4 \\ 4 & 16 \end{bmatrix}$$

Thus, the multivariate error term (i.e., the pooled within covariance matrix) is calculated as:

$$S = \frac{W_1 + W_2}{n_1 + n_2 - 2} = \frac{\begin{bmatrix} 2 & 4 \\ 4 & 14 \end{bmatrix} + \begin{bmatrix} 4 & 4 \\ 4 & 16 \end{bmatrix}}{7} = \begin{bmatrix} 6/7 & 8/7 \\ 8/7 & 30/7 \end{bmatrix}$$

Note that 6/7 is just the sample variance for variable 1, 30/7 is the sample variance for variable 2, and 8/7 is the sample covariance.

4.4.2 Calculation of the Multivariate Test Statistic

To obtain Hotelling's T^2 we need the inverse of S as follows:

$$S^{-1} = \begin{bmatrix} 1.811 & -.483 \\ -.483 & .362 \end{bmatrix}$$

From Equation 2 then, Hotelling's T^2 is

$$T^2 = \frac{n_1 n_2}{n_1 + n_2}(\bar{y}_1 - \bar{y}_2)'S^{-1}(\bar{y}_1 - \bar{y}_2)$$

$$T^2 = \frac{3(6)}{3+6}(2-5, 4-8)\begin{bmatrix} 1.811 & -.483 \\ -.483 & .362 \end{bmatrix}\begin{pmatrix} 2-5 \\ 4-8 \end{pmatrix}$$

$$T^2 = (-6,-8)\begin{pmatrix} -3.501 \\ .001 \end{pmatrix} = 21$$

The exact F transformation of T^2 is then

$$F = \frac{n_1 + n_2 - p - 1}{(n_1 + n_2 - 2)p}T^2 = \frac{9-2-1}{7(2)}(21) = 9$$

where F has 2 and 6 degrees of freedom (cf. Equation 3).

If we were testing the multivariate null hypothesis at the .05 level, then we would reject (because the critical value = 5.14) and conclude that the two groups differ on the set of two variables.

After finding that the groups differ, we would like to determine which of the variables are contributing to the overall difference; that is, a post hoc procedure is needed. This is similar to the procedure followed in a one-way ANOVA, where first an overall F test is done. If F is significant, then a post hoc technique (such as Scheffé's or Tukey's) is used to determine which specific groups differed, and thus contributed to the overall difference. Here, instead of groups, we wish to know which variables contributed to the overall multivariate significance.

Now, multivariate significance implies there is a linear combination of the dependent variables (the discriminant function) that is significantly separating the groups. We defer extensive discussion of discriminant analysis to Chapter 7. Harris (1985, p. 9) argued vigorously for focusing on such linear combinations. "Multivariate statistics can be of considerable value in suggesting new, emergent variables of this sort that may not have been anticipated—but the researcher must be prepared to think in terms of such combinations." While we agree that discriminant analysis can be of value, there are at least three factors that can mitigate its usefulness in many instances:

1. There is no guarantee that the linear combination (the discriminant function) will be a meaningful variate, that is, that it will make substantive or conceptual sense.

2. Sample size must be considerably larger than many investigators realize in order to have the results of a discriminant analysis be reliable. More details on this later.

3. The investigator may be more interested in what specific variables contributed to treatment differences, rather than on some combination of them.

4.5 Three Post Hoc Procedures

We now consider three possible post hoc approaches. One approach is to use the Roy–Bose simultaneous confidence intervals. These are a generalization of the Scheffé intervals, and are illustrated in Morrison (1976) and in Johnson and Wichern (1982). The intervals are nice in that we not only can determine whether a pair of means is different, but in addition can obtain a range of values within which the population mean differences probably lie. Unfortunately, however, the procedure is extremely conservative (Hummel & Sligo, 1971), and this will hurt power (sensitivity for detecting differences).

As Bock (1975, p. 422) noted, "Their [Roy–Bose intervals] use at the conventional 90% confidence level will lead the investigator to overlook many differences that should be interpreted and defeat the purposes of an exploratory comparative study." What Bock says applies with particularly great force to a very large number of studies in social science research where the group or effect sizes are small or moderate. In these studies, power will be poor or not adequate to begin with. To be more specific, consider the power table from Cohen (1977, p. 36) for a two-tailed t test at the .05 level of significance. For group sizes ≤20 and small or medium effect sizes through .60 standard deviations, which is a quite common class of situations, the *largest* power is .45. The use of the Roy–Bose intervals will dilute the power even further to extremely low levels.

A second, less conservative post hoc procedure is to follow a significant multivariate result by univariate t's, but to do each t test at the α/p level of significance. Then we are assured by the Bonferroni inequality that the overall type I error rate for the set of t tests will be less than α. This is a good procedure if the number of dependent variables is small (say ≤7). Thus, if there were four variables and we wished to take at most a 10% chance of one or more false rejections, this can be assured by setting $\alpha = 10/4 = .025$ for each t test. Recall that the Bonferroni inequality simply says that the overall α level for a set of tests is less than or equal to the sum of the α levels for each test.

The third post hoc procedure we consider is following a significant multivariate test at the .05 level by univariate tests, each at the .05 level. The results of a Monte Carlo study by Hummel and Sligo (1971) indicate that, if the multivariate null hypothesis is true, then this

TABLE 4.2

Experimentwise Error Rates for Analyzing Multivariate Data with Only Univariate Tests and with a Multivariate Test Followed by Univariate Tests

Sample size	Number of variables	Proportion of variance in common			
		.10	.30	.50	.70
Univariate tests only					
10	3	.145	.112	.114	.077
10	6	.267	.190	.178	.111
10	9	.348	.247	.209	.129
30	3	.115	.119	.117	.085
30	6	.225	.200	.176	.115
30	9	.296	.263	.223	.140
50	3	.138	.124	.102	.083
50	6	.230	.190	.160	.115
50	9	.324	.258	.208	.146
Multivariate test followed by univariate tests					
10	3	.044	.029	.035	.022
10	6	.046	.029	.030	.017
10	9	.050	.026	.025	.018
30	3	.037	.044	.029	.025
30	6	.037	.037	.032	.021
30	9	.042	.042	.030	.021
50	3	.038	.041	.033	.028
50	6	.037	.039	.028	.027
50	9	.036	.038	.026	.020

Note: Nominal $\alpha = .05$.

procedure keeps the overall α level under control for the set of *t* tests (see Table 4.2). This procedure has greater power for detecting differences than the two previous approaches, and this is an important consideration when small or moderate sample sizes are involved. Timm (1975) noted that if the multivariate null hypothesis is only partially true (e.g., for only three of five variables there are no differences in the population means), and the multivariate null hypothesis is likely to be rejected, then the Hummel and Sligo results are not directly applicable. He suggested use of the second approach we mentioned. Although this approach will guard against spurious results, power will be severely attenuated if the number of dependent variables is even moderately large. For example, if $p = 15$ and we wish to set overall $\alpha = .05$, then each univariate test must be done at the $.05/15 = .0033$ level of significance. Two things can be done to improve power and yet provide reasonably good protection against type I errors. First, there are several reasons (which we detail in Chapter 5) for *generally* preferring to work with a relatively small number of dependent variables (say ≤10). Second, in many cases, it may be possible to divide the dependent variables up into two or three of the following categories: (a) those variables likely to show a difference, (b) those variables (based on past research) that may show a difference, and (c) those variables that are being tested on a heuristic basis.

As an example, suppose we conduct a study limiting the number of variables to eight. There is fairly solid evidence from the literature that three of the variables should show a difference, while the other five are being tested on a heuristic basis. In this situation, as indicated in section 4.2, two multivariate tests should be done. If the multivariate test is significant for the fairly solid variables, then we would test each of the individual variables at the .05 level. Here we are not as concerned about type I errors in the follow-up phase, because there is prior reason to believe they will be significant. A separate multivariate test is done for the five heuristic variables. If this is significant, then we would employ the Timm approach, but set overall α somewhat higher for better power (especially if sample size is small or moderate). For example, set overall $\alpha = .15$, and thus test each variable for significance at the $.15/5 = .03$ level of significance.

4.6 SAS and SPSS Control Lines for Sample Problem and Selected Printout

Table 4.3 presents the complete SAS and SPSS control lines for running the two-group sample MANOVA problem. Table 4.4 gives selected printout from the SAS and SPSS runs. Note that both SAS and SPSS give all four multivariate test statistics, although in different

TABLE 4.3

SAS GLM and SPSS MANOVA Control Lines for Two-Group MANOVA Sample Problem

	SAS GLM		SPSS MANOVA
	TITLE 'MANOVA';		TITLE 'MANOVA'.
	DATA TWOGP;		DATA LIST FREE/GP Y1 Y2.
	INPUT GP Y1 Y2 @@;		BEGIN DATA.
	CARDS;	⑤	1 1 3 1 3 7 1 2 2
	1 1 3 1 3 7 1 2 2		2 4 6 2 6 8 2 6 8
	2 4 6 2 6 8 2 6 8		2 5 10 2 5 10 2 4 6
	2 5 10 2 5 10 2 4 6		END DATA.
①	PROC GLM;	⑥	MANOVA Y1 Y2 BY GP(1,2)/
②	CLASS GP;	⑦	PRINT = CELLINFO (MEANS)/.
③	MODEL Y1 Y2 = GP;		
④	MANOVA H = GP/PRINTE PRINTH;		

① The GENERAL LINEAR MODELS procedure is called. This is a very powerful and general procedure, which does univariate and multivariate analysis of variance and covariance, etc.

② The CLASS statement tells SAS which variable is the grouping variable.

③ In the MODEL statement the dependent variables are put on the left-hand side and the grouping variable(s) on the right side.

④ It is necessary to identify the effect to be used as the hypothesis matrix, which here by default is GP. After the slash a wide variety of optional output is available. We have selected PRINTE (prints the error SSCP matrix) and PRINTH (prints the matrix associated with the effect, which here is group).

⑤ The first number for each triplet is the group identification with the remaining two numbers the scores on the dependent variables.

⑥ The general form for the MANOVA command is

MANOVA	list of	BY	list of	WITH	list of
	dep. vars		factors		covariates

Since we have no covariates here, the WITH part is dropped.

⑦ This PRINT subcommand yields descriptive statistics for the groups, that is, means and standard deviations.

orders. Recall also from earlier in the chapter that for two groups they are equivalent, and therefore the multivariate F is the same for all four. I prefer the arrangement of the multivariate and univariate results given by SPSS (the lower half of Table 4.4). The multivariate tests are presented first, followed by the univariate tests. The multivariate tests show significance at the .05 level, because $.016 < .05$. The univariate F's show that both variables are contributing at the .05 level to the overall multivariate significance, because the p values (.003 and .029) are less than .05. These F's are equivalent to squared t values. Recall that for two groups $F = t^2$.

TABLE 4.4

Selected Output from SAS GLM and SPSS MANOVA for Two-Group MANOVA Sample Problem

---

SAS GLM OUTPUT

E = Error SSS & CP Matrix

	Y1	Y2
Y1	6	8
Y2	8	30

General Linear Models Procedure
Multivariate Analysis of Variance

H = Type III SS&CP Matrix for GP

	Y1	Y2
Y1	18	24
Y2	24	32

In 4.4, under CALCULATING THE MULIVARIATE ERROR TERM, we computed the W_1 and W_2 matrices (the within sums of squares and cross products matrices), and then pooled or added them in getting to the covariance matrix S, What SAS is outputting here is the $W_1 = W_2$ matrix.

Note that the diagonal elements of this hypothesis SSCP matrix are just the hypothesis mean squares for the univariate F tests.

Manova Test Criteria and Exact F Statistics for the Hypothesis of no Overall GP Effect
H = Type III SS&CP Matrix for GP   E = Error SS&CP Matrix

$S = 1$ $M = 0$ $N = 2$

Statistic	Value	F	Num DF	Den DF	Pr > F
Wilks' Lambda	0.25000000	9.0000	2	6	0.0156
Pillai's Trace	0.75000000	9.0000	2	6	0.0156
Hotelling-Lawley Trace	3.00000000	9.0000	2	6	0.0156
Roy's Greatest Root	3.00000000	9.0000	2	6	0.0156

SPSSX MANOVA OUTPUT

EFFECT .. GP
Multivariate Tests of Significance (S = 1, M = 0, N = 2)

Test Name	Value	Exact F	Hypoth. DF	Error DF	Sig. of F
Pillais	.75000	9.00000	2.00	6.00	.016
Hotelling	3.00000	9.00000	2.00	6.00	.016
Wilks	.25000	9.00000	2.00	6.00	.016
Roys	.75000				

Note .. F statistics are exact.

Effect .. GP (Cont.)
Univariate F-tests with (1, 7) D. F.

Variable	Hypoth. SS	Error SS	Hypoth. MS	Error MS	F	Sig. of F
Y1	18.00000	6.00000	18.00000	.85714	21.00000	.003
Y2	32.00000	30.00000	32.00000	4.28571	7.46667	.029

Although both variables are contributing to the multivariate significance, it needs to be emphasized that *because the univariate F's ignore how a given variable is correlated with the others in the set, they do not give an indication of the relative importance of that variable to group differentiation.* A technique for determining the relative importance of each variable to group separation is discriminant analysis, which will be discussed in Chapter 7. To obtain reliable results with discriminant analysis, however, a large subject-to-variable ratio is needed; that is, about 20 subjects per variable are required.

4.7 Multivariate Significance But No Univariate Significance

If the multivariate null hypothesis is rejected, then *generally* at least one of the univariate *t*'s will be significant, as in our previous example. This will not always be the case. It is possible to reject the multivariate null hypothesis and yet for none of the univariate *t*'s to be significant. As Timm (1975, p. 166) pointed out, "Furthermore, rejection of the multivariate test does not guarantee that there exists at least one significant univariate F ratio. For a given set of data, the significant comparison may involve some linear combination of the variables." This is analogous to what happens occasionally in univariate analysis of variance. The overall F is significant, but when, say, the Tukey procedure is used to determine which pairs of groups are significantly different, none are found. Again, all that significant F guarantees is that there is at least one comparison among the group means that is significant at or beyond the same α level: The particular comparison may be a complex one, and may or may not be a meaningful one.

One way of seeing that there will be no necessary relationship between multivariate significance and univariate significance is to observe that the tests make use of different information. For example, the multivariate test takes into account the correlations among the variables, whereas the univariate don't. Also, the multivariate test considers the differences on all variables jointly, whereas the univariate tests consider the difference on each variable separately.

We now consider a specific example, explaining in a couple of ways why multivariate significance was obtained but univariate significance was not.

Example 4.1

Kerlinger and Pedhazur (1973) present a three-group, two-dependent-variable example where the MANOVA test is significant at the .001 level, yet neither univariate test is significant, even at the .05 level. To explain this geometrically, they plot the scores for the variables in the plane (see Figure 4.1), along with the means for the groups in the plane (the problem considered as two-dimensional, i.e., multivariate). The separation of the means for the groups along each axis (i.e., when the problem is considered as two unidimensional or univariate analyses) is also given in Figure 4.1. Note that the separation of the groups in the plane is clearly greater than the separation along either axis, and in fact yielded multivariate significance. Thus, the smaller unreliable differences on each of the variables combined to produce a cumulative reliable overall difference when the variables are considered jointly.

We wish to dig a bit more deeply into this example, for there are two factors present that make it a near optimal situation for the multivariate test. First, treatments affected the dependent variables in different ways; that is, the across-groups association between the variables was weak, so each variable was adding something relatively unusual to group differentiation. This is analogous to

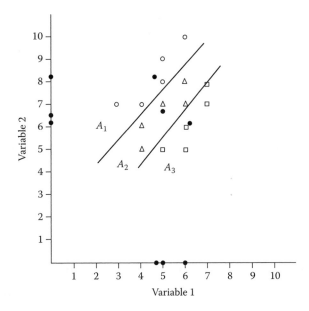

Data for Above Plot

A_1		A_2		A_2	
1	2	1	2	1	2
3	7	4	5	5	5
4	7	4	6	6	5
5	8	5	7	6	6
5	9	6	7	7	7
6	10	6	8	7	8

FIGURE 4.1

Graphical plot of scores for three-group case with multivariate significance but no univariate significance.

having low intercorrelations among the predictors in a multiple regression situation. Each predictor is then adding something relatively unusual to prediction of y. The pattern of means for the problem is presented here:

	Gp 1	Gp 2	Gp 3
Dep. 1	4.6	5.0	6.2
Dep. 2	8.2	6.6	6.2

The second factor that contributed to a particularly sensitive multivariate test is that the variables had a very strong *within*-group correlation (.88). This is important, because it produced a smaller generalized error term against which multivariate significance was judged. The error term in MANOVA that corresponds to MS_w in ANOVA is $|\mathbf{W}|$. That is, $|\mathbf{W}|$ is a measure of how much the subjects' scores vary within groups on the set of variables.

Consider the following two $\mathbf{W}$ matrices (the first matrix is from the preceding example) whose off diagonal elements differ because the correlation between the variables in the first case is .88 while in the other case it is .33.

$$\mathbf{W}_1 = \begin{bmatrix} 12.0 & 13.2 \\ 13.2 & 18.8 \end{bmatrix} \mathbf{W}_2 = \begin{bmatrix} 12.0 & 5.0 \\ 5.0 & 18.8 \end{bmatrix}$$

The multivariate error term in the first situation is $|\mathbf{W_1}| = 12\,(18.8) - 13.2^2 = 51.36$, whereas for $\mathbf{W_2}$ the error term is 200.6, almost four times greater. Thus, the size of the correlation can make a considerable difference in the magnitude of the multivariate error term. If the correlation is weak, then most of the error on the second variable cannot be accounted for by error on the first, and all that additional error becomes part of the multivariate error. On the other hand, when the correlation is strong, the second variable adds little additional error, and therefore the multivariate error term is much smaller.

Summarizing then, in the Kerlinger and Pedhazur example it was the *combination* of weak across-group association (meaning each variable was making a relatively unique contribution to group differentiation) coupled with a strong within-group correlation (producing a small multivariate error term) that yielded an excellent situation for the multivariate test.

4.8 Multivariate Regression Analysis for the Sample Problem

This section is presented to show that ANOVA and MANOVA are special cases of regression analysis, that is, of the so-called general linear model. Cohen's (1968) seminal article was primarily responsible for bringing the general linear model to the attention of social science researchers. The regression approach to MANOVA is accomplished by dummy coding group membership. This amounts, for the two-group problem, to coding the subjects in Group 1 by some numerical value, say 1, and the subjects in Group 2 by another numerical value, say 0. Thus, the data for our sample problem would look like this:

y_1	y_2	x	
1	3	1	
3	7	1	Group 1
2	2	1	
4	6	0	
4	6	0	
5	10	0	Group 2
5	10	0	
6	8	0	
6	8	0	

In a typical regression problem, as considered in the previous chapters, the predictors have been continuous variables. Here, for MANOVA, the predictor is a categorical or nominal variable, and is used to determine how much of the variance in the dependent variables is accounted for by group membership. It should be noted that values other than 1 and 0 could have been used as the dummy codes without affecting the results. For example, the subjects in Group 1 could have been coded as 1's and the subjects in Group 2 as 2's. All that is necessary is to distinguish between the subjects in the two groups by two different values.

The setup of the two-group MANOVA as a multivariate regression may seem somewhat strange since there are two dependent variables and only one predictor. In the previous chapters there has been either one dependent variable and several predictors, or several dependent variables and several predictors. However, the examination of the association is done in the same way. Recall that Wilks' Λ was the statistic for determining whether there is a significant association between the dependent variables and the predictor(s):

$$\Lambda = \frac{|\mathbf{S}_e|}{|\mathbf{S}_e + \mathbf{S}_r|}$$

where $\mathbf{S}_e$ is the error SSCP matrix, that is, the sum of square and cross products not due to regression (or the residual), and $\mathbf{S}_r$ is the regression SSCP matrix, that is, an index of how much variability in the dependent variables is due to regression. In this case, variability due to regression is variability in the dependent variables due to group membership, because the predictor is group membership.

Part of the output from SPSS for the two-group MANOVA, set up and run as a regression, is presented in Table 4.5. The error matrix $\mathbf{S}_e$ is called adjusted within-cells sum of squares and cross products, and the regression SSCP matrix is called adjusted hypothesis sum of squares and cross products. Using these matrices, we can form Wilks' Λ (and see how the value of .25 is obtained):

$$\Lambda = \frac{|\mathbf{S}_e|}{|\mathbf{S}_e + \mathbf{S}_r|} = \frac{\begin{vmatrix} 6 & 8 \\ 8 & 30 \end{vmatrix}}{\begin{vmatrix} \begin{bmatrix} 6 & 8 \\ 8 & 30 \end{bmatrix} + \begin{bmatrix} 18 & 24 \\ 24 & 32 \end{bmatrix} \end{vmatrix}}$$

$$\Lambda = \frac{\begin{vmatrix} 6 & 8 \\ 8 & 30 \end{vmatrix}}{\begin{vmatrix} 24 & 32 \\ 32 & 62 \end{vmatrix}} = \frac{116}{464} = .25$$

Note first that the multivariate F's are *identical* for Table 4.4 and Table 4.5; thus, significant separation of the group mean vectors is equivalent to significant association between group membership (dummy coded) and the set of dependent variables.

The univariate F's are also the same for both analyses, although it may not be clear to the reader why this is so.

In traditional ANOVA, the total sum of squares (ss_t) is partitioned as:

$$ss_t = ss_b + ss_w$$

whereas in regression analysis the total sum of squares is partitioned as follows:

$$ss_t = ss_{\text{reg}} + ss_{\text{resid}}$$

The corresponding F ratios, for determining whether there is significant group separation and for determining whether there is a significant regression, are:

$$F = \frac{SS_b / df_b}{SS_w / df_w} \quad \text{and} \quad F = \frac{SS_{\text{reg}} / df_{\text{reg}}}{SS_{\text{resid}} / df_{\text{resid}}}$$

TABLE 4.5

Selected Output from SPSS for Regression Analysis on Two-Group MANOVA
with Group Membership as Predictor

GP	Pillai's Trace	.750	9.000[a]	2.000	6.000	.016
	Wilks' Lambda	.250	9.000[a]	2.000	6.000	.016
	Hotelling's Trace	3.000	9.000[a]	2.000	6.000	.016
	Roy's Largest Root	3.000	9.000[a]	2.000	6.000	.016

Source	Dependent Variable	Type III Sum of Squares	df	Mean Square	F	Sig.
Corrected Model	Y1	18.000[a]	1	18.000	21.000	.003
	Y2	32.000[b]	1	32.000	7.467	.029
Intercept	Y1	98.000	1	98.000	114.333	.000
	Y2	288.000	1	288.000	67.200	.000
GP	Y1	18.000	1	18.000	21.000	.003
	Y2	32.000	1	32.000	7.467	.029
Error	Y1	6.000	7	.857		
	Y2	30.000	7	4.286		

Between-Subjects SSCP Matrix

			Y1	Y2
Hypothesis	Intercept	Y1	98.000	168.000
		Y2	168.000	288.000
	GP	Y1	18.000	24.000
		Y2	24.000	32.000
Error		Y1	6.000	8.000
		Y2	8.000	30.000

Based on Type III Sum of Squares

To see that these F ratios are equivalent, note that because the predictor variable is group membership, ss_{reg} is just the amount of variability between groups or ss_b, and ss_{resid} is just the amount of variability not accounted for by group membership, or the variability of the scores within each group (i.e., ss_w).

The regression output from SPSS also gives some information *not* on the traditional MANOVA output: the squared multiple R's for each dependent variable. Because in this case there is just one predictor, these multiple R's are just squared Pearson correlations. In particular, they are squared pt-biserial correlations because one of the variables is dichotomous (dummy coded group membership). The relationship between the pt-biserial correlation and the F statistic is given by (Welkowitz, Ewen, and Cohen, 1982):

$$r_{pb} = \sqrt{\frac{F}{F + df_w}}$$

$$r_{pb}^2 = \frac{F}{F + df_w}$$

Thus, for dependent variable 1, we have

$$r_{pb}^2 = \frac{21}{21+7} = .75$$

This squared correlation has a very meaningful and important interpretation. It tells us that 75% of the variance in the dependent variable is accounted for by group membership. Thus, we not only have a statistically significant relationship, as indicated by the F ratio, but in addition, the relationship is very strong. It should be recalled that it is important to have a measure of strength of relationship *along* with a test of significance, as significance resulting from large sample size might indicate a very weak relationship, and therefore one that may be of little practical significance.

Various textbook authors have recommended measures of association or strength of relationship measures (Cohen & Cohen, 1975; Hays, 1981; Kerlinger & Pedhazur, 1973; Kirk, 1982). We also believe that they can be useful, but they have limitations.

For example, simply because a strength of relationship indicates that, say, only 10% of variance is accounted for, does not *necessarily* imply that the result has no practical significance, as O'Grady (1982) indicated in an excellent review on measures of association. There are several factors that affect such measures. One very important factor is context: 10% of variance accounted for in certain research areas may indeed be practically significant.

A good example illustrating this point is provided by Rosenthal and Rosnow (1984). They consider the comparison of a treatment and control group where the dependent variable is dichotomous, whether the subjects survive or die. The following table is presented:

	Treatment Outcome		
	Alive	Dead	
Treatment	66	34	100
Control	34	66	100
	100	100	

Because both variables are dichotomous, the phi coefficient—a special case of the Pearson correlation for two dichotomous variables (Glass and Hopkins, 1984)—measures the relationship between them:

$$\phi = \frac{34^2 - 66^2}{\sqrt{100(100)(100)(100)}} = -.32 \Rightarrow \phi^2 = .10$$

Thus, even though the treatment-control distinction accounts for "only" 10% of the variance in the outcome, it increases the survival rate from 34% to 66%, far from trivial. The same type of interpretation would hold if we considered some less dramatic type of outcome like improvement versus no improvement, where treatment was a type of psychotherapy. Also, the interpretation is *not* confined to a dichotomous outcome measure. Another factor to consider is the design of the study. As O'Grady (1982) noted:

> Thus, true experiments will frequently produce smaller measures of explained variance than will correlational studies. At the least this implies that consideration should be given to whether an investigation involves a true experiment or a correlational approach in deciding whether an effect is weak or strong.

Another point to keep in mind is that, because most behaviors have multiple causes, it will be difficult in these cases to account for a large percent of variance with just a single cause (say treatments). Still another factor is the homogeneity of the population sampled. Because measures of association are correlational-type measures, the more homogeneous the population, the smaller the correlation will tend to be, and therefore the smaller the percent of variance accounted for can potentially be (this is the restriction-of-range phenomenon).

Finally, we focus on a topic that is generally neglected in texts on MANOVA, estimation of power. We start at a basic level, reviewing what power is, factors affecting power, and reasons that estimation of power is important. Then the notion of effect size for the univariate t test is given, followed by the multivariate effect size concept for Hotelling's T^2.

4.9 Power Analysis*

Type I error, or the level of significance (α), is familiar to all readers. This is the probability of rejecting the null hypothesis when it is true, that is, saying the groups differ when in fact they don't. The α level set by the experimenter is a subjective decision, but is usually set at .05 or .01 by most researchers to minimize the probability of making this kind of error. There is, however, another type of error that one can make in conducting a statistical test, and this is called a type II error. Type II error, denoted by β, is the probability of accepting H_0 when it is false, that is, saying the groups don't differ when they do. Now, not only can either of these errors occur, but in addition they are inversely related. Thus, as we control on type I error, type II error increases. This is illustrated next for a two-group problem with 15 subjects per group:

α	β	$1 - \beta$
.10	.37	.63
.05	.52	.48
.01	.78	.22

Notice that as we control on α more severely (from .10 to .01), type II error increases fairly sharply (from .37 to .78). Therefore, the problem for the experimental planner is achieving an appropriate balance between the two types of errors. Although we do not intend to minimize the seriousness of making a type I error, we hope to convince the reader that much more attention should be paid to type II error. Now, the quantity in the last column is the *power* of a statistical test, and is the probability of rejecting the null hypothesis when it is false. Thus, power is the probability of making a correct decision. In the preceding example if we are willing to take a 10% chance of rejecting H_0 falsely, then we have a 63% chance of finding a difference of a specified magnitude in the population (more specifics on this shortly). On the other hand, if we insist on only a 1% chance of rejecting H_0 falsely, then we have only about 2 chances out of 10 of finding the difference. This example with small sample size suggests that in this case it might be prudent to abandon the traditional α levels of .01 or .05 to a more liberal α level to improve power sharply. Of course, one does

---

* Much of the material in this section is identical to that presented in 1.2; however, it was believed to be worth repeating in this more extensive discussion of power.

not get something for nothing. We are taking a greater risk of rejecting falsely, but that increased risk is *more than balanced* by the increase in power.

There are two types of power estimation, a priori and post hoc, and very good reasons why each of them should be considered seriously. If a researcher is going to invest a great amount of time and money in carrying out a study, then he or she would certainly want to have a 70% or 80% chance (i.e., power of .70 or .80) of finding a difference if one is there. Thus, the a priori estimation of power will alert the researcher to how many subjects per group will be needed for adequate power. Later on we consider an example of how this is done in the multivariate case.

The post hoc estimation of power is important in terms of how one interprets the results of completed studies. Researchers not sufficiently sensitive to power may interpret non-significant results from studies as demonstrating that treatments made no difference. In fact, it may be that treatments did make a difference but that the researchers had poor power for detecting the difference. The poor power may result from small sample size or effect size. The following example shows how important an awareness of power can be. Cronbach and Snow had written a report on aptitude-treatment interaction research, not being fully cognizant of power. By the publication of their text *Aptitudes and Instructional Methods* (1977) on the same topic, they acknowledged the importance of power, stating in the preface. "[We] … became aware of the critical relevance of statistical power, and conse-quently changed our interpretations of individual studies and sometimes of whole bodies of literature." Why would they change their interpretation of a whole body of literature? Because, prior to being sensitive to power when they found most studies in a given body of literature had nonsignificant results, they concluded no effect existed. However, after being sensitized to power, they took into account the sample sizes in the studies, and also the magnitude of the effects. If the sample sizes were small in most of the studies with nonsignificant results, then lack of significance is due to poor power. Or, in other words, several low-power studies that report nonsignificant results of the same character *are* evi-dence for an effect.

The power of a statistical test is dependent on three factors:

1. The α level set by the experimenter
2. Sample size
3. Effect size—How much of a difference the treatments make, or the extent to which the groups differ in the population on the dependent variable(s)

For the univariate independent samples *t* test, Cohen (1977) defined the population effect size as $d = (\mu_1 - \mu_2)/\sigma$, where σ is the assumed common population standard deviation. Thus, effect size simply indicates how many standard deviation units the group means are separated by.

Power is *heavily* dependent on sample size. Consider a two-tailed test at the .05 level for the *t* test for independent samples. Suppose we have an effect size of .5 standard devia-tions. The next table shows how power changes dramatically as sample size increases.

n (subjects per group)	power
10	.18
20	.33
50	.70
100	.94

As this example suggests, when sample size is large (say 100 or more subjects per group) power is not an issue. It is when one is conducting a study where the group sizes are small ($n \leq 20$), or when one is evaluating a completed study that had small group size, that it is imperative to be very sensitive to the possibility of poor power (or equivalently, a type II error).

We have indicated that power is also influenced by effect size. For the t test, Cohen (1977) suggested as a rough rule of thumb that an effect size around .20 is small, an effect size around .50 is medium, and an effect size > .80 is large. The difference in the mean IQs between PhDs and the typical college freshmen is an example of a large effect size (about .8 of a standard deviation).

Cohen and many others have noted that *small and medium effect sizes are very common in social science research*. Light and Pillemer (1984) commented on the fact that most evaluations find small effects in reviews of the literature on programs of various types (social, educational, etc.): "Review after review confirms it and drives it home. Its importance comes from having managers understand that they should not expect large, positive findings to emerge routinely from a single study of a new program" (pp. 153–154). Results from Becker (1987) of effect sizes for three sets of studies (on teacher expectancy, desegregation, and gender influenceability) showed only three large effect sizes out of 40. Also, Light, Singer, and Willett (1990) noted that, "Meta-analyses often reveal a sobering fact: effect sizes are not nearly as large as we all might hope" (p. 195). To illustrate, they present average effect sizes from six meta-analyses in different areas that yielded .13, .25, .27, .38, .43, and .49; all in the small to medium range.

4.10 Ways of Improving Power

Given how poor power generally is with fewer than 20 subjects per group, the following four methods of improving power should be seriously considered:

1. Adopt a more lenient α level, perhaps $\alpha = .10$ or $\alpha = .15$.

2. Use one-tailed tests where the literature supports a directional hypothesis. This option is not available for the multivariate tests because they are inherently two-tailed.

3. Consider ways of reducing within-group variability, so that one has a more sensitive design. One way is through sample selection; more homogeneous subjects tend to vary less on the dependent variable(s). For example, use just males, rather than males and females, or use only 6- and 7-year-old children rather than 6- through 9-year-old children. A second way is through the use of factorial designs, which we consider in Chapter 8. A third way of reducing within-group variability is through the use of analysis of covariance, which we consider in Chapter 9. Covariates that have low correlations with each other are particularly helpful because then each is removing a somewhat different part of the within-group (error) variance. A fourth means is through the use of repeated-measures designs. These designs are particularly helpful because all individual difference due to the average response of subjects is removed

from the error term, and individual differences are the main reason for within-group variability.

4. Make sure there is a strong linkage between the treatments and the dependent variable(s), and that the treatments extend over a long enough period of time to produce a large—or at least fairly large—effect size.

Using these methods *in combination* can make a considerable difference in effective power. To illustrate, we consider a two-group situation with 18 subjects per group and one dependent variable. Suppose a two-tailed test was done at the .05 level, and that the effect size was

$$\hat{d} = (\bar{x}_1 - \bar{x}_2)/s = (8 - 4)/10 = .40,$$

where s is pooled within standard deviation. Then, from Cohen (1977, p. 36), power = .21, which is very poor.

Now, suppose that through the use of two good covariates we are able to reduce pooled within variability (s^2) by 60%, from 100 (as earlier) to 40. This is a definite realistic possibility in practice. Then our new estimated effect size would be $\hat{d} \approx 4/\sqrt{40} = .63$. Suppose in addition that a one-tail test was really appropriate, and that we also take a somewhat greater risk of a type I error, i.e., $\alpha = .10$. Then, our new estimated power changes dramatically to .69 (Cohen, 1977, p. 32).

Before leaving this section, it needs to be emphasized that how far one "pushes" the power issue depends on the *consequences* of making a type I error. We give three examples to illustrate. First, suppose that in a medical study examining the safety of a drug we have the following null and alternative hypotheses:

H_0: The drug is unsafe

H_1: The drug is safe

Here making a type I error (rejecting H_0 when true) is concluding that the drug is safe when in fact it is unsafe. This is a situation where we would want a type I error to be very small, because making a type I error could harm or possibly kill some people.

As a second example, suppose we are comparing two teaching methods, where method A is several times more expensive than method B to implement. If we conclude that method A is more effective (when in fact it is not), this will be a very costly mistake for a school district.

Finally, a classic example of the relative consequences of type I and type II errors can be taken from our judicial system, under which a defendant is innocent until proven guilty. Thus, we could formulate the following null and alternative hypotheses:

H_0: The defendant is innocent

H_1: The defendant is guilty

If we make a type I error we conclude that the defendant is guilty when he is innocent, while a type II error is concluding the defendant is innocent when he is guilty. Most would probably agree that the type I error is by far the more serious here, and thus we would want a type I error to be very small.

4.11 Power Estimation on SPSS MANOVA

Starting with Release 2.2 (1988), power estimates for a wide variety of statistical tests can be obtained using the SPSS MANOVA program with the POWER subcommand. To quote from the *SPSS User's Guide* (3rd edition), "The POWER subcommand requests observed power values based on fixed-effect assumptions for all univariate and multivariate F and T tests" (p. 601). Power can be obtained for any α level between 0 and 1, with .05 being the default value. If we wish power at the .05 level, we simply insert POWER /, or if we wish power at the .10 level, then the subcommand is POWER = F(.10)/. You will also want an effect size measure to go along with the power values, and these are obtained by putting SIGNIF (EFSIZE) in the PRINT subcommand. The effect size measure for the univariate F's is partial eta squared, which is given by

$$\eta_p^2 = (df \cdot F)/(df_h \cdot F + df_e)$$

where df_h denotes degrees of freedom for hypothesis and df_e denotes degrees of freedom for error (Cohen, 1973). The justification for the use of this measure, according to the *SPSS User's Guide* (1988), is that, "partial eta squared is an overestimate of the actual effect size. However, it is a consistent measure of effect size and is applicable to all F and t tests" (p. 602). Actually, partial η^2 and η^2 differ by very little when total sample size is about 50 or more. In terms of interpreting the partial eta squares for the univariate tests, Cohen (1977) characterized $\eta^2 = .01$ as small, $\eta^2 = .06$ as medium, and $\eta^2 = .14$ as a large effect size.

We obtained power at the .05 level for the multivariate and univariate tests, and the effect size measures for the sample problem (Table 4.3) by inserting the following subcommands after the MANOVA statement:

```
PRINT=CELLINFO(MEANS) SIGNIF(EFSIZE)/POWER/
```

The results are presented in Table 4.6, along with annotation.

4.12 Multivariate Estimation of Power

Stevens (1980) discussed estimation of power in MANOVA at some length, and in what follows we borrow heavily from his work. Next, we present the univariate and multivariate measures of effect size for the two-group problem. Recall that the univariate measure was presented earlier.

The first row gives the population values, and the second row the estimated effect sizes. Notice that the multivariate measure $\hat{D}^2$ is Hotelling's T^2 without the sample sizes (see Equation 2); that is, it is a measure of separation of the groups that is *independent* of sample size. D^2 is called in the literature the Mahalanobis distance. Note also that the multivariate measure $\hat{D}^2$ *is a natural squared generalization of the univariate measure* d, *where the means have been replaced by mean vectors and* s *(standard deviation) has been replaced by its squared multivariate generalization of within variability, the sample covariance matrix* **S**.

TABLE 4.6

SPSS MANOVA Run on Sample Problem Obtaining Power and Multivariate and Univariate Effect Size Measure

Effect		Value	F	Hypothesis df	Error df	Sig.
GP	Pillai's Trace	.750	9.000[b]	2.000	6.000	.016
	Wilks' Lambda	.250	9.000[b]	2.000	6.000	.016
	Hotelling's Trace	3.000	9.000[b]	2.000	6.000	.016
	Roy's Largest Root	3.000	9.000[b]	2.000	6.000	.016

Effect		Noncent. Parameter	Observed Power[a]
GP	Pillai's Trace	18.000	.832
	Wilks' Lambda	18.000	.832
	Hotelling's Trace	18.000	.832
	Roy's Largest Root	18.000	.832

[a] Computed using alpha = .05

Dependent Variable	Type III Sum of Squares	df	Mean Square	F	Sig.	Noncent. Parameter	Observed Power[a]
DEP1	18.000[b]	1	18.000	21.000	.003	21.000	.974
DEP2	32.000[c]	1	32.000	7.467	.029	7.467	.651
DEP1	98.000	1	98.000	114.333	.000	114.333	1.000
DEP2	288.000	1	288.000	67.200	.000	67.200	1.000
DEP1	18.000	1	18.000	21.000	.003	21.000	.974
DEP2	32.000	1	32.000	7.467	.029	7.467	.651
DEP1	6.000	7	.857				
DEP2	30.000	7	4.286				

Measures of Effect Size

Univariate	Multivariate

$$d = \frac{\mu_1 - \mu_2}{\sigma} \qquad D^2 = (\mu_1 - \mu_2)' \Sigma^{-1} (\mu_1 - \mu_2)$$

$$\hat{d} = \frac{\bar{y}_1 - \bar{y}_2}{s} \qquad \hat{D}^2 = (\bar{y}_1 - \bar{y}_2)' S^{-1} (\bar{y}_1 - \bar{y}_2)$$

Table 4.7 from Stevens (1980) provides power values for two-group MANOVA for two through seven variables, with group size varying from small (15) to large (100), and with effect size varying from small ($D^2 = .25$) to very large ($D^2 = 2.25$). Earlier, we indicated that small or moderate group and effect sizes produce inadequate power for the univariate t test. Inspection of Table 4.7 shows that a similar situation exists for MANOVA. The following from Stevens (1980, p. 731) provides a summary of the results in Table 4.7:

> For values of $D^2 \leq .64$ and $n \leq 25$, ... power is generally poor (< .45) and never really adequate (i.e., > .70) for $\alpha = .05$. Adequate power (at $\alpha = .10$) for two through seven variables at a moderate overall effect size of .64 would require about 30 subjects per group. When the overall effect size is large ($D \geq 1$), then 15 or more subjects per group is sufficient to yield power values $\geq .60$ for two through seven variables at $\alpha = .10$.

TABLE 4.7

Power of Hotelling's T^2 at $\alpha = .05$ and $.10$ for Small Through Large Overall Effect and Group Sizes

Number of variables	n^*	D^{2**} .25	.64	1	2.25
2	15	26 (32)	44 (60)	65 (77)	95***
2	25	33 (47)	66 (80)	86	97
2	50	60 (77)	95	1	1
2	100	90	1	1	1
3	15	23 (29)	37 (55)	58 (72)	91
3	25	28 (41)	58 (74)	80	95
3	50	54 (65)	93 (98)	1	1
3	100	86	1	1	1
5	15	21 (25)	32 (47)	42 (66)	83
5	25	26 (35)	42 (68)	72	96
5	50	44 (59)	88	1	1
5	100	78	1	1	1
7	15	18 (22)	27 (42)	37 (59)	77
7	25	22 (31)	38 (62)	64 (81)	94
7	50	40 (52)	82	97	1
7	100	72	1	1	1

Note: Power values at $\alpha = .10$ are in parentheses.
* Equal group sizes are assumed.
** $D^2 = (\mu_1 - \mu_2)'\Sigma^{-1}(\mu_1 - \mu_2)$
*** Decimal points have been omitted. Thus, 95 means a power of .95. Also, a value of 1 means the power is approximately equal to 1.

4.12.1 Post Hoc Estimation of Power

Suppose you wish to evaluate the power of a two-group MANOVA that was completed in a journal in your content area. Here SPSS MANOVA is not going to help. However, Table 4.7 can be used, assuming the number of dependent variables in the study is between two and seven. Actually, with a slight amount of extrapolation, the table will yield a reasonable approximation for eight or nine variables. For example, for $D^2 = .64$, five variables and $n = 25$, power = .42 at the .05 level. For the same situation, but with seven variables, power = .38. Therefore, a reasonable estimate for power for nine variables is about .34.

Now, to use Table 4.7, the value of D^2 is needed, and this almost certainly will not be reported. Very probably then, a couple of steps will be required to obtain D^2. The investigator(s) will probably report the multivariate F. From this, one obtains T^2 using Equation 3. Finally, D^2 is obtained using Equation 2. Because the right-hand side of Equation 2 without the sample sizes is D^2, it follows that $T^2 = [n_1 n_2/(n_1 + n_2)]D^2$, or $D^2 = [(n_1 + n_2)/n_1 n_2]T^2$.

We now consider two examples to illustrate how to use Table 4.7 to estimate power for studies in the literature when (a) the number of dependent variables is not explicitly given in Table 4.7, and (b) the group sizes are not equal.

Example 4.2

Consider a two-group study in the literature with 25 subjects per group that used 4 dependent variables and reports a multivariate $F = 2.81$. What is the estimated power at the .05 level? First, we convert F to corresponding T^2 value:

$$F = [(N-p-1)/(N-2)p]T^2 \quad \text{or} \quad T^2 = (N-2)pF/(N-p-1)$$

Thus, $T^2 = 48(4)2.81/45 = 11.99$. Now, because $D^2 = (NT^2)/n_1 n_2$, we have $D^2 = 50(11.99)/625 = .96$. This is a large multivariate effect size. Table 4.7 does not have power for four variables, but we can interpolate between three and five variables. Using $D^2 = 1$ in the table we find that:

Number of variables	n	$D^2 = 1$
3	25	.80
5	25	.72

Thus, a good approximation to power is .76, which is adequate power. Here, as in univariate analysis, with a large effect size, not many subjects are needed per group to have adequate power.

Example 4.3

Now consider an article in the literature that is a two-group MANOVA with five dependent variables, having 22 subjects in one group and 32 in the other. The investigators obtain a multivariate $F = 1.61$, which is not significant at the .05 level (critical value = 2.42). Calculate power at the .05 level and comment on the size of the multivariate effect measure. Here the number of dependent variables (5) is given in the table, but the group sizes are unequal. Following Cohen (1977), we use the harmonic mean as the n with which to enter the table. The harmonic mean for two groups is $\tilde{n} = 2n_1 n_2/(n_1 + n_2)$. Thus, for this case we have $\tilde{n} = 2(22)(32)/54 = 26.07$. Now, to get D^2 we first obtain T^2:

$$T^2 = (N-2)p\,F/(N-p-1) = 52(5)1.61/48 = 8.72$$

Now, $D^2 = N\,T^2/n_1 n_2 = 54(8.72)/22(32) = .67$. using $n = 25$ and $D^2 = .64$ to enter Table 4.7, we see that power = .42. Actually, power is slightly greater than .42 because $n = 26$ and $D^2 = .67$, but it would still not reach even .50. Thus, power is definitely inadequate here, but there is a solid medium multivariate effect size that may be of practical significance.

4.12.2 A Priori Estimation of Sample Size

Suppose that from a pilot study or from a previous study that used the same kind of subjects, an investigator had obtained the following pooled within-group covariance matrix for three variables:

$$\mathbf{S} = \begin{bmatrix} 16 & 6 & 1.6 \\ 6 & 9 & .9 \\ 1.6 & .9 & 1 \end{bmatrix}$$

Recall that the elements on the main diagonal of **S** are the variances for the variables: 16 is the variance for Variable 1, and so on.

To complete the estimate of D^2 the difference in the mean vectors must be estimated; this amounts to estimating the mean difference expected for each variable. Suppose that on the basis of previous literature, the investigator hypothesizes that the mean differences on variables 1 and 2 will be 2 and 1.5. Thus, they will correspond to moderate effect sizes of .5 standard derivations. Why? The investigator further expects the mean difference on Variable 3 will be .2, that is, .2 of a standard deviation, or a small effect size. How many subjects per group are required, at $\alpha = .10$, for detecting this set of differences if power = .70 is desired?

To answer this question we first need to estimate D^2:

$$\hat{D}^2 = (2, 1.5, .2) \begin{bmatrix} .0917 & -.0511 & -.1008 \\ -.0511 & .1505 & -.0538 \\ -.1008 & -.0538 & 1.2100 \end{bmatrix} \begin{pmatrix} 2.0 \\ 1.5 \\ 2 \end{pmatrix} = .3347$$

The middle matrix is the inverse of **S**. Because moderate and small univariate effect sizes produced this $\hat{D}^2$ value .3347, such a numerical value for D^2 would probably occur fairly frequently in social science research. To determine the n required for power = .70 we enter Table 4.7 for three variables and use the values in parentheses. For $n = 50$ and three variables, note that power = .65 for $D^2 = .25$ and power = .98 for $D^2 = .64$. Therefore, we have

$$\text{Power } (D^2 = .33) = \text{Power}(D^2 = .25) + [.08/.39](.33) = .72$$

4.13 Summary

In this chapter we have considered the statistical analysis of two groups on several dependent variables simultaneously. Among the reasons for preferring a MANOVA over separate univariate analyses were (a) MANOVA takes into account important information, that is, the intercorrelations among the variables, (b) MANOVA keeps the overall α level under control, and (c) MANOVA has greater sensitivity for detecting differences in certain situations. It was shown how the multivariate test (Hotelling's T^2) arises naturally from the univariate t by replacing the means with mean vectors and by replacing the pooled within-variance by the covariance matrix. An example indicated the numerical details associated with calculating T^2.

Three post hoc procedures for determining which of the variables contributed to the overall multivariate significance were considered. The Roy–Bose simultaneous confidence interval approach was rejected because it is extremely conservative, and hence has poor power for detecting differences. The approach of testing each variable at the α/p level of significance was considered a good procedure if the number of variables is small.

An example where multivariate significance was obtained, but not univariate significance, was considered in detail. Examination showed that the example was a near optimal situation for the multivariate test because the treatments affected the dependent variables in different ways (thus each variable was making a relatively unique contribution to group differentiation), whereas the dependent variables were strongly correlated within groups (providing a small multivariate error term).

Group membership for the sample problem was dummy coded, and it was run as a regression analysis. This yielded the same multivariate and univariate results as when the problem was run as a traditional MANOVA. This was done to show that MANOVA is a special case of regression analysis, that is, of the general linear model. It was noted that the regression output also provided useful strength of relationship measures for each variable (R^2's). However, the reader was warned against concluding that a result is of little practical significance simply because the R^2 value is small (say .10). Several reasons were given for this, one of the most important being context. Thus, 10% variance accounted for in some research areas may indeed be practically significant.

Power analysis was considered in some detail. It was noted that small and medium effect sizes are *very common* in social science research. Mahalanobis D^2 was presented as the multivariate effect size measure, with the following guidelines for interpretation: $D^2 =$ .25 small effect, $D^2 = .50$ medium effect, and $D^2 > 1$ large effect. Power estimation on SPSS MANOVA was illustrated. A couple of examples were given to show how to estimate multivariate power (using a table from Stevens, 1980), for studies in the literature, where only the multivariate F statistic is given.

4.14 Exercises

1. Which of the following are multivariate studies, that is, involve several correlated dependent variables?

   (a) An investigator classifies high school freshmen by sex, socioeconomic status, and teaching method, and then compares them on total test score on the Lankton algebra test.

   (b) A treatment and control group are compared on measures of reading speed and reading comprehension.

   (c) An investigator is predicting success on the job from high school GPA and a battery of personality variables.

   (d) An investigator has administered a 50-item scale to 200 college freshmen and he wished to determine whether a smaller number of underlying constructs account for most of the variance in the subjects responses to the items.

   (e) The same middle and upper class children have been measured in grades 6, 7, and 8 on reading comprehension, math ability, and science ability. The researcher wishes to determine whether there are social class differences on these variables and if the differences change over time.

2. An investigator has a 50-item scale. He wishes to compare two groups of subjects on the scale. He has heard about MANOVA, and realizes that the items will be correlated. Therefore, he decided to do such an analysis. The scale is administered to 45 subjects, and the analysis is run on SPSS. However, he finds that the analysis is aborted. Why? What might the investigator consider doing before running the analysis?

3. Suppose you come across a journal article where the investigators have a three-way design and five correlated dependent variables. They report the results in five tables, having done a univariate analysis on each of the five variables. They find four significant results at the .05 level. Would you be impressed with these results? Why, or why not? Would you have more confidence if the significant results had been hypothesized a priori? What else could they have done that would have given you more confidence in their significant results?

4. Consider the following data for a two-group, two-dependent-variable problem:

T_1		T_2	
y_1	y_2	y_1	y_2
1	9	4	8
2	3	5	6
3	4	6	7
5	4		
2	5		

(a) Compute **W**, the pooled within-SSCP matrix.

(b) Find the pooled within-covariance matrix, and indicate what each of the elements in the matrix represents.

(c) Find Hotelling's T^2.

(d) What is the multivariate null hypothesis in symbolic form?

(e) Test the null hypothesis at the .05 level. What is your decision?

5. Suppose we have two groups, with 30 subjects in each group. The means for the two criterion measures in Group 1 are 10 and 9, while the means in Group 2 are 9 and 9.5. The pooled within-sample variances are 9 and 4 for variables 1 and 2, and the pooled within-correlation is .70.

(a) Show that each of the univariate t's is not significant at .05 (two-tailed test), but that the multivariate test is significant at .05.

(b) Now change the pooled within-correlation to .20 and determine whether the multivariate test is still significant at .05. Explain.

6. Consider the following set of data for two groups of subjects on two dependent variables:

Group 1		Group 2	
y_1	y_2	y_1	y_2
3	9	8	13
5	15	4	9
5	15	4	7
4	13	2	7
I	8	9	15

(a) Analyze this data using the traditional MANOVA approach. Does anything interesting happen?

(b) Use the regression approach (i.e., dummy coding of group membership) to analyze the data and compare the results.

7. An investigator ran a two-group MANOVA with three dependent variables on SPSS. There were 12 subjects in Group 1 and 26 subjects in Group 2. The following selected output gives the results for the multivariate tests (remember that for two groups they are equivalent). Note that the multivariate F is significant at the .05 level. Estimate what power the investigator had at the .05 level for finding a significant difference.

EFFECT . . TREATS
Multivariate Tests of Significance (S = 1, M = 1/2, N = 16)

TEST NAME	VALUE	APPROX. F	HYPOTH. DF	ERROR DF	SIG. DF
PILLAIS	.33083	5.60300	3.00	34.00	.000
HOTELLINGS	.49438	5.60300	3.00	34.00	.000
WILKS	.66917	5.60300	3.00	34.00	.000
ROYS	.33083				

Hint: One would think that the value for "Hotelling's" could be used directly in conjunction with Equation 2. However, the value for Hotelling's must first be multiplied by $(N-k)$, where N is total number of subjects and k is the number of groups.

8. An investigator has an estimate of $D^2 = .61$ from a previous study that used the same 4 dependent variables on a similar group of subjects. How many subjects per group are needed to have power = .70 at $\alpha = .10$?

9. From a pilot study, a researcher has the following pooled within-covariance matrix for two variables:

$$S = \begin{bmatrix} 8.6 & 10.4 \\ 10.4 & 21.3 \end{bmatrix}$$

From previous research a moderate effect size of .5 standard deviations on Variable 1 and a small effect size of 1/3 standard deviations on Variable 2 are anticipated. For the researcher's main study, how many subjects per group are needed for power = .70 at the .05 level? At the .10 level?

10. Ambrose (1985) compared elementary school children who received instruction on the clarinet via programmed instruction (experimental group) versus those who received instruction via traditional classroom instruction on the following six performance aspects: interpretation (interp), tone, rhythm, intonation (inton), tempo (tem), and articulation (artic). The data, representing the average of two judges' ratings, are listed here, with GPID = 1 referring to the experimental group and GPID = 2 referring to the control group:

    (a) Run the two-group MANOVA on these data using SAS GLM. Is the multivariate null hypothesis rejected at the .05 level?

    (b) What is the value of Mahalanobis D^2? How would you characterize the magnitude of this effect size? Given this, is it surprising that the null hypothesis was rejected?

    (c) Setting overall $\alpha = .05$ and using the Bonferroni inequality approach, which of the individual variables are significant, and hence contributing to the overall multivariate significance?

GP	INT	TONE	RHY	INTON	TEM	ARTIC
1	4.2	4.1	3.2	4.2	2.8	3.5
1	4.1	4.1	3.7	3.9	3.1	3.2
1	4.9	4.7	4.7	5.0	2.9	4.5
1	4.4	4.1	4.1	3.5	2.8	4.0
1	3.7	2.0	2.4	3.4	2.8	2.3
1	3.9	3.2	2.7	3.1	2.7	3.6
1	3.8	3.5	3.4	4.0	2.7	3.2
1	4.2	4.1	4.1	4.2	3.7	2.8
1	3.6	3.8	4.2	3.4	4.2	3.0
1	2.6	3.2	1.9	3.5	3.7	3.1
1	3.0	2.5	2.9	3.2	3.3	3.1
1	2.9	3.3	3.5	3.1	3.6	3.4
2	2.1	1.8	1.7	1.7	2.8	1.5
2	4.8	4.0	3.5	1.8	3.1	2.2
2	4.2	2.9	4.0	1.8	3.1	2.2
2	3.7	1.9	1.7	1.6	3.1	1.6
2	3.7	2.1	2.2	3.1	2.8	1.7
2	3.8	2.1	3.0	3.3	3.0	1.7
2	2.1	2.0	2.2	1.8	2.6	1.5
2	2.2	1.9	2.2	3.4	4.2	2.7
2	3.3	3.6	2.3	4.3	4.0	3.8
2	2.6	1.5	1.3	2.5	3.5	1.9
2	2.5	1.7	1.7	2.8	3.3	3.1

11. We consider the Pope (1980) data. Children in kindergarten were measured on various instruments to determine whether they could be classified as low risk or high risk with respect to having reading problems later on in school. The variables considered are word identification (WI), word comprehension (WC) and passage comprehension (PC).

	GP	WI	WC	PC
1	1.00	5.80	9.70	8.90
2	1.00	10.60	10.90	11.00
3	1.00	8.60	7.20	8.70
4	1.00	4.80	4.60	6.20
5	1.00	8.30	10.60	7.80
6	1.00	4.60	3.30	4.70
7	1.00	4.80	3.70	6.40
8	1.00	6.70	6.00	7.20
9	1.00	6.90	9.70	7.20
10	1.00	5.60	4.10	4.30
11	1.00	4.80	3.80	5.30
12	1.00	2.90	3.70	4.20
13	2.00	2.40	2.10	2.40
14	2.00	3.50	1.80	3.90
15	2.00	6.70	3.60	5.90
16	2.00	5.30	3.30	6.10

	GP	WI	WC	PC
17	2.00	5.20	4.10	6.40
18	2.00	3.20	2.70	4.00
19	2.00	4.50	4.90	5.70
20	2.00	3.90	4.70	4.70
21	2.00	4.00	3.60	2.90
22	2.00	5.70	5.50	6.20
23	2.00	2.40	2.90	3.20
24	2.00	2.70	2.60	4.10

(a) Run the two group MANOVA on SPSS. Is it significant at the .05 level?

(b) Are any of the univariate F's significant at the .05 level?

12. Show graphically that type I error and type II error are inversely related. That is, as the area for type I error decreases the corresponding area for type II error increases.

13. The correlations among the dependent variables are embedded in the covariance matrix **S**. Why is this true?

5

k-*Group MANOVA:*
A Priori *and* Post Hoc *Procedures*

5.1 Introduction

In this chapter we consider the case where more than two groups of subjects are being compared on several dependent variables simultaneously. We first show how the MANOVA can be done within the regression model by dummy coding group membership for a small sample problem and using it as a nominal predictor. In doing this, we build on the multivariate regression analysis of two-group MANOVA that was presented in the last chapter. Then we consider the traditional analysis of variance for MANOVA, introducing the most familiar multivariate test statistic Wilks' Λ. Three post hoc procedures for determining which groups and which variables are contributing to overall multivariate significance are discussed. The first two employ Hotelling T^2's, to locate which pairs of groups differ significantly on the set of variables. The first post hoc procedure then uses univariate t's to determine which of the variables are contributing to the significant pairwise differences that are found, and the second procedure uses the Tukey simultaneous confidence interval approach to identify the variables. As a third procedure, we consider the Roy–Bose multivariate simultaneous confidence intervals.

Next, we consider a different approach to the k-group problem, that of using planned comparisons rather than an omnibus F test. Hays (1981) gave an excellent discussion of this approach for univariate ANOVA. Our discussion of multivariate planned comparisons is extensive and is made quite concrete through the use of several examples, including two studies from the literature. The setup of multivariate contrasts on SPSS MANOVA is illustrated and some printout is discussed.

We then consider the important problem of a priori determination of sample size for 3-, 4-, 5-, and 6-group MANOVA for the number of dependent variables ranging from 2 to 15, using extensive tables developed by Lauter (1978). Finally, the chapter concludes with a discussion of some considerations that mitigate generally against the use of a large number of criterion variables in MANOVA.

5.2 Multivariate Regression Analysis for a Sample Problem

In the previous chapter we indicated how analysis of variance can be incorporated within the regression model by dummy coding group membership and using it as a nominal predictor. For the two-group case, just one dummy variable (predictor) was needed, which took on the value 1 for subjects in group 1 and was 0 for the subjects in the other group.

For our three-group example, we need two dummy variables (predictors) to identify group membership. The first dummy variable (x_1) is 1 for all subjects in Group 1 and 0 for all other subjects. The other dummy variable (x_2) is one for all subjects in Group 2 and 0 for all other subjects. A third dummy variable is *not* needed because the subjects in Group 3 are identified by 0's on x_1 and x_2, i.e., not in Group 1 or Group 2. Therefore, by default, those subjects must be in Group 3. In general, for k groups, the number of dummy variables needed is $(k - 1)$, corresponding to the between degrees of freedom.

The data for our two-dependent-variable, three-group problem are presented here:

Dep. 1	Dep. 2	x_1	x_2	
2	3	1	0	
3	4	1	0	
5	4	1	0	Group 1
2	5	1	0	
4	8	0	1	
5	6	0	1	Group 2
6	7	0	1	
7	6	0	0	
8	7	0	0	
10	8	0	0	Group 3
9	5	0	0	
7	6	0	0	

Thus, cast in a regression mold, we are relating two sets of variables, the two dependent variables and the two predictors (dummy variables). The regression analysis will then determine how much of the variance on the dependent variables is accounted for by the predictors, that is, by group membership.

In Table 5.1 we present the control lines for running the sample problem as a multivariate regression on SPSS MANOVA, and the lines for running the problem as a traditional MANOVA. The reader can verify by running both analyses that the multivariate F's for the regression analysis are identical to those obtained from the MANOVA run.

5.3 Traditional Multivariate Analysis of Variance

In the k-group MANOVA case we are comparing the groups on p dependent variables simultaneously. For the univariate case, the null hypothesis is:

$$H_0 : \mu_1 = \mu_2 = \cdots = \mu_k \text{ (population means are equal)]}$$

whereas for MANOVA the null hypothesis is

$$H_0 : \boldsymbol{\mu}_1 = \boldsymbol{\mu}_2 = \cdots = \boldsymbol{\mu}_k \text{ (population mean vectors are equal)]}$$

TABLE 5.1

SPSS MANOVA Control Lines for Running Sample Problem
as Multivariate Regression and as MANOVA

	TITLE 'THREE GROUP MANOVA RUN AS MULTIVARIATE REGRESSION'.		
	DATA LIST FREE/X1 X2 DEP1 DEP2.		
	BEGIN DATA.		
①	1 0 2 3	1 0 3 4	
	1 0 5 4	1 0 2 5	
	0 1 4 8	0 1 5 6	0 1 6 7
	0 0 7 6	0 0 8 7	
	0 0 10 8	0 0 9 5	0 0 7 6
	END DATA.		
	LIST.		
	MANOVA DEP1 DEP2 WITH X1 X2/.		
	TITLE 'MANOVA RUN ON SAMPLE PROBLEM'.		
	DATA LIST FREE/GPS DEP1 DEP2.		
②	BEGIN DATA.		
	1 2 3	1 3 4	
	1 5 4	1 2 5	
	2 4 8	2 5 6	2 6 7
	3 7 6	3 8 7	3 10 8
	3 9 5	3 7 6	
	END DATA.		
	LIST.		
	MANOVA DEP1 DEP2 BY GPS(1,3)/		
	PRINT = CELLINFO(MEANS)/.		

① The first two columns of data are for the dummy variables X1 and X2, which identify group membership (cf. the data display in section 5.2).

② The first column of data identifies group membership—again compare the data display in section 5.2.

For univariate analysis of variance the F statistic ($F = MS_b/MS_w$) is used for testing the tenability of H_0. What statistic do we use for testing the multivariate null hypothesis? There is no single answer, as several test statistics are available (Olson, 1974). The one that is most widely known is Wilks' Λ, where Λ is given by:

$$\Lambda = \frac{|\mathbf{W}|}{|\mathbf{T}|} = \frac{|\mathbf{W}|}{|\mathbf{B}+\mathbf{W}|} \quad 0 \leq \Lambda \leq 1$$

$|\mathbf{W}|$ and $|\mathbf{T}|$ are the determinants of the within and total sum of squares and cross-products matrices. $\mathbf{W}$ has already been defined for the two-group case, where the observations in each group are deviated about the individual group means. Thus $\mathbf{W}$ is a measure of within-group variability and is a multivariate generalization of the univariate sum of squares within (SS_w). In $\mathbf{T}$ the observations in each group are deviated about the *grand* mean for each variable. $\mathbf{B}$ is the between sum of squares and cross-products matrix, and is the multivariate generalization of the univariate sum of squares between (SS_b). Thus, $\mathbf{B}$ is a measure of how differential the effect of treatments has been on a set of dependent variables. We define the elements of $\mathbf{B}$ shortly. We need matrices to define within, between, and total variability in the multivariate case because there is variability on each variable (these variabilities will appear on the main diagonals of the **W**, **B**, and **T** matrices) as well as covariability for each pair of variables (these will be the off diagonal elements of the matrices).

Because Wilks' Λ is defined in terms of the determinants of **W** and **T**, it is important to recall from the matrix algebra chapter (Chapter 2) that the determinant of a covariance matrix is called the *generalized variance* for a set of variables. Now, because **W** and **T** differ from their corresponding covariance matrices only by a scalar, we can think of $|\mathbf{W}|$ and $|\mathbf{T}|$ in the same basic way. Thus, the determinant neatly characterizes within and total variability in terms of *single* numbers. It may also be helpful for the reader to recall that geometrically the generalized variance for two variables is the square of the area of a parallelogram whose sides are the standard deviations for the variables, and that for three variables the generalized variance is the square of the volume of a three-dimensional parallelogram whose sides are the standard deviations for the variables. Although it is not clear why the generalized variance is the square of the area of a parallelogram, the important fact here is the area interpretation of variance for two variables.

For one variable, variance indicates how much scatter there is about the mean on a line, that is, in one dimension. For two variables, the scores for each subject on the variables defines a point in the plane, and thus generalized variance indicates how much the points (subjects) scatter in the plane in two dimensions. For three variables, the scores for the subjects define points in three space, and hence generalized variance shows how much the subjects scatter (vary) in three dimensions. An excellent extended discussion of generalized variance for the more mathematically inclined is provided in Johnson and Wichern (1982, pp. 103–112).

For univariate ANOVA the reader may recall that

$$SS_t = SS_b + SS_w$$

where SS_t is the total sum of squares.

For MANOVA the corresponding matrix analogue holds:

$$T = \mathbf{B} + \mathbf{W}$$

Total SSCP = Between SSCP + Within SSCP

Matrix   Matrix   Matrix

Notice that Wilks' Λ is an inverse criterion: the smaller the value of Λ, the more evidence for treatment effects (between group association). If there were no treatment effect, then $\mathbf{B} = 0$ and $\Lambda = \dfrac{|\mathbf{W}|}{|0 + \mathbf{W}|} = 1$, whereas if **B** were very large relative to **W** then Λ would approach 0.

The sampling distribution of Λ is very complicated, and generally an approximation is necessary. Two approximations are available: (a) Bartlett's χ^2 and (b) Rao's F. Bartlett's χ^2 is given by:

$$\chi^2 = -[(N-1)-.5(p+k)] \quad \ln \Lambda \quad p(k-1)df$$

where N is total sample size, p is the number of dependent variables, and k is the number of groups. Bartlett's χ^2 is a good approximation for moderate to large sample sizes. For smaller sample size, Rao's F is a better approximation (Lohnes, 1961), although generally the two statistics will lead to the same decision on H_0. The multivariate F given on SPSS is the Rao F. The formula for Rao's F is complicated and is presented later. We point out now, however, that the degrees of freedom for error with Rao's F can be *noninteger*, so that the reader should not be alarmed if this happens on the computer printout.

As alluded to earlier, there are certain values of p and k for which a function of Λ is exactly distributed as an F ratio (for example, $k = 2$ or 3 and any p; see Tatsuoka, 1971, p. 89).

5.4 Multivariate Analysis of Variance for Sample Data

We now consider the MANOVA of the data given earlier. For convenience, we present the data again here, with the means for the subjects on the two dependent variables in each group:

T_1		T_2		T_3	
y_1	y_2	y_1	y_2	y_1	y_2
2	3	4	8	7	6
3	4	5	6	8	7
5	4	6	7	10	8
2	5	$\bar{y}_{12} = 5$	$\bar{y}_{22} = 7$	9	5
$\bar{y}_{11} = 3$	$\bar{y}_{21} = 4$			7	6
				$\bar{y}_{13} = 8.2$	$\bar{y}_{23} = 6.4$

We wish to test the multivariate null hypothesis with the χ^2 approximation for Wilks' Λ. Recall that $\Lambda = |\mathbf{W}|/|\mathbf{T}|$, so that $\mathbf{W}$ and $\mathbf{T}$ are needed. $\mathbf{W}$ is the pooled estimate of within variability on the set of variables, that is, our multivariate error term.

5.4.1 Calculation of W

Calculation of $\mathbf{W}$ proceeds in exactly the same way as we obtained $\mathbf{W}$ for Hotelling's T^2 in the two-group MANOVA case in Chapter 4. That is, we determine how much the subjects' scores vary on the dependent variables within *each* group, and then pool (add) these together. Symbolically, then,

$$\mathbf{W} = \mathbf{W}_1 + \mathbf{W}_2 + \mathbf{W}_3$$

where $\mathbf{W}_1$, $\mathbf{W}_2$, and $\mathbf{W}_3$ are the within sums of squares and cross-products matrices for Groups 1, 2, and 3. As in the two-group chapter, we denote the elements of $\mathbf{W}_1$ by ss_1 and ss_2 (measuring the variability on the variables within Group 1) and ss_{12} (measuring the covariability of the variables in Group 1).

$$\mathbf{W}_1 = \begin{bmatrix} ss_1 & ss_{12} \\ ss_{21} & ss_2 \end{bmatrix}$$

Then, we have

$$ss_1 = \sum_{j=1}^{4}(y_{1(j)} - \bar{y}_{11})^2$$

$$= (2-3)^2 + (3-3)^2 + (5-3)^2 + (2-3)^2 = 6$$

$$ss_2 = \sum_{j=1}^{4}(y_{2(j)} - \bar{y}_{11})^2$$

$$= (3-4)^2 + (4-4)^2 + (4-4)^2 + (5-4)^2 = 2$$

$$ss_{12} = ss_{21} = \sum_{j=1}^{4}(y_{1(j)} - \bar{y}_{11})(y_{2(j)} - \bar{y}_{21})$$

$$= (2-3)(3-4) + (3-3)(4-4) + (5-3)(4-4) + (2-3)(5-4) = 0$$

Thus, the matrix that measures within variability on the two variables in Group 1 is given by:

$$\mathbf{W}_1 = \begin{bmatrix} 6 & 0 \\ 0 & 2 \end{bmatrix}$$

In exactly the same way the within SCCP matrices for groups 2 and 3 can be shown to be:

$$\mathbf{W}_2 = \begin{bmatrix} 2 & -1 \\ -1 & 2 \end{bmatrix} \quad \mathbf{W}_3 = \begin{bmatrix} 6.8 & 2.6 \\ 2.6 & 5.2 \end{bmatrix}$$

Therefore, the pooled estimate of within variability on the set of variables is given by

$$\mathbf{W} = \mathbf{W}_1 + \mathbf{W}_2 + \mathbf{W}_3 = \begin{bmatrix} 14.8 & 1.6 \\ 1.6 & 9.2 \end{bmatrix}$$

5.4.2 Calculation of T

Recall, from earlier in this chapter, that $\mathbf{T} = \mathbf{B} + \mathbf{W}$. We find the $\mathbf{B}$ (between) matrix, and then obtain the elements of $\mathbf{T}$ by adding the elements of $\mathbf{B}$ to the elements of $\mathbf{W}$.

The diagonal elements of $\mathbf{B}$ are defined as follows:

$$b_{ii} = \sum_{j=1}^{k} n_j(\bar{y}_{ij} - \bar{\bar{y}}_i)^2,$$

where n_j is the number of subjects in group j, $\bar{y}_{ij}$ is the mean for variable i in group j, and $\bar{\bar{y}}_i$ is the grand mean for variable i. Notice that for any particular variable, say Variable 1, b_{11} is simply the sum of squares between for a univariate analysis of variance on that variable.

The off-diagonal elements of **B** are defined as follows:

$$b_{mi} = b_{im} = \sum_{j=1}^{k} n_j(\bar{y}_{ij} - \bar{\bar{y}}_i)(\bar{y}_{mj} - \bar{\bar{y}}_m)$$

To find the elements of **B** we need the grand means on the two variables. These are obtained by simply adding up all the scores on each variable and then dividing by the total number of scores. Thus $\bar{\bar{y}}_1 = 68/12 = 5.67$, and $\bar{\bar{y}}_2 = 69/12 = 5.75$.

Now we find the elements of the **B** (between) matrix:

$$b_{11} = \sum_{j=1}^{3} n_j(\bar{y}_{1j} - \bar{\bar{y}}_1)^2, \text{where } \bar{\bar{y}}_1 \text{ is the mean of variable 1 ingroup } j.$$

$$= 4(3 - 5.67)^2 + 3(5 - 5.67)^2 + 5(8.2 - 5.67)^2 = 61.87$$

$$b_{22} = \sum_{j=1}^{3} n_j(\bar{y}_{2j} - \bar{\bar{y}}_2)^2$$

$$= 4(4 - 5.75)^2 + 3(7 - 5.75)^2 + 5(6.4 - 5.75)^2 = 19.05$$

$$b_{12} = b_{21} = \sum_{j=1}^{3} n_j(\bar{y}_{1j} - \bar{\bar{y}}_1)(\bar{y}_{2j} - \bar{\bar{y}}_2)$$

$$= 4(3 - 5.67)(4 - 5.75) + 3(5 - 5.67)(7 - 5.75) + 5(8.2 - 5.67)(6.4 - 5.75) = 24.4$$

Therefore, the **B** matrix is

$$\mathbf{B} = \begin{bmatrix} 61.87 & 24.40 \\ 24.40 & 19.05 \end{bmatrix}$$

and the diagonal elements 61.87 and 19.05 represent the between sum of squares that would be obtained if separate univariate analyses had been done on variables 1 and 2.

Because **T** = **B** + **W**, we have

$$\mathbf{T} = \begin{bmatrix} 61.87 & 24.40 \\ 24.40 & 19.05 \end{bmatrix} + \begin{bmatrix} 14.80 & 1.6 \\ 1.6 & 9.2 \end{bmatrix} = \begin{bmatrix} 76.72 & 26.00 \\ 26.00 & 28.25 \end{bmatrix}$$

5.4.3 Calculation of Wilks Λ and the Chi-Square Approximation

Now we can obtain Wilks' Λ:

$$\Lambda = \frac{|\mathbf{W}|}{|\mathbf{T}|} = \frac{\begin{vmatrix} 14.8 & 1.6 \\ 1.6 & 9.2 \end{vmatrix}}{\begin{vmatrix} 76.72 & 26 \\ 26 & 28.25 \end{vmatrix}} = \frac{14.8(9.2) - 1.6^2}{76.72(28.25) - 26^2} = .0897$$

Finally, we can compute the chi-square test statistic:

$$\chi^2 = -[(N-1)-.5(p+k)]\ln \Lambda, \text{ with } p\,(k-1)df$$

$$\chi^2 = -[(12-1)-.5(2+3)]\ln (.0897)$$

$$\chi^2 = -8.5[(-2.4116) = 20.4987, \text{ with } 2(3-1) = 4\ df$$

The multivariate null hypothesis here is:

$$\begin{pmatrix} \mu_{11} \\ \mu_{21} \end{pmatrix} = \begin{pmatrix} \mu_{12} \\ \mu_{22} \end{pmatrix} = \begin{pmatrix} \mu_{13} \\ \mu_{23} \end{pmatrix}$$

that is, that the population means in the three groups on Variable 1 are equal, and similarily that the population means on Variable 2 are equal. Because the critical value at .05 is 9.49, we reject the multivariate null hypothesis and conclude that the three groups differ overall on the set of two variables. Table 5.2 gives the multivariate F's and the univariate F's from the SPSS MANOVA run on the sample problem and presents the formula for Rao's F approximation and also relates some of the output from the univariate F's to the **B** and **W** matrices that we computed. After overall multivariate significance one would like to know which groups and which variables were responsible for the overall association, that is, more detailed breakdown. This is considered next.

5.5 Post Hoc Procedures

Because pairwise differences are easy to interpret and often the most meaningful, we concentrate on procedures for locating significant pairwise differences, both multivariate and univariate. We consider three procedures, from least to most conservative, in terms of protecting against type I error.

5.5.1 Procedure 1—Hotelling T^2's and Univariate t Tests

Follow a significant overall multivariate result by all pairwise multivariate tests (T^2's) to determine which pairs of groups differ significantly on the set of variables. Then use univariate t tests, each at the .05 level, to determine which of the individual variables are contributing to the significant multivariate pairwise differences. To keep the overall α for the set of pairwise multivariate tests under some control (and still maintain reasonable power) we may want to set overall $\alpha = .15$. Thus, for four groups, there will be six Hotelling T^2's, and we would do each T^2 at the $.15/6 = .025$ level of significance. This procedure has fairly good control on type I error for the first two parts, and not as good control for the last part (i.e., identifying the significant individual variables). It has the best power of the three procedures we discuss, and as long as we recognize that the individual variables identified must be treated somewhat tenuously, it has merit.

5.5.2 Procedure 2—Hotelling T^2's and Tukey Confidence Intervals

Once again we follow a significant overall multivariate result by all pairwise multivariate tests, but then we apply the Tukey simultaneous confidence interval technique to determine which of the individual variables are contributing to each pairwise significant multivariate result. This procedure affords us better protection against type I errors, especially if we set the

TABLE 5.2

Multivariate F's and Univariate F's for Sample Problem From SPSS MANOVA

EFFECT .. GPID					
MULTIVARIATE TESTS OF SIGNIFICANCE (S = 2, M = −1/2, N = 3)					
TEST NAME	VALUE	APPROX. F	HYPOTH. DF	ERROR DF	SIG. OF F
PILLAIS	1.30173	8.38990	4.00	18.00	.001
HOTELLINGS	5.78518	10.12581	4.00	14.00	.000
WILKS	.08967	9.35751	4.00	16.00	.000
ROYS	.83034				

$$\frac{1-\Lambda^{1/s}}{\Lambda^{1/s}}\frac{ms-p(k-1)/2+1}{p(k-1)}, \text{where } m = N-1-(p+k)/2 \text{ and}$$

$$s = \sqrt{\frac{p^2(k-1)^2-4}{p^2+(k-1)^2-5}}$$

is approximately distributed as F with $p(k-1)$ and $ms - p(k-1)/2 + 1$ degrees of freedom. Here Wilks' $\Lambda = .08967$, $p = 2, k = 3$ and $N = 12$. Thus, we have $m = 12 - 1 - (2 + 3)/2 = 8.5$ and

$$s = \sqrt{\{4(3-1)^2-4\}/\{4+(2)^2-5\}} = \sqrt{12/3} = 2,$$

and

$$F = \frac{1-\sqrt{.08967}}{\sqrt{.08967}}\frac{8.5(2)-2(2)/2+1}{2(3-1)} = \frac{1-.29945}{.29945} \cdot \frac{16}{4} = 9.357$$

as given on the printout. The pair of degrees of freedom is $p(k-1) = 2(3-1) = 4$ and $ms - p(k-1)/2 + 1 = 8.5(2) - 2(3-1)/2 + 1 = 16$.

UNIVARIATE F-TESTS WITH (2.9) D.F.						
VARIABLE	HYPOTH. SS	ERROR SS	HYPOTH. MS	ERROR MS	F	SIG. OF F.
y1	① 61.86667	② 14.80000	30.93333	1.64444	18.81081	.001
y2	19.05000	9.20000	9.52500	1.02222	9.31793	.006

① These are the diagonal elements of the **B** (between) matrix we computed in the example:

$$\mathbf{B} = \begin{bmatrix} 61.87 & 24.40 \\ 24.40 & 19.05 \end{bmatrix}$$

② Recall that the pooled within matrix computed in the example was

$$\mathbf{W} = \begin{bmatrix} 14.8 & 1.6 \\ 1.6 & 9.2 \end{bmatrix}$$

and these are the diagonal elements of **W**. The univariate F ratios are formed from the elements on the main diagonals of **B** and **W**. Dividing the elements of **B** by hypothesis degrees of freedom gives the hypothesis mean squares, while dividing the elements of **W** by error degrees of freedom gives the error mean squares. Then, dividing hypothesis mean squares by error mean squares yields the F ratios. Thus, for Y1 we have

$$F = \frac{30.933}{1.644} = 18.81$$

experimentwise error rate (EER) for each variable that we are applying the Tukey to such that the overall α is *at maximum* .15. Thus, depending on how large a risk of spurious results (within the .15) we can tolerate, we may set EER at .05 for each variable in a three-variable problem, at .025 for each variable in a six-variable problem, variable, or at .01 for each variable in an eight-variable study. As we show in an example shortly, the 90%, 95%, and 99% confidence intervals, corresponding to EERs of .10, .05, and .01, are easily obtained from the SAS GLM program.

5.5.3 Procedure 3—Roy–Bose Simultaneous Confidence Intervals

In exploratory research in univariate ANOVA after the null hypothesis has been rejected, one wishes to determine where the differences lie with some post hoc procedures. One of the more popular post hoc procedures is the Scheffé, with which a wide variety of comparisons can be made. For example, all pairwise comparisons as well as complex comparisons such as $\mu_1 - (\mu_2 + \mu_3)/2$ or $(\mu_1 + \mu_2) - (\mu_3 + \mu_4)$ can be tested. The Scheffé allows one to examine *any* complex comparison, as long as the sum of the coefficients for the means is 0. All these comparisons can be made with the assurance that overall type I error is controlled (i.e., the probability of one or more type I errors) at a level set by the experimenter. Importantly, however, the price one pays for being allowed to do all this data snooping is loss of power for detecting differences. This is due to the basic principle that, as one type of error (in this case type I) is controlled, the other type (type II here) increases and therefore power decreases, because power = 1 – type II error. Glass and Hopkins (1984, p. 382) noted, "The Scheffé method is the most widely presented MC (multiple comparison) method in textbooks of statistical methods; ironically it is rarely the MC method of choice for the questions of interest in terms of power efficiency."

The Roy–Bose intervals are the multivariate generalization of the Scheffé univariate intervals. After the multivariate null hypothesis has been rejected, the Roy–Bose intervals can be used to examine all pairwise group comparisons as well as all complex comparisons for *each* dependent variable. In addition to all these comparisons, one can examine pairwise and complex comparisons on various linear combinations of the variables (such as the difference of two variables). Thus, *the Roy–Bose approach controls on overall α for an enormous number of comparisons. To do so, power has to suffer, and it suffers considerably, especially for small- or moderate-sized samples.* Hummel and Sligo (1971) found the Roy–Bose procedure to be extremely conservative, and recommended generally against its use. We agree. In many studies the sample sizes are small or relatively small *and* the effect sizes are small. In these circumstances power will be far from adequate to begin with, and the use of Roy–Bose intervals will further sharply diminish the researchers' chances of finding any differences. In addition, there is the question of why one would want to examine all or most of the comparisons allowed by the Roy–Bose procedure. As Bird commented (1975, p. 344), "a completely unrestricted analysis of multivariate data, however, would be extremely unusual."

Example 5.1: Illustrating Post Hoc Procedures 1 and 2

We illustrate first the use of post hoc procedure 1 on social psychological data collected by Novince (1977). She was interested in improving the social skills of college females and reducing their anxiety in heterosexual encounters. There were three groups in her study: control group, behavioral rehearsal, and a behavioral rehearsal + cognitive restructuring group. We consider the analysis on the following set of dependent variables: (a) anxiety—physiological anxiety in a series of heterosexual encounters, (b) measure of social skills in social interactions, (c) appropriateness, and (d) assertiveness. The raw data for this problem is given inline in Table 5.3.

TABLE 5.3

SPSS MANOVA and Discriminant Control Lines on Novince Data for Locating Multivariate Group Differences

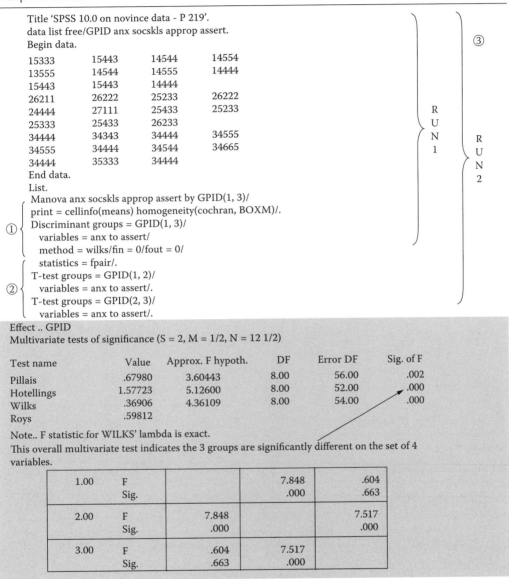

```
Title 'SPSS 10.0 on novince data - P 219'.
data list free/GPID anx socskls approp assert.
Begin data.
  15333    15443    14544    14554
  13555    14544    14555    14444
  15443    15443    14444
  26211    26222    25233    26222
  24444    27111    25433    25233
  25333    25433    26233
  34444    34343    34444    34555
  34555    34444    34544    34665
  34444    35333    34444
End data.
List.
Manova anx socskls approp assert by GPID(1, 3)/
  print = cellinfo(means) homogeneity(cochran, BOXM)/.
Discriminant groups = GPID(1, 3)/
  variables = anx to assert/
  method = wilks/fin = 0/fout = 0/
  statistics = fpair/.
T-test groups = GPID(1, 2)/
  variables = anx to assert/.
T-test groups = GPID(2, 3)/
  variables = anx to assert/.
```

① This set of control lines needed to obtained the pairwise multivariate tests.

② (T-test bracket)

③ R U N 1 / R U N 2

Effect .. GPID
Multivariate tests of significance (S = 2, M = 1/2, N = 12 1/2)

Test name	Value	Approx. F hypoth.	DF	Error DF	Sig. of F
Pillais	.67980	3.60443	8.00	56.00	.002
Hotellings	1.57723	5.12600	8.00	52.00	.000
Wilks	.36906	4.36109	8.00	54.00	.000
Roys	.59812				

Note.. F statistic for WILKS' lambda is exact.

This overall multivariate test indicates the 3 groups are significantly different on the set of 4 variables.

1.00	F			7.848	.604
	Sig.			.000	.663
2.00	F	7.848			7.517
	Sig.	.000			.000
3.00	F	.604		7.517	
	Sig.	.663		.000	

These pairwise multivariant tests, with the *p* values underneath, indicate that groups 1 & 2, and groups 2 & 3 are significantly different at the .05 level.

① This set of control lines needed to obtained the pairwise multivariate tests. FIN = 0 AND FOUT = 0 are necessary if one wishes all the dependent variables in the analysis.

② This set of control lines yields the univariate *t* tests for those pairs of groups (1 and 2, 2 and 3) that were different on the multivariate tests.

③ Actually two separate runs would be required. The first run is to determine whether there is an overall difference, and if so, which pairs of groups are different (in multivariate sense). The second run is to obtain the univariate *t*'s, to determine which of the variables are contributing to each pairwise multivariate significance.

TABLE 5.4

Univariate *t* Tests for Each of the Significant Multivariate Pairs for the Novince Data

		Levene's Test for Equality of Variances			*t* test for Equality of Means		
		F	Sig.		t	df	Sig. (2-tailed)
ANX	Equal variances assumed	.876	.361	Equal variances assumed	−3.753	20	.001
	Equal variances not assumed			Equal variances not assumed	−3.753	18.967	.001
SOCSKLS	Equal variances assumed	3.092	.094	Equal variances assumed	4.880	20	.000
	Equal variances not assumed			Equal variances not assumed	4.880	17.185	.000
APPROP	Equal variances assumed	2.845	.107	Equal variances assumed	4.881	20	.000
	Equal variances not assumed			Equal variances not assumed	4.881	17.101	.000
ASSERT	Equal variances assumed	731	.403	Equal variances assumed	3.522	20	.002
	Equal variances not assumed			Equal variances not assumed	3.522	19.115	.002

	Levene's Test for Equality of Variances				*t* test for Equality of Means		
	F	Sig.			t	df	Sig. (2-tailed)
Equal variances assumed	12.645	.002	ANX	Equal variances assumed	5.175	20	.000
Equal variances not assumed				Equal variances not assumed	5.175	12.654	.000
Equal variances assumed	.612	.443	SOCSKLS	Equal variances assumed	−4.166	20	.000
Equal variances not assumed				Equal variances not assumed	−4.166	19.644	.000
Equal variances assumed	.747	.398	APPROP	Equal variances assumed	−4.692	20	.000
Equal variances not assumed				Equal variances not assumed	−4.692	19.434	.000
Equal variances assumed	1.683	.209	ASSERT	Equal variances assumed	−4.389	20	.000
Equal variances not assumed				Equal variances not assumed	−4.389	18.546	.000

The control lines for obtaining the overall multivariate test on SPSS MANOVA and all pairwise multivariate tests (using the SPSS DISCRIMINANT program), along with selected printout, are given in Table 5.3. That printout indicates that groups 1 and 2 and groups 2 and 3 differ in a multivariate sense. Therefore, the SPSS T-TEST procedure was used to determine which of the individual variables contributed to the multivariate significance in each case. The results of the *t* tests are presented in Table 5.4, and indicate that all of the variables contribute to each multivariate significance at the .01 level of significance.

5.6 The Tukey Procedure

The Tukey procedure (Glass and Hopkins, 1984, p. 370) enables us to examine *all* pairwise group differences on a variable with experimentwise error rate held in check. The studentized range statistic (which we denote by q) is used in the procedure, and the critical values for it are in Table D of the statistical tables in Appendix A of this volume. If there are k groups and the total sample size is N, then any two means are declared significantly different at the .05 level if the following inequality holds:

$$|\overline{y}_i - \overline{y}_j| > q_{.05;k,N-k}\sqrt{\frac{MS_w}{n}}$$

where MS_w is the error term for a one-way ANOVA, and n is the common group size.

Equivalently, and somewhat more informatively, we can determine whether the population means for groups i and j (μ_i and μ_j) differ if the following confidence interval does *not* include 0:

$$\overline{y}_i - \overline{y}_j \pm q_{.05;k,N-k}\sqrt{\frac{MS_w}{n}}$$

that is,

$$\overline{y}_i - \overline{y}_j - q_{.05;k,N-k}\sqrt{\frac{MS_w}{n}} < \mu_i - \mu_j < \overline{y}_i - \overline{y}_j + q_{.05;k,N-k}\sqrt{\frac{MS_w}{n}}$$

If the confidence interval includes 0, we conclude that the population means are not significantly different. Why? Because if the interval includes 0 that means 0 is a likely value for $\mu_i - \mu_j$, which is to say it is likely that $\mu_i = \mu_j$.

Example 5.2

To illustrate numerically the Tukey procedure, we consider obtaining the confidence interval for the anxiety (ANX) variable from the Novince study in Table 5.3. In particular, we obtain the 95% confidence interval for groups 1 and 2. The mean difference, not given in Table 5.5, is –1.18. Recall that the common group size in this study is $n = 11$. MS_w, denoted by MSE in Table 5.5, is .39394 for ANX. Finally, from Table D, the critical value for the studentized range statistic is $q_{.05;3,30} = 3.49$. Thus, the confidence interval is given by

$$-1.18 - 3.49\sqrt{\frac{.39394}{11}} < \mu_1 - \mu_2 < -1.18 + 3.49\sqrt{\frac{.39394}{11}}$$

$$-1.84 < \mu_1 - \mu_2 < -.52$$

Because this interval does not cover 0, we conclude that the population means for the anxiety variable in groups 1 and 2 are significantly different. Why is the confidence interval approach more informative, as indicated earlier, than simply testing whether the means are different? Because the confidence interval not only tells us whether the means differ, but it also gives us a range of values within which the mean difference probably lies. This tells us the precision with which we have

TABLE 5.5

Tukey Procedure Printout From SAS GLM for Novince Data

The SAS System
General Linear Models Procedure
Tukey's Studentized Range (HSD) Text for variable: ANX

Note: This text controls the type I experimentwise error rate, but generally has a higher type II error rate than REGWQ.

Alpha = 0.05 df = 30 MSE = 0.393939
Critical Value of Studentized Range = 3.486
Minimum Significant Difference = 0.6598
Means with the same letter are not significantly different.

Tukey Grouping	Mean	N	GPID
A	5.4545	11	2
B	4.2727	11	1
B			
B	4.0909	11	3

Tukey's Studentized Range (HSD) Test for variable: SOCSKLS

Note: This text controls the type I experimentwise error rate, but generally has a higher type II error rate than REGWQ.

Alpha = 0.05 df = 30 MSE = 0.781818
Critical Value of Studentized Range = 3.486
Minimum Significant Difference = 0.9295
Means with the same letter are not significantly different.

Tukey Grouping	Mean	N	GPID
A	4.3636	11	1
A			
A	4.2727	11	3
B	3.5455	11	2

captured the mean difference, and can be used in judging the practical significance of a result. In the preceding example the mean difference could be anywhere in the range from −1.84 to −.52. If the investigator had decided on some grounds that a difference of at least 1 had to be established for practical significance, then the statistical significance found would not be sufficient.

The Tukey procedure assumes that the variances are homogeneous and it also assumes equal group sizes. If the group sizes are unequal, even very sharply unequal, then various studies (e.g., Dunnett, 1980; Keselman, Murray, & Rogan, 1976) indicate that the procedure is still appropriate provided that n is replaced by the harmonic mean for each pair of groups *and* provided that the variances are homogeneous. Thus, for groups i and j with sample sizes n_i and n_j, we replace n by

$$\frac{2}{\frac{1}{n_i} + \frac{1}{n_j}}$$

The studies cited earlier showed that under the conditions given, the type I error rate for the Tukey procedure is kept very close to the nominal α, and always less than nominal α (within .01 for α = .05 from the Dunnett study).

TABLE 5.6

Tukey Printout From SAS GLM for Novince Data (cont.)

Tukey's Studentized Range (HSD) Text for variable: APPROP

Note: This text controls the type I experimentwise error rate, but generally has a higher type II error rate than REGWQ.

Alpha = 0.05 df = 30 MSE = 0.618182
Critical Value of Studentized Range = 3.486
Minimum Significant Difference = 0.8265
Means with the same letter are not significantly different.

Tukey Grouping	Mean	N	GPID
A	4.2727	11	3
A			
B	4.1818	11	1
B	2.5455	11	2

Tukey's Studentized Range (HSD) Test for variable: ASSERT

Note: This text controls the type I experimentwise error rate, but generally has a higher type II error rate than REGWQ.

Alpha = 0.05 df = 30 MSE = 0.642424
Critical Value of Studentized Range = 3.486
Minimum Significant Difference = 0.8425
Means with the same letter are not significantly different.

Tukey Grouping	Mean	N	GPID
A	4.0909	11	3
A			
A	3.8182	11	1
B	2.5455	11	2

We indicated earlier that the Tukey procedure can be easily implemented using the SAS GLM procedure. Here are the SAS GLM control lines for applying the Tukey procedure to each of the four dependent variables from the Novince data.

```
data novince;
input gpid anx socskls approp assert @@;
cards;
1 5 3 3 3    1 5 4 4 3    1 4 5 4 4    1 4 5 5 4
1 3 5 5 5    1 4 5 4 4    1 4 5 5 5    1 4 4 4 4
1 5 4 4 3    1 5 4 4 3    1 4 4 4 4
2 6 2 1 1    2 6 2 2 2    2 5 2 3 3    2 6 2 2 2
2 4 4 4 4    2 7 1 1 1    2 5 4 3 3    2 5 2 3 3
2 5 3 3 3    2 5 4 3 3    2 6 2 3 3
3 4 4 4 4    3 4 3 4 3    3 4 4 4 4    3 4 5 5 5
3 4 5 5 5    3 4 4 4 4    3 4 5 4 4    3 4 6 6 5
3 4 4 4 4    3 5 3 3 3    3 4 4 4 4
proc print;
proc glm;
class gpid;
model anx socskls approp assert=gpid/alpha=.05;
means gpid/tukey;
```

Selected printout from the run is presented in Tables 5.5 and 5.6.

5.7 Planned Comparisons

One approach to the analysis of data is to first demonstrate overall significance, and then follow this up to assess the subsources of variation (i.e., which particular groups or variables were primarily responsible for the overall significance). One such procedure using pairwise T^2's has been presented. This approach is appropriate in exploratory studies where the investigator first has to establish that an effect exists. However, in many instances, there is more of an empirical or theoretical base and the investigator is conducting a confirmatory study. Here the existence of an effect can be taken for granted, and the investigator has specific questions he or she wishes to ask of the data. Thus, rather than examining all 10 pairwise comparisons for a five-group problem, there may be only three or four comparisons (that may or may not be paired comparisons) of interest. It is important to use planned comparisons when the situation justifies them, because performing a small number of statistical tests cuts down on the probability of spurious results (type I errors), which can result much more readily when a large number of tests are done.

Hays (1981) showed in univariate ANOVA that the test is more powerful when the comparison is planned. This would carry over to MANOVA. This is a very important factor weighing in favor of planned comparisons. Many studies in educational research have only 10 to 20 subjects per group. With these sample sizes, power is generally going to be poor unless the treatment effect is large (Cohen, 1977). *If we plan a small or moderate number of contrasts that we wish to test, then power can be improved considerably, whereas control on overall α can be maintained through the use of the Bonferroni Inequality.* Recall this inequality states that if k hypotheses, k planned comparisons here, are tested separately with type I error rates of $\alpha_1, \alpha_2, \ldots, \alpha_k$, then

$$\text{overall } \alpha \leq \alpha_1 + \alpha_2 + \cdots + \alpha_k$$

where overall α is the probability of one or more type I errors when all the hypotheses are true. Therefore, if three planned comparisons were tested each at $\alpha = .01$, then the probability of one or more spurious results can be no greater than .03 for the *set* of three tests.

Let us now consider two situations where planned comparisons would be appropriate:

1. Suppose an investigator wishes to determine whether each of two drugs produces a differential effect on three measures of task performance over a placebo. Then, if we denote the placebo as Group 2, the following set of planned comparisons would answer the investigator's questions:

$$\psi_1 = \mu_1 - \mu_1 \quad \text{and} \quad \psi_2 = \mu_2 - \mu_3$$

2. Second, consider the following four-group schematic design:

| | Groups | | |
Control	T_1 & T_2 combined	T_1	T_2
μ_1	μ_2	μ_3	μ_4

Note: T_1 and T_2 represent two treatments.

As outlined, this could represent the format for a variety of studies (e.g., if T_1 and T_2 were two methods of teaching reading, or if T_1 and T_2 were two counseling approaches). Then the three most relevant questions the investigator wishes to answer are given by the following planned and so-called Helmert contrasts:

1. Do the treatments as a set make a difference?

$$\psi_1 = \mu_1 - \frac{\mu_2 + \mu_3 + \mu_4}{3}$$

2. Is the combination of treatments more effective than either treatment alone?

$$\psi_2 = \mu_2 - \frac{\mu_3 + \mu_4}{2}$$

3. Is one treatment more effective than the other treatment?

$$\psi_3 = \mu_3 - \mu_4$$

Assuming equal n per group, the above two situations represent dependent versus independent planned comparisons. Two comparisons among means are *independent* if the sum of the products of the coefficients is 0. We represent the contrasts for Situation 1 as follows:

	Groups		
	1	2	3
Ψ_1	1	−1	0
Ψ_2	0	1	−1

These contrasts are dependent because the sum of products of the coefficients $\neq 0$ as shown below:

$$\text{Sum of products} = 1(0) + (-1)(1) + 0(-1) = -1$$

Now consider the contrasts from Situation 2:

	Groups			
	1	2	3	4
Ψ_1	1	$-\frac{1}{3}$	$-\frac{1}{3}$	$-\frac{1}{3}$
Ψ_2	0	1	$-\frac{1}{2}$	$-\frac{1}{2}$
Ψ_3	0	0	1	−1

Next we show that these contrasts are pairwise independent by demonstrating that the sum of the products of the coefficients in each case = 0:

$$\psi_1 \text{ and } \psi_1 : 1(0) + (-\tfrac{1}{3})(1) + (-\tfrac{1}{3})(-\tfrac{1}{2}) + (-\tfrac{1}{3})(-\tfrac{1}{2}) = 0$$

$$\psi_1 \text{ and } \psi_3 : 1(0) + (-\tfrac{1}{3})(0) + (-\tfrac{1}{3})(1) + (-\tfrac{1}{3})(-1) = 0$$

$$\psi_2 \text{ and } \psi_3 : 0(0) + (1)(0) + (-\tfrac{1}{2})(1) + (-\tfrac{1}{2})(-1) = 0$$

Now consider two general contrasts for k groups:

$$\Psi_1 = c_{11}\mu_1 + c_{12}\mu_2 + \ldots + c_{1k}\mu_k$$

$$\Psi_2 = c_{21}\mu_1 + c_{22}\mu_2 + \ldots + c_{2k}\mu_k$$

The first part of the c subscript refers to the contrast number and the second part to the group. The condition for independence in symbols then is:

$$c_{11}c_{21} + c_{12}c_{22} + \cdots + c_{1k}c_{2k} = \sum_{j=1}^{k} c_{1j}c_{2j} = 0$$

If the sample sizes are not equal, then the condition for independence is more complicated and becomes:

$$\frac{c_{11}c_{21}}{n_1} + \frac{c_{12}c_{22}}{n_2} + \cdots + \frac{c_{1k}c_{2k}}{n_k} = 0$$

It is very desirable, both statistically and substantively, to have orthogonal multivariate planned comparisons. Because the comparisons are uncorrelated, we obtain a nice additive partitioning of the total between-group association (Stevens, 1972). The reader may recall that in univariate ANOVA the between sum of squares is split into additive portions by a set of orthogonal planned comparisons (see Hays, 1981, ch. 14). Exactly the same type of thing is accomplished in the multivariate case; however, now the between matrix is split into additive portions that yield nonoverlapping pieces of information. Because the orthogonal comparisons are uncorrelated, the interpretation is clear and straightforward.

Although it is desirable to have orthogonal comparisons, the set to impose depends on the questions that are of primary interest to the investigator. The first example we gave of planned comparisons was not orthogonal, but corresponded to the important questions the investigator wanted answered. The interpretation of correlated contrasts requires some care, however, and we consider these in more detail later on in this chapter.

5.8 Test Statistics for Planned Comparisons

5.8.1 Univariate Case

The reader may have been exposed to planned comparisons for a single dependent variable, the univariate case. For k groups, with population means $\mu_1, \mu_2, \ldots, \mu_k$, a contrast among the population means is given by

$$\Psi = c_1\mu_1 + c_2\mu_2 + \cdots + c_k\mu_k$$

where the sum of the coefficients (c_i) must equal 0.

This contrast is estimated by replacing the population means by the sample means, yielding

$$\hat{\Psi} = c_1\bar{x} + c_2\bar{x}_2 + \cdots + c_k\bar{x}_k$$

To test whether a given contrast is significantly different from 0, that is, to test

$$H_0 : \Psi = 0 \quad \text{vs.} \quad H_1 : \Psi \neq 0$$

we need an expression for the standard error of a contrast. It can be shown that the variance for a contrast is given by

$$\hat{\sigma}_{\hat{\Psi}}^2 = MS_w \cdot \sum_{i=1}^{k} \frac{c_i^2}{n_i} \tag{1}$$

where MS_w is the error term from all the groups (the denominator of the F test) and n_i are the group sizes. Thus, the standard error of a contrast is simply the square root of Equation 1 and the following t statistic can be used to determine whether a contrast is significantly different from 0:

$$t = \frac{\hat{\Psi}}{\sqrt{MS_w \cdot \sum_{i=1}^{k} \frac{c_i^2}{n_i}}}$$

SPSS MANOVA reports the univariate results for contrasts as F values. Recall that because $F = t^2$, the following F test with 1 and $N - k$ degrees of freedom is equivalent to a two-tailed t test at the same level of significance:

$$F = \frac{\hat{\Psi}^2}{MS_w \cdot \sum_{i=1}^{k} \frac{c_i^2}{n_i}}$$

If we rewrite this as

$$F = \frac{\hat{\Psi}^2 \Big/ \sum_{i=1}^{k} \frac{c_i^2}{n_i}}{MS_w} \tag{2}$$

we can think of the numerator of Equation 2 as the sum of squares for a contrast, and this will appear as the hypothesis sum of squares (HYPOTH. *SS* specifically) on the SPSS printout. MS_w will appear under the heading ERROR MS.

Let us consider a special case of Equation 2. Suppose the group sizes are equal and we are making a simple paired comparison. Then the coefficient for one mean will be 1 and the coefficient for the other mean will be -1, and $\Sigma c_i^2 = 2$. Then the F statistic can be written as

$$F = \frac{n\hat{\Psi}^2/2}{MS_w} = \frac{n}{2}\hat{\Psi}(MS_w)^{-1}\hat{\Psi} \tag{3}$$

We have rewritten the test statistic in the form on the extreme right because we will be able to relate it more easily to the multivariate test statistic for a two-group planned comparison.

5.8.2 Multivariate Case

All contrasts, whether univariate or multivariate, can be thought of as fundamentally "two-group" comparisons. We are literally comparing two groups, or we are comparing one set of means versus another set of means. In the multivariate case this means that Hotelling's T^2 will be appropriate for testing the multivariate contrasts for significance.

We now have a contrast among the population mean vectors $\mu_1, \mu_2, \ldots \mu_k$, given by

$$\Psi = c_1\mu_1 + c_2\mu_2 + \cdots + c_k\mu_k$$

This contrast is estimated by replacing the population mean vectors by the sample mean vectors:

$$\hat{\Psi} = c_1\bar{x}_1 + c_2\bar{x}_2 + \cdots + c_k\bar{x}_k$$

We wish to test that the contrast among the population mean vectors is the null vector:

$$H_0 : \Psi = 0$$

Our estimate of error is **S**, the estimate of the assumed common within-group population covariance matrix Σ, and the general test statistic is

$$T^2 = \left(\sum_{i=1}^{k} \frac{c_i^2}{n_i}\right)^{-1} \hat{\Psi}'S^{-1}\hat{\Psi} \tag{4}$$

where, as in the univariate case, the n_i refer to the group sizes. Suppose we wish to contrast Group 1 against the average of groups 2 and 3. If the group sizes are 20, 15, and 12, then the term in parentheses would be evaluated as $[1^2/20 + (-.5)^2/15 + (-.5)^2/12]$. Complete evaluation of a multivariate contrast is given later in Table 5.10. Note that the first part of Equation 4, involving the summation, is exactly the same as in the univariate case (see Equation 2). Now, however, there are matrices instead of scalars. For example, the univariate error term MS_w has been replaced by the matrix **S**.

Again, as in the two-group MANOVA chapter, we have an exact F transformation of T^2, which is given by

$$F = \frac{(n_e - p + 1)}{n_e p} T^2 \quad \text{with } p \text{ and } (n_e - p + 1) \text{ degrees of freedom} \tag{5}$$

In Equation 5, $n_e = N - k$, that is, the degrees of freedom for estimating the pooled within covariance matrix. Note that for $k = 2$, (5) reduces to Equation 3 in Chapter 4.

For equal n per group and a simple paired comparison, observe that Equation 4 can be written as

$$T^2 = \frac{n}{2}\hat{\Psi}'\mathbf{S}^{-1}\hat{\Psi} \tag{6}$$

Note the analogy with the univariate case in Equation 3, except that now we have matrices instead of scalars. The estimated contrast has been replaced by the estimated mean vector contrast ($\hat{\Psi}$) and the univariate error term (MS_w) has been replaced by the corresponding multivariate error term $\mathbf{S}$.

5.9 Multivariate Planned Comparisons on SPSS MANOVA

SPSS MANOVA is set up very nicely for running multivariate planned comparisons. The following type of contrasts are automatically generated by the program: Helmert (which we have discussed), Simple, Repeated (comparing adjacent levels of a factor), Deviation, and Polynomial. Thus, if we wish Helmert contrasts, it is not necessary to set up the coefficients, the program does this automatically. All we need do is give the following CONTRAST SUBCOMMAND:

CONTRAST(FACTORNAME) = HELMERT/

We remind the reader that all subcommands are indented at least one column and begin with a keyword (in this case CONTRAST) followed by an equals sign, then the specifications, and are terminated by a slash.

An example of where Helmert contrasts are very meaningful has already been given. Simple contrasts involve comparing each group against the last group. A situation where this set of contrasts would make sense is if we were mainly interested in comparing each of several treatment groups against a control group (labeled as the last group). Repeated contrasts might be of considerable interest in a repeated measures design where a single group of subjects is measured at say five points in time (a longitudinal study). We might be particularly interested in differences at adjacent points in time. For example, a group of elementary school children is measured on a standardized achievement test in grades 1, 3, 5, 7, and 8. We wish to know the extent of change from Grade 1 to 3, from Grade 3 to 5, from Grade 5 to 7, and from Grade 7 to 8. The coefficients for the contrasts would be as follows:

Grade				
1	**3**	**5**	**7**	**8**
1	−1	0	0	0
0	1	−1	0	0
0	0	1	−1	0
0	0	0	1	−1

Polynomial contrasts are useful in trend analysis, where we wish to determine whether there is a linear, quadratic, cubic, etc., trend in the data. Again, these contrasts can be of great interest in repeated measures designs in growth curve analysis, where we wish to model the mathematical form of the growth. To reconsider the previous example, some investigators may be more interested in whether the growth in some basic skills areas such as reading and mathematics is linear (proportional) during the elementary years, or perhaps curvilinear. For example, maybe growth is linear for a while and then somewhat levels off, suggesting an overall curvilinear trend.

If none of these automatically generated contrasts answers the research questions, then one can set up contrasts using SPECIAL as the code name. Special contrasts are "tailor-made" comparisons for the group comparisons suggested by your hypotheses. In setting these up, however, remember that for k groups there are only $(k - 1)$ between degrees of freedom, so that only $(k - 1)$ nonredundant contrasts can be run. The coefficients for the contrasts are enclosed in parentheses after special:

CONTRAST(FACTORNAME) = SPECIAL(1, 1, …, 1 coefficients for contrasts)/

There *must* first be as many 1's as there are groups (see *SPSS User's Guide*, 1988, p. 590). We give an example illustrating special contrasts shortly.

Example 5.1: Helmert Contrasts

An investigator has a three-group, two-dependent variable problem with five subjects per group. The first is a control group, and the remaining two groups are treatment groups. The Helmert contrasts test each level (group) against the average of the remaining levels. In this case the two single degree-of-freedom Helmert contrasts, corresponding to the two between degrees of freedom, are very meaningful. The first tests whether the control group differs from the average of the treatment groups on the set of variables. The second Helmert contrast tests whether the treatments are differentially effective. In Table 5.7 we present the control lines along with the data as part of the command file, for running the contrasts. Recall that when the data is part of the command file it is preceded by the BEGIN DATA command and the data is followed by the END DATA command.

The means, standard deviations and pooled within-covariance matrix S are presented in Table 5.8, where we also calculate S^{-1}, which will serve as the error term for the multivariate contrasts (see Equation 4). Table 5.9 presents the output for the multivariate and univariate Helmert contrasts comparing the treatment groups against the control group. The multivariate contrast is significant at the .05 level ($F = 4.303$, $p < .042$), indicating that something is better than nothing. Note also that the F's for all the multivariate tests are the *same*, since this is a single degree of freedom comparison and thus effectively a two-group comparison. The univariate results show that each of the two variables is significant at .05, and are thus contributing to overall multivariate significance. We also show in Table 5.9 how the hypothesis sum of squares is obtained for the first univariate Helmert contrast (i.e., for Y1).

In Table 5.10 we present the multivariate and univariate Helmert contrasts comparing the two treatment groups. As the annotation indicates, both the multivariate and univariate contrasts are significant at the .05 level. Thus, the treatment groups differ on the set of variables and both variables are contributing to multivariate significance. In Table 5.10 we also show in detail how the F value for the multivariate Helmert contrast is arrived at.

TABLE 5.7

SPSS MANOVA Control Lines for Multivariate Helmert Contrasts

```
TITLE 'HELMERT CONTRASTS'.
DATA LIST FREE/GPS Y1 Y2.
BEGIN DATA.
1 5 6     1 6 7     1 6 7     1 4 5     1 5 4
2 2 2     2 3 3     2 4 4     2 3 2     2 2 1
3 4 3     3 6 7     3 3 3     3 5 5     3 5 5
END DATA.
LIST.
MANOVA Y1 Y2 BY GPS(1,3)/
    CONTRAST(GPS) = HELMERT/
  ① PARTITION(GPS)/
  ② DESIGN = GPS(1), GPS(2)/
    PRINT = CELLINFO(MEANS, COV)/.
```

① In general, for *k* groups, the between degrees of freedom could be partitioned in various ways. If we wish all single degree of freedom contrasts, as here, then we could put PARTITION(GPS) = (1, 1)/. Or, this can be abbreviated to PARTITION(GPS)/.

② This DESIGN subcommand specifies the effects we are testing for significance, in this case the two single degree of freedom multivariate contrasts. The numbers in parentheses refer to the part of the partition. Thus, GPS(1) refers to the first part of the partition (the first Helmert contrast) and GPS(2) refers to the second part of the partition, i.e., the second Helmert contrast.

TABLE 5.8

Means, Standard Deviations, and Pooled Within Covariance Matrix for Helmert Contrast Example

Cell Means and Standard Deviations
Variable .. Y1

FACTOR	CODE	Mean	Std. Dev.
GPS	1	5.200	.837
GPS	2	2.800	.837
GPS	3	4.600	1.140
For entire sample		4.200	1.373

Variable .. Y2

FACTOR	CODE	Mean	Std. Dev.
GPS	1	5.800	1.304
GPS	2	2.400	1.140
GPS	3	4.600	1.673
For entire sample		4.267	1.944

Pooled within-cells Variance-Covariance matrix

	Y1	Y2
Y1	.900	
Y2	1.150	1.933

Determinant of pooled Covariance matrix of dependent vars. = .41750

To compute the multivariate test statistic for the contrasts we need the inverse of this covariance matrix **S**; compare Equation 4.

The procedure for finding the inverse of a matrix was given in section 2.5. We obtain the matrix of cofactors and then divide by the determinant. Thus, here we have

$$\mathbf{S}^{-1} = \frac{1}{.4175}\begin{bmatrix} 1.933 & -1.15 \\ -1.15 & .9 \end{bmatrix} = \begin{bmatrix} 4.631 & -2.755 \\ -2.755 & 2.156 \end{bmatrix}$$

TABLE 5.9

Multivariate and Univariate Tests for Helmert Contrast Comparing the Control Group
Against the Two Treatment Groups

EFFECT .. GPS(l)
Multivariate Tests of Significance (S = 1, M = 0, N = 4 1/2)

Test Name	Value	Exact F	Hypoth. DF	Error DF	Sig. of F
Pillais	.43897	4.30339	2.00	11.00	.042
Hotellings	.78244	4.30339	2.00	11.00	① .042
Wilks	.56103	4.30339	2.00	11.00	.042
Roys	.43897				

Note.. F statistics are exact.

- -

EFFECT .. GPS(l) (Cont.)
Univariate F-tests with (1, 12) D. F.

Variable	Hypoth. SS	Error SS	Hypoth. MS	Error MS	F	Sig. of F
Y1	7.50000	10.80000	7.50000	.90000	8.33333	.014
Y2	17.63333	23.20000	17.63333	1.93333	9.12069	.011

The univariate contrast for Y1 is given by $\psi_1 = \mu_1 - (\mu_2 + \mu_3)/2$.
Using the boxed in means of Table 5.8, we obtain the following estimate for the contrast:
$\hat{\psi}_1 = 5.2 - (2.8 + 4.6)/2 = 1.5$.

Recall from Equation 2 that the hypothesis sum of squares is given by $\psi^2 \Big/ \sum_{i=1}^{k} \frac{c_i^2}{n_i}$. For equal group sizes, as here,

this becomes $n\psi^2 \Big/ \sum_{i=1}^{k} c_i^2$. Thus, HYPOTH $SS = \dfrac{5(1.5)^2}{1^2 + (-.5)^2 + (-.5)^2} = 7.5$.

The error term for the contrast is MS_w appears under ERROR MS and is .900. Thus, the F ratio for Y1 is 7.5/.90 = 8.333. Notice that both variables are significant at the .05 level.

---

① This indicates that the multivariate contrast $\psi_1 = \mu_1 - (\mu_2 + \mu_3)/2$ is significant at the .05 level (because .042 < .05). That is, the control group differs significantly from the average of the two treatment groups on the set of two variables.

Example 5.2: Special Contrasts

We indicated earlier that researchers can set up their own contrasts on MANOVA. We now illustrate this for a four-group, five-dependent variable example. There are two control groups, one of which is a Hawthorne control, and two treatment groups. Three very meaningful contrasts are indicated schematically below:

	T_1 (control)	T_2 (Hawthorne)	T_3	T_4
ψ_1	−.5	−.5	.5	.5
ψ_2	0	1	−.5	−.5
ψ_3	0	0	1	−1

The control lines for running these contrasts on SPSS MANOVA are presented in Table 5.11. (In this case I have just put in some data schematically and have used column input, simply to illustrate it.) As indicated earlier, note that the first four numbers in the CONTRAST subcommand are 1's, corresponding to the number of groups. The next four numbers define the first contrast, where we are comparing the control groups against the treatment groups. The following four numbers define the second contrast, and the last four numbers define the third contrast.

TABLE 5.10

Multivariate and Univariate Tests for Helmert Contrast Comparing the Two Treatment Groups

EFFECT .. GPS(2)
Multivariate Tests of Significance (S = 1, M = 0, N = 4 1/2)

Test Name	Value	Exact F	Hypoth. DF	Error DF	Sig. of F
Pillais	.43003	4.14970	2.00	11.00	.045
Hotellings	.75449	4.14970	① 2.00	11.00	.045
Wilks	.56997	4.14970	2.00	11.00	.045
Roys	.43003				

Note.. F statistics are exact.

- -

Recall from Table 5.8 that the inverse of pooled within convariance matrix is

$$S^{21} = \begin{bmatrix} 4.631 & -2.755 \\ -2.755 & 2.156 \end{bmatrix}$$

Since that is a simple contrast with equal n, we can use Equation 6:

$$T^2 = \frac{n}{2}\hat{\Psi}'S^{-1}\hat{\Psi} = \frac{n}{2}(\bar{x}_2 - \bar{x}_3)'S^{-1}(\bar{x}_2 - \bar{x}_3) = \frac{5}{2}\left[\begin{pmatrix} 2.8 \\ 2.4 \end{pmatrix} - \begin{pmatrix} 4.6 \\ 4.6 \end{pmatrix}\right]'\begin{bmatrix} 4.631 & -2.755 \\ -2.755 & 2.156 \end{bmatrix}\begin{pmatrix} -1.8 \\ -2.2 \end{pmatrix} = 9.0535$$

To obtain the value of HOTELLING given on printout above we simply divide by error df, i.e., 9.0535/12 = .75446.
To obtain the F we use Equation 5:

$$F = \frac{(n_e - p + 1)}{n_e p}T^2 = \frac{(12 - 2 + 1)}{12(2)}(9.0535) = 4.1495,$$

With degrees of freedom $p = 2$ and $(n_e - p + 1) = 11$ as given above.
EFFECT .. GPS (2) (Cont.)
Univariate F-tests with (1, 12) D. F.

Variable	Hypoth. SS	Error SS	Hypoth. MS	Error MS	F	Sig. of F
Y1	8.10000	10.80000	8.10000	.90000	9.00000	.011
Y2	12.10000	23.20000	12.10000	② 1.93333	6.25862	.028

- -

① This multivariate test indicates that treatment groups do differ significantly at the .05 level (because .045 < .05) on the *set* of two variables.
② These results indicate that both univariate contrasts are significant at .05 level, i.e., both variables are contributing to overall multivariate significance.

TABLE 5.11

SPSS MANOVA Control Lines for Special Multivariate Contrasts

```
TITLE 'SPECIAL MULTIVARIATE CONTRASTS'.
DATA LIST FREE/GPS 1 Y1 3-4 Y2 6-7(1) Y3 9-11(2)
  Y4 13-15 Y5 17-18.
BEGIN DATA.
1  28  13  476  215  74
......
4  24  31  668  355  56
END DATA.
LIST.
MANOVA Y1 TO Y5 BY GPS(1, 4)/
  CONTRAST(GPS) = SPECIAL (1  1  1  1  −.5  −.5  .5  .5
  0  1  −.5  −.5  0  0  1  −1)/
  PARTITION(GPS)/
  DESIGN = GPS(1), GPS(2), GPS(3)/
  PRINT = CELLINFO(MEAN, COV, COR)/.
```

5.10 Correlated Contrasts

The Helmert contrasts we considered in Example 5.1 are, for equal n, uncorrelated. This is important in terms of clarity of interpretation because significance on one Helmert contrast implies nothing about significance on a different Helmert contrast. For correlated contrasts this is not true. To determine the unique contribution a given contrast is making we need to partial out its correlations with the other contrasts. We illustrate how this is done on MANOVA.

Correlated contrasts can arise in two ways: (a) the sum of products of the coefficients ≠ 0 for the contrasts, and (b) the sum of products of coefficients = 0, but the group sizes are not equal.

Example 5.3: Correlated Contrasts

We consider an example with four groups and two dependent variables. The contrasts are indicated schematically here, with the group sizes in parentheses:

	T_1 & T_2 (12) combined	Hawthorne (14) control	T_1 (11)	T_2 (8)
ψ_1	0	1	−1	0
ψ_2	0	1	−.5	−.5
ψ_3	1	0	0	−1

Notice that ψ_1 and ψ_2 as well as ψ_2 and ψ_3 are correlated because the sum of products of coefficients in each case ≠ 0. However, ψ_1 and ψ_3 are also correlated since group sizes are unequal. The data for this problem are given next.

GP1		GP2		GP3		GP4	
y_1	y_2	y_1	y_2	y_1	y_2	y_1	y_2
18	5	18	9	17	5	13	3
13	6	20	5	22	7	9	3
20	4	17	10	22	5	9	3
22	8	24	4	13	9	15	5
21	9	19	4	13	5	13	4
19	0	18	4	11	5	12	4
12	6	15	7	12	6	13	5
10	5	16	7	23	3	12	3
15	4	16	5	17	7		
15	5	14	3	18	7		
14	0	18	2	13	3		
12	6	14	4				
		19	6				
		23	2				

1. We used the default method (UNIQUE SUM OF SQUARES—as of Release 2.1). This gives the unique contribution of the contrast to between variation; that is, each contrast is adjusted for its correlations with the other contrasts.
2. We used the SEQUENTIAL sum of squares option. This is obtained by putting the following subcommand right after the MANOVA statement:

METHOD = SEQUENTIAL/

With this option each contrast is adjusted *only* for all contrasts to the *left* of it in the DESIGN subcommand. Thus, if our DESIGN subcommand is

DESIGN = GPS(1), GPS(2), GPS(3)/

then the last contrast (denoted by GPS(3) is adjusted for all other contrasts, and the value of the multivariate test statistics for GPS(3) will be the *same* as we obtained for the default method (unique sum of squares). However, the value of the test statistics for GPS(2) and GPS(1) will differ from those obtained using unique sum of squares, since GPS(2) is only adjusted for GPS(1) and GPS(1) is not adjusted for either of the other two contrasts.

The multivariate test statistics for the contrasts using the unique decomposition are presented in Table 5.12, whereas the statistics for the hierarchical decomposition are given in Table 5.13. As explained earlier, the results for ψ_3 are identical for both approaches, and indicate significance at the .05 level ($F = 3.499$, $p < .04$). That is, the combination of treatments differs from T_2 alone. The results for the other two contrasts, however, are quite different for the two approaches. The unique breakdown indicates that ψ_2 is significant at .05 (treatments differ from Hawthorne control) and ψ_1 is not significant (T_1 is not different from Hawthorne control). The results in Table 5.12 for

TABLE 5.12

Multivariate Tests for Unique Contribution of Each Correlated Contrast to Between Variation*

EFFECT .. GPS (3) Multivariate Tests of Significance (S = 1, M = 0, N = 19)					
Test Name	Value	Exact F	Hypoth. DF	Error DF	Sig. of F
Pillais	.14891	3.49930	2.00	40.00	.040
Hotellings	.17496	3.49930	2.00	40.00	.040
Wilks	.85109	3.49930	2.00	40.00	.040
Roys	.14891				
Note.. F statistics are exact.					
EFFECT .. GPS (2) Multivariate Tests of Significance (S = 1, M = 0, N = 19)					
Test Name	Value	Exact F	Hypoth. DF	Error DF	Sig. of F
Pillais	.18228	4.45832	2.00	40.00	.018
Hotellings	.22292	4.45832	2.00	40.00	.018
Wilks	.81772	4.45832	2.00	40.00	.018
Roys	.18228				
Note.. F statistics are exact.					
EFFECT .. GPS (1) Multivariate Tests of Significance (S = 1, M = 0, N = 19)					
Test Name	Value	Exact F	Hypoth. DF	Error DF	Sig. of F
Pillais	.03233	.66813	2.00	40.00	.518
Hotellings	.03341	.66813	2.00	40.00	.518
Wilks	.96767	.66813	2.00	40.00	.518
Roys	.03233				
Note.. F statistics are exact.					

* Each contrast is adjusted for its correlations with the other contrasts.

TABLE 5.13

Multivariate Tests of Correlated Contrasts for Hierarchical Option of SPSS MANOVA

EFFECT .. GPS (3)
Multivariate Tests of Significance (S = 1, M = 0, N = 19)

Test Name	Value	Exact F	Hypoth. DF	Error DF	Sig. of F
Pillais	.14891	3.49930	2.00	40.00	.040
Hotellings	.17496	3.49930	2.00	40.00	.040
Wilks	.85109	3.49930	2.00	40.00	.040
Roys	.14891				

Note.. F statistics are exact.

EFFECT .. GPS (2)
Multivariate Tests of Significance (S = 1, M = 0, N = 19)

Test Name	Value	Exact F	Hypoth. DF	Error DF	Sig. of F
Pillais	.10542	2.35677	2.00	40.00	.108
Hotellings	.11784	2.35677	2.00	40.00	.108
Wilks	.89458	2.35677	2.00	40.00	.108
Roys	.10542				

Note.. F statistics are exact.

EFFECT .. GPS (1)
Multivariate Tests of Significance (S = 1, M = 0, N = 19)

Test Name	Value	Exact F	Hypoth. DF	Error DF	Sig. of F
Pillais	.13641	3.15905	2.00	40.00	.053
Hotellings	.15795	3.15905	2.00	40.00	.053
Wilks	.86359	3.15905	2.00	40.00	.053
Roys	.13641				

Note.. F statistics are exact.

Note: Each contrast is adjusted *only* for all contrasts to left of it in the DESIGN subcommand.

the hierarchical approach yield exactly the opposite conclusion. Obviously, the conclusions one draws in this study would depend on which approach was used to test the contrasts for significance. We would express a preference in general for the unique approach.

It should be noted that the unique contribution of each contrast can be obtained using the heirarchical approach; however, in this case three DESIGN subcommands would be required, with each of the contrasts ordered last in one of the subcommands:

DESIGN = GPS(1), GPS(2), GPS(3)/
DESIGN = GPS(2), GPS(3), GPS(1)/
DESIGN = GPS(3), GPS(1), GPS(2)/

All three orderings can be done in a single run.

5.11 Studies Using Multivariate Planned Comparisons

Clifford (1972) was interested in the effect of competition as a motivational technique in the classroom. The subjects were primarily white, average-IQ fifth graders, with the group about evenly divided between girls and boys. A 2-week vocabulary learning task was given under three conditions:

1. Control—a noncompetitive atmosphere in which no score comparisons among classmates were made.
2. Reward Treatment—comparisons among relatively homogeneous subjects were made and accentuated by the rewarding of candy to high-scoring subjects.
3. Game Treatment—again, comparisons were made among relatively homogeneous subjects and accentuated in a follow-up game activity. Here high-scoring subjects received an advantage in a game that was played immediately after the vocabulary task was scored.

The three dependent variables were performance, interest, and retention. The retention measure was given 2 weeks after the completion of treatments. Clifford had the following two planned comparisons:

1. Competition is more effective than noncompetition. Thus, she was testing the following contrast for significance:

$$\Psi_1 = \frac{\mu_2 + \mu_3}{2} - \mu_1$$

2. Game competition is as effective as reward with respect to performance on the dependent variables. Thus, she was predicting the following contrast would *not* be significant:

$$\Psi_2 = \mu_2 + \mu_3$$

Clifford's results are presented in Table 5.14.

As predicted, competition was more effective than noncompetition for the set of three dependent variables. Estimation of the univariate results in Table 5.14 shows that the multivariate significance is primarily due to a significant difference on the interest variable. Clifford's second prediction was also confirmed, that there was no difference in the relative effectiveness of reward versus game treatments ($F = .84, p < .47$).

A second study involving multivariate planned comparisons was conducted by Stevens (1972). He was interested in studying the relationship between parents' educational level and eight personality characteristics of their National Merit scholar children. Part of the analysis involved the following set of orthogonal comparisons (75 subjects per group):

1. Group 1 (parents' education eighth grade or less) versus Group 2 (parents' both high school graduates).
2. Groups 1 and 2 (no college) versus groups 3 and 4 (college for both parents).
3. Group 3 (both parents attended college) versus Group 4 (both parents at least one college degree).

This set of comparisons corresponds to a very meaningful set of questions: Which differences in degree of education produce differential effects on the children's personality characteristics?

TABLE 5.14

Means and Multivariate and Univariate Results for Two Planned Comparisons in Clifford Study

	df	MS	F	p
1st Planned Comparison				
(Control vs. Reward and Game)				
Multivariate Test	3/61		10.04	.0001
Univariate Tests				
Performance	1/63	.54	.64	.43
Interest	1/63	4.70	29.24	.0001
Retention	1/63	4.01	.18	.67
2nd Planned Comparison				
(Reward vs. Game)				
Multivariate Test	3/61		.84	.47
Univariate Tests				
Performance	1/63	.002	.003	.96
Interest	1/63	.37	2.32	.13
Retention	1/63	1.47	.07	.80

Variable	Means for the Groups		
	Control	Reward	Games
Performance	5.72	5.92	5.90
Interest	2.41	2.63	2.57
Retention	30.85	31.55	31.19

Another set of orthogonal contrasts that could have been of interest in this study looks like this schematically:

	Groups			
	1	2	3	4
ψ_1	1	−.33	−.33	−.33
ψ_2	0	0	1	−1
ψ_3	0	1	−.50	−.50

This would have resulted in a different meaningful, additive breakdown of the between association. However, one set of orthogonal contrasts does not have an empirical superiority over another (after all, they both additively partition the between association). In terms of choosing one set over the other, it is a matter of which set best answers the experimenter's research hypotheses.

5.12 Stepdown Analysis

We have just finished discussing one type of focused inquiry, planned comparisons, in which specific questions were asked of the data. Another type of directed inquiry in the MANOVA context, but one that focuses on the dependent variables rather than the groups, is stepdown analysis. Here, based on previous research or theory, we are able to a priori order the dependent variables, and test in that specific order for group discrimination. As an example, let the independent variable be three teaching methods and the dependent variables be the three subtest scores on a common achievement test covering the three lowest levels in Bloom's taxonomy: knowledge, comprehension, and application. An assumption of the taxonomy is that learning at a lower level is a necessary but not sufficient condition for learning at a higher level. Because of this, there is a theoretical rationale for ordering the dependent variables in the above specified way and to test first whether the methods have had a differential effect on knowledge: then, if so, whether the methods differentially affect comprehension, with knowledge held constant (used as a covariate), and so on. Because stepdown analysis is just a series of analyses of covariance, we defer a complete discussion of it to Chapter 10, after we have covered analysis of covariance in chapter 9.

5.13 Other Multivariate Test Statistics

In addition to Wilks' Λ, three other multivariate test statistics are in use and are printed out on the packages:

1. Roy's largest root (eigenvalue) of $\mathbf{BW}^{-1}$.
2. The Hotelling–Lawley trace, the sum of the eigenvalues of $\mathbf{BW}^{-1}$.
3. The Pillai–Bartlett trace, the sum of the eigenvalues of $\mathbf{BT}^{-1}$.

Notice that the Roy and Hotelling–Lawley multivariate statistics are natural generalizations of the univariate F statistic. In univariate ANOVA the test statistic is $F = MS_b/MS_w$, a measure of between- to within-association. The multivariate analogue of this is $\mathbf{BW}^{-1}$, which is a "ratio" of between- to within-association. With matrices there is no division, so we don't literally divide the between by the within as in the univariate case; however, the matrix analogue of division is inversion.

Because Wilks' Λ can be expressed as a product of eigenvalues of $\mathbf{WT}^{-1}$, *we see that all four of the multivariate test statistics are some function of an eigenvalue(s) (sum, product). Thus, eigenvalues are fundamental to the multivariate problem.* We will show in Chapter 7 on discriminant analysis that there are quantities corresponding to the eigenvalues (the discriminant functions) that are linear combinations of the dependent variables and that characterize major differences among the groups.

The reader might well ask at this point, "Which of these four multivariate test statistics should be used in practice?" This is a somewhat complicated question that, for full understanding, requires a knowledge of discriminant analysis and of the robustness of the four statistics to the assumptions in MANOVA. Nevertheless, the following will provide guidelines for the researcher. In terms of robustness with respect to type I error for the homogeneity of covariance matrices assumption, Stevens (1979) found that *any* of the following three can be used: Pillai–Bartlett trace, Hotelling–Lawley trace, or Wilks' Λ. For subgroup variance differences likely to be encountered in social science research, these three are equally quite robust, provided the group sizes are equal or approximately equal $\left(\frac{\text{largest}}{\text{smallest}} < 1.5\right)$. In terms of power, no one of the four statistics is always most powerful; which depends on how the null hypothesis is false. Importantly, however, Olson (1973) found that *power differences among the four multivariate test statistics are generally quite small* (< .06). So as a general rule, it won't make that much of a difference which of the statistics is used. But, if the differences among the groups are concentrated on the first discriminant function, which does occur quite often in practice (Bock, 1975, p. 154), then Roy's statistic technically would be preferred since it is most powerful. However, Roy's statistic should be used in this case only if there is evidence to suggest that the homogeneity of covariance matrices assumption is tenable. Finally, when the differences among the groups involve two or more discriminant functions, the Pillai–Bartlett trace is most powerful, although its power advantage tends to be slight.

5.14 How Many Dependent Variables for a Manova?

Of course, there is no simple answer to this question. However, the following considerations mitigate *generally* against the use of a large number of criterion variables:

1. If a large number of dependent variables are included without any strong rationale (empirical or theoretical), then small or negligible differences on most of them may obscure a real difference(s) on a few of them. That is, the multivariate test detects mainly error in the system, that is, in the set of variables, and therefore declares no reliable overall difference.

2. The power of the multivariate tests generally declines as the number of dependent variables is increased (DasGupta and Perlman, 1973).

3. The reliability of variables can be a problem in behavioral science work. Thus, given a large number of criterion variables, it probably will be wise to combine (usually add) highly similar response measures, particularly when the basic measurements tend individually to be quite unreliable (Pruzek, 1971). As Pruzek stated, one should always consider the possibility that his variables include errors of measurement that may attentuate F ratios and generally confound interpretations of experimental effects. Especially when there are several dependent variables whose reliabilities and mutal intercorrelations vary widely, inferences based on fallible data may be quite misleading. (p. 187)

4. Based on his Monte Carlo results, Olson had some comments on the design of multivariate experiments which are worth remembering: For example, one generally will not do worse by making the dimensionality p smaller, insofar as it is under experimenter control. Variates should not be thoughtlessly included in an analysis just because the data are available. Besides aiding robustness, a small value of p is apt to facilitate interpretation. (p. 906)

5. Given a large number of variables, one should always consider the possibility that there are a much smaller number of underlying constructs that will account for most of the variance on the original set of variables. Thus, the use of principal components analysis as a preliminary data reduction scheme before the use of MANOVA should be contemplated.

5.15 Power Analysis—a Priori Determination of Sample Size

Several studies have dealt with power in MANOVA (e.g., Ito, 1962; Pillai and Jayachandian, 1967; Olson, 1974; Lauter, 1978). Olson examined power for small and moderate sample size, but expressed the noncentrality parameter (which measures the extent of deviation from the null hypothesis) in terms of eigenvalues. Also, there were many gaps in his tables: No power values for 4, 5, 7, 8, and 9 variables or 4 or 5 groups. The Lauter study is much more comprehensive, giving sample size tables for a very wide range of situations:

1. For α = .05 or .01.
2. For 2, 3, 4, 5, 6, 8, 10, 15, 20, 30, 50, and 100 variables.
3. For 2, 3, 4, 5, 6, 8, and 10 groups.
4. For power = .70, .80, .90, and .95.

His tables are specifically for the Hotelling–Lawley trace criterion, and this might seem to limit their utility. However, as Morrison (1967) noted for large sample size, and as Olson (1974) showed for small and moderate sample size, the power differences among the four main multivariate test statistics are generally quite small. Thus, the sample size requirements for Wilks' Λ, the Pillai–Bartlett trace, and Roy's largest root will be very similar to those for the Hotelling–Lawley trace for the vast majority of situations.

Lauter's tables are set up in terms of a certain *minimum* deviation from the multivariate null hypothesis, which can be expressed in the following three forms:

1. There exists a variable i such that $\dfrac{1}{\sigma_{j=1}^2}\displaystyle\sum_{j=1}^{j}(\mu_{ij}-\mu_i)\geq q^2$ where μ_i, is the total mean and σ^2 is variance.
2. There exists a variable i such that $1/\sigma_i\left|\mu_{ij_1}-\mu_{ij_2}\right|\geq d$ for two groups j1 and j2.
3. There exists a variable i such that for all pairs of groups 1 and m we have $1/\sigma_i\left|\mu_{il}-\mu_{il}\right|>c$.

In Table E at the end of this volume we present selected situations and power values that it is believed would be of most value to social science researchers: for 2, 3, 4, 5, 6, 8, 10, and 15 variables, with 3, 4, 5, and 6 groups, and for power = .70, .80, and .90. We have also characterized the four different minimum deviation patterns as very large, large, moderate, and small effect sizes. Although the characterizations may be somewhat rough, they are reasonable in the following senses: they agree with Cohen's definitions of large, medium, and small effect sizes for one variable (Lauter included the univariate case in his tables), and with Stevens' (1980) definitions of large, medium, and small effect sizes for the two-group MANOVA case.

It is important to note that there could be several ways, other than that specified by Lauter, in which a large, moderate, or small multivariate effect size could occur. But the essential point is how many subjects will be needed for a given effect size, regardless of the combination of differences on the variables that produced the specific effect size. Thus, the tables do have broad applicability. We consider shortly a few specific examples of the use of the tables, but first we present a compact table that should be of great interest to applied researchers:

		Groups			
		3	4	5	6
	very large	12–16	14–18	15–19	16–21
EFFECT	large	25–32	28–36	31–40	33–44
SIZE	medium	42–54	48–62	54–70	58–76
	small	92–120	105–140	120–155	130–170

This table gives the range of sample sizes needed per group for adequate power (.70) at $\alpha = .05$ when there are three to six variables.

Thus, if we expect a large effect size and have four groups, 28 subjects per group are needed for power = .70 with three variables, whereas 36 subjects per group are required if there were six dependent variables.

Now we consider two examples to illustrate the use of the Lauter sample size tables in the appendix.

Example 5.4

An investigator has a four-group MANOVA with five dependent variables. He wishes power = .80 at $\alpha = .05$. From previous research and his knowledge of the nature of the treatments, he anticipates a moderate effect size. How many subjects per group will he need? Reference to Table E (for four groups) indicates that 70 subjects per group are required.

Example 5.5

A team of researchers has a five-group, seven-dependent-variable MANOVA. They wish power = .70 at $\alpha = .05$. From previous research they anticipate a large effect size. How many subjects per group are needed? Interpolating in Table E (for five groups) between six and eight variables, we see that 43 subjects per group are needed, or a total of 215 subjects.

5.16 Summary

Cohen's (1968) seminal article showed social science researchers that univariate ANOVA could be considered as a special case of regression, by dummy coding group membership. In this chapter we have pointed out that MANOVA can also be considered as a special case of regression analysis, except that for MANOVA it is multivariate regression because there are several dependent variables being predicted from the dummy variables. That is, separation of the mean vectors is equivalent to demonstrating that the dummy variables (predictors) significantly predict the scores on the dependent variables.

For exploratory research, three post hoc procedures were given for determining which of the group or variables are responsible for an overall difference. One procedure used Hotelling T^2's to determine the significant pairwise multivariate differences, and then univariate t's to determine which of the variables are contributing to the significant pairwise multivariate differences. The second procedure also used Hotelling T^2's, but then used the Tukey intervals to determine which variables were contributing to the significant pairwise multivariate differences. The third post hoc procedure, the Roy–Bose multivariate confidence interval approach (the generalization of the univariate Scheffé intervals) was discussed and rejected. It was rejected because the power for detecting differences with this approach is quite poor, especially for small or moderate sample size.

For confirmatory research, planned comparisons were discussed. The setup of multivariate contrasts on SPSS MANOVA was illustrated. Although uncorrelated contrasts are very desirable because of ease of interpretation and the nice additive partitioning they yield, it was noted that often the important questions an investigator has will yield correlated contrasts. The use of SPSS MANOVA to obtain the unique contribution of each correlated contrast was illustrated.

It was noted that the Roy and Hotelling–Lawley statistics are natural generalizations of the univariate F ratio. In terms of which of the four multivariate test statistics to use in practice, two criteria can be used: robustness and power. Wilks' Λ, the Pillai–Bartlett trace, and Hotelling–Lawley statistics are equally robust (for equal or approximately equal group sizes) with respect to the homogeneity of covariance matrices assumption, and therefore any one of them can be used. The power differences among the four statistics are in general quite small ($< .06$), so that there is no strong basis for preferring any one of them over the others on power considerations.

The important problem, in terms of experimental planning, of a priori determination of sample size was considered for three-, four-, five-, and six-group MANOVA for the number of dependent variables ranging from 2 to 15.

5.17 Exercises

1. Consider the following data for a three-group, three-dependent-variable problem:

Group 1			Group 2			Group 3		
y_1	y_2	y_3	y_1	y_2	y_3	y_1	y_2	y_3
2.0	2.5	2.5	1.5	3.5	2.5	1.0	2.0	1.0
1.5	2.0	1.5	1.0	4.5	2.5	1.0	2.0	1.5
2.0	3.0	2.5	3.0	3.0	3.0	1.5	1.0	1.0
2.5	4.0	3.0	4.5	4.5	4.5	2.0	2.5	2.0
1.0	2.0	1.0	1.5	4.5	3.5	2.0	3.0	2.5
1.5	3.5	2.5	2.5	4.0	3.0	2.5	3.0	2.5
4.0	3.0	3.0	3.0	4.0	3.5	2.0	2.5	2.5
3.0	4.0	3.5	4.0	5.0	5.0	1.0	1.0	1.0
3.5	3.5	3.5				1.0	1.5	1.5
1.0	1.0	1.0				2.0	3.5	2.5
1.0	2.5	2.0						

Run the one-way MANOVA on SPSS.

(a) What is the multivariate null hypothesis? Do you reject it at $\alpha = .05$?

(b) If you reject in part (a), then which pairs of groups are significantly different in a multivariate sense at the .05 level?

(c) For the significant pairs, which of the individual variables are contributing (at .01 level) to the multivariate significance?

2. Consider the following data from Wilkinson (1975):

Group A			Group B			Group C		
5	6	4	2	2	7	4	3	4
6	7	5	3	3	5	6	7	5
6	7	3	4	4	6	3	3	5
4	5	5	3	2	4	5	5	5
5	4	2	2	1	4	5	5	4

(a) Run a one-way MANOVA on SPSS. Do the various multivariate test statistics agree in a decision on H_0?

(b) Below are the multivariate (Roy–Bose) and univariate (Scheffé) 95% simultaneous confidence intervals for the three variables for the three paired comparisons.

Contrast	Variable	Multivariate Intervals	Univariate Intervals
A–B	1	$-.1 \le 2.4 \le 4.9$	$.7 \le 2.4 \le 4.1$
	2	$-.3 \le 3.4 \le 7.1$	$.9 \le 3.4 \le 5.6$
	3	$-4.4 \le -1.4 \le 1.6$	$-3.4 \le -1.4 \le .6$
A–C	1	$-1.9 \le .6 \le 3.1$	$-1.1 \le .6 \le 2.3$
	2	$-2.5 \le 1.2 \le 4.9$	$-1.3 \le 1.2 \le 3.7$
	3	$-3.8 \le -.8 \le 2.2$	$-2.8 \le -.8 \le 1.2$
B–C	1	$-4.3 \le -1.8 \le .7$	$-3.5 \le -1.8 \le -.1$
	2	$-5.9 \le -2.2 \le 1.5$	$-4.7 \le -2.2 \le .3$
	3	$-2.4 \le .6 \le 3.6$	$-1.4 \le .6 \le 2.6$

Note: Estimates of the contrasts are given at the center of the inequalities.

Comment on the multivariate intervals relative to the decision reached by the test statistics on H_0. Why is the situation different for the univariate intervals?

3. Stilbeck, Acousta, Yamamoto, and Evans (1984) examined differences among black, Hispanic, and white applicants for outpatient therapy, using symptoms reported on the Symptom Checklist 90–Revised. They report the following results, having done 12 univariate ANVOA.

SCL 90–R Ethnicity Main Effects

	Group					
	Black N = 48	Hispanic N = 60	White N = 57			
Dimension	$\bar{x}$	$\bar{x}$	$\bar{x}$	F	df	Significance
Somatization	53.7	53.2	53.7	.03	2,141	ns
Obsessive-Compulsive	48.7	53.9	52.2	2.75	2,141	ns
Interpersonal Sensitivity	47.3	51.3	52.9	4.84	2,141	$p < .01$
Depression	47.5	53.5	53.9	5.44	2,141	$p < .01$
Anxiety	48.5	52.9	52.2	1.86	2,141	ns
Hostility	48.1	54.6	52.4	3.82	2,141	$p < .03$
Phobic Anxiety	49.8	54.2	51.8	2.08	2,141	ns
Paranoid Ideation	51.4	54.7	54.0	1.38	2,141	ns
Psychoticism	52.4	54.6	54.2	.37	2,141	ns
Global Severity Index Positive Symptom	49.7	54.4	54.0	2.55	2,141	ns
Distress Index	49.3	55.8	53.2	3.39	2,141	$p < .04$
Positive Symptom Total	50.2	52.9	54.4	1.96	2,141	ns

(a) Could we be confident that these results would replicate? Explain.

(b) Check the article to see if the authors' a priori hypothesized differences on the specific variables for which significance was found.

(c) What would have been a better method of analysis?

4. A researcher is testing the efficacy of four drugs in inhibiting undesirable responses in mental patients. Drugs A and B are similar in composition, whereas drugs C and D are distinctly different in composition from A and B, although similar in their basic ingredients. He takes 100 patients and randomly assigns them to five groups: Gp 1—control, Gp 2—drug A, Gp 3—drug B, Gp 4—drug C, and Gp 5—drug D. The following would be four very relevant planned comparisons to test:

		Control	Drug A	Drug B	Drug C	Drug D
Contrasts	1	1	−.25	−.25	−.25	−.25
	2	0	1	1	−1	−1
	3	0	1	−1	0	0
	4	0	0	0	1	−1

(a) Show that these contrasts are orthogonal.

Now, consider the following set of contrasts, which might also be of interest in the preceding study:

		Control	Drug A	Drug B	Drug C	Drug D
Contrasts	1	1	−.25	−.25	−.25	−.25
	2	1	−.5	−.5	0	0
	3	1	0	0	−.5	−.5
	4	0	1	1	−1	−1

(b) Show that these contrasts are not orthogonal.

(c) Because neither of these two sets of contrasts are one of the standard sets that come out of SPSS MANOVA, it would be necessary to use the special contrast feature to test each set. Show the control lines for doing this for each set. Assume four criterion measures.

5. Consider the following three-group MANOVA with two dependent variables. Run the MANOVA on SPSS. Is it significant at the .05 level? Examine the univariate F's at the .05 level. Are any of them significant? How would you explain this situation?

Group 1		Group 2		Group 3	
y_1	y_2	y_1	y_2	y_1	y_2
3	7	4	5	5	5
4	7	4	6	6	5
5	8	5	7	6	6
5	9	6	7	7	7
6	10	6	8	7	8

6. A MANOVA was run on the Sesame data using SPSS for Windows 15.0. The grouping variable was viewing category (VIEWCAT). Recall that 1 means the children watched the program rarely and 4 means the children watched the program on the average of more than 5 times a week. The dependent variables were gains in knowledge of body parts, letters, and forms. These gain scores were obtained by using the COMPUTE statement to obtain difference scores, e.g., BODYDIFF = POSTBODY – PREBODY.

(a) Is the multivariate test significant at the .05 level?

(b) Are any of the univariate tests significant at the .05 level?

(c) Examine the means, and explain why the p value for LETDIFF is so small.

VIEWCAT		N		Box's Test of Equality of Covariance Matrices[a]	
VIEWCAT	1.00	54		Box's M	31.263
	2.00	60		F	1.697
	3.00	64		df1	18
	4.00	62		df2	190268
				Sig.	.033

Multivariate Tests[c]

Effect		Value	F	Hypothesis df	Error df	Sig.
Intercept	Pillai's Trace	.658	149.989[a]	3.000	234.000	.000
	Wilks' Lambda	.342	149.989[a]	3.000	234.000	.000
	Hotelling's Trace	1.923	149.989[a]	3.000	234.000	.000
	Roy's Largest Root	1.923	149.989[a]	3.000	234.000	.000
VIEWCAT	Pillai's Trace	.238	6.769	9.000	708.000	.000
	Wilks' Lambda	.764	7.405	9.000	569.645	.000
	Hotelling's Trace	.307	7.934	9.000	698.000	.000
	Roy's Largest Root	.300	23.586[b]	3.000	236.000	.000

Tests of Between-Subjects Effects

Source	Dependent Variable	Type III Sum of Squares	df	Mean Square	F	Sig.
Corrected Model	BODYDIFF	51.842[a]	3	17.281	.685	.562
	LETDIFF	6850.255[b]	3	2283.418	23.481	.000
	FORMDIFF	121.552[c]	3	40.517	2.956	.033
Intercept	BODYDIFF	3522.814	1	3522.814	139.573	.000
	LETDIFF	26040.525	1	26040.525	267.784	.000
	FORMDIFF	3416.976	1	3416.976	249.323	.000
VIEWCAT	BODYDIFF	51.842	3	17.281	.685	.562
	LETDIFF	6850.255	3	2283.418	23.481	.000
	FORMDIFF	121.552	3	40.517	2.956	.033
Error	BODYDIFF	5956.621	236	25.240		
	LETDIFF	22949.728	236	97.245		
	FORMDIFF	3234.382	236	13.705		

Dependent Variable	VIEWCAT	Mean	Std. Error	95% Confidence Interval	
				Lower Bound	Upper Bound
BODYDIFF	1.00	3.167	.684	1.820	4.514
	2.00	3.783	.649	2.506	5.061
	3.00	3.906	.628	2.669	5.143
	4.00	4.500	.638	3.243	5.757
LETDIFF	1.00	2.481	1.342	−.162	5.125
	2.00	8.350	1.273	5.842	10.858
	3.00	15.000	1.233	12.572	17.428
	4.00	15.919	1.252	13.452	18.387
FORMDIFF	1.00	2.778	.504	1.785	3.770
	2.00	3.633	.478	2.692	4.575
	3.00	3.906	.463	2.995	4.818
	4.00	4.806	.470	3.880	5.733

7. An extremely important assumption underlying both univariate and multivariate ANOVA is independence of the observations. If this assumption is violated, even to a small degree, it causes the actual α to be several times greater than the level of significance, as you can see in the next chapter. If one suspects dependent observations, as would be the case in studies involving teaching methods, then one might consider using the classroom mean as the unit of analysis. If there are several classes for each method or condition, then you want the software package to compute the means for your dependent variables from the raw data for each method. In a recent dissertation there were a total of 64 classes and about 1,200 subjects with 10 variables. Fortunately, SPSS has a procedure called AGGREGATE, which computes the mean across a group of cases and produces a new file containing one case for each group.

To illustrate AGGREGATE in a somewhat simpler but similar context, suppose we are comparing three teaching methods and have three classes for Method 1, two classes for Method 2, and two classes for Method 3. There are two dependent variables (denote them by ACH1, ACH2). The AGGREGATE control syntax is as follows:

```
TITLE 'AGGREG. CLASS DATA'.
DATA LIST FREE/METHOD CLASS ACH1 ACH2.
BEGIN DATA.
1 1 13 14 1 1 11 15 1 2 23 27 1 2 25 29 1 3 32 31 1 3 35 37
2 1 45 47 2 1 55 58 2 1 65 63 2 2 75 78 2 2 65 66 2 2 87 85
3 1 88 85 3 1 91 93 3 1 24 25 3 1 65 68 3 2 43 41 3 2 54 53 3 2 65
68 3 2 76 74
END DATA.
LIST.
AGGREGATE OUTFILE=*/
 BREAK=METHOD CLASS/
 COUNT=N/
 AVACH1 AVACH2=MEAN(ACH1, ACH2)/.
LIST.
MANOVA AVACH1 AVACH2 BY METHOD(1,3)/
 PRINT=CELLINFO(MEANS)/.
```

Run this syntax in the syntax editor and observe that the *n* for the MANOVA is 7.

8. Find an article in one of the better journals in your content area from within the last 5 years that used primarily MANOVA. Answer the following questions:

   (a) How many statistical tests (univariate or multivariate or both) were done? Were the authors aware of this, and did they adjust in any way?

   (b) Was power an issue in this study? Explain.

   (c) Did the authors address practical significance in ANY way? Explain.

9. Consider the following data for a three-group MANOVA:

Group 1		Group 2		Group 3	
y_1	y_2	y_1	y_2	y_1	y_2
2	13	3	10	6	13
3	14	7	8	4	10
5	17	6	14	9	17
7	15	9	11	3	18
8	21	11	15		
		8	10		
		5	16		

   (a) Calculate the **W** and **B** matrices.

   (b) Calculate Wilks' lambda.

   (c) What is the multivariate null hypothesis?

   (d) Test the multivariate null hypothesis at the .05 level using the chi square approximation.

6

Assumptions in MANOVA

6.1 Introduction

The reader may recall that one of the assumptions in analysis of variance is normality; that is, the scores for the subjects in each group are normally distributed. Why should we be interested in studying assumptions in ANOVA and MANOVA? Because, in ANOVA and MANOVA, we set up a mathematical model based on these assumptions, and all mathematical models are approximations to reality. Therefore, violations of the assumptions are inevitable. The salient question becomes: How radically must a given assumption be violated before it has a serious effect on type I and type II error rates? Thus, we may set our $\alpha = .05$ and think we are rejecting falsely 5% of the time, but if a given assumption is violated, we may be rejecting falsely 10%, or if another assumption is violated, may be rejecting falsely 40% of the time. For these kinds of situations, we would certainly want to be able to detect such violations and take some corrective action, but all violations of assumptions are not serious, and hence it is crucial to know *which* assumptions to be particularly concerned about, and under what conditions.

In this chapter, I consider in detail what effect violating assumptions has on type I error and power. There has been a very substantial amount of research on violations of assumptions in ANOVA and a fair amount of research for MANOVA on which to base our conclusions. First, I remind the reader of some basic terminology that is needed to discuss the results of simulation (i.e., Monte Carlo) studies, whether univariate or multivariate. The nominal α (level of significance) is the α level set by the experimenter, and is the percent of time one is rejecting falsely when *all* assumptions are met. The *actual* α is the percent of time one is rejecting falsely if one or more of the assumptions is violated. We say the F statistic is *robust* when the actual α is very close to the level of significance (nominal α). For example, the actual α's for some very skewed (nonnormal) populations were only .055 or .06, very minor deviations from the level of significance of .05.

6.2 ANOVA and MANOVA Assumptions

The three assumptions for univariate ANOVA are:

1. The observations are independent.
   (violation very serious)
2. The observations are normally distributed on the dependent variable in each group.
   (robust with respect to type I error)
   (skewness has very little effect on power, while platykurtosis attenuates power)

3. The population variances for the groups are equal, often referred to as the *homogeneity of variance* assumption.
(conditionally robust—robust if group sizes are equal or approximately equal—largest/smallest < 1.5)

The assumptions for MANOVA are as follows:

1. The observations are independent.
(violation very serious)

2. The observations on the dependent variables follow a multivariate normal distribution in each group.
(robust with respect to type I error)
(no studies on effect of skewness on power, but platykurtosis attenuates power)

3. The population covariance matrices for the p dependent variables are equal.
(conditionally robust—robust if the group sizes are equal or approximately equal—largest/smallest < 1.5)

6.3 Independence Assumption

Note that independence of observations is an assumption for both ANOVA and MANOVA. I have listed this assumption first and am emphasizing it for three reasons:

1. A violation of this assumption is *very* serious.

2. Dependent observations do occur fairly often in social science research.

3. Many statistics books do not mention this assumption, and in some cases where they do, misleading statements are made (e.g., that dependent observations occur only infrequently, that random assignment of subjects to groups will eliminate the problem, or that this assumption is usually satisfied by using a random sample).

Now let us consider several situations in social science research where dependence among the observations will be present. Cooperative learning has become very popular since the early 1980s. In this method, students work in small groups, interacting with each other and helping each other learn the lesson. In fact, the evaluation of the success of the group is dependent on the individual success of its members. Many studies have compared cooperative learning versus individualistic learning. A review of such studies in the "best" journals since 1980 found that about 80% of the analyses were done incorrectly (Hykle, Stevens, and Markle, 1993). That is, the investigators used the subject as the unit of analysis, when the very nature of cooperative learning implies dependence of the subjects' scores within each group.

Teaching methods studies constitute another broad class of situations where dependence of observations is undoubtedly present. For example, a few troublemakers in a classroom would have a detrimental effect on the achievement of many children in the classroom. Thus, their posttest achievement would be at least partially dependent on the disruptive classroom atmosphere. On the other hand, even with a good classroom atmosphere, dependence is introduced, for the achievement of many of the children will be enhanced by the positive learning situation. Therefore, in either case (positive or negative classroom atmosphere), the achievement of each child is not independent of the other children in the classroom.

Another situation I came across in which dependence among the observations was present involved a study comparing the achievement of students working in pairs at microcomputers versus students working in groups of three. Here, if Bill and John are working at the same microcomputer, then obviously Bill's achievement is partially influenced by John. The proper unit of analysis in this study is the *mean* achievement for each pair or triplet of students, as it is plausible to assume that the achievement of students working one micro is independent of that of students working at others.

Glass and Hopkins (1984) made the following statement concerning situations where independence may or may not be tenable, "Whenever the treatment is individually administered, observations are independent. But where treatments involve interaction among persons, such as discussion method or group counseling, the observations may influence each other" (p. 353).

6.3.1 Effect of Correlated Observations

I indicated earlier that a violation of the independence of observations assumption is very serious. I now elaborate on this assertion. Just a *small* amount of dependence among the observations causes the actual α to be several times greater than the level of significance. Dependence among the observations is measured by the intraclass correlation R, where:

$$R = MS_b - MS_w / [MS_b + (n-1)MS_y]$$

M_b and MS_w are the numerator and denominator of the F statistic and n is the number of subjects in each group.

Table 6.1, from Scariano and Davenport (1987), shows precisely how dramatic an effect dependence has on type I error. For example, for the three-group case with 10 subjects per group and moderate dependence (intraclass correlation = .30) the actual α is .5379. Also, for three groups with 30 subjects per group and small dependence (intraclass correlation = .10) the actual α is .4917, almost 10 times the level of significance. Notice, also, from the table, that for a fixed value of the intraclass correlation, the situation does not improve with larger sample size, but gets far worse.

6.4 What Should Be Done with Correlated Observations?

Given the results in Table 6.1 for a positive intraclass correlation, one route investigators should seriously consider if they suspect that the nature of their study will lead to correlated observations is to test at a more stringent level of significance. For the three- and five-group cases in Table 6.1, with 10 observations per group and intraclass correlation = .10, the error rates are five to six times greater than the assumed level of significance of .05. Thus, for this type of situation, it would be wise to test at $\alpha = .01$, realizing that the actual error rate will be about .05 or somewhat greater. For the three- and five-group cases in Table 6.1 with 30 observations per group and intraclass correlation = .10, the error rates are about 10 times greater than .05. Here, it would be advisable to either test at .01, realizing that the actual α will be about .10, or test at an even more stringent α level.

TABLE 6.1

Actual Type I Error Rates for Correlated Observations in a One-Way ANOVA

Number of Groups	Group Size	Intraclass Correlation								
		.00	.01	.10	.30	.50	.70	.90	.95	.99
2	3	.0500	.0522	.0740	.1402	.2374	.3819	.6275	.7339	.8800
	10	.0500	.0606	.1654	.3729	.5344	.6752	.8282	.8809	.9475
	30	.0500	.0848	.3402	.5928	.7205	.8131	.9036	.9335	.9708
	100	.0500	.1658	.5716	.7662	.8446	.8976	.9477	.9640	.9842
3	3	.0500	.0529	.0837	.1866	.3430	.5585	.8367	.9163	.9829
	10	.0500	.0641	.2227	.5379	.7397	.8718	.9639	.9826	.9966
	30	.0500	.0985	.4917	.7999	.9049	.9573	.9886	.9946	.9990
	100	.0500	.2236	.7791	.9333	.9705	.9872	.9966	.9984	.9997
5	3	.0500	.0540	.0997	.2684	.5149	.7808	.9704	.9923	.9997
	10	.0500	.0692	.3151	.7446	.9175	.9798	.9984	.9996	1.0000
	30	.0500	.1192	.6908	.9506	.9888	.9977	.9998	1.0000	1.0000
	100	.0500	.3147	.9397	.9945	.9989	.9998	1.0000	1.0000	1.0000
10	3	.0500	.0560	.1323	.4396	.7837	.9664	.9997	1.0000	1.0000
	10	.0500	.0783	.4945	.9439	.9957	.9998	1.0000	1.0000	1.0000
	30	.0500	.1594	.9119	.9986	1.0000	1.0000	1.0000	1.0000	1.0000
	100	.0500	.4892	.9978	1.0000	1.0000	1.0000	1.0000	1.0000	1.0000

If several small groups (counseling, social interaction, etc.) are involved in each treatment, and there are clear reasons to suspect that observations will be correlated within the groups but uncorrelated across groups, then consider using the *group mean* as the unit of analysis. Of course, this will reduce the effective sample size considerably; however, this will not cause as drastic a drop in power as some have feared. The reason is that the means are much more stable than individual observations and, hence, the within-group variability will be far less.

Table 6.2, from Barcikowski (1981), shows that if the effect size is medium or large, then the number of groups needed per treatment for power .80 doesn't have to be large. For example, at $\alpha = .10$, intraclass correlation $= .10$, and medium effect size, 10 groups (of 10 subjects each) are needed per treatment. For power .70 (which I consider adequate) at $\alpha = .15$, one probably could get by with about six groups of 10 per treatment. This is a rough estimate, because it involves double extrapolation.

Before we leave the topic of correlated observations, I wish to mention an interesting paper by Kenny and Judd (1986), who discussed how nonindependent observations can arise because of several factors, grouping being one of them. The following quote from their paper is important to keep in mind for applied researchers:

> Throughout this article we have treated nonindependence as a statistical nuisance, to be avoided because of the bias it introduces. … There are, however, many occasions when nonindependence is the substantive problem that we are trying to understand in psychological research. For instance, in developmental psychology, a frequently asked question concerns the development of social interaction. Developmental researchers study the content and rate of vocalization from infants for cues about the onset of interaction. Social interaction implies nonindependence between the vocalizations of interacting individuals. To study interaction developmentally, then, we should be interested

TABLE 6.2

Number of Groups per Treatment Necessary for Power > .80 in a Two-Treatment-Level Design

α level	Number per group	Intraclass Correlation for Effect Size[a]					
		.10			**.20**		
		.20	.50	.80	.20	.50	.80
	10	73	13	6	107	18	8
	15	62	11	5	97	17	8
	20	56	10	5	92	16	7
.05	25	53	10	5	89	16	7
	30	51	9	5	87	15	7
	35	49	9	5	86	15	7
	40	48	9	5	85	15	7
	10	57	10	5	83	14	7
	15	48	9	4	76	13	6
	20	44	8	4	72	13	6
.10	25	41	8	4	69	12	6
	30	39	7	4	68	12	6
	35	38	7	4	67	12	5
	40	37	7	4	66	12	5

[a] .20 = small effect size; .50 = medium effect size; .80 = large effect size.

> in nonindependence not solely as a statistical problem, but also a substantive focus in itself. … In social psychology, one of the fundamental questions concerns how individual behavior is modified by group contexts. (p. 431)

6.5 Normality Assumption

Recall that the second assumption for ANOVA is that the observations are normally distributed in each group. What are the consequences of violating this assumption? An excellent review regarding violations of assumptions in ANOVA was done by Glass, Peckham, and Sanders (1972), and provides the answer. They found that skewness has only a slight effect (generally only a few hundredths) on level of significance or power. The effects of kurtosis on level of significance, although greater, also tend to be slight.

The reader may be puzzled as to how this can be. The basic reason is the *Central Limit Theorem*, which states that the sum of independent observations having any distribution whatsoever approaches a normal distribution as the number of observations increases. To be somewhat more specific, Bock (1975) noted, "even for distributions which depart markedly from normality, sums of 50 or more observations approximate to normality. For moderately nonnormal distributions the approximation is good with as few as 10 to 20 observations" (p. 111). Because the sums of independent observations approach normality rapidly, so do the means, and the sampling distribution of F is based on means. Thus, the sampling distribution of F is only slightly affected, and therefore the critical values when sampling from normal and nonnormal distributions will not differ by much.

With respect to power, a platykurtic distribution (a flattened distribution relative to the normal distribution) does attenuate power.

6.6 Multivariate Normality

The multivariate normality assumption is a much more stringent assumption than the corresponding assumption of normality on a single variable in ANOVA. Although it is difficult to completely characterize multivariate normality, *normality on each of the variables separately is a necessary, but not sufficient, condition for multivariate normality to hold.* That is, each of the individual variables must be normally distributed for the variables to follow a multivariate normal distribution. Two other properties of a multivariate normal distribution are: (a) any linear combination of the variables are normally distributed, and (b) all subsets of the set of variables have multivariate normal distributions. This latter property implies, among other things, that all pairs of variables must be bivariate normal. Bivariate normality, for correlated variables, implies that the scatterplots for each pair of variables will be elliptical; the higher the correlation, the thinner the ellipse. Thus, as a partial check on multivariate normality, one could obtain the scatterplots for pairs of variables from SPSS or SAS and see if they are approximately elliptical.

6.6.1 Effect of Nonmultivariate Normality on Type I Error and Power

Results from various studies that considered up to 10 variables and small or moderate sample sizes (Everitt, 1979; Hopkins & Clay, 1963; Mardia, 1971; Olson, 1973) indicate that *deviation from multivariate normality has only a small effect on type I error.* In almost all cases in these studies, the actual α was within .02 of the level of significance for levels of .05 and .10.

Olson found, however, that platykurtosis does have an effect on power, and the severity of the effect increases as platykurtosis spreads from one to all groups. For example, in one specific instance, power was close to 1 under no violation. With kurtosis present in just one group, the power dropped to about .90. When kurtosis was present in all three groups, the power dropped substantially, to .55.

The reader should note that what has been found in MANOVA is consistent with what was found in univariate ANOVA, in which the F statistic was robust with respect to type I error against nonnormality, making it plausible that this robustness might extend to the multivariate case; this, indeed, is what has been found. Incidentally, there is a multivariate extension of the Central Limit Theorem, which also makes the multivariate results not entirely surprising. Second, Olson's result, that platykurtosis has a substantial effect on power, should not be surprising, given that platykurtosis had been shown in univariate ANOVA to have a substantial effect on power for small n's (Glass et al., 1972).

With respect to skewness, again the Glass et al. (1972) review indicates that distortions of power values are rarely greater than a few hundredths for univariate ANOVA, even with considerably skewed distributions. Thus, it could well be the case that multivariate skewness also has a negligible effect on power, although I have not located any studies bearing on this issue.

6.6.2 Assessing Multivariate Normality

Unfortunately, as was true in 1986, a statistical test for multivariate normality is still not available on SAS or SPSS. There are empirical and graphical techniques for checking multivariate normality (Gnanedesikan, 1977, pp. 168–175), but they tend to be difficult to implement unless some special-purpose software is used. I included a graphical test for multivariate normality in the first two editions of this text, but have decided not to do so in this edition. One of my reasons is that you can get a pretty good idea as to whether multivariate normality is roughly plausible by seeing whether the marginal distributions are normal and by checking bivariate normality.

6.7 Assessing Univariate Normality

There are three reasons that assessing univariate normality is of interest:

1. We may not have a large enough n to feel comfortable doing the graphical test for multivariate normality.

2. As Gnanadesikan (1977) has stated, "In practice, except for rare or pathological examples, the presence of joint (multivariate) normality is likely to be detected quite often by methods directed at studying the marginal (univariate) normality of the observations on each variable" (p. 168). Johnson and Wichern (1992) made essentially the same point: "Moreover, for most practical work, one-dimensional and two-dimensional investigations are ordinarily sufficient. Fortunately, pathological data sets that are normal in lower dimensional representations but nonnormal in higher dimensions are not frequently encountered in practice" (p. 153).

3. Because the Box test for the homogeneity of covariance matrices assumption is quite sensitive to nonnormality, we wish to detect nonnormality on the individual variables and transform to normality to bring the joint distribution much closer to multivariate normality so that the Box test is not unduly affected. With respect to transformations, Figure 6.1 should be quite helpful.

There are many tests, graphical and nongraphical, for assessing univariate normality. One of the most popular graphical tests is the normal probability plot, where the observations are arranged in increasing order of magnitude and then plotted against expected normal distribution values. The plot should resemble a straight line if normality is tenable. These plots are available on SAS and SPSS. One could also examine the histogram (or stem-and-leaf plot) of the variable in each group. This gives some indication of whether normality might be violated. However, with small or moderate sample sizes, it is difficult to tell whether the nonnormality is real or apparent, because of considerable sampling error. Therefore, I prefer a nongraphical test.

Among the nongraphical tests are the chi-square goodness of fit, Kolmogorov–Smirnov, the Shapiro–Wilk test, and the use of skewness and kurtosis coefficients. The chi-square test suffers from the defect of depending on the number of intervals used for the grouping, whereas the Kolmogorov–Smirnov test was shown not to be as powerful as the Shapiro–Wilk test or the combination of using the skewness and kurtosis coefficients in an extensive Monte Carlo study by Wilk, Shapiro, and Chen (1968). These investigators studied 44 different distributions, with sample sizes ranging from 10 to 50, and found that the combination of skewness and kurtosis coefficients and the Shapiro–Wilk test were the most powerful in detecting departures from normality. They also found that extreme nonnormality can be detected with sample sizes of less than 20 by using sensitive procedures (like the two just mentioned). This is important, because for many practical problems, the group sizes are quite small.

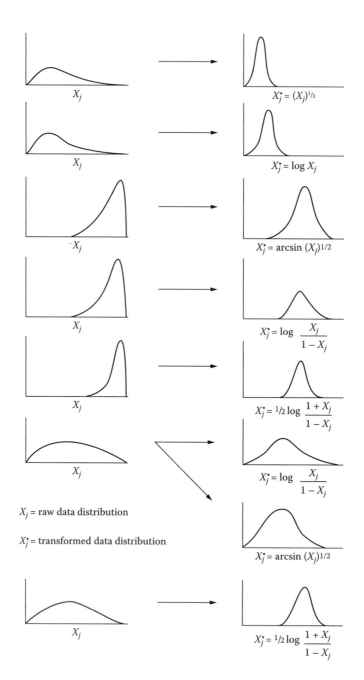

FIGURE 6.1
Distributional transformations (from Rummel, 1970).

On power considerations then, we use the Shapiro–Wilk statistic. This is easily obtained with the EXAMINE procedure in SPSS. This procedure also yields the skewness and kurtosis coefficients, along with their standard errors. All of this information is useful in determining whether there is a significant departure from normality, and whether skewness or kurtosis is primarily responsible.

Example 6.1

Our example comes from a study on the cost of transporting milk from farms to dairy plants. From a survey, cost data on $X1$ = fuel, $X2$ = repair, and $X3$ = capital (all measures on a per mile basis) were obtained for two types of trucks, gasoline and diesel. Thus, we have a two-group MANOVA, with three dependent variables. First, we ran this data through the SPSS DESCRIPTIVES program. The complete lines for doing so are presented in Table 6.3. This was done to obtain the z scores for the variables *within each group*. Converting to z scores makes it much easier to identify potential outliers. Any variables with z values substantially greater than 2 (in absolute value) need to be examined carefully. Three such observations are marked with an arrow in Table 6.3.

Next, the data was run through the SPSS EXAMINE procedure to obtain, among other things, the Shapiro–Wilk statistical test for normality for each variable in each group. The complete lines for doing this are presented in Table 6.4. These are the results for the three variables in each group:

	STATISTIC	**SIGNIFICANCE**
VARIABLE X1		
GROUP 1		
SHAPIRO-WILK	.8411	.0100
GROUP 2		
SHAPIRO-WILK	.9625	.5105
VARIABLE X2		
GROUP 1		
SHAPIRO-WILK	.9578	.3045
GROUP 2		
SHAPIRO-WILK	.9620	.4995
VARIABLE X3		
GROUP 1		
SHAPIRO-WILK	.9653	.4244
GROUP 2		
SHAPIRO-WILK	.9686	.6392

If we were testing for normality in each case at the .05 level, then only variable $X1$ deviates from normality in just Group 1. This would not have much of an effect on power, and hence we would not be concerned. We would have been concerned if we had found deviation from normality on two or more variables, and this deviation was due to platykurtosis, and would then have applied the last transformation in Figure 6.1: $[.05 \log (1 + X)]/(1 - X)$.

TABLE 6.3

Control Lines for SPSS Descriptives and Z Scores for Three Variables
in Two-Group MANOVA

TITLE 'SPLIT FILE FOR MILK DATA'.
DATA LIST FREE/GP X1 X2 X3.
BEGIN DATA.
   DATA LINES
END DATA.
SPLIT FILE BY GP.
DESCRIPTIVES VARIABLES = X1 X2 X3/SAVE/
LIST.

zx1	zx2	zx3	zx1	zx2	zx3
.87996	1.03078	.43881	−.76876	.29459	−1.32610
−1.04823	−1.29221	−1.51743	−1.28585	−1.10773	−.14901
−.47915	−1.61451	.04274	.08348	−1.46372	−1.01573
−1.66317	−.55687	−.48445	.02602	.77842	−1.78289
−.21233	−.73116	.28895	1.28523	−1.29655	1.62687
.42345	−.55687	.07753	−.24210	.38506	−1.04940
.26711	.68460	.27021	−1.74070	−.36822	.12183
.22959	1.47007	−.03754	.59578	−.15974	−.53259
→ 3.52108	1.66584	−1.68871	−.45755	−1.53846	−.65704
.09618	−.11997	.17120	−.19422	−1.12150	.39122
−.98153	−.55210	−.39079	−.16071	1.39600	2.49065
−.48332	−1.07017	−.12318	.72026	.19429	−.17097
−.41036	−.72638	.15514	−.48628	.48930	.36486
−.23109	−.46854	−.52995	−.75440	−.12237	−.10509
−.01013	1.46769	1.28446	−.86931	−.89335	−.26175
−.41245	−1.31847	−.93672	2.77425	.42047	→ .13501
−.42496	−.49241	.68234	.87826	−.99759	−.49746
−.69595	−1.29221	.70642	−.27083	1.18162	.65767
.02530	−.09132	.55923	.15529	1.35469	−1.09918
−.77307	1.41039	.64755	.36596	2.11585	1.50828
→ 2.90614	2.22689	1.95349	−1.42470	.48340	.18625
.15246	.03044	−.64502	.84953	.27886	.44392
.98211	1.25520	2.14082	.92135	−.30331	.72063
.51726	.63685	1.33531			
−.39577	−.70489	1.98293			
−.67510	−.86485	−1.42645			
−.52501	.83024	−.73868			
.10452	.12355	−1.07052			
−.56879	−1.42113	−.89925			
−.83353	−.03880	−.76812			
.30880	.74190	−1.25250			
−.83561	.41482	−.38008			
.75906	.78965	.92854			
−.63341	.25486	−.02684			
.05657	−.82188	.62881			
1.06340	−.2990	−1.37828			

TABLE 6.4

Control Lines for EXAMINE Procedure on Two-Group MANOVA

TITLE 'TWO GROUP MANOVA - 3 DEPENDENT VARIABLES'.
DATA LIST FREE/GP X1 X2 X3.
BEGIN DATA.

1 16.44 12.43 11.23	1 7.19 2.70 3.92	1 9.92 1.35 9.75
1 4.24 5.78 7.78	1 11.20 5.05 10.67	1 14.25 5.78 9.88
1 13.50 10.98 10.60	1 13.32 14.27 9.45	1 29.11 15.09 3.28
1 12.68 7.61 10.23	1 7.51 5.80 8.13	1 9.90 3.63 9.13
1 10.25 5.07 10.17	1 11.11 6.15 7.61	1 12.17 14.26 14.39
1 10.24 2.59 6.09	1 10.18 6.05 12.14	1 8.88 2.70 12.23
1 12.34 7.73 11.68	1 8.51 14.02 12.01	1 26.16 17.44 16.89
1 12.95 8.24 7.18	1 16.93 13.37 17.59	1 14.70 10.78 14.58
1 10.32 5.16 17.00	1 8.98 4.49 4.26	1 9.70 11.59 6.83
1 12.72 8.63 5.59	1 9.49 2.16 6.23	1 8.22 7.95 6.72
1 13.70 11.22 4.91	1 8.21 9.85 8.17	1 15.86 11.42 13.06
1 9.18 9.18 9.49	1 12.49 4.67 11.94	1 17.32 6.86 4.44
2 8.50 12.26 9.11	2 7.42 5.13 17.15	2 10.28 3.32 11.23
2 10.16 14.72 5.99	2 12.79 4.17 29.28	2 9.60 12.72 11.00
2 6.47 8.88 19	2 11.35 9.95 14.53	2 9.15 2.94 13.68
2 9.70 5.06 20.84	2 9.77 17.86 35.18	2 11.61 11.75 17.00
2 9.09 13.25 20.66	2 8.53 10.14 17.45	2 8.29 6.22 16.38
2 15.90 12.90 19.09	2 11.94 5.69 14.77	2 9.54 16.77 22.66
2 10.43 17.65 10.66	2 10.87 21.52 28.47	2 7.13 13.22 19.44
2 11.88 12.18 21.20	2 12.03 9.22 23.09	

END DATA.
① EXAMINE VARIABLES = X1 X2 X3 BY GP/
② PLOT = STEMLEAF NPPLOT/.

① The BY keyword will yield variety of descriptive statistics for each group: mean, median, skewness, kurtosis, etc.
② STEMLEAF will yield a stem-and-leaf plot for each variable in each group. NPPLOT yields normal probability plots, as well as the Shapiro–Wilks and Kolmogorov–Smirnov statistical tests for normality for each variable in each group.

6.8 Homogeneity of Variance Assumption

Recall that the third assumption for ANOVA is that of equal population variances. The Glass, Peckham, and Sanders (1972) review indicates that the F statistic is robust against heterogeneous variances when the group sizes are equal. I would extend this a bit further. As long as the group sizes are approximately equal (largest/smallest <1.5), F is robust. On the other hand, when the group sizes are sharply unequal *and* the population variances are different, then if the large sample variances are associated with the small group sizes, the F statistic is *liberal*. A statistic's being liberal means we are rejecting falsely too often; that is, actual α > level of significance. Thus, the experimenter may think he or she is rejecting falsely 5% of the time, but the true rejection rate (actual α) may be 11%. When the large variances are associated with the large group sizes, then the F statistic is *conservative*. This means actual α < level of significance. Many researchers would not consider this serious, but note that the smaller α will cause a decrease in power, and in many studies, one can ill afford to have the power further attenuated.

It is important to note that many of the frequently used tests for homogeneity of variance, such as Bartlett's, Cochran's, and Hartley's $F_{\max}$, are quite sensitive to non-normality. That is, with these tests, one may reject and erroneously conclude that the population variances are different when, in fact, the rejection was due to nonnormality in the underlying populations. Fortunately, Leven has a test that is more robust against nonnormality. This test is available in the EXAMINE procedure in SPSS. The test statistic is formed by deviating the scores for the subjects in each group from the group mean, and then taking the absolute values. Thus, $z_{ij} = |x_{ij} - \bar{x}_j|$, where $\bar{x}_j$ represents the mean for the jth group. An ANOVA is then done on the $\bar{z}_{ij}$'s. Although the Levene test is somewhat more robust, an extensive Monte Carlo study by Conover, Johnson, and Johnson (1981) showed that if considerable skewness is present, a modification of the Levene test is necessary for it to remain robust. The mean for each group is replaced by the median, and an ANOVA is done on the deviation scores from the group medians. This modification produces a more robust test with good power. It is available on SAS and SPSS.

6.9 Homogeneity of the Covariance Matrices*

The assumption of equal (homogeneous) covariance matrices is a very restrictive one. Recall from the matrix algebra chapter (Chapter 2) that two matrices are equal only if all corresponding elements are equal. Let us consider a two-group problem with five dependent variables. All corresponding elements in the two matrices being equal implies, first, that the corresponding diagonal elements are equal. This means that the five population variances in Group 1 are equal to their counterparts in Group 2. But all nondiagonal elements must also be equal for the matrices to be equal, and this implies that all covariances are equal. Because for five variables there are 10 covariances, this means that the 10 covariances in Group 1 are equal to their counterpart covariances in Group 2. Thus, for only five variables, the equal covariance matrices assumption requires that 15 elements of Group 1 be equal to their counterparts in Group 2.

For eight variables, the assumption implies that the eight population variances in Group 1 are equal to their counterparts in Group 2 *and* that the 28 corresponding covariances for the two groups are equal. The restrictiveness of the assumption becomes more strikingly apparent when we realize that the corresponding assumption for the univariate t test is that the variances on only *one* variable be equal.

Hence, it is very unlikely that the equal covariance matrices assumption would ever literally be satisfied in practice. The relevant question is: Will the very plausible violations of this assumption that occur in practice have much of an effect on power?

6.9.1 Effect of Heterogeneous Covariance Matrices on Type I Error and Power

Three major Monte Carlo studies have examined the effect of unequal covariance matrices on error rates: Holloway and Dunn (1967) and Hakstian, Roed, and Linn (1979) for the two-group case, and Olson (1974) for the k-group case. Holloway and Dunn considered

---

* Appendix 6.2 discusses multivariate test statistics for unequal covariance matrices.

TABLE 6.5

Effect of Heterogeneous Covariance Matrices
on Type I Error for Hotelling's T^2 ①

Number of variables	Number of Observations per Group		Degree of Heterogeneity	
	N_1	N_2 ②	$D = 3$ ③ (Moderate)	$D = 10$ (Very large)
3	15	35	.015	0
3	20	30	.03	.02
3	25	25	.055	.07
3	30	20	.09	.15
3	35	15	.175	.28
7	15	35	.01	0
7	20	30	.03	.02
7	25	25	.06	.08
7	30	20	.13	.27
7	35	15	.24	.40
10	15	35	.01	0
10	20	30	.03	.03
10	25	25	.08	.12
10	30	20	.17	.33
10	35	15	.31	.40

① Nominal $\alpha = .05$.

② Group 2 is more variable.

③ $D = 3$ means that the population variances for all variables in Group 2 are 3 times as large as the population variances for those variables in Group 1.

Source: Data from Holloway & Dunn, 1967.

both equal and unequal group sizes and modeled moderate to extreme heterogeneity. A representative sampling of their results, presented in Table 6.5, shows that *equal n's keep the actual α very close to the level of significance (within a few percentage points) for all but the extreme cases.* Sharply unequal group sizes for moderate inequality, with the larger variability in the small group, produce a liberal test. In fact, the test can become very liberal (cf. three variables, $N_1 = 35$, $N_2 = 15$, actual $\alpha = .175$). Larger variability in the group with the large size produces a conservative test.

Hakstian et al. modeled heterogeneity that was milder and, I believe, somewhat more representative of what is encountered in practice, than that considered in the Holloway and Dunn study. They also considered more disparate group sizes (up to a ratio of 5 to 1) for the 2-, 6-, and 10-variable cases. The following three heterogeneity conditions were examined:

1. The population variances for the variables in Population 2 are only 1.44 times as great as those for the variables in Population 1.

2. The Population 2 variances and covariances are 2.25 times as great as those for all variables in Population 1.

3. The Population 2 variances and covariances are 2.25 times as great as those for Population 1 for only *half* the variables.

TABLE 6.6

Effect of Heterogeneous Covariance Matrices with Six Variables on Type I Error for Hotelling's T^2

$N_1{:}N_2$①	Nominal α	Heterog. 1		Heterog. 2		Heterog. 3	
		② POS.	NEG.	POS.	NEG.	POS.	NEG. ③
18:18	.01		.006		.011		.012
	.05		.048		.057		.064
	.10		.099		.109		.114
24:12	.01	.007	.020	.005	.043	.006	.018
	.05	.035	.088	.021	.127	.028	.076
	.10	.068	.155	.051	.214	.072	.158
30:6	.01	.004	.036	.000	.103	.003	.046
	.05	.018	.117	.004	.249	.022	.145
	.10	.045	.202	.012	.358	.046	.231

① Ratio of the group sizes.
② Condition in which group with larger generalized variance has larger group size.
③ Condition in which group with larger generalized variance has smaller group size.
Source: Data from Hakstian, Roed, & Lind, 1979.

The results in Table 6.6 for the six-variable case are representative of what Hakstian et al. found. Their results are consistent with the Holloway and Dunn findings, but they extend them in two ways. First, even for milder heterogeneity, sharply unequal group sizes can produce sizable distortions in the type I error rate (cf. 24:12, Heterogeneity 2 (negative): actual α = .127 vs. level of significance = .05). Second, *severely unequal group sizes can produce sizable distortions in type I error rates, even for very mild heterogeneity* (cf. 30:6, Heterogeneity 1 (negative): actual α = .117 vs. level of significance = .05).

Olson (1974) considered only equal *n*'s and warned, on the basis of the Holloway and Dunn results and some preliminary findings of his own, that researchers would be well advised to strain to attain equal group sizes in the *k*-group case. The results of Olson's study should be interpreted with care, because he modeled primarily *extreme* heterogeneity (i.e., cases where the population variances of all variables in one group were 36 times as great as the variances of those variables in all the other groups).

6.9.2 Testing Homogeneity of Covariance Matrices: The Box Test

Box (1949) developed a test that is a generalization of the Bartlett univariate homogeneity of variance test, for determining whether the covariance matrices are equal. The test uses the *generalized variances*; that is, the determinants of the within-covariance matrices. It is very sensitive to nonnormality. Thus, one may reject with the Box test because of a lack of multivariate normality, not because the covariance matrices are unequal. Therefore, before employing the Box test, it is important to see whether the multivariate normality assumption is reasonable. As suggested earlier in this chapter, a check of marginal normality for the individual variables is probably sufficient (using the Shapiro–Wilk test). Where there is a departure from normality, find transformations (see Figure 6.1).

Box has given an χ^2 approximation and an *F* approximation for his test statistic, both of which appear on the SPSS MANOVA output, as an upcoming example in this section shows. To decide to which of these one should pay more attention, the following rule is helpful: When all group sizes are 20 and the number of dependent variables is 6, the χ^2 approximation is fine. Otherwise, the *F* approximation is more accurate and should be used.

Example 6.2

To illustrate the use of SPSS MANOVA for assessing homogeneity of the covariance matrices, I consider, again, the data from Example 1. Recall that this involved two types of trucks (gasoline and diesel), with measurements on three variables: $X1$ = fuel, $X2$ = repair, and $X3$ = capital. The raw data were provided in Table 6.4. Recall that there were 36 gasoline trucks and 23 diesel trucks, so we have sharply unequal group sizes. Thus, a significant Box test here will produce biased multivariate statistics that we need to worry about.

The complete control lines for running the MANOVA, along with getting the Box test and some selected printout, are presented in Table 6.7. It is in the PRINT subcommand that we obtain the multivariate (Box test) and univariate tests of homogeneity of variance. Note, in Table 6.7 (center), that the Box test is significant well beyond the .01 level ($F = 5.088$, $p = .000$, approximately). We wish to determine whether the multivariate test statistics will be liberal or conservative. To do this, we examine the determinants of the covariance matrices (they are called variance–covariance matrices on the printout). Remember that the determinant of the covariance matrix is the generalized variance; that is, it is the multivariate measure of within-group variability for a set of variables. In this case, the larger generalized variance (the determinant of the covariance matrix) is in Group 2, which has the smaller group size. The effect of this is to produce positively biased (liberal) multivariate test statistics. Also, although this is not presented in Table 6.7, the group effect is quite significant ($F = 16.375$, $p = .000$, approximately). It is possible, however, that this significant group effect may be mainly due to the positive bias present.

To see whether this is the case, we look for variance-stabilizing transformations that, hopefully, will make the Box test not significant, and then check to see whether the group effect is still significant. Note, in Table 6.7, that the Cochran tests indicate there are significant variance differences for $X1$ and $X3$.

The EXAMINE procedure was also run, and indicated that the following new variables will have approximately equal variances: $NEWX1 = X1** (-1.678)$ and $NEWX3 = X3** (.395)$. When these new variables, along with $X2$, were run in a MANOVA (see Table 6.8), the Box test was *not* significant at the .05 level ($F = 1.79$, $p = .097$), but the group effect was still significant well beyond the .01 level ($F = 13.785$, $p = .000$ approximately).

We now consider two variations of this result. In the first, a violation would not be of concern. If the Box test had been significant and the larger generalized variance was with the larger group size, then the multivariate statistics would be conservative. In that case, we would not be concerned, for we would have found significance at an even more stringent level had the assumption been satisfied.

A second variation on the example results that would have been of concern is if the large generalized variance was with the large group size and the group effect was *not* significant. Then, it wouldn't be clear whether the reason we did not find significance was because of the conservativeness of the test statistic. In this case, we could simply test at a more liberal level, once again realizing that the effective alpha level will probably be around .05. Or, we could again seek variance stabilizing transformations.

With respect to transformations, there are two possible approaches. If there is a known relationship between the means and variances, then the following two transformations are helpful. The square root transformation, where the original scores are replaced by $\sqrt{y_{ij}}$ will stabilize the variances if the means and variances are proportional for each group. This can happen when the data are in the form of frequency counts. If the scores are proportions, then the means and variances are related as follows: $\sigma_i^2 = \mu_i(1 - \mu_i)$. This is true because, with proportions, we have a binomial variable, and for a binominal variable the variance is this function of its mean. The arcsine transformation, where the original scores are replaced by arcsin $\sqrt{y_{ij}}$, will also stabilize the variances in this case.

TABLE 6.7

SPSS MANOVA and EXAMINE Control Lines for Milk Data and Selected Printout

```
TITLE 'MILK DATA'.
DATA LIST FREE/GP X1 X2 X3.
BEGIN DATA.
      DATA LINES
END DATA.
MANOVA X1 X2 X3 BY GP(1,2)/
  PRINT = HOMOGENEITY(COCHRAN,BOXM)/.
EXAMINE VARIABLES = X1 X2 X3 BY GP(1,3)/
  PLOT = SPREADLEVEL/.
```

generalized variance

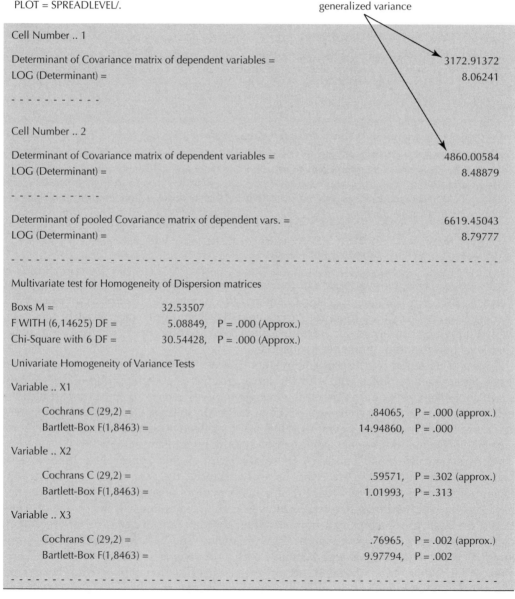

Cell Number .. 1	
Determinant of Covariance matrix of dependent variables =	3172.91372
LOG (Determinant) =	8.06241

- - - - - - - - - - -

Cell Number .. 2	
Determinant of Covariance matrix of dependent variables =	4860.00584
LOG (Determinant) =	8.48879

- - - - - - - - - -

| Determinant of pooled Covariance matrix of dependent vars. = | 6619.45043 |
| LOG (Determinant) = | 8.79777 |

- -

Multivariate test for Homogeneity of Dispersion matrices

Boxs M =   32.53507
F WITH (6,14625) DF =   5.08849,   P = .000 (Approx.)
Chi-Square with 6 DF =   30.54428,   P = .000 (Approx.)

Univariate Homogeneity of Variance Tests

Variable .. X1

        Cochrans C (29,2) =   .84065,   P = .000 (approx.)
        Bartlett-Box F(1,8463) =   14.94860,   P = .000

Variable .. X2

        Cochrans C (29,2) =   .59571,   P = .302 (approx.)
        Bartlett-Box F(1,8463) =   1.01993,   P = .313

Variable .. X3

        Cochrans C (29,2) =   .76965,   P = .002 (approx.)
        Bartlett-Box F(1,8463) =   9.97794,   P = .002

- -

TABLE 6.8

SPSS MANOVA and EXAMINE Control Lines for Milk Data Using Two Transformed Variables and Selected Printout

TITLE 'MILK DATA – X1 AND X3 TRANSFORMED'.
DATA LIST FREE/GP X1 X2 X3.
BEGIN DATA.
   DATA LINES
END DATA.
LIST.
COMPUTE NEWX1 = X1**(−1.678).
COMPUTE NEWX3 = X3**.395.
MANOVA NEWX1 X2 NEWX3 BY GP(1,2)/
  PRINT = CELLINFO(MEANS) HOMOGENEITY(BOXM,COCHRAN)/.
EXAMINE VARIABLES = NEWX1 X2 NEWX3 BY GP/
  PLOT = SPREADLEVEL/.

Multivariate test for Homogeneity of Dispersion matrices

Boxs M =	11.44292
F WITH (6,14625) DF =	1.78967, P = .097 (Approx.)
Chi-Square with 6 DF =	10.74274, P = .097 (Approx.)

EFFECT .. GP
Multivariate Tests of Significance (S = 1, M = 1/2, N = 26 1/2)

Test Name	Value	Exact F	Hypoth. DF	Error DF	Sig. of F
Pillais	.42920	13.78512	3.00	55.00	.000
Hotellings	.75192	13.78512	3.00	55.00	.000
Wilks	.57080	13.78512	3.00	55.00	.000
Roys	.42920				

Note .. F statistics are exact.

Test of Homogeneity of Variance

		Levene Statistic	df1	df2	Sig.
NEWX1	Based on Mean	1.008	1	57	.320
	Based on Median	.918	1	57	.342
	Based on Median and with adjusted df	.918	1	43.663	.343
	Based on trimmed mean	.953	1	57	.333
X2	Based on Mean	.960	1	57	.331
	Based on Median	.816	1	57	.370
	Based on Median and with adjusted df	.816	1	52.943	.370
	Based on trimmed mean	1.006	1	57	.320
NEWX3	Based on Mean	.451	1	57	.505
	Based on Median	.502	1	57	.482
	Based on Median and with adjusted df	.502	1	53.408	.482
	Based on trimmed mean	.455	1	57	.503

If the relationship between the means and the variances is not known, then one can let the data decide on an appropriate transformation (as in the previous example).

We now consider an example that illustrates the first approach, that of using a *known* relationship between the means and variances to stabilize the variances.

Example 6.3

	Group 1				Group 2				Group 3			
	Y1	Y2	Y1	Y2	Y1	Y2	Y1	Y2	Y1	Y2	Y1	Y2
	.30	5	3.5	4.0	5	4	9	5	14	5	18	8
	1.1	4	4.3	7.0	5	4	11	6	9	10	21	2
	5.1	8	1.9	7.0	12	6	5	3	20	2	12	2
	1.9	6	2.7	4.0	8	3	10	4	16	6	15	4
	4.3	4	5.9	7.0	13	4	7	2	23	9	12	5
MEANS	Y1 = 3.1		Y2 = 5.6		Y1 = 8.5		Y2 = 4		Y1 = 16		Y2 = 5.3	
VARIANCES	3.31		2.49		8.94		1.78		20		8.68	

Notice that for Y1, as the means increase (from Group 1 to Group 3) the variances also increase. Also, the ratio of variance to mean is approximately the same for the three groups: 3.31/3.1 = 1.068, 8.94/8.5 = 1.052, and 20/16 = 1.25. Further, the variances for Y2 differ by a fair amount. Thus, it is likely here that the homogeneity of covariance matrices assumption is not tenable. Indeed, when the MANOVA was run on SPSS, the Box test was significant at the .05 level ($F = 2.947$, $p = .007$), and the Cochran univariate tests for both variables were also significant at the .05 level (Y1: Cochran = .62; Y2: Cochran = .67).

Because the means and variances for Y1 are approximately proportional, as mentioned earlier, a square-root transformation will stabilize the variances. The control lines for running SPSS MANOVA, with the square-root transformation on Y1, are given in Table 6.9, along with selected printout. A few comments on the control lines: It is in the COMPUTE command that we do the transformation, calling the transformed variable *RTY1*. We then use the transformed variable *RTY1*, along with Y2, in the MANOVA command for the analysis. Note the stabilizing effect of the square root transformation on Y1; the standard deviations are now approximately equal (.587, .522, and .567). Also, Box's test is no longer significant ($F = 1.86$, $p = .084$).

6.10 Summary

We have considered each of the assumptions in MANOVA in some detail individually. I now tie together these pieces of information into an overall strategy for assessing assumptions in a practical problem.

1. Check to determine whether it is reasonable to assume the subjects are responding independently; a violation of this assumption is very serious. Logically, from the context in which the subjects are receiving treatments, one should be able to make a judgment. Empirically, the intraclass correlation can be used (for a single variable) to assess whether this assumption is tenable.

   At least four types of analyses are appropriate for correlated observations. If several groups are involved for each treatment condition, then consider using the group mean as the unit of analysis. Another method, which is probably preferable to using the group mean, is to do a hierarchical linear model analysis. The power of these models is that they are statistically correct for situations in which individual scores are not independent observations, and one doesn't waste the

TABLE 6.9

SPSS Control Lines for Three-Group MANOVA with Unequal Variances
(Illustrating Square-Root Transformation)

```
TITLE 'THREE GROUP MANOVA – TRANSFORMING Y1'.
DATA LIST FREE/GPID Y1 Y2.
BEGIN DATA.
     DATA LINES
END DATA.
COMPUTE RTY1 = SQRT(Y1).
MANOVA RTY1 Y2 BY GPID(1,3)/
   PRINT = CELLINFO(MEANS) HOMOGENEITY(COCHRAN,BOXM)/.
```

Cell Means and Standard Deviations
Variable .. RTY1

FACTOR	CODE	Mean	Std. Dev.
GPID	1	1.670	.587
GPID	2	2.873	.522
GPID	3	3.964	.568
For entire sample		2.836	1.095

Variable .. Y2

FACTOR	CODE	Mean	Std. Dev.
GPID	1	5.600	1.578
GPID	2	4.100	1.287
GPID	3	5.300	2.946
For entire sample		5.000	2.101

Univariate Homogeneity of Variance Tests
Variable .. RTY1

Cochrans C (9, 3) =	.36712,	P = 1.000
Bartlett-Box F (2, 1640) =	.06176,	P = .940

Variable .. Y2

Cochrans C (9, 3) =	.67678,	P = .014
Bartlett-Box F (2, 1640) =	3.35877,	P = .035

Multivariate test for Homogeneity of Dispersion matrices

Boxs M =	11.65338	
F WITH (6, 18168) DF =	1.73378,	P = .109 (Approx.)
Chi-Square with 6 DF =	10.40652,	P = .109 (Approx.)

information about individuals (which occurs when group or class is the unit of analysis). An in-depth explanation of these models can be found in *Hierarchical Linear Models* (Bryk and Raudenbush, 1992).

Two other methods that are appropriate were developed and validated by Myers, Dicecco, and Lorch (1981). They are presented in the textbook, *Research Design and Statistical Analysis* by Myers and Well (1991). They were shown to have approximately correct type I error rates and similar power (see Exercise 9).

2. Check to see whether multivariate normality is reasonable. In this regard, checking the marginal (univariate) normality for each variable should be adequate. The EXAMINE procedure from SPSS is very helpful. If departure from normality is found, consider transforming the variable(s). Figure 6.1 can be helpful. This comment from Johnson and Wichern (1992) should be kept in mind: "Deviations from normality are often due to one or more unusual observations (outliers)" (p. 163). Once again, we see the importance of screening the data initially and converting to z scores.

3. Apply Box's test to check the assumption of homogeneity of the covariance matrices. If normality has been achieved in Step 2 on all or most of the variables, then Box's test should be a fairly clean test of variance differences. If the Box test is not significant, then all is fine.

4. If the Box test is significant with equal n's, then, although the type I error rate will be only slightly affected, power will be attenuated to some extent. Hence, look for transformations on the variables that are causing the covariance matrices to differ.

5. If the Box test is significant with sharply unequal n's for two groups, compare the determinants of S_1 and S_2 (generalized variances for the two groups). If the larger generalized variance is with the smaller group size, T^2 will be liberal. If the larger generalized variance is with the larger group size, T^2 will be conservative.

6. For the k-group case, if the Box test is significant, examine the $|S_i|$ for the groups. If the generalized variances are largest for the groups with the smaller sample sizes, then the multivariate statistics will be liberal. If the generalized variances are largest for the groups with the larger group sizes, then the statistics will be conservative.

It is possible for the k-group case that neither of these two conditions hold. For example, for three groups, it could happen that the two groups with the smallest and the largest sample sizes have large generalized variances, and the remaining group has a variance somewhat smaller. In this case, however, the effect of heterogeneity should not be serious, because the coexisting liberal and conservative tendencies should cancel each other out somewhat.

Finally, because there are several test statistics in the k-group MANOVA case, their relative robustness in the presence of violations of assumptions could be a criterion for preferring one over the others. In this regard, Olson (1976) argued in favor of the Pillai–Bartlett trace, because of its presumed greater robustness against heterogeneous covariances matrices. For variance differences *likely to occur in practice*, however, Stevens (1979) found that the Pillai–Bartlett trace, Wilks' λ, and the Hotelling–Lawley trace are essentially equally robust.

Appendix 6.1: Analyzing Correlated Observations[*]

Much has been written about correlated observations, and that INDEPENDENCE of observations is an assumption for ANOVA and regression analysis. What is not apparent from reading most statistics books is how critical an assumption it is. Hays (1963) indicated over 40 years ago that violation of the independence assumption is very serious. Glass and Stanley (1970) in their textbook talked about the critical importance of this assumption. Barcikowski (1981) showed that even a SMALL violation of the independence assumption

---

[*] The authoritative book on ANOVA (Scheffe, 1959) states that one of the assumptions in ANOVA is statistical independence of the errors. But this is equivalent to the independence of the observations (Maxwell & Delaney, 2004, p. 110).

can cause the actual alpha level to be several times greater than the nominal level. Kreft and de Leeuw (1998) note on p. 9 , "This means that if intra-class correlation is present, as it may be when we are dealing with clustered data, the assumption of independent observations in the traditional linear model is violated." The Scariano and Davenport (1987) table (Table 6.1) shows the dramatic effect dependence can have on type I error rate. The problem is, as Burstein (1980) pointed out more than 25 years ago, is that, "Most of what goes on in education occurs within some group context." This gives rise to nested data, and hence correlated observations. More generally, nested data occurs quite frequently in social science research. Social psychology often is focused on groups. In clinical psychology, if we are dealing with different types of psychotherapy, groups are involved.

The hierarchical linear model (Chapter 15) is one way of dealing with correlated observations, and HLM is very big in the United States. The hierarchical linear model has been used extensively, certainly within the last 10 years. Raudenbush's dissertation (1984) and the subsequent book by him and Bryk (2002) promoted the use of the hierarchical linear model. As a matter of fact, Raudenbush and Bryk developed the HLM program.

Let us first turn to a simpler analysis, which makes practical sense if the effect anticipated (from previous research) or desired is at least MODERATE. With correlated data, we first compute the mean for each cluster, and then do the analysis on the means. Table 6.2, from Barcikowski (1981), shows that if the effect is moderate, then about 10 groups per treatment are only necessary at the .10 level for power = .80 when there are 10 subjects per group. This implies that about eight or nine groups per treatment would be needed for power = .70. For a large effect size, only five groups per treatment are needed for power = .80. For a SMALL effect size, the number of groups per treatment for adequate power is much too large, and impractical.

Now we consider a very important recent paper by Hedges (2007). The title of the paper is quite revealing, "Correcting a significance test for clustering." He develops a correction for the t test in the context of randomly assigning intact groups to treatments. But the results, in my opinion, have broader implications. Below we present modified information from his study, involving some results in the paper and some results not in the paper, but which I received from Dr. Hedges: (nominal alpha = .05)

M (clusters)	n (S's per cluster)	Intraclass Correlation	Actual Rejection Rate
2	100	.05	.511
2	100	.10	.626
2	100	.20	.732
2	100	.30	.784
2	30	.05	.214
2	30	.10	.330
2	30	.20	.470
2	30	.30	.553
5	10	.05	.104
5	10	.10	.157
5	10	.20	.246
5	10	.30	.316
10	5	.05	.074
10	5	.10	.098
10	5	.20	.145
10	5	.30	.189

In the above information, we have m clusters assigned to each treatment and an assumed alpha level of .05. Note that it is the n (number of subjects in each cluster), not m, that causes the alpha rate to skyrocket. Compare the actual alpha levels for intraclass correlation fixed at .10 as n varies from 100 to 5 (.626, .330, .157 and .098).

For equal cluster size (n), Hedges derives the following relationship between the t (uncorrected for the cluster effect) and t, corrected for the cluster effect:

$$t_A = ct, \text{ with h degrees of freedom.}$$

The correction factor is $c = \sqrt{[(N-2)-2(n-1)p]/(N-2)[1+(n-1)p]}$, where p represents the intraclass correlation, and $h = (N-2)/[1+(n-1)p]$ (good approximation).

To see the difference the correction factor and the reduced df can make, we consider an example. Suppose we have three groups of 10 subjects in each of two treatment groups and that p = .10. A non-corrected t = 2.72 with df = 58, and this is significant at the .01 level for a two-tailed test. The corrected t = 1.94 with h = 30.5 df, and this is NOT even significant at the .05 level for a two tailed test.

We now consider two practical situations where the results from the Hedges study can be useful. First, teaching methods is a big area of concern in education. If we are considering two teaching methods, then we will have about 30 students in each class. Obviously, just two classes per method will yield inadequate power, but the modified information from the Hedges study shows that with just two classes per method and n = 30 the actual type I error rate is .33 for intraclass correlation = .10. So, for more than two classes per method, the situation will just get worse in terms of type I error.

Now, suppose we wish to compare two types of counseling or psychotherapy. If we assign five groups of 10 subjects each to each of the two types and intraclass correlation = .10 (and it could be larger) , then actual type I error is .157, not .05 as we thought. The modified information also covers the situation where the group size is smaller and more groups are assigned to each type. Now, consider the case were 10 groups of size n = 5 are assigned to each type. If intraclass correlation = .10, then actual type I error = .098. If intraclass correlation = .20, then actual type I error = .145, almost three times what we want it to be.

Hedges (2007) has compared the power of clustered means analysis vs power of his adjusted *t* test when the effect is quite LARGE (one standard deviation). Here are some results from his comparison:

Power	n	m	Adjusted t	Cluster Means
p = .10	10	2	.607	.265
	25	2	.765	.336
	10	3	.788	.566
	25	3	.909	.703
	10	4	.893	.771
	25	4	.968	.889
p = .20	10	2	.449	.201
	25	2	.533	.230
	10	3	.620	.424
	25	3	.710	.490
	10	4	.748	.609
	25	4	.829	.689

These results show the power of cluster means analysis does not fare well when there are three or fewer means per treatment group, and this is for a large effect size (which is NOT realistic of what one will generally encounter in practice). For a medium effect size (.5 sd) Barcikowski (1981) shows that for power > .80 you will need nine groups per treatment if group size is 30 for intraclass correlation = .10 at the .05 level.

So, the bottom line is that correlated observations occur very frequently in social science research, and researchers must take this into account in their analysis. The intraclass correlation is an index of how much the observations correlate, and an estimate of it, or at least an upper bound for it, needs to be obtained, so that the type I error rate is under control. If one is going to consider a cluster means analysis, then a table from Barcikowski (1981) indicates that one should have at least seven groups per treatment (with 30 observations per group) for power = .80 at the .10 level. One could probably get by with six or five groups for power = .70. The same table from Barcikowski shows that if group size is 10 then at least 10 groups per counseling method are needed for power = .80 at the .10 level. One could probably get by with eight groups per method for power = .70. Both of these situations assume we wish to detect at least a moderate effect size. Hedges adjusted t has some potential advantages. For p = .10 his power analysis (presumably at the .05 level) shows that probably four groups of 30 in each treatment will yield adequate power (> .70). The reason I say probably is that power for a very large effect size is .968, and n = 25. The question is, for a medium effect size at the .10 level , will power be adequate? For p = .20, I believe we would need five groups per treatment.

Barcikowski (1981) has indicated that intraclass correlations for teaching various subjects are generally in the .10 to .15 range. It seems to me, that for counseling or psychotherapy methods, an intraclass correlation of .20 is prudent. Bosker and Snidjers (1999) indicated that in the social sciences intraclass correlationa are generally in the 0 to .4 range, and often narrower bounds can be found.

In finishing this appendix, I think it is appropriate to quote from Hedges conclusion:

> Cluster randomized trials are increasingly important in education and the social and policy sciences. However, these trials are often improperly analyzed by ignoring the effects of clustering on significance tests. ... This article considered only t tests under a sampling model with one level of clustering. The generalization of the methods used in this article to more designs with additional levels of clustering and more complex analyses would be desirable.

Appendix 6.2: Multivariate Test Statistics for Unequal Covariance Matrices

The two-group test statistic that should be used when the population covariance matrices are not equal, especially with sharply unequal group sizes, is

$$T_*^2 = (\bar{\mathbf{y}}_1 - \bar{\mathbf{y}}_2)' \left(\frac{\mathbf{S}_1}{n_1} + \frac{\mathbf{S}_2}{n_2} \right)^{-1} (\bar{\mathbf{y}}_1 - \bar{\mathbf{y}}_2)$$

This statistic must be transformed, and various critical values have been proposed (see Coombs, Algina, & Olson, 1996). An important Monte Carlo study comparing seven solutions to the multivariate Behrens–Fisher problem is by Christensen and Rencher (1995).

They considered 2, 5 and 10 variables (p), and the data were generated such that the population covariance matrix for group 2 was d times covariance matrix for group 1 (d was set at 3 and 9). The sample sizes for different p values are given here:

	$p = 2$	$p = 5$	$p = 10$
$n_1 > n_2$	10:5	20:10	30:20
$n_1 = n_2$	10:10	20:20	30:30
$n_1 < n_2$	10:20	20:40	30:60

Here are two important tables from their study:

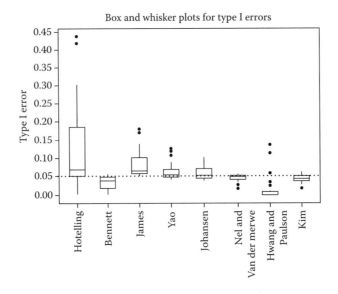

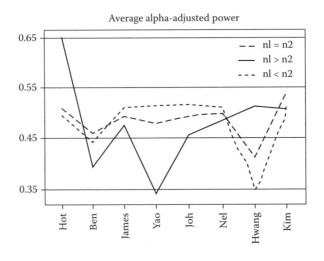

They recommended the Kim and Nel and van der Merwe procedures because they are conservative and have good power relative to the other procedures. To this writer, the Yao procedure is also fairly good, although slightly liberal. Importantly, however, all the highest error rates for the Yao procedure (including the three outliers) occurred when the variables were uncorrelated. This implies that the adjusted power of the Yao (which is somewhat low for $n_1 > n_2$) would be better for correlated variables. Finally, for test statistics for the k-group MANOVA case see Coombs, Algina, and Olson (1996) for appropriate references.

The approximate test by Nel and van der Merwe (1986) uses T_*^2 above, which is approximately distributed as $T_{p,v}^2$, with

$$v = \frac{\text{tr}(S_e)^2 + [\text{tr}(S_e)]^2}{(n_1 - 1)^{-1}\left\{\text{tr}\left(V_1^2\right) + [\text{tr}(V_1)]^2\right\} + (n_2 - 1)^{-1}\left\{\text{tr}\left(V_2^2\right) + [\text{tr}(V_2)]^2\right\}}$$

SPSS Matrix Procedure Program for Calculating Hotelling's T^2 and v (knu) for the Nel and van der Merwe Modification and Selected Printout

```
MATRIX.
COMPUTE S1 = {23.013, 12.366, 2.907; 12.366, 17.544, 4.773; 2.907, 4.773, 13.963}.
COMPUTE S2 = {4.362, .760, 2.362; .760, 25.851, 7.686; 2.362, 7.686, 46.654}.
COMPUTE V1 = S1/36.
COMPUTE V2 = S2/23.
COMPUTE TRACEV1 = TRACE(V1).
COMPUTE SQTRV1 = TRACEV1*TRACEV1.
COMPUTE TRACEV2 = TRACE(V2).
COMPUTE SQTRV2 = TRACEV2*TRACEV2.
COMPUTE V1SQ = V1*V1.
COMPUTE V2SQ = V2*V2.
COMPUTE TRV1SQ = TRACE(V1SQ).
COMPUTE TRV2SQ = TRACE(V2SQ).
COMPUTE SE = V1 + V2.
COMPUTE SESQ = SE*SE.
COMPUTE TRACESE = TRACE(SE).
COMPUTE SQTRSE = TRACESE*TRACESE.
COMPUTE TRSESQ = TRACE(SESQ).
COMPUTE SEINV = INV(SE).
COMPUTE DIFFM = {2.113, -2.649, -8.578}.
COMPUTE TDIFFM = T(DIFFM).
COMPUTE HOTL = DIFFM*SEINV*TDIFFM.
COMPUTE KNU = (TRSESQ + SQTRSE)/(1/36*(TRV1SQ + SQTRV1) + 1/23*(TRV2SQ + SQTRV2)).
PRINT S1.
PRINT S2.
PRINT HOTL.
PRINT KNU.
END MATRIX.
```

Matrix

Run MATRIX procedure

S1

23.01300000	12.36600000	2.90700000
12.36600000	17.54400000	4.77300000
2.90700000	4.77300000	13.96300000

S2

4.36200000	.76000000	2.36200000
.76000000	25.85100000	7.68600000
2.36200000	7.68600000	46.65400000

HOTL

43.17860426

KNU

40.57627238

END MATRIX

Exercises

1. Describe a situation or class of situations where dependence of the observations would be present.

2. An investigator has a treatment vs. control group design with 30 subjects per group. The intraclass correlation is calculated and found to be .15. If testing for significance at .05, estimate what the actual type I error rate is.

3. Consider a four-group, three-dependent-variable study. What does the homogeneity of covariance matrices assumption imply in this case?

4. Consider the following three MANOVA situations. Indicate whether you would be concerned in each case.

(a)

Gp 1	Gp 2	Gp 3
$n_1 = 15$	$n_2 = 15$	$n_3 = 15$
$|S_1| = 1.4$	$|S_2| = 18.6$	$|S_3| = 5.9$

Multivariate test for homogeneity of dispersion matrices

$$F = 2.98, p = .027$$

(b)

Gp 1	Gp 2
$n_1 = 21$	$n_2 = 57$
$|S_1| = 14.6$	$|S_2| = 2.4$

Multivariate test for homogeneity of dispersion matrices

$$F = 4.82, p = .008$$

(c)	**Gp 1**	**Gp 2**	**Gp 3**	**Gp 4**
	$n_1 = 20$	$n_2 = 15$	$n_3 = 40$	$n_4 = 29$
	$|\mathbf{S}_1| = 42.8$	$|\mathbf{S}_2| = 20.1$	$|\mathbf{S}_3| = 50.2$	$|\mathbf{S}_4| = 15.6$

Multivariate test for homogeneity of dispersion matrices

$$F = 3.79, p = .014$$

5. Zwick (1984) collected data on incoming clients at a mental health center who were randomly assigned to either an oriented group, who saw a videotape describing the goals and processes of psychotherapy, or a control group. She presented the following data on measures of anxiety, depression, and anger that were collected in a 1-month follow-up:

Anxiety	Depression	Anger	Anxiety	Depression	Anger
Oriented group ($n_1 = 20$)			*Control group ($n_2 = 26$)*		
285	325	165	168	190	160
23	45	15	277	230	63
40	85	18	153	80	29
215	307	60	306	440	105
110	110	50	252	350	175
65	105	24	143	205	42
43	160	44	69	55	10
120	180	80	177	195	75
250	335	185	73	57	32
14	20	3	81	120	7
0	15	5	63	63	0
5	23	12	64	53	35
75	303	95	88	125	21
27	113	40	132	225	9
30	25	28	122	60	38
183	175	100	309	355	135
47	117	46	147	135	83
385	520	23	223	300	30
83	95	26	217	235	130
87	27	2	74	67	20
			258	185	115
			239	445	145
			78	40	48
			70	50	55
			188	165	87
			157	330	67

(a) Run the EXAMINE procedure on this data, obtaining the stem-and-leaf plots and the tests for normality on each variable in each group. Focusing on the Shapiro–Wilks test and doing each test at the .025 level, does there appear to be a problem with the normality assumption?

(b) Now, recall the statement in the chapter by Johnson and Wichern that lack of normality can be due to one or more outliers. Run the Zwick data through the DESCRIPTIVES procedure twice, obtaining the z scores for the variables in each group.

(c) Note that observation 18 in group 1 is quite deviant. What are the z values for each variable? Also, observation 4 in group 2 is fairly deviant. Remove these two observations from the Zwick data set and rerun the EXAMINE procedure. Is there still a problem with lack of normality?

(d) Look at the stem-and-leaf plots for the variables. What transformation(s) from Figure 6.1 might be helpful here? Apply the transformation to the variables and rerun the EXAMINE procedure one more time. How many of the Shapiro–Wilks tests are now significant at the .025 level?

6. Many studies have compared "groups" vs. individuals, e.g., cooperative learning (working in small groups) vs. individual study, and have analyzed the data incorrectly, assuming independence of observations for subjects working within groups. Myers, Dicecco, and Lorch (1981) presented two correct ways of analyzing such data, showing that both yield honest type I error rates and have similar power. The two methods are also illustrated in the text *Research Design and Statistical Analysis* by Myers and Well (1991, pp. 327–329) in comparing the effectiveness of group study vs. individual study, where 15 students are studying individually and another 15 are in five discussion groups of size 3, with the following data:

Individual Study	Group Study
9, 9, 11, 15, 16, 12, 12, 8	(11, 16, 15) (17, 18, 19) (11, 13, 15)
15, 16, 15, 16, 14, 11, 13	(17, 18, 19) (10, 13, 13)

(a) Test for a significant difference at the .05 level with a t test, incorrectly assuming 30 independent observations.

(b) Compare the result you obtained in (a), with the result obtained in the Myers and Well book for the quasi-F test.

(c) A third correct way of analyzing the above data is to think of only 20 independent observations with the means for the group study comprising five independent observations. Analyze the data with this approach. Do you obtain significance at the .05 level?

7. In the Appendix: Analyzing correlated observations I illustrate what a difference the Hedges correction factor, a correction for clustering, can have on t with reduced degrees of freedom. I illustrate this for $p = .10$. Show that, if $p = .20$, the effect is even more dramatic.

8. Consider Table 6.6. Show that the value of .035 for $N_1 : N_2 = 24:12$ for nominal $\alpha = .05$ for the positive condition makes sense. Also, show that the value $= .076$ for the negative condition makes sense.

7

Discriminant Analysis

7.1 Introduction

Discriminant analysis is used for two purposes: (1) describing major differences among the groups in MANOVA, and (2) classifying subjects into groups on the basis of a battery of measurements. Since this text is heavily focused on multivariate tests of group differences, more space is devoted in this chapter to what is called by some "descriptive discriminant analysis." We also discuss the use of discriminant analysis for classifying subjects, limiting our attention to the two-group case. The SPSS package is used for the descriptive discriminant example, and SAS DISCRIM is used for the classification problem.

An excellent, current, and very thorough book on discriminant analysis is written by Huberty (1994), who distinguishes between predictive and descriptive discriminant analysis. In predictive discriminant analysis the focus is on classifying subjects into one of several groups, whereas in descriptive discriminant analysis the focus is on revealing major differences among the groups. The major differences are revealed through the discriminant functions. One nice feature of the book is that Huberty describes several "exemplary applications" for each type of discriminant analysis along with numerous additional applications in chapters 12 and 18. Another nice feature is that there are five special-purpose programs, along with four real data sets, on a 3.5-inch diskette that is included in the volume.

7.2 Descriptive Discriminant Analysis

Discriminant analysis is used here to break down the total between association in MANOVA into *additive* pieces, through the use of uncorrelated linear combinations of the original variables (these are the discriminant functions). An additive breakdown is obtained because the discriminant functions are derived to be uncorrelated.

Discriminant analysis has two very nice features: (a) parsimony of description, and (b) clarity of interpretation. It can be quite parsimonious in that in comparing five groups on say 10 variables, we may find that the groups differ mainly on only two major dimensions, that is, the discriminant functions. It has a clarity of interpretation in the sense that separation of the groups along one function is unrelated to separation along a different function. This is all fine, *provided* we can meaningfully name the discriminant functions and that there is adequate sample size so that the results are generalizable.

Recall that in multiple regression we found the linear combination of the predictors that was maximally correlated with the dependent variable. Here, in discriminant analysis, linear combinations are again used to distinguish the groups. Continuing through the text, it becomes clear that linear combinations are central to many forms of multivariate analysis.

An example of the use of discriminant analysis, which is discussed in complete detail later in this chapter, involved National Merit Scholars who were classified in terms of their parents' education, from eighth grade or less up to one or more college degrees, yielding four groups. The dependent variables were eight Vocational Personality variables (realistic, conventional, enterprising, sociability, etc.). The major personality differences among the scholars were revealed in one linear combination of variables (the first discriminant function), and showed that the two groups of scholars whose parents had more education were less conventional and more enterprising than the scholars whose parents had less education.

Before we begin a detailed discussion of discriminant analysis, it is important to note that discriminant analysis is a *mathematical maximization* procedure. What is being maximized is made clear shortly. The important thing to keep in mind is that any time this type of procedure is employed there is a tremendous opportunity for capitalization on chance, especially if the number of subjects is *not large* relative to the number of variables. That is, the results found on one sample may well not replicate on another independent sample. Multiple regression, it will be recalled, was another example of a mathematical maximization procedure. Because discriminant analysis is formally equivalent to multiple regression for two groups (Stevens, 1972), we might expect a similar problem with replicability of results. And indeed, as we see later, this is the case.

If the dependent variables are denoted by $y_1, y_2, \ldots, y_p$, then in discriminant analysis the row vector of coefficients a_1' is sought, which maximizes $a_1'Ba_1/a_1'Wa_1$, where B and W are the between and the within sum of squares and cross-products matrices. The linear combination of the dependent variables involving the elements of a_1' as coefficients is the best discriminant function, in that it provides for maximum separation on the groups. Note that both the numerator and denominator in the above quotient are scalars (numbers). Thus, the procedure finds the linear combination of the dependent variables, which maximizes between to within association. The quotient shown corresponds to the largest eigenvalue (ϕ_1) of the BW^{-1} matrix. The next best discriminant, corresponding to the second largest eigenvalue of BW^{-1}, call it ϕ_2, involves the elements of a_2' in the following ratio: $a_2'Ba_2/a_2'Wa_2$, as coefficients. This function is derived to be *uncorrelated* with the first discriminant function. It is the next best discriminator among the groups, in terms of separating on them. The third discriminant function would be a linear combination of the dependent variables, derived to be uncorrelated from both the first and second functions, which provides the next maximum amount of separation, and so on. The *i*th discriminant function (z_i) then is given by $z_i = a_i'y$, where y is the column vector of dependent variables.

If k is the number of groups and p is the number of dependent variables, then the number of possible discriminant functions is the minimum of p and $(k - 1)$. Thus, if there were four groups and 10 dependent variables, there would be three discriminant functions. For two groups, no matter how many dependent variables, there will be only one discriminant function. Finally, in obtaining the discriminant functions, the coefficients (the a_i) are scaled so that $a_i'a_i = 1$ for each discriminant function (the so-called unit norm condition). This is done so that there is a unique solution for each discriminant function.

7.3 Significance Tests

First, it can be shown that Wilks' Λ can be expressed as the following function of eigenvalues (ϕ_i) of $\mathbf{BW}^{-1}$ (Tatsuoka, 1971, p. 164):

$$\Lambda = \frac{1}{1+\phi_1} \frac{1}{1+\phi_2} \cdots \frac{1}{1+\phi_r}$$

where r is the number of possible discriminant functions.

Now, Bartlett showed that the following V statistic can be used for testing the significance of Λ:

$$V = [N - 1 - (p + k)/2] \cdot \sum_{i=1}^{r} \ln(1 + \phi_i)$$

where V is approximately distributed as a χ^2 with $p(k-1)$ degrees of freedom.

The test procedure for determining how many of the discriminant functions are significant is a residual procedure. First, all of the eigenvalues (roots) are tested together, using the V statistic. If this is significant, then the largest root (corresponding to the first discriminant function) is removed and a test made of the remaining roots (the first residual) to determine if this is significant. If the first residual (V_1) is not significant, then we conclude that only the first discriminant function is significant. If the first residual is significant, then we examine the second residual, that is, the V statistic with the largest two roots removed. If the second residual is not significant, then we conclude that only the first two discriminant functions are significant, and so on. In general then, when the residual after removing the first s roots is not significant, we conclude that only the first s discriminant functions are significant.

We illustrate this residual test procedure next, also giving the degrees of freedom for each test, for the case of four possible discriminant functions. The constant term, the term in brackets, is denoted by C for the sake of conciseness.

Residual Test Procedure for Four Possible
Discriminant Functions

Name	Test statistic	df
V	$C\sum_{i=1}^{4} \ln(1+\phi_i)$	$p(k-1)$
V_1	$C[\ln(1 + \phi_2) + \ln(1 + \phi_3) + \ln(1+ \phi_4)]$	$(p-1)(k-2)$
V_2	$C[\ln(1 + \phi_3) + \ln(1 + \phi_4)]$	$(p-2)(k-3)$
V_3	$C[\ln(1 + \phi_4)]$	$(p-3)(k-4)$

The general formula for the degrees of freedom for the rth residual is $(p - r)[k - (r + 1)]$.

7.4 Interpreting the Discriminant Functions

Two methods are in use for interpreting the discriminant functions:

1. Examine the standardized coefficients—these are obtained by multiplying the raw coefficient for each variable by the standard deviation for that variable.
2. Examine the discriminant function—variable correlations, that is, the correlations between each discriminant function and each of the original variables.

For both of these methods it is the largest (in absolute value) coefficients or correlations that are used for interpretation. It should be noted that these two methods can give different results; that is, some variables may have low coefficients and high correlations while other variables may have high coefficients and low correlations. This raises the question of which to use.

Meredith (1964), Porebski (1966), and Darlington, Weinberg, and Walberg (1973) argued in favor of using the discriminant function–variable correlations for two reasons: (a) the assumed greater stability of the correlations in small- or medium-sized samples, especially when there are high or fairly high intercorrelations among the variables, and (b) the correlations give a direct indication of which variables are most closely aligned with the unobserved trait that the canonical variate (discriminant function) represents. On the other hand, the coefficients are partial coefficients, with the effects of the other variables removed.

Incidentally, the use of discriminant function–variable correlations for interpretation is parallel to what is done in factor analysis, where factor–variable correlations (the so-called factor loadings) are used to interpret the factors.

Two Monte Carlo studies (Barcikowski and Stevens, 1975; Huberty, 1975) *indicate that unless sample size is large relative to the number of variables, both the standardized coefficients and the correlations are very unstable.* That is, the results obtained in one sample (e.g., interpreting the first discriminant function using variables 3 and 5) will very likely not hold up in another sample from the same population. *The clear implication of both studies is that unless the N (total sample size)/p (number of variables) ratio is quite large, say 20 to 1, one should be very cautious in interpreting the results.* This is saying, for example, that if there are 10 variables in a discriminant analysis, at least 200 subjects are needed for the investigator to have confidence that the variables selected as most important in interpreting the discriminant function would again show up as most important in another sample.

Now, given that one has enough subjects to have confidence in the reliability of the index chosen, which should be used? It seems that the following suggestion of Tatsuoka (1973), is very reasonable: "Both approaches are useful, provided we keep their different objectives in mind" (p. 280). That is, use the correlations for substantive interpretation of the discriminant functions, but use the coefficients to determine which of the variables are redundant given that others are in the set. This approach is illustrated in an example later in the chapter.

7.5 Graphing the Groups in the Discriminant Plane

If there are two or more significant discriminant functions, then a useful device for determining directional differences among the groups is to graph them in the discriminant plane. The horizontal direction corresponds to the first discriminant function, and thus lateral separation among the groups indicates how much they have been distinguished on this function. The vertical dimension corresponds to the second discriminant function and thus vertical separation tells us which groups are being distinguished in a way unrelated to the way they were separated on the first discriminant function (because the discriminant functions are uncorrelated). Because the functions are uncorrelated, it is quite possible for two groups to differ very little on the first discriminant function and yet show a large separation on the second function.

Because each of the discriminant functions is a linear combination of the original variables, the question arises as to how we determine the mean coordinates of the groups on these linear combinations. Fortunately, the answer is quite simple because it can be shown that the mean for a linear combination is equal to the linear combination of the means on the original variables. That is,

$$\bar{z}_1 = a_{11}\bar{x}_1 + a_{12}\bar{x}_2 + \cdots + a_{1p}\bar{x}_p$$

where z_1 is the discriminant function and the x_i are the original variables.

The matrix equation for obtaining the coordinates of the groups on the discriminant functions is given by:

$$\mathbf{Z} = \bar{\mathbf{X}}\mathbf{V}$$

where $\bar{\mathbf{X}}$ is the matrix of means for the original variables in the various groups and $\mathbf{V}$ is a matrix whose *columns* are the raw coefficients for the discriminant functions (the first column for the first function, etc.). To make this more concrete we consider the case of three groups and four variables. Then the matrix equation becomes:

$$_3\mathbf{Z}_2 = {}_3\bar{\mathbf{X}}_4 \, {}_4\mathbf{V}_2$$

The specific elements of the matrices would be as follows:

$$\begin{bmatrix} z_{11} & z_{12} \\ z_{21} & z_{22} \\ z_{31} & z_{32} \end{bmatrix} = \begin{bmatrix} \bar{x}_{11} & \bar{x}_{12} & \bar{x}_{13} & \bar{x}_{14} \\ \bar{x}_{21} & \bar{x}_{22} & \bar{x}_{23} & \bar{x}_{24} \\ \bar{x}_{31} & \bar{x}_{32} & \bar{x}_{33} & \bar{x}_{34} \end{bmatrix} \begin{bmatrix} a_{11} & a_{12} \\ a_{21} & a_{22} \\ a_{31} & a_{32} \\ a_{41} & a_{42} \end{bmatrix}$$

In this equation $\bar{x}_{11}$ gives the mean for variable 1 in group 1, $\bar{x}_{12}$ the mean for variable 2 in group 1, and so on. The first row of Z gives the "*x*" and "*y*" coordinates of group 1 on the two discriminant functions, the second row gives the location of group 2 in the discriminant plane, and so on.

The location of the groups on the discriminant functions appears in all three examples from the literature we present in this chapter. For plots of the groups in the plane, see the Smart study later in this chapter, and specifically Figure 7.1.

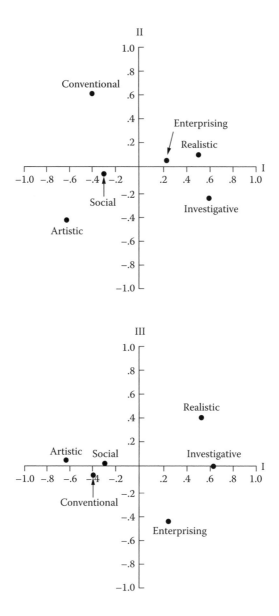

FIGURE 7.1
Position of groups for Holland's model in discriminant planes defined by functions 1 and 2 and by functions 1 and 3.

Example 7.1

The data for the example was extracted from the National Merit file (Stevens, 1972). The classification variable was the educational level of both parents of the National Merit Scholars. Four groups were formed: (a) those students for whom at least one parent had an eighth-grade education or less ($n = 90$), (b) those students both of whose parents were high school graduates ($n = 104$), (c) those students both of whose parents had gone to college, with at most one graduating ($n = 115$), and (d) those students both of whose parents had at least one college degree ($n = 75$). The dependent variables, or those we are attempting to predict from the above grouping, were a subset of the Vocational Personality Inventory (VPI): realistic, intellectual, social, conventional, enterprising, artistic, status, and aggression.

TABLE 7.1

Control Lines and Selected Output from SPSS for Discriminant Analysis

TITLE 'DISCRIMINANT ANALYSIS ON NATIONAL MERIT DATA—4 GPS—N = 384'.
DATA LIST FREE/EDUC REAL INTELL SOCIAL CONVEN ENTERP ARTIS STATUS AGGRESS
LIST
BEGIN DATA

    DATA

END DATA
DISCRIMINANT GROUPS = EDUC(1,4)/
    VARIABLES = REAL TO AGGRESS/   ①

OUTPUT

POOLED WITHIN-GROUPS CORRELATION MATRIX

	REAL	INTELL	SOCIAL	CONVEN	ENTERP	ARTIS	STATUS	AGGRESS
REAL	1.00000							
INTELL	0.44541	1.00000						
SOCIAL	0.04860	0.24193	1.00000					
CONVEN	0.32733	0.06629	0.23716	1.00000				
ENTERP	0.35377	0.10396	0.35573	0.54567	1.00000			
ARTIS	.04639	0.23030	0.48143	0.13472	0.37977	1.00000		
STATUS	−0.32954	0.06541	0.38498	0.14731	0.28262	0.40873	1.00000	
AGGRESS	0.32066	0.31931	0.49830	0.32698	0.58887	0.50353	0.43702	1.00000

GROUP MEANS

EDUC	REAL	INTELL	SOCIAL	CONVEN	ENTERP	ARTIS	STATUS	AGGRESS
1	2.35556	4.88889	5.73333	2.64444	2.63333	4.45556	8.67778	5.20000
2	2.01923	4.78846	5.42308	2.32692	2.89423	4.06731	8.41346	5.06731
3	1.96522	5.12174	5.25217	1.91304	3.63478	5.20000	8.92174	5.19130
4	1.44000	4.53333	5.10667	1.29333	2.84000	5.08000	9.08000	4.61333
TOTAL	1.96875	4.86198	5.38261	2.07552	3.04427	4.69531	8.80469	5.04688

① The GROUPS and VARIABLES subcommands are the only subcommands required for running a standard discriminant analysis. Various other options are available, such as a varimax rotation to increase interpretability, and several different types of stepwise discriminant analysis.

In Table 7.1 we present the SPSS control lines necessary to run the DISCRIMINANT program, along with some descriptive statistics, that is, the means and the correlation matrix for the VPI variables. Many of the correlations are in the moderate range (.30 to .58) and clearly significant, indicating that a multivariate analysis is dictated.

At the top of Table 7.2 is the residual test procedure involving Bartlett's chi-square tests, to determine the number of significant discriminant functions. Note that there are min $(k − 1, p)$ = min $(3,8) = 3$ possible discriminant functions. The first line has all three eigenvalues (corresponding to the three discriminant functions) lumped together, yielding a significant χ^2 at the .0004 level. This tells us there is significant overall association. Now, the largest eigenvalue of $\mathbf{BW}^{-1}$ (i.e., the first discriminant function) is removed, and we test whether the residual, the last two discriminant functions, constitute significant association. The χ^2 for this first residual is not significant ($\chi^2 =$ 14.63, $p < .40$) at the .05 level. The "After Function" column simply means after the first discriminant function has been removed. The third line, testing whether the third discriminant function is significant by itself, has a 2 in the "After Function" column. This means, "Is the χ^2 significant after the first *two* discriminant functions have been removed?" To summarize then, only the first discriminant function is significant. The details of obtaining the χ^2, using the eigenvalues of $\mathbf{BW}^{-1}$, which appear in the upper left hand corner of the printout, are given in Table 7.2.

TABLE 7.2

Tests of Significance for Discriminant Functions, Discriminant Function–Variable Correlations and Standardized Coefficients

$$73.64\% = \frac{\text{EIGENVALUE}}{\text{SUM OF EIGENVALUES}} \times 100 = \frac{.1097}{.1489} \times 100$$

CANONICAL DISCRIMINANT FUNCTIONS

Function	Eigenvalue of BW^{-1}	Percent of Variance	Cumulative Percent	Canonical Correlation :	After Function	Wilks' Lambda	Chi-Squared	D.F.	Significance
1*	0.10970	73.64	73.64	0.3144148 :	0	0.8666342	53.876	24	0.0004
2*	0.02871	19.27	92.91	0.1670684 :	1	0.9619271	14.634	14	0.4036
3*	0.01056	7.09	100.00	0.1022387 :	2	0.9895472	3.9614	6	0.4819

* MARKS THE 3 CANONICAL DISCRIMINANT FUNCTION(S) TO BE USED IN THE REMAINING ANALYSIS

STANDARDIZED CANONICAL DISCRIMINANT FUNCTION COEFFICIENTS   RESIDUAL   TEST PROCEDURE

	FUNC 1	FUNC 2	FUNC 3
REAL	0.33567	0.92803	0.55970
INTELL	−0.24881	−0.42593	0.18729
SOCIAL	0.36854	0.01669	−0.21222
CONVEN	0.79971	−0.19960	0.33530
ENTERP	−1.07691	−0.66618	0.59790
ARTIS	−0.32335	0.41416	0.205
STATUS	−0.05005	1.13509	0.38153
AGGRESS	0.41918	−0.55000	−0.27073

Let ϕ_1, ϕ_2, etc denote the eigenvalues of BW^{-1}.

$\chi^2 = [(N-1)-(p+k)/2] \Sigma_i ln(1+\phi_i)$

$\chi^2 = [(384-1)-(8+4)/2](ln(1+.11) + ln(1+.029) + ln(1+.0106))$

$\chi^2 = 377(.1429) = 53.88$, $df = p(k-1) = 8(3) = 24$

First Residual : $\chi_1^2 = 377[ln(1.029) + ln(1.0106)] = 14.64$, $df = (p-1)(k-2) = 14$

Second Residual : $\chi_2^2 = 377\, ln(1.0106) = 3.97$, $df = (p-2)(k-3) = 6$

POOLED WITHIN-GROUPS CORRELATION BETWEEN CANONICAL DISCRIMINANT FUNCTIONS AND DISCRIMINATING VARIABLES VARIABLES ARE ORDERED BY THE FUNCTION WITH LARGEST CORRELATION AND THE MAGNITUDE OF THAT CORRELATION.

	FUNC 1	FUNC 2	FUNC 3
STATUS	−0.17058	0.519084*	0.25516
ENTERP	−0.30649	−0.33095	0.74936
CONVEN	0.47878	−0.24059	0.69316
REAL	0.25946	−0.09310	0.68032
AGGRESS	0.07366	−0.13305	0.47697
INTELL	−0.01297	−0.09701	0.43467
ARTIS	−0.29829	0.27428	0.38834
SOCIAL	0.16516	0.03674	0.19227

CANONICAL DISCRIMINANT FUNCTIONS EVALUATED AT GROUP MEANS (GROUP CENTROIDS)

GROUP	FUNC 1	FUNC 2	FUNC 3
1	0.39158	−0.27492	0.00687
2	0.09873	−0.04190	−0.29200
3	−0.18324	0.27619	0.11148
4	−0.32583	−0.03558	0.22572

The eigenvalues of **BW**$^{-1}$ are .1097, .0287, and .0106. Because the eigenvalues additively partition the total association, as the discriminant functions are uncorrelated, the "Percent of Variance" is simply the given eigenvalue divided by the sum of the eigenvalues. Thus, for the first discriminant function we have:

$$\text{Percent of variance} = \frac{.1097}{.1097 + .0287 + .0106} \times 100 = 73.64\%$$

The reader should recall from Chapter 5, when we discussed "Other Multivariate Test Statistics," that the sum of the eigenvalues of $\mathbf{BW}^{-1}$ is one of the global multivariate test statistics, the Hotelling–Lawley trace. Therefore, the sum of the eigenvalues of $\mathbf{BW}^{-1}$ *is* a measure of the total association.

Because the group sizes are sharply unequal (115/75 > 1.5), it is important to check the homogeneity of covariance matrices assumption. The Box test for doing so is part of the printout, although we have not presented it. Fortunately, the Box test is not significant ($F = 1.18$, $p < .09$) at the .05 level.

The means of the groups on the first discriminant function (Table 7.2) show that it separates those children whose parents have had exposure to college (groups 3 and 4) from children whose parents have not gone to college (groups 1 and 2).

For interpreting the first discriminant function, as mentioned earlier, we use both the standardized coefficients and the discriminant function–variable correlations. We use the correlations for substantive interpretation to name the underlying construct that the discriminant function represents. The procedure has empirically clustered the variables. Our task is to determine what the variables that correlate highly with the discriminant function have in common, and thus name the function.

The discriminant function–variable correlations are given in Table 7.2. Examining these for the first discriminant function, we see that it is primarily the conventional variable (correlation = .479) that defines the function, with the enterprising and artistic variables secondarily involved (correlations of −.306 and −.298, respectively). Because the correlations are negative for these variables, the groups that scored higher on the enterprising and artistic variables, that is, those Merit Scholars whose parents had a college education, scored lower on the first discriminant function.

Now, examining the standardized coefficients to determine which of the variables are redundant given others in the set, we see that the conventional and enterprising variables are *not* redundant (coefficients of .80 and −1.08, respectively), but that the artistic variable is redundant because its coefficient is only −.32. Thus, combining the information from the coefficients and the discriminant function–variable correlations, we can say that the first discriminant function is characterizable as a conventional–enterprising continuum. Note, from the group centroid means, that it is the Merit Scholars whose parents have a college education who tend to be less conventional and more enterprising.

Finally, we can have confidence in the reliability of the results from this study since the subject/variable ratio is very large, about 50 to 1.

7.6 Rotation of the Discriminant Functions

In factor analysis, rotation of the factors often facilitates interpretation. The discriminant functions can also be rotated (varimax) to help interpret them. This is easily accomplished with the SPSS Discrim program by requesting 13 for "Options." Of course, one should rotate only statistically significant discriminant functions to ensure that the rotated functions are still significant. Also, in rotating, the maximizing property is lost; that is, the first rotated function will no longer *necessarily* account for the maximum amount of between association. The amount of between association that the rotated functions account for tends to be more evenly distributed. The SPSS package does print out how much of the canonical variance each rotated factor accounts for.

Up to this point, we have used all the variables in forming the discriminant functions. There is a procedure, called stepwise discriminant analysis, for selecting the best set of discriminators, just as one would select the "best" set of predictors in a regression analysis. It is to this procedure that we turn next.

7.7 Stepwise Discriminant Analysis

A popular procedure with the SPSS package is stepwise discriminant analysis. In this procedure the first variable to enter is the one that maximizes separation among the groups. The next variable to enter is the one that adds the most to further separating the groups, etc. It should be obvious that this procedure capitalizes on chance in the same way stepwise regression analysis does, where the first predictor to enter is the one that has the maximum correlation with the dependent variable, the second predictor to enter is the one that adds the next largest amount to prediction, and so on.

The F's to enter and the corresponding significance tests in stepwise discriminant analysis must be interpreted with caution, especially if the subject/variable ratio is small (say ≤ 5). The Wilks' Λ for the "best" set of discriminators is positively biased, and this bias can lead to the following problem (Rencher and Larson, 1980):

> Inclusion of too many variables in the subset. If the significance level shown on a computer output is used as an informal stopping rule, some variables will likely be included which do not contribute to the separation of the groups. A subset chosen with significance levels as guidelines will not likely be stable, i.e., a different subset would emerge from a repetition of the study. (p. 350)

Hawkins (1976) suggested that a variable be entered only if it is significant at the $\alpha/(k - p)$ level, where α is the desired level of significance, p is the number of variables already included and $(k - p)$ is the number of variables available for inclusion. Although this probably is a good idea if N/p ratio is small, it probably is conservative if $N/p > 10$.

7.8 Two Other Studies That Used Discriminant Analysis

7.8.1 Pollock, Jackson, and Pate Study

They used discriminant analysis to determine if five physiological variables could distinguish between three groups of runners: middle–long distance runners, marathon runners, and good runners. The variables are (1) fat weight (2) lean weight (3) VO_2 (4) blood lactic acid (5) maximum VO_2, a measure of the ability of the body to take in and process oxygen. There were 12 middle–long distance runners, eight marathon runners and eight good runners. Since min (2,5) = 2, there are just two possible discriminant functions. Selected SPSS output below shows that both functions are significant at the .05 level. The group centroids show that discriminant function 1 separates group 3 (good runners) from the elite runners, while discriminant function 2 separates group 1 (middle-long distance runners from the group 2 (marathon runners).

Test of Function(s)	Wilks'	Chi-square	df	sig
1 through 2	.166	41.310	10	.000
2	.610	11.366	4	.023

Standardized Canonical Discriminant Function Coefficients

	Function	
	1	2
Fat	.419	−.659
Lean	.695	−1.383
Maxvo2	−1.588	1.807
Lactic	.351	.813
Subvo2	.989	.404

StructureMatrix

	Function	
	1	2
Lactic	786	.179
Subvo$_2$	.208	.616
Maxvo$_2$	−.211	.561
Lean	.183	.215
Fat	.134	.169

Pooled Correlations Between Variables and Standardized Discriminant Functions

Functions at Group Centroids

	Function	
Gp	1	2
1.00	−1.177	.656
2.00	−.656	−1.151
3.00	2.420	.157

We would be worried about the reliability of the results since the N/p ratio is far less than 20/1. In fact, it is 28/5, which is less than 6/1.

7.8.2 Smart Study

A study by Smart (1976) provides a nice illustration of the use of discriminant analysis to help validate Holland's (1966) theory of vocational choice/personality. Holland's theory assumes that (a) vocational choice is an expression of personality and (b) most people can be classified as one of six primary personality types: realistic, investigative, artistic, social, enterprising, or conventional. Realistic types, for example, tend to be pragmatic, asocial, and possess strong mechanical and technical competencies, whereas social types tend to be idealistic, sociable, and possess strong interpersonal skills.

Holland's theory further states that there are six related model environments. That is, for each personality type, there is a logically related environment that is characterized in terms of the atmosphere created by the people who dominate it. For example, realistic environments are dominated by realistic personality types and are characterized primarily by the tendencies and competencies these people possess.

Now, Holland and his associates have developed a hexagonal model that defines the psychological resemblances among the six personality types and the environments. The types and environments are arranged in the following clockwise order: realistic, investigative, artistic, social, enterprising, and conventional. The closer any two environments are on the hexagonal arrangement, the stronger they are related. This means, for example, that because realistic and conventional are next to each other they should be much more similar than realistic and social, which are the farthest possible distance apart on an hexagonal arrangement.

In validating Holland's theory, Smart nationally sampled 939 academic department chairmen from 32 public universities. The departments could be classified in one of the six Holland environments. We give a sampling here: realistic—civil and mechanical engineering, industrial arts, and vocational education; investigative—biology, chemistry, psychology, mathematics; artistic—classics, music, English; social—counseling, history, sociology, and elementary education; enterprising—government, marketing, and prelaw; conventional—accounting, business education, and finance.

A questionnaire containing 27 duties typically performed by department chairmen was given to all chairmen, and the responses were factor analyzed (principal components with varimax rotation). The six factors that emerged were the dependent variables for the study, and were named: (a) faculty development, (b) external coordination, (c) graduate program, (d) internal administration, (e) instructional, and (f) program management. The independent variable was environments. The overall multivariate $F = 9.65$ was significant at the .001 level. Thus, the department chairmen did devote significantly different amounts of time to the above six categories of their professional duties. A discriminant analysis breakdown of the overall association showed there were three significant discriminant functions ($p < .001$, $p < 001$, and $p < .02$, respectively). The standardized coefficients, discussed earlier as one of the devices for interpreting such functions, are given in Table 7.3.

Using the italicized weights, Smart gave the following names to the functions: discriminant function 1—curriculum management, discriminant function 2—internal orientation, and discriminant function 3—faculty orientation. The positions of the groups on the discriminant planes defined by functions 1 and 2 and by functions 1 and 3 are given in Figure 7.1. The clustering of the groups in Figure 7.1 is reasonably consistent with Holland's hexagonal model.

In Figure 7.2 we present the hexagonal model, showing how all three discriminant functions empirically confirm different similarities and disparities that should exist, according to the theory. For example, the realistic and investigative groups should be very similar, and the closeness of these groups appears on discriminant function 1. On the other hand,

TABLE 7.3

Standardized Coefficients for Smart Study

Variables	Function 1	Function 2	Function 3
Faculty development	.22	−.20	*−.62*
External coordination	−.14	*.56*	.34
Graduate program	.36	.45	.17
Internal administration	.17	*−.58*	*.69*
Instructional	*−.82*	.15	.06
Program management	*−.46*	−.35	−.09

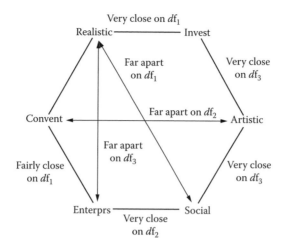

FIGURE 7.2
Empirical fit of the groups as determined by the three discriminant functions to Holland's hexagonal model; df_1, df_2, and df_3 refer to the first, second, and third discriminant functions respectively.

the conventional and artistic groups should be very dissimilar and this is revealed by their vertical separation on discriminant function 2. Also, the realistic and enterprising groups should be somewhat dissimilar and this appears as a fairly sizable separation (vertical) on discriminant function 3 in Figure 7.2.

In concluding our discussion of Smart's study, there are two important points to be made:

1. The issue raised earlier about the lack of stability of the coefficients is *not* a problem in this study. Smart had 932 subjects and only six dependent variables, so that his subject/variable ratio was very large.

2. Smart did not use the discriminant function–variable correlations in combination with the coefficients to interpret the discriminant functions, as it was unnecessary to do so. Smart's dependent variables were principal components, which are uncorrelated, and for uncorrelated variables the interpretation from the two approaches is identical, because the coefficients and correlations are equal (Thorndike, 1976)

7.8.3 Bootstrapping

Bootstrapping is a computer intensive technique developed by Efron in 1979. It can be used to obtain standard errors for any parameters. The standard errors are NOT given by SPSS or SAS for the discriminant function coefficients. These would be very useful in knowing which variables to focus on. Arbuckle and Wothke (1999) devote *three* chapters to bootstrapping. Although they discuss the technique in the context of structural equation modeling, it can be useful in the discriminant analysis context. As they note (p. 359), "Bootstrapping is a completely different approach to the problem of estimating standard errors … with bootstrapping, lack of an explicit formula for standard errors is never a problem." When bootstrapping was developed, computers weren't that fast (relatively speaking). Now, they are much, much faster, and the technique is easily implemented, even on a notebook computer at home, as I have done.

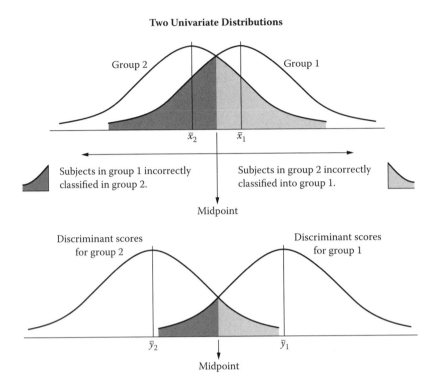

FIGURE 7.3
Two univariate distributions and two discriminant score distributions with incorrectly classified cases indicated. For this multivariate problem we have indicated much greater separation for the groups than in the
univariate example. The amounts of incorrect classifications are indicated by the shaded and lined areas as in
univariate example; $\hat{y}_1$ and $\hat{y}_2$ are the means for the two groups on the discriminant function.

7.9 The Classification Problem

The classification problem involves classifying subjects (entities in general) into the one of
several groups that they most closely resemble on the basis of a set of measurements. We
say that a subject most closely resembles group i if the vector of scores for that subject is
closest to the vector of means (centroid) for group i. Geometrically, the subject is closest
in a distance sense (Mahalanobis distance) to the centroid for that group. Recall that in
Chapter 3 (on multiple regression) we used the Mahalanobis distance to measure outliers
on the set of predictors, and that the distance for subject i is given as:

$$D_i^2 = (\mathbf{x}_i - \bar{\mathbf{x}})'\mathbf{S}^{-1}(\mathbf{x} - \bar{\mathbf{x}}),$$

where $\mathbf{x}_i$ is the vector of scores for subject i, $\bar{\mathbf{x}}$ is the vector of means, and $\mathbf{S}$ is the covariance
matrix. It may be helpful to review the section on Mahalanobis distance in Chapter 3, and
in particular a worked-out example of calculating it in Table 3.11.

Our discussion of classification is brief, and focuses on the two-group problem. For a
thorough discussion see Johnson and Wichern (1988), and for a good review of discriminant analysis see Huberty (1984).

Let us now consider several examples from different content areas where classifying subjects into groups is of practical interest:

1. A bank wants a reliable means, on the basis of a set of variables, to identify low-risk versus high-risk credit customers.

2. A reading diagnostic specialist wishes a means of identifying in kindergarten those children who are likely to encounter reading difficulties in the early elementary grades from those not likely to have difficulty.

3. A special educator wants to classify handicapped children as either learning disabled, emotionally disturbed, or mentally retarded.

4. A dean of a law school wants a means of identifying those likely to succeed in law school from those not likely to succeed.

5. A vocational guidance counselor, on the basis of a battery of interest variables, wishes to classify high school students into occupational groups (artists, lawyers, scientists, accountants, etc.) whose interests are similar.

6. A clinical psychologist or psychiatrist wishes to classify mental patients into one of several psychotic groups (schizophrenic, manic-depressive, catatonic, etc.).

7.9.1 The Two-Group Situation

Let $\mathbf{x}' = (x_1, x_2, ..., x_p)$ denote the vector of measurements on the basis of which we wish to classify a subject into one of two groups, G_1 or G_2. Fisher's (1936) idea was to transform the multivariate problem into a univariate one, in the sense of finding the linear combination of the x's (a single composite variable) that will maximally discriminant the groups. This is, of course, the single discriminant function. It is assumed that the two populations are multivariate normal and have the same covariance matrix. Let $\mathbf{z} = a_1x_1 + a_2x_2 + ... + a_px_p$ denote the discriminant function, where $\mathbf{a}' = (a_1, a_2, ..., a_p)$ is the vector of coefficients. Let $\bar{\mathbf{x}}_1$ and $\bar{\mathbf{x}}_2$ denote the vectors of means for the subjects on the p variables in groups 1 and 2. The location of group 1 on the discriminant function is then given by $\bar{y}_1 = \mathbf{a}' \bar{\mathbf{x}}_1$ and the location of group 2 by $\bar{y}_2 = \mathbf{a}' \bar{\mathbf{x}}_2$. The midpoint between the two groups on the discriminant function is then given by $m = (\bar{y}_1 + \bar{y}_2)/2$.

If we let z_i denote the score for the ith subject on the discriminant function, then the *decision rule* is as follows:

If $z_i \geq m$, then classify subject in group 1.

If $z_i < m$, then classify subject in group 2.

As we see in Example 7.2, the stepwise discriminant analysis program prints out the scores on the discriminant function for each subject and the means for the groups on the discriminant function (so that we can easily determine the midpoint m). Thus, applying the preceding decision rule, we are easily able to determine why the program classified a subject in a given group. In this decision rule, we assume the group that has the higher mean is designated as group 1.

This midpoint rule makes intuitive sense and is easiest to see for the single-variable case. Suppose there are two normal distributions with equal variances and means 55 (group 1) and 45. The midpoint is 50. If we consider classifying a subject with a score of 52, it makes sense to put the person into group 1. Why? Because the score puts the subject much closer to what is typical for group 1 (i.e., only 3 points away from the mean), whereas this score is nowhere near as typical for a subject from group 2 (7 points from the mean). On the other hand, a subject with a score of 48.5 is more appropriately placed in group 2 because that person's score is closer to what is typical for group 2 (3.5 points from the mean) than what is typical for group 1 (6.5 points from the mean).

In Figure 7.3 we illustrate the percentages of subjects that would be misclassified in the univariate case and when using discriminant scores.

Example 7.2

We consider again the Pope, Lehrer, and Stevens (1980) data used in Chapter 6. Children in kindergarten were measured with various instruments to determine whether they could be classified as low risk or high risk with respect to having reading problems later on in school. The variables we considered here are word identification (WI), word comprehension (WC), and passage comprehension (PC). The group sizes are sharply unequal and the homogeneity of covariance matrices assumption here was not tenable at the .05 level, so that a quadratic rule may be more appropriate. But we are using this example just for illustrative purposes.

In Table 7.4 are the control lines for obtaining the classification results on SAS DISCRIM using the ordinary discriminant function. The hit rate, that is, the number of correct classifications, is quite good, especially as 11 of the 12 high risk subjects have been correctly classified.

Table 7.5 gives the means for the groups on the discriminant function (.46 for low risk and −1.01 for high risk), along with the scores for the subjects on the discriminant function (these are listed under CAN.V, an abbreviation for canonical variate). The histogram for the discriminant scores shows that we have a fairly good separation, although there are several (9) misclassifications of low-risk subjects' being classified as high risk.

TABLE 7.4

SAS DISCRIM Control Lines and Group Probabilities for Low-Risk and High-Risk Subjects

```
data pope;
input gprisk wi wc pc @@;
lines;
1   5.8    9.7  8.9   1  10.6  10.9 11    1   8.6  7.2  8.7
1   4.8    4.6  6.2   1   8.3  10.6  7.8  1   4.6  3.3  4.7
1   4.8    3.7  6.4   1   6.7   6.0  7.2  1   7.1  8.4  8.4
1   6.2    3.0  4.3   1   4.2   5.3  4.2  1   6.9  9.7  7.2
1   5.6    4.1  4.3   1   4.8   3.8  5.3  1   2.9  3.7  4.2
1   6.1    7.1  8.1   1  12.5  11.2  8.9  1   5.2  9.3  6.2
1   5.7   10.3  5.5   1   6.0   5.7  5.4  1   5.2  7.7  6.9
1   7.2    5.8  6.7   1   8.1   7.1  8.1  1   3.3  3.0  4.9
1   7.6    7.7  6.2   1   7.7   9.7  8.9
2   2.4    2.1  2.4   2   3.5   1.8  3.9  2   6.7  3.6  5.9
2   5.3    3.3  6.1   2   5.2   4.1  6.4  2   3.2  2.7  4.0
2   4.5    4.9  5.7   2   3.9   4.7  4.7  2   4.0  3.6  2.9
2   5.7    5.5  6.2   2   2.4   2.9  3.2  2   2.7  2.6  4.1
proc discrim data = pope testdata = pope testlist;
class gprisk;
var wi wc pc;
```

TABLE 7.4 *(continued)*

SAS DISCRIM Control Lines and Group Probabilities for Low-Risk and High-Risk Subjects

Obs	From GPRISK	CLASSIFIED into GPRISK	Posterior Probability of Membership in GPRISK	
			1	2
1	1	1	0.9317	0.0683
2	1	1	0.9840	0.0160
3	1	1	0.8600	0.1400
4	1	2[a]	0.4365	0.5635
5	1	1	0.9615	0.0385
6	1	2[a]	0.2511	0.7489
7	1	2[a]	0.3446	0.6554
8	1	1	0.6880	0.3120
9	1	1	0.8930	0.1070
10	1	2[a]	0.2557	0.7443
11	1	2[a]	0.4269	0.5731
12	1	1	0.9260	0.0740
13	1	2[a]	0.3446	0.6554
14	1	2[a]	0.3207	0.6793
15	1	2[a]	0.2295	0.7705
16	1	1	0.7929	0.2071
17	1	1	0.9856	0.0144
18	1	1	0.8775	0.1225
19	1	1	0.9169	0.0831
20	1	1	0.5756	0.4244
21	1	1	0.7906	0.2094
22	1	1	0.6675	0.3325
23	1	1	0.8343	0.1657
24	1	2[a]	0.2008	0.7992
25	1	1	0.8262	0.1738
26	1	1	0.9465	0.0535
27	2	2	0.0936	0.9064
28	2	2	0.1143	0.8857
29	2	2	0.3778	0.6222
30	2	2	0.3098	0.6902
31	2	2	0.4005	0.5995
32	2	2	0.1598	0.8402
33	2	2	0.4432	0.5568
34	2	2	0.3676	0.6324
35	2	2	0.2161	0.7839
36	2	1[a]	0.5703	0.4297
37	2	2	0.1432	0.8568
38	2	2	0.1468	0.8532

Number of Observations and Percent into GPRISK:

From GPRISK		1	2	Total
1	low-risk	17	9	26
		65.38	34.62	100.00
2	high-risk	1	11	12
		8.33	91.67	100.00

We have 9 low-risk subjects misclassified as high-risk.

There is only 1 high-risk subject misclassified as low-risk.

[a] Misclassified observation.

TABLE 7.5

Means for Groups on Discriminant Function, Scores for Cases on Discriminant Function, and Histogram for Discriminant Scores

Group		Mean coordinates		Symbol for cases	Symbol for mean
Low risk	①	0.46	0.00	L	1
High risk		−1.01	0.00	H	2

	Low risk		②		
Group case	CAN.V	Case	CAN.V	Case	CAN.V
1	1.50	11	−0.47	21	0.63
2	2.53	12	1.44	22	0.20
3	0.96	13	−0.71	23	0.83
4	−0.44	14	−0.78	24	−1.21
5	1.91	15	−1.09	25	0.79
6	−1.01	16	0.64	26	1.68
7	−0.71	17	2.60		
8	0.27	18	1.07		
9	1.17	19	1.36		
10	−1.00	20	−0.06		

Group high risk			
Case	CAN.V	Case	CAN.V
27	−1.81	37	−1.49
28	−1.66	38	−1.47
29	−0.81		
30	−0.82		
31	−0.55		
32	−1.40		
33	−0.43		
34	−0.64		
35	−1.15		
36	−0.08		

Histogram for discriminant function scores   Only misclassification for high risk subjects (case 36)

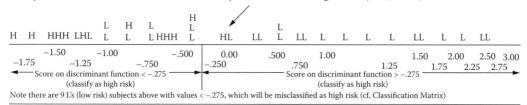

Note there are 9 L's (low risk) subjects above with values < −.275, which will be misclassified as high risk (cf, Classification Matrix)

① These are the means for the groups on the discriminant function. thus, this midpoint is

$$\frac{.46 + (-1.01)}{2} = -.275$$

② The scores listed under CAN.V (for canonical variate) are the scores for the subjects on the discriminant function.

7.9.3 Assessing the Accuracy of the Maximized Hit Rates

The classification procedure is set up to maximize the hit rates, that is, the number of correct classifications. This is analogous to the maximization procedure in multiple regression, where the regression equation was designed to maximize predictive power. We saw how misleading the prediction on the derivation sample could be. There is the same need here to obtain a more realistic estimate of the hit rate through use of an "external" classification analysis. That is, an analysis is needed in which the data to be classified are *not* used in constructing the classification function. There are two ways of accomplishing this:

1. We can use the *jackknife* procedure of Lachenbruch (1967). Here, each subject is classified based on a classification statistic derived from the remaining $(n-1)$ subjects. This is the procedure of choice for small or moderate sample sizes, and is obtained by specifying CROSSLIST as an option in the SAS DISCRIM program (see Table 7.6). The jackknifed probabilities and classification results for the Pope data are given in Table 7.6. The probabilities are different from those obtained with the discriminant function (Table 7.4), but for this data set the classification results are identical.

2. If the sample size is large, then we can randomly split the sample and cross validate. That is, we compute the classification function on one sample and then check its hit rate on the other random sample. This provides a good check on the external validity of the classification function.

7.9.4 Using Prior Probabilities

Ordinarily, we would assume that any given subject has a priori an equal probability of being in any of the groups to which we wish to classify, and the packages have equal prior probabilities as the default option. Different a priori group probabilities can have a substantial effect on the classification function, as we will show shortly. The pertinent question is, "How often are we justified in using unequal a priori probabilities for group membership?" If indeed, based on content knowledge, one can be confident that the different sample sizes result *because* of differences in population sizes, then prior probabilities

TABLE 7.6

SAS DISCRIM Control Lines and Selected Printout for Classifying the Pope Data with the Jackknife Procedure

```
data pope;
input gprisk wi wc pc @@;
lines;
1   5.8    9.7   8.9   1   10.6   10.9  11    1   8.6   7.2   8.7
1   4.8    4.6   6.2   1    8.3   10.6   7.8  1   4.6   3.3   4.7
1   4.8    3.7   6.4   1    6.7    6.0   7.2  1   7.1   8.4   8.4
1   6.2    3.0   4.3   1    4.2    5.3   4.2  1   6.9   9.7   7.2
1   5.6    4.1   4.3   1    4.8    3.8   5.3  1   2.9   3.7   4.2
1   6.1    7.1   8.1   1   12.5   11.2   8.9  1   5.2   9.3   6.2
1   5.7   10.3   5.5   1    6.0    5.7   5.4  1   5.2   7.7   6.9
1   7.2    5.8   6.7   1    8.1    7.1   8.1  1   3.3   3.0   4.9
1   7.6    7.7   6.2   1    7.7    9.7   8.9
2   2.4    2.1   2.4   2    3.5    1.8   3.9  2   6.7   3.6   5.9
2   5.3    3.3   6.1   2    5.2    4.1   6.4  2   3.2   2.7   4.0
2   4.5    4.9   5.7   2    3.9    4.7   4.7  2   4.0   3.6   2.9
2   5.7    5.5   6.2   2    2.4    2.9   3.2  2   2.7   2.6   4.1
proc discrim data = pope testdata = pope testlist;
class gprisk;
var wi wc pc;
```

When the CROSSLIST option is listed, the program prints the cross validation classification results for each observation. Listing this option invokes the jackknife procedure (see SAS/STAT *User's Guide*, Vol. 1, p. 688).

TABLE 7.6 *(continued)*

Cross-validation Results using Linear Discriminant Function
Generalized Squared Distance Function:

$$D_j^2(X) = (X - \bar{X}_{(x)j})' \text{cov}(X)(X - \bar{X}_{(x)j})$$

Posterior Probability of Membership in each GPRISK:

$$\Pr(j \mid X) = \exp(-.5\, D_j^2(X)) / \text{SUM} \exp(-.5\, D_k^2(X))$$

Obs	GPRSK	Into GPRISK	1	2
1	1	1	0.9315	0.0685
2	1	1	0.9893	0.0107
3	1	1	0.8474	0.1526
4	1	2[a]	0.4106	0.5894
5	1	1	0.9634	0.0366
6	1	2[a]	0.2232	0.7768
7	1	2[a]	0.2843	0.7157
8	1	1	0.6752	0.3248
9	1	1	0.8873	0.1127
10	1	2[a]	0.1508	0.8492
11	1	2[a]	0.3842	0.6158
12	1	1	0.9234	0.0766
13	1	2[a]	0.2860	0.7140
14	1	2[a]	0.3004	0.6996
15	1	2[a]	0.1857	0.8143
16	1	1	0.7729	0.2271
17	1	1	0.9955	0.0045
18	1	1	0.8639	0.1361
19	1	1	0.9118	0.0882
20	1	1	0.5605	0.4395
21	1	1	0.7740	0.2260
22	1	1	0.6501	0.3499
23	1	1	0.8230	0.1770
24	1	2[a]	0.1562	0.8438
25	1	1	0.8113	0.1887
26	1	1	0.9462	0.0538
27	2	2	0.1082	0.8918
28	2	2	0.1225	0.8775
29	2	2	0.4710	0.5290
30	2	2	0.3572	0.6428
31	2	2	0.4485	0.5515
32	2	2	0.1679	0.8321
33	2	2	0.4639	0.5361
34	2	2	0.3878	0.6122
35	2	2	0.2762	0.7238
36	2	1[a]	0.5927	0.4073
37	2	2	0.1607	0.8393
38	2	2	0.1591	0.8409

[a] Misclassified observation.

are justified. However, several researchers have urged caution in using anything but equal priors (Lindeman, Merenda, and Gold, 1980; Tatsuoka, 1971).

To use prior probability in the SAS DISCRIM program is easy (see *SAS/STAT User's Guide*, Vol. 1, p. 694).

Example 7.3: National Merit Data–Cross-Validation

We consider a second example to illustrate randomly splitting the sample and cross-validating the classification function with SPSS for Windows 10.0. The 10.0 applications guide (p. 290) states:

> You can ask SPSS to compute classification functions for a subset of each group and then see how the procedure classifies the unused cases. This means that new data may be classified using functions derived from the original groups. More importantly, for model building, this means it is easy to design your own cross-validation.

We have randomly selected 100 cases from the National Merit data three times (labeled select, select2, and select3) and then cross-validated the classification function in each case on the remaining 65 cases. This is the percent correct for the cases not selected. Some screens from SPSS 10.0 for Windows that are relevant are presented in Table 7.7. For the screen in the middle, one must click on (select) SUMMARY TABLE to get the results given in Table 7.8. The results are presented in Table 7.8. Note that the percent correctly classified in the first case is actually higher (this is unusual, but can happen). In the second and third case, the percent correctly classified in the unselected cases drops off (from 68% to 61.5% for second case and from 66% to 60% for the third case). The raw data, along with the random samples (labeled select, select2, and select3), are on the CD (labeled MERIT3).

7.10 Linear vs. Quadratic Classification Rule

A more complicated classification rule is available. However, the following comments should be kept in mind before using it. Johnson and Wichern (1982) indicated:

> The quadratic … rules are appropriate if normality appears to hold but the assumption of equal covariance matrices is seriously violated. However, the assumption of normality seems to be more critical for quadratic rules than linear rules (p. 504).

Huberty (1984) stated, "The stability of results yielded by a linear rule is greater than results yielded by a quadratic rule when small samples are used and when the normality condition is not met" (p. 165).

7.11 Characteristics of a Good Classification Procedure

One obvious characteristic of a good classification procedure is that the hit rate be high; we should have mainly correct classifications. But another important consideration, some-times lost sight of, is the cost of misclassification (financial or otherwise). The cost of mis-classifying a subject from group A in group B may be greater than misclassifying a subject from group B in group A. We give three examples to illustrate:

TABLE 7.7

SPSS 10.0 Screens for Random Splits of National Merit Data

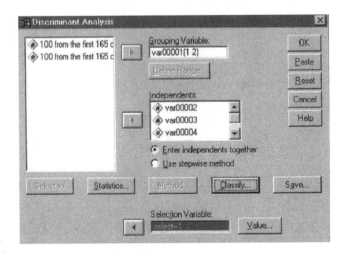

TABLE 7.8

Three Random Splits of National Merit Data and Cross-Validation Results

Classification Results[a,b]						
				Predicted Group Membership		
			VAR00001	**1.00**	**2.00**	**Total**
Cases Selected	Original	Count	1.00	37	21	58
			2.00	17	25	42
		%	1.00	63.6	36.2	100.0
			2.00	40.5	59.5	100.0
Cases Not Selected	Original	Count	1.00	15	17	32
			2.00	6	27	33
		%	1.00	46.9	53.1	100.0
			2.00	18.2	81.8	100.0

[a] 62.0% of selected original grouped cases correctly classified.
[b] 64.6% of unselected original grouped cases correctly classified.

Classification Results[a,b]						
				Predicted Group Membership		
			VAR00001	**1.00**	**2.00**	**Total**
Cases Selected	Original	Count	1.00	33	22	55
			2.00	10	35	45
		%	1.00	60.0	40.0	100.0
			2.00	22.2	77.8	100.0
Cases Not Selected	Original	Count	1.00	19	16	35
			2.00	9	21	30
		%	1.00	54.3	45.7	100.0
			2.00	30.0	70.0	100.0

[a] 68.0% of selected original grouped cases correctly classified.
[b] 61.5% of unselected original grouped cases correctly classified.

Classification Results[a,b]						
				Predicted Group Membership		
			VAR00001	**1.00**	**2.00**	**Total**
Cases Selected	Original	Count	1.00	39	18	57
			2.00	16	27	43
		%	1.00	68.4	31.6	100.0
			2.00	37.2	62.8	100.0
Cases Not Selected	Original	Count	1.00	19	14	33
			2.00	12	20	32
		%	1.00	57.6	42.4	100.0
			2.00	37.5	62.5	100.0

[a] 66.0% of selected original grouped cases correctly classified.
[b] 60.0% of unselected original grouped cases correctly classified

1. A medical researcher wishes classify subjects as low risk or high risk in terms of developing cancer on the basis of family history, personal health habits, and environmental factors. Here, saying a subject is low risk when in fact he is high risk is more serious than classifying a subject as high risk when he is low risk.

2. A bank wishes to classify low- and high-risk credit customers. Certainly, for the bank, misclassifying high-risk customers as low risk is going to be more costly than misclassifying low-risk as high-risk customers.

3. This example was illustrated previously, of identifying low-risk versus high-risk kindergarten children with respect to possible reading problems in the early elementary grades. Once again, misclassifying a high-risk child as low risk is more serious than misclassifying a low-risk child as high risk. In the former case, the child who needs help (intervention) doesn't receive it.

7.11.1 The Multivariate Normality Assumption

Recall that linear discriminant analysis is based on the assumption of multivariate normality, and that quadratic rules are also sensitive to a violation of this assumption. Thus, in situations where multivariate normality is particularly suspect, for example when using some discrete dichotomous variables, an alternative classification procedure is desirable. Logistic regression (Press & Wilson, 1978) is a good choice here; it is available on SPSS (in the Loglinear procedure).

7.12 Summary

1. Discriminant analysis is used for two purposes: (a) for describing major differences among groups, and (b) for classifying subjects into groups on the basis of a battery of measurements.

2. The major differences among the groups are revealed through the use of uncorrelated linear combinations of the original variables, that is, the discriminant functions. Because the discriminant functions are uncorrelated, they yield an additive partitioning of the between association.

3. Use the discriminant function–variable correlations to name the discriminant functions and the standardized coefficients to determine which of the variables are redundant.

4. About 20 subjects per variable are needed for reliable results, to have confidence that the variables selected for interpreting the discriminant functions would again show up in an independent sample from the same population.

5. Stepwise discriminant analysis should be used with caution.

6. For the classification problem, it is assumed that the two populations are multivariate normal and have the same covariance matrix.

7. The hit rate is the number of correct classifications, and is an optimistic value, because we are using a mathematical maximization procedure. To obtain a more realistic estimate of how good the classification function is, use the jackknife procedure for small or moderate samples, and randomly split the sample and cross validate with large samples.

8. If the covariance matrices are unequal, then a quadratic classification procedure should be considered.

9. There is evidence that linear classification is more reliable when small samples are used and normality does not hold.

10. The cost of misclassifying must be considered in judging the worth of a classification rule. Of procedures A and B, with the same overall hit rate, A would be considered better if it resulted in less "costly" misclassifications.

Exercises

1. Run a discriminant analysis on the data from Exercise 1 in chapter 5 using the DISCRIMINANT program.

   (a) How many discriminant functions are there?

   (b) Which of the discriminant functions are significant at the .05 level?

   (c) Show how the chi-square values for the residual test procedure are obtained, using the eigenvalues on the printout.

   Run a discriminant analysis on this data again, but this time using SPSS MANOVA. Use the following PRINT subcommand:

   PRINT = ERROR(SSCP) SIGNIF(HYPOTH) DISCRIM(RAW)/

   ERROR(SSCP) is used to obtain the error sums of square and cross products matrix, the **W** matrix. SIGNIF(HYPOTH) is used to obtain the hypothesis SSCP, the **B** matrix here, while DISCRIM(RAW) is used to obtain the raw discriminant function coefficients.

   (d) Recall that **a′** was used to denote the vector of raw discriminant coefficients. By plugging the coefficients into **a′Ba/a′Wa** show that the value is equal to the largest eigenvalue of **BW**$^{-1}$ given on the printout.

2. (a) Given the results of the Smart study, which of the four multivariate test statistics do you think would be most powerful?

   (b) From the results of the Stevens study, which of the four multivariate test statistics would be most powerful?

3. Press and Wilson (1978) examined population change data for the 50 states. The percent change in population from the 1960 Census to the 1970 Census for each state was coded as 0 or 1, according to whether the change was below or above the median change for all states. This is the grouping variable. The following demographic variables are to be used to explain the population changes: (a) per capita income (in $1,000), (b) percent birth rate, (c) presence or absence of a coastline, and (d) percent death rate.

   (a) Run the discriminant analysis, forcing in all predictors, to see how well the states can be classified (as below or above the median). What is the hit rate?

   (b) Run the jackknife classification. Does the hit rate drop off appreciably?

Data for Exercise 3

State	Population Change	Income	Births	Coast	Deaths
Arkansas	0	2.878	1.8	0	1.1
Colorado	1	3.855	1.9	0	.8
Delaware	1	4.524	1.9	1	.9
Georgia	1	3.354	2.1	1	.9
Idaho	0	3.290	1.9	0	.8
Iowa	0	3.751	1.7	0	1.0
Mississippi	0	2.626	2.2	1	1.0
New Jersey	1	4.701	1.6	1	.9
Vermont	1	3.468	1.8	0	1.0
Washington	1	4.053	1.8	1	.9
Kentucky	0	3.112	1.9	0	1.0
Louisiana	1	3.090	2.7	1	1.3
Minnesota	1	3.859	1.8	0	.9
New Hampshire	1	3.737	1.7	1	1.0
North Dakota	0	3.086	1.9	0	.9
Ohio	0	4.020	1.9	0	1.0
Oklahoma	0	3.387	1.7	0	1.0
Rhode Island	0	3.959	1.7	1	1.0
South Carolina	0	2.990	2.0	1	.9
West Virginia	0	3.061	1.7	0	1.2
Connecticut	1	4.917	1.6	1	.8
Maine	0	3.302	1.8	1	1.1
Maryland	1	4.309	1.5	1	.8
Massachusetts	0	4.340	1.7	1	1.0
Michigan	1	4.180	1.9	0	.9
Missouri	0	3.781	1.8	0	1.1
Oregon	1	3.719	1.7	1	.9
Pennsylvania	0	3.971	1.6	1	1.1
Texas	1	3.606	2.0	1	.8
Utah	1	3.227	2.6	0	.7
Alabama	0	2.948	2.0	1	1.0
Alaska	1	4.644	2.5	1	1.0
Arizona	1	3.665	2.1	0	.9
California	1	4.493	1.8	1	.8
Florida	1	3.738	1.7	1	1.1
Nevada	1	4.563	1.8	0	.8
New York	0	4.712	1.7	1	1.0
South Dakota	0	3.123	1.7	0	2.4
Wisconsin	1	3.812	1.7	0	.9
Wyoming	0	3.815	1.9	0	.9
Hawaii	1	4.623	2.2	1	.5
Illinois	0	4.507	1.8	0	1.0
Indiana	1	3.772	1.9	0	.9
Kansas	0	3.853	1.6	0	1.0
Montana	0	3.500	1.8	0	.9
Nebraska	0	3.789	1.8	0	1.1
New Mexico	0	3.077	2.2	0	.7
North Carolina	1	3.252	1.9	1	.9
Tennessee	0	3.119	1.9	0	1.0
Virginia	1	3.712	1.8	1	.8

8

Factorial Analysis of Variance

8.1 Introduction

In this chapter we consider the effect of two or more independent or classification variables (e.g., sex, social class, treatments) on a set of dependent variables. Four schematic two-way designs, where just the classification variables are shown, are given here:

	Treatments		
	1	2	3
Male			
Female			

	Teaching Methods		
	1	2	3
Urban			
Suburban			
Rural			

	Drugs			
	1	2	3	4
Schizop.				
Depressives				

Intelligence	Stimulus Complexity		
	Easy	Average	Hard
Average			
Super			

We indicate what the advantages of a factorial design are over a one-way design. We also remind the reader what an interaction means, and distinguish between the two types of interaction (ordinal and disordinal). The univariate equal cell size (balanced design) situation is discussed first. Then we tackle the much more difficult disproportional (non-orthogonal or unbalanced) case. Three different ways of handling the unequal n case are considered; it is indicated why we feel one of these methods is generally superior. We then discuss a multivariate factorial design, and finally the interpretation of a three-way interaction. The control lines for running the various analyses are given, and selected printout from SPSS MANOVA is discussed.

8.2 Advantages of a Two-Way Design

1. A two-way design enables us to examine the *joint* effect of the independent variables on the dependent variable(s). We cannot get this information by running two separate one-way analyses, one for each of the independent variables. If one of the independent variables is treatments and the other some individual difference characteristic (sex, IQ, locus of control, age, etc.), then a significant interaction tells us that the superiority of one treatment over another is *moderated* by

271

the individual difference characteristic. (An interaction means that the effect one independent variable has on a dependent variable is not the same for all levels of the other independent variable.) This moderating effect can take two forms:

(a) The degree of superiority changes, but one subgroup always does better than another. To illustrate this, consider the following ability by teaching methods design:

	Methods of Teaching		
	T_1	T_2	T_3
High ability	85	80	76
Low ability	60	63	68

The superiority of the high-ability students changes from 25 for T_1 to only 8 for T_3, but high-ability students always do better than low-ability students. Because the order of superiority is maintained, this is called an *ordinal* interaction.

(b) The superiority reverses; that is, one treatment is best with one group, but another treatment is better for a different group. A study by Daniels and Stevens (1976) provides an illustration of this more dramatic type of interaction, called a *disordinal* interaction. On a group of college undergraduates, they considered two types of instruction: (1) a traditional, teacher-controlled (lecture) type and (2) a contract for grade plan. The subjects were classified as internally or externally controlled, using Rotter's scale. An internal orientation means that those subjects perceive that positive events occur as a consequence of their actions (i.e., they are in control), whereas external subjects feel that positive and/or negative events occur more because of powerful others, or due to chance or fate. The design and the means for the subjects on an achievement posttest in psychology are given here:

		Instruction	
		Contract for Grade	Teacher Controlled
	Internal	50.52	38.01
Locus of control			
	External	36.33	46.22

The moderator variable in this case is locus of control, and it has a substantial effect on the efficacy of an instructional method. When the subjects' locus of control is matched to the teaching method (internals with contract for grade and externals with teacher controlled) they do quite well in terms of achievement; where there is a mismatch, achievement suffers.

This study also illustrates how a one-way design can lead to quite misleading results. Suppose Daniels and Stevens had just considered the two methods, ignoring locus of control. The means for achievement for the contract for grade plan and for teacher controlled are 43.42 and 42.11, nowhere near significance. The conclusion would have been that teaching methods don't make a difference. The factorial study shows, however, that methods definitely do make a difference—a quite positive difference if subject locus of control is matched to teaching methods, and an undesirable effect if there is a mismatch.

The general area of matching treatments to individual difference characteristics of subjects is an interesting and important one, and is called aptitude–
treatment interaction research. A thorough and critical analysis of many
studies in this area is covered in the excellent text *Aptitudes and Instructional
Methods* by Cronbach and Snow (1977).

2. A second advantage of factorial designs is that they can lead to more powerful
   tests by reducing error (within-cell) variance. If performance on the dependent
   variable is related to the individual difference characteristic (the blocking variable), then the reduction can be substantial. We consider a hypothetical sex ×
   treatment design to illustrate:

	T_1		T_2	
Males	18, 19, 21	(2.5)	17, 16, 16	(1.3)
	20, 22		18, 15	
Females	11, 12, 11	(1.7)	9, 9, 11	(2.2)
	13, 14		8, 7	

Notice that *within* each cell there is very little variability. The within-cell variances quantify this, and are given in parentheses. The pooled within-cell error
term for the factorial analysis is quite small, 1.925. On the other hand, if this had
been considered as a two-group design, the variability is considerably greater, as
evidenced by the within-*group* (treatment) variances for T_1 and T_2 of 18.766 and
17.6, and a pooled error term for the *t* test of 18.18.

8.3 Univariate Factorial Analysis

8.3.1 Equal Cell *n* (Orthogonal) Case

When there are equal numbers of subjects in each cell in a factorial design, then the sum of
squares for the different effects (main and interactions) are uncorrelated (orthogonal). This
is important in terms of interpreting results, because significance for one effect implies
nothing about significance on another. This helps for a clean and clear interpretation of
results. It puts us in the same nice situation we had with uncorrelated planned comparisons, which we discussed in chapter 5.

Overall and Spiegel (1969), in a classic paper on analyzing factorial designs, discussed
three basic methods of analysis:

Method 1: Adjust each effect for all other effects in the design to obtain its unique
contribution (regression approach).

Method 2: Estimate the main effects ignoring the interaction, but estimate the interaction effect adjusting for the main effects (experimental method).

Method 3: Based on theory or previous research, establish an ordering for the
effects, and then adjust each effect only for those effects preceding it in
the ordering (hierarchical approach).

For equal cell size designs all three of these methods yield the same results, that is, the same F *tests.* Therefore, it will not make any difference, in terms of the conclusions a researcher draws, as to which of these methods is used on one of the packages. *For unequal cell sizes, however, these methods can yield quite different results,* and this is what we consider shortly. First, however, we consider an example with equal cell size to show two things: (a) that the methods do indeed yield the same results, and (b) to demonstrate, using dummy coding for the effects, that the effects are uncorrelated.

Example 8.1: Two-Way Equal Cell *n*

Consider the following 2 × 3 factorial data set:

		B		
		1	2	3
A	1	3, 5, 6	2, 4, 8	11, 7, 8
	2	9, 14, 5	6, 7, 7	9, 8, 10

In Table 8.1 we give the control lines for running the analysis on SPSS MANOVA. In the MANOVA command we indicate the factors after the keyword BY, with the beginning level for each factor first in parentheses and then the last level for the factor. The DESIGN subcommand lists the effects we wish to test for significance. In this case the program *assumes* a full factorial model by default, and therefore it is not necessary to list the effects.

Method 3, the hierarchical approach, means that a given effect is adjusted for all effects to its left in the ordering. The effects here would go in the following order: FACA, FACB, FACA by FACB. Thus, the A main effect is not adjusted for anything. The B main effect is adjusted for the A main effect, and the interaction is adjusted for both main effects.

We also ran this problem using Method 1, the default method starting with Release 2.1, to obtain the unique contribution of each effect, adjusting for all other effects. Note, however, that the *F* ratios for both methods are identical (see Table 8.1). Why? Because the effects are uncorrelated for equal cell size, and therefore no adjustment takes place. Thus, the *F* for an effect "adjusted" is the same as an effect unadjusted.

To show that the effects are indeed uncorrelated we dummy coded the effects in Table 8.2 and ran the problem as a regression analysis. The coding scheme is explained there. Predictor A1 represents the A main effect, predictors B1 and B2 represent the B main effect, and predictors A1B1 and A1B2 represent the interaction. We are using all these predictors to explain variation on *y*. Note that the correlations between predictors representing *different* effects are all 0. This means that those effects are accounting for distinct parts of the variation on *y*, or that we have an orthogonal partitioning of the *y* variation.

In Table 8.3 we present the stepwise regression results for the example with the effects entered as the predictors. There we explain how the sum of squares obtained for each effect is exactly the same as was obtained when the problem was run as a traditional ANOVA in Table 8.1.

Example 8.2: Two-Way Disproportional Cell Size

The data for our disproportional cell size example is given in Table 8.5, along with the dummy coding for the effects, and the correlation matrix for the effects. Here there definitely are correlations among the effects. For example, the correlations between A1 (representing the A main effect) and B1 and B2 (representing the B main effect) are −.163 and −.275. This contrasts with the equal cell *n*

TABLE 8.1

Control Lines and Selected Output for Two-Way Equal Cell N ANOVA on SPSS

```
TITLE 'TWO WAY ANOVA EQUAL N P 294'.
DATA LIST FREE/FACA FACB DEP.
BEGIN DATA.
1 1 3     1 1 5     1 1 6
1 2 2     1 2 4     1 2 8
1 3 11    1 3 7     1 3 8
2 1 9     2 1 14    2 1 5
2 2 6     2 2 7     2 2 7
2 3 9     2 3 8     2 3 10
END DATA.
LIST.
GLM DEP BY FACA FACB/
    PRINT = DESCRIPTIVES/.
```

Tests of Significance for DEP using UNIQUE sums of squares

Source of Variation	SS	DF	MS	F	Sig of F
WITHIN CELLS	75.33	12	6.28		
FACA	24.50	1	24.50	3.90	.072
FACB	30.33	2	15.17	2.42	.131
FACA BY FACB	14.33	2	7.17	1.14	.352
(Model)	69.17	5	13.83	2.20	.122
(Total)	144.50	17	8.50		

Tests of Significance for DEP using SEQUENTIAL Sums of Squares

Source of Variation	SS	DF	MS	F	Sig of F
WITHIN CELLS	75.33	12	6.28		
FACA	24.50	1	24.50	3.90	.072
FACB	30.33	2	15.17	2.42	.131
FACA BY FACB	14.33	2	7.17	1.14	.352
(Model)	69.17	5	13.83	2.20	.122
(Total)	144.50	17	8.50		

Note: The screens for this problem can be found in Appendix 3.

case where the correlations among the effects were all 0 (Table 8.2). Thus, for disproportional cell sizes the sources of variation are confounded (mixed together). To determine how much unique variation on y a given effect accounts for we must adjust or partial out how much of that variation is explainable because of the effect's correlations with the other effects in the design. Recall that in chapter 5 the same procedure was employed to determine the unique amount of between variation a given planned comparison accounts for out of a set of correlated planned comparisons.

In Table 8.4 we present the control lines for running the disproportional cell size example, along with Method 1 (unique sum of squares) results and Method 3 (hierarchical or called sequential on the printout) results. The F ratios for the interaction effect are the same, but the F ratios for the main effects are quite different. For example, if we had used the default option (Method 3) we would have declared a significant B main effect at the .05 level, but with Method 1 (unique decomposition) the B main effect is not significant at the .05 level. Therefore, with unequal n designs the method used can clearly make a difference in terms of the conclusions reached in the study. This raises the question of which of the three methods should be used for disproportional cell size factorial designs.

TABLE 8.2

Regression Analysis of Two-Way Equal *n* ANOVA with Effects Dummy Coded and Correlation Matrix for the Effects

TITLE 'DUMMY CODING OF EFFECTS FOR EQUAL N 2 WAY ANOVA'.
DATA LIST FREE/Y A1 B1 B2 A1B1 A1B2.
BEGIN DATA.

```
3 1 1 0 1 0              5 1 1 0 1 0              6 1 1 0 1 0
2 1 0 1 0 1              4 1 0 1 0 1              8 1 0 1 0 1
11 1 1 −1 −1 −1 −1       7 1 −1 −1 −1 −1          8 1 −1 −1 −1 − 1
9 −1 1 0 −1 0            14 −1 1 0 −1 0           5 −1 1 0 −1 0
6 −1 0 1 0 −1            7 −1 0 1 0 −1            7 −1 0 1 0 −1
9 −1 −1 −1 1 1           8 −1 −1 −1 1 1           10 −1 −1 −1 1 1
```

END DATA.
LIST.
REGRESSION DESCRIPTIVES = DEFAULT/
    VARIABLES = Y TO A1B2/
    DEPENDENT = Y/
    METHOD = ENTER/.

Y	A1	① B1	B2	A1B1	A1B2
3.00	1.00	1.00	.00	1.00	.00
5.00	1.00	1.00	.00	1.00	.00
6.00	1.00	1.00	.00	1.00	.00
2.00	1.00	.00	1.00	.00	1.00
4.00	1.00	.00	1.00	.00	1.00
8.00	1.00	.00	1.00	.00	1.00
11.00	1.00	−1.00	−1.00	−1.00	−1.00
7.00	1.00	−1.00	−1.00	−1.00	−1.00
8.00	1.00	−1.00	−1.00	−1.00	−1.00
9.00	−1.00	1.00	.00	−1.00	.00
14.00	−1.00	1.00	.00	−1.00	.00
5.00	−1.00	1.00	.00	−1.00	.00
6.00	−1.00	.00	1.00	.00	−1.00
7.00	−1.00	.00	1.00	.00	−1.00
7.00	−1.00	.00	1.00	.00	−1.00
9.00	−1.00	−1.00	−1.00	1.00	1.00
8.00	−1.00	−1.00	−1.00	1.00	1.00
10.00	−1.00	−1.00	−1.00	1.00	1.00

Correlations

	Y	A1	B1	B2	A1B1	A1B2
Y	1.000	−.412	−.264	−.456	−.312	−.120
A1	−.412	1.000	.000	.000	.000	.000
B1	−.264	② .000	1.000	.500	.000	.000
B2	−.456	.000	.500	1.000	.000	.000
A1B1	−.312	.000	.000	.000	1.000	.500
A1B2	−.120	.000	.000	.000	.500	1.000

① The S's in the first level of B are coded as 1s on the first dummy variable (A1 here), with the S's for all other levels of B, except the last, coded as 0s. The S's in the last level of B are coded as −1s. Similarly, the S's on the second level of B are coded as 1s on the second dummy variable (B2 here), with the S's for all other levels of B, except the last, coded as 0's. Again, the S's in the last level of B are coded as −1s. To obtain the elements for the interaction dummy variables, i.e., A1B1 and A1B2, multiply the corresponding elements of the dummy variables composing the interaction variable. Thus, to obtain the elements of A1B1 multiply the elements of A1 by the elements of B1.

② Note that the correlations between variables representing *different* effects are all 0. The only nonzero correlations are for the two variables that jointly represent the B main effect (B1 and B2), and for the two variables (A1B1 and A1B2) that jointly represent the AB interaction effect.

TABLE 8.3

Stepwise Regression Results for Two-Way Equal *n* ANOVA with the Effects Entered as the Predictors

Step No.	1				
Variable Entered		A1			
Analysis of Variance					
		Sum of Squares	DF	Mean Square	F Ratio
Regression		24.499954	1	24.49995	3.27
Residual		120.00003	16	7.500002	

Step No.	2				
Variable Entered		B2			
Analysis of Variance					
		Sum of Squares	DF	Mean Square	F Ratio
Regression		54.583191	2	27.29160	4.55
Residual		89.916794	15	8.994452	

Step No.	3				
Variable Entered		B1			
Analysis of Variance					
		Sum of Squares	DF	Mean Square	F Ratio
Regression		54.833206	3	18.27773	2.85
Residual		89.666779	14	6.404770	

Step No.	4				
Variable Entered		A1B1			
Analysis of Variance					
		Sum of Squares	DF	Mean Square	F Ratio
Regression		68.916504	4	17.22913	2.98
Residual		75.683481	13	5.814114	

Step No.	5				
Variable Entered		A1B2			
Analysis of Variance					
		Sum of Squares	DF	Mean Square	F Ratio
Regression		69.166489	5	13.83330	2.20
Residual		75.333496	12	6.277791	

Note: The sum of squares (*SS*) for regression for A1, representing the A main effect, is the same as the *SS* for FACA in Table 8.1. Also, the *additional SS* for B1 and B2, representing the B main effect, is $54.833 - 24.5 = 30.333$, the same as *SS* for FACB in Table 8.1. Finally, the additional *SS* for A1B1 and A1B2, representing the AB interaction, is $69.166 - 54.833 = 14.333$, the same as *SS* for FACA by FACB in Table 8.1.

TABLE 8.4

Control Lines for Two-Way Disproportional Cell n ANOVA on SPSS with the Sequential and Unique Sum of Squares F Ratios

```
TITLE 'TWO WAY UNEQUAL N'.
DATA LIST FREE/FACA FACB DEP.
BEGIN DATA.
1 1 3      1 1 5      1 1 6
1 2 2      1 2 4      1 2 8
1 3 11     1 3 7      1 3 8      1 3 6      1 3 9
2 1 9      2 1 14     2 1 5      2 1 11
2 2 6      2 2 7      2 2 7      2 2 8      2 2 10    2 2 5     2 2 6
2 3 9      2 3 8      2 3 10
END DATA.
LIST.
UNIANOVA DEP BY FACA FACB/
   METHOD = SSTYPE(1)/
   PRINT = DESCRIPTIVES/.
```

Tests of Between-Subjects Effects

Dependent Variable: DEP

Source	Type I Sum of Squares	df	Mean Square	F	Sig.
Corrected Model	78.877[a]	5	15.775	3.031	.035
Intercept	1354.240	1	1354.240	260.211	.000
FACA	23.221	1	23.221	4.462	.048
FACB	38.878	2	19.439	3.735	.043
FACA * FACB	16.778	2	8.389	1.612	.226
Error	98.883	19	5.204		
Total	1532.000	25			
Corrected Total	177.760	24			

Tests of Between-Subjects Effects

Dependent Variable: DEP

Source	Type III Sum of Squares	df	Mean Square	F	Sig.
Corrected Model	78.877[a]	5	15.775	3.031	.035
Intercept	1176.155	1	1176.155	225.993	.000
FACA	42.385	1	42.385	8.144	.010
FACB	30.352	2	15.176	2.916	.079
FACA * FACB	16.778	2	8.389	1.612	.226
Error	98.883	19	5.204		
Total	1532.000	25			
Corrected Total	177.760	24			

[a] R Squared = .444 (Adjusted R Squared = .297)

TABLE 8.5

Dummy Coding of the Effects for the Disproportional Cell *n* ANOVA and
Correlation Matrix for the Effects

	Design B		
A	3, 5, 6	2, 4, 8	11, 7, 8, 6, 9
	9, 14, 5, 11	6, 7, 7, 8, 10, 5, 6	9, 8, 10

A1	B1	B2	A1B1	A1B2	Y
1.00	1.00	.00	1.00	.00	3.00
1.00	1.00	.00	1.00	.00	5.00
1.00	1.00	.00	1.00	.00	6.00
1.00	.00	1.00	.00	1.00	2.00
1.00	.00	1.00	.00	1.00	4.00
1.00	.00	1.00	.00	1.00	8.00
1.00	−1.00	−1.00	−1.00	−1.00	11.00
1.00	−1.00	−1.00	−1.00	−1.00	7.00
1.00	−1.00	−1.00	−1.00	−1.00	8.00
1.00	−1.00	−1.00	−1.00	−1.00	6.00
1.00	−1.00	−1.00	−1.00	−1.00	9.00
−1.00	1.00	.00	−1.00	.00	9.00
−1.00	1.00	.00	−1.00	.00	14.00
−1.00	1.00	.00	−1.00	.00	5.00
−1.00	1.00	.00	−1.00	.00	11.00
−1.00	.00	1.00	.00	−1.00	6.00
−1.00	.00	1.00	.00	−1.00	7.00
−1.00	.00	1.00	.00	−1.00	7.00
−1.00	.00	1.00	.00	−1.00	8.00
−1.00	.00	1.00	.00	−1.00	10.00
−1.00	.00	1.00	.00	−1.00	5.00
−1.00	.00	1.00	.00	−1.00	6.00
−1.00	−1.00	−1.00	1.00	1.00	9.00
−1.00	−1.00	−1.00	1.00	1.00	8.00
−1.00	−1.00	−1.00	1.00	1.00	10.00

For A main effect → A1

For B main effect → B1, B2

For AB interaction effect → A1B1, A1B2

Correlation:

	A1	B1	B2	A1B1	A1B2	Y
A1	1.000	−.163	−.275	−.072	.063	−.361
B1	−.163	1.000	.495	.059	.112	−.148
B2	−.275	.495	1.000	.139	−.088	−.350
A1B1	−0.72	0.59	1.39	1.000	.458	−.332
A1B2	.063	.112	−.088	.488	1.000	−.089
Y	−.361	−.148	−.350	−.332	−.089	1.000

Note: The correlations between variables representing different effects are boxed in. Contrast
with the situation for equal cell size, as presented in Table 8.2.

8.3.2 Which Method Should Be Used?

Overall and Spiegel (1969) recommended Method 2 as generally being most appropriate. I do not agree, believing that Method 2 would rarely be the method of choice, since it estimates the main effects ignoring the interaction. Carlson and Timm's comment (1974) is appropriate here: "We find it hard to believe that a researcher would consciously design a factorial experiment and then ignore the factorial nature of the data in testing the main effects" (p. 156).

We feel that Method 1, where we are obtaining the unique contribution of each effect, is generally more appropriate. This is what Carlson and Timm (1974) recommended, and what Myers (1979) recommended for experimental studies (random assignment involved), or as he put it, "whenever variations in cell frequencies can reasonably be assumed due to chance."

Where an a priori ordering of the effects can be established (Overall & Spiegel, 1969, give a nice psychiatric example), Method 3 makes sense. This is analogous to establishing an a priori ordering of the predictors in multiple regression. Pedhazur (1982) gave the following example. There is a 2 × 2 design in which one of the classification variables is race (black and white) and the other classification variable is education (high school and college). The dependent variable is income. In this case one can argue that race affects one's level of education, but obviously not vice versa. Thus, it makes sense to enter race first to determine its effect on income, then to enter education to determine how much it adds in predicting income. Finally, the race × education interaction is entered.

8.4 Factorial Multivariate Analysis of Variance

Here, we are considering the effect of two or more independent variables on a set of dependent variables. To illustrate factorial MANOVA we use an example from Barcikowski (1983). Sixth-grade students were classified as being of high, average, or low aptitude, and then within each of these aptitudes, were randomly assigned to one of five methods of teaching social studies. The dependent variables were measures of attitude and achievement. These data resulted:

| | **Method of Instruction** | | | | |
	1	2	3	4	5
High	15, 11	19, 11	14, 13	19, 14	14, 16
	9, 7	12, 9	9, 9	7, 8	14, 8
		12, 6	14, 15	6, 6	18, 16
Average	18, 13	25, 24	29, 23	11, 14	18, 17
	8, 11	24, 23	28, 26	14, 10	11, 13
	6, 6	26, 19		8, 7	
Low	11, 9	13, 11	17, 10	15, 9	17, 12
	16, 15	10, 11	7, 9	13, 13	13, 15
			7, 9	7, 7	9, 12

Of the 45 subjects who started the study, five were lost for various reasons. This resulted in a disproportional factorial design. To obtain the unique contribution of each effect, the unique sum of squares decomposition was run on SPSS MANOVA. The control lines for doing so are given in Table 8.6. The results of the multivariate and univariate tests of the

TABLE 8.6

Control Lines for Factorial MANOVA on SPSS

TITLE 'TWO WAY MANOVA
DATA LIST FREE/FACA FACB ATTIT ACHIEV.
BEGIN DATA.

1 1 15 11	1 1 9 7	
1 2 19 11	1 2 12 9	1 2 12 6
1 3 14 13	1 3 9 9	1 3 14 15
1 4 19 14	1 4 7 8	1 4 6 6
1 5 14 16	1 5 14 8	1 15 18 16
2 1 18 13	2 1 8 11	2 1 6 6
2 2 25 24	2 2 24 23	2 2 26 19
2 3 29 23	2 3 28 26	
2 4 11 14	2 4 14 10	2 4 8 7
2 5 18 17	2 5 11 13	
3 1 11 9	3 1 16 15	
3 2 13 11	3 2 10 11	
3 3 17 10	3 3 7 9	3 3 7 9
3 4 15 9	3 4 13 13	3 4 7 7
3 5 17 12	3 5 13 15	3 5 9 12

END DATA.
LIST.
GLM ATTIT ACHIEV BY FACA FACB/
    PRINT = DESCRIPTIVES/.

effects are presented in Table 8.7. All of the multivariate effects are significant at the .05 level. We use the F's associated with Wilks to illustrate (aptitude by method: $F = 2.19$, $p < .018$; method: $F = 2.46$, $p < .025$; and aptitude: $F = 5.92$, $p < .001$). Because the interaction is significant, we focus our interpretation on it. The univariate tests for this effect on attitude and achievement are also both significant at the .05 level. Use of simple effects revealed that it was the attitude and achievement of the average aptitude subjects under methods 2 and 3 that were responsible for the interaction.

8.5 Weighting of the Cell Means

In experimental studies that wind up with unequal cell sizes, it is reasonable to assume equal population sizes and equal cell weighting are appropriate in estimating the grand mean. However, when sampling from intact groups (sex, age, race, socioeconomic status [SES], religions) in nonexperimental studies, the populations may well differ in size, and the sizes of the samples may reflect the different population sizes. In such cases, equally weighting the subgroup means will not provide an unbiased estimate of the combined (grand) mean, whereas weighting the means will produce an unbiased estimate. *The BMDP4V program is specifically set up to provide either equal or unequal weighting of the cell means.* In some situations one may wish to use both weighted and unweighted cell means in a single factorial design, that is, in a semiexperimental design. In such designs one of the factors is an attribute factor (sex, SES, race, etc.) and the other factor is treatments.

TABLE 8.7

Multivariate Tests[c]

Effect		Value	F	Hypothesis df	Error df	Sig.
Intercept	Pillai's Trace	.965	329.152[a]	2.000	24.000	.000
	Wilks' Lambda	.035	329.152[a]	2.000	24.000	.000
	Hotelling's Trace	27.429	329.152[a]	2.000	24.000	.000
	Roy's Largest Root	27.429	329.152[a]	2.000	24.000	.000
FACA	Pillai's Trace	.574	5.031	4.000	50.000	.002
	Wilks' Lambda	.449	5.917[a]	4.000	48.000	.001
	Hotelling's Trace	1.179	6.780	4.000	46.000	.000
	Roy's Largest Root	1.135	14.187[b]	2.000	25.000	.000
FACB	Pillai's Trace	.534	2.278	8.000	50.000	.037
	Wilks' Lambda	.503	2.463[a]	8.000	48.000	.025
	Hotelling's Trace	.916	2.633	8.000	46.000	.018
	Roy's Largest Root	.827	5.167[b]	4.000	25.000	.004
FACA * FACB	Pillai's Trace	.757	1.905	16.000	50.000	.042
	Wilks' Lambda	.333	2.196[a]	16.000	48.000	.018
	Hotelling's Trace	1.727	2.482	16.000	46.000	.008
	Roy's Largest Root	1.551	4.847[b]	8.000	25.000	.001

[a] Exact statistic
[b] The statistic is an upper bound on F that yields a lower bound on the significance level.
[c] Design: Intercept+FACA+FACB+FACA * FACB

Tests of Between-Subjects Effects

Source	Dependent Variable	Type III Sum of Squares	df	Mean Square	F	Sig.
Corrected Model	ATTIT	972.108[a]	14	69.436	3.768	.002
	ACHIEV	764.608[b]	14	54.615	5.757	.000
Intercept	ATTIT	7875.219	1	7875.219	427.382	.000
	ACHIEV	6156.043	1	6156.043	648.915	.000
FACA	ATTIT	256.508	2	128.254	6.960	.004
	ACHIEV	267.558	2	133.779	14.102	.000
FACB	ATTIT	237.906	4	59.477	3.228	.029
	ACHIEV	189.881	4	47.470	5.004	.004
FACA * FACB	ATTIT	503.321	8	62.915	3.414	.009
	ACHIEV	343.112	8	42.889	4.521	.002
Error	ATTIT	460.667	25	18.427		
	ACHIEV	237.167	25	9.487		
Total	ATTIT	9357.000	40			
	ACHIEV	7177.000	40			
Corrected Total	ATTIT	1432.775	39			
	ACHIEV	1001.775	39			

[a] R Squared = .678 (Adjusted R Squared = .498)
[b] R Squared = .763 (Adjusted R Squared = .631)

Suppose for a given situation it is reasonable to assume there are twice as many middle SES in a population as lower SES, and that two treatments are involved. Forty lower SES are sampled and randomly assigned to treatments, and 80 middle SES are selected and assigned to treatments. Schematically then, the setup of the weighted and unweighted means is:

		T_1	T_2	Unweighted means
SES	Lower	$n_{11} = 20$	$n_{12} = 20$	$(\mu_{11} + \mu_{12})/2$
	Middle	$n_{21} = 40$	$n_{22} = 40$	$(\mu_{21} + \mu_{22})/2$

Weighted Means	$\dfrac{n_{11}\mu_{11} + n_{21}\mu_{21}}{n_{11} + n_{21}}$	$\dfrac{n_{12}\mu_{12} + n_{22}\mu_{22}}{n_{12} + n_{22}}$

8.6 Three-Way Manova

This section is included to show how to set up the control lines for running a three-way MANOVA, and to indicate a procedure for interpreting a three-way interaction. We take the previous aptitude by method example and add sex as an additional factor. Then assuming we will use the same two dependent variables, the *only* change that is required in the control lines presented in Table 8.6 is that the MANOVA command becomes:

```
Manova Attit Achiev by Aptitude(1,3) Method(1,5) Sex(1,2)
```

We wish to focus our attention on the interpretation of a three-way interaction, if it were significant in such a design. First, what does a significant three-way interaction mean for a single variable? If the three factors are denoted by A, B, and C, then *a significant ABC interaction implies that the two-way interaction profiles for the different levels of the third factor are different.* A nonsignificant three-way interaction means that the two-way profiles are the same; that is, the differences can be attributed to sampling error.

Example 8.3

Consider a sex (a) by treatments (b) by race (c) design. Suppose that the two-way design (collapsed on race) looked like this:

	Treatments	
	1	2
Males	60	50
Females	40	42

This profile reveals a significant sex main effect and a significant ordinal interaction. But it does not tell the whole story. Let us examine the profiles for blacks and whites separately (we assume equal *n* per cell):

	Whites				Blacks	
	T_1	T_2			T_1	T_2
M	65	50		M	55	50
F	40	47		F	40	37

We see that for whites there clearly is an ordinal interaction, whereas for blacks there is no interaction effect. The two profiles are distinctly different. The point is, race further moderates the sex-by-treatments interaction.

In the context of aptitude–treatment interaction (ATI) research, Cronbach (1975) had an interesting way of characterizing higher order interactions:

> When ATIs are present, a general statement about a treatment effect is misleading because the effect will come or go depending on the kind of person treated. . . . An ATI result can be taken as a general conclusion only if it is not in turn moderated by further variables. If Aptitude×Treatment×Sex interact, for example, then the Aptitude×Treatment effect does not tell the story. Once we attend to interactions, we enter a hall of mirrors that extends to infinity. (p. 119)

Thus, to examine the nature of a significant three-way multivariate interaction, one might first determine which of the individual variables are significant (by examining the univariate F's). Then look at the two-way profiles to see how they differ for those variables that are significant.

8.7 Summary

The advantages of a factorial design over a one way are discussed. For equal cell n, all three methods that Overall and Spiegel (1969) mention yield the same F tests. For unequal cell n (which usually occurs in practice), the three methods can yield quite different results. The reason for this is that for unequal cell n the effects are correlated. There is a consensus among experts that for unequal cell size the regression approach (which yields the UNIQUE contribution of each effect) is generally preferable. The regression approach is the default option in SPSS. In SAS, type III sum of squares is the unique sum of squares. A significant three-way interaction implies that the two-way interaction profiles are different for the different levels of the third factor.

Exercises

1. Consider the following 2 × 4 equal cell size MANOVA data set (two dependent variables):

B

	6, 10	13, 16	9, 11	21, 19
	7, 8	11, 15	8, 8	18, 15
	9, 9	17, 18	14, 9	16, 13
A				
	11, 8	10, 12	4, 12	11, 10
	7, 6	11, 13	10, 8	9, 8
	10, 5	14, 10	11, 13	8, 15

(a) Run the factorial MANOVA on SPSS using the default option.

(b) Which of the multivariate tests for the three different effects is(are) significant at the .05 level?

(c) For the effect(s) that show multivariate significance, which of the individual variables (at .025 level) are contributing to the multivariate significance?

(d) Run the above data on SPSS using METHOD = SSTYPE (SEQUENTIAL). Are the results different? Explain.

2. An investigator has the following 2 × 4 MANOVA data set for two dependent variables:

B

		13, 16	9, 11	21, 19
	7, 8	11, 15	8, 8	18, 15
		17, 18	14, 9	16, 13
			13, 11	
A				
	11, 8	10, 12	14, 12	11, 10
	7, 6	11, 13	10, 8	9, 8
	10, 5	14, 10	11, 13	8, 15
	6, 12			17, 12
	9, 7			13, 14
	11, 14			

(a) Run the factorial MANOVA on SPSS.

(b) Which of the multivariate tests for the three effects is(are) significant at the .05 level?

(c) For the effect(s) that show multivariate significance, which of the individual variables is(are) contributing to the multivariate significance at the .025 level?

(d) Is the homogeneity of the covariance matrices assumption for the cells tenable at the .05 level?

(e) Run the factorial MANOVA on the data set using sequential sum of squares option of SPSS. Are the F ratios different? Explain.

(f) Dummy code group (cell) membership and run as a regression analysis, in the process obtaining the correlations among the effects, as illustrated in Tables 9.2 and 9.5.

3. Consider the following hypothetical data for a sex×age×treatment factorial MANOVA on two personality measures:

   (a) Run the three-way MANOVA on SPSS.

   (b) Which of the multivariate effects are significant at the .025 level? What is the overall α for the set of multivariate tests?

   (c) Is the homogeneity of covariance matrices assumption tenable at the .05 level?

   (d) For the multivariate effects that are significant, which of the individual variables are significant at the .01 level? Interpret the results.

	Age	\multicolumn{2}{c	}{Treatments 1}	2	3
Males	14	8, 19 5, 18 9, 16 7, 25 4, 20 4, 17 3, 21	2, 23 3, 27 8, 20	6, 16 9, 12 13, 24 5, 20
	17	9, 22 11, 15 8, 14	4, 30 7, 25 8, 28 13, 23	5, 15 5, 16 9, 23 8, 27
Females	14	10, 17 12, 18 8, 14 7, 22	8, 26 2, 29 10, 23 7, 17	3, 21 7, 17 4, 15 9, 22 12, 23
	17	9, 13 5, 19 6, 18 8, 15 12, 20 11, 1	5, 14 11, 13 4, 21 8, 18	10, 14 15, 18 9, 19

9

Analysis of Covariance

9.1 Introduction

Analysis of covariance (ANCOVA) is a statistical technique that combines regression analysis and analysis of variance. It can be helpful in nonrandomized studies in drawing more accurate conclusions. However, precautions have to be taken, or analysis of covariance can be misleading in some cases. In this chapter we indicate what the purposes of covariance are, when it is most effective, when the interpretation of results from covariance is "cleanest," and when covariance should not be used. We start with the simplest case, one dependent variable and one covariate, with which many readers may be somewhat familiar. Then we consider one dependent variable and several covariates, where our previous study of multiple regression is helpful. Finally, multivariate analysis of covariance is considered, where there are several dependent variables and several covariates. We show how to run a multivariate analysis of covariance (MANCOVA) on SPSS and on SAS and explain the proper order of interpretation of the printout. An extension of the Tukey post hoc procedure, the Bryant–Paulson, is also illustrated.

9.1.1 Examples of Univariate and Multivariate Analysis of Covariance

What is a covariate? A potential covariate is any variable that is significantly correlated with the dependent variable. That is, we assume a *linear* relationship between the covariate (x) and the dependent variable (y). Consider now two typical univariate ANCOVAs with one covariate. In a two-group pretest–posttest design, the pretest is often used as a covariate, because how the subjects score before treatments is generally correlated with how they score after treatments. Or, suppose three groups are compared on some measure of achievement. In this situation IQ is often used as a covariate, because IQ is usually at least moderately correlated with achievement.

The reader should recall that the null hypothesis being tested in ANCOVA is that the adjusted population means are equal. Since a linear relationship is assumed between the covariate and the dependent variable, the means are adjusted in a linear fashion. We consider this in detail shortly in this chapter. Thus, in interpreting printout, for either univariate or MANCOVA, it is the adjusted means that need to be examined. It is important to note that SPSS and SAS do not automatically provide the adjusted means; they must be requested.

Now consider two situations where MANCOVA would be appropriate. A counselor wishes to examine the effect of two different counseling approaches on several personality variables. The subjects are pretested on these variables and then posttested 2 months later. The pretest scores are the covariates and the posttest scores are the dependent variables.

Second, a teacher educator wishes to determine the relative efficacy of two different methods of teaching 12th-grade mathematics. He uses three subtest scores of achievement on a posttest as the dependent variables. A plausible set of covariates here would be grade in math 11, an IQ measure, and, say, attitude toward education. The null hypothesis that is tested in MANCOVA is that the adjusted population mean vectors are equal. Recall that the null hypothesis for MANOVA was that the population mean vectors are equal.

Four excellent references for further study of covariance are available: an elementary introduction (Huck, Cormier, & Bounds, 1974), two good classic review articles (Cochran, 1957; Elashoff, 1969), and especially a very comprehensive and thorough text by Huitema (1980).

9.2 Purposes of Covariance

ANCOVA is linked to the following two basic objectives in experimental design:

1. Elimination of systematic bias
2. Reduction of within group or error variance

The best way of dealing with systematic bias (e.g., intact groups that differ systematically on several variables) is through random assignment of subjects to groups, thus equating the groups on all variables within sampling error. If random assignment is not possible, however, then covariance can be helpful in reducing bias.

Within-group variability, which is primarily due to individual differences among the subjects, can be dealt with in several ways: sample selection (subjects who are more homogeneous will vary less on the criterion measure), factorial designs (blocking), repeated-measures analysis, and ANCOVA. Precisely how covariance reduces error is considered soon. Because ANCOVA is linked to both of the basic objectives of experimental design, it certainly is a useful tool if properly used and interpreted.

In an experimental study (random assignment of subjects to groups) the main purpose of covariance is to reduce error variance, because there will be no systematic bias. However, if only a small number of subjects (say ≤ 10) can be assigned to each group, then chance differences are more possible and covariance is useful in adjusting the posttest means for the chance differences.

In a nonexperimental study the main purpose of covariance is to adjust the posttest means for initial differences among the groups that are very likely with intact groups. It should be emphasized, however, that even the use of several covariates does *not* equate intact groups, that is, does not eliminate bias. Nevertheless, the use of two or three appropriate covariates can make for a much fairer comparison.

We now give two examples to illustrate how initial differences (systematic bias) on a key variable between treatment groups can confound the interpretation of results. Suppose an experimental psychologist wished to determine the effect of three methods of extinction on some kind of learned response. There are three intact groups to which the methods are applied, and it is found that the average number of trials to extinguish the response is least for Method 2. Now, it may be that Method 2 is more effective, or it may be that the subjects in Method 2 didn't have the response as thoroughly ingrained as the subjects in the other two groups. In the latter case, the response would be easier to extinguish, and it wouldn't be clear whether it was the method that made the difference or the fact that the response was easier to extinguish that made Method 2 look better. The effects of the two are confounded or mixed together. What is needed here is a measure of degree of learning at the start of the extinction trials (covariate). Then, if there are initial differences between the groups, the posttest means will be adjusted to take this into account. That is, covariance will adjust the posttest means to what they would be if all groups had started out *equally* on the covariate.

As another example, suppose we are comparing the effect of four stress situations on blood pressure, and find that Situation 3 was significantly more stressful than the other three situations. However, we note that the blood pressure of the subjects in Group 3 under minimal stress is greater than for subjects in the other groups. Then, as in the previous example, it isn't clear that Situation 3 is necessarily most stressful. We need to determine whether the blood pressure for Group 3 would still be higher if the means for all four groups were adjusted, assuming equal average blood pressure initially.

9.3 Adjustment of Posttest Means and Reduction of Error Variance

As mentioned earlier, ANCOVA adjusts the posttest means to what they would be if all groups started out equally on the covariate, at the grand mean. In this section we derive the general equation for linearly adjusting the posttest means for one covariate. Before we do that, however, it is important to discuss one of the assumptions underlying the analysis of covariance. That assumption for one covariate requires *equal population regression slopes* for all groups. Consider a three-group situation, with 15 subjects per group. Suppose that the scatterplots for the three groups looked as given here:

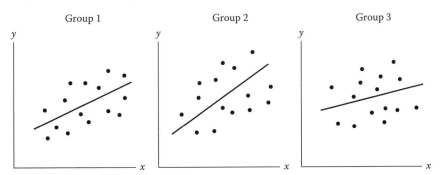

Recall from beginning statistics that the x and y scores for each subject determine a point in the plane. Requiring that the slopes be equal is equivalent to saying that the nature of the linear relationship is the *same* for all groups, or that the rate of change in y as a function of x is the same for all groups. For these scatterplots the slopes are different, with the slope being the largest for Group 2 and smallest for Group 3. But the issue is whether the *population* slopes are different and whether the sample slopes differ sufficiently to conclude that the population values are different. With small sample sizes as in these scatterplots, it is dangerous to rely on visual inspection to determine whether the population values are equal, because of considerable sampling error. Fortunately, there is a statistic for this, and later we indicate how to obtain it on SPSS and SAS. In deriving the equation for the adjusted means we are going to assume the slopes are equal. What if the slopes are not equal? Then ANCOVA is *not* appropriate, and we indicate alternatives later on in the chapter.

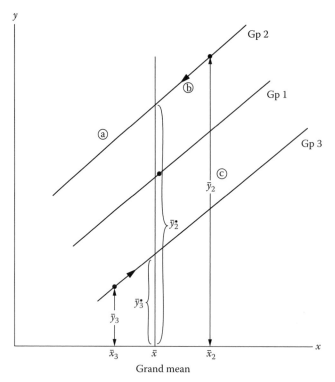

(a) positive correlation assumed between x and y

(b) The arrows on the regression lines indicate that the adjusted
means can be obtained by sliding the mean up (down) the
regression line until it hits the line for the grand mean.

(c) $\bar{y}_2$ is actual mean for Gp 2 and $\bar{y}_2^*$ represents the adjusted mean.

FIGURE 9.1
Regression lines and adjusted means for three-group analysis of covariance.

The details of obtaining the adjusted mean for the ith group (i.e., any group) are given in
Figure 9.1. The general equation follows from the definition for the slope of a straight line
and some basic algebra.

In Figure 9.2 we show the adjusted means geometrically for a hypothetical three-group
data set. A positive correlation is assumed between the covariate and the dependent variable, so that a higher mean on x implies a higher mean on y. Note that because Group 3
scored below the grand mean on the covariate, its mean is adjusted upward. On the other
hand, because the mean for Group 2 on the covariate is *above* the grand mean, covariance
estimates that it would have scored lower on y if its mean on the covariate was lower (at
grand mean), and therefore the mean for Group 2 is adjusted downward.

9.3.1 Reduction of Error Variance

Consider a teaching methods study where the dependent variable is chemistry achievement and the covariate is IQ. Then, within each teaching method there will be considerable
variability on chemistry achievement due to individual differences among the students in
terms of ability, background, attitude, and so on. A sizable portion of this within-variability, however, is due to differences in IQ. That is, chemistry achievement scores differ partly

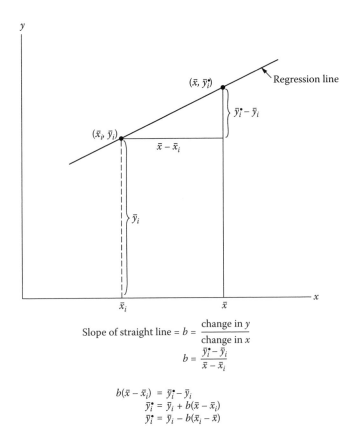

$$\text{Slope of straight line} = b = \frac{\text{change in } y}{\text{change in } x}$$

$$b = \frac{\bar{y}_i^* - \bar{y}_i}{\bar{x} - \bar{x}_i}$$

$$b(\bar{x} - \bar{x}_i) = \bar{y}_i^* - \bar{y}_i$$
$$\bar{y}_i^* = \bar{y}_i + b(\bar{x} - \bar{x}_i)$$
$$\bar{y}_i^* = \bar{y}_i - b(\bar{x}_i - \bar{x})$$

FIGURE 9.2
Deriving the general equation for the adjusted means in covariance.

because the students differ in IQ. If we can statistically remove this part of the within-variability, a smaller error term results, and hence a more powerful test. We denote the correlation between IQ and chemistry achievement by r_{xy}. Recall that the square of a correlation can be interpreted as "variance accounted for." Thus, for example, if $r_{xy} = .71$, then $(.71)^2 = .50$, or 50% of the within-variability on chemistry achievement can be accounted for by variability on IQ.

We denote the within-variability on chemistry achievement by MS_w, the usual error term for ANOVA. Now, symbolically, the part of MS_w that is accounted for by IQ is $MS_w r_{xy}^2$. Thus, the within-variability that is left after the portion due to the covariate is removed, is

$$MS_w - MS_w r_{xy}^2 = MS_w \left(1 - r_{xy}^2\right) \tag{1}$$

and this becomes our new error term for analysis of covariance, which we denote by MS_w^*. Technically, there is an additional factor involved,

$$MS_w^* = MS_w \left(1 - r_{xy}^2\right)\left\{1 + 1/(f_e - 2)\right\} \tag{2}$$

where f_e is error degrees of freedom. However, the effect of this additional factor is slight as long as $N \geq 50$.

To show how much of a difference a covariate can make in increasing the sensitivity of an experiment, we consider a hypothetical study. An investigator runs a one-way ANOVA (three groups with 20 subjects per group), and obtains $F = 200/100 = 2$, which is not significant, because the critical value at .05 is 3.18. He had pretested the subjects, but didn't use the pretest as a covariate because the groups didn't differ significantly on the pretest (even though the correlation between pretest and posttest was .71). This is a common mistake made by some researchers who are unaware of the other purpose of covariance, that of reducing error variance. The analysis is redone by another investigator using ANCOVA. Using the equation that we just derived for the new error term for ANCOVA he finds:

$$MS_w^* \approx 100[1 - (.71)^2] = 50$$

Thus, the error term for ANCOVA is only half as large as the error term for ANOVA. It is also necessary to obtain a new MS_b for ANCOVA; call it MS_b^*. Because the formula for MS_b^* is complicated, we do not pursue it. Let us assume the investigator obtains the following F ratio for covariance analysis:

$$F^* = 190/50 = 3.8$$

This is significant at the .05 level. Therefore, the use of covariance can make the difference between not finding significance and finding significance. Finally, we wish to note that MS_b^* can be smaller or larger than MS_b, although in a randomized study the expected values of the two are equal.

9.4 Choice of Covariates

In general, any variables that theoretically should correlate with the dependent variable, or variables that have been shown to correlate on similar types of subjects, should be considered as possible covariates. The ideal is to choose as covariates variables that of course are significantly correlated with the dependent variable *and* that have low correlations among themselves. If two covariates are highly correlated (say .80), then they are removing much of the *same* error variance from y; x_2 will not have much incremental validity. On the other hand, if two covariates (x_1 and x_2) have a low correlation (say .20), then they are removing relatively distinct pieces of the error variance from y, and we will obtain a much greater total error reduction. This is illustrated here graphically using Venn diagrams, where the circle represents error variance on y.

x_1 and x_2 Low correl. x_1 and x_2 High correl.

Solid lines—part of variance on y that x_1 accounts for.

Dashed lines—part of variance on y that x_2 accounts for.

The shaded portion in each case represents the incremental validity of x_2, that is, the part of error variance on y it removes that x_1 did not.

If the dependent variable is achievement in some content area, then one should always consider the possibility of at least three covariates:

1. A measure of ability in that specific content area
2. A measure of general ability (IQ measure)
3. One or two relevant noncognitive measures (e.g., attitude toward education, study habits, etc.)

An example of this was given earlier, where we considered the effect of two different teaching methods on 12th-grade mathematics achievement. We indicated that a plausible set of covariates would be grade in math 11 (a previous measure of ability in mathematics), an IQ measure, and attitude toward education (a noncognitive measure).

In studies with small or relatively small group sizes, it is particularly imperative to consider the use of two or three covariates. Why? Because for small or medium effect sizes, which are *very common* in social science research, power will be poor for small group size. Thus, one should attempt to reduce the error variance as much as possible to obtain a more sensitive (powerful) test.

Huitema (1980, p. 161) recommended limiting the number of covariates to the extent that the ratio

$$\frac{C+(J-1)}{N} < .10 \tag{3}$$

where C is the number of covariates, J is the number of groups, and N is total sample size. Thus, if we had a three-group problem with a total of 60 subjects, then $(C + 2)/60 < .10$ or $C < 4$. We should use less than four covariates. If the above ratio is $> .10$, then the estimates of the adjusted means are likely to be unstable. That is, if the study were cross-validated, it could be expected that the equation used to estimate the adjusted means in the original study would yield very different estimates for another sample from the same population.

9.4.1 Importance of Covariate's Being Measured before Treatments

To avoid confounding (mixing together) of the treatment effect with a change on the covariate, one should use only pretest or other information gathered before treatments begin as covariates. If a covariate that was measured after treatments is used and that variable was affected by treatments, then the change on the covariate may be correlated with change on the dependent variable. Thus, when the covariate adjustment is made, you will remove part of the treatment effect.

9.5 Assumptions in Analysis of Covariance

Analysis of covariance rests on the same assumptions as analysis of variance plus three additional assumptions regarding the regression part of the covariance analysis. That is, ANCOVA also assumes:

1. A linear relationship between the dependent variable and the covariate(s).*

2. Homogeneity of the regression slopes (for one covariate), that is, that the slope of the regression line is the same in each group. For two covariates the assumption is parallelism of the regression planes, and for more than two covariates the assumption is homogeneity of the regression hyperplanes.

3. The covariate is measured without error.

Because covariance rests partly on the same assumptions as ANOVA, any violations that are serious in ANOVA (such as the independence assumption) are also serious in ANCOVA. Violation of *all three* of the remaining assumptions of covariance is also serious. For example, if the relationship between the covariate and the dependent variable is curvilinear, then the adjustment of the means will be improper. In this case, two possible courses of action are:

1. Seek a transformation of the data that is linear. This is possible if the relationship between the covariate and the dependent variable is monotonic.

2. Fit a polynomial ANCOVA model to the data.

There is always measurement error for the variables that are typically used as covariates in social science research, and measurement error causes problems in both randomized and nonrandomized designs, but is more serious in nonrandomized designs. As Huitema (1980) noted, "In the case of randomized designs, … the power of the ANCOVA is reduced relative to what it would be if no error were present, but treatment effects are not biased. With other designs the effects of measurement error in x (covariate) are likely to be serious" (p. 299).

When measurement error is present on the covariate, then treatment effects can be seriously biased in nonrandomized designs. In Figure 9.3 we illustrate the effect measurement error can have when comparing two *different* populations with analysis of covariance. In the hypothetical example, with no measurement error we would conclude that Group 1 is superior to Group 2, whereas with considerable measurement error the opposite conclusion is drawn. This example shows that if the covariate means are not equal, then the difference between the adjusted means is partly a function of the reliability of the covariate. Now, this problem would not be of particular concern if we had a very reliable covariate such as IQ or other cognitive variables from a good standardized test. If, on the other hand, the covariate is a noncognitive variable, or a variable derived from a nonstandardized instrument (which might well be of questionable reliability), then concern would definitely be justified.

A violation of the homogeneity of regression slopes can also yield misleading results if covariance is used. To illustrate this, we present in Figure 9.4 the situation where the assumption is met and two situations where the assumption is violated. Notice that with homogeneous slopes the estimated superiority of Group 1 at the grand mean is an accurate estimate of Group 1's superiority for all levels of the covariate, since the lines are parallel. On the other hand, for Case 1 of heterogeneous slopes, the superiority of Group 1 (as estimated by covariance) is *not* an accurate estimate of Group 1's superiority for other values of the covariate. For $x = a$, Group 1 is only slightly better than Group 2, whereas for $x = b$, the superiority of Group 1 is seriously underestimated

---

* Nonlinear analysis of covariance is possible (cf. Huitema, chap. 9, 1980), but is rarely done.

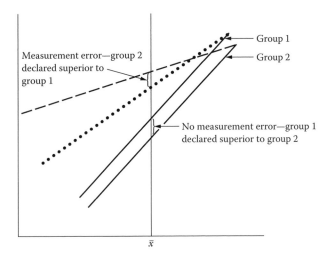

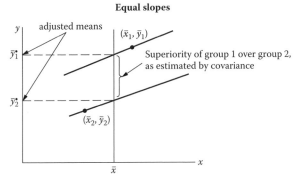

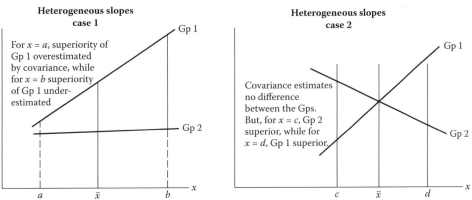

FIGURE 9.3
Effect of measurement error on covariance results when comparing subjects from two different populations.

FIGURE 9.4
Effect of heterogeneous slopes on interpretation in ANCOVA.

by covariance. The point is, *when the slopes are unequal there is a covariate by treatment interaction.* That is, how much better Group 1 is depends on which value of the covariate we specify.

For Case 2 of heterogeneous slopes, use of covariance would be totally misleading. Covariance estimates no difference between the groups, while for $x = c$, Group 2 is quite superior to Group 1. For $x = d$, Group 1 is superior to Group 2. We indicate later in the chapter, in detail, how the assumption of equal slopes is tested on SPSS.

9.6 Use of ANCOVA with Intact Groups

It should be noted that some researchers (Anderson, 1963; Lord, 1969) have argued strongly against using ANCOVA with intact groups. Although we do not take this position, it is important that the reader be aware of the several limitations or possible dangers when using ANCOVA with intact groups. First, even the use of several covariates will *not* equate intact groups, and one should never be deluded into thinking it can. The groups may still differ on some unknown important variable(s). Also, note that equating groups on one variable may result in accentuating their differences on other variables.

Second, recall that ANCOVA adjusts the posttest means to what they would be if all the groups had started out equal on the covariate(s). You then need to consider whether groups that are equal on the covariate would ever exist in the real world. Elashoff (1969) gave the following example:

> Teaching methods *A* and *B* are being compared. The class using *A* is composed of high-ability students, whereas the class using *B* is composed of low-ability students. A covariance analysis can be done on the posttest achievement scores holding ability constant, as if *A* and *B* had been used on classes of equal and average ability. ... It may make no sense to think about comparing methods *A* and *B* for students of average ability, perhaps each has been designed specifically for the ability level it was used with, or neither method will, in the future, be used for students of average ability. (p. 387)

Third, the assumptions of linearity and homogeneity of regression slopes need to be satisfied for ANCOVA to be appropriate.

A fourth issue that can confound the interpretation of results is differential growth of subjects in intact or self selected groups on some dependent variable. If the natural growth is much greater in one group (treatment) than for the control group and covariance finds a significance difference after adjusting for any pretest differences, then it isn't clear whether the difference is due to treatment, differential growth, or part of each. Bryk and Weisberg (1977) discussed this issue in detail and propose an alternative approach for such growth models.

A fifth problem is that of measurement error. Of course, this same problem is present in randomized studies. But there the effect is merely to attenuate power. In nonrandomized studies measurement error can seriously bias the treatment effect. Reichardt (1979), in an extended discussion on measurement error in ANCOVA, stated:

> Measurement error in the pretest can therefore produce spurious treatment effects when none exist. But it can also result in a finding of no intercept difference when a true treatment effect exists, or it can produce an estimate of the treatment effect which is in the opposite direction of the true effect. (p. 164)

It is no wonder then that Pedhazur (1982, p. 524), in discussing the effect of measurement error when comparing intact groups, said:

> The purpose of the discussion here was only to alert you to the problem in the hope that you will reach two obvious conclusions: (1) that efforts should be directed to construct measures of the covariates that have very high reliabilities and (2) that ignoring the problem, as is unfortunately done in most applications of ANCOVA, will not make it disappear.

Porter (1967) developed a procedure to correct ANCOVA for measurement error, and an example illustrating that procedure was given in Huitema (1980, pp. 315–316). This is beyond the scope of our text.

Given all of these problems, the reader may well wonder whether we should abandon the use of covariance when comparing intact groups. But other statistical methods for analyzing this kind of data (such as matched samples, gain score ANOVA) suffer from many of the same problems, such as seriously biased treatment effects. The fact is that inferring cause–effect from intact groups is treacherous, regardless of the type of statistical analysis. Therefore, the task is to do the best we can and exercise considerable caution, or as Pedhazur (1982) put it, "But the conduct of such research, indeed all scientific research, requires sound theoretical thinking, constant vigilance, and a thorough understanding of the potential and limitations of the methods being used" (p. 525).

9.7 Alternative Analyses for Pretest–Posttest Designs

When comparing two or more groups with pretest and posttest data, the following three other modes of analysis are possible:

1. An ANOVA is done on the difference or gain scores (posttest–pretest).
2. A two-way repeated-measures (this will be covered in Chapter 13) ANOVA is done. This is called a one between (the grouping variable) and one within (pretest–posttest part) factor ANOVA.
3. An ANOVA is done on residual scores. That is, the dependent variable is regressed on the covariate. Predicted scores are then subtracted from observed dependent scores, yielding residual scores ($\hat{e}_i$). An ordinary one-way ANOVA is then performed on these residual scores. Although some individuals feel this approach is equivalent to ANCOVA, Maxwell, Delaney, and Manheimer (1985) showed the two methods are not the same and that analysis on residuals should be avoided.

The first two methods are used quite frequently, with ANOVA on residuals being done only occasionally. Huck and McLean (1975) and Jennings (1988) compared the first two methods just mentioned, along with the use of ANCOVA for the pretest–posttest control group design, and concluded that ANCOVA is the preferred method of analysis. Several comments from the Huck and McLean article are worth mentioning. First, they noted that with the repeated-measures approach it is the *interaction F* that is indicating whether the treatments had a differential effect, and not the treatment main effect. We consider two patterns of means to illustrate.

	Situation 1			Situation 2	
	Pretest	**Posttest**		**Pretest**	**Posttest**
Treatment	70	80	Treatment	65	80
Control	60	70	Control	60	68

In situation 1 the treatment main effect would probably be significant, because there is a difference of 10 in the row means. However, the difference of 10 on the posttest just transferred from an initial difference of 10 on the pretest. There is no differential change in the treatment and control groups here. On the other hand, in Situation 2, even though the treatment group scored higher on the pretest, it increased 15 points from pre to post, whereas the control group increased just 8 points. That is, there was a *differential* change in performance in the two groups. But recall from Chapter 4 that one way of thinking of an interaction effect is as a "difference in the differences." This is exactly what we have in Situation 2, hence a significant interaction effect.

Second, Huck and McLean (1975) noted that the interaction F from the repeated-measures ANOVA is *identical* to the F ratio one would obtain from an ANOVA on the gain (difference) scores. Finally, whenever the regression coefficient is not equal to 1 (generally the case), the error term for ANCOVA will be smaller than for the gain score analysis and hence the ANCOVA will be a more sensitive or powerful analysis.

Although not discussed in the Huck and McLean paper, we would like to add a measurement caution against the use of gain scores. It is a fairly well known measurement fact that the reliability of gain (difference) scores is generally not good. To be more specific, *as the correlation between the pretest and posttest scores approaches the reliability of the test, the reliability of the difference scores goes to 0.* The following table from Thorndike and Hagen (1977) quantifies things:

Correlation between tests	Average Reliability of Two Tests					
	.50	**.60**	**.70**	**.80**	**.90**	**.95**
.00	.50	.60	.70	.80	.90	.95
.40	.17	.33	.50	.67	.83	.92
.50	.00	.20	.40	.60	.80	.90
.60		.00	.25	.50	.75	.88
.70			.00	.33	.67	.83
.80				.00	.50	.75
.90					.00	.50
.95						.00

If our dependent variable is some noncognitive measure, or a variable derived from a nonstandardized test (which could well be of questionable reliability), then a reliability of about .60 or so is a definite possibility. In this case, if the correlation between pretest and posttest is .50 (a realistic possibility), the reliability of the difference scores is only .20. On the other hand, this table also shows that if our measure is quite reliable (say .90), then the difference scores will be reliable for moderate pre–post correlations. For example, for reliability = .90 and pre–post correlation = .50, the reliability of the differences scores is .80.

9.8 Error Reduction and Adjustment of Posttest Means for Several Covariates

What is the rationale for using several covariates? First, the use of several covariates will result in greater error reduction than can be obtained with just one covariate. The error reduction will be substantially greater if the covariates have relatively low intercorrelations among themselves (say <.40). Second, with several covariates, we can make a better adjustment for initial differences between intact groups.

For one covariate, the amount of error reduction was governed primarily by the magnitude of the correlation between the covariate and the dependent variable (see Equation 2). For several covariates, the amount of error reduction is determined by the magnitude of the multiple correlation between the dependent variable and the set of covariates (predictors). This is why we indicated earlier that it is desirable to have covariates with low intercorrelations among themselves, for then the multiple correlation will be larger, and we will achieve greater error reduction. Also, because R^2 has a variance accounted for interpretation, we can speak of the percentage of *within* variability on the dependent variable that is accounted for by the set of covariates.

Recall that the equation for the adjusted posttest mean for one covariate was given by:

$$\bar{y}_i^* = \bar{y}_i - b(\bar{x}_i - \bar{x}), \tag{3}$$

where b is the estimated common regression slope.

With several covariates $(x_1, x_2, \ldots, x_k)$ we are simply regressing y on the set of x's, and the adjusted equation becomes an extension:

$$\bar{y}_j^* = \bar{y}_j - b_1(\bar{x}_{1j} - \bar{x}_1) - b_2(\bar{x}_{2j} - \bar{x}_2) - \cdots - b_k(\bar{x}_{kj} - \bar{x}_k) \tag{4}$$

where the b_i are the regression coefficients, $\bar{x}_{1j}$ is the mean for the covariate 1 in group j, $\bar{x}_{2j}$ is the mean for covariate 2 in group j, and so on, and the $\bar{x}_i$ are the grand means for the covariates. We next illustrate the use of this equation on a sample MANCOVA problem.

9.9 MANCOVA—Several Dependent Variables and Several Covariates

In MANCOVA we are assuming there is a significant relationship between the set of dependent variables and the set of covariates, or that there is a significant regression of the y's on the x's. This is tested through the use of Wilks' Λ. We are also assuming, for more than two covariates, homogeneity of the regression hyperplanes. The null hypothesis that is being tested in MANCOVA is that the adjusted population mean vectors are equal:

$$H_0 : \boldsymbol{\mu}_{1_{adj}} = \boldsymbol{\mu}_{2_{adj}} = \boldsymbol{\mu}_{3_{adj}} = \cdots = \boldsymbol{\mu}_{J_{adj}}$$

In testing the null hypothesis in MANCOVA, adjusted W and T matrices are needed; we denote these by $\mathbf{W}^*$ and $\mathbf{T}^*$. In MANOVA, recall that the null hypothesis was tested using Wilks' Λ. Thus, we have:

MANOVA　　MANCOVA

Test

Statistic　　$\Lambda = \dfrac{|\mathbf{W}|}{|\mathbf{T}|}$　　$\Lambda^* = \dfrac{|\mathbf{W}^*|}{|\mathbf{T}^*|}$

The calculation of $\mathbf{W}^*$ and $\mathbf{T}^*$ involves considerable matrix algebra, which we wish to avoid. For the reader who is interested in the details, however, Finn (1974) had a nicely worked out example.

In examining the printout from the statistical packages it is important to *first* make two checks to determine whether covariance is appropriate:

1. Check to see that there is a significant relationship between the dependent variables and the covariates.
2. Check to determine that the homogeneity of the regression hyperplanes is satisfied.

If either of these is not satisfied, then covariance is not appropriate. In particular, if number 2 is not met, then one should consider using the Johnson–Neyman technique, which determines a region of nonsignificance, that is, a set of x values for which the groups do not differ, and hence for values of x outside this region one group is superior to the other. The Johnson–Neyman technique was excellently described by Huitema (1980), where he showed specifically how to calculate the region of nonsignificance for one covariate, the effect of measurement error on the procedure, and other issues. For further extended discussion on the Johnson–Neyman technique see Rogosa (1977, 1980).

Incidentally, if the homogeneity of regression slopes is rejected for several groups, it does not automatically follow that the slopes for all groups differ. In this case, one might follow up the overall test with additional homogeneity tests on all combinations of pairs of slopes. Often, the slopes will be homogeneous for many of the groups. In this case one can apply ANCOVA to the groups that have homogeneous slopes, and apply the Johnson–Neyman technique to the groups with heterogeneous slopes. Unfortunately, at present, none of the major statistical packages (SPSS or SAS) has the Johnson–Neyman technique.

9.10 Testing the Assumption of Homogeneous Hyperplanes on SPSS

Neither SPSS or SAS automatically provides the test of the homogeneity of the regression hyperplanes. Recall that, for one covariate, this is the assumption of equal regression slopes in the groups, and that for two covariates it is the assumption of parallel regression planes. To set up the control lines to test this assumption, it is necessary to understand what a violation of the assumption means. As we indicated earlier (and displayed in Figure 9.4), a violation means there is a covariate-by-treatment interaction. Evidence that the assumption is met means the interaction is not significant.

Thus, what is done on SPSS is to set up an effect involving the interaction (for one covariate), and then test whether this effect is significant. If so, this means the assumption is *not* tenable. This is one of those cases where we don't want significance, for then the assumption is tenable and covariance is appropriate.

If there is more than one covariate, then there is an interaction effect for each covariate. We lump the effects together and then test whether the combined interactions are significant. Before we give two examples, we note that BY is the keyword used by SPSS to denote an interaction and + is used to lump effects together.

Example 9.1: Two Dependent Variables and One Covariate

We call the grouping variable TREATS, and denote the dependent variables by $Y1$ and $Y2$, and the covariate by $X1$. Then the control lines are

ANALYSIS = $Y1$, $Y2$/
DESIGN = $X1$, TREATS, $X1$ BY TREATS/

Example 9.2: Three Dependent Variables and Two Covariates

We denote the dependent variables by $Y1$, $Y2$, and $Y3$ and the covariates by $X1$ and $X2$. Then the control lines are

ANALYSIS = $Y1$, $Y2$, $Y3$/
DESIGN = $X1 + X2$, TREATS,$X1$ BY TREATS + $X2$ BY TREATS/

These two control lines will be embedded among many others in running a multivariate MANCOVA on SPSS, as the reader can see in the computer examples we consider next. With the previous two examples and the computer examples, the reader should be able to generalize the set-up of the control lines for testing homogeneity of regression hyperplanes for any combination of dependent variables and covariates. With factorial designs, things are more complicated. We present two examples to illustrate.

9.11 Two Computer Examples

We now consider two examples to illustrate (a) how to set up the control lines to run a multivariate analysis of covariance on both SPSS MANOVA and on SAS GLM, and (b) how to interpret the output, including that which checks whether covariance is appropriate. The first example uses artificial data and is simpler, having just two dependent variables and one covariate, whereas the second example uses data from an actual study and is more complex, involving two dependent variables and two covariates.

Example 9.3: MANCOVA on SAS GLM

This example has two groups, with 15 subjects in Group 1 and 14 subjects in Group 2. There are two dependent variables, denoted by POSTCOMP and POSTHIOR in the SAS GLM control lines and on the printout, and one covariate (denoted by PRECOMP). The control lines for running the MANCOVA analysis are given in Table 9.1, along with annotation.

TABLE 9.1

SAS GLM Control Lines for Two-Group MANCOVA:
Two Dependent Variables and One Covariate

```
      TITLE 'MULTIVARIATE ANALYSIS OF COVARIANCE';
      DATA COMP;
      INPUT GPID PRECOMP POSTCOMP POSTHIOR @@;
      CARDS;
      1 15 17 3 1 10 6 3 1 13 13 1 1 14 14 8
      1 12 12 3 1 10 9 9 1 12 12 3 1 8 9 12
      1 12 15 3 1 8 10 8 1 12 13 1 1 7 11 10
      1 12 16 1 1 9 12 2 1 12 14 8
      2 9 9 3 2 13 19 5 2 13 16 11 2 6 7 18
      2 10 11 15 2 6 9 9 2 16 20 8 2 9 15 6
      2 10 8 9 2 8 10 3 2 13 16 12 2 12 17 20
      2 11 18 12 2 14 18 16
      PROC PRINT;
      PROC REG;
①    MODEL POSTCOMP POSTHIOR = PRECOMP;
      MTEST;
     ⎡PROC GLM;
②    ⎢CLASSES GPID;
     ⎢MODEL POSTCOMP POSTHIOR = PRECOMP GPID PRECOMP*GPID;
     ⎣MANOVA H = PRECOMP*GPID;
     ⎡PROC GLM;
③    ⎢CLASSES GPID;
     ⎢MODEL POSTCOMP POSTHIOR = PRECOMP GPID;
     ⎣MANOVA H = GPID;
④    LSMEANS GPID/PDIFF;
```

---

① PROC REG is used to examine the relationship between the two dependent variables and the covariate. The MTEST is needed to obtain the multivariate test.

② Here GLM is used along with the MANOVA statement to obtain the multivariate test of no overall PRECOMP BY GPID interaction effect.

③ GLM is used again, along with the MANOVA statement, to test whether the adjusted population mean vectors are equal.

④ This statement is needed to obtain the adjusted means.

Table 9.2 presents the two multivariate tests for determining whether MANCOVA is appropriate, that is, whether there is a significant relationship between the two dependent variables and the covariate, and whether there is no covariate by group interaction effect. The multivariate test at the top of Table 9.2 indicates there is a significant relationship ($F = 21.4623$, $p < .0001$). Also, the multivariate test in the middle of the table shows there is *not* a covariate-by-group interaction effect ($F = 1.9048$, $p < .1707$). Therefore, multivariate analysis of covariance is appropriate. In Figure 9.5 we present the scatter plots for POSTCOMP, along with the slopes and the regression lines for each group.

The multivariate null hypothesis tested in covariance is that the adjusted population mean vectors are equal, that is,

$$H_0 : \begin{pmatrix} \mu_{11}^* \\ \mu_{21}^* \end{pmatrix} = \begin{pmatrix} \mu_{12}^* \\ \mu_{22}^* \end{pmatrix}$$

TABLE 9.2

Multivariate Tests for Significant Regression, for Covariate-by-Treatment Interaction, and for Group Difference

Multivariate Test:					
Multivariate Statistics and Exact F Statistics					
S = 1		M = 0	N = 12		
Statistic	Value	F	Num DF	Den DF	Pr > F
Wilks' Lambda	0.37722383	21.4623	2	26	0.0001
Pillar's Trace	0.62277617	21.4623	2	26	0.0001
Hotelling-Lawley Trace	1.65094597	21.4623	2	26	0.0001
Roy's Greatest Root	1.65094597	21.4623	2	26	0.0001

MANOVA Test Criteria and Exact F Statistics for the Hypothesis of no Overall PRECOMP*GPID Effect

H = Type III SS&CP Matrix for PRECOMP*GPID   E = Error SS&CPMatrix

	S = 1	M = 0	N = 11		
Statistic	Value	F	Num DF	Den DF	Pr > F
Wilks' Lambda	0.86301048	1.9048	2	24	0.1707
Pillar's Trace	0.13698952	1.9048	2	24	0.1707
Hotelling-Lawley Trace	0.15873448	1.9048	2	24	0.1707
Roy's Greatest Root	0.15873448	1.9048	2	24	0.1707

MANOVA Test Criteria and Exact F Statistics for the Hypothesis of no Overall GPID Effect

H = Type III SS&CP Matrix for GPID   E = Error SS&CP Matrix

	S = 1	M = 0	N = 11.5		
Statistic	Value	F	Num DF	Den DF	Pr > F
Wilks' Lambda	0.64891393	6.7628	2	25	0.0045
Pillar's Trace	0.35108107	6.7628	2	25	0.0045
Hotelling-Lawley Trace	0.54102455	6.7628	2	25	0.0045
Roy's Greatest Root	0.54102455	6.7628	2	25	0.0045

The multivariate test at the bottom of Table 9.2 shows that we reject the multivariate null hypothesis at the .05 level, and hence we conclude that the groups differ on the *set* of two adjusted means. The univariate ANCOVA follow-up F's in Table 9.3 ($F = 5.26$ for POSTCOMP, $p < .03$, and $F = 9.84$ for POSTHIOR, $p < .004$) show that both variables are contributing to the overall multivariate significance. The adjusted means for the variables are also given in Table 9.3.

Can we have confidence in the reliability of the adjusted means? From Huitema's inequality we need $C + (J - 1)/N < .10$. Because here $J = 2$ and $N = 29$, we obtain $(C + 1)/29 < .10$ or $C < 1.9$. Thus, we should use fewer than two covariates for reliable results, and we have used just one covariate.

Example 9.4: MANCOVA on SPSS MANOVA

Next, we consider a social psychological study by Novince (1977) that examined the effect of behavioral rehearsal and of behavioral rehearsal plus cognitive restructuring (combination treatment) on reducing anxiety and facilitating social skills for female college freshmen. There was also a control group (Group 2), with 11 subjects in each group. The subjects were pretested and posttested on four measures, thus the pretests were the covariates. For this example we use only two of the measures: avoidance and negative evaluation. In Table 9.4 we present the control lines for running the MANCOVA, along with annotation explaining what the various subcommands are

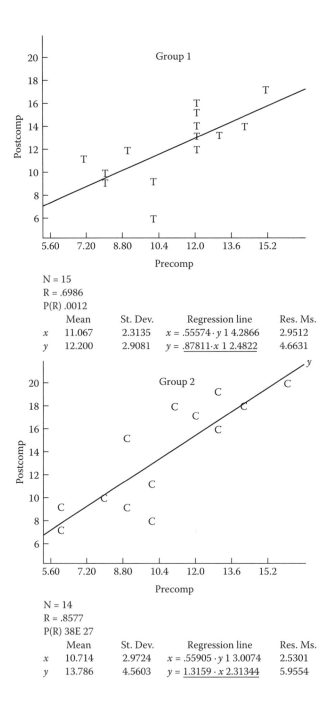

FIGURE 9.5
Scatterplots and regression lines for POSTCOMP vs. covariate in two groups. The fact that the univariate test for POSTCOMP in Table 9.2 is not significant ($F = 1.645$, $p < .211$) means that the differences in slopes here (.878 and 1.316) are simply due to sampling error, i.e., the homogeneity of slopes assumption is tenable for this variable.

TABLE 9.3

Univariate Tests for Group Differences and Adjusted Means

Source	DF	Type I SS	Mean Square	F Value	Pr > F
PRECOMP	1	237.68956787	237.68956787	43.90	0.000
GPID	1	28.49860091	28.49860091	5.26	0.0301

Source	DF	Type III SS	Mean Square	F Value	Pr > F
PRECOMP	1	17.66221238	17.66221238	0.82	0.3732
GPID	1	28.4986091	28.49860091	5.26	0.0301

Source	DF	Type I SS	Mean Square	F Value	Pr > F
PRECOMP	1	17.66221238	17.66221238	0.82	0.3732
GPID	1	211.59023436	211.59023436	9.84	0.0042

Source	DF	Type I SS	Mean Square	F Value	Pr > F
PRECOMP	1	10.20072260	10.20072260	0.47	0.4972
GPID	1	211.59023436	211.59023436	9.84	0.0042

General Linear Models Procedure
Least Squares Means

GPID	POSTCOMP LSMEAN	Pr > |T| H0: LSMEAN1 = LSMEAN2
1	12.0055476	0.0301
2	13.9940562	

GPID	POSTHIOR LSMEAN	Pr > |T| H0: LSMEAN1 = LSMEAN2
1	5.0394385	0.0042
2	10.4577444	

doing. The least obvious part of the setup is obtaining the test of the homogeneity of the regression planes. Tables 9.5, 9.6, and 9.7 present selected output from the MANCOVA run on SPSS. Table 9.5 presents the means on the dependent variables (posttests and the adjusted means). Table 9.6 contains output for determining whether covariance is appropriate for this data. First in Table 9.6 is the multivariate test for significant association between the dependent variables and the covariates (or significant regression of y's on x's). The multivariate $F = 11.78$ (corresponding to Wilks' Λ) is significant well beyond the .01 level. Now we make the second check to determine whether covariance is appropriate, that is, whether the assumption of homogeneous regression planes is tenable. The multivariate test for this assumption is under

EFFECT .. PREAVOID BY GPID + PRENEG BY GPID

Because the multivariate $F = .427$ (corresponding to Wilks' Λ), the assumption is quite tenable. Recall that a violation of this assumption implies no interaction. We then test to see whether this interaction is different from zero.

The main result for the multivariate analysis of covariance is to test whether the adjusted population mean vectors are equal, and is at the top of Table 9.7. The multivariate $F = 5.185$ ($p = .001$) indicates significance at the .01 level. The univariate ANCOVAs underneath indicate that both variables (AVOID and NEGEVAL) are contributing to the multivariate significance.

Also in Table 9.7 we present the regression coefficients for AVOID and NEGEVAL (.60434 and .30602), which can be used to obtain the adjusted means.

TABLE 9.4

SPSS MANOVA Control Lines for Example 4: Two Dependent Variables and Two Covariates

```
TITLE 'NOVINCE DATA - 3 GP ANCOVA-2 DEP VARS AND 2 COVS'.
DATA LIST FREE/GPID AVOID NEGEVAL PREAVOID PRENEG.
BEGIN DATA.
1  91  81  70 102      1 107 132 121  71      1 121  97  89  76      1  86  88  80  85
1 137 119 123 117      1 138 132 112 106      1 133 116 126  97
1 127 101 121  85      1 114 138  80 105      1 118 121 101 113      1 114  72 112  76
2 107  88 116  97      2  76  95  77  64      2 116  87 111  86      2 126 112 121 106
2 104 107 105 113      2  96  84  97  92      2 127  88 132 104      2  99 101  98  81
2  94  87  85  96      2  92  80  82  88      2 128 109 112 118
3 121 134  96  96      3 140 130 120 110      3 148 123 130 111      3 147 155 145 118
3 139 124 122 105      3 121 123 119 122      3 141 155 104 139      3 143 131 121 103
3 120 123  80  77      3 140 140 121 121      3  95 103  92  94
END DATA.
LIST.
MANOVA AVOID NEGEVAL PREAVOID PRENEG BY GPID(1,3)/
① ANALYSIS AVOID NEGEVAL WITH PREAVOID PRENEG/
② PRINT = PMEANS/
  DESIGN/
③ ANALYSIS = AVOID NEGEVAL/
  DESIGN = PREAVOID + PRENEG, GPID, PREAVOID BY GPID + PRENEG BY GPID/.
```

① Recall that the keyword WITH precedes the covariates in SPSS.
② This subcommand is needed to obtain the adjusted means.
③ These subcommands are needed to test the equality of the regression planes assumption. We set up the interaction effect for each covariate and then use the + to lump the effects together.

TABLE 9.5

Means on Posttests and Pretests for MANCOVA Problem

VARIABLE .. PREVOID		
FACTOR	CODE	OBS. MEAN
TREATS	1	104.00000
TREATS	2	103.27273
TREATS	3	113.63635
VARIABLE .. PRENEG		
FACTOR	CODE	OBS. MEAN
TREATS	1	93.90909
TREATS	2	95.00000
TREATS	3	109.18182
VARIABLE .. AVOID		
FACTOR	CODE	OBS. MEAN
TREATS	1	116.98090
TREATS	2	105.90909
TREATS	3	132.27273
VARIABLE .. NEGEVAL		
FACTOR	CODE	OBS. MEAN
TREATS	1	108.81818
TREATS	2	94.36364
TREATS	3	131.00000

TABLE 9.6

Multivariate Tests for Relationship Between Dependent Variables and Covariates and Test for Parallelism of Regression Hyperplanes

EFFECT .. WITHIN CELLS Regression
Multivariate Tests of Significance (S = 2, M = −1/2, N = 12 1/2)

Test Name	Value	Approx. F	Hypoth. DF	Error DF	Sig. of F
Pillais	.77175	8.79662	4.00	56.00	.000
Hotellings	2.30665	14.99323	4.00	52.00	.000
Wilks	.28520	11.77899	①4.00	54.00	.000
Roys	.68911				

Note .. F statistic for WILKS' Lambda is exact.

- -

Univariate F-tests with (2,28) D. F.

Variable	Hypoth. SS	Error SS	Hypoth. MS	Error MS	F	Sig. of F
AVOID	5784.89287	2617.10713	2892.44644	93.46811	30.94581	.000
NEGEVAL	2158.21221	6335.96961	1079.10610	226.28463	4.76880	.017

EFFECT .. PREAVOID BY GPID + PRENEG BY GPID
Multivariate Tests of Significance (S = 2, M = 1/2, N = 10 1/2)

Test Name	Value	Approx. F	Hypoth. DF	Error DF	Sig. of F
Pillais	.13759	.44326	8.00	48.00	.889
Hotellings	.14904	.40986	8.00	44.00	.909
Wilks	.86663	②.42664	8.00	46.00	.899
Roys	.09156				

Note.. F statistic for WILKS' Lambda is exact.

① This multivariate test indicates there is a significant relationship between the two dependent variables and the two covariates.
② This indicates that the assumption of equal regression planes is tenable.

Can we have confidence in the reliability of the adjusted means? Huitema's inequality suggests we should be somewhat leery, because the inequality suggests we should just use one covariate.

* Parallelism Test with Crossed Factors

MANOVA YIELD BY PLOT(1,4) TYPEFERT(1,3) WITH FERT
    /ANALYSIS YIELD
    DESIGN FERT, PLOT, TYPEFERT, PLOT BY TYPEFERT, FERT BY PLOT + FERT BY TYPEFERT
    + FERT BY PLOT BY TYPEFERT.

* This example tests whether the regression of the dependent Variable *Y* on the two variables X1 and X2 is the same across all the categories of the factors AGE and TREATMNT.

MANOVA Y BY AGE(l,5) TREATMNT(1,3) WITH X1, X2
    /ANALYSIS = Y
    /DESIGN = POOL(X1,X2),
              AGE, TREATMNT, AGE BY TREATMNT,
              POOL(X1,X2) BY AGE + POOL(X1,X2) BY TREATMNT
              + POOL(X1,X2) BY AGE BY TREATMNT.

TABLE 9.7

Multivariate and Univariate Covariance Results and Regression Coefficients
for the Avoidance Variable

EFFECT .. GPID
Multivariate Tests of Significance (S = 2, M = −1/2, N = 12 1/2)

Test Name	Value	Approx. F	Hypoth. DF	Error DF	Sig. of F
Pillais	.48783	4.51647	4.00	56.00	.003
Hotellings	.89680	5.82919	4.00	52.00	.001
Wilks	.52201	5.18499 ①	4.00	54.00	.001
Roys	.46674				

Note .. F statistic for WILKS' Lambda is exact.

- -

Univariate F-tests with (2, 28) D. F.

Variable	Hypoth. SS	Error SS	Hypoth. MS	Error MS	F	Sig. of F
AVOID	1335.84547	2617.10713	667.92274	93.46811	7.14600 ②	.003
NEGEVAL	4010.78058	6335.96961	2005.39029	226.28463	8.86225	.001

Dependent variable .. AVOID

COVARIATE	B	Beta	Std. Err.	t-Value	Sig. of t
PREAVOID	③ .60434	.58193	.101	5.990	.000
PRENEG	.30602	.26587	.119	2.581	.015

① This is the main result, indicating that the adjusted population mean vectors are significantly different at the
   .05 level (F 55.185, p5.001).
② These are the F's that would result if a separate analysis of covariance was done of each dependent variable.
   The probabilities indicate each is significant at the .05 level.
③ These are the regression coefficients that are used in obtaining the adjusted means for AVOID.

9.12 Bryant–Paulson Simultaneous Test Procedure

Because the covariate(s) used in social science research are essentially always random, it
is important that this information be incorporated into any post hoc procedure following
ANCOVA. This is *not* the case for the Tukey procedure, and hence it is not appropriate as a
follow-up technique following ANCOVA. The Bryant–Paulson (1976) procedure was derived
under the assumption that the covariate is a random variable and hence is appropriate in
ANCOVA. It is a generalization of the Tukey technique. Which particular Bryant–Paulson
(BP) statistic we use to determine whether a pair of means are significantly different depends
on whether the study is a randomized or non-randomized design and on how many covariates there are (one or several). In Table 9.8 we have the test statistic for each of the four cases.
Note that if the group sizes are unequal, then the harmonic mean is employed.

We now illustrate use of the Bryant–Paulson procedure on the computer example.
Because this was a randomized study with four covariates, the appropriate statistic from
Table 9.8 is

$$BP = \frac{\bar{Y}_i^* - \bar{Y}_j^*}{\sqrt{MS_w^*\left[1 + \frac{1}{(J-1)}\,TR\left(\mathbf{B}_\lambda\,\mathbf{W}_\lambda^{-1}\right)\right]\Big/n}}$$

TABLE 9.8

Bryant–Paulson Statistics for Detecting Significant Pairwise Differences in Covariance Analysis for One and for Several Covariates ①

One Covariate	Many Covariates ②
RANDOMIZED STUDY	

$$\frac{\bar{Y}_i^* - \bar{Y}_j^*}{\sqrt{MW_w^*[1 + MS_{B_x}/SS_{w_x}]/n}}$$

$$\frac{\bar{Y}_i^* - \bar{Y}_j^*}{\sqrt{MS_w^*\left[1 + \frac{1}{(J-1)}TR\left(\mathbf{B}_\lambda\,\mathbf{W}_\lambda^{-1}\right)\right]/n}}$$

WHERE

$\bar{Y}_i^*$ IS THE ADJUSTED MEAN FOR GROUP i

MS_{B_x} IS THE MEAN BETWEEN SQUARE ON THE COVARIATE

SS_{w_x} IS THE SUM OF SQUARES WITHIN ON THE COVARIATE

MS_w^* IS THE ERROR TERM FOR COVARIANCE

N IS THE COMMON GROUP SIZE. IF UNEQUAL n, USE THE HARMONIC MEAN

$\mathbf{B}_x$ IS THE BETWEEN SSCP MATRIX

$\mathbf{W}_x$ IS THE WITHIN SSCP MATRIX

TR $(B_x W_x^{-1})$ IS THE HOTELLING- LAWLEY TRACE.

THIS IS GIVEN ON THE SPSS MANOVA PRINTOUT

NON-RANDOMIZED STUDY

$$\frac{\bar{Y}_i^* - \bar{Y}_j^*}{\sqrt{MS_w^*(2/n+[(\bar{X}_i - \bar{X}_j)^2/SS_{w_x}])/2}}$$

$$(\bar{Y}_i^* - \bar{Y}_j^*)\Big/ \sqrt{\frac{MS_w^*[(2/n)+\mathbf{d}'\mathbf{W}_x^{-1}\mathbf{d}]}{2}}$$

WHERE $\bar{X}_i$ IS THE MEAN FOR THE COVARIATE IN GROUP i. NOTE THAT THE ERROR TERM MUST BE COMPUTED *SEPARATELY* FOR EACH PAIRWISE COMPARISON.

$\mathbf{d}'$ IS THE ROW VECTOR OF DIFFERENCES BETWEEN THE ith and jth GROUPS ON THE COVARIATES.

① The Bryant–Paulson statistics were derived under the assumption that the covariates are random variables, which is almost always the case in practice.
② Degrees of freedom for error is $N-J-C$, where C is the number of covariates.

Is there a significant difference between the adjusted means on avoidance for groups 1 and 2 at the .95 simultaneous level?

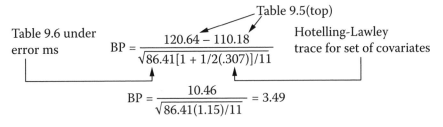

We have not presented the Hotelling–Lawley trace as part of the selected output for the second computer example. It is the part of the output related to the last ANALYSIS subcommand in Table 9.4 comparing the groups on the set of covariates. Now, having computed the value of the test statistic, we need the critical value. The critical values are given in Table G in Appendix A. Table G is entered at $\alpha = .05$, with $df_e = N - J - C = 33 - 3 - 4 = 26$, and for four covariates. The table extends to only three covariates, but the value for three will be a good approximation. The critical value for $df = 24$ with three covariates is 3.76, and the critical value for $df = 30$ is 3.67. Interpolating, we find the critical value = 3.73. Because the value of the BP statistic is 3.49, there is not a significant difference.

9.13 Summary

1. In analysis of covariance a linear relationship is assumed between the dependent variable(s) and the covariate(s).

2. Analysis of covariance is directly related to the two basic objectives in experimental design of (a) eliminating systematic bias and (b) reduction of error variance. Although ANCOVA does not eliminate bias, it can reduce bias. This can be helpful in nonexperimental studies comparing intact groups. The bias is reduced by adjusting the posttest means to what they would be if all groups had started out equally on the covariate(s), that is, at the grand mean(s). There is disagreement among statisticians about the use of ANCOVA with intact groups, and several precautions were mentioned in Section 9.6.

3. The main reason for using ANCOVA in an experimental study (random assignment of subjects to groups) is to reduce error variance, yielding a more powerful test. When using several covariates, greater error reduction will occur when the covariates have low intercorrelations among themselves.

4. Limit the number of covariates (C) so that

$$\frac{C+(J-1)}{N} < .10$$

where J is the number of groups and N is total sample size, so that stable estimates of the adjusted means are obtained.

5. In examining printout from the statistical packages, first make two checks to determine whether covariance is appropriate: (a) Check that there is a significant relationship between the dependent variables and the covariates, and (b) check that the homogeneity of the regression hyperplanes assumption is tenable. If either of these is not satisfied, then covariance is not appropriate. In particular, if (b) is not satisfied, then the Johnson–Neyman technique should be used.

6. Measurement error on the covariate causes loss of power in randomized designs, and can lead to seriously biased treatment effects in nonrandomized designs. Thus, if one has a covariate of low or questionable reliability, then true score ANCOVA should be contemplated.

7. Use the Bryant–Paulson procedure for determining where there are significant pairwise differences. This technique assumes the covariates are random variables, almost always the case in social science research, and with it one can maintain the overall alpha level at .05 or .01.

Exercises

1. Scandura (1984) examined the effects of a leadership training treatment on employee work outcomes of job satisfaction (HOPPOCKA), leadership relations (LMXA), performance ratings (ERSA), and actual performance—quantity (QUANAFT) and quality of work (QUALAFT). Thus, there were five dependent variables. The names in parentheses are the names used for the variables that

appear on selected printout we present here. Because previous research had indicated that the characteristics of the work performed—motivating potential (MPS), work load (OL1), and job problems (DTT)—are related to these work outcomes, these three variables were used as covariates. Of 100 subjects, 35 were randomly assigned to the leadership treatment condition and 65 to the control group. During the 26 weeks of the study, 11 subjects dropped out, about an equal number from each group. Scandura ran the two-group multivariate analysis of covariance on SPSS.

(a) Show the control lines for running the MANCOVA on SPSS such that the adjusted means and the test for homogeneity of the regression hyperplanes are also obtained. Assume free format for the variables.

(b) At the end of this chapter we present selected printout from Scandura's run. From the printout determine whether ANCOVA is appropriate.

(c) If covariance is appropriate, then determine whether the multivariate test is significant at the .05 level.

(d) If the multivariate test is significant, then which of the individual variables, at the .01 level, are contributing to the multivariate significance?

(e) What are the adjusted means for the significant variable(s) found in (d)? Did the treatment group do better than the control (assume higher is better)?

Selected Output from Scandura's Run

EFFECT .. WITHIN CELLS REGRESSION						
MULTIVARIATE TESTS OF SIGNIFICANCE (S = 3, M = 1/2, N = 36)						
TEST NAME	VALUE		APPROX. F	HYPOTH. DF	ERROR DF	SIG. OF F
PILLAIS	.32175		1.82605	15.00	228.00	.032
HOTELLINGS	.29799		1.92804	15.00	218.00	.022
WILKS	.69999		1.88208	15.00	204.68	.027
ROYS	.23303					
UNIVARIATE F-TESTS WITH (3,78) D.F.						
VARIABLE	SQ. MUL. R	MUL. R	ADJ. R-SQ.	HYPOTH. MS	ERROR MS	F	SIG. OF F
HOPPOCKA	.05146	.22684	.01497	16.04757	11.37763	1.41045	.246
LNXA	.07412	.27225	.03851	33.51239	16.10126	2.08135	.109
ERSA	.13167	.36287	.09827	158.04864	39.58010	3.94260	.011
QUANAFT	.05930	.24351	.02312	.01169	.00713	1.63889	.187
QUALAFT	.14992	.38719	.11722	.00975	.00213	4.58530	.005
REGRESSION ANALYSIS FOR WITHIN CELLS ERROR TEAM						
EFFECT .. MPS BY TRIMT2+OLI BY TRIMT2 +DTT BY TRIMT2						
MULTIVARIATE TESTS OF SIGNIFICANCE (S = 3, M = 1/2, N = 34 1/2)						
PILLAIS	.18417		.95491	15.00	219.00	.504
HOTELLINGS	.20597		.95662	15.00	209.00	.503
WILKS	.82318		.95619	15.00	196.40	.503
ROYS	.13308					

UNIVARIATE F-TESTS WITH (3,75) D.F.

VARIABLE	HYPOTH. SS	ERROR SS	HYPOTH. MS	ERROR MS	F	SIG. OF F
HOPPOCKA	22.41809	865.03704	7.47270	11.53383	.64789	.587
LMXA	21.18137	1234.71668	7.06046	16.46289	.42887	.733
ERSA	249.38711	2837.86037	83.12904	37.83814	2.19696	.095
QUANAFT	.00503	.55127	.00168	.00735	.22812	.877
QUALAFT	.00263	.16315	.00088	.00218	.40343	.751

EFFECT .. TRTMT2

MULTIVARIATE TESTS OF SIGNIFICANCE (S = 1, M = 1 1/2, N = 34 1/2)

TEST NAME	VALUE	APPROX. F	HYPOTH. DF	ERROR DF	SIG. OF F
PILLAIS	.15824	2.66941	5.00	71.00	.029
HOTELLINGS	.18799	2.66941	5.00	71.00	.029
WILKS	.84176	2.66941	5.00	71.00	.029
ROYS	.15824				

UNIVARIATE F-TESTS WITH (1,75) D.F.

VARIABLE	HYPOTH. SS	ERROR SS	F	SIG. OF F
HOPPOCKA	32.81297	865.03704	2.84493	.096
LMXA	.20963	1234.71668	.01273	.910
ERSA	87.59018	2837.86037	2.31486	.132
QUANAFT	.80222	.55127	11.18658	.001
QUALAFT	.00254	.16315	1.16651	.284

ADJUSTED AND ESTIMATED MEANS VARIABLE .. HOPPOCKA

FACTOR	CODE	OBS. MEAN	ADJ. MEAN
TRTMT2	LMX TREA	19.23077	19.31360
TRTMT2	CONTROL	17.98246	17.94467

VARIABLE .. LMXA

FACTOR	CODE	OBS. MEAN	ADJ. MEAN
TRTMT2	LMX TREA	19.03846	19.23177
TRTMT2	CONTROL	19.21053	19.12235

VARIABLE .. ERSA

FACTOR	CODE	OBS. MEAN	ADJ. MEAN
TRMTMT2	LMX TREA	34.34615	34.76489
TRTMT2	CONTROL	32.71930	32.52830

VARIABLE .. QUANAFT

FACTOR	CODE	OBS. MEAN	ADJ. MEAN
TRTMT2	LMX TREA	.38846	.39188
TRMTMT2	CONTROL	.32491	.32335

VARIABLE E .. QUALAFT

FACTOR	CODE	OBS. MEAN	ADJ. MEAN
TRTMT2	LMX TREA	.05577	.05330
TRTMT2	CONTROL	.06421	.06534

2. Consider the following data from a two-group MANCOVA with two dependent variables (Y1 and Y2) and one covariate (X):

GPS	X	Y1	Y2
1.00	12.00	13.00	3.00
1.00	10.00	6.00	5.00
1.00	11.00	17.00	2.00
1.00	14.00	14.00	8.00
1.00	13.00	12.00	6.00
1.00	10.00	6.00	8.00
1.00	8.00	12.00	3.00
1.00	8.00	6.00	12.00
1.00	12.00	12.00	7.00
1.00	10.00	12.00	8.00
1.00	12.00	13.00	2.00
1.00	7.00	14.00	10.00
1.00	12.00	16.00	1.00
1.00	9.00	9.00	2.00
1.00	12.00	14.00	10.00
2.00	9.00	7.00	3.00
2.00	16.00	13.00	5.00
2.00	11.00	14.00	5.00
2.00	8.00	13.00	18.00
2.00	10.00	11.00	12.00
2.00	7.00	15.00	9.00
2.00	16.00	17.00	4.00
2.00	9.00	9.00	6.00
2.00	10.00	8.00	4.00
2.00	8.00	10.00	1.00
2.00	16.00	16.00	3.00
2.00	12.00	12.00	17.00
2.00	15.00	14.00	4.00
2.00	12.00	18.00	11.00

Run the MANCOVA on SAS GLM. Is MANCOVA appropriate? Explain. If it is appropriate, then are the adjusted mean vectors significantly different at the .05 level?

3. Consider a three-group study (randomized) with 24 subjects per group. The correlation between the covariate and the dependent variable is .25, which is statistically significant at the .05 level. Is covariance going to be very useful in this study? Explain.

4. For the Novince example, determine whether there are any significant differences on SOCINT at the .95 simultaneous confidence level using the Bryant–Paulson procedure.

5. Suppose we were comparing two different teaching methods and that the covariate was IQ. The homogeneity of regression slopes is tested and rejected, implying a covariate-by-treatment interaction. Relate this to what we would have found had we blocked on IQ and run a factorial design (IQ by methods) on achievement.

6. As part of a study by Benton, Kraft, Groover, and Plake (1984), three tasks were employed to ascertain differences between good and poor undergraduate writers on recall and manipulation of information: an ordered letters task, an iconic memory task, and a letter reordering task. In the following table are means and standard deviations for the percentage of correct letters recalled on the three dependent variables. There were 15 subjects in each group.

	Good Writers		Poor Writers	
Task	*M*	*SD*	*M*	*SD*
Ordered letters	57.79	12.96	49.71	21.79
Iconic memory	49.78	14.59	45.63	13.09
Letter reordering	71.00	4.80	63.18	7.03

The following is from their results section (p. 824):

The data were then analyzed via a multivariate analysis of covariance using the background variables (English usage ACT subtest, composite ACT, and grade point average) as covariates, writing ability as the independent variable, and task scores (correct recall in the ordered letters task, correct recall in the iconic memory task, and correct recall in the letter reordering task) as the dependent variables. The global test was significant, $F(3, 23) = 5.43$, $p < .001$. To control for experimentwise type I error rate at .05, each of the three univariate analyses was conducted at a per comparison rate of .017. No significant difference was observed between groups on the ordered letters task, univariate $F(1, 25) = 1.92$, $p > .10$. Similarly, no significant difference was observed between groups on the iconic memory task, univariate $F < 1$.

However, good writers obtained significantly higher scores on the letter reordering task than the poor writers, univariate $F(1, 25) = 15.02$, $p < .001$.

(a) From what was said here, can we be confident that covariance is appropriate here?

(b) The "global" multivariate test referred to is not identified as to whether it is Wilks' Λ, Roy's largest root, and so on. Would it make a difference as to which multivariate test was employed in this case?

(c) Benton et al. talked about controlling the experimentwise error rate at .05 by conducting each test at the .017 level of significance. Which post hoc procedure that we discussed in chapter 4 were they employing here?

(d) Is there a sufficient number of subjects for us to have confidence in the reliability of the adjusted means?

7. Consider the NOVINCE data, which is on the website. Use SOCINT and SRINV as the dependent variables and PRESOCI and PRESR as the covariates.

(a) Determine whether MANCOVA is appropriate. Do each check at the .05 level.

(b) What is the multivariate null hypothesis in this case. Is it tenable at the .05 level?

8. What is the main reason for using covariance in a randomized study?

10

Stepdown Analysis

10.1 Introduction

In this chapter we consider a type of analysis that is similar to stepwise regression analysis (Chapter 3). The stepdown analysis is similar in that in both analyses we are interested in how much a variable "adds." In regression analysis the question is, "How much does a predictor add to predicting the dependent variable above and beyond the previous predictors in the regression equation?" The corresponding question in stepdown analysis is, "How much does a given dependent variable add to discriminating the groups, above and beyond the previous dependent variables for a given a priori ordering?"

Because the stepdown analysis requires an a priori ordering of the dependent variables, there must be some theoretical rationale or empirical evidence to dictate a given ordering. If there is such a rationale, then the stepdown analysis determines whether the groups differ on the first dependent variable in the ordering. The stepdown F for the first variable is the same as the univariate F. For the second dependent variable in the ordering, the analysis determines whether the groups differ on this variable with the first dependent variable used as a covariate in adjusting the effects for Variable 2. The stepdown F for the third dependent variable in the ordering indicates whether the groups differ on this variable after its effects have been adjusted for variables 1 and 2, i.e., with variables 1 and 2 used as covariates, and so on. Because the stepdown analysis is just a series of analyses of covariance (ANCOVA), the reader should examine Section 9.2 on purposes of covariance before going any farther in this chapter.

10.2 Four Appropriate Situations for Stepdown Analysis

To make the foregoing discussion more concrete, we consider an example. Let the independent variable be three different teaching methods, and the three dependent variables be the three subtest scores on a common achievement test covering the three lowest levels in Bloom's taxonomy: knowledge, comprehension, and application. An assumption of the taxonomy is that learning at a lower level is a necessary but not sufficient condition for learning at a higher level. Because of this, there is a theoretical rationale for ordering the variables as given above. The analysis will determine whether methods are differentially affecting learning at the most basic level, knowledge. At this point the analysis is the same as doing a univariate ANOVA on the single dependent variable knowledge. Next, the stepdown analysis will indicate whether the effect has extended itself to the next higher level, comprehension, with the differences at the knowledge level eliminated. The stepdown F

for comprehension is *identical* to what one would obtain if a univariate analysis of covariance was done with comprehension as the dependent variable and knowledge as the covariate. Finally, the analysis will show whether methods have had a significant effect on application, with the differences at the two lower levels eliminated. The stepdown *F* for the analysis variable is the *same one* that would be obtained if a univariate ANCOVA was done with analysis as the dependent variable and knowledge and comprehension as the covariates. Thus, the stepdown analysis not only gives an indication of how comprehensive the effect of the independent variable is, but also details which aspects of a grossly defined variable (such as achievement) have been differentially affected.

A second example is provided by Kohlberg's theory of moral development. Kohlberg described six stages of moral development, ranging from premoral to the formulation of self-accepted moral principles, and argued that attainment of a higher stage should depend on attainment of the preceding stages. Let us assume that tests are available for determining which stage a given individual has attained. Suppose we were interested in determining the extent to which lower-, middle-, and upperclass adults differ with respect to moral development. With Kohlberg's hierarchial theory we have a rationale for ordering from premoral as the first dependent variable on up to self-accepted principles as the last dependent variable in the ordering. The stepdown analysis will then tell us whether the social classes differ on premoral level of development, then whether the social classes differ on the next level of moral development with the differences at the premoral level eliminated, and so on. In other words, the analysis will tell us where there are differences among the classes with respect to moral development and how far up the ladder of moral development those differences extend.

As a third example where the stepdown analysis would be particularly appropriate, suppose an investigator wishes to determine whether some conceptually newer measures (among a set of dependent variables) are adding anything beyond what the older, more proven variables contribute, in relation to some independent variable. This case provides an empirical rationale for ordering the newer measures last, to allow them to demonstrate their incremental importance to the effect under investigation. Thus, in the previous example, the stepdown *F* for the first new conceptual measure in the ordering would indicate the importance of that variable, with the effects of the more proven variables eliminated. The utility of this approach in terms of providing evidence on variables that are redundant is clear.

A fourth instance in which the stepdown *F*'s are particularly valuable is in the analysis of repeated-measures designs, where time provides a natural logical ordering for the measures.

10.3 Controlling on Overall Type I Error

The stepdown analysis can control very effectively and in a precise way against Type I error. To show how Type I error can be controlled for the stepdown analysis, it is necessary to note that *if* H_0 *is true (i.e., the population mean vectors are equal), then the stepdown F's are statistically independent* (Roy and Bargmann, 1958). How then is the overall α level set for the stepdown *F*'s for a set of *p* variables? Each variable is assigned an α level, the *i*th variable being assigned α_i. Thus, $(1 - \alpha_1)$ is the probability of no Type I error for Variable 1, $(1 - \alpha_2)$ is the probability of no Type I error for Variable 2, and so on. Now, because the tests are statistically independent, these probabilities can be multiplied. Therefore, the probability of *no* Type I errors for *all p* tests is $(1 - \alpha_1) \times (1 - \alpha_2) \ldots (1 - \alpha_p)$. Using the symbol π, which denotes "product of," this expression can be written more concisely as $\pi_{i=1}^{p}(1 - \alpha_i)$. Finally, our overall α level is:

$$\text{Overall } \alpha = 1 - \prod_{i=1}^{p}(1-\alpha_i).$$

This is the probability of *at least one* stepdown F exceeding its critical value when H_0 is true.

Because we have one exact estimate of the probability of overall Type I error, when employing the stepdown F's it is unnecessary to perform the overall multivariate significance test. We can adopt the rule that the multivariate null hypothesis will be rejected if at least one of the stepdown F's is significant.

Recall that one of the primary reasons for the multivariate test with correlated dependent variables was the difficulty of accurately estimating overall Type I error. As Bock and Haggard noted (1968), "Because all variables have been obtained from the same subjects, they are correlated in some arbitrary and unknown manner, and the separate F tests are not statistically independent. No exact probability that at least one of them will exceed some critical value on the null hypothesis can be calculated" (p. 102).

10.4 Stepdown F's For Two Groups

To obtain the stepdown F's for the two-group case, the pooled within variance matrix **S** must be factored. That is, the square root or Cholesky factor of **S** must be found. What this means is that **S** is expressed as a product of a lower triangular matrix (all 0s above the main diagonal) and an upper triangular matrix (all 0s below the main diagonal). For three variables, it would look as follows:

$$\underset{\mathbf{S}}{\begin{bmatrix} s_1^2 & s_{12} & s_{13} \\ s_{21} & s_2^2 & s_{23} \\ s_{31} & s_{32} & s_3^2 \end{bmatrix}} = \underset{\mathbf{R}}{\begin{bmatrix} t_{11} & 0 & 0 \\ t_{21} & t_{22} & 0 \\ t_{31} & t_{32} & t_{33} \end{bmatrix}} \underset{\mathbf{R}'}{\begin{bmatrix} t_{11} & t_{12} & t_{13} \\ 0 & t_{22} & t_{23} \\ 0 & 0 & t_{33} \end{bmatrix}}$$

Now, for two groups the stepdown analysis yields a nice *additive breakdown* of Hotelling's T^2. The first term in the sum (which is an F ratio) gives the contribution of Variable 1 to group discrimination, the second term (which is the stepdown F for the second variable in the ordering) the contribution of Variable 2 to group discrimination, and so on. To at least partially show how this additive breakdown is achieved, recall that Hotelling's T^2 can be written as:

$$T^2 = n_1 n_2 / (n_1 + n_2) \mathbf{d}' \mathbf{S}^{-1} \mathbf{d}$$

where **d** is the vector of mean differences on the variables for the two groups. Because factoring the covariance matrix **S** means writing it as $\mathbf{S} = \mathbf{R}\,\mathbf{R}'$, it can be shown that T^2 CAN then be rewritten as

$$T^2 = n_1 n_2 / (n_1 + n_2)(\mathbf{R}^{-1}\mathbf{d})'(\mathbf{R}^{-1}\mathbf{d})$$

But $\mathbf{R}^{-1}_{(p \times p)}\mathbf{d}_{(p \times 1)}$ is just a column vector and the transpose of this column vector is a row vector that we denote by $\mathbf{w}' = (w_1, w_2, \ldots, w_p)$. Thus, $T^2 = n_1 n_2/(n_1 + n_2)\mathbf{w}'\,\mathbf{w}$. But $\mathbf{w}'\,\mathbf{w} = w_1^2 + w_2^2 + \cdots + w_p^2$.

Therefore, we get the following additive breakdown of T^2:

$$T^2 = \frac{n_1 n_2}{n_1 + n_2}w_1^2 + \frac{n_1 n_2}{n_1 + n_2}w_2^2 + \cdots + \frac{n_1 n_2}{n_1 + n_2}w_p^2$$

$$T^2 = \quad\quad F_1 \quad\quad + \quad\quad F_2 \quad\quad + \ldots + \quad\quad F_p$$

univariate F for	stepdown F for	stepdown F for
first variable	second variable	last variable in
in the ordering	in ordering	the ordering

We now consider an example to illustrate numerically the breakdown of T^2. In this example we just give the factors $\mathbf{R}$ and $\mathbf{R}'$ of $\mathbf{S}$ without showing the details, as most of our readers are probably not interested in the details. Those who are interested, however, can find the details in Finn (1974).

Example 10.1

Suppose there are two groups of subjects ($n_1 = 50$ and $n_2 = 43$) measured on three variables. The vector of differences on the means ($\mathbf{d}$) and the pooled within covariance matrix $\mathbf{S}$ are as follows:

$$\mathbf{d}' = (3.7, 2.1, 2.3), \; \mathbf{S} = \begin{bmatrix} 38.10 & 14.59 & 1.63 \\ 14.59 & 31.26 & 2.05 \\ 1.63 & 2.05 & 16.72 \end{bmatrix}$$

$$\mathbf{S} = \begin{bmatrix} 6.173 & 0 & 0 \\ 2.634 & 5.067 & 0 \\ .264 & .282 & 4.071 \end{bmatrix}\begin{bmatrix} 6.173 & 2.364 & .264 \\ 0 & 5.067 & .282 \\ 0 & 0 & 4.071 \end{bmatrix}$$

Now, to obtain the additive breakdown for T^2 we need $\mathbf{R}^{-1}\mathbf{d}$. This is:

$$\mathbf{R}^{-1}\mathbf{d} = \begin{bmatrix} .162 & 0 & 0 \\ -.076 & .197 & 0 \\ -.005 & -.014 & .25 \end{bmatrix}\begin{bmatrix} 3.7 \\ 2.1 \\ 2.3 \end{bmatrix} = \begin{bmatrix} .60 \\ .133 \\ .527 \end{bmatrix} = \mathbf{w}$$

We have not shown the details but $\mathbf{R}^{-1}$ is the inverse of $\mathbf{R}$. The reader can check this by multiplying the two matrices. The product is indeed the identity matrix (within rounding error). Thus,

$$T^2 = \frac{50(43)}{93}(.60, .133, .527)\begin{pmatrix} .60 \\ .133 \\ .527 \end{pmatrix}$$

$$T^2 = 25.904(.36 + .018 + .278)$$

$$T^2 = \quad 9.325 \quad + \quad\quad .466 \quad\quad + \quad\quad\quad 7.201$$

| contribution | contribution of variable 2 with | contribution of variable 3 to group discrimination *above* |
| of variable 1 | effects of variable 1 removed | *and beyond* what the first 2 variables contribute |

Each of the above numbers is just the value for the stepdown F (F^*) for the corresponding variable. Now, suppose we had set the probability of a type I error at .05 for the first variable and at .025 for the other two variables. Then, the probability of at least one type I error is $1 - (1 - .05)(1 - .025)(1 - .025) = 1 - .903 = .097$. Thus, there is about a 10% chance of falsely concluding that at least one of the variables contributes to group discrimination, when in fact it does not. What is our decision for each of the variables?

F_1^* = 9.325 (crit. value = 3.95), reject and conclude variable 1 significantly
.05; 1, 91   contributes to group discrimination

F_2^* = .466 < 1, so this can't be significant
.025; 1, 90

F_3^* = 7.201 (crit. value = 5.22), reject and conclude variable 3 makes a significant
.025; 1, 89   contribution to group discrimination above and beyond what first two criterion
                variables do.

Notice that the degrees of freedom for error decreases by one for each successive stepdown F, just as we lose one degree of freedom for each covariate used in analysis of covariance. The general formula for degrees of freedom for error (df_{w^*}) for the ith stepdown F then is $df_{w^*} = df_w - (i - 1)$, where $df_w = N - k$, that is, the ordinary formula for df in a one-way univariate analysis of variance.

Thus df_{w^*} for the third variable here is $df_{w^*} = 91 - (3 - 1) = 89$.

10.5 Comparison of Interpretation of Stepdown F's vs. Univariate F's

To illustrate the difference in interpretation when using univariate F's following a significant multivariate F vs. the use of stepdown F's, we consider an example. A different set of four variables that Novince (1977) analyzed in her study is presented in Table 10.1, along with the control lines for obtaining the stepdown F's on SPSS MANOVA.

The control lines are of exactly the same form as were used in obtaining a one-way MANOVA in Chapter 5. The only difference is that the last line SIGNIF(STEPDOWN)/ is included to obtain the stepdown F's. In Table 10.2 we present the multivariate tests, along with the univariate F's and the stepdown F's. Even though, as mentioned earlier in this chapter, it is *not* necessary to examine the multivariate tests when using stepdown F's, it was done here for illustrative purposes. This is one of those somewhat infrequent situations where the multivariate tests would not agree in a decision at the .05 level. In this case, 96% of between variation was concentrated in the first discriminant function, in which case the Pillai trace is known to be least powerful (Olson, 1976).

Using the univariate F's for interpretation, we would conclude that each of the variables is significant at the .05 level, because all the exact probabilities are < .05. That is, when each variable is considered separately, not taking into account how it is correlated with the others, it significantly separates the groups.

However, if we are able to establish a logical ordering of the criterion measures and thus use the stepdown F's, then it is clear that *only the first two* variables make a significant contribution (assuming the nominal levels had been set at .05 for the first variable and .025 for the other three variables). Variables 3 and 4 are redundant; that is, given 1 and 2, they do not make a significant contribution to group discrimination above and beyond what the first two variables do.

TABLE 10.1

Control Lines and Data for Stepdown Analysis on SPSS MANOVA for Novince Data

TITLE 'STEPDOWN F S ON NOVINCE DATA'.
DATA LIST FREE/TREATS JRANX JRNEGEVA JRGLOA JRSOCSKL.
BEGIN DATA.

```
1 2 2.5 2.5 3.5       1 1.5 2 1.5 4.5      1 2 3 2.5 3.5
1 2.5 4 3 3.5         1 1 2 1 5            1 1.5 3.5 2.5 4
1 4 3 3 4             1 3 4 3.5 4          1 3.5 3.5 3.5 2.5
1 1 1 1 4             1 1 2.5 2 4.5
2 1.5 3.5 2.5 4       2 1 4.5 2.5 4.5      2 3 3 3 4
2 4.5 4.5 4.5 3.5     2 1.5 4.5 3.5 3.5    2 2.5 4 3 4
2 3 4 3.5 3           2 4 5 5 1            2 3.5 3 3.5 3.5
2 1.5 1.5 1.5 4.5     2 3 4 3.5 3
3 1 2 1 4             3 1 2 1.5 4.5        3 1.5 1 1 3.5
3 2 2.5 2 4           3 2 3 2.5 4.5        3 2.5 3 2.5 4
3 2 2.5 2.5 4         3 1 1 1 5            3 1 1.5 1.5 5
3 1.5 1.5 1.5 5       3 2 3.5 2.5 4
```

END DATA.
LIST.
MANOVA JRANX TO JRSOCSKL BY TREATS(1 ,3)/
PRINT = CELLINFO(MEANS) SIGNIF(STEPDOWN)/.

TABLE 10.2

Multivariate Tests, Univariate F's and Stepdown F's for Novince Data

EFFECT .. TREATS
MULTIVARIATE TESTS OF SIGNIFICANCE (S = 2, M = 1/2, N = 12 1/2)

Test Name	Value	Approx. F	Hypoth. DF	Error DF	Sig. of F
Pillais	.42619	1.89561	8.00	56.00	.079
Hotellings	.69664	2.26409	8.00	52.00	.037
Wilks	.58362	2.08566	8.00	54.00	.053
Roys	.40178				

Note .. F statistic for WILKS' Lambda is exact.

- -

Univariate F-tests with (2,30) D. F.

Variable	Hypoth. SS	Error SS	Hypoth. MS	Error MS	F	Sig. of F
JRANX	6.01515	26.86364	3.00758	.89545	3.35871	.048
JRNEGEVA	14.86364	25.36364	7.43182	.84545	8.79032	.001
JRGLOA	12.56061	21.40909	6.28030	.71364	8.80042	.001
JRSOCSKL	3.68182	16.54545	1.84091	.55152	3.33791	.049

Roy-Bargman Stepdown F - tests

Variable	Hypoth. MS	Error MS	Stepdown F	Hypoth. DF	Error DF	Sig. of F
JRANX	3.00758	.89545	3.35871	2	30	.048
JRNEGEVA	2.99776	.66964	4.47666	2	29	.020
JRGLOA	.05601	.06520	.85899	2	28	.434
JRSOCSKL	.03462	.32567	.10631	2	27	.900

10.6 Stepdown *F*'s for *K* Groups—Effect of Within and Between Correlations

For more than two groups two matrices must be factored, and obtaining the stepdown *F*'s becomes more complicated (Finn, 1974). We do not worry about the details, but instead concentrate on two factors (the within and between correlations), which will determine how much a stepdown *F* for a given variable will differ from the univariate *F* for that variable.

The within-group correlation for variables x and y can be thought of as the weighted average of the individual group correlations. (This is not exactly technically correct, but will yield a value quite close to the actual value and it is easier to understand conceptually.) Consider the data from Exercise 5.1 in Chapter 5, and in particular variables y_1 and y_2. Suppose we computed r_{y1y2} for subjects in Group 1 only, then r_{y1y2} for subjects in Group 2 only, and finally r_{y1y2} for subjects in Group 3 only. These correlations are .637, .201, and .754 respectively, as the reader should check.

$$r_{y1y2(w)} = \frac{n_1 \cdot r_{(1)} + n_2 \cdot r_{(2)} + n_3 \cdot r_{(3)}}{N}$$

$$= \frac{11(.637) + 8(.201) + 10(.754)}{29} = .56$$

In this case we have taken the weighted average, because the groups' sizes were unequal. Now, the actual within (error) correlation is .61, which is quite close to the .56 we obtained.

How does one obtain the between correlation for x and y? The formula for $r_{xy(B)}$ is identical in form to the formula used for obtaining the simple Pearson correlation between two variables. That formula is:

$$r = \frac{\sum_i (x_i - \bar{x})(y_i - \bar{y})}{\sqrt{\sum_i (x_i - \bar{x})^2 \sum_i (y_i - \bar{y})^2}}$$

The formula for $r_{xy(B)}$ is obtained by replacing x_i and y_i by $\bar{x}_i$ and $\bar{y}_i$ (group means) and by replacing $\bar{x}$ and $\bar{y}$ by the grand means of $\bar{\bar{x}}$ and $\bar{\bar{y}}$. Also, for the between correlation the summation is over *groups*, not individuals. The formula is:

$$r_{xy(B)} = \frac{\sum (\bar{x}_i - \bar{\bar{x}})(\bar{y}_i - \bar{\bar{y}})}{\sqrt{\sum (\bar{x}_i - \bar{\bar{x}})^2 \sum (\bar{y}_i - \bar{\bar{y}})^2}}$$

Now that we have introduced the within and between correlations, and keeping in mind that stepdown analysis is just a series of analyses of covariance, the following from Bock and Haggard (1968, p. 129) is important:

> The results of an analysis of covariance depend on the extent to which the correlation of the concomitant and the dependent variables is concentrated in the errors (i.e., within group correlation) or in the effects of the experimental conditions (between correlation). If the concomitant variable is correlated appreciably with the errors, but little or not at all with the effects, the analysis of covariance increases the power of the statistical tests to detect differences .... If the concomitant variable is correlated with the experimental effects as much or more than with the errors, the analysis of covariance will show that the effect observed in the dependent variable can be largely accounted for by the concomitant variable (covariate).

Thus, the stepdown F's can differ considerably from the univariate F's and in *either* direction. If a given dependent variable in the ordering is correlated more within groups with the previous variables in the ordering than between groups, then the stepdown F for that variable will be larger than the univariate F, because more within variability will be removed from the variable by the covariates (i.e., previous dependent variables) than between-groups variability. If, on the other hand, the dependent variable is correlated strongly between groups with the previous dependent variables in the ordering, then we would expect its stepdown F to be considerably smaller than the univariate F. In this case, the mean sum of squares between for the variable is markedly reduced; its effect in discriminating the groups is strongly tied to the previous dependent variables or can be accounted for by them.

Specific illustrations of each of the above situations are provided by two examples from Morrison (1976, p. 127 and p. 154, #3). Our focus is on the first two dependent variables in the ordering for each problem. For the first problem, those variables were called information and similarities, while for the second problem they were simply called variable A and variable B. For each pair of variables, the correlation was high (.762 and .657). In the first case, however, the correlation was concentrated in the experimental condition (between correlation), while in the second it was concentrated in the errors (within-group correlation). A comparison of the univariate and stepdown F's shows this very clearly: for similarities (2nd variable in ordering) the univariate $F = 12.04$, while the stepdown $F = 1.37$. Thus, most of the between association for the similarities variable can be accounted for by its high correlation with the first variable in the ordering, that is, information. On the other hand, for the other situation the univariate $F = 6.4$ for variable B (2nd variable in ordering), and the stepdown $F = 24.03$. The reason for this striking result is that variable B and variable A (first variable in ordering) are highly correlated *within* groups, and thus most of the error variance for variable B can be accounted for by variance on variable A. Thus, the error variance for B in the stepdown F is much smaller than the error variance for B in the univariate F. The much smaller error coupled with the fact that A and B had a lower correlation across the groups resulted in a much larger stepdown F for B.

10.7 Summary

One could always routinely printout the stepdown F's. This can be dangerous, however, to users who may try to interpret these when not appropriate. In those cases (probably most cases) where a logical ordering can't be established, one should either not attempt to interpret the stepdown F's or do so very cautiously.

Some investigators may try several different orderings of the dependent variables to gather additional information. Although this may prove useful for future studies, it should be kept in mind that the different orderings are *not* independent. Although for a single ordering the overall α can be exactly estimated, for several orderings the probability of spurious results is unknown.

It is important to distinguish between the stepdown analysis, where a single a priori ordering of the dependent variables enables one to exactly estimate the probability of at least one false rejection and so-called stepwise procedures (as previously described in the multiple regression chapter). In these latter stepwise procedures the variable that is the best discriminator among the groups is entered first, then the procedure finds the next best discriminator, and so on. In such a procedure, especially with small or moderate sample sizes, there is a substantial hazard of capitalization on chance. That is, the variables that happen to have the highest correlations with the criterion (in multiple regression) or happen to be the best discriminators in the *particular* sample are those that are chosen. Very often, however, in another independent sample (from the population) some or many of the same variables may not be the best.

Thus, the stepdown analysis approach possesses two distinct advantages over such stepwise procedures: (a) It rests on a solid theoretical or empirical foundation—necessary to order the variables—and (b) the probability of one or more false rejections can be exactly estimated—statistically very desirable. The stepwise procedure, on the other hand, is likely to produce results that will not replicate and are therefore of dubious scientific value.

11

Exploratory and Confirmatory Factor Analysis

11.1 Introduction

Consider the following two common classes of research situations:

1. Exploratory regression analysis: An experimenter has gathered a moderate to large number of predictors (say 15 to 40) to predict some dependent variable.
2. Scale development: An investigator has assembled a set of items (say 20 to 50) designed to measure some construct (e.g., attitude toward education, anxiety, sociability). Here we think of the items as the variables.

In both of these situations the number of simple correlations among the variables is very large, and it is quite difficult to summarize by inspection precisely what the pattern of correlations represents. For example, with 30 variables, there are 435 simple correlations. Some means is needed for determining if there is a small number of underlying constructs that might account for the main sources of variation in such a complex set of correlations.

Furthermore, if there are 30 variables (whether predictors or items), we are undoubtedly not measuring 30 different constructs; hence, it makes sense to find some variable reduction scheme that will indicate how the variables cluster or hang together. Now, if sample size is not large enough (how large N needs to be is discussed in Section 11.7), then we need to resort to a logical clustering (grouping) based on theoretical or substantive grounds. On the other hand, with adequate sample size an empirical approach is preferable. Two basic empirical approaches are (a) principal components analysis and (b) factor analysis. In both approaches linear combinations of the original variables (the factors) are derived, and often a small number of these account for most of the variation or the pattern of correlations. In factor analysis a mathematical model is set up, and the factors can only be estimated, whereas in components analysis we are simply transforming the original variables into the new set of linear combinations (the principal components).

Both methods often yield similar results. We prefer to discuss principal components for several reasons:

1. It is a psychometrically sound procedure.
2. It is simpler mathematically, relatively speaking, than factor analysis. And a main theme in this text is to keep the mathematics as simple as possible.
3. The factor indeterminacy issue associated with common factor analysis (Steiger, 1979) is a troublesome feature.
4. A thorough discussion of factor analysis would require hundreds of pages, and there are other good sources on the subject (Gorsuch, 1983).

Recall that for discriminant analysis uncorrelated linear combinations of the original variables were used to additively partition the association between the classification variable and the set of dependent variables. Here we are again using uncorrelated linear combinations of the original variables (the principal components), but this time to additively partition the variance for a set of variables.

In this chapter we consider in some detail two fundamentally different approaches to factor analysis. The first approach, just discussed, is called exploratory factor analysis. Here the researcher is attempting to determine how many factors are present and whether the factors are correlated, and wishes to name the factors. The other approach, called confirmatory factor analysis, rests on a solid theoretical or empirical base. Here, the researcher "knows" how many factors there are and whether the factors should be correlated. Also, the researcher generally forces items to load only on a specific factor and wishes to "confirm" a hypothesized factor structure with data. There is an overall statistical test for doing so. First, however, we turn to the exploratory mode.

11.2 Exploratory Factor Analysis

11.2.1 The Nature of Principal Components

If we have a single group of subjects measured on a set of variables, then principal components partition the total variance (i.e., the sum of the variances for the original variables) by first finding the linear combination of the variables that accounts for the maximum account of variance:

$$y_1 = a_{11}x_1 + a_{12}x_2 + \cdots + a_{1p}x_p$$

y_1 is called the first principal component, and if the coefficients are scaled such that $\mathbf{a}_1'\mathbf{a}_1 = 1$ [where $\mathbf{a}_1' = (a_{11}, a_{12}, \ldots, a_{1p})$] then the variance of y_1 is equal to the *largest* eigenvalue of the sample covariance matrix (Morrison, 1967, p. 224). The coefficients of the principal component are the elements of the eigenvector corresponding to the largest eigenvalue.

Then the procedure finds a second linear combination, *uncorrelated* with the first component, such that it accounts for the next largest amount of variance (after the variance attributable to the first component has been removed) in the system. This second component y_2 is

$$y_2 = a_{21}x_1 + a_{22}x_2 + \cdots a_{2p}x_p$$

and the coefficients are scaled so that $\mathbf{a}_2'\mathbf{a}_2 = 1$, as for the first component. The fact that the two components are constructed to be uncorrelated means that the Pearson correlation between y_1 and y_2 is 0. The coefficients of the second component are simply the elements of the eigenvector associated with the second largest eigenvalue of the covariance matrix, and the sample variance of y_2 is equal to the second largest eigenvalue.

The third principal component is constructed to be uncorrelated with the first two, and accounts for the third largest amount of variance in the system, and so on. Principal components analysis is therefore still another example of a mathematical maximization procedure, where each successive component accounts for the maximum amount of the variance that is left.

Thus, through the use of principal components, a set of correlated variables is transformed into a set of uncorrelated variables (the components). The hope is that a much smaller number of these components will account for most of the variance in the original set of variables, and of course that we can meaningfully interpret the components. By most of the variance we mean about 75% or more, and often this can be accomplished with five or fewer components.

The components are interpreted by using the component-variable correlations (called *factor loadings*) that are largest in absolute magnitude. For example, if the first component loaded high and positive on variables 1, 3, 5, and 6, then we would interpret that component by attempting to determine what those four variables have in common. *The component procedure has empirically clustered the four variables, and the job of the psychologist is to give a name to the construct that underlies variability and thus identify the component substantively.*

In the preceding example we assumed that the loadings were all in the same direction (all positive). Of course, it is possible to have a mixture of high positive and negative loadings on a particular component. In this case we have what is called a *bipolar* factor. For example, in components analyses of IQ tests, the second component may be a bipolar factor contrasting verbal abilities against spatial-perceptual abilities.

Social science researchers would be used to extracting components from a correlation matrix. The reason for this standardization is that scales for tests used in educational, sociological, and psychological research are usually arbitrary. If, however, the scales are reasonably commensurable, performing a components analysis on the *covariance* matrix is preferable for statistical reasons (Morrison, 1967, p. 222). The components obtained from the correlation and covariance matrices are, in general, *not* the same. The option of doing the components analysis on either the correlation or covariance matrix is available on SAS and SPSS.

A precaution that researchers contemplating a components analysis with a small sample size (certainly any n around 100) should take, especially if most of the elements in the sample correlation matrix are small, is to apply Bartlett's sphericity test (Cooley & Lohnes, 1971, p. 103). This procedure tests the null hypothesis that the variables in the *population* correlation matrix are uncorrelated. If one fails to reject with this test, then there is no reason to do the components analysis because the variables are already uncorrelated. The sphericity test is available on both the SAS and SPSS packages.

11.3 Three Uses for Components as a Variable Reducing Scheme

We now consider three cases in which the use of components as a variable reducing scheme can be very valuable.

1. The first use has already been mentioned, and that is to determine empirically how many dimensions (underlying constructs) account for most of the variance on an instrument (scale). The original variables in this case are the items on the scale.

2. In a multiple regression context, if the number of predictors is large relative to the number of subjects, then we may wish to use principal components on the predictors to reduce markedly the number of predictors. If so, then the N/variable ratio increases considerably and the possibility of the regression equation's holding up under cross-validation is much better (see Herzberg, 1969). We show later in the chapter (Example 11.3) how to do this on SAS and SPSS.

    The use of principal components on the predictors is also one way of attacking the multicollinearity problem (correlated predictors). Furthermore, because the new predictors (i.e., the components) are uncorrelated, the order in which they enter the regression equation makes no difference in terms of how much variance in the dependent variable they will account for.

3. In the chapter on k-group MANOVA we indicated several reasons (reliability consideration, robustness, etc.) that generally mitigate against the use of a large number of criterion variables. Therefore, if there is initially a large number of potential criterion variables, it probably would be wise to perform a principal components analysis on them in an attempt to work with a smaller set of new criterion variables. We show later in the chapter (in Example 11.4) how to do this for SAS and SPSS. It must be recognized, however, that the components are *artificial* variables and are not necessarily going to be interpretable. Nevertheless, there are techniques for improving their interpretability, and we discuss these later.

11.4 Criteria for Deciding on How Many Components to Retain

Four methods can be used in deciding how many components to retain:

1. Probably the most widely used criterion is that of Kaiser (1960): Retain only those components whose eigenvalues are greater than 1. Unless something else is specified, this is the rule that is used by SPSS, but not by SAS. Although using this rule generally will result in retention of only the most important factors, blind use could lead to retaining factors that may have no practical significance (in terms of percent of variance accounted for).

    Studies by Cattell and Jaspers (1967), Browne (1968), and Linn (1968) evaluated the accuracy of the eigenvalue > 1 criterion. In all three studies, the authors determined how often the criterion would identify the correct number of factors from matrices with a known number of factors. The number of variables in the studies ranged from 10 to 40. Generally, the criterion was accurate to fairly accurate, with gross overestimation occurring only with a large number of variables (40) *and* low communalities (around .40). The criterion is more accurate when the number of variables is small (10 to 15) or moderate (20 to 30) and the communalities are high (>.70). The communality of a variable is the amount of variance on a variable accounted for by the set of factors. We see how it is computed later in this chapter.

2. A graphical method called the *scree test* has been proposed by Cattell (1966). In this method the magnitude of the eigenvalues (vertical axis) is plotted against their ordinal numbers (whether it was the first eigenvalue, the second, etc.). Generally what happens is that the magnitude of successive eigenvalues drops

off sharply (steep descent) and then tends to level off. The recommendation is to retain all eigenvalues (and hence components) in the sharp descent *before* the first one on the line where they start to level off. In one of our examples we illustrate this test. This method will generally retain components that account for large or fairly large and distinct amounts of variances (e.g., 31%, 20%, 13%, and 9%). Here, however, blind use might lead to not retaining factors which, although they account for a smaller amount of variance, might be practically significant. For example, if the first eigenvalue at the break point accounted for 8.3% of variance and then the next three eigenvalues accounted for 7.1%, 6%, and 5.2%, then 5% or more might well be considered significant in some contexts, and retaining the first and dropping the next three seems somewhat arbitrary. The scree plot is available on SPSS (in FACTOR program) and in the SAS package. Several studies have investigated the accuracy of the scree test. Tucker, Koopman, and Linn (1969) found it gave the correct number of factors in 12 of 18 cases. Linn (1968) found it to yield the correct number of factors in seven of 10 cases, whereas Cattell and Jaspers (1967) found it to be correct in six of eight cases.

A later, more extensive study on the number of factors problem (Hakstian, Rogers, & Cattell, 1982) adds some additional information. They note that for $N > 250$ and a mean communality $\geq .60$, either the Kaiser or Scree rules will yield an accurate estimate for the number of true factors. They add that such an estimate will be just that much more credible if the Q/P ratio is $<.30$ (P is the number of variables and Q is the number of factors). With mean communality .30 or $Q/P > .3$, the Kaiser rule is less accurate and the Scree rule much less accurate.

3. There is a statistical significance test for the number of factors to retain that was developed by Lawley (1940). However, as with all statistical tests, it is influenced by sample size, and large sample size may lead to the retention of too many factors.

4. Retain as many factors as will account for a specified amount of total variance. Generally, one would want to account for at least 70% of the total variance, although in some cases the investigator may not be satisfied unless 80 to 85% of the variance is accounted for. This method could lead to the retention of factors that are essentially variable specific, that is, load highly on only a single variable.

So what criterion should be used in deciding how many factors to retain? *Since the Kaiser criterion has been shown to be quite accurate when the number of variables is <30 and the communalities are >.70, or when N > 250 and the mean communality is ≥.60, we would use it under these circumstances.* For other situations, use of the scree test with an $N > 200$ will probably not lead us too far astray, provided that most of the communalities are reasonably large.

In all of the above we have assumed that we will retain only so many components, which will hopefully account for a sizable amount of the total variance and simply discard the rest of the information, that is, not worry about the 20 or 30% of the variance that is not accounted for. However, it seems to us that in some cases the following suggestion of Morrison (1967, p. 228) has merit:

> Frequently, it is better to summarize the complex in terms of the first components with large and markedly distinct variances and include as highly specific and unique variates those responses which are generally independent in the system. Such unique responses could probably be represented by high loadings in the later components but only in the presence of considerable noise from the other unrelated variates.

In other words, if we did a components analysis on, say, 20 variables and only the first four components accounted for large and distinct amounts of variance, then we should summarize the complex of 20 variables in terms of the four components *and* those particular variables that had high correlations (loadings) with the latter components. In this way more of the total information in the complex is retained, although some parsimony is sacrificed.

11.5 Increasing Interpretability of Factors by Rotation

Although the principal components are fine for summarizing most of the variance in a large set of variables with a small number of components, often the components are not easily interpretable. The components are artificial variates designed to maximize variance accounted for, not designed for interpretability. Two major classes of rotations are available:

1. Orthogonal (rigid) rotations—here the new factors are still uncorrelated, as were the original components.
2. Oblique rotations—here the new factors will be correlated.

11.5.1 Orthogonal Rotations

We discuss two such rotations:

1. Quartimax—Here the idea is to clean up the variables. That is, the rotation is done so that each variable loads mainly on one factor. Then that variable can be considered to be a relatively pure measure of the factor. The problem with this approach is that most of the variables tend to load on a single factor (producing the so called "g" factor in analyses of IQ tests), making interpretation of the factor difficult.
2. Varimax—Kaiser (1960) took a different tack. He designed a rotation to clean up the factors. That is, with his rotation, each factor tends to load high on a smaller number of variables and low or very low on the other variables. This will generally make interpretation of the resulting factors easier. The varimax rotation is the default option in SPSS.

It should be mentioned that when the varimax rotation is done, the *maximum variance property* of the original components is destroyed. The rotation essentially reallocates the loadings. Thus, the first rotated factor will no longer *necessarily* account for the maximum amount of variance. The amount of variance accounted for by each rotated factor has to be recalculated. You will see this on the printout from SAS and SPSS. Even though this is true, and somewhat unfortunate, it is more important to be able to interpret the factors.

11.5.2 Oblique Rotations

Numerous oblique rotations have been proposed: for example, oblimax, quartimin, maxplane, orthoblique (Harris–Kaiser), promax, and oblimin. Promax and orthoblique are available on SAS, and oblimin is available on SPSS.

Many have argued that correlated factors are much more reasonable to assume in most cases (Cliff, 1987; Pedhazur & Schmelkin, 1991; *SAS STAT User's Guide*, Vol. 1, p. 776, 1990), and therefore oblique rotations are quite reasonable. The following from Pedhazur and Schmelkin (1991) is interesting:

> From the perspective of construct validation, the decision whether to rotate factors orthogonally or obliquely reflects one's conception regarding the structure of the construct under consideration. It boils down to the question: Are aspects of a postulated multidimensional construct intercorrelated? The answer to this question is relegated to the status of an assumption when an orthogonal rotation is employed.… The preferred course of action is, in our opinion, to rotate both orthogonally and obliquely. When, on the basis of the latter, it is concluded that the correlations among the factors are negligible, the interpretation of the simpler orthogonal solution becomes tenable. (p. 615)

It has also been argued that there is no such thing as a "best" oblique rotation. The following from the *SAS STAT User's Guide* (Vol. 1, 1990) strongly expresses this view:

> You cannot say that any rotation is better than any other rotation from a statistical point of view; all rotations are equally good statistically. Therefore, the choice among different rotations must be based on nonstatistical grounds. … If two rotations give rise to different interpretations, those two interpretations must not be regarded as conflicting. Rather, they are two different ways of looking at the same thing, two different points of view in the common factor space. (p. 776)

In the two computer examples we simply did the components analysis and a varimax rotation, that is, an orthogonal rotation. The solutions obtained may or may not be the most reasonable ones. We also did an oblique rotation (promax) on the Personality Research Form using SAS. Interestingly, the correlations among the factors were very small (all <.10 in absolute value), suggesting that the original orthogonal solution is quite reasonable. We leave it to the reader to run an oblique rotation (oblimin) on the California Psychological Inventory using SPSS, and to compare the orthogonal and oblique solutions.

The reader needs to be aware that when an oblique solution is more reasonable, interpretation of the factors becomes more complicated. Two matrices need to be examined:

1. Factor pattern matrix—The elements here are analogous to standardized regression coefficients from a multiple regression analysis. That is, a given element indicates the importance of that variable to the factor with the influence of the other variables partialled out.

2. Factor structure matrix—The elements here are the simple correlations of the variables with the factors; that is, they are the factor loadings.

For orthogonal factors these two matrices are the same.

11.6 What Loadings Should Be Used for Interpretation?

Recall that a loading is simply the Pearson correlation between the variable and the factor (linear combination of the variables). Now, certainly any loading that is going to be used to interpret a factor should be statistically significant at a minimum. The formula for the standard error of a correlation coefficient is given in elementary statistics books as

$1/\sqrt{N-1}$ and one might think it could be used to determine which loadings are significant. But, in components analysis (where we are maximizing again), and in rotating, there is considerable opportunity for capitalization on chance. This is especially true for small or moderate sample sizes, or even for fairly large sample size (200 or 300) if the number of variables being factored is large (say 40 or 50). Because of this capitalization on chance, the formula for the standard error of correlation can *seriously underestimate* the actual amount of error in the factor loadings.

A study by Cliff and Hamburger (1967) showed that the standard errors of factor loadings for orthogonally rotated solutions in all cases were considerably greater (150 to 200% in most cases) than the standard error for an ordinary correlation. Thus, a rough check as to whether a loading is statistically significant can be obtained by *doubling* the standard error, that is, doubling the critical value required for significance for an ordinary correlation. This kind of statistical check is most crucial when sample size is small, or small relative to the number of variables being factor analyzed. When sample size is quite large (say 1,000), or large relative to the number of variables ($N = 500$ for 20 variables), then significance is ensured. It may be that doubling the standard error in general is too conservative, because for the case where a statistical check is more crucial ($N = 100$), the errors were generally less than 1½ times greater. However, because Cliff and Hamburger (1967, p. 438) suggested that the sampling error might be greater in situations that aren't as clean as the one they analyzed, it probably is advisable to be conservative until more evidence becomes available.

Given the Cliff and Hamburger results, we feel it is time that investigators stopped blindly using the rule of interpreting factors with loadings greater than |.30|, and take sample size into account. Also, because in checking to determine which loadings are significant, many statistical tests will be done, it is advisable to set the α level more stringently for each test. This is done to control on overall α, that is, the probability of at least one false rejection. We would recommend testing each loading for significance at $\alpha = .01$ (two-tailed test). To aid the reader in this task we present in Table 11.1 the critical values for a simple correlation at $\alpha = .01$ for sample size ranging from 50 to 1,000. *Remember that the critical values in Table 11.1 should be doubled, and it is the doubled value that is used as the critical value for testing the significance of a loading.* To illustrate the use of Table 11.1, suppose a factor analysis had been run with 140 subjects. Then, only loadings $>2(.217) = .434$ in absolute value would be declared statistically significant. If sample size in this example had been 160, then interpolation between 140 and 180 would give a very good approximation to the critical value.

Once one is confident that the loadings being used for interpretation are significant (because of a significance test or because of large sample size), then the question becomes which loadings are large enough to be practically significant. For example, a loading of .20 could well be significant with large sample size, but this indicates only 4% shared variance between the variable and the factor. It would seem that one would want in general a variable to share *at least* 15% of its variance with the construct (factor) it is going to be used to

TABLE 11.1

Critical Values for a Correlation Coefficient
at $\alpha = .01$ for a Two-Tailed Test

n	CV	n	CV	n	CV
50	.361	180	.192	400	.129
80	.286	200	.182	600	.105
100	.256	250	.163	800	.091
140	.217	300	.149	1000	.081

help name. This means using only loadings that are about .40 or greater for interpretation purposes. To interpret what the variables with high loadings have in common, i.e., to name the factor (construct), a substantive specialist is needed.

11.7 Sample Size and Reliable Factors

Various rules have been suggested in terms of the sample size required for reliable factors. Many of the popular rules suggest that sample size be determined as a function of the number of variables being analyzed, ranging anywhere from two subjects per variable to 20 subjects per variable. And indeed, in a previous edition of this text, I suggested five subjects per variable as the minimum needed. However, a Monte Carlo study by Guadagnoli and Velicer (1988) indicated, contrary to the popular rules, that the most important factors are component saturation (the absolute magnitude of the loadings) and absolute sample size. Also, number of variables per component is somewhat important. Their recommendations for the applied researcher were as follows:

1. Components with four or more loadings above .60 in absolute value are reliable, regardless of sample size.
2. Components with about 10 or more low (.40) loadings are reliable as long as sample size is greater than about 150.
3. Components with only a few low loadings should not be interpreted unless sample size is at least 300.

An additional reasonable conclusion to draw from their study is that any component with at least three loadings above .80 will be reliable.

These results are nice in establishing at least some empirical basis, rather than "seat-of-the-pants" judgment, for assessing what components we can have confidence in. However, as with any study, they cover only a certain set of situations. For example, what if we run across a component that has two loadings above .60 and six loadings of at least .40; is this a reliable component? My guess is that it probably would be, but at this time we don't have a strict empirical basis for saying so.

The third recommendation of Guadagnoli and Velicer, that components with only a few low loadings be interpreted tenuously, doesn't seem that important to me. The reason is that a factor defined by only a few loadings is not much of a factor; as a matter of fact, we are as close as we can get to the factor's being variable specific.

Velicer also indicated that when the *average* of the four largest loadings is >.60 or the *average* of the three largest loadings is >.80, then the factors will be reliable (personal communication, August, 1992). This broadens considerably when the factors will be reliable.

11.8 Four Computer Examples

We now consider four examples to illustrate the use of components analysis and the varimax rotation in practice. The first two involve popular personality scales: the California Psychological Inventory and the Personality Research Form. Example 11.1 shows how to input a correlation matrix using the SPSS FACTOR program, and Example 11.2 illustrates correlation matrix input for the SAS FACTOR program. Example 11.3 shows how to do a components analysis on a set of predictors and then pass the new predictors (the factor scores) to a regression program for both SAS and SPSS. Example 11.4 illustrates a components analysis and varimax rotation on a set of dependent variables and then passing the factor scores to a MANOVA program for both SAS and SPSS.

Example 11.1: California Psychological Inventory on SPSS

The first example is a components analysis of the California Psychological Inventory followed by a varimax rotation. The data was collected on 180 college freshmen (90 males and 90 females) by Smith (1975). He was interested in gathering evidence to support the uniqueness of death anxiety as a construct. Thus, he wanted to determine to what extent death anxiety could be predicted from general anxiety, other personality variables (hence the use of the CPI), and situational variables related to death (recent loss of a love one, recent experiences with a deathly situation, etc.). In this use of multiple regression Smith was hoping for a *small R²*; that is, he wanted only a small amount of the variance in death anxiety scores to be accounted for by the other variables.

Table 11.2 presents the SPSS control lines for the factor analysis, along with annotation explaining what several of the commands mean. Table 11.3 presents part of the printout from SPSS. The printout indicates that the first component (factor) accounted for 37.1% of the total variance. This is arrived at by dividing the eigenvalue for the first component (6.679), which tells how much variance that component accounts for, by the total variance (which for a correlation matrix is just the sum of the diagonal elements, or 18 here). The second component accounts for $2.935/18 \times 100 = 16.3\%$ of the variance, and so on.

As to how many components to retain, Kaiser's rule of using only those components whose eigenvalues are greater than 1 would indicate that we should retain only the first four components (which is what has been done on the printout; remember Kaiser's rule is the default option for SPSS). Thus, as the printout indicates, we account for 71.4% of the total variance. Cattell's screen test (see Table 11.3) would not agree with the Kaiser rule, because there are only three eigenvalues (associated with the first three factors) before the breaking point, the point where the steep descent stops and the eigenvalues start to level off. The results of a study by Zwick and Velicer (1986) would lead us to use only three factors here. These three factors, as Table 11.3 shows, account for 65.2% of the total variance.

Table 11.4 gives the unrotated loadings and the varimax rotated loadings. From Table 11.1, the critical value for a significant loading is 2(.192) = .384. Thus, this is an absolute minimum value for us to be confident that we are dealing with nonchance loadings. The original components are somewhat difficult to interpret, especially the first component, because 14 of the loadings are "significant." Therefore, we focus our interpretation on the rotated factors. The variables that we use in interpretation are boxed in on Table 11.4. The first rotated factor still has significant loadings on 11 variables, although because one of these (.410 for CS) is just barely significant, and is also substantially less than the other significant loadings (the next smallest is .535), we disregard it for interpretation purposes. Among the adjectives that characterize high scores on the other 10 variables, from the CPI manual, are: calm, patient, thorough, nonaggressive, conscientious, cooperative, modest, diligent, and organized. Thus, this first rotated factor appears to be a "conforming, mature, inward tendencies" dimension. That is, it reveals a low-profile individual, who is conforming, industrious, thorough, and nonaggressive.

The loadings that are significant on the second rotated factor are also strong loadings (the smallest is .666): .774 for dominance, .666 for capacity for status, .855 for sociability, .780 for social presence, and .879 for self-acceptance. Adjectives from the CPI manual used to characterize high scores on these variables are: aggressive, ambitious, spontaneous, outspoken, self-centered, quick, and enterprising. Thus, this factor appears to describe an "aggressive, outward tendencies" dimension. High scores on this dimension reveal a high-profile individual who is aggressive, dynamic, and outspoken.

TABLE 11.2

SPSS Factor Control Lines for Principal Components on California Psychological Inventory

```
TITLE 'PRINCIPAL COMPONENTS ON CPI'.
MATRIX DATA VARIABLES=DOM CAPSTAT SOCIAL SOCPRES SELFACP WELLBEG RESPON SOCLIZ SELFCTRL TOLER
GOODIMP COMMUNAL ACHCONF ACHINDEP INTELEFF PSYMIND FLEX FEMIN/CONTENTS=N_SCALAR CORR/.
BEGIN DATA.
 180
1.000
 .467  1.000
 .681   .600  1.000
 .447   .585   .643  1.000
 .610   .466   .673   .612  1.000
 .236   .324   .339   .357   .077  1.000
 .401   .346   .344   .081   .056   .518  1.000
 .214   .179   .242   .003  -.029   .517   .632  1.000
-.062   .105  -.001  -.130  -.352   .619   .476   .544  1.000
 .227   .465   .295   .330   .004   .698   .502   .517   .575  1.000
 .238   .392   .367   .178   .023   .542   .381   .367   .697   .501  1.000
 .189   .146   .227   .159   .117   .336   .380   .384   .084   .192  -.001  1.000
 .401   .374   .479   .296   .154   .676   .567   .589   .633   .588   .610   .307  1.000
 .075   .400   .140   .289  -.027   .513   .369   .280   .464   .359   .460   .175   .465  1.000
 .314   .590   .451   .457   .192   .671   .500   .442   .456   .720   .716   .333   .616   .688  1.000
 .167   .337   .239   .336   .011   .463   .217   .182   .410   .502   .502  -.060   .393   .519   .466  1.000
 .148   .203  -.028   .236   .037   .051  -.155  -.300  -.043   .079   .218  -.149  -.120   .393   .199   .276  1.000
 .099   .061  -.069  -.158  -.097  -.038   .275   .159   .215   .032   .091   .139   .071   .033  -.031  -.145  -.344  1.000
END DATA.
FACTOR MATRIX IN(COR=*)/ ①
 CRITERIA=FACTORS(3)/ ②
 PRINT=CORRELATION DEFAULT/
 PLOT=EIGEN/
 FORMAT=BLANK(.384)/. ③
```

① To read in matrices in FACTOR the matrix subcommand is used. The keyword IN specifies the file from which the matrix is read. The CORR=* means we are reading the correlation matrix from the active file.

② This subcommand means we are requesting three factors.

③ The BLANK .384 is very useful for zeroing in on the most important loadings. It means that all loadings less than .384 in absolute value will not be printed.

TABLE 11.3

Eigenvalues, Communalities, and Scree Plot for CPI from SPSS Factor Analysis Program

FINAL STATISTICS:

VARIABLE	COMMUNALITY	*	FACTOR	EIGENVALUE	① PCT of VAR	CUM PCT
		*				
DOM	.64619	*	1	6.67904	37.1	37.1
CAPSTAT	.61477	*	2	2.93494	16.3	53.4
SOCIAL	.79929	*	3	2.11381	11.7	② 65.2
SOCPRES	.72447	*				
SELFACP	.79781	*				
WELLBEG	.69046	*				
RESPON	.65899	*				
SOCLIZ	.68243	*				
SELFCTRL	.83300	*				
TOLER	.75739	*				
GOODIMP	.50292	*				
COMMUNAL	.31968	*				
ACHCONF	.72748	*				
ACHINDEP	.69383	*				
INTELEFF	.73794	*				
PSYMIND	.55269	*				
FLEX	.66568	*				
FEMIN	.32275	*				

Scree plot

① The eigenvalue indicates the amount of variance accounted for by each factor.
② The three factors account for 65.2% of total variance.

TABLE 11.4

Unrotated Components Loadings and Varimax Rotated Loadings for California Psychological Inventory

FACTOR MATRIX:	FACTOR 1	FACTOR 2	FACTOR 3
INTELEFF	.84602		
ACHCONF	.81978		
TOLER	.81618		
WELLBEG	.80596		
ACHINDEP	.67844		−.45209
RESPON	.67775		.38887
GOODIMP	.67347		
CAPSTAT	.64991	.43580	
SOCLIZ	.61110		.41036
SOCIAL	.60980	.60145	.
PSYMIND	.57314		−.47158
SELFACP		.82106	
SELFCTRL	.60942	−.67659	
SOCPRES	.51248	.66551	
DOM	.50137	.55616	
FLEX			−.76714
FEMIN			.49437 .
COMMUNAL			.43941

VARIMAX CONVERGED IN 5 ITERATIONS.

ROTATED FACTOR MATRIX:	FACTOR 1	FACTOR 2	FACTOR 3
TOLER	.85516		
SELFCTRL	.80528		
ACHINDEP	.80019		
WELLBEG	.78605		
INTELEFF	.77170		
ACHCONF	.70442		
GOODIMP	.68552		
PSYMIND	.66676		
SELFACP		.87923	
SOCIAL		.85542	
SOCPRES		.77968	
DOM		.77396	
CAPSTAT	.40969	.66550	
FLEX			−.76248
SOCLIZ	.53450		.62776
RESPON	.53971		.56861
FEMIN			.56029
COMMUNAL			.47917

Note: Only three factors are displayed in this table, because there is evidence that the Kaiser criterion (the default in SPSS—which yields four factors) can yield too many factors (Zwick & Velicer, 1986), while the scree test is usually within 1 or 2 of true number of factors. Note also that all loadings less than |.384| have been set equal to 0 (see Table 11.2). Both of these are changes from the third edition of this text. To obtain just the three factors indicated by the scree test, you need to insert in the control lines in Table 11.2 after the Print subcommand the following subcommand: CRITERIA MINEIGEN(2)/CRITERIA = FACTORS(3)/

Factor 3 is somewhat dominated by the flexibility variable (loading = −.76248), although the loadings for socialization, responsibility, femininity, and communality are also fairly substantial (ranging from .628 to .479). Low scores on flexibility from the CPI manual characterize an individual as cautious, guarded, mannerly, and overly deferential to authority. High scores on femininity reflect an individual who is patient, gentle, and respectful and accepting of others. Factor 3 thus seems to be measuring a "demure inflexibility in intellectual and social matters."

Before proceeding to another example, we wish to make a few additional points. Nunnally (1978, pp. 433–436) indicated, in an excellent discussion, several ways in which one can be fooled by factor analysis. One point he made that we wish to elaborate on is that of ignoring the simple correlations among the variables after the factors have been derived; that is, not checking the correlations among the variables that have been used to define a factor, to see if there is communality among them in the simple sense. As Nunnally noted, in some cases, variables used to define a factor may have simple correlations near 0.

For our example this is not the case. Examination of the simple correlations in Table 11.2 for the 10 variables used to define Factor 1 shows that most of the correlations are in the moderate to fairly strong range. The correlations among the five variables used to define Factor 2 are also in the moderate to fairly strong range.

An additional point concerning Factor 2 is of interest. The empirical clustering of the variables coincides almost exactly with the logical clustering of the variables given in the CPI manual. The only difference is that Wellbeg is in the logical cluster but not in the empirical cluster (i.e., not on the factor).

Example 11.2: Personality Research Form on SAS

We now consider the interpretation of a principal components analysis and varimax rotation on the Personality Research Form for 231 undergraduate males from a study by Golding and Seidman (1974). The control lines for running the analysis on the SAS FACTOR program and the correlation matrix are presented in Table 11.5. It is important to note here that SAS is different from the other major package (SPSS) in that (a) a varimax rotation is *not* a default option—the default is no rotation, and (b) the Kaiser criterion (retaining only those factors whose eigenvalues are >1) is not a default option. In Table 11.5 we have requested the Kaiser criterion be used by specifying MINEIGEN = 1.0, and have requested the varimax rotation by specifying ROTATE = VARIMAX.

To indicate to SAS that we are inputting a correlation matrix, the TYPE = CORR in parentheses after the name for the data set is necessary. The TYPE = 'CORR' on the next line is also required. Note that the name for each variable precedes the correlations for it with all the other variables. Also, note that there are 14 periods for the ABASE variable, 13 periods for the ACH variable, 12 periods for AGGRESS, and so on. These periods need to be inserted. Finally, the correlations for each row of the matrix must be on a separate record. Thus, although we may need two lines for the correlations of ORDER with all other variables, once we put the last correlation there (which is a 1) we must start the correlations for the next variable (PLAY) on a *new* line. The same is true for the SPSS FACTOR program.

The CORR in this statement yields the correlation matrix for the variables. The FUZZ = .34 prints correlations and factor loadings with absolute value less than .34 as missing values. Our purpose in using FUZZ is to think of values <|.34| as chance values, and to treat them as 0. The SCREE is inserted to obtain Cattell's scree test, useful in determining the number of factors to retain.

The first part of the printout appears in Table 11.6, and the output at the top indicates that according to the Kaiser criterion only four factors will be retained because there are only four eigenvalues >1. Will the Kaiser criterion accurately identify the true number of factors in this case? To answer this question it is helpful to refer back to the Hakstian et al. (1982) study cited earlier. They noted that for N > 250 and a mean communality >.60, the Kaiser criterion is accurate. Because the total of the communality estimates in Table 11.6 is given as 9.338987, the mean communality here is 9.338987/15 = .622. Although N is not >250, it is close (N = 231), and we feel the Kaiser rule will be accurate.

TABLE 11.5
SAS Factor Control Lines for Components Analysis and Varimax Rotation on the Personality Research Form

```
DATA PRF(TYPE = CORR);
TYPE = 'CORR';
INPUT NAME $ ABASE ACH AGGRESS AUTON CHANGE COGSTR DEF DOMIN
ENDUR EXHIB HARAVOD IMPLUS NUTUR ORDER PLAY;
CARDS;
ABASE      1.0   ...
ACH        .01   1.0   ...
AGGRESS   −.32  −.08   1.0   ...
AUTON      .13   .03   .04   1.0   ...
CHANGE     .15   .09   .06   .28   1.0   ...
COGSTR    −.23   .22   .02  −.17  −.27   1.0   ...
DEF       −.42   .06   .57   .04  −.01   .14   1.0   ...
DOMIN     −.22   .37   .25   .08   .17  −.05   .32   1.0   ...
ENDUR      .01   .65  −.11   .09   .03   .20   .02   .39   1.0   ...
EXHIB     −.09   .13   .28  −.07   .15  −.24   .10   .52   .08   1.0   ...
HARAVOD   −.22  −.02  −.01  −.28  −.33   .45   .08  −.21  −.08  −.22   1.0   ...
IMPLUS     .14  −.16   .30   .16   .33  −.46   .14   .07  −.23   .34  −.31   1.0   ...
NUTUR      .33   .30  −.23  −.24   .03  −.05  −.19   .16   .20   .22  −.04   .04   1.0   ...
ORDER     −.11   .29   .01  −.13  −.17   .53   .09   .08   .27  −.11   .22  −.35   0.0   1.0   ...
PLAY       .05  −.25   .27  −.02   .12  −.31  −.02   .11  −.27   .43  −.26   .48  −.10  −.25   1.0
PROC FACTOR CORR FUZZ = .34 MINEIGEN = 1.0 REORDER ROTATE = VARIMAX SCREE;
```

TABLE 11.6
Eigenvalues and Scree Plot from the SAS Factor Program for Personality Research Form

Eigenvalues of the Correlation Matrix: Total = 15 Average = 1								
	1	2	3	4	5	6	7	8
Eigenvalue	3.1684	2.4821	2.2464	1.4422	0.8591	0.8326	0.6859	0.6047
Difference	0.6862	0.2358	0.8042	0.5830	0.0266	0.1466	0.0812	0.0636
Proportion	0.2112	0.1655	0.1498	0.0961	0.0573	0.0555	0.0457	0.0403
Cumulative	0.2112	0.3767	0.5265	0.6226	0.6799	0.7354	0.7811	0.8214
	9	10	11	12	13	14	15	
Eigenvalue	0.5411	0.4382	0.4060	0.3826	0.3283	0.3108	0.2717	
Difference	0.1029	0.0322	0.0234	0.0543	0.0175	0.0391		
Proportion	0.0361	0.0292	0.0271	0.0255	0.0219	0.0207	0.0181	
Cumulative	0.8575	0.8867	0.8867	0.9393	0.9612	0.9819	1.0000	

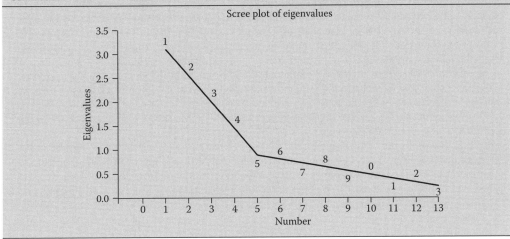

Scree plot of eigenvalues

The scree plot in Table 11.6 also supports using four factors, because the break point occurs at the fifth eigenvalue. That is, the eigenvalues level off from the fifth eigenvalue on. To further support the claim of four true factors, note that the Q/P ratio is $4/15 = .267 < .30$, and Hakstian et al. (1982) indicated that when this is the case the estimate of the number of factors will be just that much more credible.

To interpret the four factors, the sorted, rotated loadings in Table 11.7 are very useful. Referring back to Table 11.1, we see that the critical value for a significant loading at the .01 level is $2(.17)$ $= .34$. So, we certainly would not want to pay any attention to loadings less than .34 in absolute value. That is why we have had SAS print those loadings as a period. This helps to sharpen our focus on the salient loadings. The loadings that most strongly characterize the first three factors (and are of the same order of magnitude) are boxed in on Table 11.7. In terms of interpretation, Factor 1 represents an "unstructured, free spirit tendency," with the loadings on Factor 2 suggesting a "structured, hard driving tendency" construct. Factor 3 appears to represent a "non-demeaning aggressive tendency," while the loadings on Factor 4, which are dominated by the very high loading on autonomy, imply a "somewhat fearless tendency to act on one's own."

As mentioned in the first edition of this text, it would help if there were a statistical test, even a rough one, for determining when one loading on a factor is significantly greater than another loading on the same factor. This would then provide a more solid basis for including one variable in the interpretation of a factor and excluding another, assuming we can be confident that both are nonchance loadings. I remain unaware of such a test.

Example 11.3: Regression Analysis on Factor Scores—SAS and SPSS

We mentioned earlier in this chapter that one of the uses of components analysis is to reduce the number of predictors in regression analysis. This makes good statistical and conceptual sense for several reasons. First, if there is a fairly large number of initial predictors (say 15), we are undoubtedly not measuring 15 different constructs, and hence it makes sense to determine what the main constructs are that we are measuring. Second, this is desirable from the viewpoint of scientific parsimony. Third, we reduce from 15 initial predictors to, say, four new predictors (the components or rotated factors), our N/k ratio increases dramatically and this helps cross-validation prospects considerably. Fourth, our new predictors are uncorrelated, which means we have eliminated multicollinearity, which is a major factor in causing unstable regression equations. Fifth, because the new predictors are uncorrelated, we can talk about the unique contribution of each predictor in accounting for variance on y; that is, there is an unambiguous interpretation of the importance of each predictor.

We illustrate the process of doing the components analysis on the predictors and then passing the factor scores (as the new predictors) for a regression analysis for both SAS and SPSS using the National Academy of Science data introduced in Chapter 3 on multiple regression. Although there is not a compelling need for a factor analysis here because there are just six predictors, this example is simply meant to show the process. The new predictors, that is, the retained factors, will then be used to predict quality of the graduate psychology program. The control lines for doing both the factor analysis and the regression analysis for both packages are given in Table 11.8.

Note in the SAS control lines that the output data set from the principal components procedure contains the original variables *and* the factor scores for the first two components. It is this data set that we are accessing in the PROC REG procedure. Similarly, for SPSS the factor scores for the first two components are saved and *added* to the active file (as they call it), and it is this file that the regression procedure is dealing with.

So that the results are comparable for the SAS and SPSS runs, a couple of things *must* be done. First, as mentioned in Table 11.8, one must insert STANDARD into the control lines for SAS, so that the components have a variance of 1, as they have by default for SPSS. Second, because SPSS does a varimax rotation by default and SAS does not, we must insert the subcommand ROTATION=NOROTATE into the SPSS control lines so that is the principal components scores that are being used by the regression procedure in each case. If one does not insert the NOROTATE subcommand, then the regression analysis will use the *rotated* factors as the predictors.

TABLE 11.7

Factor Loading and Rotated, Sorted Loadings for Personality Research Form

Factor Pattern

	FACTOR 1	FACTOR 2	FACTOR 3	FACTOR 4
IMPLUS	0.76960	•	•	•
PLAY	0.66312	•	•	•
CHANGE	0.46746	•	•	−0.36271
HARMAVOD	−0.58060	•	−0.35665	•
ORDER	−0.60035	•	•	•
COGSTR	−0.73891	•	•	•
DOMIN	•	0.80853	•	•
ACH	•	0.61394	0.48781	•
ENDUR	•	0.57943	0.49114	•
EXHIB	0.48854	0.53279	•	0.44574
ABASE	•	−0.37413	0.62691	•
NUTUR	•	•	0.60007	0.52851
DEF	•	0.54265	−0.56778	•
AGGRESS	•	0.45762	−0.61053	•
AUTON	•	•	•	−0.77911

NOTE: Values less than 0.34 have been printed as (•).

Variance explained by each

FACTOR 1	FACTOR 2	FACTOR 3	FACTOR 4
3.168359	2.482114	2.246351	1.442163

Final Community Estimates: Total = 9.338987

ABASE	ACH	AGGRESS	AUTON	CHANGE	COGSTR	DEF	DOMIN
0.567546	0.715861	0.670982	0.701144	0.448672	0.624114	0.644643	0.701961

ENDUR	EXHIB	HARMAVOD	IMPLUS	NUTUR	ORDER	PLAY
0.713278	0.724334	0.537959	0.502875	0.659155	0.452917	0.573546

Rotated Factor Pattern

	FACTOR 1	FACTOR 2	FACTOR 3	FACTOR 4
PLAY	0.73149	•	•	•
IMPLUS	0.73013	•	•	•
EXHIB	0.66060	0.47003	•	•
ORDER	−0.53072	•	•	•
COGSTR	−0.66102	•	•	•
ASH	•	0.78676	•	•
ENDUR	•	0.75731	•	•
DOMIN	•	0.71173	0.35986	•
NUTUR	•	0.51149	−0.50100	•
DEF	•	•	0.79311	•
AGGRESS	•	•	0.76624	•
ABASE	•	•	−0.71271	•
AUTON	•	•	•	0.83214
CHANGE	•	•	•	0.57560
HARMAVOD	−0.44237	•	•	−0.53376

Variance explained by each

FACTOR 1	FACTOR 2	FACTOR 3	FACTOR 4
2.891095	2.405032	2.297653	1.745206

TABLE 11.8

SAS and SPSS Control Lines for Components Analysis on National Academy of Science Data and Then Passing Factor Scores for a Regression Analysis

	SAS

    DATA REGRESS;
    INPUT QUALITY NFACUL NGRADS PCTSUPP PCTGRT NARTIC PCTPUB @@;
    CARDS;
    DATA IN BACK OF TEXT
① PROC PRINCOMP N = 2 STANDARD OUT = FSCORES;
② VAR = NFACUL NGRADS PCTSUPP PCTGRT NARTIC PCTPUB; PROC REG DATA = FSCORES;
③ MODEL QUALITY = PRIN1 PRIN2;
    SELECTION = STEPWISE;
    PROC PRINT DATA = FSCORES;

	SPSS

    DATA LIST FREE/QUALITY NFACUL NGRADS PCTSUPP PCTGRT NARTIC
        PCTPUB.
    BEGIN DATA.
        DATA IN BACK OF TEXT
    END DATA.
④ FACTOR VARIABLES = NFACUL TO PCTPUB/
⑤   ROTATION = NOROTATE/
⑥   SAVE REG (ALL FSCORE)/.
    LIST.
    REGRESSION DESCRIPTIVES = DEFAULT/
⑦   VARIABLES = QUALITY FSCOREl FSCORE2/
        DEPENDENT = QUALITY/
        METHOD = STEPWISE/.

① The N = 2 specifies the number of components to be computed; here we just want two. STANDARD is necessary for the components to have variance of 1; otherwise the variance will equal the eigenvalue for the component (see *SAS STAT User's Guide,* Vol. 2, p. 1247). The OUT data set (here called FSCORES) contains the original variables and the component scores.

② In this VAR statement we "pick off" just those variables we wish to do the components analysis on, that is, the predictors.

③ The principal component variables are denoted by default as PRIN1, PRIN2, etc.

④ Recall that TO enables one to refer to a consecutive string of variables more concisely.

⑤ By default in SPSS the VARIMAX rotation would be done, and the factor scores obtained would be those for the rotated factors. Therefore, we specify NOROTATE so that no rotation is done.

⑥ There are three different methods for computing factor scores, but for components analysis they all yield the same scores. Thus, we have used the default method REG (regression method).

⑦ In saving the factor scores we have used the rootname FSCORE; the maximum number of characters for this name is 7. This rootname is then used along with a number to refer to consecutive factor scores. Thus, FSCORE1 for the factor scores on component 1, FSCORE2 for the factor scores on component 2, etc.

Example 11.4: MANOVA on Factor Scores—SAS and SPSS

In Table 11.9 we illustrate a components analysis on a hypothetical set of seven variables, and then pass the first two components to do a two-group MANOVA on these "new" variables. Because the components are uncorrelated, one might argue for performing just three univariate tests, for in this case an exact estimate of overall α is available from $1 - (1 - .05)^3 = .145$. Although an exact estimate is available, the multivariate approach covers a possibility that the univariate approach would miss, that is, the case where there are small nonsignificant differences on each of the variables, but cumulatively (with the multivariate test) there is a significant difference.

TABLE 11.9

SAS and SPSS Control Lines for Components Analysis on Set of Dependent Variables and Then Passing Factor Scores for Two-Group MANOVA

SAS

```
DATA MANOVA;
INPUT GP X1 X2 X3 X4 X5 X6 X7;
CARDS;
1  23   4  45  43  34   8  89  1  34  46  54  46  27   6   93
1  31  34  45  43  56   5  78  1  36   8  65  57  56   3  104
1  43  56  67  54  67  78  92  1  23  43  54  76  54   2  112
2  21  32  65  47  65  56  69  2  34  54  32  45  67  65   74
2  31  23  43  45  76  86  61  2  17  23  43  25  46  65   66

PROC PRINCOMP N = 2 STANDARD OUT = FSCORES;
VAR X1 X2 X3 X4 X5 X6 X7;
PROC GLM DATA = FSCORES;
MODEL PRIN1 PRIN2 = GP;
MANOVA H = GP;
PROC PRINT DATA = FSCORES;
```

SPSS

```
DATA LIST FREE/GP X1 X2 X3 X4 X5 X6 X7.
BEGIN DATA.
1  23   4  45  43  34   8  89  1  34  46  54  46  27   6   93
1  31  34  45  43  56   5  78  1  36   8  65  57  56   3  104
1  43  56  67  54  67  78  92  1  23  43  54  76  54   2  112
2  21  32  65  47  65  56  69  2  34  54  32  45  67  65   74
2  31  23  43  45  76  86  61  2  17  23  43  25  46  65   66

END DATA.
FACTOR VARIABLES = X1 TO X7/
    ROTATION = NOROTATE/
    SAVE REG (ALL FSCORE)/.
LIST.
MANOVA FSCORE1 FSCORE2 BY GP(I,2)/.
```

Also, if we had done an oblique rotation, and hence were passing correlated factors, then the case for a multivariate analysis is even more compelling because an exact estimate of overall α is not available. Another case where some of the variables would be correlated is if we did a factor analysis and retained three factors and two of the original variables (which were relatively independent of the factors). Then there would be correlations between the original variables retained and between those variables and the factors.

11.9 The Communality Issue

In principal components analysis we simply transform the original variables into linear combinations of these variables, and often three or four of these combinations (i.e., the components) account for most of the total variance. Also, we used 1's in the diagonal of the correlation matrix. Factor analysis per se differs from components analysis in two ways: (a) The hypothetical factors that are derived can only be *estimated* from the original variables, whereas in components analysis, because the components are specific linear combinations, no estimate is involved, and (b) numbers less than 1, called communalities, are put in the main diagonal of the correlation matrix in factor analysis. A relevant question is, "Will different factors emerge if 1's are put in the main diagonal (as in components analysis) than will emerge if communalities (the squared multiple correlation of each variable with all the others is one of the most popular) are placed in the main diagonal?"

The following quotes from five different sources give a pretty good sense of what might be expected in practice. Cliff (1987) noted that, "the choice of common factors or components methods often makes virtually no difference to the conclusions of a study" (p. 349). Guadagnoli and Velicer (1988) cited several studies by Velicer et al. that "have demonstrated that principal components solutions differ little from the solutions generated from factor analysis methods" (p. 266).

Harman (1967) stated, "As a saving grace, there is much evidence in the literature that for all but very small sets of variables, the resulting factorial solutions are little affected by the particular choice of communalities in the principal diagonal of the correlation matrix" (p. 83). Nunnally (1978) noted, "It is very safe to say that if there are as many as 20 variables in the analysis, as there are in nearly all exploratory factor analyses, then it does not matter what one puts in the diagonal spaces" (p. 418). Gorsuch (1983) took a somewhat more conservative position: "If communalities are reasonably high (e.g., .7 and up), even unities are probably adequate communality estimates in a problem with more than 35 variables" (p. 108). A general, somewhat conservative conclusion from these is that when the number of variables is moderately large (say >30), and the analysis contains virtually no variables expected to have low communalities (e.g., .4), then practically any of the factor procedures will lead to the same interpretations. Differences can occur when the number of variables is fairly small (<20), and some communalities are low.

11.10 A Few Concluding Comments

We have focused on an internal criterion in evaluating the factor solution, i.e., how interpretable the factors are. However, an important external criterion is the reliability of the solution. If the sample size is large, then one should randomly split the sample to check the consistency (reliability) of the factor solution on both random samples. In checking to determine whether the same factors have appeared in both cases it is not sufficient to just examine the factor loadings. One needs to obtain the correlations between the factor scores for corresponding pairs of factors. If these correlations are high, then one may have confidence of factor stability.

Finally, there is the issue of "factor indeterminancy" when estimating factors as in the common factor model. This refers to the fact that the factors are not uniquely determined. The importance of this for the common factor model has been the subject of much hot debate in the literature. We tend to side with Steiger (1979), who stated, "My opinion is that indeterminacy and related problems of the factor model counterbalance the model's theoretical advantages, and that the elevated status of the common factor model (relative to, say, components analysis) is largely undeserved" (p. 157).

11.11 Exploratory and Confirmatory Factor Analysis

The principal component analyses presented previously in this chapter are a form of what are commonly termed *exploratory factor analyses* (EFAs). The purpose of exploratory analysis is to identify the factor structure or model for a set of variables. This often involves determining how many factors exist, as well as the pattern of the factor loadings. Although most EFA programs allow for the number of factors to be specified in advance, it is not possible in these programs to force variables to load only on certain factors. EFA is generally considered to be more of a theory-generating than a theory-testing procedure. In contrast, *confirmatory factor analysis* (CFA) is generally based on a strong theoretical or empirical foundation that allows the researcher to specify an exact factor model in advance. This model usually specifies which variables will load on which factors, as well as such things as which factors are correlated. It is more of a theory-testing procedure than is EFA. Although, in practice, studies may contain aspects of both exploratory and confimatory analyses, it is useful to distinguish between the two techniques in terms of the situations in which they are commonly used. The following table displays some of the general differences between the two approaches.

Exploratory—Theory Generating	Confirmatory—Theory Testing
Heuristic—weak literature base	Strong theory or strong empirical base
Determine the number of factors	Number of factors fixed *a priori*
Determine whether the factors are correlated or uncorrelated	Factors fixed *a priori* as correlated or uncorrelated
Variables free to load on all factors	Variables fixed to load on a specific factor or factors

Let us consider an example of an EFA. Suppose a researcher is developing a scale to measure self-concept. The researcher does not conceptualize specific self-concept factors in advance, and simply writes a variety of items designed to tap into various aspects of self-concept. An EFA or components analysis of these items may yield three factors that the researcher then identifies as physical (PSC), social (SSC), and academic (ASC) self-concept. The researcher notes that items with large loadings on one of the three factors tend to have very small loadings on the other two, and interprets this as further support for the presence of three distinct factors or dimensions underlying self-concept.

A less common variation on this EFA example would be one in which the researcher had hypothesized the three factors *a priori* and intentionally written items to tap each dimension. In this case, the EFA would be carried out in the same way, except that the researcher might specify in advance that three factors should be extracted. Note, however, that in both of these EFA situations, the researcher would *not* be able to force items to load on certain factors, even though in the second example the pattern of loadings was hypothesized in advance. Also, there is no overall statistical test to help the researcher determine whether the observed pattern of loadings confirms the three factor structure. Both of these are limitations of EFA.

Before we turn to how a CFA would be done for this example, it is important to consider examples of the types of situations in which CFA would be appropriate; that is, situations in which a strong theory or empirical base exists.

11.11.1 Strong Theory

The four-factor model of self-concept (Shavelson, Hubner, and Stanton, 1976), which includes general self-concept, academic self-concept, English self-concept, and math self-concept, has a strong underlying theory. This model was presented and tested by Byrne (1994).

11.11.2 Strong Empirical Base

The "big five" factors of personality—extraversion, agreeableness, conscientiousness, neuroticism, and intellect—is an example. Goldberg (1990), among others, provided some strong empirical evidence for the five-factor trait model of personality. The five-factor model is not without its critics; see, for example, Block (1995). Using English trait adjectives obtained from three studies, Goldberg employed five different EFA methods, each one rotated orthogonally and obliquely, and found essentially the same five uncorrelated factors or personality in each analysis. Another confirmatory analysis of these five personality factors by Church and Burke (1994) again found evidence for the five factors, although these authors concluded that some of the factors may be correlated.

The Maslach Burnout Inventory was examined by Byrne (1994), who indicated that considerable empirical evidence exists to suggest the existence of three factors for this instrument. She conducted a confirmatory factor analysis to test this theory.

In this chapter we consider what are called by many people "measurement models." As Jöreskog and Sörbom put it (1993, p. 15), "The purpose of a measurement model is to describe how well the observed indicators serve as a measurement instrument for the latent variables."

Karl Jöreskog (1967, 1969; Jöreskog & Lawley, 1968) is generally credited with overcoming the limitations of exploratory factor analysis through his development of confirmatory factor analysis. In CFA, researchers can specify the structure of their factor models *a priori*, according to their theories about how the variables ought to be related to the factors. For example, in the second EFA situation just presented, the researcher could constrain the ASC items to load on the ASC factor, and to have loadings of zero on the other two factors; the other loadings could be similarly constrained.

Figure 11.1 gives a pictorial representation of the hypothesized three-factor structure. This type of representation, usually referred to as a *path model*, is a common way of showing the hypothesized or actual relationships among observed variables and the factors they were designed to measure.

The path model shown in Figure 11.1 indicates that three factors are hypothesized, as represented by the three circles. The curved arrows connecting the circles indicate that all three factors are hypothesized to be correlated. The items are represented by squares and are connected to the factors by straight arrows, which indicate causal relationships.

In CFA, each observed variable has an error term associated with it. These error terms are similar to the residuals in a regression analysis in that they are the part of each observed variable that is not explained by the factors. In CFA, however, the error terms also contain measurement error due to the lack of reliability of the observed variables.

The error terms are represented by the symbol δ in Figure 11.1 and are referred to in this chapter as *measurement errors*. The straight arrows from the δ's to the observed variables indicate that the observed variables are influenced by measurement error in addition to being influenced by the factors.

We could write equations to specify the relationships of the observed variables to the factors and measurement errors. These equations would be written as:

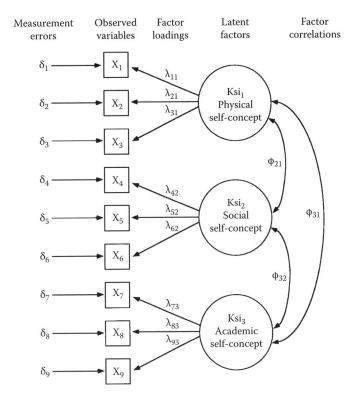

FIGURE 11.1
Three-factor self-concept model with three indicators per factor.

$$X = \lambda\xi + \delta$$

where the symbol λ stands for a factor loading and the symbol ξ represents the factor itself. This is similar to the regression equation

$$Y = \beta X + e$$

where β corresponds to λ and e corresponds to δ. One difference between the two equations is that in the regression equation, X and Y are both observed variables, whereas in the CFA equation, X is an observed variable but ξ is a latent factor. One implication of this is that we cannot obtain solutions for the values of λ and δ through typical regression methods. Instead, the correlation or covariance matrix of the observed variables is used to find solutions for elements of the matrices. This matrix is usually symbolized by **S** for a sample matrix and Σ for a population matrix. The relationships between the elements of **S** or Σ and the elements of λ, ξ, and δ can be obtained by expressing each side of the equation

$$X = \lambda\xi + \delta$$

as a covariance matrix. The algebra is not presented here (cf. Bollen, 1989, p. 35), but results in the following equality:

$$\Sigma = \lambda\phi\lambda' + \theta\delta$$

where ϕ is a matrix of correlations or covariances among the factors (ξs) and $\theta\delta$ is a matrix of correlations or covariances among the measurement error terms. Typically, $\theta\delta$ is a diagonal matrix, containing only the variances of the measurement errors. This matrix equation shows that the covariances among the X variables (Σ) can be broken down into the CFA matrices λ, ϕ, and $\theta\delta$. It is this equation that is solved to find values for the elements of λ, ϕ, and $\theta\delta$.

As the first step in any CFA, the researcher must therefore fully specify the structure or form of the matrices λ, ϕ, and $\theta\delta$ in terms of which elements are to be included. In our example, the λ matrix would be specified to include only the loadings of the three items designated to measure each factor, represented in Figure 11.1 by the straight arrows from the factors to the variables. The ϕ matrix would include all of the factor correlations, represented by the curved arrows between each pair of factors in Figure 11.1. Finally, one measurement error variance for each item would be estimated.

These specifications are based on the researcher's theory about the relationships among the observed variables, latent factors, and measurement errors. This theory may be based on previous empirical research, the current thinking in a particular field, the researcher's own hypotheses about the variables, or any combination of these. It is essential that the researcher be able to base a model on theory, however, because, as we show later, it is not always possible to distinguish between different models on statistical grounds alone. In many cases, theoretical considerations are the only way in which one model can be distinguished from another.

In the following sections, two examples using the LISREL program's (Jöreskog & Sörbom, 1986, 1988, 1993) new simplified language, known as SIMPLIS, are presented and discussed in order to demonstrate the steps involved in carrying out a CFA. Because CFAs always involve the analysis of a covariance or correlation matrix, we begin in Section 11.12 with a brief introduction to the PRELIS program that has been designed to create matrices that LISREL can easily use.

11.12 PRELIS

The PRELIS program is sometimes referred to as a "preprocessor" for LISREL. The PRELIS program is usually used by researchers to prepare covariance or correlation matrices that can be analyzed by LISREL. Although correlation and covariance matrices can be output from statistics packages such as SPSS or SAS, the PRELIS program has been especially designed to prepare data in a way that is compatible with the LISREL program, and has several useful features.

PRELIS 1 was introduced in 1986, and was updated in 1993 with the introduction of PRELIS 2. PRELIS 2 offers several features that were unavailable in PRELIS 1, including facilities for transforming and combining variables, recoding, and more options for handling missing data. Among the missing data options is an imputation procedure in which values obtained from a case with a similar response pattern on a set of matching variables are substituted for missing values on another case (see Jöreskog & Sörbom, 1996, p. 77 for more information). PRELIS 2 also offers tests of univariate and multivariate normality. As Jöreskog and Sörbom noted (1996, p. 168), "For each continuous variable, PRELIS 2 gives tests of zero skewness and zero kurtosis. For all continuous variables, PRELIS 2 gives tests of zero multivariate skewness and zero multivariate kurtosis." Other useful features of the

TABLE 11.10

PRELIS Command Lines for Health Beliefs Model Example

Title: Amlung Dissertation: Health Belief Model; Correlated Factors	
da ni=27 no=527	①
ra fi=a:\amlung.dta fo	②
(27f1.0)	
la	③
sus1 sus2 sus3 sus4 sus5 ser1 ser2 ser3 ser4 ser5 ser6 ser7 ser8 ben1	
ben4 ben7 ben10 ben11 ben12 ben13 bar1 bar2 bar3 bar4 bar5 bar6 bar7	
mi all (0)	④
co all	⑤
ou cm=amlung.cov	⑥

① The da (data) line specifies that there are 27 variables (ni=27) and 527 observations. The number of observations need not be included here—PRELIS will count them if this information is not given.

② The raw data (ra) are read from a file called "amlung.dta" that is on a disk on the a drive. The command "fo" indicates that a FORTRAN type format will be given on the next line. This must be enclosed in parentheses. The format 27f1.0 means that there are 27 variables, each taking up one column, with no decimals.

③ Names of up to 8 characters can be given to the variables.

④ Missing values for all variables are coded as 0.

⑤ The variables are all declared to be continuous (co).

⑥ A covariance matrix (cm) is requested, which will be written to a file called "amlung.cov."

PRELIS 2 program include facilities for conducting bootstrapping procedures and Monte Carlo or simulation studies. These procedures are described in the PRELIS 2 manual (Jöreskog & Sörbom, 1996, Appendix C, pp. 185–206). Another improvement implemented in PRELIS 2 has to do with the computation of the weight matrix needed for weighted least squares (WLS) estimation. The weight matrix computed in PRELIS 1 was based on a simplifying assumption that was later found to yield inaccurate results. This has been corrected in PRELIS 2.

Although LISREL can read in raw data, it has no facilities for data screening or for handling missing values. For this reason, most researchers prefer to use programs such as PRELIS to create their covariance matrix, which can then be easily read into LISREL. The PRELIS program can read in raw data and compute various covariance matrices as well as various types of correlation matrices (Pearson, polychoric, polyserial, tetrachoric, etc.). At the same time, PRELIS will compute descriptive statistics, handle missing data, perform data transformations such as recoding or transforming variables, and provide tests of normality assumptions.

Table 11.10 shows the PRELIS command lines used to create the covariance matrix used by Amlung (1996) in testing two competing CFA models of the Health Belief Model (HBM). In this study, Amlung reanalyzed data from Champion and Miller's 1996 study in which 527 women responded to items designed to measure the four theoretically derived HBM dimensions of seriousness, susceptibility, benefits, and barriers. Through preliminary reliability analyses and EFAs, Amlung selected 27 of the HBM items with which to test two CFA models.

The PRELIS language is not case sensitive; either upper- or lowercase letters can be used. Note that unless the raw data are in free format, with at least one space between each variable, a FORTRAN format, enclosed in parentheses, must be given in the line directly after the "ra" line. This is indicated by the keyword "fo" on the "ra" line. Those readers who are unfamiliar with this type of format are encouraged to refer to the examples given in the PRELIS manual.

In addition to the covariance matrix, which is written to an external file, an output file containing descriptive statistics and other useful information is created when the PRELIS program is run. Selected output for the HBM example is shown in Table 11.11.

As can be seen in Table 11.11, some of the HBM items have fairly high levels of non-normality. PRELIS provides statistical tests of whether the distributions of the individual variables are significantly skewed and kurtotic. For example, in looking at the first part of the table, we can see that the variable SER1 has a skewness value of -2.043 and a kurtosis value of 7.157. In the next section of the table we see that these skewness and kurtosis values resulted in highly significant z values of -4.603 and 9.202, respectively. These values indicate that the distribution of the item SER1 deviates significantly from normality with regard to both skewness and kurtosis. This is confirmed by the highly significant

TABLE 11.11

PRELIS 2 Output for Health Belief Model

TOTAL SAMPLE SIZE = 527
UNIVARIATE SUMMARY STATISTICS FOR CONTINUOUS VARIABLES

VARIABLE	MEAN	S. DEV.	SKEW	KURT	MIN	FREQ	MAX	FREQ
SUS1	2.528	0.893	0.448	0.131	1.000	52	5.000	13
SUS2	2.512	0.843	0.315	0.204	1.000	51	5.000	9
SUS3	2.615	0.882	0.216	−0.419	1.000	43	5.000	6
SUS4	2.510	0.953	0.638	−0.124	1.000	51	5.000	15
SUS5	2.493	1.032	0.685	−0.240	1.000	65	5.000	22
SER1	4.539	0.657	−2.043	7.157	1.000	5	5.000	314
SER2	4.220	0.837	−1.331	2.310	1.000	7	5.000	216
SER3	3.421	1.054	−0.261	−0.712	1.000	16	5.000	82
SER4	2.979	1.124	0.089	−1.090	1.000	36	5.000	42
SER5	3.789	0.891	−0.707	0.155	1.000	4	5.000	99
SER6	2.643	1.126	0.374	−0.695	1.000	78	5.000	33
SER7	3.268	1.085	−0.180	−1.057	1.000	17	5.000	58
SER8	2.421	0.952	0.811	0.439	1.000	63	5.000	20
BEN1	3.824	0.671	−0.765	1.780	1.000	3	5.000	57
BEN4	3.715	0.729	−0.865	0.617	2.000	46	5.000	40
BEN7	3.486	0.804	−0.417	0.263	1.000	7	5.000	38
BEN10	4.021	0.679	−1.121	3.180	1.000	3	5.000	100
BEN11	3.888	0.804	−1.114	1.779	1.000	6	5.000	90
BEN12	3.759	0.898	−0.897	0.586	1.000	8	5.000	84
BEN13	4.066	0.627	−1.258	5.096	1.000	4	5.000	100
BAR1	2.408	0.996	0.587	−0.303	1.000	82	5.000	12
BAR2	2.125	0.818	0.896	0.812	1.000	95	5.000	2
BAR3	1.943	0.763	0.947	1.478	1.000	138	5.000	2
BAR4	1.913	0.644	0.811	2.328	1.000	118	5.000	1
BAR5	1.937	0.731	0.977	2.072	1.000	131	5.000	3
BAR6	3.224	1.116	−0.368	−0.968	1.000	34	5.000	44
BAR7	1.808	0.616	1.220	5.601	1.000	142	5.000	4

TABLE 11.11 (continued)

PRELIS 2 Output for Health Belief Model

TEST OF UNIVARIATE NORMALITY FOR CONTINUOUS VARIABLES

	SKEWNESS		KURTOSIS		SKEWNESS AND KURTOSIS	
	Z-SCORE	P-VALUE	Z-SCORE	P-VALUE	CHI-SQUARE	P-VALUE
SUS1	2.813	0.002	0.742	0.229	8.466	0.015
SUS2	2.401	0.008	1.041	0.149	6.848	0.033
SUS3	1.971	0.024	−2.361	0.009	9.458	0.009
SUS4	3.235	0.001	−0.472	0.318	10.685	0.005
SUS5	3.320	0.000	−1.138	0.128	12.316	0.002
SER1	−4.630	0.000	9.202	0.000	106.113	0.000
SER2	−4.115	0.000	5.694	0.000	49.351	0.000
SER3	−2.184	0.014	−5.186	0.000	31.659	0.000
SER4	1.082	0.140	−12.904	0.000	167.682	0.000
SER5	−3.357	0.000	0.841	0.200	11.979	0.003
SER6	2.601	0.005	−4.983	0.000	31.597	0.000
SER7	−1.768	0.039	−11.794	0.000	142.221	0.000
SER8	3.521	0.000	1.889	0.029	15.965	0.000
BEN1	−3.450	0.000	4.933	0.000	36.237	0.000
BEN4	−3.598	0.000	2.445	0.007	18.920	0.000
BEN7	−2.730	0.003	1.269	0.102	9.061	0.011
BEN10	−3.909	0.000	6.672	0.000	59.792	0.000
BEN11	−3.902	0.000	4.931	0.000	39.536	0.000
BEN12	−3.642	0.000	2.352	0.009	18.797	0.000
BEN13	−4.047	0.000	8.151	0.000	82.823	0.000
BAR1	3.134	0.001	−1.540	0.062	12.192	0.002
BAR2	3.641	0.000	2.978	0.001	22.125	0.000
BAR3	3.706	0.000	4.420	0.000	33.270	0.000
BAR4	3.521	0.000	5.717	0.000	45.085	0.000
BAR5	3.744	0.000	5.372	0.000	42.876	0.000
BAR6	−2.583	0.005	−9.443	0.000	95.833	0.000
BAR7	4.011	0.000	8.446	0.000	87.425	0.000

TEST OF MULTIVARIATE NORMALITY FOR CONTINUOUS VARIABLES

SKEWNESS		KURTOSIS		SKEWNESS AND KURTOSIS	
Z-SCORE	P-VALUE	Z-SCORE	P-VALUE	CHI-SQUARE	P-VALUE
83.599	0.000	36.469	0.000	8318.704	0.000

chi-square value of 106.113, which is a combined test of both skewness and kurtosis. Finally, tests of multivariate skewness and kurtosis, both individually and in combination, are given. For the HBM data, these tests indicate significant departures from multivariate normality that may bias the tests of fit for this model (see, e.g., West, Finch, & Curran, 1995; Muthén & Kaplan, 1992).

In section 11.13 a LISREL 8 example using the HBM data is presented in order to demonstrate the steps involved in carrying out a CFA. The next sections explain each step in more detail.

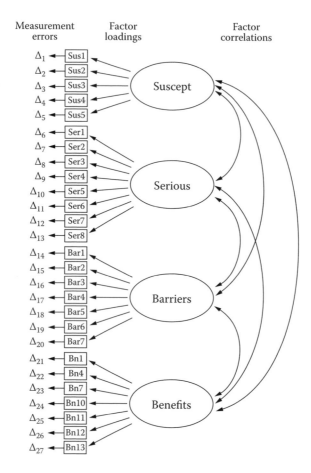

FIGURE 11.2
Model 1: Correlated factors for the health belief model.

11.13 A LISREL Example Comparing Two *a priori* Models

In this section, the new SIMPLIS language of the LISREL program is used to analyze data from the common situation in which one wishes to test a hypothesis about the underlying factor structure of a set of observed variables. The researcher usually has several hypotheses about the nature of the matrices λ (factor loadings), ϕ (factor correlations), and $\theta\delta$ (measurement error variances and covariances). Common hypotheses are that the items load on the appropriate factors, the factors are correlated in a certain way, or are uncorrelated, that the measurement errors are uncorrelated, or, in some cases, that some of these are correlated. These hypotheses can all be tested simultaneously using CFA methods.

In our example, the observed variables are the 27 HBM items. Amlung (1996) wanted to compare the fit of two models. In the first model, based on studies by Kegeles (1963) and Maiman et al. (1977), all the factors were free to correlate. The second model, based more on theoretical considerations (Rosenstock, 1974), allowed for correlations among only two pairs of factors. These two models are shown in Figure 11.2 and Figure 11.3 respectively. For simplicity, the measurement errors are omitted in Figure 11.3.

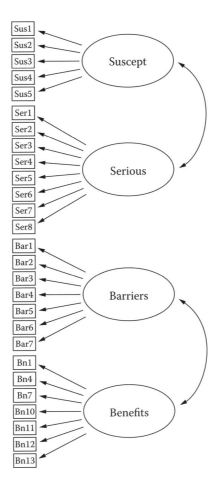

FIGURE 11.3
Model 2: Health Belief Model with two pairs of correlated factors.

The LISREL 8 SIMPLIS language program for Model 2 is shown in Table 11.12.

In both models, items were allowed to load only on the factor on which they were written to measure. This is accomplished in LISREL 8 by the first four lines under the keyword "relationships" shown in Table 11.12. As can be seen from the figures, all factors were hypothesized to correlate in the first model, whereas in the second only the two pairs of factors Seriousness and Susceptibility and Benefits and Barriers were allowed to correlate. Because *in LISREL 8 factors are all correlated by default*, this was accomplished by including the four lines under "relationships" that set the other correlations to zero. To run the first model, in which all factors were allowed to correlate, one would need to delete only those four lines from the LISREL 8 program. Finally, the measurement error variances are always included by default in LISREL 8.

Table 11.13 shows the estimates of the factor loadings and measurement error variances for Model 2. The standard error of each parameter estimate and a so-called *t* value obtained by dividing the estimate by its standard error are shown below each one. Table 11.14 shows the factor correlations for Model 2, along with their standard errors and *t* values.

Values of *t* greater than about |2.0| are commonly taken to be significant. Of course, these values are greatly influenced by the sample size, which is quite large in this example.

TABLE 11.12

SIMPLIS Command Lines for HBM with Two Pairs of Correlated Factors

title: Amlung Dissertation: Model with 2 pairs of correlated factors
observed variables:
sus1 sus2 sus3 sus4 sus5 ser1 ser2 ser3 ser4 ser5 ser6 ser7 ser8 ben1
ben4 ben7 ben10 ben11 ben12 ben13 bar1 bar2 bar3 bar4 bar5 bar6 bar7 ①
covariance matrix from file: AMLUNG.COV ②
sample size 527
latent variables: suscept serious benefits barriers ③
relationships: ④
sus1 sus2 sus3 sus4 sus5 = suscept
ser1 ser2 ser3 ser4 ser5 ser6 ser7 ser8 = serious
ben1 ben4 ben7 ben10 ben11 ben12 ben13 = benefits
bar1 bar2 bar3 bar4 bar5 bar6 bar7 = barriers
set the correlation of benefits and serious to 0 ⑤
set the correlation of benefits and suscept to 0
set the correlation of suscept and barriers to 0
set the correlation of barriers and serious to 0
end of problem

① Up to 8 characters can be used to name each observed variable.
② Here, the matrix created by PRELIS 2 is used by the LISREL 8 program.
③ Names (8 characters or less) are given to the latent variables (factors).
④ Here, under relationships, we link the observed variables to the factors.
⑤ In these four lines, the correlations among certain pairs of factors are set to zero.

Although all of the *t* values for the parameters in Model 2 are statistically significant, it is evident that the items on the Benefits scale have loadings that are much lower than those of the other scales. Several other items, such as Ser1, also have very low loadings. We saw in our PRELIS output that the distribution of Ser1 was quite nonnormal. This probably resulted in a lack of variance for this item, which in turn has caused its low loading.

The factor correlations are of particular interest in this study. Amlung (1996) hypothesized that only the two factor pairs Seriousness/Susceptibility and Benefits/Barriers would be significantly correlated. The results shown in Table 11.14 support the hypothesis that these two pairs of factors are significantly correlated. To see whether these were the only pairs with significant correlations, we must look at the factor correlations obtained from Model 1, in which all of the factors were allowed to correlate. These factor correlations, along with their standard errors and *t* values, are shown in Table 11.15.

Although the highest factor correlations are found between the factors Barriers/Benefits, and Seriousness/Susceptibility, all other factor pairs, with the exception of Seriousness/Benefits, are significantly correlated. None of the factor correlations are particularly large in magnitude, however, and the statistical significance may be due primarily to the large sample size. Based on our inspection of the parameter values and *t* statistics, support for Model 2 over Model 1 appears to be somewhat equivocal. However, note that these statistics are tests of *individual* model parameters. There are also statistics that test all model parameters simultaneously. Many such statistics, commonly called *overall fit* statistics, have been developed. These are discussed in more detail in Section 11.15. For now, we consider only the chi-square test and the goodness-of-fit index (GFI).

The chi-square statistic in CFA tests the hypothesis that the model fits, or is consistent with, the pattern of covariation of the observed variables. If this hypothesis were rejected, it would mean that the hypothesized model is not reasonable, or does not fit with our data. Therefore, contrary to the usual hypothesis testing procedures, we do *not* want to reject

TABLE 11.13

Factor Loadings and Measurement Error Variances with Standard Errors and *t* Values for Health Belief Model 2

LISREL ESTIMATES (MAXIMUM LIKELIHOOD)	
① ②	
sus1 = 0.79*suscept, Errorvar. = 0.18, R* = 0.78	ben1 = 0.29*benefits, Errorvar. = 0.37, R* = 0.18
(0.031) ③ (0.015) ③	(0.031) (0.024)
25.28 ④ 12.09 ④	9.36 15.48
sus2 = 0.77*suscept, Errorvar. = 0.12, R* = 0.83	ben4 = 0.35*benefits, Errorvar. = 0.41, R* = 0.23
(0.029) (0.012)	(0.033) (0.027)
26.79 10.38	10.78 15.20
sus3 = 0.74*suscept, Errorvar. = 0.23, R* = 0.70	ben7 = 0.20*benefits, Errorvar. = 0.61, R* = 0.059
(0.032) (0.017)	(0.038) (0.038)
23.38 13.42	5.17 16.01
sus4 = 0.77*suscept, Errorvar. = 0.31, R* = 0.66	ben10 = 0.49*benefits, Errorvar. = 0.22, R* = 0.53
(0.035) (0.022)	(0.028) (0.018)
22.15 13.99	17.73 12.37
sus5 = 0.81*suscept, Errorvar. = 0.42, R* = 0.61	ben11 = 0.62*benefits, Errorvar. = 0.27, R* = 0.59
(0.038) (0.029)	(0.032) (0.024)
20.98 14.40	19.00 11.35
ser1 = 0.18*serious, Errorvar. = 0.40, R* = 0.075	ben12 = 0.62*benefits, Errorvar. = 0.42, R* = 0.48
(0.031) (0.025)	(0.037) (0.032)
5.76 15.90	16.70 13.04
ser2 = 0.47*serious, Errorvar. = 0.48, R* = 0.31	ben13 = 0.41*benefits, Errorvar. = 0.22, R* = 0.43
(0.037) (0.033)	(0.026) (0.016)
12.48 14.48	15.61 13.62
ser3 = 0.67*serious, Errorvar. = 0.67, R* = 0.40	bar1 = 0.75*barriers, Errorvar. = 0.43, R* = 0.56
(0.046) (0.049)	(0.038) (0.031)
14.61 13.60	19.50 13.94
ser4 = 0.70*serious, Errorvar. = 0.78, R* = 0.38	bar2 = 0.53*barriers, Errorvar. = 0.39, R* = 0.42
(0.049) (0.057)	(0.033) (0.026)
14.19 13.79	15.91 14.97
ser5 = 0.56*serious, Errorvar. = 0.48, R* = 0.40	bar3 = 0.64*barriers, Errorvar. = 0.17, R* = 0.71
(0.039) (0.035)	(0.028) (0.014)
14.60 13.60	23.10 11.86
ser6 = 0.63*serious, Errorvar. = 0.87, R* = 0.32	bar4 = 0.48*barriers, Errorvar. = 0.19, R* = 0.55
(0.050) (0.060)	(0.025) (0.013)
12.66 14.41	19.17 14.06
ser7 = 0.75*serious, Errorvar. = 0.62, R* = 0.48	bar5 = 0.62*barriers, Errorvar. = 0.15, R* = 0.73
(0.046) (0.049)	(0.026) (0.013)
16.27 12.65	23.60 11.42
ser8 = 0.45*serious, Errorvar. = 0.70, R* = 0.23	bar6 = 0.33*barriers, Errorvar. = 1.14, R* = 0.089
(0.043) (0.047)	(0.050) (0.071)
10.41 15.09	6.67 16.05
	bar7 = 0.42*barriers, Errorvar. = 0.20, R* = 0.47
	(0.025) (0.014)
	17.19 14.67

① Factor loading.
② Measurement error variance.
③ Standard error.
④ *t* Value.

TABLE 11.14

Factor Correlations, Standard Errors, and
t Values for Health Belief Model 2

CORRELATION MATRIX OF INDEPENDENT VARIABLES				
	suscept	serious	benefits	barriers
suscept	1.00 ①			
serious	0.24 ②	1.00		
	(0.05) ③			
	4.92 ④			
benefits	— ⑤	—	1.00	
barriers	—	—	−0.27	1.00
			(0.05)	
			−5.66	

① Factor variances were set equal to 1.0 in order to give a metric
   to the factors.
② Factor correlation.
③ Standard error.
④ *t* Value.
⑤ Indicates that this correlation was not estimated.

TABLE 11.15

Factor Correlations, Standard Errors,
and *t* Values for HBM Model 1

CORRELATION MATRIX OF INDEPENDENT VARIABLES				
	suscept	serious	benefits	barriers
suscept	1.00			
serious	0.24 ①	1.00		
	(0.05) ②			
	4.93 ③			
benefits	−0.16	−0.02	1.00	
	(0.05)	(0.05)		
	−3.37	−0.43		
barriers	0.15	0.20	−0.27	1.00
	(0.05)	(0.05)	(0.05)	
	3.33	4.14	−5.66	

① Factor correlation.
② Standard error.
③ *t* Value.

the null hypothesis. Unfortunately, the chi-square statistic used in CFA is very sensitive to sample size, such that, with a large enough sample size, almost any hypothesis will be rejected. This dilemma, which is discussed in more detail in Section 11.15, has led to the development of many other statistics designed to assess overall model fit in some way. One of these is the goodness-of-fit index (GFI) produced by the LISREL program. This index is roughly analogous to the multiple R^2 value in multiple regression in that it represents the overall amount of the covariation among the observed variables that can be accounted for by the hypothesized model.

TABLE 11.16

Goodness-of-Fit Statistics for Model 1 (All Factors Correlated)

CHI-SQUARE WITH 318 DEGREES OF FREEDOM = 1147.45 (P = 0.0)
ROOT MEAN SQUARE ERROR OF APPROXIMATION (RMSEA) = 0.070
P-VALUE FOR TEST OF CLOSE FIT (RMSEA < 0.05) = 0.00000037
EXPECTED CROSS-VALIDATION INDEX (ECVI) = 2.41
ECVI FOR SATURATED MODEL = 1.44
INDEPENDENCE AIC = 6590.16
MODEL AIC = 1267.45
ROOT MEAN SQUARE RESIDUAL (RMR) = 0.047
STANDARDIZED RMR = 0.063
GOODNESS OF FIT INDEX (GFI) = 0.86
ADJUSTED GOODNESS OF FIT INDEX (AGFI) = 0.83
PARSIMONY GOODNESS OF FIT INDEX (PGFI) = 0.72
NORMED FIT INDEX (NFI) = 0.82
NON-NORMED FIT INDEX (NNFI) = 0.85
PARSIMONY NORMED FIT INDEX (PNFI) = 0.75

TABLE 11.17

Goodness-of-Fit Statistics for Model 2 (Two Pairs of Correlated Factors)

CHI-SQUARE WITH 322 DEGREES OF FREEDOM = 1177.93 (P = 0.0)
ROOT MEAN SQUARE ERROR OF APPROXIMATION (RMSEA) = 0.071
P-VALUE FOR TEST OF CLOSE FIT (RMSEA < 0.05) = 0.00000038
EXPECTED CROSS-VALIDATION INDEX (ECVI) = 2.45
ECVI FOR SATURATED MODEL = 1.44
INDEPENDENCE AIC = 6590.16
MODEL AIC = 1289.93
ROOT MEAN SQUARE RESIDUAL (RMR) = 0.062
STANDARDIZED RMR = 0.081
GOODNESS OF FIT INDEX (GFI) = 0.85
ADJUSTED GOODNESS OF FIT INDEX (AGFI) = 0.83
PARSIMONY GOODNESS OF FIT INDEX (PGFI) = 0.73
NORMED FIT INDEX (NFI) = 0.82
NON-NORMED FIT INDEX (NNFI) = 0.85
PARSIMONY NORMED FIT INDEX (PNFI) = 0.75

Values of the chi-square statistic and GFI obtained for Models 1 and 2, as well as many other overall fit indices produced by the LISREL 8 program, are presented in Table 11.16 and Table 11.17, respectively.

The chi-square values for Models 1 and 2 are 1147.45 and 1177.93, respectively, with 318 and 322 degrees of freedom. Both chi-square values are highly significant, indicating that neither model adequately accounts for the observed covariation among the HBM items. The GFI values for the two models are almost identical at .86 and .85 for Models 1 and 2, respectively. In many cases, models that provide a good fit to the data have GFI values above .9, so again the two models tested here do not seem to fit well. The large chi-square values may be due, at least in part, to the large sample size, rather than to any substantial misspecification of the model. However, it is also possible that the model is misspecified in some fundamental way. For example, one or more of the items may actually load on more than one of the factors, instead of loading on only one, as specified in our model. Before making any decisions about the two models, we must examine such possibilities. We learn more about how to do this in the following sections, in which model identification, estimation, assessment, and modification are discussed more thoroughly.

11.14 Identification

The topic of identification is complex, and a thorough treatment is beyond the scope of this chapter. The interested reader is encouraged to consult Bollen (1989).

Identification of a CFA model is a prerequisite for obtaining correct estimates of the parameter values. A simple algebraic example can be used to illustrate this concept. Given the equations $X + Y = 5$, we cannot obtain *unique* solutions for X and Y, because an infinite number of values for X and Y will produce the same solution (5 and 0, 100 and −95, 2.5 and 2.5, etc.). However, if we impose another constraint on our solution by specifying that $2X = 4$, we can obtain one and only one solution: $X = 2$ and $Y = 3$. After imposing the additional constraint, we have two unknowns, X and Y, and two pieces of information, $X + Y = 5$, and $2X = 4$. Note that in the first situation with two unknowns and only one piece of information, the problem was not that we could not find a solution, but that we could find too many solutions. When this is the case, there is no way of determining which solution is "best" without imposing further constraints. Identification refers, therefore, to whether the parameters of a model can be *uniquely* determined.

Models that have more unknown parameters than pieces of information are called unidentified or *underidentified* models, and cannot be solved uniquely. Models with just as many unknowns as pieces of information are referred to as *just-identified* models, and can be solved, but cannot be tested statistically. Models with more information than unknowns are called *overidentified* models, or sometimes simply identified models, and can be solved uniquely. In addition, as we show in Section 11.15, overidentified models can be tested statistically.

As we have seen, one condition for identification is that the number of unknown parameters must be less than or equal to the number of pieces of information. In CFA, the unknown parameters are the factor loadings, factor correlations, and measurement error variances (and possibly covariances) that are to be estimated, and the information available to solve for these is the elements of the covariance matrix for the observed variables. In the HBM example, the number of parameters to be estimated for Model 1 would be the 27 factor loadings, plus the six factor correlations, plus the 27 measurement error variances, for a total of 60 parameters. In Model 2, we estimated only two factor correlations, giving us a total of 56 parameters for that model. The number of unique values in a covariance matrix is equal to $p(p + 1)/2$, where p is the number of observed variables. This number represents the number of covariance elements below the diagonal plus the number of variance elements. Above-diagonal elements are not counted because they must be the same as the below-diagonal elements. For the 27 items in our HBM example, the number of elements in the covariance matrix would be $(27 \times 28)/2$, or 378. Because the number of pieces of information is much greater than the number of parameters to be estimated, we should have enough information to identify these two models.

Bollen (1989) gave several rules that enable researchers to determine the identification status of their models. In general, CFA models should be identified if they have at least three items for each factor. However, there are some situations in which this will not be the case, and applied researchers should be alert for signs of underidentification. These include factor loadings or correlations that seem to have the wrong sign or are much smaller or larger in magnitude than what was expected, negative variances, and correlations greater than 1.0 (for further discussion see Wothke, 1993).

One more piece of information is necessary in order to assure identification of CFA models: each factor must have a unit of measurement. Because the factors are unobservable, they have no inherent scale. Instead, they are usually assigned scales in a convenient metric. One common way of doing this is to set the variances of the factors equal to one (Bentler, 1992a, p. 22). In the LISREL 8 program, this is done automatically. Note that one consequence of this is that the matrix ϕ will contain the factor correlations rather than the factor covariances.

Once the identification of a model has been established, estimation of the factor loadings, factor correlations, and measurement error variances can proceed. The estimation process is the subject of the next section.

11.15 Estimation

Recall that in CFA it is hypothesized that the relationships among the observed variables can be explained by the factors. The researchers' hypotheses about the form of these relationships are represented by the structure of the factor loadings, factor correlations, and measurement error variances. Thus, the relationship between the observed variables and the researchers' hypotheses or model is represented by the equation $\Sigma = \lambda\phi\lambda' + \theta\delta$. Estimation is concerned with finding the values for λ, ϕ, and $\theta\delta$ that will best reproduce the matrix Σ. This is analogous to the situation in multiple regression in which values of β are sought that will reproduce the original Y values as closely as possible.

In reality, we do not have the population matrix Σ, but rather the sample matrix **S**. It is this sample matrix that is compared to the matrix reproduced by the estimates of the parameters in λ, ϕ, and $\theta\delta$, referred to as $\Sigma(\theta)$.

In practice, our model will probably not reproduce S perfectly. The best we can usually do is to find parameter estimates that result in matrix $\overline{\Sigma}$ that is close to S. A function that measures how close $\overline{\Sigma}$ is to S is called a *discrepancy* or *fit function*, and is usually symbolized as $F(S;\overline{\Sigma})$. Many different fit functions are available in CFA programs, but probably the most commonly used is the maximum likelihood function, defined as:

$$F(\mathbf{S}; \Sigma(\theta)) = \mathrm{tr}(\mathbf{S}\Sigma(\theta)^{-1}) + \left\lceil \ln\left|\Sigma(\theta)\right| - \ln\left|\mathbf{S}\right| \right\rceil - p$$

where tr stands for the trace of a matrix, defined as the sum of its diagonal elements, and p is the number of variables.

The criterion for finding estimates of the parameters in λ, ϕ, and $\theta\delta$ is that they result in values of the fit function $F(\mathbf{S};\Sigma(\theta))$ that are as small as possible. In maximum likelihood terminology, we are trying to find parameter estimates that will *maximize* the likelihood that the differences between **S** and $\Sigma(\theta)$ are due to random sampling fluctuations, rather than to some type of model misspecification. Although the maximum likelihood criterion involves maximizing a quantity rather than minimizing one, it is similar in purpose to the least squares criterion in multiple regression, in which the quantity $\Sigma(Y - Y')^2$ is minimized.

Unlike the least squares criterion, however, the criterion used in maximum likelihood estimation of CFA parameters cannot usually be solved algebraically. Instead, computer programs have been developed that use an iterative process for finding the parameter estimates. In an iterative solution, a set of initial values for the parameters of λ, ϕ, and $\theta\delta$ are used as starting points. The matrix $\Sigma(\theta) = \lambda\phi\lambda' + \theta\delta$ is then calculated based on these values, and is compared with $\mathbf{S}$. If $\Sigma(\theta)$ does not match $\mathbf{S}$, one or more of the initial values is changed in such a way as to improve the fit, and $\Sigma(\theta)$ is recomputed. This process continues until $\Sigma(\theta)$ is sufficiently close to $\mathbf{S}$, or until no further improvements can be made that are within the constraints of the hypothesized model. The final values obtained are taken as the estimates of the elements of λ, ϕ, and $\theta\delta$.

The value of the fit function $F(\mathbf{S};\Sigma(\theta))$ that is based on these final values can be used to determine how well the hypothesized model fits the observed matrix $\mathbf{S}$. The topic of assessing model fit is taken up in the next section. Before concluding our discussion about estimation, however, a few words concerning the appropriate sample size are essential. Several studies have focused on the question of how large a sample should be in order to obtain accurate results in maximum likelihood CFA. Most have recommended minimum sample sizes of 200, although smaller sample sizes may be adequate for models with a relatively small number of parameters to be estimated (see, e.g., Anderson & Gerbing, 1984; Boomsma, 1982). For models with many paths to be estimated, larger sample sizes are needed.

11.16 Assessment of Model Fit

The appropriate way to assess the fit of CFA models has been a subject of debate since the 1970s. A plethora of fit statistics has been developed and discussed in the literature. In this chapter, I focus only on the most commonly used fit statistics and present some general guidelines for model assessment. For more detailed information, the reader is directed to the excellent presentations in Bollen (1989), Bollen and Long (1993), Hayduk (1987), and Loehlin (1992).

It is useful to divide statistics for assessing the fit of a model, commonly called *fit statistics*, into two categories: those that measure the overall fit of the model, and those that are concerned with individual model parameters, such as factor loadings or correlations.

Probably the most well-known measure of overall model fit is the chi-square (χ^2) statistic, which was presented briefly in Section 11.13. This statistic is calculated as

$$(n-1)F(\mathbf{S};\Sigma(\theta))$$

and is distributed as a chi-square with degrees of freedom equal to the number of elements in $\mathbf{S}$, $p(p+1)/2$ minus the number of parameters estimated, if certain conditions are met. These conditions include having a large enough sample size and variables that follow a multivariate normal distribution. Notice that, for a just-identified model, the degrees of freedom are zero, because the number of parameters estimated are equal to the number of elements in $\mathbf{S}$. This means that just-identified models cannot be tested. However, recall that just-identified models will *always* exactly reproduce $\mathbf{S}$ perfectly; therefore a test of such a model would be pointless, as we already know the answer.

The chi-square statistic can be used to test the hypothesis that $\Sigma = \Sigma(\theta)$, or that the original population matrix is equal to the matrix reproduced from one's model. Remember that, contrary to the general rule in hypothesis testing, the researcher would *not* want to reject the null hypothesis, as finding $\Sigma \neq \Sigma(\theta)$ would mean that the hypothesized model parameters were unable to reproduce **S**. Thus, smaller rather than larger chi-square values are indicative of a good fit.

From the chi-square formula we can see that, as n increases, the value of chi-square will increase to the point at which, for a large enough value of n, even trivial differences between Σ and $\Sigma(\theta)$ will be found significant. Largely because of this, as early as 1969 Jöreskog recommended that the chi-square statistic be used more as a descriptive index of fit rather than as a statistical test. Accordingly, Jöreskog and Sörbom (1993) included other fit indices in the LISREL output. The GFI was introduced in Section 11.12. This index was defined by Jöreskog and Sörbom as:

$$\text{GFI} = 1 - \frac{F(\mathbf{S}; \Sigma(\theta))}{F(\mathbf{S}; \Sigma(0))}$$

where $F(\mathbf{S}; \Sigma(0))$ is the value of the fit function for a null model in which all parameters except the variances of the variables have values of zero. In other words, the null model is one that posits no relationships among the variables. The GFI can be thought of as the amount of the overall variance and covariance in **S** that can be accounted for by $\Sigma(\theta)$ and is roughly analogous to the multiple R^2 in multiple regression. The adjusted GFI (AGFI) is given as

$$\text{AGFI} = 1 - \frac{p(p+1)}{2df}(1 - \text{GFI})$$

(Jöreskog & Sörbom, 1993), where p represents the number of variables in the model and df stands for degrees of freedom. The AGFI adjusts the GFI for degrees of freedom, resulting in lower values for models with more parameters. The rationale behind this adjustment is that models can always be made to reproduce **S** more closely by adding more parameters to the model. The ultimate example of this is the just-identified model, which always reproduces **S** exactly because it includes all possible parameters. In our HBM examples, Model 1 resulted in values of .86 and .83 for the GFI and AGFI, and the corresponding values for Model 2 were .85 and .83. The AGFI was not substantially lower than the GFI for these models because the number of parameters estimated was not overly large, given the number of pieces of information (covariance elements) that were available to estimate them.

Another measure of overall fit is the difference between the matrices **S** and $\Sigma(\theta)$. These differences are called *residuals* and can be obtained as output from CFA computer programs. *Standardized* residuals are residuals that have been standardized to have a mean of zero and a standard deviation of one, making them easier to interpret. Standardized residuals larger than $|2.0|$ are usually considered to be suggestive of a lack of fit.

Bentler and Bonett (1980) introduced a class of fit indexes commonly called *comparative fit indexes*. These indexes compare the fit of the hypothesized model to a baseline or null model, in order to determine the amount by which the fit is improved by using the hypothesized model instead of the a model. The most commonly used null model is that described earlier in which the variables are completely uncorrelated.

The normed fit index (NFI; Bentler & Bonett, 1980) can be computed as

$$\chi_0^2 - \chi_1^2 / \chi_0^2$$

where χ_0^2 and χ_1^2 are the χ^2 values for the null and hypothesized models, respectively. The NFI represents the increment in fit obtained by using the hypothesized model relative to the fit of the null model. Values range from zero to one, with higher values indicative of a greater improvement in fit.

Bentler and Bonett's nonnormed fit index (NNFI) can be calculated as

$$NNFI = \frac{(\chi_0^2/df_0 - \chi_1^2/df_1)}{(\chi_0^2/df_0 - 1)}$$

where χ_0^2 and χ_1^2 are as before and df_0 and df_1 are the degrees of freedom for the null and hypothesized models, respectively. This index is referred to as nonnormed because it is not constrained to have values between zero and one, as is common for comparative fit indexes. The NNFI can be interpreted as the increment in fit per degree of freedom obtained by using the hypothesized model, relative to the best possible fit that could be obtained by using the hypothesized model. As with the NFI, higher values are suggestive of more improvement in fit. Although NFI and NNFI values greater than .9 have typically been considered indicative of a good fit, this rule of thumb has recently been called into question (see, e.g., Hu & Bentler, 1995). Values of the NFI and NNFI were .82 and .85, respectively, for both HBM models, indicating that these two models resulted in identical improvements in fit over a null model.

Because a better fit can always be obtained by adding more parameters to the model, James, Mulaik, and Brett (1982) suggested a modification of the NFI to adjust for the loss of degrees of freedom associated with such improvements in fit. This parsimony adjustment is obtained by multiplying the NFI by the ratio of degrees of freedom of the hypothesized model to those of the null model. A similar adjustment to the GFI was suggested by Mulaik et al. (1989). These two parsimony-adjusted indices are implemented in LISREL 8 as the parsimony goodness-of-fit index (PGFI) and the parsimony normed fit index (PNFI). For the two HBM models, the values of the PGFI and PNFI were .72 and .75, respectively, for Model 1, and .73 and .75 for Model 2. Because the two models differed by only four degrees of freedom, the parsimony adjustments had almost identical effects on them.

Several researchers (see, e.g., Cudeck & Henly, 1991) suggested that it may be unrealistic to suppose that the null hypothesis $\Sigma = \Sigma(\theta)$ will hold exactly, even in the population, because this would mean that the model can correctly specify all of the relationships among the variables. The lack of fit of the hypothesized model to the population is known as the *error of approximation*. The root mean square error of approximation (Steiger, 1990) is a standardized measure of error of approximation

$$RMSEA = \sqrt{\max\left\{\left(\frac{f(\theta)}{df} - \frac{1}{n}\right), 0\right\}}$$

where $F(\theta)$ is the maximum likelihood fit function discussed earlier, and df and n are as before.

MacCallum (1995, pp. 29–30), in arguing for RMSEA, discussed the disconfirmability of a model:

> A model is disconfirmable to the degree that it is possible for the model to be inconsistent with observed data ... if a model is not disconfirmable to any reasonable degree, then a finding of good fit is essentially useless and meaningless. Therefore, in the model specification process, researchers are very strongly encouraged to keep in mind the

principle of disconfirmability and to construct models that are not highly parametrized .... Researchers are thus strongly urged to consider an index such as the root mean square error of approximation (RMSEA), which is essentially a measure of lack of fit per degree of freedom.

Based on their experience, Browne and Cudeck (1993) suggested that RMSEA values of .05 or less indicate a close approximation and that values of up to .08 suggest a reasonable fit of the model in the population. For our two HBM models, the RMSEA values were .07 and .071 for Models 1 and 2, respectively.

Finally, Browne and Cudeck (1989) proposed a single-sample cross-validation index developed to assess the degree to which a set of parameter estimates estimated in one sample would fit if used in another similar sample. This index is roughly analogous to the adjusted or "shrunken" R^2 value obtained in multiple regression. It is given as the ECVI, or expected cross-validation index, in the LISREL program. Because the ECVI is based on the chi-square statistic, smaller values are desired, which would indicate a greater likelihood that the model would cross-validate in another sample. A similar index is reported as part of the output from the LISREL 8 as well as the EQS (Bentler, 1989, 1992a) program. This is the Akaike (1987) Information Criterion (AIC), calculated as $\chi^2 - 2df$. As with the ECVI, smaller values of the AIC represent a greater likelihood of cross-validation. In a recent study by Bandalos (1993), values of the ECVI and AIC were compared with the values obtained by carrying out an actual two-sample cross-validation procedure in CFA. It was found that, although both indices provided very accurate estimates of the actual two-sample cross-validation values, the ECVI was slightly more accurate, especially with smaller sample sizes.

Thus far, the overall fit indices for the two HBM models have not provided us with a compelling statistical basis for preferring one model over the other. Values of the GFI, AGFI, NFI, NNFI, the parsimony-adjusted indices, and the RMSEA are almost identical for these two models. However, these two models are *nested* models, meaning that one can be obtained from the other by eliminating one or more paths. More specifically, Model 2 is nested within Model 1 because we can obtain the former from the latter by eliminating four of the factor correlations. The difference between the chi-square values of two nested models is itself distributed as a chi-square statistic, with degrees of freedom equal to the difference between the degrees of freedom for the two models. For Model 1, the chi-square value and degrees of freedom were 1147.45 and 318, while the corresponding values for Model 2 were 1177.93 and 322. The chi-square difference test is thus 30.38 with four degrees of freedom. The chi-square critical value at the .05 level of significance is 9.488. We would therefore find the chi-square difference statistically significant, which indicates that Model 2 (with a significantly higher chi-square value) fit significantly *worse* than Model 1.

In addition to the overall fit indices, individual parameter values should be scrutinized closely. Computer programs such as LISREL and EQS provide tests of each parameter estimate, computed by dividing the parameter estimate by its standard error. (These are referred to as *t* tests in LISREL.) These values can be used to test the hypothesis that the parameter value is significantly different from zero. The actual values of the parameter estimates should also be examined to determine whether any appear to be out of range. Out-of-range parameter values may take the form of negative variances in ϕ or $\theta\delta$, factor correlations greater than one, parameter estimates that seem much too high or too low, or parameter estimates that have the opposite sign from what was expected. Models resulting in any of these problems should be studied carefully to determine the cause of the error. One possible reason for problems of this type is that the model is not identified. However, it may also be that the researcher has inadvertently set the model up incorrectly.

It should be clear from this discussion that the assessment of model fit is not a simple process, nor is there a definitive answer to the question of how well a model fits the data. However, *several criteria with which most experts are in agreement have been developed over the years*. These have been discussed by Bollen and Long (1993) and are summarized here.

1. Hypothesize *at least* one model *a priori*, based on the best theory available. Often, theoretical knowledge in an area may be ambiguous or contradictory, and more than one model may be tenable. The relative fit of the different models can be compared using such indexes as the NFI, NNFI, PNFI, ECVI, and AIC.

2. Do not rely on the chi-square statistic as the only basis for assessing fit. The use of several indexes is encouraged.

3. Examine the values of individual parameter estimates in addition to assessing the overall fit.

4. Assessment of model fit should be made in the context of prior studies in the area. In fields in which little research has been done, less stringent standards may be acceptable than in areas in which well-developed theory is available.

5. As in any statistical analysis, data should be screened for outliers and for violations of distributional assumptions. Multivariate normality is one assumption underlying the use of maximum likelihood estimation in CFA.

The following quote from MacCallum (1995) concerning model fit touches on several issues that researchers must bear in mind during the process of model specification and evaluation, and thus makes a fitting conclusion to this section:

> A critical principle in model specification and evaluation is the fact that all of the models that we would be interested in specifying and evaluating are wrong to some degree. Models at their best can be expected to provide only a close approximation to observed data, rather than an exact fit. In the case of SEM, the real-world phenomena that give rise to our observed correlational data are far more complex than we can hope to represent using a linear structural equation model and associated assumptions. Thus we must define as an optimal outcome a finding that a particular model fits our observed data closely and yields a highly interpretable solution. Furthermore, one must understand that even when such an outcome is obtained, one can conclude only that the particular model is a plausible one. There will virtually always be other models that fit the data to exactly the same degree, or very nearly so, thereby representing models with different substantive interpretation but equivalent fit to the observed data. The number of such models may be extremely large, and they can be distinguished only in terms of their substantive meaning. (p. 17)

11.17 Model Modification

It is not uncommon in practice to find large discrepancies between **S** and $\Sigma(\theta)$, indicating that the hypothesized model was unable to accurately reproduce the original covariance matrix. Assuming that the hypothesized model was based on the best available theory, changes based on theoretical considerations may not be feasible. Given this state of affairs, the researcher may opt to modify the model in a post hoc fashion by adding or deleting parameters suggested by the fit statistics obtained. Statistics are available from both the LISREL and EQS programs that suggest possible changes to the model that will improve fit.

Two caveats are in order before we begin our discussion of these statistics. First, as in any post hoc statistical analysis, modifications made on the basis of information derived from a given sample cannot properly be tested on that same sample. This is because the results obtained from any sample data will have been fitted to the idiosyncrasies of that data, and may not generalize to other samples. For this reason, *post hoc model modifications must be regarded as tentative until they have been replicated on a different sample.* The second point that must be kept in mind is that the modifications suggested by programs such as LISREL and EQS can only tell us what additions or deletions of parameters will result in a better *statistical* fit. These modifications may or may not be defensible from a theoretical point of view. Changes that cannot be justified theoretically should be made.

Bollen (1989), in discussing modification of models, wrote:

> Researchers with inadequate models have many ways—in fact, too many ways—in which to modify their specification. An incredible number of major or minor alterations are possible, and the analyst needs some procedure to narrow the choices. The empirical means can be helpful, but they can also lead to nonsensical respecifications. Furthermore, empirical means work best in detecting simple alterations and are less helpful when major changes in structure are needed. The potentially richest source of ideas for respecification is the theoretical or substantive knowledge of the researcher. (pp. 296–297)

With these caveats, we can turn our attention to the indices that may be useful in suggesting possible model modifications. One obvious possibility is to delete parameters that are nonsignificant. For example, a factor loading may be found for which the reported t value in LISREL is less than $|2.0|$, indicating that the value of that loading is not significantly different from zero. Deleting a parameter from the model will not result in a better fit, but will gain a degree of freedom, resulting in a lower critical value. However, if the same data are used to both obtain and modify the model, this increase in degrees of freedom is not justified. This is because the degree of freedom has already been used to obtain the estimate in the original model. In subsequent analyses on other data sets, however, the researcher could omit the parameter, thus gaining a degree of freedom and obtaining a simpler model. Simpler models are generally preferred over more complex models for reasons of parsimony.

Another type of model modification that might be considered is to add parameters to the model. For example, a variable that had been constrained to load on only one factor might be allowed to have loadings on two factors. In the LISREL program, modification indexes (MIs) are provided. These are estimates of the decrease in the chi-square value that would result if a given parameter, such as a factor loading, were to be added to the model. MIs are available for all parameters that were constrained to be zero in the original model. They are accompanied by the expected parameter change (EPC) statistics. These represent the value a given parameter would have if it were added to the model. As is the case with the deletion of parameters, parameters should be added one at a time, with the model being reestimated after each addition. In the EQS program, the Lagrange Multiplier (LM) statistics serve the same function as the MIs in LISREL. EQS also provides multivariate LM statistics that take into account the correlations among the parameters.

The modification indexes for the factor loading and measurement error variance matrices from Model 1 of the HBM data are shown in Table 11.18. Because all of the factor correlations were included in that model, no modification indexes were computed for these.

TABLE 11.18

Modification Indexes for Health Belief Model 1

THE MODIFICATION INDICES SUGGEST TO ADD THE			
PATH TO	FROM	DECREASE IN CHI-SQUARE	NEW ESTIMATE
ser1	benefits	8.9	0.09
ser1	barriers	21.5	−0.14
ser8	suscept	13.9	0.15
ser8	benefits	14.1	−0.16
ser8	barriers	12.6	0.15
bar2	serious	10.9	0.11
bar2	benefits	11.4	−0.11
bar3	benefits	9.1	0.07

THE MODIFICATION INDICES SUGGEST TO ADD AN ERROR COVARIANCE			
BETWEEN	AND	DECREASE IN CHI-SQUARE	NEW ESTIMATE
sus2	sus1	26.8	0.07
sus3	sus2	16.1	0.05
sus4	sus2	44.2	−0.09
sus5	sus2	11.5	−0.05
sus5	sus4	93.1	0.18
ser2	ser1	56.6	0.16
ser3	ser2	65.4	0.24
ser4	sus1	12.4	−0.07
ser4	ser3	77.2	0.35
ser5	ser3	24.9	−0.15
ser5	ser4	21.7	−0.15
ser6	ser1	18.0	−0.12
ser6	ser2	24.5	−0.16
ser6	ser3	13.3	−0.15
ser7	ser2	19.7	−0.13
ser7	ser3	29.3	−0.20
ser7	ser4	17.9	−0.17
ser7	ser5	33.9	0.18
ser7	ser6	42.3	0.26
ser8	ser2	19.5	−0.12
ser8	ser7	8.2	0.10
ben4	ben1	70.8	0.15
ben7	ben1	9.6	0.07
ben10	ben1	9.2	−0.04
ben11	ser4	8.2	−0.07
ben12	ser5	9.7	−0.07
ben12	ben11	23.1	0.11
ben13	ben4	10.9	−0.05
ben13	ben10	41.1	0.09
bar1	ben1	8.1	−0.05
bar3	ser1	13.7	−0.05
bar3	bar1	44.2	0.11
bar4	bar1	26.2	−0.08
bar4	bar3	21.1	−0.05
bar5	bar4	17.2	0.04
bar6	bar4	15.8	0.09
bar7	bar4	26.3	0.05

The MIs suggest that the largest drop in chi-square (93.1) would be obtained if we were to add a measurement error covariance for items 4 and 5 on the Susceptibility scale. Several other large MIs have been obtained for pairs of measurement error covariances. However, most researchers share the view of Hoyle and Panter (1995), who stated that correlated errors of measurement are among the most problematic types of post hoc modifications because they are rarely theoretically justified and are unlikely to replicate. The need for correlated measurement errors is an indication that the factor model has been unable to account for all of the covariation among the variables. This may occur if, for example, more factors are needed or if method variance is present. These possibilities should be evaluated before any decision is made with regard to freeing these measurement error covariances.

If changes are made on the basis of MIs, the model must be reestimated following each change, as it is likely that the other parameter estimates and their MI values, as well as the chi-square value, would also change. This is the reason for the common recommendation that only one modification be made to a model at a time. Finally, no model modifications should be made unless they are theoretically defensible.

Section 11.20 provides a discussion of some concerns that have been voiced about current practices in CFA studies. One of these pertains to the use of MIs in making post hoc model modifications; the other has to do with the issue of equivalent or alternative models. Before discussing these issues, however, we consider two more examples: one that has been analyzed using the LISREL 8 program and one using the EQS (Bentler, 1989) program.

11.18 LISREL 8 Example

In this example, the observed variables are items from a measure of test anxiety known as the Reactions to Tests (RTT) scale. The RTT was developed by Sarason (1984) to measure the four hypothesized dimensions of worry, tension, test-irrelevant thinking, and bodily symptoms. The data are drawn from a study of the scale by Benson and Bandalos (1992) in which the items were found to be approximately normally distributed. For simplicity, only three items from each scale are used.

The factor structure tested is shown in Figure 11.4. As can be seen from the figure, each of the three items for each scale is hypothesized to load only on the scale it was written to measure, and the factors are hypothesized to correlate with each other. The 12 diagonal elements of $\theta\delta$, or the measurement error variances, are included in the model. The absence of curved arrows connecting the δ's in Figure 11.4 means that the measurement errors were not hypothesized to be correlated.

The SIMPLIS command lines are shown in Table 11.19. For those readers who do not have access to LISREL 8 and the new SIMPLIS command language, the LISREL 7 commands for this problem are shown in the Appendix to this chapter.

Table 11.20 shows the estimates of the factor loadings with their standard errors and *t* values in matrix format rather than the equation format used for the Health Belief examples. This format is used in older versions of the LISREL program and is preferred by some researchers. Table 11.21 presents similar information for the factor correlations. To conserve space, estimates of the measurement error variances are not shown.

An inspection of the *t* values for these parameter estimates reveals that all are significant with the exception of the correlation between the tension and test-irrelevant thinking factors, which has a *t* value of 1.76. There are no unreasonable parameter estimates such as negative variances or correlations greater than 1. All of the parameter estimates appear to be in the expected range of values and to have the expected signs. This is important because unreasonable values usually indicate a problem with the model, such as a lack of identification.

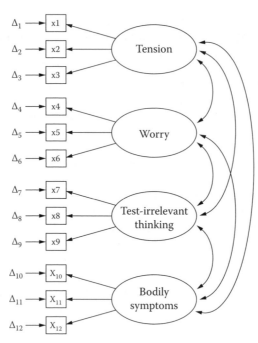

FIGURE 11.4
Four-factor test anxiety model with three indicators per factor.

The significance of the factor loadings is of special interest as these indicate that the items did have significant loadings on the factors they were intended to measure. The lack of a significant correlation between tension and test-irrelevant thinking is not surprising; other studies have also found the test-irrelevant thinking factor to be the most distinct of the four factors. The magnitudes and statistical significance of the remaining factor correlations support the hypothesis that the four factors are distinct, yet related, dimensions of test anxiety.

Our inspection of the parameter values and *t* statistics indicate support for the hypothesized four-factor structure. Some selected tests of overall fit are shown in Table 11.22.

The chi-square value of 88.396 with 48 degrees of freedom is significant with a probability of .0003, indicating that the model does not adequately account for the observed covariation among the variables. However, many of the other fit indexes suggest that the fit of the model is fairly good. It may be that the significant chi-square is, at least in part, due to the fairly large sample size, rather than to any serious misspecification of the model.

Setting the loadings equal to 0 does not make them 0. Thus, previous empirical work should be done to ensure that the items are relatively pure measures of the constructs they are designed to measure. In Table 11.23 we have allowed TEN1, WOR1, IRTHK1, and BODY1 to load on all four factors, to see if they are relatively pure measures of TEN, WOR, IRTHK, and BODY. We have done the same for TEN2 and such, and for TEN3 and such. The loadings on the other factors are in almost all cases close to 0, which is reassuring.

11.19 EQS Example

Having presented an example using the LISREL 8 program, I now discuss one using Bentler's (1989) EQS program. This chapter is not intended as a comprehensive guide to the program, however. The interested reader should consult the program manual or the excellent reference on this program by Byrne (1994).

TABLE 11.19

SIMPLIS Command Lines for Test Anxiety Example

TITLE: FOUR FACTOR STRUCTURE FOR ANXIETY
OBSERVED VARIABLES: TEN1 TEN2 TEN3 WOR1 WOR2 WOR3 IRTHK1
IRTHK2 IRTHK3 BODY1 BODY2 BODY3   ①
COVARIANCE MATRIX:

.7821

.5602   .9299   ②

.5695   .6281   .9751

.1969   .2599   .2362   .6352

.2289   .2835   .3079   .4575   .7943

.2609   .3670   .3575   .4327   .4151   .6783

.0556   .0740   .0981   .2094   .2306   .2503   .6855

.0025   .0279   .0798   .2047   .2270   .2257   .4224   .6952

.0180   .0753   .0744   .1892   .2352   .2008   .4343   .4514   .6065

.1617   .1919   .2892   .1376   .1744   .1845   .0645   .0731   .0921   .4068

.2628   .3047   .4043   .1742   .2066   .2547   .1356   .1336   .1283   .1958   .7015

.2966   .3040   .3919   .1942   .1864   .2402   .1073   .0988   .0599   .2233   .3033   .5786

SAMPLE SIZE: 318
LATENT VARIABLES: TENSION WORRY TIRT BODY   ③
RELATIONSHIPS:
TEN1 TEN2 TEN3 = TENSION   ④
WOR1 WOR2 WOR3 = WORRY
IRTHK1 IRTHK2 IRTHK3 = TIRT
BODY1 BODY2 BODY3 = BODY
END OF PROBLEM

① Up to 8 characters can be used to name each observed variable.
② Only the lower half of the covariance matrix need be inserted.
③ Names (8 characters or less) are given to the latent variables (factor).
④ Here, under relationships, we link the observed variables to the factors.

In this example, the data given later in Exercise 7 of this chapter have been reanalyzed using the EQS program. Although the data presented in Exercise 7 are in the form of a correlation matrix, the inclusion of the standard deviations makes it possible for the program to calculate a covariance matrix, which, you will recall, is preferred for use in CFA. The data consist of 10 communication skills measured on 159 deaf rehabilitation candidates. A two-factor solution was obtained. In this example, the data has been reanalyzed using this two-factor solution as the hypothesized model in order to demonstrate the similarities of, and differences between, the EFA solution presented earlier and the CFA procedures. I emphasize that the reanalysis cannot be used as a test of the factor structure reported earlier because the same data are being used in both the confirmatory and exploratory analyses. If our objective were to test the structure obtained from the EFA, a new set of data would have to be obtained. This analysis is therefore introduced only for the purpose of contrasting the exploratory and confirmatory procedures.

The EQS command lines are presented in Table 11.24. The factor loadings are shown in Table 11.25, along with their standard errors and *t* values. The measurement error variances are included in a separate matrix labeled "variances of independent variables." To conserve space, and because our primary interest is in the factor loadings, this matrix is not reproduced here.

An inspection of the *t* values for the factor loadings reveals that all are statistically significant. They also appear to be reasonable and of the expected magnitude and direction. The factor loadings differ somewhat from those from the EFA, but these differences do not appear to be substantial. Recall that in the original EFA, each variable actually had loadings on both factors, but loadings less than .30 were not reported. In the current analysis, loadings less than .30 were

TABLE 11.20

Factor Loadings, Standard Errors, and *t* Values for Test Anxiety Example

LISREL ESTIMATES (MAXIMUM LIKELIHOOD)				
	LAMBDA-X (factor loadings)			
	tension	worry	tirt	body
TEN1	.69 ①	— ④	—	—
	(.04) ②			
	15.59 ③			
TEN2	.76	—	—	—
	(.05)			
	16.01			
TEN3	.84	—	—	—
	(.05)			
	17.70			
WOR1	—	.64	—	—
		(.04)		
		16.18		
WOR2	—	.66	—	—
		(.05)		
		14.51		
WOR3	—	.67	—	—
		(.04)		
		16.30		
IRTHK1	—	—	.64	—
			(.04)	
			15.47	
IRTHK2	—	—	.67	—
			(.04)	
			16.09	
IRTHK3	—	—	.67	—
			(.04)	
			17.69	
BODY1	—	—	—	.38
				(.04)
				10.51
BODY2	—	—	—	.54
				(.05)
				11.52
BODY3	—	—	—	.56
				(.04)
				13.29

① Factor loading.
② Standard error.
③ *t* Value.
④ — Indicates a factor loading that was constrained to equal zero by the program.

TABLE 11.21

Factor Correlations, Standard Errors, and *t* Values for Test Anxiety Example

	PHI (factor correlations)			
	tension	worry	tirt	body
tension	1.00 ①			
worry	.55 ②	1.00		
	(.05) ③			
	11.01 ④			
tirt	.11	.49	1.00	
	(.06)	(.05)		
	1.76	9.28		
body	.78	.59	.29	1.00
	(.04)	(.05)	(.07)	
	18.73	10.89	4.25	

① Factor variances were set to equal 1.0 in order to give a metric to the factors.
② Factor correlation.
③ Standard error.
④ *t* Value.

TABLE 11.22

Goodness-of-Fit Statistics for Test Anxiety Example

CHI-SQUARE WITH 48 DEGREES OF FREEDOM = 88.396 (P = 0.000345)
GOODNESS OF FIT INDEX (GFI) = 0.957
ADJUSTED GOODNESS OF FIT INDEX (AGFI) = 0.929
EXPECTED CROSS-VALIDATION INDEX (ECVI) = 0.477
90 PERCENT CONFIDENCE INTERVAL FOR ECVI = (0.397; 0.564)
ECVI FOR SATURATED MODEL = 0.492
INDEPENDENCE AIC = 1634.054
MODEL AIC = −7.604
NORMED FIT INDEX (NFI) = 0.95
NON-NORMED FIT INDEX (NNFI) = 0.967
PARSIMONY NORMED FIT INDEX = 0.691

constrained to be zero. This probably accounts for most of the discrepancies between the two sets of factor loadings.

To ascertain whether the two-factor model represents a good fit to the data, the fit statistics must be considered. Some of these are presented in Table 11.26.

Overall, the fit statistics do not suggest a good fit to the data. The chi-square value is highly significant, indicating that the model has not adequately reproduced the original covariance matrix. Both the NFI and the NNFI are well below .9. The AIC value of 262.6 for our model is considerably lower than the independence model AIC value of 1602.04, but this indicates only that the hypothesized model represents a considerable improvement over a model in which the variables are hypothesized to be uncorrelated.

The results of the LM and Wald tests are often useful in identifying the sources of model misfit. The LM test is equivalent to the modification index (MI) in LISREL and represents the amount by which the overall chi-square value should decrease if a parameter were to be added to the model. In contrast, values of the Wald test represent the amount by which the overall chi-square value will increase if a parameter were to be dropped from the model. The LM and Wald tests are thus

TABLE 11.23

Loadings with TEN1, WOR1, IRTHK1, and BODY1 Free to Load on All Factors; TEN2, WOR2, IRTHK2, and BODY2 Free to Load on All Factors; and TEN3, WOR3, IRTHK3, and BODY3 Free to Load on All Factors

	TENSION	WORRY	TIRT	BODY		TENSION	WORRY	TIRT	BODY		TENSION	WORRY	TIRT	BODY
TEN1	0.98 (0.17) 5.92	−0.01 (0.08) −0.11	−0.01 (0.06) −0.12	−0.31 (0.17) −1.87	TEN1	0.68 (0.04) 15.44	— 	— 	— 	TEN1	0.70 (0.04) 15.85	— 	— 	—
TEN2	0.75 (0.05) 15.81	— 	— 	— 	TEN2	0.98 (0.14) 6.90	0.15 (0.08) 1.96	0.00 (0.06) −0.03	−0.35 (0.15) −2.39	TEN2	0.80 (0.05) 16.70	— 	— 	—
TEN3	0.83 (0.05) 17.50	— 	— 	— 	TEN3	0.83 (0.05) 17.41	— 	— 	— 	TEN3	0.58 (0.08) 7.12	−0.08 (0.06) −1.26	−0.02 (0.06) −0.34	0.38 (0.08) 4.50
WOR1	−0.18 (0.12) −1.50	0.94 (0.11) 8.20	−0.14 (0.07) −1.97	−0.10 (0.13) −0.80	WOR1	— 	0.64 (0.04) 16.13	— 	— 	WOR1	— 	0.68 (0.04) 16.82	— 	—
WOR2	— 	0.65 (0.05) 14.07	— 	— 	WOR2	0.01 (0.09) 0.11	0.65 (0.07) 8.80	0.04 (0.05) 0.84	−0.03 (0.10) −0.28	WOR2	— 	0.67 (0.05) 14.57	— 	—
WOR3	— 	0.65 (0.04) 15.50	— 	— 	WOR3	— 	0.67 (0.04) 16.37	— 	— 	WOR3	0.11 (0.07) 1.63	0.50 (0.06) 8.82	0.05 (0.05) 1.02	0.11 (0.07) 1.51

Matrix 1

	IRTHK1	IRTHK2	IRTHK3	BODY1	BODY2	BODY3
IRTHK1	0.09 (0.10) 0.87					
IRTHK2	0.05 (0.06) 0.75	0.63 (0.06) 11.46				
IRTHK3	—	0.67 (0.04) 16.09	0.67 (0.04) 17.69			
BODY1	-0.17 (0.14) -1.26	0.02 (0.07) 0.34	-0.03 (0.06) -0.47	0.55 (0.15) 3.54		
BODY2	—	—	—	0.53 (0.05) 11.24	—	
BODY3	—	—	—	0.53 (0.04) 12.47	—	—

Matrix 2

	IRTHK1	IRTHK2	IRTHK3	BODY1	BODY2	BODY3
IRTHK1	—					
IRTHK2	0.64 (0.04) 15.42	0.13 (0.09) 1.55				
IRTHK3	0.64 (0.05) 12.67	—	—			
BODY1	0.68 (0.04) 17.76	0.39 (0.04) 10.56	0.09 (0.07) 1.35	—		
BODY2	0.10 (0.05) 1.77	0.43 (0.12) 3.67	-0.06 (0.06) -1.17	0.55 (0.05) 11.36	—	
BODY3	0.57 (0.04) 13.09	0.57 (0.04) 13.09	0.02 (0.07) 0.28	0.00 (0.10) 0.01	—	—

Additional matrix values

	IRTHK1	IRTHK2	IRTHK3	BODY1	BODY2	BODY3
IRTHK1	—					
IRTHK2	0.64 (0.04) 15.20	—				
IRTHK3	0.66 (0.04) 15.83	—	—			
BODY1	0.74 (0.06) 12.84	—	—	—		
BODY2	—	—	—	—	—	
BODY3	-0.08 (0.06) -1.34	-0.09 (0.07) -1.27	—	—	—	—

Other estimates: -0.14 (0.08) -1.79; 0.01 (0.06) 0.20; 0.12 (0.10) 1.14; -0.03 (0.07) -0.48; 0.39 (0.04) 10.50; 5.39

TABLE 11.24

Command Lines for EQS CFA of Bolton Data

EXAMPLE 2: BOLTON DATA;	
/SPECS	①
CAS = 159;VARS = 10;ME = ML;MA = COV;	
/EQUATIONS	
V1 =　　　　　　1.000*F2 + E1;	
V2 =　　　　　　1.000*F2 + E2;	
V3 = 1.000*F1 + 1.000*F2 + E3;	
V4 = 1.000*F1 + 1.000*F2 + E4;	
V5 = 1.000*F1　　　　　+ E5;	②
V6 = 1.000*F1　　　　　+ E6;	
V7 =　　　　　　1.000*F2 + E7;	
V8 = 1.000*F1 + 1.000*F2 + E8;	
V9 = 1.000*F1　　　　　+ E9;	
V10 = 1.000*F1　　　　+ E10;	
/VARIANCES	
E1 TO E10 = .500*;	③
F1 TO F2 = 1.000;	

```
    /MATRIX
       1.0
        .59    1.0
        .30    .34   1.0
        .16    .24    .62   1.0
       -.02   -.13    .28    .37   1.0
        .00   -.05    .42    .51    .90   1.0
        .39    .61    .70    .59    .05    .20   1.0
        .17    .29    .57    .88    .30    .46    .60   1.0           ④
       -.04   -.14    .28    .33    .93    .86    .04    .28   1.0
       -.04   -.08    .42    .50    .87    .94    .17    .45    .90   1.0
    /STANDARD DEVIATIONS
        .45   1.06   1.17   1.11   1.50   .144   1.31   1.04
       /LMTEST; /WTEST;
       /END
```

① ME = ML means that the method of estimation (ME) is maximum likelihood covariance matrix (COV).

② These lines give the structure for the factor loadings. The asterisks design

③ The measurement error variances (E1) must be given starting values; here fixed at 1.00.

④ Only the lower half of the correlation matrix is required, along with the start

tests of whether parameters should be added to or deleted from the model, respectively. The results of the Wald and LM tests are presented in Table 11.27.

The results of the Wald test indicate that there are no model parameters that could be dropped without significantly worsening overall model fit. This is not surprising, as all parameter estimates were found to be highly significant.

The EQS program computes both univariate and multivariate forms of the LM test. The multivariate LM is generally preferred because it takes into account the correlations among the parameters. It may be that two parameters have high values for the univariate LM tests, but that these two parameters are highly correlated with one another. In such a case, adding both parameters will not decrease the overall chi-square value much more than would adding only one. The multivariate LM tests take the intercorrelations among the parameters into account in computing the estimated

TABLE 11.25

Factor Loadings, Standard Errors, and *t* Values for CFA of Bolton Data

MEASUREMENT EQUATIONS WITH STANDARD ERRORS AND TEST STATISTICS

$$V1 = V1 = \quad .302 \ ① \ *F2 \quad + \quad 1.000 \ ④ \ E1$$
$$.081 \ ②$$
$$3.711 \ ③$$
$$V2 = V2 = \quad .461*F2 \quad + \quad 1.000 \ E2$$
$$.079$$
$$5.863$$
$$V3 = V3 = \quad .349*F1 \quad + \quad .585*F2 \quad + \quad 1.000 \ E3$$
$$.068 \qquad\qquad .069$$
$$5.150 \qquad\qquad 8.527$$
$$V4 = V4 = \quad .428*F1 \quad + \quad .796*F2 \quad + \quad 1.000 \ E4$$
$$.056 \qquad\qquad .057$$
$$7.613 \qquad\qquad 14.022$$
$$V5 = V5 = \quad .934*F1 \quad + \quad 1.000 \ E5$$
$$.060$$
$$15.560$$
$$V6 = V6 = \quad .960*F1 \quad + \quad 1.000 \ E6$$
$$.059$$
$$16.382$$
$$V7 = V7 = \quad .728*F2 \quad + \quad 1.000 \ E7$$
$$.071$$
$$10.276$$
$$V8 = V8 = \quad .371*F1 \quad + \quad .815*F2 \quad + \quad 1.000 \ E8$$
$$.057 \qquad\qquad .059$$
$$6.530 \qquad\qquad 13.883$$
$$V9 = V9 = \quad .930*F1 \quad + \quad 1.000 \ E9$$
$$.060$$
$$15.464$$
$$V10 = V10 = .965*F1 \quad + \quad 1.000 \ E10$$
$$.058$$
$$16.518$$

① Factor loading.
② Factor correlation.
③ *t* Value.
④ Values of 1.000 here serve only to indicate that the measurement error was included in the model, and should not be interpreted as parameter estimates.

TABLE 11.26

Goodness-of-Fit Statistics from CFA of Bolton Data

GOODNESS OF FIT SUMMARY
INDEPENDENCE AIC = 1602.04359
MODEL AIC = 262.60282
CHI-SQUARE = 326.603 BASED ON 32 DEGREES OF FREEDOM
PROBABILITY VALUE FOR THE CHI-SQUARE STATISTIC IS LESS THAN 0.001
BENTLER-BONETT NORMED FIT INDEX = .807
BENTLER-BONETT NONNORMED FIT INDEX = .748

TABLE 11.27

Results of Wald and LM Tests From CFA of Bolton Data

WALD TEST (FOR DROPPING PARAMETERS)
NONE OF THE FREE PARAMETERS IS DROPPED IN THIS PROCESS.

LAGRANGE MULTIPLIER TEST (FOR ADDING PARAMETERS)
ORDERED UNIVARIATE TEST STATISTICS:

NO	PARAMETER	CHI-SQUARE	PROBABILITY	PARAMETER CHANGE
1	V9,F2 ①	22.643 ②	.000 ③	−.159 ④
2	V6,F2	15.386	.000	.110
3	V5,F2	13.986	.000	−.123
4	V10,F2	10.107	.001	.087
5	V7,F1	5.646	.017	.177
6	V2,F1	3.651	.056	−.145
7	F2,F1	.882	.348	.098
8	V1,F1	.434	.510	−.052
9	F2,F2	.000	1.000	.000
10	F1,F1	.000	1.000	.000

MULTIVARIATE LAGRANGE MULTIPLIER TEST BY SIMULTANEOUS PROCESS IN STAGE 1

STEP	PARAMETER	CUMULATIVE MULTIVARIATE STATISTICS			UNIVARIATE INCREMENT	
		CHI-SQUARE	D.F.	PROB	CHI-SQUARE	PROB
1	V9,F2	22.643	1	.000	22.643	.000
2	V5,F2	45.826	2	.000	23.183	.000
3	V7,F1	53.946 ⑤	3	.000	8.119 ⑥	.004

① V9,F2 represents the loading of variable 9 on factor 2.
② Amount by which the overall chi-square value would decrease if the parameter V9,F2 were added to the model.
③ Probability of the associated chi-square value with 1 degree of freedom.
④ Value that the associated parameter would have if added to the model.
⑤ Total amount by which the overall chi-square value would decrease if the three parameters V9,F2, V5,F2, and V7,F1 were all added to the model.
⑥ Amount of the decrease in chi-square that would be accounted for by adding the parameter V7,F1 to the model.

decrease in the overall chi-square. This is why some parameters that are included in the univariate LM tests are not included in the multivariate test. For example, the parameter V6,F2 has a univariate value of 15.386, indicating that if variable 6 were allowed to load on factor 2, the overall chi-square value would decrease by 15.386. However, note that this decrease in chi-square would result only if that were the only parameter added to the model. The fact that the parameter V6,F2 is not included in the multivariate LM test probably indicates that it is so highly correlated with one or more of the other parameters that it would not result in a large decrease if other parameters were also added. The results of the multivariate LM test indicate that the greatest decrease in the overall chi-square value would occur if variables 9 and 5 were allowed to load on factor 2 and variable 7 were allowed to load on factor 1. Of course, these changes should be made only if they can be supported by theory.

Overall, then, the structure obtained from the EFA for these 10 items cannot be shown to fit the data optimally. Even the addition of the three-factor loadings described in the preceding paragraph would not result in a nonsignificant chi-square value. It may be that more than two factors are needed, or that the factors should be allowed to correlate. At this point, however, the researcher should carefully consider whether any proposed changes in the model can be justified theoretically.

11.20 Some Caveats Regarding Structural Equation Modeling

Covariance structure modeling (CSM) or structural equation modeling (SEM) techniques, which include CFA, have been used extensively since the 1980s. They have been touted as one of the most important advances in quantitative methodology in many years. One of the advantages of these techniques is that they allow for measurement error to be taken into account, which traditional procedures do not. Although these techniques are very sophisticated mathematically, they can now be implemented easily with the latest releases of programs such as LISREL and EQS. The availability of Windows versions of these programs has made their implementation still easier. However, Cliff (1983, 1989), among others, has cautioned researchers that the sophistication of these techniques and the facility with which they can now be applied should not blind researchers to some basic research principles.

One of these principles concerns the issue of capitalization on chance, which has been a major theme of this book. MacCallum, Roznowski, and Necowitz (1992) reported a compelling study on this issue. As noted earlier, it is not uncommon in practice for researchers to modify their models in a post hoc fashion, based on indices such as the LISREL MIs, or the LM and Wald tests given by the EQS program. This process of post hoc model modification is often called a *specification search*. What most researchers appear to be unaware of is that this is a *data-driven* process that is very susceptible to capitalization on chance. Because of this, modifications made in this way are likely to be very unstable, and are unlikely to cross-validate. This is particularly true when sample size is small, the number of modifications is large, and the modifications are not theoretically defensible (MacCallum, 1986). As MacCallum et al. (1992), noted:

> *Model modification in practice is usually done with no substantive justification and no cross-validation, often involves a substantial number of modifications, and is often based on samples that may be too small for such analyses...* . We consider this to be an unfortunate state of affairs, representing a dangerous and misleading methodological trend (p. 494, italics added).

The MacCallum et al. (1992) study found that no searches were based on a sequence of four modifications that resulted in the same modified models when sample size was 250 or less. Only when the sample size reached 400 was there *some* consistency. Unfortunately, most studies reported in the literature have sample sizes between 100 and 350.

A recent Monte Carlo study by Hutchinson (1994) is right on target in having investigated the stability of post hoc model modifications for some CFA models. Two population models were created involving two- and four-factor oblique factor structures. In each model, all factors had four primary indicators (with population loadings varying from .60 to .80) and two secondary population loadings of .40. Four levels of misspecification were imposed on the two models by incorrectly setting certain loadings to zero. I discuss only the first two levels of misspecification here. For Model 1, the first level had two secondary loadings incorrectly set to zero, and the second level had one primary and one secondary loading incorrectly set to zero. For the four-factor model, Level 1 misspecification involved incorrectly setting four secondary loadings to zero, and Level 2 had two primary and two secondary loadings incorrectly set to zero.

Sample sizes of 200, 400, 800, and 1,200 were chosen. One hundred samples were generated for each model and sample size combination, for a total of 800 samples. Hutchinson found that:

TABLE 11.28

Number of Times (Out of 100) Population Models Recovered

	Level of misspecification			
	Two-factor model		Four-factor model	
n	1	2	1	2
200	23	26	19	30
400	64	78	64	71
800	94	93	96	99
1,200	94	93	100	100

Conditions with marked declines in values of MIs were also those that exhibited greater modification consistency …. When values of MIs seem to gradually decrease, even if still statistically significant, it suggests that there may be a number of specification errors present, but none of substantial size. Errors of this type are more likely to reflect chance characteristics of the data. Consequently, in practice one should probably try to limit modifications to correction of noticeably large specification errors which would be more likely to replicate in other samples (p. 25).

Table 11.28 shows that if the specification errors are relatively minor, a sample size of 400 gives one a good chance (from 64% to 78%) of recovering a known population model. More severe misspecification requires at least 800 subjects to obtain similar results.

Another problem encountered in SEM analyses is that researchers too often seem to interpret the finding that their model fits the data as meaning it is the *only* model that can do so. Various individuals (Bollen, 1989, p. 71; Cliff, 1983; Jöreskog, 1993, p. 298) noted that there are always other models that can fit the data as well, if not better, than the one originally hypothesized. These alternative models represent competing hypotheses that must be ruled out if the originally hypothesized model is to be supported.

In a 1993 paper, MacCallum, Wegener, Uchino, and Fabrigar discussed this issue in the context of mathematically equivalent models. These are models that cannot be distinguished from the originally hypothesized model on the basis of their goodness of fit. For example, in CFA, one model with items that load on more than one factor and another model with items that load on only one factor but have correlated measurement errors may fit equally well in terms of their chi-square values, even though they represent fundamentally different hypotheses. In cases like this, there is no statistical basis for choosing one model over another, and such decisions must be made on the basis of theoretical considerations. In their 1993 study, MacCallum et al. catalogued all applications of CSM in three prominent journals (*Journal of Educational Psychology, Journal of Applied Psychology*, and *Journal of Personality and Social Psychology*) for the years 1988 through 1991. For these articles the median number of equivalent models was quite large, as shown here:

Journal	Number of articles	Percent with equivalent models	Median number of models
Educ. Psych	14	86	16.5
Appl. Psych	19	74	12.0
Personality & Social Psych	20	100	21.0

They selected one article from each of these three journals and presented an analysis of three of the plausible equivalent models for each case. As MacCallum et al. (1993) noted:

> Importantly, the presented equivalent models have theoretical implications that differ substantially from the models preferred by the authors of the published applications. We know of no compelling evidence that would suggest that these equivalent models are theoretically less plausible than the original models.... The gravity of this issue for empirical research is increased by the fact that the phenomenon of equivalent models has been virtually ignored in practice. Of the 72 published applications examined by Becker (1990) and the additional 53 studies considered in this article, only *one* study contained an explicit acknowledgment of the existence of even a single equivalent model.... *Without adequate consideration of alternative equivalent models, support for one model from a class of equivalent models is suspect at best and potentially groundless and misleading.* (p. 196)

When taken in conjunction with their 1992 paper, the picture painted by MacCallum and his colleagues is a bleak one with regard to the amount of confidence one is justified in placing in the results of many CSM studies. What then should be done in CSM studies to enhance meaningfulness and generalizability? First, if post hoc model modifications are to be made, sample size must be adequate (probably 400 subjects for most studies, although this will depend on the size of the model). Also, no modifications should be made without a clear theoretical justification. Any model obtained as a result of such modifications should be treated *very tentatively* until the model has been validated on an independent sample of data. This is the issue of cross-validation, which has been stressed in this text, and which several prominent CSM researchers (Breckler, 1990; Browne & Cudeck, 1989; Cudeck & Browne, 1983; Jöreskog, 1993; MacCallum et al., 1992) have indicated is crucial in CSM research.

The problem of equivalent or alternative models must also be seriously considered in CSM studies. Although Jöreskog (1993, p. 295) indicated that the consideration of several *a priori* models is rare in practice, Bollen and Long (1993, p. 7), in the same volume, stated that one point of consensus among CSM researchers is that "it is better to consider several alternative models than to examine only a single model." While not all alternative models will be plausible, those that are should be estimated along with the originally hypothesized model. The values of such indexes as the AIC, ECVI, PGFI, and PNFI can then be used as a basis for comparing the fit of the various models.

In concluding this section, the following from Cliff (1987) is important. Most of all, one wonders at the personal arrogance and disrespect for the scientific process that is shown by some of these authors. Do they really think causal relations are established by a simple statistical analysis of a few, often adventitiously available, variables?

11.21 Summary

1. Principal components are uncorrelated, linear combinations of the original variables. They therefore provide for an *additive* partitioning of the total variance.

2. When there is a large number of variables, say 30, the number of correlations is high (435 for 30), and it is very difficult to summarize by inspection precisely what this pattern of correlations represents. Principal components analysis is a means of "boiling down" the main sources of variation in such a complex set of correlations, and often a small number of components will account for most of the variance.

3. Three uses for components analysis as a variable reducing scheme are: (a) determining the number of dimensions underlying a test, (b) reducing the number of predictors, prior to a regression analysis, and (c) reducing the number of dependent variables, prior to a MANOVA.

4. The absolute magnitude and number of loadings are crucial in determining reliable components. Components with at least four loadings $> |.60|$, or with at least three loadings $> |.80|$ are reliable. Also, components with at least 10 loadings $> |.40|$ are reliable for $N > 150$.

5. I suggest *doubling* the critical value for an ordinary correlation and using that, at the .01 level, to determine whether a loading is significant.

6. For increasing interpretability of factors, there are two basic types of rotations: (a) orthogonal—the rotated factors are still uncorrelated—and (b) oblique—the rotated factors are correlated.

7. When uncorrelated factors are appropriate, the varimax rotation generally is quite useful in improving interpretability. Often, however, oblique or correlated factors are more reasonable to assume. There are many different oblique rotations. No one of them should be considered superior, but rather they represent different ways of looking at the factors in the factor space.

8. With respect to using communality estimates in the main diagonal of the matrix being factor analyzed (rather than 1's), several sources suggest that when the number of variables is > 30 and only a few variables have low communalities, then practically any one of the factor procedures leads to the same conclusions. When the number of variables is < 20 and some of the communalities are low, then differences can occur.

9. Complete control lines were given for both SAS and SPSS for saving factor scores and then passing them to another program for regression analysis and for doing a MANOVA.

11.22 Exercises

1. The notion of a linear combination of variables and how much variance that linear combination accounts for is fundamental not only in principal components analysis but also in other forms of multivariate analysis such as discriminant analysis and canonical correlation. We indicated in this chapter that the variances for the successive components are equal to eigenvalues of covariance (correlation) matrix. However, the variance for a linear combination is defined more fundamentally in terms of the variances and covariances of the variables which make up the composite. We denote the matrix of variances and covariances for a set of p variables as:

$$
S = \begin{bmatrix} s_1^2 & s_{12} & \cdots & s_{1p} \\ s_{21} & s_2^2 & \cdots & s_{2p} \\ \vdots & \vdots & & \vdots \\ s_{p1} & s_{p2} & & s_p^2 \end{bmatrix}
$$

The variance of a linear combination is defined as:

$$
\mathrm{var}(a_{11}x_1 + a_{12}x_2 + \cdots + a_{1p}x_p) = \mathrm{var}(\mathbf{a'x}) = \mathbf{a'Sa},
$$

where $\mathbf{a'} = (a_{11}, a_{12}, \ldots, a_{1p})$.

(a) Write out what the formula for the variance of a linear combination of two and three variables will be.

(b) The covariance matrix S for a set of three variables was:

$$
S = \begin{bmatrix} 451.4 & 271.2 & 168.7 \\ & 171.7 & 103.3 \\ \text{symm} & & 66.7 \end{bmatrix}
$$

and the first principal component of S was

$$
y_1 = .81x_1 + .50x_2 + .31x_3
$$

What is the variance of y_1?

2. Golding and Seidman (1974) measured 231 undergraduate males enrolled in an undergraduate psychology course on the *Strong Vocational Interest Blank for Men*, and obtained the following correlation matrix on the 22 basic interest scales: public speaking, law/politics, business management, sales, merchandising, office practice, military activities, technical supervision, mathematics, science, mechanical, nature, agriculture, adventure, recreational leadership, medical service, social service, religious activities, teaching, music, art, and writing.

	1	2	3	4	5	6	7	8	9	10	11	12	13	14	15	16	17	18	19	20	21	22
1	1.0																					
2	.77	1.0																				
3	53	50	1.0																			
4	54	44	74	1.0																		
5	54	48	91	82	1.0																	
6	30	28	72	63	75	1.0																
7	16	20	28	19	26	31	1.0															
8	36	34	79	56	70	63	38	1.0														
9	−11	−05	08	02	05	20	03	14	1.0													
10	−10	−09	−03	−07	−08	02	15	05	50	1.0												
11	−02	−07	22	23	21	27	29	37	44	62	1.0											
12	14	−02	04	05	07	−03	23	11	−04	37	31	1.0										
13	09	−01	06	10	09	−03	24	11	−10	08	21	73	1.0									
14	21	18	15	15	14	−01	16	13	13	11	28	12	31	1.0								
15	16	21	22	22	22	23	29	18	03	−07	09	10	32	41	1.0							
16	23	24	09	12	12	05	19	08	08	41	24	33	05	12	10	1.0						
17	38	36	13	21	14	10	07	00	−19	−04	−07	23	09	−01	18	29	1.0					
18	32	17	18	22	17	27	17	13	−01	12	14	33	19	00	19	20	47	1.0				
19	37	23	29	35	28	30	15	20	−03	18	16	36	12	−02	12	22	51	41	1.0			
20	22	04	−01	05	06	−05	−22	−06	01	22	11	31	00	−05	−28	26	27	37	42	1.0		
21	19	−01	−06	04	05	−13	−15	−10	02	22	12	49	17	02	−22	23	26	25	34	73	1.0	
22	49	26	04	16	10	−08	−10	−06	−23	−04	−12	28	09	08	−02	15	42	31	42	57	62	1.0

Run a components analysis on this matrix. Also, do a varimax rotation, and compare the interpretations.

3. In which, if either, of the following cases would it be advisable to apply Bartlett's sphericity test before proceeding with a components analysis?

Case 1

1	.31	.45	.18	.56	.41	.50	
	1	.27	.36	.04	.30	.21	
		1	.63	.16	.41	.25	
			1	.28	.15	.32	125 subjects
				1	.46	.53	
					1	.39	
						1	

Case 2

1	.29	.18	.04	.11	.15	
	1	.07	.40	.12	.03	
		1	.23	.06	.13	111 subjects
			1	−.08	−.14	
				1	.12	
					1	

The actual sphericity test statistic is:

$$\chi^2 = -\left(N - 1 - \frac{2p+5}{6}\right)\ln|\mathbf{R}|, \text{ with } 1/2\,p(p-1)\,df$$

However, Lawley has shown that a good approximation to this statistic is:

$$\chi^2 = \left(N - 1 - \frac{2p+5}{6}\right)\sum\sum r_{ij}^2,$$

where the sum extends only over the correlations (r_{ij}) above the main diagonal.

Use the Lawley approximation for the two cases given here to determine whether you would reject the null hypothesis of uncorrelated variables in the population.

4. Consider the following correlation matrix:

$$\mathbf{R} = \begin{bmatrix} 1 & .6579 & .0034 \\ & 1 & -.0738 \\ & & 1 \end{bmatrix}$$

A principal components analysis on this matrix produced the following factor structure, that is, component–variable correlations:

	Principal Components		
Variables	1	2	3
1	.906	.112	.408
2	.912	−.005	−.411
3	−.097	.994	−.048

We denote the column of component–variable correlations for the first component by $\mathbf{h}_1$, for the second component by $\mathbf{h}_2$, and for the third component by $\mathbf{h}_3$. Show that the original correlation matrix $\mathbf{R}$ will be reproduced, within rounding error, by $\mathbf{h}_1\mathbf{h}_1' + \mathbf{h}_2\mathbf{h}_2' + \mathbf{h}_3\mathbf{h}_3'$. As you are doing this, observe what part of $\mathbf{R}$ the matrix $\mathbf{h}_1\mathbf{h}_1'$ reproduces, etc.

5. Consider the following principal components solution on five variables and the corresponding varimax rotated solution. Only the first two components are given, because the eigenvalues corresponding to the remaining components were very small (<.3).

			Varimax solution	
Variables	Comp 1	Comp 2	Factor 1	Factor 2
1	.581	.806	.016	.994
2	.767	−.545	.941	−.009
3	.672	.726	.137	.980
4	.932	−.104	.825	.447
5	.791	−.558	.968	−.006

(a) Find the percent of variance accounted for by each principal component.

(b) Find the percent of variance accounted for by each varimax rotated factor.

(c) Compare the variance accounted for by Component 1 (2) with variance accounted for by each corresponding rotated factor.

(d) Compare the total percent of variance accounted for by the two components with the total percent of variance accounted for by the two rotated factors.

6. Consider the following correlation matrix for the 12 variables on the General Aptitude Test Battery (GATB):

NAMES	1.000											
ARITh	.697	1.000										
DIM	.360	.366	1.00									
VOCAB	.637	.580	.528	1.00								
TOOLS	.586	.471	.554	.425	1.00							
MATH	.552	.760	.468	.616	.369	1.000						
SHAPES	.496	.411	.580	.444	.531	.400	1.00					
MARK	.561	.501	.249	.465	.444	.407	.387	1.000				
PLACE	.338	.297	.276	.211	.292	.300	.323	.494	1.00			
TURN	.349	.247	.279	.209	.336	.234	.401	.540	.773	1.00		
ASMBL	.390	.319	.358	.267	.361	.208	.444	.439	.468	.476	1.00	
DASMBL	.354	.325	.234	.283	.267	.311	.428	.422	.453	.482	.676	1.00

(a) Run a components analysis and varimax rotation on the SAS factor program.

(b) Interpret the components and the varimax rotated factors.

(c) Use the oblique rotation PROMAX, and interpret the oblique factors.

(d) What are the correlations among the oblique factors?

(e) Which factors seem more reasonable to use here?

7. Bolton (1971) measured 159 deaf rehabilitation candidates on 10 communication skills, of which six were reception skills in unaided hearing, aided hearing, speech reading, reading, manual signs, and fingerspellings. The other four communication skills were expression skills: oral speech, writing, manual signs, and fingerspelling. Bolton did what is called a principal axis analysis, which is identical to a components analysis, except that the factors are extracted from a correlation matrix with communality estimates on the main diagonal rather than 1's, as in components analysis. He obtained the following correlation matrix and varimax factor solution:

Correlation Matrix of Communication Variables for 159 Deaf Persons

	C_1	C_2	C_3	C_4	C_5	C_6	C_7	C_8	C_9	C_{10}	M	S
C_1	*39*										1.10	0.45
C_2	59	*55*									1.49	1.06
C_3	30	34	*61*								2.56	1.17
C_4	16	24	62	*81*							2.63	1.11
C_5	−02	−13	28	37	*92*						3.30	1.50
C_6	00	−05	42	51	90	*94*					2.90	1.44
C_7	39	61	70	59	05	20	*71*				2.14	1.31
C_8	17	29	57	88	30	46	60	*78*			2.42	1.04
C_9	−04	−14	28	33	93	86	04	28	*92*		3.25	1.49
C_{10}	−04	−08	42	50	87	94	17	45	90	*94*	2.89	1.41

Note: The italicized diagonal values are squared multiple correlations.

Varimax Factor Solution for 10 Communication
Variables for 159 Deaf Persons

		I	II
C_1	Hearing (unaided)		49
C_2	Hearing (aided)		66
C_3	Speech reading	32	70
C_4	Reading	45	71
C_5	Manual signs	94	
C_6	Fingerspelling	94	
C_7	Speech		86
C_8	Writing	38	72
C_9	Manual signs	94	
C_{10}	Fingerspelling	96	
Percent of common variance		53.8	39.3

Note: Factor loadings less than .30 are omitted.

(a) Interpret the varimax factors. What does each of them represent?

(b) Does the way the variables that defined Factor 1 correspond to the way they are correlated? That is, is the empirical clustering of the variables by the principal axis technique consistent with the way those variables "go together" in the original correlation matrix?

8. (a) As suggested in the chapter, do the SPSS oblique rotation OBLIMIN on the California Psychological Inventory.

(b) Do the oblique factors seem to be easier to interpret than the uncorrelated, varimax factors?

(c) What are the correlations among the oblique factors?

(d) Which factors, correlated or uncorrelated, would you prefer here?

9. (a) Consider again the factor analysis of the CPI, and in particular, the first two rotated factors presented in Table 11.4. Can we have confidence in the reliability of these factors according to the Monte Carlo results of Guadagnoli and Velicer (1988)?

(b) Now consider the rotated factor loadings for the SAS run on the Personality Research Form given in Table 11.7. Can we have confidence in the reliability of the four rotated factors according to the Guadagnoli and Velicer study? For which factor(s) is the evidence strong, but not totally conclusive?

10. Look at the tables that follow. The first involves an exploratory factor analysis on Tellegen's three-factor model, that is, a principal axis analysis (squared multiple correlations were used as the communality estimates in the main diagonal) followed by a varimax rotation. The second is an exploratory factor analysis on the "big five" model, that is, a principal axis analysis followed by a varimax rotation. Note that those scales that should load on each factor according to the models have been boxed in.

(a) Concerning Tellegen's model in the top table, do we have a good fit for Factor 1? How about for Factors 2 and 3?

(b) Concerning the big five model (NEO scales), for which factors does there seem to be a good fit? For which factor(s) is the fit not so good? (Note: These tables are from Church and Burke, copyright © 1994, by the American Psychological Association. Reprinted with permission.)

Varimax-Rotated Factor Matrix for Multidimensional
Personality Questionnaire (MPQ) Scales

MPQ scale	Factors			h^2
	1	2	3	
Well being	**−.55**	−.04	**.37**	.43
Social potency	−.03	.23	**.50**	.30
Achievement	−.07	.22	**.67**	.50
Social closeness	**−.49**	.05	−.02	.24
Stress reaction	**.44**	.01	−.03	.19
Alienation	**.66**	−.16	.12	.48
Aggression	**.42**	**−.38**	.19	.36
Control	−.04	**.76**	.12	.59
Harmavoidance	−.09	**.54**	−.23	.35
Traditionalism	−.03	**.41**	−.05	.17
Absorption	.12	−.19	**.31**	.15

Note: Factor loadings greater than | .30 | are shown in boldface.

Varimax-Rotated Factor Matrix for NEO Scales

NEO scale	Factors					h^2
	1	2	3	4	5	
Neuroticism facets						
Anxiety	**.79**	−.01	.07	−.02	−.04	63
Hostility	**.43**	**−.56**	.03	.14	.06	.53
Depression	**.76**	−.17	.05	−.16	−.05	.64
Self-consciousness	**.73**	.02	−.16	−.14	−.16	.60
Impulsiveness	**.45**	.00	.23	−.05	**.39**	.40
Vulnerability	**.66**	−.18	−.14	−.28	.07	.57
Extraversion facets						
Warmth	−.06	**.65**	.15	.25	**.37**	.65
Gregariousness	−.10	.20	−.02	.02	**.60**	.41
Assertiveness	**−.36**	−.18	.14	**.61**	.21	.60
Activity	−.08	.07	−.02	**.53**	.08	.30
Excitement-seeking	−.01	05	.14	.04	**.56**	.33
Positive emotions	−.12	**.59**	.22	.27	**.35**	.61
Openness facets						
Fantasy	.15	.05	**.54**	−.11	.20	.37
Aesthetics	.13	.20	**.63**	.04	−.01	.45
Feelings	.17	**.45**	**.50**	.23	.13	.55
Actions	−.24	−.02	**.48**	−.15	.16	.33
Ideas	−.18	−.06	**.63**	.16	−.13	.48
Values	−.04	.18	**.43**	.03	.11	.23
Agreeableness	−.08	**.80**	.19	.01	.05	.69
Conscientiousness	−.13	**.32**	−.05	**.65**	−.25	.60

Note: Factor loadings greater than | .30 | are shown in boldface. Primary loadings hypothesized in the NEO Big Five model are shown in boxes.

11. Consider the following confirmatory factor analysis output from LISREL 8.

    (a) Draw the path diagram, labeling all "variables" clearly.

    (b) Are the variables loading significantly (test each at the .01 level) on the factor they were supposed to measure?

    (c) Does the chi square test indicate a good fit at the .05 level?

    (d) Does the value of RMSEA indicate a good fit?

    (e) The modification indices near the end indicate that we could reduce the chi square statistic considerably by adding an error covariance for TURN and PLACE and an error covariance for DASMBL and ASMBL. Should we consider doing this?

SIMPLIS INPUT FILE

TITLE : GATB – THREE CORRELATED FACTORS
OBSERVED VARIABLES: NAMES ARITH DIM VOCAB TOOLS MATH
SHAPES MARK PLACE TURN ASMBL DASMBL
CORRELATION MATRIX:

1.00
.697 1.00
.360 .366 1.00
.637 .580 .528 1.00
.586 .471 .554 .425 1.00
.552 .760 .468 .616 .369 1.00
.496 .411 .580 .444 .531 .400 1.00
.561 .501 .249 .465 .444 .407 .387 1.00
.338 .297 .276 .211 .292 .300 .323 .494 1.00
.349 .247 .279 .209 .336 .234 .401 .540 .773 1.00
.390 .319 .358 .267 .361 .208 .444 .439 .468 .476 1.00
.354 .325 .234 .283 .267 .311 .428 .422 .453 .482 .676 1.00

SAMPLE SIZE=200
LATENT VARIABLES=FACTOR1 FACTOR2 FACTOR3
RELATIONSHIPS:
ARITH MATH NAMES VOCAB=FACTOR1
TURN PLACE DASMBL ASMBL=FACTOR2
DIM SHAPES TOOLS=FACTOR3
END OF PROBLEM

OUTPUT

GATB – THREE CORRELATED
CORRELATION MATRIX TO BE ANALYZED

	NAMES	ARITH	DIM	VOCAB	TOOLS	MATH
NAMES	1.00					
ARITH	0.70	1.00				
DIM	0.36	0.37	1.00			
VOCAB	0.64	0.58	0.53	1.00		
TOOLS	0.59	0.47	0.55	0.42	1.00	
MATH	0.55	0.76	0.47	0.62	0.37	1.00
SHAPES	0.50	0.41	0.58	0.44	0.53	0.40
PLACE	0.34	0.30	0.28	0.21	0.29	0.30
TURN	0.35	0.25	0.28	0.21	0.34	0.23
ASMBL	0.39	0.32	0.36	0.27	0.36	0.21
DASMBL	0.35	0.32	0.23	0.28	0.27	0.31

CORRELATION MATRIX TO BE ANALYZED

	SHAPES	PLACE	TURN	ASMBL	DASMBL
SHAPES	1.00				
PLACE	0.32	1.00			
TURN	0.40	0.77	1.00		
ASMBL	0.44	0.47	0.48	1.00	
DASMBL	0.43	0.45	0.48	0.68	1.00

GATB – THREE CORRELATED
Number of Iterations = 11

LISREL ESTIMATES (MAXIMUM LIKELIHOOD)

NAMES = 0.79*FACTOR1, Errorvar. = 0.37, R^2 = 0.63
    (0.061)   (0.047)
    12.88   7.93

ARITH = 0.86*FACTOR1, Errorvar. = 0.25, R^2 = 0.75
    (0.059)   (0.040)
    14.71   6.36

DIM = 0.74*FACTOR3, Errorvar. = 0.46, R^2 = 0.54
    (0.067)   (0.061)
    11.07   7.46

VOCAB = 0.74*FACTOR1, Errorvar. = 0.45, R^2 = 0.55
    (0.063)   (0.053)
    11.74   8.50

TOOLS = 0.74*FACTOR3, Errorvar. = 0.46, R^2 = 0.54
    (0.067)   (0.061)
    11.08   7.45

MATH = 0.81*FACTOR1, Errorvar. = 0.34, R^2 = 0.66
    (0.061)   (0.045)
    13.34   7.62

SHAPES = 0.76*FACTOR3, Errorvar. = 0.42, R^2 = 0.58
    (0.066)   (0.060)
    11.54   7.05

PLACE = 0.84*FACTOR2, Errorvar. = 0.29, R^2 = 0.71
    (0.062)   (0.049)
    13.66   6.00

TURN = 0.86*FACTOR2, Errorvar. = 0.26, R^2 = 0.74
    (0.061)   (0.048)
    14.12   5.39

ASMBL = 0.63*FACTOR2, Errorvar = 0.60, R^2 = 0.40
    (0.068)   (0.067)
    9.31   9.00

DASMBL = 0.62*FACTOR2, Errorvar. = 0.62, R^2 = 0.38
    (0.068)   (0.068)
    9.13   9.05

GOODNESS OF FIT STATISTICS

CHI-SQUARE WITH 41 DEGREES OF FREEDOM = 225.61 (P = 0.0)
ESTIMATED NON-CENTRALITY PARAMETER (NCP) = 184.61

MINIMUM FIT FUNCTION VALUE = 1.13
POPULATION DISCREPANCY FUNCTION VALUE (F0) = 0.93
ROOT MEAN SQUARE ERROR OF APPROXIMATION (RMSEA) = 0.15
P-VALUE FOR TEST OF CLOSE FIT (RMSEA < 0.05) = 0.00000037

EXPECTED CROSS-VALIDATION INDEX (ECVI) = 1.38
ECVI FOR SATURATED MODEL = 0.66
ECVI FOR INDEPENDENCE MODEL = 6.43

CHI-SQUARE FOR INDEPENDENCE MODEL WITH 55 DEGREES OF FREEDOM = 1257.96
INDEPENDENCE AIC = 1279.96
MODEL AIC = 275.61
SATURATED AIC = 132.00
INDEPENDENCE CAIC = 1327.24
MODEL CAIC = 383.07
SATURATED CAIC = 415.69

ROOT MEAN SQUARE RESIDUAL (RMR) = 0.078
STANDARDIZED RMR = 0.078
GOODNESS OF FIT INDEX (GFI) = 0.84
ADJUSTED GOODNESS OF FIT INDEX (AGFI) = 0.74
PARSIMONY GOODNESS OF FIT INDEX (PGFI) = 0.52

NORMED FIT INDEX (NFI) = 0.82
NON-NORMED FIT INDEX (NNFI) = 0.79
PARSIMONY NORMED FIT INDEX (PNFI) = 0.61
COMPARATIVE FIT INDEX (CFI) = 0.85
INCREMENTAL FIT INDEX (IFI) = 0.85
RELATIVE FIT INDEX (RFI) = 0.76

CRITICAL N (CN) = 58.29

CONFIDENCE LIMITS COULD NOT BE COMPUTED DUE TO TOO SMALL P-VALUE
FOR CHI-SQUARE

GATB – THREE CORRELATED

SUMMARY STATISTICS FOR FITTED RESIDUALS
SMALLEST FITTED RESIDUAL = −0.09
MEDIAN FITTED RESIDUAL = 0.00
LARGEST FITTED RESIDUAL = 0.29
STEMLEAF PLOT
- 0 | 993777777666666555
- 0 | 332222000000000000
  0 | 1111123444
  0 | 55556668899
  1 | 0034
  1 | 6778
  2 |
  2 | 9

SUMMARY STATISTICS FOR STANDARDIZED RESIDUALS
SMALLEST STANDARDIZED RESIDUAL = −5.36
MEDIAN STANDARDIZED RESIDUAL = 0.00
LARGEST STANDARDIZED RESIDUAL = 8.83

STEMLEAF PLOT
- 4 | 410
- 2 | 5200420
- 0 | 98876643396443000000000000
  0 | 34678000111356778
  2 | 00362336
  4 | 54
  6 | 5
  8 | 8

LARGEST NEGATIVE STANDARDIZED RESIDUALS
RESIDUAL FOR	DIM AND	ARITH	−3.01
RESIDUAL FOR	VOCAB AND	ARITH	−4.13
RESIDUAL FOR	MATH AND	NAMES	−5.36
RESIDUAL FOR	ASMBL AND	PLACE	−3.22
RESIDUAL FOR	ASMBL AND	TURN	−3.98
RESIDUAL FOR	DASMBL AND	PLACE	−3.50
RESIDUAL FOR	DASMBL AND	TURN	−3.03

LARGEST POSITIVE STANDARDIZED RESIDUALS
RESIDUAL FOR	VOCAB AND	DIM	3.33
RESIDUAL FOR	TOOLS AND	NAMES	4.48
RESIDUAL FOR	MATH AND	ARITH	5.44
RESIDUAL FOR	TURN AND	PLACE	8.83
RESIDUAL FOR	ASMBL AND	NAMES	3.21
RESIDUAL FOR	ASMBL AND	SHAPES	3.55
RESIDUAL FOR	DASMBL AND	NAMES	2.58
RESIDUAL FOR	DASMBL AND	SHAPES	3.28
RESIDUAL FOR	DASMBL AND	ASMBL	7.48

THE MODIFICATION INDICES SUGGEST TO ADD THE

PATH TO	FROM	DECREASE IN CHI-SQUARE	NEW ESTIMATE
ARITH	FACTOR3	9.3	−0.28
ASMBL	FACTOR3	12.0	0.29

THE MODIFICATION INDICES SUGGEST TO ADD AN ERROR COVARIANCE

BETWEEN	AND	DECREASE IN CHI-SQUARE	NEW ESTIMATE
DIM	NAMES	14.5	−0.14
DIM	ARITH	8.0	−0.09
VOCAB	ARITH	17.1	−0.16
VOCAB	DIM	16.4	0.16
TOOLS	NAMES	18.7	0.16
MATH	NAMES	28.8	−0.21
MATH	ARITH	29.5	0.22
MATH	DIM	8.8	0.11
MATH	TOOLS	10.0	−0.11
TURN	PLACE	78.0	0.60
ASMBL	PLACE	10.4	−0.15
ASMBL	TURN	15.8	−0.19
DASMBL	PLACE	12.3	−0.17
DASMBL	TURN	9.2	−0.14
DASMBL	ASMBL	56.0	0.37

12. Consider the following confirmatory factor analysis output from LISREL 8.
    (a) Draw the path diagram, labeling all "variables" clearly.
    (b) Are VISUAL and VERBAL significantly correlated at the .01 level?
    (c) Are the indicators for VERBAL significantly linked to it at the .01 level?
    (d) Does the chi square test indicate a good fit at the .05 level?
    (e) Do some of the other indices (e.g., AGFI and NNFI) also indicate a good fit?

SIMPLIS INPUT FILE

```
TITLE : THREE FACTOR FROM JORESKOG
OBSERVED VARIABLES: VISPERC CUBES LOZENGES PARCOMP SENCOMP WORD ADD
COUNT SCCAPS
CORRELATION MATRIX:
1.00
.318  1.00
.436  .419  1.00
.335  .234  .323  1.00
.304  .157  .283  .722  1.00
.326  .195  .350  .714  .685  1.00
.116  .057  .056  .203  .246  .170  1.00
.314  .145  .229  .095  .181  .113  .585  1.00
.489  .239  .361  .309  .345  .280  .408  .512  1.00
SAMPLE SIZE: 145
LATENT VARIABLES: VISUAL VERBAL SPEED
RELATIONSHIPS:
VISPERC CUBES LOZENGES SCCAPS=VISUAL
PARCOMP SENCOMP WORD=VERBAL
ADD COUNT SCCAPS=SPEED
END OF PROBLEM
```

OUTPUT

THREE FACTOR FROM
CORRELATION MATRIX TO BE ANALYZED

	VISPERC	CUBES	LOZENGES	PARCOMP	SENCOMP	WORD
VISPERC	1.00					
CUBES	0.32	1.00				
LOZENGES	0.44	0.42	1.00			
PARCOMP	0.34	0.23	0.32	1.00		
SENCOMP	0.30	0.16	0.28	0.72	1.00	
WORD	0.33	0.20	0.35	0.71	0.68	1.00
ADD	0.12	0.06	0.06	0.20	0.25	0.17
COUNT	0.31	0.14	0.23	0.10	0.18	0.11
SCCAPS	0.49	0.24	0.36	0.31	0.34	0.28

CORRELATION MATRIX TO BE ANALYZED

	ADD	COUNT	SCCAPS
ADD	1.00		
COUNT	0.58	1.00	
SCCAPS	0.41	0.51	1.00

THREE FACTOR FROM
Number of Iterations = 8

LISREL ESTIMATES (MAXIMUM LIKELIHOOD)

VISPERC = 0.71*VISUAL, Errorvar.= 0.50, R^2 = 0.50
　(0.087)　　　　　　(0.090)
　　8.16　　　　　　　5.53

CUBES = 0.48*VISUAL, Errorvar.= 0.77, R^2 = 0.23
　(0.091)　　　　　　(0.10)
　　5.33　　　　　　　7.62

LOZENGES = 0.65*VISUAL, Errorvar.= 0.58, R^2 = 0.42
　(0.087)　　　　　　(0.091)
　　7.43　　　　　　　6.34

PARCOMP = 0.87*VERBAL, Errorvar.= 0.25, R^2 = 0.75
　(0.070)　　　　　　(0.051)
　12.37　　　　　　　4.81

SENCOMP = 0.83*VERBAL, Errorvar.= 0.31, R^2 = 0.69
　(0.071)　　　　　　(0.054)
　11.61　　　　　　　5.80

WORD = 0.83*VERBAL, Errorvar.= 0.32, R^2 = 0.68
　(0.072)　　　　　　(0.054)
　11.51　　　　　　　5.91

ADD = 0.68*SPEED, Errorvar.= 0.54, R^2 = 0.46
　(0.089)　　　　　　(0.093)
　　7.68　　　　　　　5.76

COUNT = 0.86*SPEED, Errorvar.= 0.26, R^2 = 0.74
　(0.092)　　　　　　(0.11)
　　9.37　　　　　　　2.31

SCCAPS = 0.46*VISUAL + 0.42*SPEED, Errorvar.= 0.47, R^2 = 0.53
　(0.089)　　　　　　(0.088)　(0.073)
　　5.15　　　　　　　4.73　　6.42

CORRELATION MATRIX OF INDEPENDENT VARIABLES

	VISUAL	VERBAL	SPEED
VISUAL	1.00		
VERBAL	0.56		1.00
	(0.08)		
	6.87		
SPEED	0.39	0.22	1.00
	(0.10)	(0.10)	
	3.73	2.32	

GOODNESS OF FIT STATISTICS

CHI-SQUARE WITH 23 DEGREES OF FREEDOM = 29.01 (P = 0.18)
ESTIMATED NON-CENTRALITY PARAMETER (NCP) = 6.01
90 PERCENT CONFIDENCE INTERVAL FOR NCP = (0.0 ; 23.96)
MINIMUM FIT FUNCTION VALUE = 0.20
POPULATION DISCREPANCY FUNCTION VALUE (F0) = 0.042
90 PERCENT CONFIDENCE INTERVAL FOR F0 = (0.0 ; 0.17)
ROOT MEAN SQUARE ERROR OF APPROXIMATION (RMSEA) = 0.043
90 PERCENT CONFIDENCE INTERVAL FOR RMSEA = (0.0 ; 0.085)
P-VALUE FOR TEST OF CLOSE FIT (RMSEA < 0.05) = 0.57

EXPECTED CROSS-VALIDATION INDEX (ECVI) = 0.51
90 PERCENT CONFIDENCE INTERVAL FOR ECVI = (0.47 ; 0.63)
ECVI FOR SATURATED MODEL = 0.62
ECVI FOR INDEPENDENCE MODEL = 3.57

CHI-SQUARE FOR INDEPENDENCE MODEL WITH 36 DEGREES OF FREEDOM = 496.67
INDEPENDENCE AIC = 514.67
MODEL AIC = 73.01
SATURATED AIC = 90.00
INDEPENDENCE CAIC = 550.46
MODEL CAIC= 160.50
SATURATED CAIC = 268.95

ROOT MEAN SQUARE RESIDUAL (RMR) = 0.045
STANDARDIZED RMR = 0.045
GOODNESS OF FIT INDEX (GFI) = 0.96
ADJUSTED GOODNESS OF FIT INDEX (AGFI) = 0.92
PARSIMONY GOODNESS OF FIT INDEX (PGFI) = 0.49

NORMED FIT INDEX (NFI) = 0.94
NON-NORMED FIT INDEX (NNFI) = 0.98
PARSIMONY NORMED FIT INDEX (PNFI) = 0.60
COMPARATIVE FIT INDEX (CFI) = 0.99
INCREMENTAL FIT INDEX (IFI) = 0.99
RELATIVE FIT INDEX (RFI) = 0.91

CRITICAL N (CN) = 207.70

THREE FACTOR FROM

SUMMARY STATISTICS FOR FITTED RESIDUALS
SMALLEST FITTED RESIDUAL = −0.12
MEDIAN FITTED RESIDUAL = 0.00
LARGEST FITTED RESIDUAL = 0.12

STEMLEAF PLOT
 - 10 | 6
  - 8 |
  - 6 | 21171
  - 4 | 52
  - 2 | 7444
  - 0 | 8787210000000000000
    0 | 22791
    2 | 2

```
  4 | 5016
  6 | 17
  8 |
 10 | 5
 12 | 0
```

SUMMARY STATISTICS FOR STANDARDIZED RESIDUALS
SMALLEST STANDARDIZED RESIDUAL = −1.96
MEDIAN STANDARDIZED RESIDUAL = 0.00

13. For exercise 2, use ONLY the first 15 variables. Obtain three factors for the following runs:

    (a) Run a components analysis and varimax rotation.

    (b) Run a components analysis and oblique rotation.

    (c) Which of the above solutions would you prefer?

14. Consider the RMSEA's in Tables 11.16 and 11.17. Do they offer us a clear choice as to which model is to be preferred?

15. Consider the following part of the quote from Pedhazur and Schmelkin (1991), "... It boils down to the question: Are aspects of a postulated multidimensional construct intercorrelated? The answer to this question is relegated to the status of an assumption when an orthogonal rotation is employed."

    (a) What did they mean by the last part of this statement?

12

Canonical Correlation

12.1 Introduction

In Chapter 3, we examined breaking down the association between two sets of variables using multivariate regression analysis. This is the appropriate technique if our interest is in prediction, and if we wish to focus our attention primarily on the individual variables (both predictors and dependent), rather than on linear combinations of the variables. *Canonical correlation* is another means of breaking down the association for two sets of variables, and *is appropriate if the wish is to parsimoniously describe the number and nature of mutually independent relationships existing between the two sets*. This is accomplished through the use of pairs of linear combinations that are uncorrelated.

Because the combinations are uncorrelated, we will obtain a very nice additive partitioning of the total between association. Thus, there are several similarities to principal components analysis (discussed in Chapter 11). Both are variable reduction schemes that use uncorrelated linear combinations. In components analysis, generally the first few linear combinations (the components) account for most of the total variance in the original set of variables, whereas in canonical correlation the first few pairs of linear combinations (the so-called *canonical variates*) generally account for most of the between association. Also, in interpreting the principal components, we used the correlations between the original variables and the components. In canonical correlation, the correlations between the original variables and the canonical variates will again be used to name the canonical variates.

One could consider doing canonical regression. However, as Darlington et al. (1973) stated, investigators are generally not interested in predicting linear combinations of the dependent variables.

Let us now consider a couple of situations where canonical correlation would be useful. An investigator wishes to explore the relationship between a set of personality variables (say, as measured by the Cattell 16 PF scale or by the California Psychological Inventory) and a battery of achievement test scores for a group of high school students. The first pair of canonical variates will tell us what type of personality profile (as revealed by the linear combination and named by determining which of the original variables correlate most highly with this linear combination) is maximally associated with a given profile of achievement (as revealed by the linear combination for the achievement scores). The second pair of canonical variates will yield an uncorrelated personality profile that is associated with a different pattern of achievement, and so on.

As a second example, consider the case where a single group of subjects is measured on the *same* set of variables at two different points in time. We wish to investigate the stability of the personality profiles of female college subjects from their freshman to their senior years. Canonical correlation analysis will reveal which dimension of personality is most stable or reliable. This dimension would be named by determining which of the original variables correlate most highly with the canonical variates corresponding to the largest canonical correlation. Then the analysis will find an uncorrelated dimension of personality that is next most reliable. This dimension is named by determining which of the original variables has the highest correlations with the second pair of canonical variates, and so on. This type of *multivariate reliability analysis* using canonical correlation has been in existence for some time. Merenda, Novack, and Bonaventure (1976) did such an analysis on the subtest scores of the California Test of Mental Maturity for a group of elementary school children.

12.2 The Nature of Canonical Correlation

To focus more specifically on what canonical correlation does, consider the following hypothetical situation. A researcher is interested in the relationship between "job success" and "academic achievement." He has two measures of job success: (a) the amount of money the individual is making, and (b) the status of the individual's position. He has four measures of academic achievement: (a) high school GPA, (b) college GPA, (c) number of degrees, and (d) ranking of the college where the last degree was obtained. We denote the first set of variables by x's and the second set of variables (academic achievement) by y's.

The canonical correlation procedure first finds two linear combinations (one from the job success measures and one from the academic achievement measures) that have the maximum possible Pearson correlation. That is,

$$u_1 = a_{11}x_1 + a_{12}x_2 \quad \text{and} \quad v_1 = b_{11}y_1 + b_{12}y_2 + b_{13}y_3 + b_{14}y_4$$

are found such that $r_{u_1 v_1}$ is maximum. Note that if this were done with data, the a's and b's would be known numerical values, and a single score for each subject on each linear composite could be obtained. These two sets of scores for the subjects are then correlated just as we would perform the calculations for the scores on two individual variables, say x and y. The maximized correlation for the scores on two linear composites ($r_{u_1 v_1}$) is called the *largest canonical correlation*, and we denote it by R_1.

Now, the procedure searches for a second pair of linear combinations, *uncorrelated* with the first pair, such that the Pearson correlation between this pair is the next largest possible. That is,

$$u_2 = a_{21}x_1 + a_{22}x_2 \quad \text{and} \quad v_2 = b_{21}y_1 + b_{22}y_2 + b_{23}y_3 + b_{24}y_4$$

are found such that $r_{u_2 v_2}$ is maximum. This correlation, because of the way the procedure is set up, will be less than $r_{u_1 v_1}$. For example, $r_{u_1 v_1}$ might be .73 and $r_{u_2 v_2}$ might be .51. We denote the second largest canonical correlation by R_2.

When we say that this second pair of canonical variates is uncorrelated with the first pair we mean that (a) the canonical variates *within* each set are uncorrelated, that is, $r_{u_1 u_2} = 0$, and (b) the canonical variates are uncorrelated *across* sets, that is, $r_{u_1 v_2} = r_{v_1 u_2} = 0$.

For this example, there are just two possible canonical correlations and hence only two pairs of canonical variates. In general, if one has p variables in one set and q in the other set, the number of possible canonical correlations is min $(p,q) = m$ (see Tatsuoka, 1971, p. 186, for the reason). Therefore, for our example, there are only min $(2,4) = 2$ canonical correlations. To determine how many of the possible canonical correlations indicate statistically significant relationships, a residual test procedure identical in form to that for discriminant analysis is used. Thus, canonical correlation is still another example of a mathematical maximization procedure (as were multiple regression and principal components), which partitions the total between association through the use of uncorrelated pairs of linear combinations.

12.3 Significance Tests

First, we determine whether there is *any* association between the two sets with the following test statistic:

$$V = -\{(N-1.5)-(p+q)/2\} \sum_{i=1}^{m} \ln(1-R_i^2)$$

where N is sample size, and R_i denotes the ith canonical correlation. V is approximately distributed as a χ^2 statistic with pq degrees of freedom. If this overall test is significant, then the largest canonical correlation is removed and the residual is tested for significance. If we denote the term in braces by k, then the first residual test statistic (V_1) is given by:

$$V_1 = -k \cdot \sum_{i=2}^{m} \ln(1-R_i^2)$$

V_1 is distributed as a χ^2 with $(p-1)(q-1)$ degrees of freedom. If V_1 is not significant, then we conclude that only the largest canonical correlation is significant. If V_1 is significant, then we continue and examine the next residual (which has the two largest roots removed), V_2, where:

$$V_2 = -k \cdot \sum_{i=3}^{m} \ln(1-R_i^2)$$

V_2 is distributed as a χ^2 with $(p-2)(q-2)$ degrees of freedom. If V_2 is not significant, then we conclude that only the two largest canonical correlations are significant.

If V_2 is significant, we examine the next residual, and so on. In general, then, when the residual after removing the first s canonical correlations is not significant, we conclude that only the first s canonical correlations are significant. The degree of freedom for the ith residual is $(p-i)(q-i)$.

When we introduced canonical correlation, it was indicated that the canonical variates additively partition the association. The reason they do is because the variates are uncorrelated both within and across sets. As an analogy, recall that when the predictors are uncorrelated in multiple regression, we obtain an additive partitioning of the variance on the dependent variable.

The sequential testing procedure has been criticized by Harris (1976). However, a Monte Carlo study by Mendoza, Markos, and Gonter (1978) has refuted Harris's criticism. Mendoza et al. considered the case of a total of 12 variables, six variables in each set, and chose six population situations. The situations varied from three strong population canonical correlations (η_i), .9, .8, and .7, to three weak population canonical correlations (.3, .2, and .1), to a null condition (all population canonical correlations = 0). The last condition was inserted to check on the accuracy of their generation procedure. One thousand sample matrices, varying in size from 25 to 100, were generated from each population, and the number of significant canonical correlations declared by Bartlett's test (the one we have described) and three other tests were recorded.

Strong population canonical correlations (.9, .8, and .7) will be detected more than 90% of the time with as small a sample size as 50. For a more moderate population canonical correlation (.50), a sample size of 100 is needed to detect it about 67% of the time. A weak population canonical correlation (.30), which is probably *not* worth detecting because it would be of little practical value, requires a sample size of 200 to be detected about 60% of the time. It is fortunate that the tests are conservative in detecting weaker canonical correlations, given the tenuous nature of trying to accurately interpret the canonical variates associated with smaller canonical correlations (Barcikowski and Stevens, 1975), as we show in the next section.

12.4 Interpreting the Canonical Variates

The two methods in use for interpreting the canonical variates are the same as those used for interpreting the discriminant functions:

1. Examine the standardized coefficients.
2. Examine the canonical variate–variable correlations.

For both of these methods, it is the largest (in absolute value) coefficients or correlations that are used. I now refer the reader back to the corresponding section in the chapter on discriminant analysis, because all of the discussion there is relevant here and will not be repeated.

I do add, however, some detail from the Barcikowski and Stevens (1975) Monte Carlo study on the stability of the coefficients and the correlations, since it was for canonical correlation. They sampled eight correlation matrices from the literature and found that *the number of subjects per variable necessary to achieve reliability in determining the most important variables for the two largest canonical correlations was very large, ranging from 42/1 to 68/1. This is a somewhat conservative estimate, and if we were just interpreting the largest canonical correlation, then a ratio of about 20/1 is sufficient for accurate interpretation.* However, it doesn't seem likely, in general, that in practice there will be just one significant canonical correlation. The association between two sets of variables is likely to be more complex than that.

To impress on the reader the danger of misinterpretation if the subject to variable ratio is not large, we consider the *second* largest canonical correlation for a 31-variable example from our study. Suppose we were to interpret the left canonical variate using the canonical variate–variable correlations for 400 subjects. This yields a subject to variable ratio of about 13 to 1, a ratio many readers might feel is large enough. However, the frequency rank table (i.e., a ranking of how often each variable was ranked from most to least important) that resulted is presented here:

Var.	Total number of times less than third	Rank			Population value
		1	2	3	
1	76	4	11	9	.43
2	43	34	7	16	.64
3	86	1	4	9	.10
4	74	6	12	8	.16
5	60	19	16	5	.07
6	92	2	4	2	.09
7	78	1	5	16	.34
8	64	11	13	12	.40
9	72	6	13	9	.27
10	55	16	15	14	.62

Variables 2 and 10 are clearly the most important. Yet, with an *n* of 400, about 50% of the time each of them is *not* identified as being one of the three most important variables for interpreting the canonical variate. Furthermore, Variable 5, which is clearly not an important variable in the population, is identified 40% of the time as one of the three most important variables.

In view of the above reliability results, an investigator considering a canonical analysis on a fairly large number of variables (say 20 in one set and 15 in the other set) should consider doing a components analysis on *each* set to reduce the total number of variables dramatically, and then relate the two sets of components via canonical correlation. This should be done even if the investigator has 300 subjects, for this yields a subject to variable ratio less than 10 to 1 with the *original* set of variables. The practical implementation of this procedure, as seen in Section 12.7, can be accomplished efficiently and elegantly with the SAS package.

12.5 Computer Example Using SAS CANCORR

To illustrate how to run canonical correlation on SAS CANCORR and how to interpret the output, we consider data from a study by Lehrer and Schimoler (1975). This study examined the cognitive skills underlying an inductive problem-solving method that has been used to develop critical reasoning skills for educable mentally retarded (EMR) children. A total of 112 EMR children were given the Cognitive Abilities Test, which consists of four subtests measuring the following skills: oral vocabulary (CAT1), relational concepts (CAT2), multimental concepts (one that doesn't belong) CAT3, and quantitative concepts (CAT4). We relate these skills via canonical correlation to seven subtest scores from the Children's Analysis of Social Situations (CASS), a test that is a modification of the Test of Social Inference. The CASS was developed as a means of assessing inductive reasoning processes. For the CASS, the children respond to a sample picture and various pictorial stimuli at various levels: CASS1— labeling—identification of a relevant object; CASS2—detail—represents a further elaboration of an object; CASS3—low-level inference—a guess concerning a picture based on obvious clues; CASS4—high-level inference; CASS5—prediction—a statement concerning future outcomes of a situation; CASS6—low-level generalization—a rule derived from the context of a picture, but that is specific to the situation in that picture; and CASS7—high-level inference—deriving a rule that extends beyond the specific situation.

TABLE 12.1

Correlation Matrix for Cognitive Ability Variables and Inductive Reasoning Variables

CAT1	1.000									
CAT2	.662	1.000								
CAT3	.661	.697	1.000							
CAT4	.641	.730	.703	1.000						
CASS1	.131	−.112	.033	.040	1.000					
CASS2	.253	.031	.185	.149	.641	1.000				
CASS3	.332	.133	.197	.132	.574	.630	1.000			
CASS4	.381	.304	.304	.382	.312	.509	.583	1.000		
CASS5	.413	.313	.276	.382	.254	.491	.491	.731	1.000	
CASS6	.520	.485	.450	.466	.034	.117	.294	.595	.534	1.000
CASS7	.434	.392	.380	.390	.065	.100	.203	.328	.355	.508	1.000

TABLE 12.2

SAS CANCORR Control Lines for Canonical Correlation Relating Cognitive Abilities Subtests to Subtests From Children's Analysis of Social Situations

```
TITLE 'CANONICAL CORRELATION';
DATA CANCORR(TYPE = CORR);
TYPE = 'CORR';
INPUT NAME $  CAT1  CAT2  CAT3  CAT4  CASS1 CASS2 CASS3 CASS4 CASS5 CASS6 CASS7;
CARDS;
```

CAT1	1.00 ...									
CAT2	.662	1.00 ...								
CAT3	.661	.697	1.00 ...							
CAT4	.641	.730	.703	1.00 ...						
CASS1	.131	−.112	.033	.040	1.00 ...					
CASS2	.253	.031	.185	.149	.641	1.00 ...				
CASS3	.332	.133	.197	.132	.574	.630	1.00 ...			
CASS4	.381	.304	.304	.382	.312	.509	.583	1.00 ...		
CASS5	.413	.313	.276	.382	.254	.491	.491	.731	1.00 ...	
CASS6	.520	.485	.450	.466	.034	.117	.294	.595	.534	1.00 ...
CASS7	.434	.392	.380	.390	.065	.100	.203	.328	.355	.508	1.00

```
PROC CANCORR EDF = 111 CORR;
VAR  CAT1  CAT2  CAT3  CAT4;
WITH  CASS1  CAS2  CASS3  CASS4  CASS5  CASS6  CASS7;
```

In Table 12.1 we present the correlation matrix for the 11 variables, and in Table 12.2 give the control lines from SAS CANCORR for running the canonical correlation analysis, along with the significance tests.

Table 12.3 has the standardized coefficients and canonical variate–variable correlations that we use jointly to interpret the pair of canonical variates corresponding to the only significant canonical correlation. These coefficients and loadings are boxed in on Table 12.3. For the cognitive ability variables (CAT), note that all four variables have uniformly strong loadings, although the loading for CAT1 is extremely high (.953). Using the standardized coefficients, we see that CAT2 through CAT4 are redundant, because their coefficients are considerably lower than that for CAT1. For the CASS variables, the loadings on CASS4 through CASS7 are clearly the strongest and of uniform magnitude. Turning to the

TABLE 12.3

Standardized Coefficients and Canonical Variate–Variable Loadings

Standardized Canonical Coefficients for the 'VAR' Variables

	VI	V	V3	V$
CAT1	0.6331	−0.9449	−0.0508	−0.9198
CAT2	0.1660	1.1759	−1.0730	−0.3528
CAT3	0.1387	−0.5642	−0.3944	1.4179
CAT4	0.1849	0.4858	.5341	0.0334

Standardized Canonical Coefficients for the 'WITH' Variables

	W1	W2	W3	W4
CASS1	−0.1513	−0.3613	0.8506	−0.3307
CASS2	0.2444	−0.5973	−0.0118	1.0508
CASS3	0.1144	−0.4815	−1.0841	−0.6960
CASS4	−0.0954	0.6193	0.6808	0.4785
CASS5	0.1416	0.2564	0.4075	−1.1752
CASS6	0.6355	−0.1473	−0.3623	0.3471
CASS7	0.3681	0.0394	0.0008	0.2202

Correlations Between the 'VAR' Variables and Their Canonical Variables

	V1	V2	V3	V4
CAT1	0.9532	−0.2281	−0.0384	−0.1947d
CAT2	0.8168	0.5117	−0.2616	0.0510
CAT3	0.8025	−0.0287	−0.1004	0.5874
CAT4	0.8091	0.3430	0.4418	0.1802

Correlations Between the 'WITH' Variables and Their Canonical Variables

	W1	W2	W3	W4
CASS1	0.1228	−0.7646	0.5245	−0.1798
CASS2	0.3517	−0.7044	0.3548	0.1294
CASS3	0.4570	−0.6136	−0.1126	−0.3752
CASS4	0.6509	0.0345	0.3907	−0.0760
CASS5	0.6796	0.0230	0.3899	−0.4717
CASS6	0.8984	0.1544	−0.0304	0.0231
CASS7	0.7477	0.0778	0.0187	0.0785

coefficients for those variables, we see that CASS4 and CASS5 are redundant, because they clearly have the smallest coefficients. Thus, the only significant linkage between the two sets of variables relates oral vocabulary (CAT1) to the children's ability to generalize in social situations, particularly low-level generalization. We now consider a study from the literature that used canonical correlation analysis.

12.6 A Study That Used Canonical Correlation

A study by Tetenbaum (1975) addressed the issue of the validity of student ratings of teachers. She noted that current instruments generally list several teaching behaviors and ask the student to rate the instructor on each of them. The assumption is made that all students focus on the same teaching behavior, and furthermore, that when focusing on the same behavior, students perceive it in the same way. Tetenbaum noted that principles from social perception theory (Warr and Knapper, 1968) make both of these assumptions questionable. She argued that the social psychological needs of the students would influence their ratings, stating, "It was reasoned that in the process of rating a teacher the student focuses on the need-related aspects of the perceptual situation and bases his judgment on those areas of the teacher's performance most relevant to his own needs" (p. 418).

To assess student needs, the *Personality Research Form* was administered to 405 graduate students. The entire scale was not administered because some of the needs were not relevant to an academic setting. The part administered was then factor analyzed and a four-factor solution was obtained. For each factor, the three subscales having the highest loadings (.50) were selected to represent that factor, with the exception of one subscale (dominance), which had a high loading on more than one factor, and one subscale (harm avoidance), which was not felt to be relevant to the classroom setting. The final instrument consisted of 12 scales, three scales representing each of the four obtained factors: Factor I, Cognitive Structure (CS), Impulsivity (IM), Order (OR); Factor II, Endurance (EN), Achievement (AC), Understanding (UN); Factor III, Affiliation (AF), Autonomy (AU), Succorance (SU); Factor IV, Aggression (AG), Defendance (DE), Abasement (AB). These factors were named Need for Control, Need for Intellectual Striving, Need for Gregariousness-Defendance, and Need for Ascendancy, respectively.

Student ratings of teachers were obtained on an instrument constructed by Tetenbaum that consisted of 12 vignettes, each describing a college classroom in which the teacher was engaged in a particular set of behaviors. The particular behaviors were designed to correspond to the four need factors; that is, within the 12 vignettes, there were three replications for each of the four teacher orientations. For example, in three teacher vignettes, the orientation was aimed at meeting control needs. In these vignettes, the teachers attempted to control the classroom environment by organizing and structuring all lessons and assignments by stressing order, neatness, clarity, and logic; and by encouraging deliberation of thought and moderation of emotion so that the students would know what was expected of them.

Tetenbaum hypothesized that specific student needs (e.g., control needs) would be related to teacher orientations that met those needs. The 12 need variables (Set 1) were related to the 12 rating variables (Set 2) via canonical correlation. Three significant canonical correlations were obtained: $R_1 = .486$, $R_2 = .389$, and $R_3 = .323$ ($p < .01$ in all cases). Tetenbaum chose to use the canonical variate–variable correlations to interpret the variates. These are presented in Table 12.4. Examining the underlined correlations for the first pair (i.e., for the largest canonical correlation), we see that it clearly reflects the congruence between the intellectual striving needs and ratings on the corresponding vignettes, as well as the congruence between the ascendancy needs and ratings. The second pair of canonical variates (corresponding to the second largest canonical correlation) reflects the congruence between the control needs and the ratings. Note that the correlation for impulsivity is negative, because a low score on this variable would imply a high rating for a teacher who exhibits order and moderation of emotion. The interpretation of the third pair of canonical variates is not as clean as it was for the first two pairs. Nevertheless, the correspondence between gregariousness–dependency needs and ratings is revealed, a correspondence that did *not* appear for the first two pairs. However, there are "high" loadings on other needs and ratings as well. The interested reader is referred to Tetenbaum's article for a discussion of why this may have happened.

TABLE 12.4

Canonical Variate–Variable Correlations for Tetenbaum Study

		Canonical Variables				
First Pair		**Second Pair**		**Third Pair**		
Needs	**Ratings**	**Needs**	**Ratings**	**Needs**	**Ratings**	
.111	.028	.614	.453	−.018	−.325	⎫
−.099	−.051	−.785	.491	.078	−.397	⎬ Control
.065	.292	.774	.597	−.050	.059	⎭
−.537	−.337	.210	.263	.439	.177	⎫
−.477	−.294	.252	.125	.500	.102	⎬ Intellectual Striving
−.484	−.520	−.005	.154	.452	.497	⎭
−.134	−.233	−.343	−.210	−.354	−.335	⎫
.270	−.141	.016	.114	.657	−.468	⎬ Gregarious
−.271	−.072	−.155	−.175	−.414	−.579	⎭
−.150	.395	.205	.265	.452	.211	⎫
.535	.507	−.254	.034	.421	.361	⎬ Ascendancy
.333	.673	−.312	−.110	.289	.207	⎭

Note: Correlations > |.3| are underlined.

In summary, then, the correspondence that Tetenbaum hypothesized between student needs and ratings was clearly revealed by canonical correlation. Two of the need–rating correspondences were revealed by the first canonical correlation, a third correspondence (for control needs) was established by the second canonical correlation, and finally the gregariousness need–rating correspondence was revealed by the third canonical correlation.

Through the use of factor analysis, the author in this study was able to reduce the number of variables to 24 and achieve a fairly large subject to variable ratio (about 17/1). Based on our Monte Carlo results, one could interpret the largest canonical correlation with confidence; however, the second and third canonical correlations should be interpreted with some caution.

12.7 Using SAS for Canonical Correlation on Two Sets of Factor Scores

As indicated previously, if there is a large or fairly large number of variables in each of two sets, it is desirable to do a factor analysis on each set of variables for two reasons:

1. To obtain a more parsimonious description of what each set of variables is really measuring.
2. To reduce the total number of variables that will appear in the eventual canonical correlation analysis so that a much larger subject/variable ratio is obtained, making for more reliable results.

TABLE 12.5

SAS Control Lines for a Components Analysis on Each of Two Sets of Variables and Then a Canonical Correlation Analysis on the Two Sets of Factor Scores

DATA NATACAD;
INPUT QUALITY NFACUL NGRADS PCTSUPP PCTGRT NARTIC PCTPUB;
CARDS;
DATA
① ⎡ PRINCOMP N = 2 OUT = FSCORE1;
⎣ VAR NFACUL NGRADS PCTSUPP;
② ⎡ PROC PRINCOMP N = 3 PREFIX = PCTSET2 OUT = FSCORE2;
⎣ VAR PCTGRT NARTIC PCTPUB;
③   PRINT DATA = FSCORE2;
⎡ PROC CANCORR CORR;
④ ⎢ VAR PRIN1 PRIN2;
⎣ WITH PCSET21 PCSET22 PCSET23;

① The principal components procedure is called and a components analysis is done on only the three variables indicated.

② The components procedure is called again, this time to do a components analysis on the PCTGRT, NARTIC and PCTPUB variables. To distinguish the names for the components retained for this second analysis, we use the PREFIX option.

③ This statement is to obtain a listing of the data for all the variables, that is, the original variables, the factor scores for the two components for the first analysis, and the factor scores for the three components from the second analysis.

④ The canonical correlation procedure is called to determine the relationship between the two components from the first analysis and the three components from the second analysis.

The practical implementation of doing the component analyses and then passing the factor scores for a canonical correlation can be accomplished quite efficiently and elegantly with the SAS package. To illustrate, we use the National Academy of Science data from Chapter 3. Those data were based on 46 observations and involved the following seven variables: QUALITY, NFACUL, NGRADS, PCTSUPP, PCTGRT, NARTIC, and PCTPUB. We use SAS to do a components analysis on NFACUL, NGRADS, and PCTSUPP and then do a separate component analysis on PCTGRT, NARTIC, and PCTPUB. Obviously, with such a small number of variables in each set, a factor analysis is really not needed, but this example is for pedagogical purposes only. Then we use the SAS canonical correlation program (CANCORR) to relate the two sets of factor scores. The complete SAS control lines for doing both component analyses and the canonical correlation analysis on the factor scores are given in Table 12.5.

Now, let us consider a more realistic example, that is, where factor analysis is really needed. Suppose an investigator has 15 variables in set X and 20 variables in set Y. With 250 subjects, she wishes to run a canonical correlation analysis to determine the relationship between the two sets of variables. Recall from Section 12.4 that at least 20 subjects per variable are needed for reliable results, and the investigator is not near that ratio. Thus, a components analysis is run on each set of variables to achieve a more adequate ratio and to determine more parsimoniously the main constructs involved for each set of variables. The components analysis and varimax rotation are done for each set. On examining the output for the two component analyses, using Kaiser's rule and the scree test in combination, she decides to retain three factors for set X and four factors for set Y. In addition, from examination of the output, the investigator finds that the communalities for variables 2 and 7 are low. That is, these variables are relatively independent of what the three factors are measuring, and thus she decides to retain these original variables for the eventual canonical analysis. Similarly, the communality for Variable 12 in set Y is low, and that variable will also be retained for the canonical analysis.

We denote the variables for set X by X1, X2, X3, ... , X15 and the variables for set Y by Y1, Y2, Y3, ... , Y20. The complete control lines in this case are:

```
DATA REAL;
INPUT   X1 X2 X3 X4 X5 X6 X7 X8 X9 X10 X11 X12 X13 X14 X15
Y1 Y2 Y3 Y4 Y5 Y6 Y7 Y8 Y9 Y10 Y11 Y12 Y13 Y14 Y15 Y16 Y17
Y18 Y19 Y20;
CARDS;

    DATA

PROC FACTOR ROTATE = VARIMAX N = 3 SCREE OUT = FSCORES1;
VAR X1 – X15;
PROC DATASETS;
MODIFY FSCORES1;
RENAME FACTOR1 = SET1FAC1 FACTOR2 = SET1FAC2 FACTOR 3 = SET1FAC3;
PROC FACTOR ROTATE = VARIMAX N = 4 SCREE OUT = FSCORES2;
VAR Y1 – Y20;
PROC PRINT DATA = FSCORES2;
PROC CANCORR CORR;
VAR SET1FAC1 SET1FAC2 SET1FAC3 X2 X7;
WITH FACTOR1 FACTOR2 FACTOR3 FACTOR4 Y12;
```

12.8 The Redundancy Index of Stewart and Love

In multiple regression, the squared multiple correlation represents the proportion of criterion variance accounted for by the optimal linear combination of the predictors. In canonical correlation, however, a squared canonical correlation tells us only the amount of variance that the two canonical variates share, and does not necessarily indicate considerable variance overlap between the two sets of variables. The canonical variates are derived to maximize the correlation between them, and thus, we can't necessarily expect each canonical variate will extract much variance from its set. For example, the third canonical variable from set X may be close to a last principle component, and thus extract negligible variance from set X. That is, it may not be an important factor for battery X. Stewart and Love (1968) realized that interpreting squared canonical correlations as indicating the amount of informational overlap between two batteries (sets of variables) was not appropriate, and developed their own index of redundancy.

The essence of the Stewart and Love idea is quite simple. First, determine how much variance in Y the first canonical variate (C_1) accounts for. How this is done will be indicated shortly. Then multiply the extracted variance (we denote this by VC_1) by the square of the canonical correlation between C_1 and the corresponding canonical variate (P_1) from set X. This product then gives the amount of variance in set Y that is predictable from the first canonical variate for set X. Next, the amount of variance in Y that the second canonical variate (C_2) for Y accounts for is determined, and is multiplied by the square of the canonical correlation between C_2 and the corresponding canonical variate (P_2) from set X. This product gives the amount of variance in set Y predictable from the second canonical variate for set X. This process is repeated for all possible canonical correlations. Then the products are added (since the respective pairs of canonical variates are uncorrelated) to determine the redundancy in set Y, given set X, which we denote by $R_{Y/X}$. If the square of the ith canonical correlation is denoted by λ_i, then $R_{Y/X}$ is given by:

$$R_{Y/X} = \sum_{i=1}^{h} \lambda_i \ VC_i$$

where h is the number of possible canonical correlations.

The amount of variance canonical variate i extracts from set Y is given by:

$$VC_1 = \frac{\Sigma \text{ squared canonical variate} - \text{variable correlations}}{q \text{ (number of variables in set } Y)}$$

There is an important point I wish to make concerning the redundancy index. It is equal to the average squared multiple correlation for predicting the variables in one set from the variables in the other set. To illustrate, suppose we had four variables in set X and three variables in set Y, and we computed the multiple correlation for each y variable *separately* with the four predictors. Then, if these multiple correlations are squared and the sum of squares divided by 3, this number is equal to $R_{Y/X}$. This fact hints at a problem with the redundancy index, as Cramer and Nicewander (1979) noted:

> Moreover, the redundancy index is not multivariate in the strict sense because it is unaffected by the intercorrelations of the variables being predicted. The redundancy index is only multivariate in the sense that it involves several criterion variables (p. 43).

This is saying we would obtain the same amount of variance accounted for with the redundancy index for three y variables that are highly correlated as we would for three y variables that have low intercorrelations (other factors being held constant). This is very undesirable in the same sense as it would be undesirable if, in a multiple regression context, the multiple correlation were unaffected by the magnitude of the intercorrelations among the predictors.

This defect can be eliminated by first orthogonalizing the y variables (e.g., obtaining a set of uncorrelated variables, such as principal components or varimax rotated factors), and then computing the average squared multiple correlation between the uncorrelated y variables and the x variables. In this case we could, of course, compute the redundancy index, but it is unnecessary since it is equal to the average squared multiple correlation.

Cramer and Nicewander recommended using the *average squared canonical correlation* as the measure of variance accounted for. Thus, for example, if there were two canonical correlations, simply square each of them and then divide by 2.

12.9 Rotation of Canonical Variates

In Chapter 11 on principal components, it was stated that often the interpretation of the components can be difficult, and that a rotation (e.g., varimax) can be quite helpful in obtaining factors that tend to load high on only a small number of variables and therefore are considerably easier to interpret. In canonical correlations, the same rotation idea can be employed to increase interpretability. The situation, however, is much more complex, since two sets of factors (the successive pairs of canonical variates) are being simultaneously rotated. Cliff and Krus (1976) showed mathematically that such a procedure is sound, and the practical implementation of the procedure is possible in multivariance (Finn, 1978). Cliff and Krus also demonstrated, through an example, how interpretation is made clearer through rotation.

When such a rotation is done, the variance will be spread more evenly across the pairs of canonical variates; that is, the maximization property is lost. Recall that this is what happened when the components were rotated. But we were willing to sacrifice this property for increased interpretability. Of course, only the canonical variates corresponding to *significant* canonical correlations should be rotated, in order to ensure that the rotated variates still correspond to significant association (Cliff and Krus, 1976).

12.10 Obtaining More Reliable Canonical Variates

In concluding this chapter, I mention five approaches that will increase the probability of accurately interpreting the canonical variates, that is, the probability that the interpretation made in the given sample will hold up in another sample from the same population. The first two points have already been made, but are repeated as a means of summarizing:

1. Have a very large (1,000 or more) number of subjects, or a large subject to variable ratio.
2. If there is a large or fairly large number of variables in each set, then perform a components analysis on each set. Use only the components (or rotated factors) from each set that account for most of the variance in the canonical correlation analysis. In this way, an investigator, rather than doing a canonical analysis on a total of, say, 35 variables with 300 subjects, may be able to account for most of the variance in each of the sets with a total of 10 components, and thus achieve a much more favorable subject to variable ratio (30/1). The components analysis approach is one means of attacking the multicollinearity problem, which makes accurate interpretation difficult.
3. Ensure at least a moderate to large subject to variable ratio by judiciously selecting a priori a small number of variables for each of the two sets that will be related.
4. Another way of dealing with multicollinearity is to use canonical ridge regression. With this approach the coefficients are biased, but their variance will be much less, leading to more accurate interpretation. Monte Carlo studies (Anderson and Carney, 1974; Barcikowski and Stevens, 1978) of the effectiveness of ridge canonical regression show that it can yield more stable canonical variate coefficients and canonical variate–variable correlations. Barcikowski and Stevens examined 11 different correlation matrices that exhibited varying degrees of within and between multicollinearity. They found that, in general, ridge became more effective as the degree of multicollinearity increased. Second, ridge canonical regression was particularly effective with small subject to variable ratios. These are precisely the situations where the greater stability is desperately needed.

5. Still another approach to more accurate interpretation of canonical variates was presented by Weinberg and Darlington (1976), who used biased coefficients of 0 and 1 to form the canonical variates. This approach makes interpretation of the most important variables, those receiving 1's in the canonical variates, relatively easy.

12.11 Summary

Canonical correlation is a parsimonious way of breaking down the association between two sets of variables through the use of linear combinations. In this way, because the combinations are uncorrelated, we can describe the number and nature of independent relationships existing between two sets of variables. That canonical correlation does indeed give a parsimonious description of association that can be seen by considering the case of five variables in set X and 10 variables in set Y. To obtain an overall picture of the association using simple correlations would be very difficult, because we would have to deal with 50 fragmented between correlations. Canonical correlation, on the other hand, consolidates or channels all the association into five uncorrelated "big pieces," that is, the canonical correlations.

Two devices are available for interpreting the canonical variates: (a) standardized coefficients, and (b) canonical variate–variable correlations. Both of these are quite unreliable unless the n/total number of variables ratio is very large: at least 42/1 if interpreting the largest two canonical correlations, and about 20/1 if interpreting only the largest canonical correlation. The correlations should be used for substantive interpretation of the canonical variates, that is, for naming the constructs, and the coefficients are used for determining which of the variables are redundant. Because of the probably unattainably large n required for reliable results (especially if there are a fairly large or large number of variables in each set), several suggestions were given for obtaining reliable results with the n available, or perhaps just a somewhat larger n. The first suggestion involved doing a components analysis and varimax rotation on each set of variables and then relating the components or rotated factors via canonical correlation. An efficient, practical implementation of this procedure, using the SAS package, was illustrated.

Some other means of obtaining more reliable canonical variates were:

1. Selecting a priori a small number of variables from each of the sets, and then relating these. This would be an option to consider if the n was not judged to be large enough to do a reliable components analysis—for example, if there were 20 variables in set X and 30 variables in set Y and $n = 120$.

2. The use of canonical ridge regression.

3. The use of the technique developed by Weinberg and Darlington.

A study from the literature that used canonical correlation was discussed in detail.

The redundancy index, for determining the variance overlap between two sets of variables, was considered. It was indicated that this index suffers from the defect of being unaffected by the intercorrelations of the variables being predicted. This is undesirable in the same sense as it would be undesirable if the multiple correlation were unaffected by the intercorrelations of the predictors.

Finally, in evaluating studies from the literature that have used canonical correlation, remember it isn't just the n in a vacuum that is important. The n/total number of variables ratio, along with the degree of multicollinearity, must be examined to determine how much confidence can be placed in the results. Thus, not a great deal of confidence can be placed in the results of a study involving a total of 25 variables (say 10 in set X and 15 in set Y) based on 200 subjects. Even if a study had 400 subjects, but did the canonical analysis on a total of 60 variables, it is probably of little scientific value because the results are unlikely to replicate.

12.12 Exercises

1. Name four features that canonical correlation and principal components analysis have in common.

2. Suppose that a canonical correlation analysis on two sets of variables yielded r canonical correlations. Indicate schematically what the matrix of intercorrelations for the canonical variates would look like.

3. Shin (1971) examined the relationship between creativity and achievement. He used Guilford's battery to obtain the following six creativity scores: ideational fluency, spontaneous flexibility, associational fluency, expressional fluency, originality, and elaboration. The Kropp test was used to obtain the following six achievement variables: knowledge, comprehension, application, analysis, synthesis, and evaluation. Data from 116 11th-grade suburban high school students yielded the correlation matrix on the following page.

   Examine the association between the creativity and achievement variables via canonical correlation, and from the printout answer the following questions:

   (a) How would you characterize the strength of the relationship between the two sets of variables from the simple correlations?

   (b) How many of the canonical correlations are significant at the .05 level?

   (c) Use the canonical variable loadings to interpret the canonical variates corresponding to the largest canonical correlation.

   (d) How large an n is needed for reliable interpretation of the canonical variates in (c)?

   (e) Considering all the canonical correlations, what is the value of the redundancy index for the creativity variables given the achievement variables? Express in words what this number tells us.

   (f) Cramer and Nicewander (1979) argued that the *average* squared canonical correlation should be used as the measure of association for two sets of variables, stating, "This index has a clear interpretation, being an arithmetic mean, and gives the proportion of variance of the average of the canonical variates of the y variables predictable from the x variables" (p. 53). Obtain the Cramer–Nicewander measure for the present problem, and compare its magnitude to that obtained for the measure in (e). Explain the reason for the difference and, in particular, the direction of the difference.

	IDEAFLU	FLEXIB	ASSOCFLU	EXPRFLU	ORIG	ELAB	KNOW	COMPRE	APPLIC	ANAL	SYNTH	EVAL
IDEAFLU	1.000											
FLEXIB	0.710	1.000										
ASSOCFLU	0.120	0.120	1.000									
EXPRFLU	0.340	0.450	0.430	1.000								
ORIG	0.270	0.330	0.240	0.330	1.000							
ELAB	0.210	0.110	0.420	0.460	0.320	1.000						
KNOW	0.130	0.270	0.210	0.390	0.270	0.380	1.000					
COMPRE	0.180	0.240	0.150	0.360	0.330	0.260	0.620	1.000				
APPLIC	0.080	0.140	0.090	0.250	0.130	0.230	0.440	0.660	1.000			
ANAL	0.100	0.160	0.090	0.250	0.120	0.280	0.580	0.660	0.640	1.000		
SYNTH	0.130	0.230	0.420	0.500	0.410	0.470	0.460	0.470	0.370	0.530	1.000	
EVAL	0.080	0.150	0.360	0.280	0.210	0.260	0.300	0.240	0.190	0.290	0.580	1.000

4. Shanahan (1984) examined the nature of the reading–writing relationship through canonical correlation analysis. Measures of writing ability (*t* unit, vocabulary diversity, episodes, categories, information units, spelling, phonemic accuracy, and visual accuracy) were related to reading measures of vocabulary, word recognition, sentence comprehension, and passage comprehension. Separate canonical correlation analyses were done for 256 second graders and 251 fifth graders.

(a) How many canonical correlations will there be for each analysis?

(b) Shanahan found that for second graders there were only two significant canonical correlations, and he only interpreted the largest one. Given his sample size, was he wise in doing this?

(c) For fifth graders there was only one significant canonical correlation. Given his sample size, can we have confidence in the reliability of the results?

(d) Shanahan presents the following canonical variate–variable correlations for the largest canonical correlation for both the second- and fifth-grade samples. If you have an appropriate content background, interpret the results and then compare your interpretation with his.

Canonical Factor Structures for the Grade 2 and Grade 5 Samples: Correlations of Reading and Writing Variables with Canonical Variables

| | Canonical variable | | | |
| | 2nd Grade | | 5th Grade | |
	Reading	Writing	Reading	Writing
Writing				
t-Unit	.32	.41	.19	.25
Vocabulary diversity	.46	.59	.47	.60
Episodes	.25	.32	.20	.26
Categories	.37	.48	.33	.43
Information units	.36	.46	.24	.30
Spelling	.74	.95	.71	.92
Phonemic accuracy	.60	.77	.67	.86
Visual accuracy	.69	.89	.68	.88
Reading				
Comprehension	.81	.63	.79	.61
Cloze	.86	.66	.80	.62
Vocabulary	.65	.51	.89	.69
Phonics	.88	.68	.85	.66

5. Estabrook (1984) examined the relationship among the 11 subtests on the Wechsler Intelligence Scale for Children–Revised (WISC–R) and the 12 subtests on the Woodcock–Johnson Tests of Cognitive Ability for 152 learning disabled children. He seemed to acknowledge sample size as a problem in his study, stating, "The primary limitation of this study is the size of the sample.... However, a more conservative criterion of $100(p + q) + 50$ (where p and q refer to the number of variables in each set) has been suggested by Thorndike." Is this really a conservative criterion according to the results of Barcikowski and Stevens (1975)?

13

Repeated-Measures Analysis

13.1 Introduction

Recall that the two basic objectives in experimental design are the elimination of systematic bias and the reduction of error (within group or cell) variance. The main reason for within-group variability is individual differences among the subjects. Thus, even though the subjects receive the same treatment, their scores on the dependent variable can differ considerably because of differences on IQ, motivation, SES, and so on. One statistical way of reducing error variance is through analysis of covariance, which was discussed in Chapter 9.

Another way of reducing error variance is through blocking on a variable such as IQ. Here, the subjects are first blocked into more homogeneous subgroups, and then randomly assigned to treatments. For example, the subjects may be in blocks with only 9-point IQ ranges: 91–100, 101–110, 111–120, 121–130, and 131–140. The subjects within each block may score more similarly on the dependent variable, and the average scores for the subjects between blocks can be fairly large. But all of this variability between blocks is removed from the within-variability, yielding a much more sensitive (powerful) test.

In repeated-measures designs, blocking is carried to its extreme. That is, *we are blocking on each subject. Thus, variability among the subjects due to individual differences is completely removed from the error term.* This makes these designs much more powerful than completely randomized designs, where different subjects are randomly assigned to the different treatments. Given the emphasis in this text on power, one should seriously consider the use of repeated-measures designs where appropriate and practical. And there are many situations where such designs are appropriate. The simplest example of a repeated-measures design the reader may have encountered in a beginning statistics course—that is, the correlated or dependent samples *t* test. Here, the same subjects are pretested and posttested (measured repeatedly) on a dependent variable with an intervening treatment. The subjects are used as their own controls. Another class of repeated measures situations occurs when we are comparing the *same* subjects under several different treatments (drugs, stimulus displays of different complexity, etc.).

Repeated measures is also the natural design to use when the concern is with performance trends over time. For example, Bock (1975) presented an example comparing boys' and girls' performance on vocabulary over grades 8 through 11. Here we are also concerned with the mathematical form of the trend, that is, whether it is linear, quadratic, cubic, and so on.

Another distinct advantage of repeated-measures designs, because the same subjects are being used repeatedly, is that far fewer subjects are required for the study. For example, if three treatments are involved in a completely randomized design, we may require

45 subjects (15 subjects per treatment). With a repeated-measures design we would need only 15 subjects. This can be a very important practical advantage in many cases, since numerous subjects are not easy to come by in areas such as counseling, school psychology, clinical psychology, and nursing.

In this chapter, consideration is given to repeated-measures designs of varying complexity. We start with the simplest design: a single group of subjects measured under various treatments (conditions), or at different points in time. Schematically, it would look like this:

	Treatments				
	1	2	3	...	k
1					
2					
Subjects :					
n					

We then consider a one between and one within design. Many texts use the terms *between* and *within* in referring to repeated measures factors. A between variable is simply a grouping or classification variable such as sex, age, social class. A within variable is one on which the subjects have been measured repeatedly (such as time). Some authors even refer to repeated-measures designs as within designs (Keppel, 1983). An example of a one between and one within design would be:

	Treatments		
	1	2	3
Males			
Females			

where the same males and females are measured under all three treatments.

Another useful application of repeated measures occurs in combination with a one-way ANOVA design. In a one-way design involving treatments, the subjects are posttested to determine which treatment is best. If we are interested in the lasting or residual effects of treatments, then we need to measure the subjects at least a few more times. Huck, Cormier, and Bounds (1974) presented an example in which three teaching methods are compared, but in addition the subjects are again measured 6 weeks and 12 weeks later to determine the residual effect of the methods on achievement. A repeated-measures analysis of such data *could* yield a quite different conclusion as to which method might be preferred. Suppose the pattern of means looked as follows:

	POSTTEST	SIX WEEKS	12 WEEKS
METHOD 1	66	64	63
METHOD 2	69	65	59
METHOD 3	62	56	52

Just looking at a one-way ANOVA on posttest scores (if significant) could lead one to conclude that method 2 is best. Examination of the pattern of achievement over time, however, shows that, for lasting effect, method 1 is to be preferred, because after 12 weeks the achievement for method 1 is superior to method 2 (63 vs. 59). What we have here is an example of a method-by-time interaction.

In the above example, teaching method is the between variable and time is the within, or repeated measures factor. The reader should be aware that three other names are used to describe a one between and one within design by some authors: split plot, Lindquist Type I, and two-way ANOVA, with repeated measures on one factor. Our computer example in this chapter involves verbal recall after 1, 2, 3, 4, and 5 days for two treatment groups.

Next, we consider a one between and two within repeated-measures design, using the following example. Two groups of subjects are administered two types of drugs at each of three doses. The study aims to estimate the relative potency of the drugs in inhibiting a response to a stimulus. Schematically, the design is as follows:

		Drug 1			Drug 2		
Dose		1	2	3	1	2	3
Gp 1							
Gp 2							

Each subject is measured six times, for each dose of each drug. The two within variables are dose and drug.

Then, we consider a two between and a one within design from a study comparing the relative efficacy of a behavior modification approach to dieting versus a behavior modification approach + exercise on weight loss for a group of overweight women. The weight loss is measured 2, 4, and 6 months after the diets begin. The design is:

		WGTLOSS1	WGTLOSS2	WGTLOSS3
GROUP	AGE			
CONTROL	20–30 YRS			
CONTROL	30–40 YRS			
BEH. MOD.	20–40 YRS			
BEH. MOD.	30–40 YRS			
BEH. MOD. + EXER.	20–30 YRS			
BEH. MOD. + EXER.	30–40 YRS			

This is a two between design, because we are subdividing the subjects on the basis of both treatment and age; that is, we have two grouping variables.

For each of these designs we indicate the complete control lines for running both the univariate and multivariate approaches to repeated-measures analysis on both SPSS and SAS, and explain selected printout.

Finally, we consider profile analysis, in which two or more groups of subjects are compared on a battery of tests. The analysis determines whether the profiles for the groups are parallel. If the profiles are parallel, then the analysis will determine whether the profiles are coincident.

Although increased precision and economy of subjects are two distinct advantages of repeated-measures designs, such designs also have potentially serious disadvantages, unless care is taken. When several treatments are involved, the order in which treatments are administered might make a difference in the subjects' performance. Thus, it is important to *counterbalance* the order of treatments.

For two treatments, this would involve randomly assigning half of the subjects to get treatment *A* first, and the other half to get treatment *B* first, which would look like this schematically:

Order of administration

1	2
A	B
B	A

It is balanced because an equal number of subjects have received each treatment in each position.

For three treatments, counterbalancing involves randomly assigning one third of the subjects to each of the following sequences:

Order of administration of treatments

A	B	C
B	C	A
C	A	B

This is balanced because an equal number of subjects have received each treatment in each position. This type of design is called a Latin Square.

Also, it is important to allow sufficient time between treatments to minimize carryover effects, which certainly could occur if treatments were drugs. How much time is necessary is, of course, a substantive, not a statistical question. A nice discussion of these two problems is found in Keppel (1983) and Myers (1979).

13.2 Single-Group Repeated Measures

Suppose we wish to study the effect of four drugs on reaction time to a series of tasks. Sufficient time is allowed to minimize the effect that one drug may have on the subject's response to the next drug. The following data is from Winer (1971):

S's	Drugs 1	2	3	4	Means
1	30	28	16	34	27
2	14	18	10	22	16
3	24	20	18	30	23
4	38	34	20	44	34
5	26	28	14	30	24.5
	26.4	25.6	15.6	32	24.9 (grand mean)

We will analyze this set of data in three different ways: (a) as a completely randomized design (pretending there are different subjects for the different drugs), (b) as a univariate repeated-measures analysis, and (c) as a multivariate repeated-measures analysis. The purpose of including the completely randomized approach is to contrast the error variance that results against the markedly smaller error variance that results in the repeated measures approach. The multivariate approach to repeated-measures analysis may be new to our readers, and a specific numerical example will help in understanding how some of the printout on the packages is arrived at.

13.2.1 Completely Randomized Analysis for the Drug Data

This simply involves doing a one-way ANOVA. Thus, we compute the sum of squares between (SS_b) and the sum of squares within (SS_w):

$$SS_b = n \sum_{j=1}^{4} (\bar{y}_j - \bar{y})^2 = 5[(26.4 - 24.9)^2 + (25.6 - 24.9)^2 + (15.6 - 24.9)^2$$

$$+ (32 - 24.9)^2]$$

$$SS_b = 698.2$$

$$SS_w = (30 - 26.4)^2 + (14 - 26.4)^2 + \cdots + (26 - 26.4)^2 + \cdots$$

$$+ (34 - 32)^2 + (22 - 32)^2 + \cdots + (30 - 32)^2 = 793.6$$

Thus, $MS_b = 698.2/3 = 232.73$ and $MS_w = 793.6/16 = 49.6$ and our $F = 232.73/49.6 = 4.7$, with three and 16 degrees of freedom. This is not significant at the .01 level, because the critical value is 5.29.

13.2.2 Univariate Repeated-Measures Analysis for Drug Data

Note from the column of means for the drug of data that the subjects' average responses to the four drugs differ considerably (ranging from 16 to 34). We quantify this variability through the so-called sum of squares for blocks (SS_{bl}), where we are blocking on the subjects. The error variability that was calculated above is split up into two parts, $SS_w = SS_{bl} + SS_{res}$, where SS_{res} stands for sum of squares residual. Denote the number of repeated measures by k.

Now we calculate the sum of squares for blocks:

$$SS_{bl} = k \sum_{i=1}^{5} (\bar{y}_i - \bar{y})^2$$

$$= 4[(27 - 24.9)^2 + (16 - 24.9)^2 + \cdots + (24.5 - 24.9)^2]$$

$$SS_{bl} = 680.8$$

Our errors term for the repeated-measures analysis is formed from $SS_{res} = SS_w - SS_{bl} = 793.6 - 680.8 = 112.8$. Note that the vast portion of the within variability is due to individual differences (680.8 out of 793.6), and that we have removed all of this from our error term for the repeated-measures analysis. Now,

$$MS_{res} = SS_{res}/(n-1)(k-1) = 112.8/4(3) = 9.4$$

and $F = MS_b/MS_{res} = 232.73/9.4 = 24.76$, with $(k-1) = 3$ and $(n-1)(k-1) = 12$ degrees of freedom. This is significant well beyond the .01 level, and is approximately five times as large as the F obtained under the completely randomized design.

13.3 The Multivariate Test Statistic for Repeated Measures

Before we consider the multivariate approach, it is instructive to go back to the t test for correlated (dependent) samples. The subjects are pretested and posttested, and difference (d_1) scores are formed:

S's	Pretest	Posttest	d_i
1	7	10	3
2	5	4	−1
3	6	8	2
. . . .			
n	3	7	4

The null hypothesis here is

$$H_0: \mu_1 = \mu_2 \text{ or equivalently that } \mu_1 - \mu_2 = 0$$

The t test for determining the tenability of H_0 is

$$t = \frac{\bar{d}}{s_d / \sqrt{n}}$$

where $\bar{d}$ is the average difference score and s_d is the standard deviation for the difference scores. It is important to note that the analysis is done on the difference variable d_i.

In the multivariate case for repeated measures the test statistic for k *repeated measures is formed from the (k–1) difference variables and their variances and covariances.* The transition here from univariate to multivariate parallels that for the two-group independent samples case:

Independent Samples	Dependent Samples
$t = \dfrac{(\bar{y}_1 - \bar{y}_2)^2}{s^2(1/n_1 + 1/n_2)}$	$t^2 = \dfrac{\bar{d}^2}{s_d^2/n}$
$t^2 = \dfrac{n_1 n_2}{n_1 + n_2}(\bar{y}_1 - \bar{y}_2)(s^2)^{-1}(\bar{y}_1 - \bar{y}_2)$	$t^2 = n\bar{d}(s_d^2)^{-1}\bar{d}$
In obtaining the multivariate statistic we replace the means by mean vectors and the pooled within-variance (s^2) by pooled within-covariance matrix.	To obtain the multivariate statistic we replace the mean difference by a vector of mean differences and the variance of difference scores by the matrix of variances and covariances on the (k–1) created difference variables.
$T^2 \dfrac{n_1 n_2}{n_1 + n_2}(\bar{y}_1 - \bar{y}_2)'\mathbf{S}^{-1}(\bar{y}_1 - \bar{y}_2)$	$T^2 = n\, \mathbf{y}_d'\, \mathbf{S}_d^{-1}\, \mathbf{y}_d$
$\mathbf{S}$ is the pooled within covariance matrix, i.e., the measure of error variability.	$\mathbf{y}_d'$ is the row vector of mean difference on the (k–1) difference variables, i.e., $\mathbf{y}_d' = (\bar{y}_1 - \bar{y}_2,\ \bar{y}_2 - \bar{y}_3,\ ...,\ \bar{y}_{k-1} - \bar{y}_k)$ and $\mathbf{S}_d$ is the matrix of variances and covariances on the (k–1) difference variables, i.e., the measure of error variability.

We now calculate the preceding multivariate test statistic for dependent samples (repeated measures) on the drug data. This should help to clarify the somewhat abstract development thus far.

13.3.1 Multivariate Analysis of the Drug Data

The null hypothesis we are testing for the drug data is that the drug population means are equal, or in symbols:

$$H_0 : \mu_1 = \mu_2 = \mu_3 = \mu_4$$

But this is equivalent to saying that $\mu_1 - \mu_2 = 0$, $\mu_2 - \mu_3 = 0$, and $\mu_3 - \mu_4 = 0$. (The reader is asked to show this in one of the exercises.) We create three difference variables on the adjacent repeated measures ($y_1 - y_2$, $y_2 - y_3$ and $y_3 - y_4$) and test H_0 by determining whether the means on all three of these difference variables are simultaneously 0. Here we display the scores on the difference variables:

	$y_1 - y_2$	$y_2 - y_3$	$y_3 - y_4$
	2	12	−18
	−4	8	−12
	4	2	−12
	4	14	−24
	−2	14	−16
Means	.8	10	−16.4
Variances	13.2	26	24.8

Thus, the row vector of mean differences here is

$$\mathbf{y}_d' = (.8, 10, -16.4)$$

We need to create $\mathbf{S}_d$, the matrix of variances and covariances on the difference variables. We already have the variances, but need to compute the covariances. The calculation for the covariance for the first two difference variables is given next and calculation of the other two is left as an exercise.

$$s_{y1-y2,y2-y3} = \frac{(2-.8)(12-10)+(-4-.8)(8-10)+\cdots+(-2-.8)(14-10)}{4} = -3$$

Recall that in computing the covariance for two variables the scores for the subjects are simply deviated about the means for the variables. The matrix of variances and covariances is

$$\mathbf{S}_d = \begin{matrix} & y_1-y_2 \quad y_2-y_3 \quad y_3-y_4 \\ & \begin{bmatrix} 13.2 & -3 & -8.6 \\ -3 & 26 & -19 \\ -8.6 & -19 & 24.8 \end{bmatrix} \end{matrix}$$

covariance for $(y_1 - y_2)$ & $(y_3 - y_4)$

covariance for $(y_2 - y_3)$ & $(y_3 - y_4)$

Therefore,

$$
T^2 = 5(.8, 10, -16.4) \overset{\mathbf{S}_d^{-1}}{\begin{bmatrix} .458 & .384 & .453 \\ .384 & .409 & .446 \\ .453 & .446 & .539 \end{bmatrix}} \overset{\mathbf{y}_d}{\begin{pmatrix} .8 \\ 10 \\ -16.4 \end{pmatrix}}
$$

with $\mathbf{y}_d'$ labeling the row vector.

$$
T^2 = (-16.114, -14.586, -20.086) \begin{pmatrix} .8 \\ 10 \\ -16.4 \end{pmatrix} = 170.659
$$

There is an exact F transformation of T^2, which is

$$
F = \frac{n-k+1}{(n-1)(k-1)} T^2, \text{ with } (k-1) \text{ and } (n-k+1)df
$$

Thus,

$$
F = \frac{5-4+1}{4(3)} (170.659) = 28.443, \text{ with 3 and } 2df
$$

This is significant at the .05 level, exceeding the critical value of 19.16. The critical value is very large here, because the error degrees of freedom is extremely small (2). We conclude that the drugs are different in effectiveness.

13.4 Assumptions in Repeated-Measures Analysis

The three assumptions for a single-group univariate repeated-measures analysis are:

1. Independence of the observations
2. Multivariate normality
3. Sphericity (sometimes called circularity)*

The first two assumptions are also required for the multivariate approach, but the sphericity assumption is not necessary. The reader should recall from Chapter 6 that a violation of the independence assumption is very serious in independent samples ANOVA and MANOVA, and it is also serious here. Just as ANOVA and MANOVA are fairly robust against violation of multivariate normality, so that also carries over here.

---

* For many years it was thought that a stronger condition, called uniformity (compound symmetry) was necessary. The uniformity condition required that the population variances for all treatments be equal and also that all population covariances are equal. However, Huynh and Feldt (1970) and Rouanet and Lepine (1970) showed that sphericity is an exact condition for the F test to be valid. Sphericity requires only that the variances of the differences for *all* pairs of repeated measures be equal.

What is the sphericity condition? Recall that in testing the null hypothesis for the previous numerical example, we transformed from the original four repeated measures to three new variables, which were then used jointly in the multivariate approach. In general, if there are k repeated measures, then we transform to $(k-1)$ new variables. There are other choices for the $(k-1)$ variables than the adjacent differences used in the drug example, which will yield the *same* multivariate test statistic. This follows from the invariance property of the multivariate statistic (Morrison, 1976, p. 145).

Suppose that the $(k-1)$ new variates selected are orthogonal (uncorrelated) and are scaled such that the sum of squares of the coefficients for each variate is 1. Then we have what is called an *orthonormal* set of variates. If the transformation matrix is denoted by $\mathbf{C}$ and the population covariance matrix for the original repeated measures by Σ, then the sphericity assumption says that the covariance matrix for the new (transformed) variables is a diagonal matrix, with equal variances on the diagonal:

$$
\mathbf{C}'\,\Sigma\,\mathbf{C} = \sigma^2 \mathbf{I} =
\begin{array}{c}
\\ 1 \\ 2 \\ 3 \\ \vdots \\ k-1
\end{array}
\overset{\textit{Transformed Variables}}{
\begin{array}{cccccc}
1 & 2 & 3 & \cdots & k-1 \\
\end{array}
}
\left[
\begin{array}{ccccc}
\sigma^2 & 0 & 0 & \cdots & 0 \\
0 & \sigma^2 & 0 & \cdots & 0 \\
0 & 0 & \sigma^2 & & \\
\vdots & \vdots & \vdots & \ddots & \\
0 & 0 & & & \sigma^2
\end{array}
\right]
$$

Saying that the off diagonal elements are 0 means that the covariances for all transformed variables are 0, which implies that the correlations are 0.

Box (1954) showed that if the sphericity assumption is not met, then the F ratio is positively biased (we are rejecting falsely too often). In other words, we may set our α level at .05, but may be rejecting falsely 8% or 10% of the time. The extent to which the covariance matrix deviates from sphericity is reflected in a parameter called ϵ (Greenhouse & Geisser, 1959). We give the formula for $\hat{\epsilon}$ in one of the exercises. If sphericity is met, then $\epsilon = 1$, while for the worst possible violation the value of $\epsilon = 1/(k-1)$, where k is the number of treatments. To adjust for the positive bias, Greenhouse and Geisser suggested altering the degrees of freedom from

$$(k-1) \text{ and } (k-1)(n-1) \text{ to } 1 \text{ and } (n-1)$$

Doing this makes the test *very* conservative, because adjustment is made for the worst possible case, and we don't recommend it. A more reasonable approach is to estimate ϵ. SPSS MANOVA and SAS GLM both print out $\hat{\epsilon}$. Then, adjust the degrees of freedom from

$$(k-1) \text{ and } (k-1)(n-1) \text{ to } \hat{\epsilon}(k-1) \text{ and } \hat{\epsilon}(k-1)(n-1).$$

Results from Collier, Baker, Mandeville, and Hayes (1967) and Stoloff (1967) show that this approach keeps the actual alpha very close to the level of significance.

Huynh and Feldt (1976) found that even multiplying the degrees of freedom by $\hat{\epsilon}$ is somewhat conservative when the true value of ϵ is above about .70. They recommended using the following for those situations:

$$\bar{\epsilon} \frac{n(i-1)\hat{\epsilon} - 2}{(i-1)[(n-1)-(i-1)\hat{\epsilon}]}$$

The Huynh and Feldt epsilon is printed out by both SPSS MANOVA and SAS GLM.

The Greenhouse–Geisser estimator tends to *underestimate* ϵ, especially when ϵ is close to 1, while the Huynh–Feldt estimator tends to *overestimate* ϵ (Maxwell & Delaney, 1990). Because of these facts, our recommendation is to use the average of the estimators as the estimate of ϵ. If one wishes to be somewhat conservative, then one could always go with the Greenhouse–Geisser estimate.

There are various tests for sphericity, and in particular the Mauchley test (Kirk, 1982, p. 259) is used in Release 4.0 of SPSS. However, based on the results of Monte Carlo studies (Keselman, Rogan, Mendoza, & Breen, 1980; Rogan, Keselman, & Mendoza, 1979), we don't recommend using these tests. The studies just described showed that the tests are highly sensitive to departures from multivariate normality and from their respective null hypotheses.

13.5 Computer Analysis of the Drug Data

We now consider the univariate and multivariate repeated-measures analysis of the drug data that was worked out in numerical detail earlier in the chapter. The SPSS for Windows 10.0 screens for running the analysis are given in Table 13.1. In the top screen one would scroll over to Repeated Measures and click, and the screen in the middle of Table 13.1 will appear. Click where factor1 is and type in DRUG. Then click within Number of Levels and type 4. The Add light will go on. Click on it to add DRUG(4) to the box. The Define will light up; click on it and the screen at the bottom will appear. Click on the forward arrow and y1 will go in position 1. Highlight y2, click on the forward arrow, and y2 will go into position 2. Do the same for y3 and y4. Then click on OK (which will light up), and the analysis will be run. The means and standard deviations for the variables are given in Table 13.2. Selected printout from the analysis is given in Table 13.3. Note that the multivariate test is significant at the .05 level ($F = 28.41$, $p < .034$), and that the F value agrees, within rounding error, with the F calculated earlier ($F = 28.25$). The unadjusted univariate test is significant at .05, based on 3 and 12 degrees of freedom. However, the *adjusted* univariate F is also easily significant at .05 ($p < .001$), based on 1.81 and 7.26 *df*.

We wish to note that this example is not a good situation for the multivariate approach, because sample size is so small (five subjects). That is, this is not a favorable situation for the multivariate approach in terms of statistical power. We discuss this further later on in the chapter.

We indicated earlier that the multivariate test statistic for repeated measures is based on the $(k - 1)$ transformed variables, not on the original k variables. SPSS GLM creates a specific set of orthonormalized transformed variables on which the multivariate test statistic is based, although the reader should recall that there are many choices for the $(k - 1)$ transformed variables that will yield the *same* multivariate test value.

The program uses orthogonal polynomials (linear, quadratic, and cubic) for the drug data problem, as Table 13.3 shows.

TABLE 13.1

SPSS 10.0 Screens for Single-Group Repeated Measures

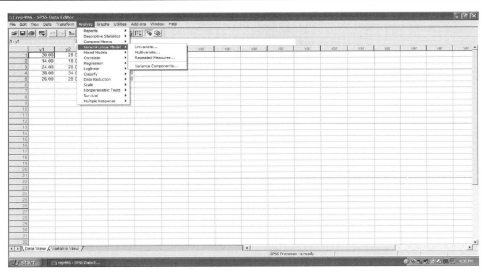

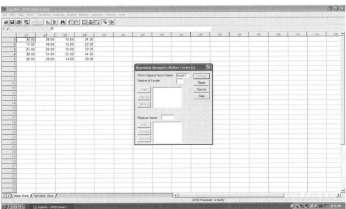

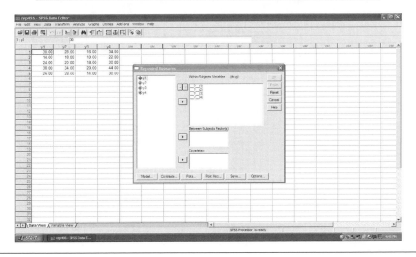

TABLE 13.2

Means and Standard Deviations for Single-Group Repeated Measures

Cell Means and Standard Deviations		
VARIABLE .. Y1		
	MEAN	**STD. DEV.**
FOR ENTIRE SAMPLE	26.40000	8.76356
VARIABLE .. Y2		
	MEAN	**STD. DEV.**
FOR ENTIRE SAMPLE	25.60000	6.54217
VARIABLE.. Y3		
	MEAN	**STD. DEV.**
FOR ENTIRE SAMPLE	15.60000	3.84708
VARIABLE .. Y4		
	MEAN	**STD. DEV.**
FOR ENTIRE SAMPLE	32.00000	8.00000

TABLE 13.3

Selected SPSS GLM Printout for Single-Group Repeated Measures Drug Data

Multivariate Tests[b]					
Effect	Value	F	Hypothesis df	Error df	Sig.
DRUG					
Pillai's Trace	.977	28.412[a]	3.000	2.000	.034
Wilks' Lambda	.023	28.412[a]	3.000	2.000	.034
Hotelling's Trace	42.618	28.412[a]	3.000	2.000	.034
Roy's Largest Root	42.618	28.412[a]	3.000	2.000	.034

[a] Exact statistic
[b] Design: Intercept
Within Subjects Design: DRUG

Mauchly's Test of Sphericity[b]

Measure: MEASURE_1

Within Subjects Effect	Mauchly's W	Approx. Chi-Square	df	Sig.
DRUG	.186	4.572	5	.495

	Epsilon[a]		
Within Subjects Effect	Greenhouse-Geisser	Huynh-Feldt	Lower-bound
DRUG	.605	1.000	.333

TABLE 13.3 (continued)

Selected SPSS GLM Printout for Single-Group Repeated Measures Drug Data

Measure: MEASURE_1

Source		Type III Sum of Squares	df	Mean Square	F	Sig.
DRUG	Sphericity Assumed	698.200	3	232.733	24.759	.000
	Greenhouse-Geisser	698.200	1.815	384.763	24.759	.001
	Huynh-Feldt	698.200	3.000	232.733	24.759	.000
	Lower-bound	698.200	1.000	698.200	24.759	.008
Error(DRUG)	Sphericity Assumed	112.800	12	9.400		
	Greenhouse-Geisser	112.800	7.258	15.540		
	Huynh-Feldt	112.800	12.000	9.400		
	Lower-bound	112.800	4.000	28.200		

Tests of Within-Subjects Contrasts

Measure: MEASURE_1

Source	DRUG	Type III Sum of Squares	df	Mean Square	F	Sig.
DRUG	Linear	11.560	1	11.560	3.074	.154
	Quadratic	369.800	1	369.800	26.797	.007
	Cubic	316.840	1	316.840	29.778	.005
Error(DRUG)	Linear	15.040	4	3.760		
	Quadratic	55.200	4	13.800		
	Cubic	42.560	4	10.640		

DRUG[a]

Measure: MEASURE_1

	DRUG		
Dependent Variable	Linear	Quadratic	Cubic
Y1	−.671	.500	−.224
Y2	−.224	−.500	.671
Y3	.224	−.500	−.671
Y4	.671	.500	.224

13.6 Post Hoc Procedures in Repeated-Measures Analysis

As in a one-way independent samples ANOVA, if an overall difference is found, one would almost always want to determine which specific treatments or conditions differed. This entails a *post hoc* procedure. There are several reasons for preferring pairwise procedures: (a) They are easily interpreted, (b) they are quite meaningful, and (c) some of these procedures are fairly powerful. The Tukey procedure is appropriate in repeated-measures designs, provided that the sphericity assumption is met. Recall that for the drug data the sphericity assumption was met (Table 13.3). We now apply the Tukey procedure, setting overall $\alpha = .05$; that is, we take at most a 5% chance of one or more false rejections. Some readers may have encountered the Tukey procedure in an intermediate statistics course. The studentized range statistic (which we denote by q) is used in the procedure. If there are k samples and the total sample size is N, then any two means are declared significantly different at the .05 level if the following inequality holds:

$$\left| \bar{y}_i - \bar{y}_j \right| > q_{.05;k,N-k} \sqrt{\frac{MS_w}{n}}$$

where MS_w is the error term in a one-way ANOVA, and n is the common group size.

The modification of the Tukey for the one-sample repeated measures is

$$\left| \bar{y}_i - \bar{y}_j \right| > q_{.05;k,(n-1)(k-1)} \sqrt{\frac{MS_{res}}{n}}$$

where $(n - 1)(k - 1)$ is the error degrees of freedom (replacing $N - k$, the error df for independent samples ANOVA), and MS_{res} is the error term for repeated measures, replacing MS_w (the error term for ANOVA).

13.6.1 Tukey Procedure Applied to the Drug Data

The drug means, from Table 13.2, are

	Drugs		
1	2	3	4
26.4	25.6	15.6	32

If we set overall $\alpha = .05$, then the appropriate studentized range value is $q_{.05;\ k,(n-1)(k-1)} = q_{.05,4,12} = 4.20$. The error term for the drug data from Table 13.3 is 9.40, and the number of subjects is $n = 5$. Thus, two drugs will be declared significantly different if

$$\left| \bar{y}_i - \bar{y}_j \right| > 4.20 \sqrt{\frac{9.4}{5}} = 5.76$$

Reference to the means above shows that the following pairs of drugs differ: drugs 1 and 3, drugs 2 and 3, drugs 3 and 4, and drugs 2 and 4.

There are several other pairwise post hoc procedures that Maxwell (1980) discusses. One can employ the Tukey, but with separate error terms. The Roy–Bose intervals can be used. In Chapter 4, we recommended against the use of these because of their extreme conservativeness, and the same applies here. Still another approach is to use multiple *dependent t* tests, but employing the Bonferroni inequality to keep overall α under control. For example, if there are five treatments, then there will be 10 paired comparisons. If we wish overall α to equal .05, then we simply do each dependent t test at the $.05/10 = .005$ level of significance. In general, if there are k treatments, then to keep overall α at .05, do each test at the $.05/[k(k - 1)/2]$ level of significance (because for k treatments there are $k(k - 1)/2$ paired comparisons).

Maxwell (1980), using a Monte Carlo approach, compared the following five pairwise post hoc procedures in terms of how well they control on overall α when the sphericity assumption is violated:

1. Tukey
2. Roy–Bose
3. Bonferroni (multiple dependent t tests)
4. Tukey, with separate error terms on $(n - 1)$ df
5. Tukey, with separate error term on $(n - 1)(k - 1)$ df

Results from Maxwell concerning the effect of violation of sphericity on Type I error for 3, 4, and 5 treatments and for sample sizes of 8 and 15 are given in Table 13.4. This table shows, as expected, that the Roy–Bose approach is too conservative. It also shows that *the Bonferroni approach keeps the actual α < nominal α in all cases, even when there is a severe violation of the sphericity assumption* (e.g., for $k = 3$ the min ϵ = .50, and one of the conditions modeled had ϵ = .54). Because of this, Maxwell recommended the Bonferroni approach for post hoc pairwise comparisons in repeated-measures analysis if the sphericity assumption is violated. Maxwell also studied the power of the five approaches, and found the Tukey to be most powerful. Also, when ϵ > .70 in Table 13.4, the deviation of actual α from nominal α is less than .02 for the Tukey procedure. This, coupled with the fact that the Tukey tends to be most powerful, would lead us to prefer the Tukey when ϵ > .70. When ϵ < .70, however, then we agree with Maxwell that the Bonferroni approach should be used.

13.7 Should We Use the Univariate Or Multivariate Approach?

In terms of controlling on Type I error, there is no real basis for preferring the multivariate approach, because use of the modified test (i.e., multiplying the degrees of freedom by $\hat{\epsilon}$) yields an "honest" error rate. The choice then involves a question of power. If sphericity holds, then the univariate approach is more powerful. When sphericity is violated, however, then the situation is much more complex. Davidson (1972) stated, "When small but reliable effects are present with the effects being highly variable … the multivariate test is far more powerful than the univariate test" (p. 452). And O'Brien and Kaiser (1985), after mentioning several studies that compared the power of the multivariate and modified univariate tests, state, "*Even though a limited number of situations have been investigated, this work found that no procedure is uniformly more powerful or even usually the most powerful*" (p. 319). Maxwell and Delaney (1990, pp. 602–604) present a nice extended discussion concerning the relative power of the univariate and multivariate approaches. They note that:

> All other things being equal, the multivariate test is relatively less powerful than the mixed model test (the univariate approach) as n decreases…. This statement implies that if the multivariate test has a power advantage for a certain pattern of population means and covariances, the magnitude of the advantage tends to decrease for smaller n and to increase for larger n (p. 602).

Based on the above statement, they further state, "As a rough rule of thumb, we would suggest that the *multivariate approach should probably not be used if n is less than a+10* (a is number of levels for repeated measures)" (p. 602, emphasis added). I feel that the above statements should be seriously considered, and would generally not advocate use of the multivariate approach if one has only a handful of observations more than the number of

TABLE 13.4

Type I Error Rates for Various Pairwise Multiple Comparison Procedures in Repeated-Measures Analysis under Different Violations of Sphericity Assumption

n	ϵ	Type I error rates for $k = 3$				
		WSD	SCI	BON	SEP1	SEP2
15	1.00	.041	.026	.039	.046	.058
15	0.86	.043	.026	.036	.045	.058
15	0.74	.051	.025	.033	.040	.054
15	0.54	.073	.021	.033	.040	.045
8	1.00	.046	.035	.050	.065	.089
8	0.86	.048	.030	.042	.052	.082
8	0.74	.054	.028	.038	.050	.076
8	0.54	.078	.026	.036	.044	.064

$$\min \epsilon = 1/(3 - 1) = .50$$

n	ϵ	Type I error rates for $k = 4$				
		WSD	SCI	BON	SEP1	SEP2
15	1.00	.045	.019	.043	.056	.080
15	1.00	.044	.020	.044	.056	.083
15	0.53	.081	.014	.030	.042	.064
15	0.49	.087	.018	.036	.050	.073
8	1.00	.045	.010	.048	.070	.128
8	1.00	.048	.013	.048	.072	.126
8	0.53	.084	.011	.042	.061	.104
8	0.49	.095	.011	.032	.054	.108

$$\min \epsilon = 1/(4 - 1) = .333$$

n	ϵ	Type I error rates for $k = 5$				
		WSD	SCI	BON	SEP1	SEP2
15	1.000	.050	.007	.040	.065	.109
15	0.831	.061	.009	.044	.066	.108
15	0.752	.067	.008	.042	.060	.106
15	0.522	.081	.010	.038	.058	.092
8	1.000	.048	.003	.044	.071	.172
8	0.831	.058	.004	.044	.074	.162
8	0.752	.060	.002	.042	.072	.156
8	0.522	.076	.003	.044	.066	.137

Note: WSD, Tukey procedure; SCI, Roy–Bose; BON, Bonferroni; SEP1, Tukey with separate error term and $(n - 1)$ *df*; SEP2, Tukey with separate error term and $(n - 1)(k - 1)$ *df*.

repeated measures, because of power considerations. However, I still tend to agree with Barcikowski and Robey (1984) that, given an exploratory study, *both* the adjusted univariate and multivariate tests be routinely used because they may differ in the treatment effects they will discern. In such a study half, the experimentwise level of significance might be set for each test. Thus, if we wish overall alpha to be .05, do each test at the .025 level of significance.

13.8 Sample Size for Power = .80 in Single-Sample Case

Although the classic text on power analysis by Cohen (1977) has power tables for a variety of situations (*t* tests, correlation, chi-square tests, differences between correlations, differences between proportions, one-way and factorial ANOVA, etc.), it does *not* provide tables for repeated-measures designs. Some work has been done in this area, most of it confined to the single sample case. The PASS program (2002) does calculate power for more complex repeated-measures designs. The following is taken from the PASS 2002 User's Guide – II (p. 1127):

> This module calculates power for repeated-measures designs having up to three within factors and three between factors. It computes power for various test statistics including the F test with the Greenhouse-Geisser correction, Wilks' lambda, Pillai-Bartlett trace, and Hotelling-Lawley trace.

Barcikowski and Robey (1985) have given power tables for various alpha levels for the single group repeated-measures design. Their tables assume a common correlation for the repeated measures, which generally will not be tenable (especially in longitudinal studies); however, a later paper by Green (1990) indicated that use of an estimated *average* correlation (from all the correlations among the repeated measures) is fine. Selected results from their work are presented in Table 13.5, which indicates sample size needed for power = .80 for small, medium, and large effect sizes at alpha = .01, .05, .10, and .20 for two through seven repeated measures. We give two examples to show how to use the table.

Example 13.1

An investigator has a three treatment design: that is, each of the subjects is exposed to three treatments. He uses $r = .80$ as his estimate of the average correlation of the subjects' responses to the three treatments. How many subjects will he need for power = .80 at the .05 level, if he anticipates a medium effect size?

Reference to Table 13.5 with correl = .80, effect size = .35, $k = 3$, and $\alpha = .05$, shows that only 14 subjects are needed.

Example 13.2

An investigator will be carrying out a longitudinal study, measuring the subjects at five points in time. She wishes to detect a large effect size at the .10 level of significance, and estimates that the average correlation among the five measures will be about .50. How many subjects will she need?

Reference to Table 13.5 with correl = .50, effect size = .57, $k = 5$, and $\alpha = .10$, shows that 11 subjects are needed.

13.9 Multivariate Matched Pairs Analysis

It was mentioned in Chapter 4 that often in comparing intact groups the subjects are matched or paired on variables known or suspected to be related to performance on the dependent variable(s). This is done so that if a significant difference is found, the investigator can be more confident it was the treatment(s) that "caused" the difference. In Chapter 4 we gave a univariate example, where kindergarteners were compared against nonkindergarteners on first-grade readiness, after they were matched on IQ, SES, and number of children in the family.

TABLE 13.5

Sample Sizes Needed for Power = .80 in a Single-Group Repeated Measures

Average corr.	Effect size[a]	\multicolumn{6}{c}{Number of repeated measures}					
		2	3	4	5	6	7
\multicolumn{8}{c}{$\alpha = .01$}							
.30	.12	404	324	273	238	214	195
	.30	68	56	49	44	41	39
	.49	28	24	22	21	21	21
.50	.14	298	239	202	177	159	146
	.35	51	43	38	35	33	31
	.57	22	19	18	18	18	18
.80	.22	123	100	86	76	69	65
	.56	22	20	19	18	18	18
	.89	11	11	11	12	12	13
\multicolumn{8}{c}{$\alpha = .05$}							
.30	.12	268	223	192	170	154	141
	.30	45	39	35	32	30	29
	.49	19	17	16	16	16	16
.50	.14	199	165	142	126	114	106
	.35	34	30	27	25	24	23
	.57	14	14	13	13	13	14
.80	.22	82	69	60	54	50	47
	.56	15	14	13	13	14	14
	.89	8	8	8	9	10	10
\multicolumn{8}{c}{$\alpha = .10$}							
.30	.12	209	178	154	137	125	116
	.30	35	31	28	26	25	24
	.49	14	14	13	13	13	13
.50	.14	154	131	114	102	93	87
	.35	26	24	22	20	20	19
	.57	11	11	11	11	11	12
.80	.22	64	55	49	44	41	39
	.56	12	11	11	11	12	12
	.89	6	7	7	8	9	9
\multicolumn{8}{c}{$\alpha = .20$}							
.30	.12	149	130	114	103	94	87
	.30	25	23	21	20	19	19
	.49	10	10	10	10	11	11
.50	.14	110	96	85	76	70	65
	.35	19	17	16	16	15	15
	.57	8	8	8	9	9	10
.80	.22	45	40	36	33	31	30
	.56	8	8	9	9	10	10
	.89	4	5	6	7	8	8

[a] These are small, medium, and large effect sizes, and are obtained from the corresponding effect size measures for independent samples ANOVA (i.e., .10, .25, and .40) by dividing by $\sqrt{1 - \text{correl}}$. Thus, for example, .14=.10/$\sqrt{1 - .50}$, and .57=.40/$\sqrt{1 - .50}$.

TABLE 13.6

Control Lines for Multivariate Matched-Pairs Analysis on SPSS MANOVA and Selected Output

```
TITLE 'KVET DATA- MULT. MATCHED PAIRS'.
DATA LIST FREE/READ1 READ2 LANG1 LANG2 MATH1 MATH2
BEGIN DATA.
62 67 72 66 67 35   95 87 99 96 82 82
66 66 96 87 74 63   87 91 87 82 98 85
70 74 69 73 85 63   96 99 96 76 74 61
85 99 99 71 91 60   54 60 69 80 66 71
82 83 69 99 63 66   69 60 87 80 69 71
55 61 52 74 55 67   87 87 88 99 95 82
91 99 99 99 99 87   78 72 66 76 52 74
78 62 79 69 54 65   72 58 74 69 59 58
85 99 99 75 66 61
END DATA.
COMPUTE READIFF = READ1-READ2.
COMPUTE LANGDIFF = LANG1-LANG2.
COMPUTE MATHDIFF = MATH1-MATH2.
LIST.
MANOVA READIFF LANGDIFF MATHDIFF/
    PRINT = CELLINFO(MEANS)/.
```

EFFECT.. CONSTANT

Multivariate Tests of Significance (S = 1, M = 1/2, N = 6)

Test Name	Value	Exact F Hypoth.	DF	Error DF	Sig. of F
Pillais	.16341	.91155	3.00	14.00	.460
Hotellings	.19533	.91155	3.00	14.00	.460
Wilks	.83659	.91155	3.00	14.00	.460
Roys	.16341				

Note: F statistics are exact.

- -

EFFECT .. CONSTANT (Cont.)

Univariate F-tests with (1,16) D.F.

Variable	Hypoth. SS	Error SS	Hypoth. MS	Error MS	F	Sig. of F.
READIFF	8.47059	1219.52941	8.47059	76.22059	.11113	.743
LANGDIFF	49.47059	3777.52941	49.47059	236.09559	.20954	.653
MATHDIFF	564.94118	3489.05882	564.94118	218.06618	2.59069	127

Now consider a multivariate example, that is, where there are several dependent variables. Kvet (1982) was interested in determining whether excusing elementary school children from regular classroom instruction for the study of instrumental music affected sixth-grade reading, language, and mathematics achievement. These were the three dependent variables. Instrumental and noninstrumental students from four public school districts were used in the study. We consider the analysis from just one of the districts. The instrumental and noninstrumental students were matched on the following variables: sex, race, IQ, cumulative achievement in fifth grade, elementary school attended, sixth-grade classroom teacher, and instrumental music outside the school.

Table 13.6 shows the control lines for running the analysis on SPSS MANOVA. Note that three COMPUTE statements are used to create the three difference variables, on which the multivariate analysis will be done, and that it is these difference variables that are used in the MANOVA line. We are testing whether these three difference variables (considered jointly) differ significantly from the 0 vector, that is, whether the differences on all three variables are jointly 0.

Again we obtain a T^2 value, as for the single sample multivariate repeated-measures analysis; however, the exact F transformation is somewhat different:

$$F = \frac{N-p}{(N-1)p} T^2, \text{ with } p \text{ and } (N-p)df$$

where N is the number of matched pairs and p is the number of difference variables.

The printout in Table 13.6 shows that the instrumental group does not differ from the noninstrumental group on the set of three difference variables ($F = .9115$, $p < .46$). Thus, the classroom time taken by the instrumental group did not adversely affect their achievement in these three basic academic areas.

13.10 One Between and One Within Factor—A Trend Analysis

We now consider a slightly more complex design, adding a grouping (between) variable. An investigator interested in verbal learning randomly assigns 16 subjects to two treatments. She obtains recall scores on verbal material after 1, 2, 3, 4, and 5 days. Treatments is the grouping variable. She expects there to be a significant effect over time, but wishes a more focused assessment. She wants to mathematically model the form of the decline in verbal recall. For this, trend analysis is appropriate and in particular orthogonal (uncorrelated) polynomials are in order. If the decline in recall is essentially constant over the days, then a significant linear (straight line) trend, or first-degree polynomial, will be found. On the other hand, if the decline in recall is slow over the first 2 days and then drops sharply over the remaining 3 days, a quadratic trend (part of a parabola), or second-degree polynomial, will be found. Finally, if the decline is slow at first, the drops off sharply for the next few days and finally levels off, we will find a cubic trend, or third-degree polynomial. We illustrate each of these cases:

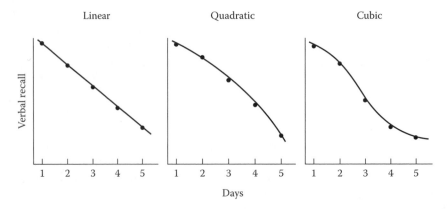

The fact that the polynomials are uncorrelated means that the linear, quadratic, cubic, and quartic components are partitioning distinct (different) parts of the variation in the data.

In Table 13.7 we present the SAS and SPSS control lines for running the trend analysis on this verbal recall data. In Chapter 5, in discussing planned comparisons, we indicated that

TABLE 13.7

SAS and SPSS Control Lines for One Between and One Within Repeated-Measures Analysis

SAS	SPSS
TITLE '1 BETW & 1 WITHIN';	TITLE '1 BETW & 1 WITHIN'.
DATA TREND;	DATA LIST FREE/GPID Y1 Y2 Y3 Y4 Y5.
INPUT GPID Y1 Y2 Y3 Y4 Y5;	BEGIN DATA.
CARDS;	1 26 20 18 11 10
1 26 20 18 11 10	1 34 35 29 22 23
1 34 35 29 22 23	1 41 37 25 18 15
1 41 37 25 18 15	1 29 28 22 15 13
1 29 28 22 15 13	1 35 34 27 21 17
1 35 34 27 21 17	1 28 22 17 14 10
1 28 22 17 14 10	1 38 34 28 25 22
1 38 34 28 25 22	1 43 37 30 27 25
1 43 37 30 27 25	2 42 38 26 20 15
2 42 38 26 20 15	2 31 27 21 18 13
2 31 27 21 18 13	2 45 40 33 25 18
2 45 40 33 25 18	2 29 25 17 13 8
2 29 25 17 13 8	2 39 32 28 22 18
2 29 32 28 22 18	2 33 30 24 18 7
2 33 30 24 18 7	2 34 30 25 24 23
2 34 30 25 24 23	2 37 31 25 22 20
2 37 31 25 22 20	END DATA.
PROC GLM;	MANOVA Y1 TO Y5 BY GPID (1,2)/
CLASS GPID;	③ WSFACTOR = DAY(5)/
MODEL Y1 Y2 Y3 Y4 Y5 = GPID;	④ CONTRAST (DAY) = POLYNOMIAL/
① REPEATED DAYS 5 (1 2 3 4 5)	③ WSDESIGN = DAY/
② POLYNOMIAL/SUMMARY;	⑤ RENAME = MEAN, LINEAR, QUAD,
	CUBIC, QUART/
	PRINT = TRANSFORM CELLINFO(MEANS)
	⑥ SIGNIF(AVERF UNIV)/
	ANALYSIS(REPEATED)/
	⑦ DESIGN = GPID/.

① The REPEATED statement is fundamental for running repeated-measures designs on SAS. The general form is REPEATED factor name levels (level values) transformation/options; Note that the level values are in parentheses. We are interested in polynomial contrasts on the repeated measures, so that is what has been requested. Other transformations are available (HELMERT, PROFILE, etc.—see *SAS User's Guide: Statistics*, Version 5, p. 454).

② SUMMARY here produces ANOVA tables for each contrast defined by the within subjects factors.

③ Recall again that the WSFACTOR (within subject factor) and the WSDESIGN (within subject design) subcommands are fundamental for running multivariate repeated-measures analysis on SPSS.

④ If we wish trend analysis on the DAY repeated measure variable, then all we need do is request POLYNOMIAL on the CONTRAST subcommand.

⑤ In this RENAME subcommand we are giving meaningful names to the polynomial contrasts being generated.

⑥ We *must* put UNIV within the SIGNIF keyword for the univariate tests to be printed out in repeated-measures designs, and the univariate tests are *the* main thing of interest here, because they indicate whether there is a linear trend, a quadratic trend, etc.

⑦ It is important to realize that with SPSS MANOVA there is a design subcommand (WSDESIGN) for the within or repeated measures factor(s) and a *separate* DESIGN subcommand for the between (grouping) factor(s).

TABLE 13.8

Means and Standard Deviations for One Between and One Within Repeated Measures

CELL MEANS AND STANDARD DEVIATIONS				
VARIABLE . . Y1				
FACTOR	CODE	MEAN	STD. DEV.	N
GPID	1	34.250	6.228	8
GPID	2	36.250	5.523	8
FOR ENTIRE SAMPLE		35.250	5.779	16
VARIABLE . . Y2				
FACTOR	CODE	MEAN	STD. DEV.	N
GPID	1	30.875	6.728	8
GPID	2	31.625	5.097	8
FOR ENTIRE SAMPLE		31.250	5.779	16
VARIABLE . . Y3				
FACTOR	CODE	MEAN	STD. DEV.	N
GPID	1	24.500	4.986	8
GPID	2	24.875	4.704	8
FOR ENTIRE SAMPLE		24.687	4.686	16
VARIABLE . . Y4				
FACTOR	CODE	MEAN	STD. DEV.	N
GPID	1	19.125	5.592	8
GPID	2	20.250	3.882	8
FOR ENTIRE SAMPLE		19.687	4.686	16
VARIABLE . . Y5				
FACTOR	CODE	MEAN	STD. DEV.	N
GPID	1	16.875	5.890	8
GPID	2	15.250	5.651	8
FOR ENTIRE SAMPLE		16.062	5.639	16

several types of contrasts are available in SPSS MANOVA (Helmert, special, polynomial, etc.), and we also illustrated the use of the Helmert and special contrasts; here the polynomial contrast option is used. Recall these are built into the program, so that all we need do is request them, which is what has been done in the CONTRAST subcommand.

When several groups are involved, as in our verbal recall example, an *additional* assumption is homogeneity of the covariance matrices on the repeated measures for the groups. In our example, the group sizes are equal, and in this case a violation of the equal covariance matrices assumption is not serious. That is, the test statistic is robust (with respect to Type I error) against a violation of this assumption (see Stevens, 1986, chap. 6). However, if the group sizes are substantially unequal, then a violation is serious, and Stevens (1986) indicated in Table 6.5 what should be added to test the assumption.

Table 13.8 gives the means and standard deviations for the two groups on the five repeated measures. In Table 13.9 we present selected, annotated output from SPSS MANOVA for the trend analysis. Results from that table show that the groups do not differ significantly ($F = .04$, $p < .837$) and that there is not a significant group by days interaction ($F = 1.2$, $p < .323$). There is, however, a quite significant days main effect, and in particular, the LINEAR and CUBIC trends are significant at the .05 level ($F = 239.14$, $p < .000$, and $F = 10.51$, $p < .006$, respectively). The linear trend is by far the most pronounced, and a graph of the means for the data in

TABLE 13.9

Selected Printout from SPSS MANOVA for the Trend Analysis on the Verbal Recall Data

Orthonormalized Transformation Matrix (Transposed)

	MEAN	LINEAR	QUAD	CUBIC	QUART	
Y1	.447	−.632	.535	−.316	.120	
Y2	.447	−.316	−.267	.632	−.478	
Y3	.447	.000	−.535	.000	.717	①
Y4	.447	.316	−.267	−.632	−.478	
Y5	.447	.632	.535	.316	.120	

EFFECT . . GPID BY DAY (Cont.)
Univariate F-tests with (1,14) D. F.

Variable	Hypoth. SS	Error SS	Hypoth. MS	Error MS	F	Sig. of F	
LINEAR	18.90625	233.58750	18.90625	16.68482	1.13314	.305	
QUAD	1.00446	53.81250	1.00446	3.84375	.26132	.617	②
CUBIC	7.65625	33.03750	7.65625	2.35982	3.24442	.093	
QUART	1.35804	18.26250	1.35804	1.30446	1.04107	.325	

EFFECT . . DAY (Cont.)
Univariate F-tests with (1,14) D. F.

Variable	Hypoth. SS	Error SS	Hypoth. MS	Error MS	F	Sig. of F	
LINEAR	3990.00625	233.58750	3990.00625	16.68482	239.13988	.000	
QUAD	6.11161	53.81250	6.11161	3.84375	1.59001	.228	③
CUBIC	24.80625	33.03750	24.80625	2.35982	10.51192	.006	
QUART	4.25089	18.26250	4.25089	1.30446	3.25873	.093	

① The last four columns of numbers are the coefficients for orthogonal polynomials, although they may look strange since each column is scaled such that the sum of the squared coefficients equals 1. Textbooks typically present the coefficients for 5 levels as follows:

Linear	−2	−1	0	1	2
Quadratic	2	−1	−2	−1	2
Cubic	−1	2	0	−2	1
Quartic	1	−4	6	−4	1

Compare, for example, *Fundamentals of Experimental Design*, Myers, 1979, p. 548.

② None of the interaction effects is significant at the .05 level.
③ Both the linear and cubic effects are significant at the .05 level, although the linear is by far the strongest effect.

The screens for this problem are in Appendix D.

Figure 13.1 shows this, although a cubic curve (with a few bends) will fit the data slightly better.

In concluding this example, the following from Myers (1979) is important:

> Trend or orthogonal polynomial analyses should never be routinely applied whenever one or more independent variables are quantitative.... *It is dangerous to identify statistical components freely with psychological processes.* It is one thing to postulate a cubic component of *A*, to test for it, and to find it significant, thus substantiating the theory. It is another matter to assign psychological meaning to a significant component that has not been postulated on a priori grounds. (p. 456)

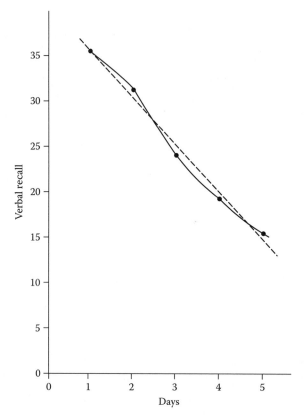

FIGURE 13.1
Linear and cubic plots for verbal recall data.

Now, suppose an investigator is in a part confirmatory and part exploratory study. He is conducting trend analyses on three different variables *A, B,* and *C,* and will be doing a total of 10 statistical tests. From previous research he is able to predict a linear trend on variable *A,* and from theoretical considerations he predicts a quadratic trend for variable *C.* He wishes to confirm these expectations; this is the confirmatory part of the study. He also wishes to determine if trends of any other nature are significant on variables *A, B,* and *C;* this is the exploratory part of the study. A simple, but reasonable way of maintaining control on overall Type I error and yet having adequate power (at least for the predicted trends) would be to test each anticipated significant effect at the .05 level and test all other effects at the .005 level. Then, by the Bonferroni inequality, he is assured that

$$\text{overall } a < .05 + .05 + 8(.005) = .14$$

13.11 Post Hoc Procedures for the One Between and One Within Design

In the one between and one within, or mixed model repeated-measures design, we have both the assumption of sphericity *and* homogeneity of the covariance matrices for the different levels of the between factor. This combination of assumptions has been called multisample sphericity. Keselman and Keselman (1988) conducted a Monte Carlo study examining how well four post hoc procedures controlled overall alpha under various violations of multisample sphericity. The four procedures were: the Tukey, a modified Tukey employing a nonpooled estimate of error, a Bonferroni *t* statistic, and a *t* statistic with a multivariate critical value. These procedures were also used in the Maxwell (1980) study of post hoc procedures for the single group repeated-measures design.

Keselman and Keselman set the number of groups at three and considered four and eight levels for the within (repeated) factor. They considered both equal and unequal group sizes for the between factor. Recall that ϵ quantifies departure from sphericity, and $\epsilon = 1$ means sphericity, with $1/(k-1)$ indicating maximum departure from sphericity. They investigated $\epsilon = .75$ (a relatively mild departure) and $\epsilon = .40$ (a severe departure for the four level case, given the minimum value there would be .33). Selected results from their study are presented here for the four level within factor case.

		Tukey (pooled)	Bonferroni	Multivariate
$\epsilon = .75$	equal covariance matrices and gp sizes	6.34	3.46	1.70
	unequal covariance matrices, but equal group sizes	7.22	4.32	2.48
	unequal covariance matrices and gp sizes—larger variability with smaller group size	14.78	11.38	7.04
$\epsilon = .40$	equal covariance matrices and gp sizes	11.36	2.38	1.16
	unequal covariance matrices, but equal group sizes	10.08	2.70	1.56
	unequal covariance matrices and gp sizes—larger variability with smaller group size	17.80	6.34	3.94

The group sizes for the values presented here were 13, 10, and 7. The entries in the body of the table are to be compared against an overall alpha of .05.

The above results show that the Bonferroni approach keeps the overall alpha less than .05, provided you do not have *both* unequal group sizes and unequal covariance matrices. If you want to be confident that you will be rejecting falsely no more than your level of significance, then this is the procedure of choice. In my opinion, the Tukey procedure is acceptable for $\epsilon = .75$, as long as there are *equal* group sizes. For the other cases, the error rates for the Tukey are at least double the level of significance, and therefore not acceptable.

Recall that the pooled Tukey procedure for the single group repeated-measures design was to reject if

$$\left| \bar{x}_i - \bar{x}_j \right| > q_{.05;k,(n-1)(k-1)} \sqrt{MS_{res}/n} \tag{1}$$

where n is the number of subjects, k is the number of levels and MS_{res} is the error term (Equation 1).

For the one between and one within design with J groups and k within levels, we declare two marginal means (means for the repeated measures levels over the J groups) different if

$$\left| \bar{x}_i - \bar{x}_j \right| > q_{.05;k,(N-J)(k-1)} \sqrt{MS_{kxs/J}/N} \tag{2}$$

where the mean square is the within subjects error term for the mixed model and N is total number of subjects.

13.12 One Between and Two Within Factors

We consider both the univariate and multivariate analyses of a one between and two within repeated measures data set from Elashoff (1981). Two groups of subjects were given three different doses of two drugs. There are several different questions of interest in this study. Will the drugs be differentially effective for different groups? Is the effectiveness of the drugs dependent on dose level? Is the effectiveness of the drugs dependent both on dose level and on the group?

The SPSS screens for obtaining the univariate and multivariate results are presented in Table 13.10. The data is given below. The first score is group ID, the second is for drug 1, dose 1, the third score is for drug 1, dose 2, etc.

1 19 22 28 16 26 22	2 16 20 24 30 34 36
1 11 19 30 12 18 28	2 26 26 26 24 30 32
1 20 24 24 24 22 29	2 22 27 23 33 36 45
1 21 25 25 15 10 26	2 16 18 29 27 26 34
1 18 24 29 19 26 28	2 19 21 20 22 22 21
1 17 23 28 15 23 22	2 20 25 25 29 29 33
1 20 23 23 26 21 28	2 21 22 23 27 26 35
1 14 20 29 25 29 29	2 17 20 22 23 26 28

In Table 13.11 are the means and standard deviations for the six variables. In Table 13.12 are the multivariate tests for the various effects. Note that DRUG, DRUG*GP and DOSE are significant at the .05 level. In Tables 13.13 and 13.14 we present the univariate tests for the various effects. Note that the same effects are significant, even when sphericity is not assumed.

Let us examine why the DRUG, DRUG*GP and DOSE effects are significant. We take the means from Table 13.11 and insert them into the design, yielding:

		DRUG				
		1			2	
DOSE	1	2	3	1	2	3
GROUP 1	17.50	22.50	27.0	19.0	21.88	26.50
GROUP 2	19.63	22.38	24.0	26.88	28.63	33.0

Now, collapsing on dose, the group × drug design means are obtained:

	DRUG	
	1	2
GROUP 1	22.33	22.46
GROUP 2	22.00	29.50

The mean in cell 11 (22.33) is simply the average of 17.5, 22.5, and 27, while the mean in cell 12 (22.46) is the average of 19, 21.88, and 26.5, and so on. It is now apparent that the outlier cell mean of 29.5 is what "caused" all the significance. For some reason Drug 2 was not as effective with Group 2 in inhibiting the response. We have indicated previously,

TABLE 13.10

SPSS for Windows 10.0 Screens for One Between and Two Within Repeated Measures

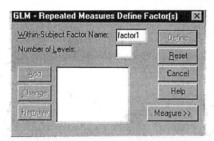

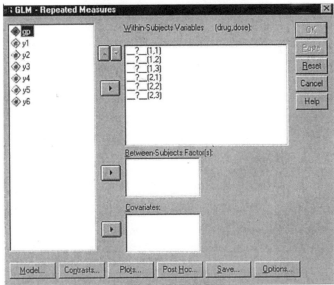

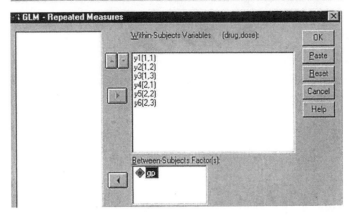

especially in connection with multiple regression, how influential an individual subject's score can be in affecting the results. This example shows the same type of thing, only now the outlier is a mean.

Finally, Table 13.15 presents only the univariate results from SAS GLM. Actually, the univariate tests would be preferred here because both Greenhouse–Geisser epsilons are >.70.

TABLE 13.11

Means and Standard Deviations for One Between and Two Repeated Measures

CELL MEANS AND STANDARD DEVIATIONS			
VARIABLE .. Y1			
FACTOR	CODE	MEAN	STD. DEV.
GPID	1	17.50000	3.42261
GPID	2	19.62500	3.42000
FOR ENTIRE SAMPLE		18.56250	3.48270
VARIABLE .. Y2			
FACTOR	CODE	MEAN	STD. DEV.
GPID	1	22.50000	2.07020
GPID	2	22.37500	3.24863
FOR ENTIRE SAMPLE		22.43750	2.63233
VARIABLE .. Y3			
FACTOR	CODE	MEAN	STD. DEV.
GPID	1	27.00000	2.61861
GPID	2	24.00000	2.72554
FOR ENTIRE SAMPLE		25.50000	3.01109
VARIABLE .. Y4			
FACTOR	CODE	MEAN	STD. DEV.
GPID	1	19.00000	5.34522
GPID	2	26.87500	3.75832
FOR ENTIRE SAMPLE		22.93750	6.03842
VARIABLE .. Y5			
FACTOR	CODE	MEAN	STD. DEV.
GPID	1	21.87500	5.89037
GPID	2	28.62500	4.62717
FOR ENTIRE SAMPLE		25.25000	6.19139
VARIABLE .. Y6			
FACTOR	CODE	MEAN	STD. DEV.
GPID	1	26.50000	2.92770
GPID	2	33.00000	6.84523
FOR ENTIRE SAMPLE		29.75000	6.09371

13.13 Two Between and One Within Factors

To illustrate how to run a two between and one within factor repeated-measures design we consider hypothetical data from a study comparing the relative efficacy of a behavior modification approach to dieting versus a behavior modification plus exercise approach (combination treatment) on weight loss for a group of overweight women. There is also a control group in this study. First, six each of women between 20 and 30 years old are randomly assigned to one of the three groups. Then, six each of women between 30 to

TABLE 13.12

Multivariate Tests for All Effects for Elashoff Data

Multivariate Tests[b]				
Effect		Value	F	Sig.
DRUG	Pillai's Trace	.482	13.001[a]	.003
	Wilks' Lambda	.518	13.001[a]	.003
	Hotelling's Trace	.929	13.001[a]	.003
	Roy's Largest Root	.929	13.001[a]	.003
DRUG * GP	Pillai's Trace	.465	12.163[a]	.004
	Wilks' Lambda	.535	12.163[a]	.004
	Hotelling's Trace	.869	12.163[a]	.004
	Roy's Largest Root	.869	12.163[a]	.004
DOSE	Pillai's Trace	.795	25.261[a]	.000
	Wilks' Lambda	.205	25.261[a]	.000
	Hotelling's Trace	3.886	25.261[a]	.000
	Roy's Largest Root	3.886	25.261[a]	.000
DOSE * GP	Pillai's Trace	.183	1.452[a]	.270
	Wilks' Lambda	.817	1.452[a]	.270
	Hotelling's Trace	.223	1.452[a]	.270
	Roy's Largest Root	.223	1.452[a]	.270
DRUG * DOSE	Pillai's Trace	.126	.937[a]	.417
	Wilks' Lambda	.874	.937[a]	.417
	Hotelling's Trace	.144	.937[a]	.417
	Roy's Largest Root	.144	.937[a]	.417
DRUG * DOSE * GP	Pillai's Trace	.143	1.086[a]	.366
	Wilks' Lambda	.857	1.086[a]	.366
	Hotelling's Trace	.167	1.086[a]	.366
	Roy's Largest Root	.167	1.086[a]	.366

[a] Exact statistic

40 years old are randomly assigned to one of the three groups. The investigator wishes to determine whether age might moderate the effectiveness of the diet approach. Weight loss is measured 2 months, 4 months, and 6 months after the program begins. Schematically, the design is as follows:

		WGTLOSS1	WGTLOSS2	WGTLOSS3
GROUP	AGE			
CONTROL	20–30 YRS			
CONTROL	30–40 YRS			
BEH. MOD.	20–30 YRS			
BEH. MOD.	30–40 YRS			
BEH. MOD. + EXER.	20–30 YRS			
BEH. MOD. + EXER.	30–40 YRS			

TABLE 13.13

Univariate Tests for Most Effects for Elashoff Data

Source		Type III Sum of Squares	df	Mean Square	F	Sig.
DRUG	Sphericity Assumed	348.844	1	348.844	13.001	.003
	Greenhouse-Geisser	348.844	1.000	348.844	13.001	.003
	Huynh-Feldt	348.844	1.000	348.844	13.001	.003
	Lower-bound	348.844	1.000	348.844	13.001	.003
DRUG * GP	Sphericity Assumed	326.344	1	326.344	12.163	.004
	Greenhouse-Geisser	326.344	1.000	326.344	12.163	.004
	Huynh-Feldt	326.344	1.000	326.344	12.163	.004
	Lower-bound	326.344	1.000	326.344	12.163	.004
Error(DRUG)	Sphericity Assumed	375.646	14	26.832		
	Greenhouse-Geisser	375.646	14.000	26.832		
	Huynh-Feldt	375.646	14.000	26.832		
	Lower-bound	375.646	14.000	26.832		
DOSE	Sphericity Assumed	758.771	2	379.385	36.510	.000
	Greenhouse-Geisser	758.771	1.757	431.768	36.510	.000
	Huynh-Feldt	758.771	2.000	379.385	36.510	.000
	Lower-bound	758.771	1.000	758.771	36.510	.000
DOSE * GP	Sphericity Assumed	42.271	2	21.135	2.034	.150
	Greenhouse-Geisser	42.271	1.757	24.054	2.034	.156
	Huynh-Feldt	42.271	2.000	21.135	2.034	.150
	Lower-bound	42.271	1.000	42.271	2.034	.176
Error(DOSE)	Sphericity Assumed	290.958	28	10.391		
	Greenhouse-Geisser	290.958	24.603	11.826		
	Huynh-Feldt	290.958	28.000	10.391		
	Lower-bound	290.958	14.000	20.783		

Treatment and age are the two grouping or between variables and time (over which the weight loss is measured) is the within variable. The SPSS MANOVA control lines for running the analysis are given in Table 13.16.

Selected results from SPSS MANOVA are given in Table 13.17. Looking first at the between subject effects at the top of the table, we see that only the diet main effect is significant at the .05 level ($F = 4.30, p < .023$).

Next, at the bottom of the printout, under

TESTS INVOLVING 'WGTLOSS' WITHIN SUBJECT EFFECT

we find that both wgtloss ($F = 84.57, p = .000$) and the diet by wgtloss interaction ($F = 4.88, p = .002$) are significant. Remember that these AVERAGED TESTS OF SIGNIFICANCE, as they are called by SPSS, are in fact the univariate approach to repeated measures. SPSS MANOVA does not print out by default the adjusted univariate tests (although they may

TABLE 13.14

Univariate Tests for Drug by Dose and Drug by Dose by GP Interaction and Transformation Matrix

DRUG * DOSE	Sphericity Assumed	12.063	2	6.031	.514
	Greenhouse-Geisser	12.063	1.459	8.265	.472
	Huynh-Feldt	12.063	1.703	7.085	.493
	Lower-bound	12.063	1.000	12.063	.423
DRUG * DOSE * GP	Sphericity Assumed	14.812	2	7.406	.444
	Greenhouse-Geisser	14.812	1.459	10.149	.413
	Huynh-Feldt	14.812	1.703	8.700	.428
	Lower-bound	14.812	1.000	14.812	.376
Error(DRUG*DOSE)	Sphericity Assumed	247.792	28	8.850	
	Greenhouse-Geisser	247.792	20.432	12.127	
	Huynh-Feldt	247.792	23.836	10.396	
	Lower-bound	247.792	14.000	17.699	

		DRUG	DOSE		DRUG LINEAR DOSE	
		Linear	Linear	Quadratic	Linear	Quadratic
Y1	.408	−.408	−.500	.289	.500	−.289
Y2	.408	−.408	.000	−.577	.000	.577
Y3	.408	−.408	.500	.289	−.500	−.289
Y4	.408	.408	−.500	.289	−.500	.289
Y5	.408	.408	.000	−.577	.000	−.577
Y6	.408	.408	.500	.289	.500	.289

be obtained by simply inserting GG AND HF in the SIGNIF part of the PRINT subcommand), but do note in the printout that "epsilons may be used to adjust degrees of freedom for the averaged results." In this case, we needn't be concerned about adjusting because the Greenhouse-Geisser epsilon of .7749 and even more so, the Huynh-Feldt epsilon of .94883 indicate that sphericity is not a problem here. In this regard, note that the Mauchley test for sphericity is "highly" significant ($p = .008$) and seems to strongly indicate that sphericity is not tenable; however, on the basis of Monte Carlo studies, we recommend against using such statistical tests of sphericity.

In interpreting the significant effects, we construct from the means on the printout, the cell means for diets by wgtloss combined over the age groups:

		WGTLOSS			
		1	2	3	ROW MEANS
	1	4.50	3.33	2.083	3.304
DIETS	2	5.33	3.917	2.250	3.832
	3	6.00	5.917	2.250	4.722
COLUMN MEANS		5.278	4.389	2.194	

TABLE 13.15

Univariate Analyses from SAS GLM for One Between and Two Within

UNIVARIATE TESTS OF HYPOTHESES FOR WITHIN SUBJECT EFFECTS

SOURCE	DF	TYPE III SS		MEAN SQUARE	F VALUE		PR > F
DRUG	1	348.84375000		348.84375000	13.00		0.0029
DRUG*GPID	1	326.34375000		326.34375000	12.16	③	0.0036
ERROR (DRUG)	14	375.64583333	⑤	26.83184524			

SOURCE	DF	TYPE III SS		MEAN SQUARE	F VALUE		PR > F
DOSE	2	758.77083333		379.38541667	36.51		0.0001
DOSE*GPID	2	42.27083333		21.13541667	2.03	④	0.1497
ERROR (DOSE)	28	290.95833333	⑤	10.39136905			

GREENHOUSE-GEISSER EPSILON = 0.8787
HUYNH-FELDT EPSILON = 1.0667

SOURCE	DF	TYPE III SS		MEAN SQUARE	F VALUE	PR > F
DRUG*DOSE	2	12.06250000		6.03125000	0.68	0.5140
DRUG*DOSE*GPID	2	14.81250000		7.40625000	0.84	0.4436
ERROR (DRUG*DOSE)	28	247.79166667	⑤	8.84970238		

GREENHOUSE-GEISSER EPSILON = 0.7297 ①
HUYNH-FELDT EPSILON = 0.8513

TESTS OF HYPOTHESES FOR BETWEEN SUBJECTS EFFECTS

SOURCE	DF	TYPE III SS		MEAN SQUARE	F VALUE		PR > F
GPID	1	270.01041667		270.01041667	7.09	②	0.0185
ERROR (DOSE)	14	532.97916667	⑤	38.06994048			

① Since both $\hat{\epsilon}$'s are >.70, the univariate approach is preferred, since the type I error rate is controlled and it is more powerful than the multivariate approach.

② Groups differ significantly at the .05 level, since .0185 < .05.

③ & ④ The drug main effect and drug by group interaction are significant at the .05 level, while the dose main effect is also significant at the .05 level.

⑤ Note that four different error terms are involved in this design; an additional complication with complex repeated-measures designs. The error terms are boxed.

TABLE 13.16

Control Lines for a Two Between and One Within Design on SPSS MANOVA

```
TITLE 'TWO BETWEEN AND ONE WITHIN'.
DATA LIST FREE/DIET AGE WGTLOSS1 WGTLOSS2 WGTLOSS3.
BEGIN DATA.
1 1 4 3 3    1 1 4 4 3    1 1 4 3 1    1 1 3 2 1
1 1 5 3 2    1 1 6 5 4    1 2 6 5 4    1 2 5 4 1
1 2 3 3 2    1 2 5 4 1    1 2 4 2 2    1 2 5 2 1
2 1 6 3 2    2 1 5 4 1    2 1 7 6 3    2 1 6 4 2
2 1 3 2 1    2 1 5 5 4    2 2 4 3 1    2 2 4 2 1
2 2 6 5 3    2 2 7 6 4    2 2 4 3 2    2 2 7 4 3
3 1 8 4 2    3 1 3 6 3    3 1 7 7 4    3 1 4 7 1
3 1 9 7 3    3 1 2 4 1    3 2 3 5 1    3 2 6 5 2
3 2 6 6 3    3 2 9 5 2    3 2 7 9 4    3 2 8 6 1
END DATA.
LIST.
MANOVA WGTLOSS1 TO WGTLOSS3 BY DIET(1,3) AGE(1,2)/
    WSFACTOR = WGTLOSS(3)/
    WSDESIGN = WGTLOSS/
    PRINT = CELLINFO(MEANS) SIGNIF(UNIV,AVERF)/
    DESIGN.
```

Graphing the cell means shows rather nicely why the interaction effect was obtained:

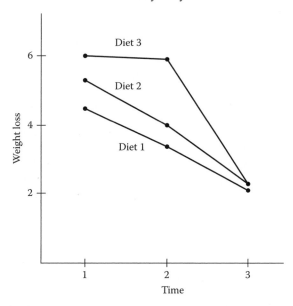

Recall that graphically an interaction is evidenced by nonparallel lines. In this graph one can see that the profiles for Diets 1 and 2 are essentially parallel; however, the profile for Diet 3 is definitely not parallel with profiles for Diets 1 and 2. And, in particular, it is the weight loss at Time 2 that is making the profile for Diet 3 distinctly nonparallel.

TABLE 13.17

Selected Printout from SPSS MANOVA for Two Between and One Within Repeated-Measures Design

Tests of Between-Subjects Effects.

Tests of Significance for T1 using UNIQUE sums of squares

Source of Variation	SS	DF	MS	F	Sig of F
WITHIN+RESIDUAL	128.83	30	4.29		
DIET	36.91	2	18.45	4.30	.023
AGE	.23	1	.23	.05	.818
DIET BY AGE	.80	2	.40	.09	.912

- -

Tests involving 'WGTLOSS' Within-Subject Effect.

Mauchly sphericity test, W =	.71381
Chi-square approx. =	9.77706 with 2 D. F.
Significance =	.008
Greenhouse-Geisser Epsilon =	.77749
Huynh-Feldt Epsilon =	.94883
Lower-bound Epsilon =	.50000

AVERAGED Tests of Significance that follow multivariate tests are equivalent to univariate or split-plot or mixed-model approach to repeated measures.
Epsilons may be used to adjust d.f. for the AVERAGED results.

Tests involving 'WGTLOSS' Within-Subject Effect.

AVERAGED Tests of Significance for WGTLOSS using UNIQUE sums of squares

Source of Variation	SS	DF	MS	F	Sig of F
WITHIN+RESIDUAL	64.33	60	1.07		
WGTLOSS	181.35	2	90.68	84.57	.000
DIET BY WGTLOSS	20.93	4	5.23	4.88	.002
AGE BY WGTLOSS	1.80	2	.90	.84	.438
DIET BY AGE BY WGTLOSS	1.59	4	.40	.37	.828

The main effect for diet is telling us that the population row means are not equal, and from the preceding sample row means with the Tukey procedure, we conclude that Diet 3 is significantly more effective than Diet 1 over time. The weightloss main effect indicates that the population column means are not equal. The sample column means suggest, and the Tukey procedure for repeated measures confirms, that there is significantly greater weight loss after 2 and 4 months than there is after 6 months.

13.14 Two Between and Two Within Factors

This is a very complex design, an example of which appears in Bock (1975, pp. 483–484). The data was from a study by Morter, who was concerned about the comparability of the first and second responses on the form definiteness and form appropriateness variables of the Holtzman Inkblot procedure for a preadolescent group of subjects. The two between variables were grade level (4 and 7) and IQ, (high and low); thus there was a crossed design on

TABLE 13.18

Control Lines for Two Between and Two Within Repeated Measures on SPSS Manova

---

TITLE 'TWO BETWEEN AND TWO WITHIN'.
DATA LIST FREE/GRADE IQ FD1 FD2 FA1 FA2.
BEGIN DATA.

1	1	2	1	0	2		1	1	−7	−2	−2	−5		1	1	−3	−1	−3 −1
1	1	1	1	0	−3		1	1	1	−1	−4	−2		1	1	−7	1	−4 −3
1	2	0	−4	−9	−7		1	2	−1	−9	−9	−4		1	2	−6	−6	3 −4
1	2	−2	−4	−4	−5		1	2	−2	−1	−3	−3		1	2	−9	−9	−3 1
2	1	3	4	2	−3		2	1	−1	−1	−3	−3		2	1	2	2	2 0
2	1	2	0	−2	0		2	1	0	−1	2	2		2	1	3	3	−4 −2
2	1	−1	2	2	−1		2	1	−3	−2	3	−2						
2	2	−3	−2	5	2		2	2	2	3	−2	−3		2	2	2	4	1 3
2	2	3	2	−5	−5		2	2	−4	−3	−3	−3		2	2	6	4	−9 −9
2	2	2	1	−3	0		2	2	−1	−4	−2	0		2	2	−2	−1	2 −2
2	2	−2	4	−1	0													

END DATA.
LIST.
① MANOVA FD1 TO FA2 BY GRADE(1,2) IQ(1,2)/
   WSFACTOR = FORM(2),TIME(2)/
   WSDESIGN/
② PRINT = TRANSFORM CELLINFO(MEANS) HOMOGENEITY(BOXM) SIGNIF(AVERF)/
   DESIGN/.

---

①		FORM	FD		FA	
		TIME	1	2	1	2
GRADE 4	HI IQ					
	LOW IQ					
GRADE 7	HI IQ					
	LOW IQ					

② Again, as for the examples in Tables 13.7 and 13.11, there is a within *S*'s design subcommand for the repeated measures factors, and a separate DESIGN subcommand for the between (grouping) factors. If we assume a full factorial model, as would be true in exploratory research, then these subcommands can be abbreviated to WSDESIGN/ and DESIGN/.

the subjects. The two within variables were form and time, with the design being crossed on the measures. The schematic layout for the design is given at the bottom of Table 13.18, which also gives the control lines for running the analysis on SPSS MANOVA, along with the data.

It may be quite helpful for the reader to compare the control lines for this example with those for the one between and two within example in Table 13.10, as they are quite similar. The main difference here is that there is an additional between variable, hence an additional factor after the keyword BY in the MANOVA command and three between effects in the DESIGN subcommand. The reader is referred to Bock (1975) for an interpretation of the results.

13.15 Totally Within Designs

There are research situations where the *same* subjects are measured under various treatment combinations, that is, where the same subjects are in each cell of the design. This may be particularly the case when not many subjects are available. We consider three examples to illustrate.

Example 13.3

A researcher in child development is interested in observing the same group of preschool children (all 4 years of age) in two situations at two different times (morning and afternoon) of the day. She is concerned with the extent of their social interaction, and will measure this by having two observers independently rate the amount of social interaction. The average of the two ratings will serve as the dependent variable. The within factors here are situation and time of day. There are four scores for each child: social interaction in Situation 1 in the morning and afternoon, and social interaction in Situation 2 in the morning and afternoon. We denote the four scores by Y1, Y2, Y3, and Y4.

Such a totally within repeated-measures design is easily set up on SPSS MANOVA. The control lines are given here:

```
TITLE 'TWO WITHIN DESIGN'.
DATA LIST FREE/Y1 Y2 Y3 Y4.
BEGIN DATA.

        DATA LINES

END DATA.
MANOVA Y1 TO Y4/
   WSFACTOR = SIT(2),TIME(2)/
   WSDESIGN/
   PRINT = TRANSFORM CELLINFO(MEANS)/
   ANALYSIS(REPEATED)/.
```

Note in this example that *only univariate* tests will be printed out by SPSS for all three effects. This is because there is only one degree of freedom for each effect, and hence only one transformed variable for each effect.

Example 13.4

Suppose in an ergonomic study we are interested in the effects of day of the work week and time of the day (AM or PM) on various measures of posture. We select 30 computer operators and for this example we consider just one measure of posture called shoulder flexion. We then have a two-factor totally within design that looks as follows:

	Monday		Wednesday		Friday	
	AM	PM	AM	PM	AM	PM
1						
2						
3						
.						
.						
.						
30						

Example 13.5

A social psychologist is interested in determining how self-reported anxiety level for 35–45 year old men varies as a function of situation, who they are with, and how many people are involved. A questionnaire will be administered to 20 such men, asking them to rate their anxiety level (on a Likert scale from 1 to 7) in three situations (going to the theater, going to a football game, and going to a dinner party), with primarily friends and primarily strangers, and with a total of six people and with 12 people. Thus, the men will be reporting anxiety for 12 different contexts. This is a three within, crossed repeated-measures design, where situation (three levels) is crossed with nature of group (two levels) and with number in group (two levels).

13.16 Planned Comparisons in Repeated-Measures Designs

Planned comparisons can also be easily set up on SPSS MANOVA for repeated-measures designs, although the WSFACTOR (within subject factor) subcommand must be included to indicate that the contrasts are being done on a repeated measures variable. To illustrate, we consider the setup of Helmert contrasts on a single group repeated-measures design with data again from Bock (1975). The study involved the effect of three drugs on the duration of sleep of 10 mental patients. The drugs were given orally on alternate evenings, and the hours of sleep were compared with an intervening control night. Each of the drugs was tested a number of times with each patient. Thus, there are four levels for treatment, the control condition, and the three drugs. The first drug (Level 2) was of a different type from the other two, which were of a similar type. Therefore, Helmert contrasts were appropriate. The control lines for running the contrasts, along with the significance tests for the contrasts, are given in Table 13.19.

There is an important additional point to be made regarding planned comparisons with repeated-measures designs. SPSS MANOVA requires that the comparisons be orthogonal for within subject factors. *If a nonorthogonal set of contrasts is input, then MANOVA will orthogonalize them.**

13.16.1 Nonorthogonal Contrasts in SPSS

In the previous editions I simply referred readers to Appendix B in the back, which is directly from SPSS. However, I have become convinced that more elaboration is needed. It is important to note, as SPSS points out, that the program is structured so that orthogonal contrasts are needed in repeated measures. Let us consider an example to illustrate. This example, which involves *nonorthogonal* contrasts, will be run as repeated measures AND in a way that preserves the nonorthogonality of the contrasts. The control lines for each analysis are given below.

```
NONORTHOGONAL CONTRASTS
RUN AS REPEATED MEASURES
TITLE ' NON-ORTHOGONAL CONTRASTS'.
DATA LIST FREE /Y1 Y2 Y3 Y4
BEGIN DATA.
 .6 1.3 2.5 2.1  3   1.4 3.8 4.4  4.7 4.5 5.8 4.7
6.2 6.1 6.1 6.7  3.2 6.6 7.6 8.3  2.5 6.2 8   8.2
2.8 3.6 4.4 4.3  1.1 1.1 5.7 5.8  2.9 4.9 6.3 6.4
5.5 4.3 5.6 4.6
END DATA.
MANOVA Y1 TO Y4/
WSFACTOR=DRUGS(4)/
CONTRAST(DRUGS)=SPECIAL(1 1 1 1 1 1
-1 -1 1 -.5 -.5 0 0 1 -.5 -.5)/
PRINT=TRANSFORM/
WSDESIGN=DRUGS/
ANALYSIS(REPEATED)/.
```

```
NONORTHOGONAL CONTRASTS
RUN ACCORDING TO APPENDIX C
TITLE ' NON-ORTHOGONAL CONTRASTS'.
DATA LIST FREE/Y1 Y2 Y3 Y4.
BEGIN DATA.
 .6 1.3 2.5 2.1  3   1.4 3.8 4.4  4.7 4.5 5.8 4.7
6.2 6.1 6.1 6.7  3.2 6.6 7.6 8.3  2.5 6.2 8   8.2
2.8 3.6 4.4 4.3  1.1 1.1 5.7 5.8  2.9 4.9 6.3 6.4
5.5 4.3 5.6 4.6
END DATA.
MANOVA Y1 TO Y4/
TRANSFORM=SPECIAL(1 1 1 1 1 -1 -1 1 -.5 -.5 0
0 1 -.5 -.5)/
PRINT=TRANSFORM/
ANALYSIS=(T1/T2 T3 T4)/.
```

---

* There is a way to get around this problem. See Appendix B.

TABLE 13.19

Control Lines for Helmert Contrasts in a Single-Group Repeated-Measures Design and
Tests of Significance

```
TITLE 'HELMERT CONTRASTS FOR REPEATED MEASURES'.
DATA LIST FREE/Y1 Y2 Y3 Y4.
BEGIN DATA.
 .6 1.3 2.5 2.1    3  1.4 3.8 4.4    4.7 4.5 5.8 4.7
6.2 6.1 6.1 6.7   3.2 6.6 7.6 8.3    2.5 6.2 8  8.2
2.8 3.6 4.4 4.3   1.1 1.1 5.7 5.8    2.9 4.9 6.3 6.4
5.5 4.3 5.6 4.8
END DATA.
LIST.
MANOVA Y1 TO Y4/
   WSFACTOR=DRUGS(4)/
   CONTRAST(DRUGS)=HELMERT/
   WSDESIGN=DRUGS/
   RENAME=MEAN, HELMERT1, HELMERT2, HELMERT3/
   PRINT=TRANSFORM CELLINFO(MEANS)/
   ANALYSIS(REPEATED)/.
```

Orthonormalized Transformation Matrix (Transposed)

	MEAN	HELMERT1	HELMERT2	HELMERT3
Y1	.500	.866	.000	.000
Y2	.500	−.289	.816	.000
Y3	.500	−.289	−.408	.707
Y4	.500	−.289	−.408	−.707

Estimates for HELMERT1

- - - Individual univariate .9500 confidence intervals

DRUGS

Parameter	Coeff.	Std. Err.	t-Value	Sig. t	Lower −95%	CL- Upper
1	−1.5588457	.52620	−2.96245	.01590	−2.74920	−.36849

Estimates for HELMERT2

- - - Individual univariate .9500 confidence intervals

DRUGS

Parameter	Coeff.	Std. Err.	t-Value	Sig. t	Lower −95%	CL- Upper
1	−1.2859821	.32960	−3.90160	.00361	−2.03160	−.54037

Estimates for HELMERT3

- - - Individual univariate .9500 confidence intervals

DRUGS

Parameter	Coeff.	Std. Err.	t-Value	Sig. t	Lower −95%	CL- Upper
1	.007071068	.13517	.05231	.95942	−.29872	.31286

When nonorthogonal contrasts are run in a repeated-measures design, as above, they are transformed into orthogonal contrasts so that the multivariate test is correct. To see what contrasts the program is actually testing one MUST refer to the transformation matrix. SPSS warns of this:

MANOVA automatically orthonormalizes contrast matrices for WSFACTORS. If the special contrasts that were requested are nonorthogonal, the contrasts actually fitted are not the contrasts requested. See the transformation matrix for the actual contrasts fitted.

Notice that in the control lines to the right, any reference to repeated measures is removed, such as WSFACTOR, WSDESIGN and ANALYSIS(REPEATED). In the repeated measures run the contrasts are transformed into an orthogonal set, as the matrix below shows

	T1	T2	T3	T4
Y1	.5000	.254	.828	.000
Y2	.5000	−.085	−.276	.816
Y3	.5000	.592	−.483	−.408
Y4	.5000	−.761	−.069	−.408

In the other case, the contrasts that are input are tested. The multivariate test is the SAME in both cases (F = 5.53737, p = .029), but the univariate tests for T2, T3, and T4 (the transformed variables) in the non-repeated measures run are respectively F = 16.86253, 7.35025 and 15.22245.

It is *very important that separate* error terms are used for testing each of the planned comparisons for significance. Boik (1981) showed that for even a very slight deviation from sphericity (ϵ = .90), the use of a pooled error term can result in a Type I error rate quite different from the level of significance. For ϵ = .90 Boik showed, if testing at α = .05, that the actual alpha for single degree of freedom contrasts ranged from .012 to .097. In some cases, the pooled error term will underestimate the amount of error and for other contrasts the error will be overestimated, resulting in a conservative test. Fortunately, in SPSS MANOVA the error terms are separate for the contrasts (see Table 13.19). As O'Brien and Kaiser (1985) noted, "The MANOVA approach handles sets of contrasts in such a way that each contrast in the set remains linked with just its specific error term. As a result, we avoid all problems associated with general (average) error terms" (p. 319).

13.17 Profile Analysis

In profile analysis the interest is in comparing the performance of two or more groups on a battery of test scores (interest, achievement, personality). It is assumed that the tests are scaled similarly, or that they are commensurable. In profile analysis there are three questions to be asked of the data in the following order:

1. Are the profiles parallel? If the answer to this is yes for two groups, it would imply that one group scored uniformly better than the other on all variables.

2. If the profiles are parallel, then are they coincident? In other words, did the groups score the same on each variable?

3. If the profiles are coincident, then are the profiles level? In other words, are the means on all variables equal to the same constant.

Next, we present *hypothetical* examples of parallel and nonparallel profiles: (the variables represent achievement in content areas).

If the profiles are not parallel, then there is a group-by-variable interaction. That is, how much better one group does than another depends on the variable.

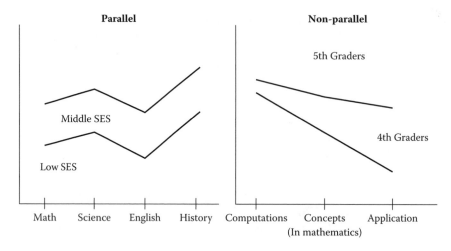

Why is it necessary that the tests be scaled similarly in order to have the results of a profile analysis meaningfully interpreted? To illustrate, suppose we compared two groups on three variables, A, B, and C, two of which were on a 1 to 5 scale and the other on a 1 to 30 scale, that is, not scaled similarly. Suppose the following graph resulted, suggesting nonparallel profiles:

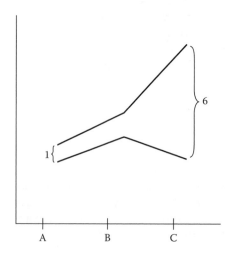

But the nonparallelism is a scaling artifact. The magnitude of superiority of Group 1 for Test *A* is 1/5, which is exactly the same order of superiority on Test *C*, 6/30 = 1/5. A way of dealing with this problem if the tests are scaled differently is to first convert to some type of standard score (e.g., z or T) before proceeding with the profile analysis.

We now consider the running and interpretation of a profile analysis on SPSS MANOVA, using some data from Johnson and Wichern (1982).

Example 13.6

In a study of love and marriage, a sample of husbands and wives were asked to respond to the following questions:

1. What is the level of passionate love you feel for your partner?
2. What is the level of passionate love that your partner feels for you?
3. What is the level of companionate love that you feel for your partner?
4. What is the level of companionate love that your partner feels for you?

The responses to all four questions were on a Likert-type scale from 1 (none at all) to 5 (a tremendous amount). We wish to determine whether the profiles for the husbands and wives are parallel. There were 30 husbands and 30 wives who responded. The control lines for running the analysis on SPSS are given in Table 13.20. The raw data are given at the end of this chapter.

The test of parallelism appears in Table 13.21 and shows that parallelism is tenable at the .01 level, because the exact probability of .057 is greater than .01. Now, it is meaningful to proceed to the second question in profile analysis, and ask whether the profiles are coincident. The test for this is given in Table 13.22 and shows that the profiles can be considered coincident, that is, the same. In other words, the differences for husbands and wives on the four variables can be considered to be due to sampling error. Finally, we ask whether husbands and wives scored the same on all four tests, that is, the question of equal scale means. The test for equal scale means in Table 13.21 indicates this is not tenable. Reference to the univariate tests at the bottom of Table 13.21 shows that it is the difference in the way the subjects responded to scales 2 and 3 that was primarily responsible for the rejection of equal scale means. Note from the means at the top of Table 13.22 that the subjects scored somewhat higher on Variable 3 than on Variable 2.

TABLE 13.20

Control Lines for Profile Analysis of Husband and Wife Ratings

```
TITLE 'PROFILE ANALYSIS ON HUSBAND AND WIFE RATINGS'.
DATA LIST FREE/SPOUSE PASS YOU PASSPART COMPYOU COMPPART.
BEGIN DATA.

       DATA LINES

END DATA.
REPORT VARS = PASSYOU PASSPART COMPYOU COMPPART/
   BREAK = SPOUSE/
   SUMMARY = MEAN/. ①
MANOVA PASSYOU TO COMPPART BY SPOUSE(1,2)/
   TRANSFORM = REPEATED/
   RENAME = AVERAGE DIF2AND1 DIF3AND2 DIF4AND3/
   PRINT = TRANSFORM/
   ANALYSIS = (DIF2AND1,DIF3AND2,DIF4AND3/ AVERAGE)/ ②
   DESIGN/.
```

① The BREAK subcommand indicates what variable will define the subgroups (in this case husbands and wives). The SUMMARY subcommand tells the program what summary statistics we want printed for each subgroup; in this case we only want the means.

② This subcommand defines two analyses. The first analysis, on the 3 difference variables before the / within the parentheses, answers questions 1 and 3 for the profile analysis. The second analysis, on the average variable, answers the question of coincident profiles. The general setup then of the ANALYSIS subcommand for k repeated measures in profile analysis would be

$$\text{ANALYSIS} = (\text{DIF2AND1, DIF3AND2, } \dots \text{ , DIFKANDK-1/ AVERAGE})/$$

For example, if k = 7, then the ANALYSIS subcommand would be:

ANALYSIS = (DIF2AND1, DIF3AND2, DIF4AND3, DIF5AND4, DIF6AND5, DIF7AND6/ AVERAGE)/

TABLE 13.21

Tests of Parallelism of Profiles for Husband and Wife Ratings

Order of Variables for Analysis

Variates   Covariates

DIF2AND1
DIF3AND2
DIF4AND3

3 Dependent Variables
0 Covariates

- -

Note. . TRANSFORMED variables are in the variates column.

Transformation Matrix (Transposed)

	AVERAGE	DIF2AND1	DIF3AND2	DIF4AND3
PASSYOU	.250	1.000	.000	.000
PASSPART	.250	−1.000	1.000	.000
COMPYOU	.250	.000	−1.000	1.000
COMPPART	.250	.000	.000	−1.000

EFFECT . . SPOUSE
Multivariate Tests of Significance (S = 1, M = 1/2, N = 27)

Test Name	Value	Exact F	Hypoth. DF	Error DF	Sig. of F
Pillais	.12474	2.66027	3.00	56.00	.057
Hotellings	.14251	2.66027	3.00	56.00	.057
Wilks'	.87526	2.66027	3.00	56.00	.057
Roys	.12474				

Note. . F statistics are exact.

- -

EFFECT . . SPOUSE (Cont.)
Univariate F-tests with (1,58) D. F.

Variable	Hypoth. SS	Error SS	Hypoth. MS	Error MS	F	Sig. of F
DIF2AND1	.81667	40.16667	.81667	.69253	1.17925	.282
DIF3AND2	.26667	50.46667	.26667	.87011	.30647	.582
DIF4AND3	.41667	4.56667	.41667	.07874	5.29197	.025

TABLE 13.22

Tests of Coincidence of the Profiles and Equal Scale Means

PROFILE ANALYSIS				
SPOUSE	PASSYOU	PASSPART	COMPYOU	COMPPART
1.00				
Mean	3.90	3.97	4.33	4.40
2.00				
Mean	3.83	4.13	4.63	4.53

Tests of Significance for AVERAGE using UNIQUE sums of squares

Source of Variation	SS	DF	MS	F	Sig of F
WITHIN CELLS	9.04	58	.16		
SPOUSE	.27	1	.27	1.71	.196
(Model)	.27	1	.27	1.71	.196
(Total)	9.31	59	.16		

R-Squared = .029
Adjusted R-Squared = .012

13.18 Doubly Multivariate Repeated-Measures Designs

In this section we consider a complex, but, not unusual in practice, repeated-measures design, in which the same subjects are measured on several variables at each point in time, or on several variables for each treatment or condition. The following are three examples:

1. We are interested in tracking elementary school children's achievement in math and reading, and we have their standardized test scores obtained in grades 2, 4, 6, and 8. Here we have data for two variables, each measured at four points in time.

2. As a second example of a doubly multivariate problem. Suppose we have 53 subjects measured on five types of tests on three occasions. In this example, there are also two between variables (group and gender).

3. A study by Wynd (1992) investigated the effect of stress reduction in preventing smoking relapse. Subjects were randomly assigned to an experimental group or control group. They were then invited to three abstinence-booster sessions (three-part treatment) provided at 1-, 2-, and 3-month intervals. After each of these sessions, they were measured on three variables: imagery, stress, and smoking rate.

Why are the data from the above three situations considered to be *doubly* multivariate? Recall from Chapter 4 that I defined a multivariate problem as one involving several correlated dependent variables. In these cases, the problem is doubly multivariate because there is a correlational structure *within* each measure and a different correlational structure *across* the measures. For item 1, the children's scores on math ability will be correlated across the grades, as will their verbal scores, but, in addition, there will be some correlation between their math and verbal scores.

13.19 Summary

1. Repeated-measures designs are much more powerful than completely randomized designs, because the variability due to individual differences is removed from the error term, and individual differences are the major reason for error variance.

2. Two major advantages of repeated-measures designs are increased precision (because of the smaller error term), and the fact that many fewer subjects are needed than in a completely randomized design. Two potential disadvantages are that the order of treatments may make a difference (this can be dealt with by counterbalancing) and carryover effects.

3. Either a univariate or a multivariate approach can be used for repeated-measures analysis. The assumptions for a single-group univariate repeated-measures analysis are (a) independence of the observations, (b) multivariate normality, and (c) sphericity (also called circularity). For the multivariate approach, the first two assumptions are still needed, but the sphericity assumption is *not* needed. Sphericity requires that the variances of the differences for *all pairs* of repeated measures be equal. Although statistical tests of sphericity exist, they are not recommended.

4. Under a violation of sphericity the Type I error rate for the univariate approach is inflated. However, a modified (adjusted) univariate approach, obtained by multiplying each of the degrees of freedom by $\hat{\epsilon}$, yields an honest Type I error rate.

5. Because both the modified (adjusted) univariate approach and the multivariate approach control the Type I error rate, the choice between them involves the issue of the power of the tests. As neither the adjusted univariate test or the multivariate test is usually most powerful, it is recommended that generally both tests be used, because they may differ in the treatment effects they will detect. The multivariate test, however, probably should be avoided when $n < k + 10$, because under this condition its power will tend to be low.

6. If the sphericity assumption is tenable, then the Tukey procedure is a good post hoc technique for locating significant pairwise differences. If the sphericity assumption is not met, then the Bonferroni approach should be used. That is, do multiple *correlated t* tests, but use the Bonferroni inequality to keep the overall alpha level under control.

7. When several groups are involved, then an additional assumption is multisample sphericity, that is, that the covariance matrices for the groups on the transformed variables are equal. This can be checked with a test found in Anderson (1958, p. 259), which is available in SAS GLM. You should, however, remember our earlier caution on statistical tests for sphericity.

8. Designs with only within subject factors are fairly common in certain areas of research. These are designs where the *same* subjects are involved in every treatment combination or in each situation. Totally within designs are easily set up on SPSS.

9. In testing contrasts with repeated-measures designs it is imperative that a *different* error term be used for each contrast, because Boik (1981) showed that if a pooled error term is used the actual alpha will be quite different from the presumed level of significance.

10. In profile analysis we are comparing two or more groups of subjects on a battery of tests. It is assumed that the tests are scaled similarly. If they are not, then the scores must be converted to some type of standard score (e.g., z or T) for the analysis to be meaningful. Nonparallel profiles means there is a group-by-variable interaction; that is, how much better one group does than another depends on the variable.

13.20 Exercises

1. In the multivariate analysis of the drug data we stated that H_0: $\mu_1 = \mu_2 = \mu_3 = \mu_4$ is equivalent to saying that $\mu_1 - \mu_2 = 0$ and $\mu_2 - \mu_3 = 0$ and $\mu_3 - \mu_4 = 0$. Show this is true.

2. Consider the following data set from a single-sample repeated-measures design with three repeated measures:

		Treatments	
S's	1	2	3
1	5	6	1
2	3	4	2
3	3	7	1
4	6	8	3
5	6	9	3
6	4	7	2
7	5	9	2

(a) Do a univariate repeated-measures analysis, using the procedure employed in the text. Do you reject at the .05 level?

(b) Do a multivariate repeated-measures analysis by hand (i.e., using a calculator) with the following difference variables: y_1-y_2 and y_2-y_3.

(c) Run the data on SPSS, obtaining both the univariate and multivariate results, to check the answers you obtained in (a) and (b).

(d) Note the $(k - 1)$ transformed variables SPSS uses in testing for the multivariate approach, and yet the same multivariate F is obtained. What point that we mentioned in the text does this illustrate?

(e) Assume the sphericity assumption is tenable and employ the Tukey post hoc procedure at the .05 level to determine which pairs of treatments differ.

3. A school psychologist is testing the effectiveness of a stress management approach in reducing the state and trait anxiety for college students. The subjects are pretested and matched on these variables and then randomly assigned within each pair to either the stress management approach or to a control group. The following data are obtained:

	Stress Management		Control	
Pairs	State	Trait	State	Trait
1	41	38	46	35
2	48	41	47	50
3	34	33	39	36
4	31	40	28	38
5	26	23	35	19
6	37	31	40	30
7	44	32	46	45
8	53	47	58	53
9	46	41	47	48
10	34	38	39	39
11	33	39	36	41
12	50	45	54	40

(a) Test at the .05 level, using the multivariate matched pairs analysis, whether the stress management approach was successful.

(b) Which of the variables are contributing to multivariate significance?

4. Suppose that in the Elashoff drug example the two groups of subjects had been given the three different doses of two drugs under two different conditions. Then we would have a one between and three within design. What modifications in the control lines from Table 13.10 would be necessary to run this analysis?

5. Show that the covariance for the difference variables $(y_1 - y_2)$ and $(y_3 - y_4)$ in the drug data example is −8.6, and that the covariance for $(y_2 - y_3)$ and $(y_3 - y_4)$ is −19.

6. The extent of the departure from the sphericity assumption is measured by

$$\hat{\varepsilon} = \frac{k^2 (\bar{s}_{ii} - \bar{s})^2}{(k-1)\left(\sum\sum s_{ij}^2 - 2k \sum_i \bar{s}_i^2 + k^2 \bar{s}^2 \right)}$$

where
  $\bar{s}$ is the mean of all entries in the covariance matrix **S**
  $\bar{s}_{ii}$ is mean of entries on main diagonal of **S**
  $\bar{s}_i$ is mean of all entries in row i of **S**
  $\bar{s}_{ij}$ is ijth entry of **S**

Find $\hat{\varepsilon}$ for the following two covariance matrices:

(a) $$\mathbf{S} = \begin{bmatrix} 76.8 & 53.2 & 29.2 & 96 \\ 53.2 & 42.8 & 15.8 & 47 \\ 29.2 & 15.8 & 14.8 & 27 \\ 69 & 47 & 27 & 64 \end{bmatrix} \text{(answer } \hat{\varepsilon} = .605)$$

(b) $$\mathbf{S} = \begin{bmatrix} 4 & 3 & 2 \\ 3 & 5 & 2 \\ 2 & 2 & 6 \end{bmatrix} \text{(answer } \hat{\varepsilon} = .83)$$

7. Trend analysis was run on the Roy and Pothoff (1964) data. It consists of growth measurements for 11 girls (coded as 1) and 16 boys at ages 8, 10, 12, and 14. Since some of the data is suspect (as the SAS manual notes), we have deleted observations 19 and 20 before running the analysis. Following is part of the SPSS printout:

Cell Means and Standard Deviations
Variable .. Y8

FACTOR	CODE	Mean	Std. Dev.	N
GENDER	1	21.182	2.125	11
GENDER	2	22.786	2.614	14
For entire sample		22.080	2.499	25

Variable .. Y10

FACTOR	CODE	Mean	Std. Dev.	N
GENDER	1	22.227	1.902	11
GENDER	2	24.214	1.958	14
For entire sample		23.340	2.144	25

Variable .. Y12

FACTOR	CODE	Mean	Std. Dev.	N
GENDER	1	23.091	2.365	11
GENDER	2	25.429	2.401	14
For entire sample		24.400	2.618	25

Variable .. Y14

FACTOR	CODE	Mean	Std. Dev.	N
GENDER	1	24.091	2.437	11
GENDER	2	27.714	2.119	14
For entire sample		26.120	2.877	25

Estimates for LINEAR
- - - Individual univariate .9500 confidence intervals

YEAR

Parameter	Coeff.	Std. Err.	t-Value	Sig. t	Lower −95%	CL-Upper
1	2.86115062	.31159	9.18254	.00000	2.21659	3.50572

GENDER BY YEAR

Parameter	Coeff.	Std. Err.	t-Value	Sig. t	Lower −95%	CL-Upper
2	−.71655815	.31159	−2.29971	.03088	−1.36112	−.07199

Estimates for QUAD
- - - Individual univariate .9500 confidence intervals

YEAR

Parameter	Coeff.	Std. Err.	t-Value	Sig. t	Lower −95%	CL-Upper
1	.202922078	.19471	1.04218	.30816	−.19987	.60571

GENDER BY YEAR

Parameter	Coeff.	Std. Err.	t-Value	Sig. t	Lower −95%	CL-Upper
2	−.22564935	.19471	−1.15890	.25839	−.62844	.17714

Estimates for CUBIC						
--- Individual univariate .9500 confidence intervals						
Year						
Parameter	Coeff.	Std. Err.	t-Value	Sig. t	Lower –95%	CL-Upper
1	.179321036	.18478	.97046	.34191	–.20292	.56157
GENDER BY YEAR						
Parameter	Coeff.	Std. Err.	t-Value	Sig. t	Lower –95%	CL-Upper
2	–.10817342	.18478	–.58542	.56397	–.49042	.27407

(a) Are there any significant (at .05 level) interactions (linear by gender, etc.)?

(b) Are there any significant (at .05 level) year effects?

8. Consider the following covariance matrix:

$$\begin{matrix} & & y_1 & y_2 & y_3 \\ & y_1 & 1.0 & .5 & 1.5 \\ \mathbf{S} = & y_2 & .5 & 3.0 & 2.5 \\ & y_3 & 1.5 & 2.5 & 5.0 \end{matrix}$$

Calculate the variances of the three difference variables: $y_1 - y_2$, $y_1 - y_3$ and $y_2 - y_3$. What do you think $\hat{\epsilon}$ will be equal to in this case?

9. Consider the following real data, where the dependent variable is Beck depression score:

	WINTER	SPRING	SUMMER	FALL
1	7.50	11.55	1.00	1.21
2	7.00	9.00	5.00	15.00
3	1.00	1.00	.00	.00
4	.00	.00	.00	.00
5	1.06	.00	1.10	4.00
6	1.00	2.50	.00	2.00
7	2.50	.00	.00	2.00
8	4.50	1.06	2.00	2.00
9	5.00	2.00	3.00	5.00
10	2.00	3.00	4.21	3.00
11	7.00	7.35	5.88	9.00
12	2.50	2.00	.01	2.00
13	11.00	16.00	13.00	13.00
14	8.00	10.50	1.00	11.00

(a) Run this on SPSS or SAS as a single group repeated measures. Is it significant at the .05 level, assuming sphericity?

(b) Is the adjusted univariate test significant at the .05 level?

(c) Is the multivariate test significant at the .05 level?

10. Marketing researchers are conducting a study to evaluate both consumer beliefs and the stability of those beliefs about the following four brands of toothpaste: Crest, Colgate, Ultra Brite, and Gleem. The beliefs to be assessed are (1) good taste, (2) cavity prevention, and (3) breath protection. They also wish to determine the extent to which the beliefs are moderated by sex and by age (20–35, 36–50, and 51 and up). The subjects will be asked their beliefs at two points in time separated by a 2-month interval.

    (a) Set up schematically the appropriate repeated-measures design.

    (b) Show the control lines necessary for running this design on SPSS MANOVA to obtain both the univariate and multivariate tests.

11. A researcher is interested in how self-reported anxiety for tenured male statisticians varies as a function of several factors. A questionnaire will be administered to 40 such statisticians, asking them to rate their anxiety in eight situations: at home and in the office, time of the day (morning or afternoon) and day of the week (Monday or Wednesday). The researcher also wishes to determine if anxiety varies as a function of how many teenagers are in the house (none, 1 or 2, more than 2).
    Show the complete SPSS MANOVA control lines for running this analysis.

12. Consider the following data for a single group repeated-measures design:

$$k = 4, n = 8, \varepsilon = .70, \alpha = .0!$$

    (a) Find the critical values for the unadjusted test, for the Greenhouse-Geisser test and for the conservative test.

    (b) Suppose an investigator had obtained F = 3.29 for the above case and had applied the unadjusted test. What type of error would he make?

    (c) Suppose a different investigator had obtained F = 4.03 and applied the conservative test. What type of error would he make?

13. Two types of pipe coating are compared for resistance to rusting. Two pipes, one with each type of coating, were buried together in 15 different locations, providing a natural pairing. Corrosion was measured by two variables: maximum depth of pit in thousandths of an inch and number of pits. Part of the analysis from SPSS MANOVA is shown below:

MULT MATCHED PAIRS-RENCHER 152

* * * * * * Analysis of Variance--design 1 * * * * * *

EFFECT . . CONSTANT
Multivariate Tests of Significance (S =1, M =0, N =5 1/2

Test Name	Value	Exact F	Hypoth. DF	Error DF	Sig. of F
Pillais	.43591	5.02306	2.00	13.00	.024
Hotellings	.77278	5.02306	2.00	13.00	.024
Wilks	.56409	5.02306	2.00	13.00	.024
Roys	.43591				

Note. . F statistics are exact.

EFFECT . . CONSTANT (Cont.)
Univariate F-tests with (1, 14) D. F.

Variable	Hypoth. SS	Error SS	Hypoth. MS	Error MS	F	Sig. of F
DEPDIFF	960.00000	1702.00000	960.00000	121.57143	7.89659	.014
NOPITDIF	141.06667	304.93333	141.06667	21.78095	6.47661	.023

(a) Is the multivariate test significant at the .05 level?

(b) Are either of the univariate tests significant at the .05 level?

14. An investigator has access to the following correlation matrix, where the measures are taken at 2-month intervals:

	Y1	Y2	Y3	Y4
Y1	1.00			
Y2	.54	1.00		
Y3	.28	.45	1.00	
Y4	.17	.23	.31	1.00

He will make use of this data in conducting a study with similar subjects on the same measure. How many subjects will he need if he wishes power of .80 to detect a medium effect size at the .05 level of significance?

15. Find an article from one of the better journals in your content area from within the last 5 years that used a repeated-measures design. Answer the following questions:

(a) What type (in terms of between and within factors) of design was used?

(b) Did the authors do a multivariate analysis?

(c) Did the authors do a univariate analysis? Was it the unadjusted or adjusted univariate test?

(d) Was any mention made of the relative power of the adjusted univariate vs. multivariate approach?

16. A researcher is interested in the smoking behavior of a group of 30 professional men, 10 of whom are 30–40, 10 are 41–50 and the remaining 10 are 51–60. She wishes to determine whether how much they smoke is influenced by the time of day (morning or afternoon) and by context (at home or in the office). The men are observed in each of the above four situations and the number of cigarettes smoked is recorded. She also wishes to determine whether the age of the men influences their smoking behavior.

(a) What type of a repeated-measures design is this?

(b) Show the complete SPSS MANOVA control lines (put DATA for the data lines) for running the analysis.

14

Categorical Data Analysis: The Log Linear Model

14.1 Introduction

The reader may recall from introductory statistics that one of the most elementary statistical tests is the two-way chi square. This test is appropriate if the subjects, or more generally, entities, have been cross-classified in two ways and the data is in the form of frequency counts. As an example, suppose we have taken a sample of 66 adults and wish to determine whether sex of adults is related to their approval or lack of approval of a television series. The results are as follows:

	Approval	No Approval
Male	22	16
Female	9	19

The null hypothesis for a two-way chi-square is that the modes of classification are independent. In this case we have:

H_o: Sex is independent of approval of the television series. Based on the null hypothesis, expected cell frequencies (e_{ij}) are computed from

$$e_{ij} = \frac{(\text{row total})(\text{column total})}{n} (n \text{ is sample size})$$

and compared against the observed frequencies (o_i) with the following chi-square statistic:

$$\chi^2 = \sum \frac{(o_{ij} - e_{ij})^2}{e_{ij}}$$

Although this is simple to handle statistically, how would we analyze the data if we also wished to examine the effect of location as a possible moderator variable on approval of the series, and had the following three-way contingency table?

	Rural 1		Urban 2	
	Approval 1	No Approval 2	Approval 1	No Approval 2
Female 1	3	7	6	12
Male 2	5	15	17	1

Note that we have put numbers for the levels of each factor. We will see that this makes it easier to identify the cell ID, especially for four- and five-way tables. What most researchers have done in the past with such multiway contingency tables is to run several two-way analyses. This was encouraged by the statistical packages, which easily produced the chi squares for all two-way tables. But, for the following two reasons, the reader should see that this is as unsatisfactory as having a three- or four-way ANOVA and doing only several two-way ANOVAs:

1. It doesn't enable one to detect three-factor or higher order interactions.
2. It doesn't allow for the simultaneous examination of the pairwise relationships.

The log linear model is a way of handling multiway (i.e., more complex) contingency tables in a statistically sound way. Major advances by statisticians such as Goodman and Mosteller and their students in the 1960s and 1970s made the log linear model accessible for applied workers. The model is available on both SAS and SPSS.

Agresti (1990) is an excellent, comprehensive theoretical textbook on categorical data analysis, while Wickens (1989) and Kennedy (1983) are very good applied texts, written especially for social science researchers. Kennedy drew many analogies between log linear analysis and analysis of variance.

Multiway contingency tables are fairly common, especially with survey data. Shown next are two four-way tables.

A group of 362 patients receiving psychiatric care were cross-classified according to four clinical indexes, yielding this table:

| | | Acute depression | | | |
| | | Yes | | No | |
Validity	Solidity	Introvert	Extrovert	Introvert	Extrovert
	Rigid	15	23	25	14
Energetic	Hysteric	9	14	46	47
	Rigid	30	22	22	8
Psychasthenic	Hysteric	32	16	27	12

In a study of the relationship between car size and accident injuries, accidents were classified according to type of accident, severity, and whether the driver was ejected.

| | | Accident Type | | | |
| | | Collision | | Rollover | |
Car weight	Driver ejected	Not severe	Severe	Not severe	Severe
Small	No	350	150	60	112
	Yes	26	23	19	80
Standard	No	1878	1022	148	404
	Yes	111	161	22	265

As the reader can see, the material in this chapter differs in several respects from that of all other chapters in the book:

1. The data now consist of frequency counts, rather than a score(s) for each subject on some dependent variable(s).

2. Although a linear model ($\mu_{ij} = \mu + \alpha_i + \beta_j + \alpha\beta_{ij}$ for ANOVA), or a linear combination of parameters for multiple regression was used in previous chapters, in multiway contingency tables the natural model is *multiplicative*. The *logarithm* is used to obtain a *linear* function of the parameters, hence the name log linear.

3. In log linear analysis, we are fitting a *series* of models to the data, whereas in ANOVA or regression one generally thinks of fitting *a* model to the data. Also, in log linear analysis we need to reverse our thinking on tests of significance. In log linear analysis, a test statistic that is not significant is good in the sense that the given model fits the data. In ANOVA or regression one generally wishes the statistic to be significant, indicating a significant main effect or interaction, or that a predictor variable contributes to significant variation on the dependent variable.

4. In multivariate analysis of variance, discriminant analysis, and repeated measures analysis, the assumed underlying distribution was the multivariate normal, whereas with frequency data the appropriate distribution is the multinomial.

The first topic covered in the chapter concerns the sampling distributions, binomial and multinomial, that describe qualitative data, and the linkage of the multinomial to the two-way chi-square. The log linear model is then developed for the two-way chi-square (where it is not needed, but easiest to explain) and three-way tables, where the important concept of hierarchical models is introduced. Computer analysis is considered for two three-way data sets, where the process of model selection is illustrated. The notions of partial and marginal association are explained. Conditions under which it is valid to collapse to two-way tables are considered and the fundamental concept of the odds (cross-product) ratio is discussed. A measure, the normed fit index, which can be very helpful in assessing model adequacy in very small or very large samples is considered. This measure is independent of sample size. The importance of cross-validating the model(s) selected on an independent sample is emphasized. Three methods of selecting models for higher dimensional tables are given, and a computer analysis is illustrated for a four-way table. The SPSS statistical package is illustrated. Finally, the use of contrasts (both planned and post hoc) in log linear analysis is discussed and an example given.

14.2 Sampling Distributions: Binomial and Multinomial

The simplest case is where there are just two possible outcomes: heads or tails for flipping a coin, in favor or not in favor of a bond issue, obtaining a 6 or not obtaining a 6 in rolling a die. The event is dichotomous and we are interested in the probability of f_1 "successes" in n trials. It is assumed that the trials are *independent*—that is, what happens in any given trial is not dependent on what happened on a previous trial(s). This is important, as independence is needed to multiply probabilities and obtain the following Binomial Law:

$$P(f_1/n) = \frac{n!}{f_1!(n-f_1)!} P_1^{f_1} P_2^{n-f_1}$$

where P_1 is the probability of success and P_2 is the probability of failure, and $n! = n(n-1)(n-2)\ldots 2(1)$.

Example 14.1

What is the probability of obtaining three 6's in rolling a die four times? Because the probability of any face coming up for a fair die is 1/6, the probability of obtaining a 6 is 1/6 and the probability of not obtaining a 6 is 5/6. Because $n = 4$, $n! = 4! = 4\ 3\ 2\ 1 = 24$. Therefore,

$$P(3/4) = \frac{4!}{3!1!}(.1667)^3(.8333)^1 = 4(.0039) = .0156$$

Thus, the probability of obtaining three 6s is less than 2%, quite small, as you might have suspected.

The binomial distribution has been introduced first because it is of historical interest and because it is a special case of a more general distribution, the multinomial, which applies to k possible outcomes for a given trial. Let P_1 be the probability of the outcome's being in category 1, P_2 the probability of the outcome's being in category 2, P_3 the probability of its being in category 3, and so on. Then it can be shown that the probability of exactly f_1 occurrences in category 1, f_2 occurrences in category 2, and so on is given by

$$P(f_1, f_2, \ldots, f_k \,/\, n) = \frac{n!}{f_1! f_2! \cdots f_k!} P_1^{f_1} P_2^{f_2} \cdots P_k^{f_k}$$

This is the *multinomial law,* and it is important because it provides the *exact* sampling distribution for two-way and higher way contingency tables. The chi-square test statistics that are presented in introductory statistics books for the one- and two-way chi-square are approximations to the multinomial distribution. Before we relate the multinomial distribution to the two-way chi-square, we give a few examples of its application in somewhat simpler situations.

Example 14.2

A die is thrown 10 times. What is the probability that a 1 will occur twice, a 3 three times, and anything else the other five times?

Here, $n = 10$ (number of trials), $f_1 = 2$, $f_2 = 3$, and $f_3 = 5$. Furthermore, the probability of a 1 is $P_1 = .1667$, the probability of a 3 is $P_2 = .1667$, and the probability of anything else is $P_3 = .667$. Therefore,

$$P(2, 3, 5/10) = \frac{10!}{2!3!5!}(.1667)^2(.1667)^3(.667)^5$$

$$= 2520(.00013)(.132) = .043$$

Example 14.3

A city has 60% Democrats, 30% Republicans, and 10% independents. If six individuals are chosen at random, what is the probability of getting two Democrats, one Republican, and three independents?

Here, $f_1 = 2$, $f_2 = 1$, and $f_3 = 3$, and the probability is:

$$P(2, 1, 3/6) = \frac{6!}{2!1!3!}(.60)^2(.30)^1(.1)^3 = .0065$$

To calculate the exact probabilities in each of these examples, we needed to know the probability of the outcome in each category. In the first two examples, this information was obtained from the fact that the probability of any face of a fair die's coming up is 1/6, whereas in Example 14.3, the probability of the outcome in each category (Democrat, Republican, or independent) was available from population information. To apply the multinomial law in the contingency table context, whether two-way, three-way, or other, we consider the cells as the categories, and think of it as a one-way layout. For example, with a 2 × 3 table, think of it as a one-way layout with six categories, or for a 2 × 2 × 3 table, think of it as a one-way layout with 12 categories. To calculate the probability of a certain frequency of subjects' falling in each of the six cells of a 2 × 3 table, however, we must know the probability of the subject's being in each cell (category). How does one obtain those probabilities? We consider an example to illustrate.

Example 14.4

A survey researcher is interested in determining how adults in a school district would vote on a bond issue. He also wants to determine whether sex moderates the response. A sample of 40 adults yields the following observed cell frequencies:

	Favor	Oppose	Row Probs
Male	10	5	.375 = 15/40
Female	6	19	.625 = 25/40
Column Probs	.40	.60	

The null hypothesis being tested here is that sex is independent of type of response. But independence means that the probability of being in a given cell (category) is simply the product of the subject's being in the ith row times the probability of the subject's being in the jth column. From these row and column probabilities, then, it is a simple matter to obtain the probability of a subject's being in each cell:

$$P_{11} = .375(.4) = .15, P_{12} = .375(.6) = .225$$

$$P_{21} = .625(.4) = .25, P_{22} = .625(.6) = .375$$

Therefore, the probability of obtaining this *specific* set of observed cell frequencies, assuming that the variables are independent, is given by the multinomial law as:

$$P(10,5,6,19/40) = \frac{40!}{10!5!6!19!}(.15)^{10}(.225)^{6}(.25)^{6}(.375)^{19}$$

To obtain the sampling distribution for hypothesis testing purposes, we would have to obtain the multinomial probabilities for all possible outcomes, a very tedious task at best. For example, for the two situations that follow:

	Favor	Oppose		Favor	Oppose
Male	11	4	Male	9	6
Female	5	20	Female	7	18

the following probabilities would need to be calculated:

$$P(11,4,5,20 / 40) = \frac{40!}{11!4!5!20!}(.15)^{11}(.225)^{4}(.25)^{5}(.375)^{20}$$

$$P(9,6,7,18 / 40) = \frac{40!}{9!6!7!18!}(.15)^{9}(.225)^{6}(.25)^{7}(.375)^{18}$$

Fortunately, however, when sample size is fairly large, the chi-square distribution provides a good approximation to the exact multinomial distribution, and can be used for testing hypotheses about frequency counts.

14.3 Two-Way Chi-Square–Log Linear Formulation

Although the log linear model is not really needed for the two-way chi-square, it provides a simple setting in which to introduce some of the fundamental notions associated with log linear analysis for higher order designs. We illustrate three main ideas:

1. Fitting a set of models to the data.
2. The notion of effects for the log linear model.
3. The notion of hierarchial models.

We use a two-way ANOVA (to which the reader has been exposed), and then consider the parallel development for the two-way chi-square.

Our two-way chi-square involves 100 university undergraduates cross-tabulated to determine whether there is an association between sex and attitude toward a constitutional amendment, and the two-way ANOVA examines the effect of sex and social class on achievement. The data for both are presented:

	Chi Square			ANOVA		
	Attitude			Social Class		
	Opposed	Support		Lower	Middle	Row
Female	33	7	Female	60	50	55
Male	37	23	Male	40	30	35
			Column Means	50	40	45

The reader may recall that in ANOVA we can model the population cell means as a linear combination of effects as follows:

$$\mu_{ij} = \mu + \alpha_i + \beta_j + \alpha\beta_{ij}$$

and therefore the estimated cell means are given as

$$\overline{x}_{ij} \;=\; \overline{x} \;+\; \hat{\alpha}_i \;+\; \hat{\beta}_j \;+\; \hat{\alpha\beta}_{ij}$$
$$\text{grand} \qquad \text{main effects} \qquad \text{interaction}$$
$$\text{mean}$$

where the estimated *main effects* for sex are given by:

$$\hat{\alpha}_1 = 55 - 45 = 10 \text{ and } \hat{a}_2 = 35 - 45 = -10$$

that is, row mean – grand mean for each level of sex.

The main effects for social class are given by:

$$\hat{\beta}_1 = 50 - 45 = 10 \text{ and } \hat{\beta}_2 = 40 - 45 = -5$$

that is, column mean – grand mean in each case.

The *interaction effects* measure that part of the cell means that cannot be explained by an overall effect and the main effects. Therefore, the estimated interaction effect for the *ij*th cell is:

$$\phi_{ij} = \text{cell mean} - \text{grand mean} - \text{main effect of A} - \text{main effect of B}$$

$$= \overline{x}_{ij} - \overline{x} - (\overline{x}_i - \overline{x}) - (\overline{x}_j - \overline{x}) = \overline{x}_{ij} - \overline{x} - \overline{x}_j + \overline{x}$$

Recall also that for fixed effects models the interaction effects for every row and column must sum to 0. Thus, for this example, once we obtain the estimated interaction effect for cell 11, the others will be determined. The interaction effect for cell 11 is

$$\phi_{11} = 60 - 55 - 50 + 45 = 0$$

Because of this, all the other cell interaction effects are 0.

Although ANOVA is not typically presented this way in textbooks, we could consider fitting various models to the data, ranging from a very simple model (grand mean), to a model involving a single main effect, a model involving all main effects, and finally the model with all effects. We could arrange these as a *hierarchical* set of models:

$$(1) \quad \overline{x}_{ij} = \overline{x}(\text{most restricted})$$

$$(2) \quad \overline{x}_{ij} = \overline{x} + \hat{\alpha}_i$$

$$(3) \quad \overline{x}_{ij} = \overline{x} + \hat{\alpha}_i + \hat{\beta}_j$$

$$(4) \quad \overline{x}_{ij} = \overline{x} + \hat{\alpha}_i + \hat{\beta}_j + \hat{\alpha\beta}_{ij}(\text{least restricted})$$

The arrangement is hierarchical, because as we proceed from most restricted to least restricted, the more restricted models become subsets of the lesser restricted models. For example, the most restricted model is a subset of Model 2, because Model 2 has the grand mean plus another effect, whereas Model 2 is a subset of Model 3, because Model 3 has all the effects in Model 2 plus β_j.

Now let us return to the two-way chi-square. To express the expected cell frequencies here as a *linear* function of parameters we need to take the natural log of the expected frequencies. It is important to see why this is necessary. The reason is that for multidimensional contingency tables the *multiplicative* model is the natural one. To see why the multiplicative model is natural, it is easiest to illustrate with something to which the reader has already been exposed. In the two-way chi-square we are testing whether the two modes of classification are independent (this is the null hypothesis). But independence implies that the probability of an observation's being in the *i*th row and the *j*th column is simply the *product* of the probability of being in the *i*th row (p_i) times the probability of being in the *j*th column (p_j), that is,

$$p_{ij} = p_i \cdot p_j$$

Recall that the expected cell frequency e_{ij} is given by $e_{ij} = Np_{ij} = Np_i.p_j$. For our 2×2 example, let us denote the row totals by o_{i+} and the column totals by o_{+j}. It then follows that $p_i = o_{i+}/N$ and $p_j = o_{+j}/N$, that is, the probability of being in the ith row is simply the number of observations in that row divided by the total number of observations, and similarly for columns. Therefore, we can rewrite the expected cell frequencies as:

$$e_{ij} = \frac{No_{i+}o_{+j}}{N \cdot N}(o_{i+}o_{+j})/N$$

and the expected frequencies are expressed as a multiplicative model. Using logs, however, we can transform the model to one that is *linear in the logs of the expected cell frequencies.* At this point, it is important to recall the following rules regarding logs:

$$\ln(ab) = \ln a + \ln b(\text{log of product} = \text{sum of logs})$$

$$\ln(a/b) = \ln a - \ln b(\text{log of quotient} = \text{difference in logs})$$

$$\ln a^b = b \ln a$$

Now let us return to the expression for the expected cell frequencies under the main effects model and rewrite it in additive form using properties of logs:

$$e_{ij} = o_{i+}o_{+j}/N$$

$$\ln e_{ij} = \ln o_{i+}o_{+j}/N$$

$$\ln e_{ij} = \ln o_{i+}o_{+j} - \ln N(\text{log of quotient} = \text{diff. in logs})$$

$$\ln e_{ij} = \ln o_{i+} + \ln o_{+j} - \ln N(\text{log of prod.} = \text{sum of logs})$$

Thus, for cell 11 we have

$$\ln 28 = \ln 40 + \ln 70 - \ln 100$$

We now wish to define estimated effects for the two-way chi-square that are analogous to what was done for the two-way ANOVA. In this case, however, we will be deviating the row and column *frequencies* about the grand mean of the expected frequencies.

$$\text{Main Effects for A} = \underset{\text{row mean}}{\frac{\Sigma \ln e_{ij}}{J}} - \underset{\text{grand mean}}{\frac{\Sigma\Sigma \ln e_{ij}}{IJ}}$$

$$\text{Main Effects for B} = \underset{\text{column mean}}{\frac{\Sigma \ln e_{ij}}{I}} - \underset{\text{grand mean}}{\frac{\Sigma\Sigma \ln e_{ij}}{IJ}}$$

$$\text{Interaction Effects} = \ln e_{ij} - \frac{\Sigma \ln e_{ij}}{J} - \frac{\Sigma \ln e_{ij}}{I} + \frac{\Sigma\Sigma \ln e_{ij}}{IJ}$$

Now let us apply these formulas to obtain the main effects for the attitude data presented at the beginning of this section. In the following table are given the natural logs of the expected frequencies under independence (the main effects model), along with the average natural logs for rows and columns. The effect parameters are then simply deviations of these averages from the grand mean of the natural logs.

| | Attitude | | Row | Row |
	Opposed	Support	Means	Effects
Female	3.332	2.485	2.909	−.202
	(28)	(12)		
Male	3.738	2.890	3.314	.203
Column Means	3.535	2.688	3.111	
Column Effects	.424	−.423	(grand mean)	

Both the sex main effect and joint main effect models were run on the SPSS HILOGLINEAR procedure for the attitude data. The control lines for doing this, along with selected printout (including the parameter estimates), are given in Table 14.1. Note that only a single value is given for each parameter estimate for the main effect model in Table 14.1. The other value is immediately obtained, because the sum of the effects in each case must equal 0.

14.4 Three-Way Tables

When the subjects are cross-classified on three variables, then the log linear model can be used to test for a three-way interaction, as well as for all two-way interactions and main effects. As with the two-way table, the natural log of the expected cell frequencies is expressed as a linear combination of effect parameters. In the two computer examples to be considered, we fit a series of models to the data, which range in complexity from just the grand mean to a model with one or more main effects, to a model with main effects and some two-way interactions, and finally to the *saturated* model (the model with all effects in it).

The other point to remember from the previous section is that we are examining only hierarchical models. A series of hierarchical models for a three-way table with factors A, B, and C is given in Table 14.2. Model 1 is called the most restricted model because only one parameter (the grand mean) is used to fit the data, and Model 8 is called the least restricted or saturated model because all parameters are used to fit the data and they will fit the data perfectly. Recall also that the models are called hierarchical because the more restricted models are subsets of the less restricted models. For example, Model 2 is a subset of Model 4 because all the parameters in Model 2 are in Model 4. Similarly, Model 5 is a subset of Model 7 because all parameters in Model 5 are in Model 7, which in addition has the AC and BC interaction parameters.

For Example 14.5, which uses Head Start data, we use basic probability theory to compute the expected cell frequencies for various models, showing how some of the printout from the package is obtained. The reader will see that two test statistics (the likelihood ratio χ^2 and the Pearson χ^2) appear on the SPSS printout for testing each model for goodness of fit. The form of the Pearson χ^2 is exactly the same as for the two-way chi-square.

TABLE 14.1

SPSS Control Lines for Main Effects Model, Selected Printout, and Expected Values for Models

```
TITLE 'LOG LINEAR MAIN EFFECT MODELS'.
DATA LIST FREE/SEX ATTITUDE FREQ.
WEIGHT BY FREQ.
BEGIN DATA.
1 1 33   1 2 7   2 1 37   2 2 23
END DATA.
LOGLINEAR SEX(1,2) ATTITUDE(1,2)/
 PRINT=ESTIM/
 DESIGN=SEX/
 PRINT=ESTIM/
 DESIGN=SEX,ATTITUDE/.
```

Goodness-of-Fit test statistics

Likelihood Ratio Chi Square = 21.65063	DF = 2	P = .000
Pearson Chi Square = 20.16667	DF = 2	P = .000

Estimates for Parameters

SEX

Parameter	Coeff.	Std. Err.	Z-Value	Lower 95 CI	Upper 95 CI
1	−.202732554	.10206	−1.98637	−.40277	−.00269

Goodness-of-Fit test statistics

Likelihood Ratio Chi Square = 5.19406	DF = 1	P = .023
Pearson Chi Square = 4.96032	DF = 1	P = .026

Estimates for Parameters

SEX

Parameter	Coeff.	Std. Err.	Z-Value	Lower 95 CI	Upper 95 CI
1	−.202732553	.10206	−1.98637	−.40277	−.00269

ATTITUDE

Parameter	Coeff.	Std. Err.	Z-Value	Lower 95 CI	Upper 95 CI
2	.4236488279	.10911	3.88281	.20980	.63750

TABLE 14.2

A Set of Hierarchical Models for a General Three-Way Table (Factors A, B, and C)

Model no.	Log linear model	Bracket notation
1	$\ln \epsilon_{ijk} = \lambda$	
2	$\ln \epsilon_{ijk} = \lambda + \alpha_A$	[A]
3	$\ln \epsilon_{ijk} = \lambda + \alpha_A + \beta_B$	[A][B]
4	$\ln \epsilon_{ijk} = \lambda + \alpha_A + \beta_B + \gamma_C$	[A][B][C]
5	$\ln \epsilon_{ijk} = \lambda + \alpha_A + \beta_B + \gamma_C + \phi_{AB}$	[A][B][C][AB]
6	$\ln \epsilon_{ijk} = \lambda + \alpha_A + \beta_B + \gamma_C + \phi_{AB} + \phi_{AC}$	[A][B][C][AB][AC]
7	$\ln \epsilon_{ijk} = \lambda + \alpha_A + \beta_B + \gamma_C + \phi_{AB} + \phi_{AC} + \phi_{BC}$	[A][B][C][AB][AC][BC]
8	$\ln \epsilon_{ijk} = \lambda + \alpha_A + \beta_B + \gamma_C + \phi_{AB} + \phi_{AC} + \phi_{BC} + \phi_{ABC}$	[A][B][C][AB][AC][BC][ABC]

Note: λ, the α's, β's, γ's, and ϕ's are parameters (population values). They, of course, must be estimated. Recall, from earlier in the chapter, that for a two-way table the estimated main effect for ith row of factor A is given by α_i = average of natural logs − grand mean of natural logs of expected freqs for row i of expected freqs for all cells and the estimated main effect for the jth column of factor B is given by β_j = average of natural logs − grand mean of natural logs of expected freqs for jth col. of expected freqs for all cells. The estimated effects for this three-way table would proceed in an analogous fashion.

The complication is that when we get into three- or higher way tables, the computation of the expected frequencies becomes increasingly more difficult, depending on the model fitted. In fact, for certain models, probability theory can't be used to obtain the expected frequencies; rather, an iterative routine is needed to obtain them. This is true for Model 7 in Table 14.2 (see Bishop, Fienberg, and Holland, 1975, pp. 83–84).

The data presented at the beginning of this chapter on approval versus nonapproval of a television series have a significant three-way interaction present, and give us an opportunity to discuss what this means in a contingency table, and to relate it to the interpretation of a three-way interaction in ANOVA.

Example 14.5

This study involves 246 preschool children, 60 of whom were in Head Start and the other 186 in a control group. They were classified as to the educational level of their parents (9th, 10th and 11th, or 12th grade) and as to whether they failed or passed a test, yielding the following table.

		Test	
Education	Treatment	Fail	Pass
Ninth	Head	11(111)	0(112)
	Cont	56(121)	15(122)
Tenth/Eleventh	Head	14(211)	8(212)
	Cont	44(221)	14(222)
Twelfth	Head	17(311)	10(312)
	Cont	35(321)	22(322)

The cell identification is in parentheses. The first number refers to the level of education, the second to the level for treatment, and the third to the level for test. This data was run on SPSS for Windows 10.5. The control syntax for doing so is presented in Table 14.3. Note that I am testing several designs in one run, and that two test statistics are for testing each model for fit. Selected printout is also given in Table 14.3. The Pearson test statistic indicates that only the last model fits the data at the .05 level.

The results from the two statistics are generally quite similar, and we could use either. However, we use the Pearson temporarily for three reasons. First, the formula for it is intuitively easier to understand. Second, it is easier to compute than the likelihood ratio statistic. And third, there is evidence that the Pearson statistic is more accurate, especially when total sample size is small (Fienberg, 1980; Milligan, 1980). For example, Fienberg (1980) indicated that when $n = 100$ and one is testing for no second-order interaction in a $3 \times 3 \times 3$ table at the .05 level, the actual $\alpha = .056$ for the Pearson and the actual $\alpha = .104$ for the likelihood ratio test statistic. We said we will use the Pearson statistic temporarily, because when we get to *comparing models* there are technical reasons for preferring the likelihood ratio test statistic.

The program (SPSS) assumes that you realize if an interaction term is in the model, like [TEST*TREAT] for the present case, then all lower order relatives are also *automatically* included in that model. This implies in this case that the model specified by only TEST*TREAT really is the model [TEST*TREAT, TEST, TREAT]. As another illustration, the model [TREAT, TEST*EDUC] actually has the following effects in it: TREAT, EDUC, TEST, TEST*EDUC.

TABLE 14.3

SPSS Control Syntax and Selected Printout for Head Start Data

```
TITLE ' LOGLINEAR MODELS ON HEADSTART DATA'.
DATA LIST FREE/EDUC TREAT TEST FREQ.
WEIGHT BY FREQ.
BEGIN DATA.
1 1 1 11   1 1 2 0    1 2 1 56   1 2 2 15
2 1 1 14   2 1 2 8    2 2 1 44   2 2 2 14
3 1 1 17   3 1 2 10   3 2 1 35   3 2 2 22
END DATA.
HILOGLINEAR EDUC(1,3) TREAT(1,2) TEST(1,2)/
 DESIGN=TEST/
 DESIGN=TEST TREAT/
 DESIGN=TEST TREAT EDUC/
 DESIGN=TREAT TEST*EDUC/
 DESIGN=TEST*EDUC TREAT*EDUC/.
```

DESIGN 2 has generating class

TEST

TREAT

Goodness-of-fit test statistics

Likelihood ratio chi square = 23.34029	DF = 9	P = .005
Pearson chi square = 18.54478	DF = 9	P = .029

DESIGN 3 has generating class

TEST

TREAT

EDUC

Goodness-of-fit statistics

Likelihood ratio chi square = 23.24271	DF = 7	P = .002
Pearson chi square = 18.31816	DF = 7	P = .011

DESIGN 4 has generating class

TREAT

TEST*EDUC

Goodness-of-fit test statistics

Likelihood ratio chi square = 15.06273	DF = 5	P = .010
Pearson chi square = 11.62014	DF = 5	P = .040

DESIGN 5 has generating class

TEST*EDUC

TREAT*EDUC

Goodness-of-fit test statistics

Likelihood ratio chi square = 5.98764	DF = 3	P = .112
Pearson chi square = 4.05887	DF = 3	P = .255

Now we wish to show the reader how the Pearson values in Table 14.3 are obtained for each of the models. We consider the following five models, in increasing complexity.

1. TEST—single main effect model
2. TEST, TREAT—two main effects in the model
3. TEST, TREAT, EDUC—all main effects (model of independence of factors)
4. TREAT, TEST*EDUC—all main effects and a single interaction effect
5. TEST*EDUC, TREAT*EDUC—all main effects and two interaction effects

14.4.1 TEST—Single Main Effect Model

Here, we are assuming the expected cell frequencies will vary only from FAIL to PASS, and that the expected frequencies will *not* vary by educational level or by treatment group. With six cells for each level of test, the expected frequencies are given by:

$$E_{ijk} = \frac{f_k}{6} = \frac{n \cdot p_k}{6}$$

where f_k is the frequency of observations in level k for TEST and p_k is the probability of being in level k of TEST. Because the frequency for level 1 of TEST = f_1 = 177, the expected frequencies for the 6 cells within FAIL = E_{ij1} = 177/6 = 29.5. The number of observations for level 2 (PASS) of TEST = f_2 = 69. Therefore, E_{ij2} = 69/6 = 11.5. Hence, the table of observed and expected frequencies is as follows:

		Test	
Education	Treatment	Fail 1	Pass 2
Ninth 1	Head 1	11(29.5)	0(11.5)
	Cont 2	56(29.5)	15(11.5)
Tenth/Eleventh 2	Head 1	14(29.5)	8(11.5)
	Cont 2	44(29.5)	14(11.5)
Twelfth 3	Head 1	17(29.5)	10(11.5)
	Cont 2	35(29.5)	22(11.5)

As mentioned at the beginning of the chapter, putting numbers for the levels of each factor makes cell ID much easier; compare Table 14.3. The Pearson chi-square statistic is calculated as:

$$\chi^2 = \frac{(11-29.5)^2}{29.5} + \frac{(0-11.5)^2}{11.5} + \frac{(56-29.5)^2}{29.5} + \cdots + \frac{(22-11.5)^2}{11.5}$$

$$\chi^2 = 80.958$$

The likelihood ratio chi-square statistic is

$$L^2 = 2\Sigma o_i \ln(o_i/e_i) = 2[11\ln(11/29.5) + 0\ln(0/11.5)$$

$$+ 56\ln(56/29.5) + \cdots + 22\ln(22/11.5)]$$

14.4.2 TEST, TREAT—Main Effects Model

Here, we are assuming that both TEST and TREAT have a systematic, although *independent*, effect in determining the expected cell frequencies, and that the expected cell frequencies do not differ over educational level, because this effect is not in the model. Thus, the expected frequencies can be found by lumping educational levels together and applying the same formula used for the two-way chi-square, but then dividing by 3 to distribute the resulting expected frequencies over the three educational levels. The formula is

$$E_{ijk} = \frac{f_j f_k}{3n} = \frac{np_j p_k}{3}$$

where f_j is the frequency or observations for level j of treatment and f_k is the frequency of observations for level k of TEST. Next, we present the combined observed frequencies for the three educational levels, along with the calculated expected frequencies, given in parentheses:

	TEST		COLUMN
	FAIL	PASS	TOTAL
HEAD	42 (43.17)	18 (16.83)	60
CONT	135 (133.83)	51 (52.17)	186
ROW TOTAL	177	69	246

Now, to obtain the expected cell frequencies for each cell in the three-way design, we simply divide each of these expected cell frequencies by 3, distributing them equally over the three educational levels. Thus, the chi-square for this main effects model becomes:

$$\chi^2 = \frac{(11-14.39)^2}{14.39} + \frac{(0-5.61)^2}{5.61} + \frac{(56-44.61)^2}{44.61} + \cdots + \frac{(35-44.61)^2}{44.61} + \frac{(22-17.39)^2}{17.39} = 18.546$$

as given on the printout in Table 14.3.

14.4.3 TEST, TREAT, EDUC—Independence Model

Here, we are assuming that TEST, TREAT, and EDUC all determine the expected cell frequencies, although they exert their influence independently of one another. Recall from basic probability theory that if independence is assumed, we can multiply probabilities. Therefore, to find the probability that a given subject falls in some cell we simply multiply the probability of the subject's being in the ith level for EDUC (p_i) by the probability of the subject's being in jth level for TREAT (p_j) by the probability of the subject's being in kth level for TEST (p_k). To determine the expected number of subjects in any cell we simply multiply by total sample size. Thus, the formula for obtaining the expected cell frequencies becomes:

$$E_{ijk} = np_i p_j p_k$$

Next is the three-way table with level probabilities for each factor in parentheses (which is the number of observations in that level divided by total sample size) and the expected cell frequencies.

		TEST	
		FAIL (.72)	PASS (.28)
Ninth (.333)	HEAD (.244)	11 (14.39)	0 (5.6)
	CONT (.756)	56 (44.59)	15 (17.34)
Tenth/Eleventh (.325)	HEAD (.244)	14 (14.05)	8 (5.46)
	CONT (.756)	44 (43.52)	14 (16.924)
Twelfth (.341)	HEAD (.244)	17 (14.74)	10 (5.73)
	CONT (.756)	35 (45.66)	22 (17.76)

From the earlier formula then, note that $E_{111} = 14.39 = 246\,(.333)\,(.244)\,(.72)$, and $E_{322} = 17.76 = 246\,(.341)\,(.756)\,(.28)$.

Thus, the chi-square statistic for this model is:

$$\chi^2 = \frac{(11-14.39)^2}{14.39} + \frac{(0-5.6)^2}{5.6} + \frac{(56-44.59)^2}{44.59} + \cdots + \frac{(35-45.66)^2}{45.66} + \frac{(22-17.76)^2}{17.76}$$

$$\chi^2 = 18.35$$

as given on the printout in Table 14.3.

14.4.4 TREAT, TEST*EDUC—Model

For this model, because we are considering hierarchical models, all main effects are in the model as well as the marginal interaction TEST*EDUC. To obtain the expected cell frequencies, we need the marginal table of frequencies for TE (i.e., f_{ik}). But these need to be adjusted for the effect of R, which is operating independently of T and E because there are no TR or ER interactions in the model. Because R is operating independently, we simply multiply the f_{ik} by the probability of the subject's being in either level of R. Therefore, the formula is

$$E_{ijk} = p_j f_{ik}$$

The two-way table of frequencies for test by educational level (TE), collapsed over the two treatment groups, is

	FAIL	PASS
Ninth	67	15
Tenth/Eleventh	58	22
Twelfth	52	32

Also, $p_1 = .244$ (probability of being in the HEAD group) and $p_2 = .756$ (probability of being in the control group). Next, we present the table of observed and expected frequencies:

		FAIL	PASS
Ninth	HEAD (.244)	11 (16.35)	0 (3.66)
	CONT (.756)	56 (50.65)	15 (11.34)
Tenth/Eleventh	HEAD (.244)	14 (14.13)	8 (5.37)
	CONT (.756)	44 (43.85)	14 (16.63)
Twelfth	HEAD (.244)	17 (12.69)	10 (7.81)
	CONT (.756)	35 (39.31)	22 (24.19)

Therefore, from the earlier formula, we have, for example

$$E_{111} = .244(67) = 16.35 \text{ and } E_{322} = .756(32) = 24.19$$

The Pearson chi-square statistic for this model is thus:

$$\chi^2 = \frac{(11-16.35)^2}{16.35} + \frac{(0-3.66)^2}{3.66} + \frac{(56-50.65)^2}{50.65} + \cdots + \frac{(35-39.31)^2}{39.31} + \frac{(22-24.19)^2}{24.19}$$

14.4.5 TEST*EDUC, TREAT*EDUC—Model

Because we are fitting interactions, the probabilities of being in a given cell for the collapsed TEST*EDUC and TREAT*EDUC tables is relevant. However, an adjustment for the probability of being in level i of EDUC is necessary. The collapsed tables are

	TEST*EDUC			TREAT*EDUC	
	FAIL	PASS		HEAD	CONT
Ninth	67	15	Ninth	11	71
Tenth/Eleventh	58	22	Tenth/Eleventh	22	58
Twelfth	52	32	Twelfth	27	57

The expected cell frequencies are calculated as:

$$E_{ijk} = \frac{np_{ik}p_{ij}}{p_i} = \frac{f_{ik}f_{ij}}{f_i}$$

and thus a few sample expected frequencies are calculated as

$$E_{111} = 67(11)/82 = 8.99$$

$$E_{222} = 22(58)/80 = 15.95$$

and the full table of observed and expected cell frequencies is

		TEST	
		FAIL	PASS
Ninth	HEAD	11 (8.99)	0 (2.01)
	CONT	56 (58.01)	15 (12.99)
Tenth/Eleventh	HEAD	14 (15.95)	8 (6.05)
	CONT	44 (42.05)	14 (15.95)
Twelfth	HEAD	17 (16.714)	10 (10.286)
	CONT	35 (35.286)	22 (21.714)

Computation of the Pearson chi-square statistic yields 4.05, within rounding error of the value on the printout.

14.5 Model Selection

Examination of Table 14.3 reveals, using the Pearson values, that only the model [TEST*EDUC, TREAT*EDUC] fits the data at the .05 level. It can also be shown that the model [TEST*TREAT, TEST*EDUC, TREAT*EDUC] also fits the data at the .05 level. Generally, when one has more than one model that fits the data, the most parsimonious model is chosen. That is, we prefer the simplest model that fits the data, which in this case would be [TEST*EDUC, TREAT*EDUC].

Generally, in comparing two or more *hierarchical* models that fit the data, the likelihood-ratio chi-square statistic is used. The difference between the two chi-squares is referred to as the chi-square distribution with degrees of freedom equal to the difference in the degrees of freedom for the two models. There was no need to do this in the previous example because the likelihood ratio χ^2 for the more complicated model differed only very slightly from the χ^2 for the simpler model (5.97 vs. 5.99).

To illustrate how to use the likelihood χ^2 statistic for comparing models, we consider the results from a log linear analysis of a three-way table from Kennedy (1983, p. 108). Here are the likelihood ratio χ^2's:

MODEL	DF	LIKELIHOOD CHISQ	PROB
T	6	42.91	.0000
E	6	46.58	.0000
S	6	8.39	.2109
T, E	5	42.55	.0000
E, S	5	8.03	.1546
S, T	5	4.36	.4984
T, E, S	4	4.00	.4057
TE	4	40.12	.0000
TS	4	3.34	.5032
ES	4	7.99	.0920
T, ES	3	3.96	.2655
E, TS	3	2.98	.3953
S, TE	3	1.57	.6664
TE, TS	2	0.54	.7623
TS, ES	2	2.94	.2304
ES, TE	2	1.53	.4655
TE, TS, ES	1	0.54	.4620

First, we compare models [S] and [S,T], both of which fit the data at the .05 level. The difference in the likelihood chi-squares is 8.39 − 4.36 = 4.03, and the difference in the degrees of freedom for the two models is 6 − 5 = 1. Because the critical value at the .05 level is 3.84, the difference is significant, indicating that [S,T] is the preferred model. Now let us compare the models [S,T] and [S,TE]. The difference in the chi-squares is 4.36 − 1.57 = 2.79, and the difference in degrees of freedom is 5 − 3 = 2. This chi-square is not significant because the critical value is 5.99, indicating that adding the TE interaction term and main effect E does not provide a better fit, and we should therefore stick with the simpler model, [S,T]. It is very important to note that comparing models with the likelihood chi-square is meaningful only when they are hierarchically related—when one model is a subset of the other model. Note that this was the case in both of the earlier examples. In the first case the model [S] is a subset of the model [S,T], and in the second case the model [S,T] is a subset of the model [S,TE], in that the latter model actually contains the terms: S,T,E, and TE. On the other hand, we cannot compare the models [E,S] and [TS], because the first model is not a subset of the second.

One of the advantages of hierarchical models is the availability of this test for comparing models. With nonhierarchical models a statistical test for the difference between models does not exist. For this and other reasons, all the major texts on categorical data analysis deal almost exclusively with hierarchical models. If you find the need to use a nonhierarchical model, they can be obtained from the SPSS LOGLINEAR program and from the SAS CATMOD program.

Before we turn to the next computer example, it is helpful to distinguish between three different types of association:

1. Marginal association—this is the association that exists between two variables A and B when we collapse over the levels of a third variable C.
2. Partial association—the association that exists between A and B after the effects of C are taken into account. If there is association between A and B for each level of C, then partial association exists.*
3. Differential association—when the nature of the association between A and B is different for the levels of C. This is evidence for a significant three-way interaction.

Example 14.6

Example 6 considers the following data:

	Rural		Urban	
	Approval	No Approval	Approval	No Approval
Female	3	7	6	12
Male	5	15	17	1

Note that the nature of the association between sex and approval is quite different for the rural and urban areas, especially for males. We can see shortly that there is a significant three-way interaction for this data. The interpretation of a three-way interaction in ANOVA is somewhat analogous, except that in ANOVA means (rather than frequencies) are involved. Consider a sex × treatment × social class design with the following profiles of means for the social classes:

	Lower		Middle	
	Treat 1	Treat 2	Treat 1	Treat 2
Males	60	53	71	65
Females	42	50	58	54

Here we have a three-way interaction because there is a strong ordinal interaction for lower social class (males do much better than females for Treat 1 but only slightly better for Treat 2) and no interaction for the middle social class. That is, the profiles of means for the social class are significantly different.

---

* Agresti (1990, pp. 135–141) has two nice examples to show that partial association doesn't imply marginal association and vice versa.

14.6 Collapsibility

In our analysis of the Head Start data (Table 14.3), it was found that the three-way interaction was not significant, and that the model [TE,RE] provided the most parsimonious fit to the data. The next natural step might appear to be that of reporting two way tables for TEST*EDUC and TREAT*EDUC, collapsing over the third variable, and discussing the results from these tables. But the question arises as to when we can validly collapse across a third variable. Bishop, Fienberg, and Holland (1975, pp. 41–42) presented an example, which we discuss shortly, to show that under certain conditions collapsing can lead to misleading interpretations.

Let A, B, and C be the factors for a three-way design. Then we can validly collapse AB over C if the following are met:

1. The three-way interaction is not significant, that is, ABC = 0.
2. Either A or B is independent of C, that is, AC = 0 or BC = 0.

Similarily, we can validly collapse AC over B if ABC = 0 and either AB = 0 or BC = 0. Finally, BC can be collapsed over A if ABC = 0 and either AB = 0 or AC = 0.

Returning to the Head Start example, we see that summarizing and discussing results from the TEST*EDUC table (collapsed over TREAT) and the TREAT*EDUC table (collapsed over TEST) will be valid if TEST*TREAT*EDUC = 0, which we know to be the case, and if either TEST*TREAT = 0 or EDUC*TREAT = 0 for the first case. For the second case, collapsing will be valid if TEST*TREAT or EDUC*TEST = 0. So for this particular example we can validly collapse in both cases if TEST*TREAT = 0. To determine if this is the case we take the data and combine over educational levels, yielding the following table for TEST*TREAT:

	Fail	Pass
Head Start	42	18
	(43.17)	(16.83)
Control	135	51
	(133.83)	(52.17)

The values in parentheses are the expected values. Calculation of the chi-square yields $\chi^2 = .149$, which is clearly not significant. Thus, TEST is independent of TREAT and we can validly collapse in both cases.

Now we return to the Bishop et al. study (1975) mentioned earlier, which related survival of infants (variable 1) to the amount of prenatal care received by the mothers (variable 2). The mothers attended one of two clinics (variable 3). The three-dimensional table was:

Clinic	Amount of care	Infant survival	
		Died	Survived
A	Less	3	176
	More	4	293
B	Less	17	197
	More	2	23

Let us examine the relationship between care and survival *within* each clinic using the cross-product ratios. We find $\hat{\alpha}_A = 3(293)/4(176) = 1.2$ and $\hat{\alpha}_B = 17(23)/2(197) = 1$. Both of these are very close to 1, indicating that survival is unrelated to amount of care. Now, suppose someone had combined (collapsed) the information from the two clinics to examine the relationship between survival and amount of care. The combined table is:

		Died	Survived
		\multicolumn{2}{c}{Infant survival}	
Amount of care	Less	20	373
	More	6	316

The cross-product ratio for this table is 2.8, a considerable deviation from 1, indicating that survival is related to amount of care. This is erroneous, however, because it is not valid to collapse here. To validly collapse, clinic would need to be independent of either amount of care or survival, but in fact, clinic is dependent on both of these. The two-way table for clinic by survival is:

	Died	Survived
Clinic A	7	469
Clinic B	19	220

The chi square for this table is 19.06, which is significant at the .05 level. The reader should show that amount of care is also dependent on clinic.

Example 14.6

This example involves the survey data presented at the beginning of the chapter, which examined the effect of sex and geographic location on reaction to a television series.

	Rural		Urban	
	Approval	No Approval	Approval	No Approval
Female	3	7	6	12
Male	5	15	17	1

Inspection of these data reveals that the pattern of responses for rural males is very different from that for urban males. These data were run on SPSS for Windows 10.0. The backward elimination procedure indicates, as we suspected, that we need a three-way interaction to explain the data. This is presented in Table 14.4. We also used the CROSSTABS procedure in SPSS to obtain the two way profiles for each location, along with the chi-square statistic for each location. The chi-squares indicate that gender is independent of approval for location 1 (rural), but that gender is related to approval for location 2 (urban): $\chi^2 = 14.57$. These results are also presented in Table 14.4.

TABLE 14.4

Backward Elimination and CROSSTAB Results on Location from SPSS for Windows for Gender ×
Location × Approval Data

DESIGN 1 has generating class

GENDER*LOCATION*APPROV

Note: For saturated models .500 has been added to all observed cells.
This value may be changed by using the CRITERIA = DELTA subcommand.

If Deleted Simple Effect is	DF	L. R. Chisq change	Prob	Iter
GENDER*LOCATION*APPROV	1	8.037	.0046	5

GENDER*APPROV*LOCATION Crosstabulation

Count

Location			Approv		
			1.00	2.00	Total
1.00	GENDER	1.00	3	7	10
		2.00	5	15	20
	Total		8	22	30
2.00	GENDER	1.00	6	12	18
		2.00	17	1	18
	Total		23	13	36

Chi-Square Tests

Location		Value	Df	Asymp. sig. (2-sided)	Exact sig. (2-sided)	Exact sig. (1-sided)
1.00	Pearson chi-square	.085[b]	1	.770		
	Continuity correction[a]	.000	1	1.000		
	Likelihood ratio	.084	1	.772		
	Fisher's exact test				1.000	.548
	Linear-by-linear association	.082	1	.774		
	N of valid cases	30				
2.00	Pearson chi-square	14.569[c]	1	.000		
	Continuity correction[a]	12.040	1	.001		
	Likelihood ratio	16.453	1	.000		
	Fisher's exact test				.000	.000
	Linear-by-linear association	14.164	1	.000		
	N of valid cases	36				

[a] Computed only for a 2 × 2 table.
[b] 1 cell (25.0%) has expected count less than 5. The minimum expected count is 2.67.
[c] 0 cells (.0%) have expected count less than 5. The minimum expected count is 6.50.

14.7 The Odds (Cross-Product) Ratio

At this point we wish to introduce a concept that many texts and authors use heavily in discussing log linear analysis, the odds ratio. For a 2 × 2 table the odds ratio is estimated as the product of the observed diagonal frequencies divided by the product of the non-diagonal frequencies:

$$\hat{\alpha} = (o_{11}o_{22})/(o_{12}o_{21})$$

If $\hat{\alpha}$ equals 1, then the variables (modes of classification) are independent. As a simple example to illustrate, consider:

	Success	Failure
Treat 1	10	30
Treat 2	5	15

Here $\hat{\alpha} = 10(15)/30(5) = 1$. Note that the ratio of successes to failures is the *same* for both treatments; that is, it is independent of treatment. Or to put it in odds terms, the odds of succeeding are 1 in 4 regardless of treatment.

If the odds ratio is sufficiently deviant from 1, then we conclude that the modes of classification are dependent or associated. There is a statistical test for this, but we do not present it.

Let us use the odds ratio to characterize the differential association for rural and urban subjects in the previous example. For rurals the odds ratio is $\hat{\alpha}_1 = 3(15)/5(7) = 1.28$, and for urban subjects the odds ratio is given by $\hat{\alpha}_2 = 6(1)/17(2) = .03$. The ratio being near 1 for rurals implies independence, and the odds ratio being near 0 for urbans implies dependence. There is a statistical test for determining whether two such odds ratios are significantly different (Fienberg, 1980, p. 37). Significance for that test implies a three-way interaction effect. The test statistic is

$$z = \frac{\ln \hat{\alpha}_1 - \ln \hat{\alpha}_2}{\sqrt{s\hat{\alpha}_1^2 + s\hat{\alpha}_2^2}}$$

where $s_{\hat{\alpha}_1}^2$ is the estimated variance of $\ln \hat{\alpha}_1$, and is given by

$$s_{\hat{\alpha}_1}^2 = 1/o_{11} + 1/o_{12} + 1/o_{21} + 1/o_{22}$$

If the three-way interaction is 0, then z has an approximate normal distribution with mean 0 and standard deviation of 1. Let us use this statistic to test the three-way interaction effect for the survey data. First, the denominator is just the square root of the sum of the reciprocals of the cell sizes:

$$\sqrt{s_{\hat{\alpha}_1}^2 + s_{\hat{\alpha}_2}^2} = \sqrt{1/3 + 1/5 + 1/7 + 1/15 + 1/6 + 1/17 + 1/12 + 1/1}$$

$$= \sqrt{2.045} = 1.43$$

Therefore, $z = (\ln 1.28 - \ln .03)/1.43 = 2.625$. We would reject at the .05 level, because the critical values are ±1.96, and conclude that there is a significant three-way interaction.

14.8 Normed Fit Index and Residual Analysis

Recall our discussion in Chapter 1 on the strong effect sample size has on tests of significance. If sample size is large enough, almost any effect, whether in ANOVA, regression, or log linear analysis, will be declared significant. On the other hand, with small sample size, important effects may not be declared significant because of inadequate power. Bonnett and Bentler (1983) commented on this problem in the context of model selection in log linear analysis:

> Sample size also has an undesirable effect on exploratory analyses when the formal test is the only criterion for model selection; overrestricted models tend to be selected in very small samples and underrestricted models tend to be selected in very large samples. Given the sample size dependency of the formal tests, goodness of fit information that is *independent* of sample size will surely be informative. (p. 156, emphasis added)

Bonnett and Bentler described a normed fit index $\hat{\Delta}$ that was originally proposed by Goodman (1970). We write it as follows:

$$\hat{\Delta} = \frac{\chi^2(\text{base model}) - \chi^2(\text{model being tested})}{\chi^2(\text{base model})}$$

Numerically, $\hat{\Delta}$ is bounded between 0 and 1, and it indicates the *percent improvement* in goodness of fit of the model being tested over the base model. The choice of base model is not fixed. It could be the model involving only the grand mean, or it could be the simpler of two models, both of which "fit" the data. To illustrate the latter, consider the following Pearson χ^2's from a run of data from Kennedy (1983, p. 108):

Model	DF	CHI Square	Prob
T	6	39.53	.0000
E	6	46.45	.0000
S	6	8.00	.2381
T, E	5	39.19	.0000
E, S	5	7.91	.1614
S, T	5	4.58	.4688
T, E, S	4	4.13	.3883
TE	4	37.03	.0000
TS	4	3.28	.5121
ES	4	7.83	.0979
T, ES	3	3.99	.2622
E, TS	3	2.93	.4025
S, TE	3	1.60	.6588
TE, TS	2	.53	.7656
TS, ES	2	2.90	.2345
ES, TE	2	1.52	.4675
TE, TS, ES	1	.53	.4653

From this table it is clear that most of the models fit the data at the .05 level. The simplest model that fits the data involves the single main effect S. The next simplest, which involves a substantial drop in the chi square value, is the main effects model [S,T]. Using Goodman's $\hat{\Delta}$ we calculate percent improvement in goodness of fit for [S,T] over S:

$$\hat{\Delta} = (8 - 4.58)/8 = .43$$

Thus, we might prefer to adopt the model (S,T), although it is slightly more complicated, because of a substantial improvement in fit.

14.9 Residual Analysis

In Chapter 3 on multiple regression we discussed the importance of residual analysis in assessing violations of assumptions and goodness of fit, and in identifying outliers. In log linear work, analysis of residuals is also useful, for example, in identifying perhaps a single cell or small group of cells that may be responsible for a given model's not fitting the data. The first point we need to make clear is that comparison of raw residuals could be quite misleading. Equal raw residuals may reflect quite different discrepancies if the expected values are different. For example, if the expected frequency for one cell is 100 and for another 10, and the raw residuals are 110 – 100 = 10 and 20 – 10 = 10, then it is intuitively clear that the deviation of 10 in the latter case reflects a larger percentage deviation. A means is needed of standardizing the residuals so that they can be meaningfully compared. Several types of standardized residuals have been developed. The one we illustrate is given on the SPSS output, and is due to Haberman (1973). It is given by

$$\text{Standardized residual} = \frac{\substack{\text{observed} \\ \text{frequency}} - \substack{\text{expected} \\ \text{frequency}}}{\sqrt{\text{expected frequency}}} = r_{ij}$$

Haberman has shown that if the conditions for the χ^2 approximation are met, then the distribution of the r_{ij} is approximately normal, with a mean = 0 and a variance approaching 1. Thus, we can think of the r_{ij} as roughly standard normal deviates. Therefore, 95% of them should lie between –2 and 2. Hence, any cell with a $|r_{ij}| > 2$ could be considered to be a "significant" residual, because these should occur only about 5% of the time. In a large table, one or two large residuals could be expected and should not be cause for alarm. However, a pattern of significant standardized residuals in a large table, or at least a few significant residuals in smaller tables, may well indicate the need for an additional term(s) in the model.

14.10 Cross-Validation

We have been concerned previously in this chapter with selection of a model that fits the data well, and many procedures have been developed for this purpose. There are simultaneous procedures that test whether all effects of order k are 0, and tests of partial and marginal association. There are also backward and forward stepwise procedures (Fienberg, 1980), analogous to what is done in stepwise regression. Thus, although there are many procedures for selecting a "good" model, the acid test is the generalizability of the model. That is, how well will the model chosen fit on an independent sample? This leads us once again into cross-validation, which was emphasized in regression analysis and in discriminant analysis.

Interestingly, many of the texts dealing with log linear analysis (Agresti, 1990; Fienberg, 1980) don't even mention cross-validation, or only allude to it briefly. However, Bonnett and Bentler (1983) pointed to the importance of cross-validation in log linear analysis, and a small study by Stevens (1984) indicates there is reason for concern. Stevens randomly halved 15 real data sets (the n for 13 of the sets was very large (> 361). Those models that were most parsimonious and fit quite well ($p > .20$) were selected and then cross-validated on the other half of the random split. In seven of the 15 sets, the model(s) chosen did *not* cross-validate. What makes this of even greater concern is that the original sample sizes were quite large.

The model selected in Table 14.3 for the Head Start data was actually one half of a random split of that data. Recall that the model selected was [TEST*EDUC, TREAT*EDUC]. The control lines for validating the model on the other half of the random split are given in Table 14.5.

TABLE 14.5

SPSS Control Lines for Validating the Head Start Data and Selected Printout

```
    TITLE ' VALIDATION ON HEADSTART DATA'.
    DATA LIST FREE/EDUC TREAT TEST FREQ.
    WEIGHT BY FREQ.
    BEGIN DATA.
    1 1 1 5    1 1 2 1    1 2 1 63   1 2 2 16
①   2 1 1 9    2 1 2 5    2 2 1 39   2 2 2 13
    3 1 1 11   3 1 2 13   3 2 1 41   3 2 2 19
    END DATA.
    HILOGLINEAR EDUC(1,3) TREAT(1,2) TEST(1,2)/
②     DESIGN=TEST*EDUC TREAT*EDUC/.
```

Goodness-of-fit test statistics		
Likelihood ratio chi square = 4.27726	DF = 3	P = .233
Pearson chi square = 4.36327	③ DF = 3	P = .225

① Recall from Table 14.3 that the frequencies for the derivation sample were:

11	0	56	15
14	8	44	14
17	10	35	22

② In this design subcommand we are fitting a specific model to the data. Recall from Table 14.3 that this model fit the other random part of the data.

③ Because this $p > .05$, it indicates that the model cross-validated at the .05 level.

14.11 Higher Dimensional Tables—Model Selection

When we consider four- or five-way tables, the number of potential models increases rapidly into the thousands, and the packages no longer enable one to test all models. Some type of screening procedure is needed to limit the number of models to be tested from a practical point of view. Three ways of selecting models are:

1. Stepwise procedures—these are analogous to the corresponding procedures in multiple regression. Here, effects are successively added or deleted according to some level of significance. The backward selection procedure is available in SPSS for Windows, and we illustrate that later in this section.

2. Use a two-stage procedure suggested by Brown (1976). In the first stage, global tests are examined that determine whether all *k*-factor interactions are simultaneously 0. Thus, for a four-way table, these would determine whether all main effects are 0, whether all two-way interactions are 0, whether all three-way interactions are 0, and finally whether the four-way interaction is 0. Then, for those sets of interactions that are significant in Stage 1, examine specific effects for significant partial and marginal association. Retain for the final model only those specific effects for which *both* the partial and marginal association are significant at some preassigned significance level.

3. Compare all effects against their standard errors and retain for the final model only those effects whose standardized values (i.e., effect/standard error) exceed some critical value. For a five-way table with 31 effects, it probably would be wise to either test at the .01 level, or to use the Bonferroni inequality with overall α at .10 or .15.

Example 14.8

We illustrate a variation of the Brown procedure using one of the four-way data sets presented at the beginning of the chapter. That set involved 362 patients receiving psychiatric care who were classified according to four clinical indices. We fit some models, using SPSS for Windows 10.0, to a random split of this data. Later, we validate these models using the other half of the random split. Suppose we have decided a priori to do each global test at the .05 level and each individual test at the .01 level. Examination of the global tests reveals that all two-way interactions are not 0 (Pearson = 31.54). Although the test for the three-way interactions is not significant at the .05 level, it is close enough to warrant further scrutiny. This is because, as Benedetti and Brown (1978) noted, "A single large effect may go undetected in the presence of many small effects."

Now, examining the individual effects in Table 14.7, we see that VALID* DEPRESS, SOLID* DEPRESS and VALID*STABIL are all significant at the .01 level. Also, VALID*SOLID*DEPRESS needs to be considered. Thus, we entertain the following two models for cross validation purposes:

Model 1: VALID*DEPRESS, SOLID*DEPRESS, VALID*STABIL
Model 2: VALID*DEPRESS, SOLID*DEPRESS, VALID*STABIL, VALID*SOLID*DEPRESS

The control lines for validating these two models and the data for the other half of the random split are given in Table 14.8. Unfortunately, the Pearson χ^2's at the bottom of the table indicate that neither model cross-validates at the .05 level (remember that the probabilities need to be *greater* than .05 for adequate fit at the .05 level).

TABLE 14.6

Frequency Table for Four-Way Clinical Data

VALID		DEPRESS	STABIL	
			INT 1	EXT 2
ENERG 1	RIGID	YES 1	11	13
	1	NO 2	10	⑨
	HYST	YES 1	5	5
	2	NO 2	19	24
PSY 2	RIGID	YES 1	19	8
	1	NO 2	⑬	4
	HYST	YES 1	16	10
	2	NO 2	10	5

Note how much easier cell ID is when the levels for each factor are given. For the circled entries, the cell ID's are easily identified as 1122 and 2121; cf Table 14.9.

TABLE 14.7

Tests of Partial Association for Four-Way Clinical Data from SPSS for Windows 15.0

			Tests of PARTIAL associations
DF	Partial Chisq	Prob	Effect Name
1	6.532	.0106	VALID*SOLID*DEPRESS
1	.277	.5984	VALID*SOLID*STABIL
1	.127	.7217	VALID*DEPRESS*STABIL
1	.208	.6484	SOLID*DEPRESS*STABIL
1	.000	.9962	VALID*SOLID
1	12.648	.0004	VALID*DEPRESS
1	6.849	.0089	SOLID*DEPRESS
1	8.360	.0038	VALID*STABIL
1	.914	.3391	SOLID*STABIL
1	.281	.5958	DEPRESS*STABIL
1	.669	.4134	VALID
1	.271	.6028	SOLID
1	.271	.6028	DEPRESS
1	3.464	.0627	STABIL

Note: The partial association tests are conditional tests of the particular k factor interaction, adjusted for all other effects of the same order. Thus, if we had three factors A, B, and C, the partial association test for AB examines the difference in fit for the model (AB, AC, BC) versus the model (AC, BC).

TABLE 14.8

SPSS Control Syntax and Selected Printout for Validating Two
Models for the Validity × Solidity × Depression × Stability Data

TITLE 'CLINICAL DATA – VALIDATING TWO MODELS'.
DATA LIST FREE/VALID SOLID DEPRES STABIL FREQ.
WEIGHT BY FREQ.
BEGIN DATA.
1 1 1 1 4   1 1 1 2 10   1 1 2 1 15   1 1 2 2 5
1 2 1 1 4   1 2 1 2 9   1 2 2 1 27   1 2 2 2 23
2 1 1 1 11   2 1 1 2 14   2 1 2 1 9   2 1 2 2 4
2 2 1 1 16   2 2 1 2 6   2 2 2 1 17   2 2 2 2 7
END DATA.
HILOGLINEAR VALID(1,2) SOLID(1,2) DEPRES(1,2) STABIL(1,2)/
  DESIGN=STABIL*VALID DEPRES*SOLID DEPRES*VALID/
  DESIGN=STABIL*VALID DEPRES*SOLID*VALID/.

Goodness-of-fit test statistics		
Likelihood ratio chi square = 16.10411	DF = 8	P = .041
Pearson chi square = 15.54164	DF = 8	P = .049
Goodness-of-fit test statistics		
Likelihood ratio chi square = 15.60793	DF = 6	P = .016
Pearson chi square = 15.34973	DF = 6	P = .018

To illustrate the backward selection procedure, we ran the clinical data on SPSS for Windows 10.0. The control lines for doing so are given in Table 14.9. Tables 14.10 and 14.11 contain selected printout from SPSS showing the seven steps needed before a final model was arrived at. The final model is the same as Model 2 found with the variation of the Brown procedure.

Although we do not show an example illustrating Procedure 3, that of comparing all effects against their standard errors, Fienberg (1980, pp. 84–88) presented an example of this approach.

TABLE 14.9

SPSS HILOGLINEAR Control Lines for Backward Elimination
on the Clinical (Four-Way) Data

TITLE ' FOUR LOG LINEAR ON CLINICAL DATA'.
DATA LIST FREE /VALID SOLID DEPRESS STABIL FREQ.
WEIGHT BY FREQ.
BEGIN DATA.
1 1 1 1 11   1 1 1 2 13   1 1 2 1 10   1 1 2 2 9
1 2 1 1 5   1 2 1 2 5   1 2 2 1 19   1 2 2 2 24
2 1 1 1 19   2 1 1 2 8   2 1 2 1 13   2 1 2 2 4
2 2 1 1 16   2 2 1 2 10   2 2 2 1 10   2 2 2 2 5
END DATA.
HILOGLINEAR VALID(1,2) SOLID(1,2) DEPRESS(1,2) STABIL(1,2)/
  METHOD=BACKWARD/
  DESIGN/.

TABLE 14.10

Selected Printout from SPSS HILOGLINEAR for Backward Elimination on Clinical Data

If Deleted Simple Effect is	DF	L.R. Chisq Change	Prob
VALID*SOLID*DEPRESS*STABIL ①	1	.094	.7594

Step 1

The best model has generating class
VALID*SOLID*DEPRESS
VALID*SOLID*STABIL
VALID*DEPRESS*STABIL ②
SOLID*DEPRESS*STABIL

Likelihood ratio chi square = .09382   DF = 1   P = .759

If Deleted Simple Effect is	DF	L.R. Chisq Change	Prob
VALID*SOLID*DEPRESS	1	6.532	.0106
VALID*SOLID*STABIL	1	.277	.5984
VALID*DEPRESS*STABIL	1	③ .127	.7217
SOLID*DEPRESS*STABIL	1	.208	.6484

Step 2

The best model has generating class
VALID*SOLID*DEPRESS
VALID*SOLID*STABIL ④
SOLID*DEPRESS*STABIL

Likelihood ratio chi square = .22066   DF = 2   P = .896

If Deleted Simple Effect is	DF	L.R. Chisq Change	Prob
VALID*SOLID*DEPRESS	1	6.792	.0092
VALID*SOLID*STABIL	1	.215	.6428
SOLID*DEPRESS*STABIL	1	⑤ .181	.6706

Step 3

The best model has generating class
VALID*SOLID*DEPRESS
VALID*SOLID*STABIL ⑥
DEPRESS*STABIL

Likelihood ratio chi square = .40156   DF = 3   P = .940

If Deleted Simple Effect is	DF	L.R. Chisq Change	Prob
VALID*SOLID*DEPRESS	1	7.709	.0055
VALID*SOLID*STABIL	1	.128	.7202
DEPRESS*STABIL	1	.212	.6455

Step 4

The best model has generating class
VALID*SOLID*DEPRESS
DEPRESS*STABIL
VALID*STABIL
SOLID*STABIL

Likelihood ratio chi square = .52983   DF = 4   P = .971

① First, the four-way interaction is tested, and the change in chi-square is far short of significance, so that this effect can be safely dropped from the model.

② At this point, all four three-way interactions are tested. The three-way interaction that causes the *smallest* change in chi-square (assuming the change is not significant) is deleted from the model. The smallest change is for VALID*DEPRESS*STABIL (see ③). Note in STEP 2 (see ④) that this effect is no longer in the model.

③ Again, the effect that has the smallest change in chi-square is deleted from the model; here it is SOLID*DEPRESS*STABIL. Note that this effect is not present in STEP 3 (see ⑥).

TABLE 14.11

More Selected Printout from SPSS HILOGLINEAR for Backward Elimination on Clinical Data

If Deleted Simple Effect is	DF	L.R. Chisq Change	Prob
VALID*SOLID*DEPRESS	1	7.795	.0052
DEPRESS*STABIL	1	.297	.5857
VALID*STABIL	1	8.376	.0038
SOLID*STABIL	1	.929	.3350

Step 5

The best model has generating class

VALID*SOLID*DEPRESS
VALID*STABIL
SOLID*STABIL

Likelihood ratio chi square = .82687   DF = 5   P = .975

- -

If Deleted Simple Effect is	DF	L.R. Chisq Change	Prob
VALID*SOLID*DEPRESS	1	7.779	.0053
VALID*STABIL	1	8.137	.0043
SOLID*STABIL	1	.757	.3844

Step 6

The best model has generating class

VALID*SOLID*DEPRESS
VALID*STABIL

Likelihood ratio chi square = 1.58355   DF = 6   P = .954

- -

If Deleted Simple Effect is	DF	L.R. Chisq Change	Prob
VALID*SOLID*DEPRESS	1	① 7.779	.0053
VALID*STABIL	1	8.482	.0036

Step 7

The best model has generating class

VALID*SOLID*DEPRESS
VALID*STABIL

Likelihood ratio chi square = 1.58355   DF = 6   P = .954

① In STEP 6, when each of the effects is deleted from the model, there is a significant change in the chi-square value at the .01 level. That is why in STEP 7 the final model consists of these effects, and all lower order derivatives because of the hierarchy principle, since neither of them can be deleted.

In concluding this section, a couple of caveats are in order. The first concerns *overfitting*, which can occur because of fitting too many parameters to the data. Both Bishop et al. (1975, p. 324) and Marascuilo and Busk (1987, p. 452) issued warnings on situations where a model appears to fit so well that the chi-square value is considerably smaller than the associated degrees of freedom. Marascuilo and Busk recommended that if several models fit a set of data (some extremely well), one should choose the model with the chi-square value that is approximately equal to the associated degrees of freedom. Overfitting could well be the reason, or one of the reasons, that many results in log linear analysis do not cross-validate.

The other caveat is that there is *no best* method of model selection (Fienberg, 1980, p. 56), nor is any of the methods guaranteed to find the best possible model. As Freeman (1987) noted, "The analyst can only rely on his or her judgment in deciding which model is the one that is most appropriate for … the data" (p. 214).

14.12 Contrasts for the Log Linear Model

Recall that in ANOVA and MANOVA we used contrasts of two types:

1. Post hoc—These were used with procedures, such as Scheffe's or Tukey's, to identify which specific groups were responsible for global significance.
2. Planned—Here we set up a priori specific comparisons among population means, which might well correspond to specific hypotheses being tested.

In both of these cases, the contrasts were on means and the condition for a contrast was that the sum of the coefficients equal 0. The same type of contrasts can be utilized in log linear analysis, thanks to work by Goodman (1970), except now we will be contrasting observed cell frequencies. We denote a contrast by L, and the estimated contrast by $\hat{L}$. An estimated contrast would look like this:

$$\hat{L} = c_1 \ln o_1 + c_2 \ln o_2 + c_3 \ln o_3 + \cdots + c_k \ln o_k$$

where $\Sigma c_i = 0$ and the o_i denote the observed frequencies. The squared standard error for a contrast is given by:

$$s_{\hat{L}}^2 = \sum_{i=1}^{k} c_i^2 / o_i$$

For large sample size, it has been shown that $z = \hat{L}/\hat{s}_L$ is normally distributed with mean = 0 and standard deviation = 1 if the null hypothesis is true. For planned comparisons, one uses this fact, along with the Bonferroni inequality, to easily test the contrasts with overall α under control. For post hoc analysis with contrasts, that is, to determine which cells accounted for a significant main effect or interaction, the critical values are given by S, where $s = \sqrt{\chi^2_{\text{df(effect)}}}$. If it were a main effect with 3 degrees of freedom, then $s = \sqrt{\chi^2_{.05;3}} = \sqrt{7.815} = 2.80$, and if it were an interaction with 2 degrees of freedom, then $s = \sqrt{\chi^2_{.05;2}} = \sqrt{5.99} = 2.45$.

Example 14.9: Post Hoc Contrasts

To illustrate the use of contrasts, we consider data from a survey of a large American city where the respondents were asked the question, "Are the radio and TV networks doing a good job, just a fair job, or a poor job?" Responses were further broken down by color of respondent and the year in which the question was asked, yielding the following table:

Year	Color	Good	Fair	Poor	Total
		Response			
1959	Black	81	23	4	108
	White	325	253	54	632
1971	Black	224	144	24	382
	White	600	636	158	1394

The data were run on SPSS for Windows 10.0, with backward elimination as the default. Selected printout in Table 14.12 shows that the three-way interaction can be deleted, but that all two-way interactions are needed for adequate fit ($p = .168$). Because all two-way interactions are significant, it is not valid to collapse. Rather, the contrasts need to be done on the individual cell

TABLE 14.12

RADIOTV DATA: Selected Printout from SPSS for Windows

Backward Elimination (p = .050) for DESIGN 1 with generating class

   YEAR*COLOR*RESPONSE

Likelihood ratio chi square = .00000   DF = 0   P = 1.000

- -

If Deleted Simple Effect is	DF	L.R. Chisq Change	Prob
YEAR*COLOR*RESPONSE	2	3.566	.1682

Step 1

  The best model has generating class

    YEAR*COLOR
    YEAR*RESPONSE
    COLOR*RESPONSE

  Likelihood ratio chi square = 3.56559   DF = 2   P = .168

- -

If Deleted Simple Effect is	DF	L.R. Chisq Change	Prob
YEAR*COLOR	1	23.677	.0000
YEAR*RESPONSE	2	21.385	.0000
COLOR*RESPONSE	2	45.776	.0000

Step 2

  The best model has generating class

    YEAR*COLOR
    YEAR*RESPONSE
    COLOR*RESPONSE

  Likelihood ratio chi square = 3.56559   DF = 2   P = .168

frequencies. We examine the Color-by-Response interaction more closely with contrasts. Next we present the Color-by-Response profiles for each year, along with the expected frequencies in parentheses:

	1959			1971		
	Good	Fair	Poor	Good	Fair	Poor
Black	81 (59)	23 (40)	4 (9)	224 (181)	144 (171)	24 (40)
White	325 (347)	253 (236)	54 (49)	600 (643)	636 (609)	158 (142)
	$\chi^2 = 21.3, p < .05$			$\chi^2 = 26.76, p < .05$		

Examination of the expected frequencies shows why we obtained the strong Color-by-Response interaction for each year. Note that more Blacks than expected (under independence) rate the networks GOOD for each year and fewer Blacks than expected rate the networks FAIR or POOR, whereas the reverse is true for Whites. To see where the larger discrepancies are, after adjusting for differing expected frequencies, we present next the standardized results:

	1959			1971		
	Good	Fair	Poor	Good	Fair	Poor
Black	2.86	−2.69	−1.6	3.20	−2.06	−2.53
White	−1.18	1.11	.714	−1.70	1.09	1.34

These residuals suggest that the following contrasts may indicate significant subsources of variation:

$$\hat{L}_1 = \ln 23 - \ln 253 - (\ln 144 - \ln 636)$$

$$\hat{L}_2 = \ln 81 - \ln 325 - (\ln 224 - \ln 600)$$

The latter contrast determines whether the gap between Blacks and Whites in responding GOOD is the same for the 2 years. Now we test the significance of each contrast:

$$\hat{L} = 3.125 - 5.533 - 4.97 + 6.455 = -.913$$

$$s_{\hat{L}_1}^2 = 1/23 + 1/253 + 1/144 + 1636 = .056$$

Therefore, the z statistic for this contrast is:

$$z_1 = -.913 / \sqrt{.056} = -3.85$$

For Contrast 2, we have:

$$\hat{L} = 4.39 - 5.78 - 5.41 + 6.4 = -.40$$

$$s_{\hat{L}_1}^2 = 1/81 + 1/325 + 1/225 + 1/600 = .0212$$

Thus, the z statistic for Contrast 2 is:

$$z_2 = -.40 / \sqrt{.0212} = -2.74$$

Both of these contrasts are significant at the .05 level, because the critical values are $\sqrt{\chi_{.05;2}} = \sqrt{5.99} = 2.45$.

14.13 Log Linear Analysis for Ordinal Data

We have treated all the factors as categorical or nominal in this chapter, and if we are talking about sex, race, religion, and such, then this is perfectly appropriate. Often, however, we have ordinal information, such as age, educational level, or achievement. With ordinal information, the analysis becomes more complicated, but using the underlying information in the ordering yields a more powerful analysis. For those who wish to pursue this further, Agresti supplied a good book (1984) and several articles on the topic. Also, in a book written more for social scientists, Wickens (1989) offerred a nice, extended chapter on handling ordered categories.

14.14 Sampling and Structural (Fixed) Zeros

One must distinguish between two types of zero observed frequencies in multidimensional contingency tables. Sampling zeros can occur in large tables because of relatively small sample size. No subjects are found in some of the cells because the sample size was either not large enough or not comprehensive enough. These are different from structural zeros that can occur because no individuals of the type are possible for a given cell (e.g., male obstetrical patients).

Sampling zeros do not occur very often with social science data; when they do occur, there are a couple ways of handling them. First, one may be able to remove the zeros by combining levels for a factor. Second, one may add a small positive constant to each cell, which is a conservative measure. Goodman (1970) recommended adding .5 for saturated models, and SPSS LOGLINEAR by default adds .5 to each cell. Agresti (1990, pp. 249–250) has discussed adding a constant to cells, and notes that:

> For unsaturated models, this usually smooths the data too much... . When there is a problem with existence or computations, it is often adequate to add an extremely small constant... . This alleviates the problem but avoids over-smoothing the data before the fitting process.

I would recommend adding a very small constant, such as .0001.

If there are structural zeros or cells one wishes to identify as structural zeros, then this can be handled (see *SPSS Advanced Statistics*, 1997, pp. 53–55 and 209–210). We do not pursue this further here; however, Fienberg (1980, Chapter 8) gave a nice discussion of several applications of structurally incomplete tables.

14.15 Summary

This chapter deals with an extension of the two-way chi square; where the subjects are cross classified on more than two variables. Recall that in the two-way chi square the data are frequency counts. Because the data are "cruder," this calls for a different statistical model. Using the natural log, we transform the model to one that is linear in the logs of the expected frequencies. Hence, it is called the loglinear model. Two very prominent statisticians, Goodman and Mosteller, and their students made the loglinear model accessible on SAS and SPSS. We use the SPSS HILOGLINEAR program to illustrate three- and four-way analyses. We distinguish between three different types of association (marginal, partial, and differential). We discuss the important notion of collapsibility, i.e., when it is valid to collapse on one or more factors. The odds (cross product) ratio, which is used by many authors, is discussed. The topic of cross validation, which is a major theme in this text, is brought up. This gets at whether the model found on a given set of data will fit on an INDEPENDENT set of data.

14.16 Exercises

1. Plackett (1974) presented the following data on a random sample of diabetic patients:

		Family History of Diabetes			
		Yes		No	
Dependence on Insulin Injections		Yes	No	Yes	No
Age at Onset	<45	6	1	16	2
	>45	6	36	8	48

   Run SPSS backward selection on this data. What model is selected?

2. McLean (1980) investigated the graduation rates of Black and White students in two Southern universities: historically one was Black, the other White. Research indicated that, in general, Black students tend to complete their undergraduate degree programs at a lower rate than White students. McLean, however, suspected that the differential rate of completion was moderated in part by the type of institution attended. Specifically, he suspected that differences between Black and White completion would be more pronounced in White universities than Black universities. He obtained the following data (G—graduated and NG—not graduated):

		Black Univ (W)		Black Univ (B)		White Univ (W)		White Univ (B)	
		G	NG	G	NG	G	NG	G	NG
ABIL	HI	10	22	55	90	114	146	5	5
	LO	4	18	71	222	46	66	3	19

   (a) Use Brown's procedure and backward selection to determine which models fit the data.

   (b) Does the evidence tend to support McLean's hunch that differential rate of completion is moderated by the type of institution attended?

3. In a survey of a large American city, respondents were asked the question: "Are the radio and TV networks doing a good job, just a fair job, or a poor job?" Data for the responses to this question were broken down by color of the respondent, and the question was asked in two separate years.

	Color					
	Black			White		
Response	Good	Fair	Poor	Good	Fair	Poor
1959	81	23	4	325	253	54
1971	224	144	24	600	636	158

(a) Run SPSS backward selection on this data. What model is selected?

(b) Is it valid to collapse here, or do we need to use contrasts?

4. The table below results from a survey of seniors in high school in a nonurban area of Dayton, Ohio. They were asked, among other issues, whether they drank alcohol, whether they smoked cigarettes, and whether they had smoked marijuana.

Alcohol (*A*), Cigarette (*C*), and Marijuana (*M*) Use for High School Seniors

		Marijuana Use	
Alcohol Use	Cigarette Use	Yes	No
Yes	Yes	911	538
	No	44	456
No	Yes	3	43
	No	2	279

(a) Using the SPSS HILOGLINEAR program, determine whether the model of complete independence fits the data at the .05 level.

(b) Set up the appropriate probability model for complete independence, calculate the expected frequencies using this model, and then show how the Pearson chi-square value on the printout was obtained.

5. The following data from Demo and Parker (1987) classifies subjects by race, gender, GPA, and self-esteem.

		Black 1		White 2	
Gender	Cumulative GPA	High 1 self-esteem	Low 2 self-esteem	High 1 self-esteem	Low 2 self-esteem
Males 1	High 1	15	9	17	10
	Low 2	26	17	22	26
Females 2	High 1	13	22	22	32
	Low 2	24	23	3	17

(a) Run backward elimination on the SPSS HILOGLINEAR program. What model is selected?

(b) One of the effects in the final model is SEX*ESTEEM. Is it valid to collapse over race and GPA in interpreting this effect? Explain.

6. The data below were used in a study of parole success involving 5,587 parolees in Ohio between 1965 and 1972 (a 10% sample of all parolees during this period). The study involved a dichotomous response—success (no major parole violation) or failure (returned to prison)—based on a 1-year follow-up. The predictors of parole success included here are type of committed offense, age, prior record, and alcohol or drug dependency. The data were randomly split into two parts. The counts for the second part of the random split are given in parentheses, and these data are to be used as the validation sample.

| | No Drug or Alcohol Dependency | | | | Drug or Alcohol Dependency | | | |
| | 25 or older | | Under 25 | | 25 or older | | Under 25 | |
	Person offense	Other offense	Person offense	Other offense	Person offense	Other offense	Person offense	Other offense
	No Prior Sentence of Any Kind							
Success	48	34	37	49	38	28	35	57
	(44)	(34)	(29)	(58)	(47)	(38)	(37)	(53)
Failure	1	5	7	11	3	8	5	18
	(1)	(7)	(7)	(5)	(1)	(2)	(4)	(24)
	Prior Sentence							
Success	117	259	131	319	197	435	107	291
	(111)	(253)	(131)	(320)	(202)	(392)	(103)	(294)
Failure	23	61	20	89	38	194	27	101
	(27)	(55)	(25)	(93)	(46)	(215)	(34)	(102)

(a) Run backward elimination on this data. What model is selected?

(b) Determine whether the model selected in (a) fits on the validation sample at the .05 level.

7. In Section 14.6 we indicated that if A, B, and C are the factors for a three-way design, then we can validly collapse AB over C if the following are met:

(a) The three-way interaction is not significant, that is, ABC=0.

(b) Either A or B is independent of C, that is, AC =0 or BC =0.

What would be the generalization of these for more than three factors? That is, what conditions would have to be met, for example, to validly collapse AB over C and D in a four-way design?

8. Wermuth (1976b) reported the following four-way table. The variables are age of mother (A), length of gestation (G) in days, infant survival (I), and number of cigarettes smoked per day during the prenatal period (S).

| | | | Infant Survival | |
Age	Smoking	Gestation	No	Yes
<30	<5	≤260	50	315
		>260	24	4012
	5+	≤260	9	40
		>260	6	459
30+	<5	≤260	41	147
		>260	14	1594
	5+	≤260	4	11
		>260	1	124

Source: Reprinted with permission from the Biometric
Society (Wermuth 1976b).

Use backward elimination on SPSS to determine which model fits the data.

9. Consider the following data for a three-way table:

Clinic	Treatment	Success	Failure
1	A	18	12
	B	12	8
2	A	2	8
	B	8	32

(a) Calculate the odds ratios for each clinic separately. What do these show?

(b) Now, lump the clinic data together and compute the odds ratio. What do you conclude?

(c) What do parts (a) and (b) of this exercise show about the relationship between marginal association and partial association?

10. For a four-way table (ABCD) is the AB partial association the same as the AB marginal association for the following models?

(a) [AB, BCD]

(b) [AB,AD,BC,CD]

11. The following table represents the association between smoking status and a breathing test result, by age, for Caucasians in certain industrial plants in Houston in 1974–1975.

| | | Breathing Test | |
Age	Smoking	Normal	Not Normal
<45	Never Smoked	574	34
	Current Smoker	682	57
>45	Never Smoked	164	4
	Current Smoker	245	74

(a) Test the model [SMOKE,AGE] for fit at the .05 level.

(b) Test the model[AGE*BREATH,SMOKE*BREATH] for fit at the.05 level.

(c) Run backward elimination. What model fits the data?

Appendix 14.1: Log Linear Analysis Using Windows for Survey Data

We illustrate for Exercise 14.3. This was survey research, where the subjects were cross-classified on three variables: year, color, and response. The data for the study, as they appear in the SPSS editor, are:

	Year	Color	Response	Freq
1	1.00	1.00	1.00	81.00
2	1.00	1.00	2.00	23.00
3	1.00	1.00	3.00	4.00
4	1.00	2.00	1.00	325.00
5	1.00	2.00	2.00	253.00
6	1.00	2.00	3.00	54.00
7	2.00	1.00	1.00	224.00
8	2.00	1.00	2.00	144.00
9	2.00	1.00	3.00	24.00
10	2.00	2.00	1.00	600.00
11	2.00	2.00	2.00	636.00
12	2.00	2.00	3.00	158.00

So, again, the first step is to type the data in and save it as a file; we call the file LOG3WAY. SAV. Then we click on Analyze and scroll down to LOGLINEAR in the dropdown menu. The screen looks as follows:

When we click on MODEL SELECTION the following screen appears:

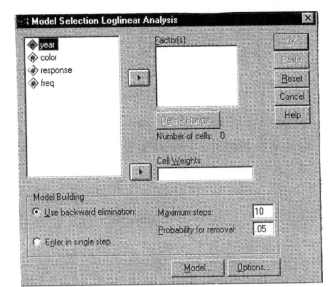

Click on YEAR, then click on the arrow to move it into the Factor(s) box. When this is done, the DEFINE RANGE box will light up asking you to define the range, which is 1 for the minimum and 2 for the maximum. Then click on CONTINUE and move COLOR into the factor box and define its range. Do the same for RESPONSE. After you have entered all three factors the box appears as follows:

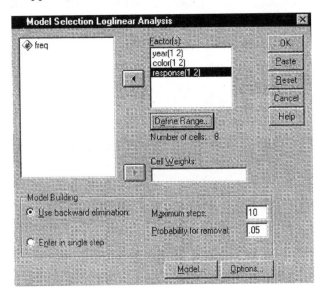

At this point click on DATA and then click on WEIGHT CASES from the dropdown menu. The following appears:

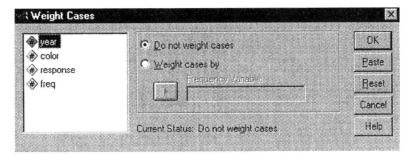

Click on WEIGHT CASES BY and make FREQ the Frequency Variable. Then click on OK. To run the analysis click on OK. Following is part of the output:

---

* * * * * * * * *HIERARCHICAL LOG LINEAR * * * * * * * * * *

Backward Elimination (p = .050) for DESIGN 1 with generating class

    YEAR*COLOR*RESPONSE

Likelihood ratio chi square = .00000   DF = 0   P = 1.000

- -

If Deleted Simple Effect is	DF	L.R. Chisq Change	Prob	Iter
YEAR*COLOR*RESPONSE	2	3.566	.1682	4

Step 1

  The best model has generating class

    YEAR*COLOR
    YEAR*RESPONSE
    COLOR*RESPONSE

Likelihood ratio chi square = 3.56559   DF = 2   P = .168

- -

If Deleted Simple Effect is	DF	L.R. Chisq Change	Prob	Iter
YEAR*COLOR	1	23.677	.0000	2
YEAR*RESPONSE	2	21.385	.0000	2
COLOR*RESPONSE	2	45.776	.0000	2

Step 2

  The best model has generating class

    YEAR*COLOR
    YEAR*RESPONSE
    COLOR*RESPONSE

Likelihood ratio chi square = 3.56559   DF = 2   P = .168

15

Hierarchical Linear Modeling

Natasha Beretvas

University of Texas at Austin

15.1 Introduction

In the social sciences, nested data structures are very common. As Burstein (1980) noted, "Most of what goes on in education occurs within some group context." Nested data (which yields correlated observations) occurs whenever subjects are clustered together in groups, as is frequently found in social science research. For example, students in the same school will be more alike than students from different schools. Responses of patients to counseling for those patients clustered together in therapy groups will depend to some extent on the patients' group's dynamics, resulting in a within-therapy group dependency (Kreft & deLeeuw, 1998). Yet *one of the assumptions made in many of the statistical techniques (including regression, ANOVA, etc.) used in the social sciences (and covered in this text) is that the observations are independent.*

Kenny and Judd (1986, p. 431) noted that while non-independence is commonly treated as a nuisance, there are still "many occasions when nonindependence is the substantive problem that we are trying to understand in psychological research." These authors refer to researchers interested in studying social interaction. Kenny and Judd note that social interaction by definition implies non-independence. If a researcher is interested in studying social interaction, or even a plethora of other social psychology constructs, the nonindependence is not so much a statistical problem to be surmounted as a focus of interest.

Additional examples of dependent data can be found for employees working together in organizations, and even citizens within nations. These scenarios, as well as students nested within schools and patients within therapy groups, provide examples of two-level designs. The first level comprises the units that are grouped together at the second level. For instance, students (level one) would be considered as nested within schools (level two), and patients (level one) are nested within counseling groups (level two).

Examples of this nestedness of clustering do not always involve only two levels. A commonly encountered three-level design found in educational research involves students (level one) nested within classrooms (level two), clustered within schools (level three). Individuals (level one) are "nested" within families (level two) that are clustered in neighborhoods (level three). Patients (level one) are frequently counseled in groups (level two) that are clustered within counseling centers (level three). There is an endless list of such groupings. When data are clustered in these ways, use of multilevel modeling should be considered.

In the late 1970s, estimation techniques and programs were developed to facilitate use of multilevel modeling (Raudenbush & Bryk, 2002; Arnold, 1992). Before this time, researchers would tend to use single-level regression models to investigate relationships between relevant variables describing the different levels, despite the violation of the assumption of independence. This would be problematic for a variety of reasons.

15.2 Problems Using Single-Level Analyses of Multilevel Data

A researcher might be interested in the relationship between students' test scores and characteristics of the schools they attended. The dataset might consist of student and school descriptors from students who were randomly selected from a random selection of schools. When investigating the question of interest, a researcher choosing to ignore the inherent dependency in his or her data would have two analytical choices (other than the use of multilevel modeling). The researcher could aggregate the student data to the school level and use school data as the level of analysis. This would mean that the outcome in a single-level regression might have been the school's average student score, with predictors consisting of school descriptors and average school characteristics summarized across students within each school. One of the primary problems with such an analysis is that valuable information is lost concerning variability of students' scores *within* schools, statistical power is decreased, and the ecological validity of the inferences has been compromised (Hox, 2002; Kreft and de Leeuw, 1998).

Alternatively, the researcher could disaggregate the student- and school-level data. This modeling would have involved using students as the unit of analysis and ignoring the non-independence of students' scores within each school. In the single-level regression that would be used with disaggregated data, the outcome would be the student's test score, with predictors including student and school characteristics. The problem in this analysis is that values for school descriptors would be the same across students within the same school. Using this disaggregated data, and thus ignoring the non-independence of the students' scores within each school, artificially deflates the estimated variability of the school descriptor. This would then affect the validity of the statistical significance test of the relationship between the student outcome and the school descriptor, and inflate the associated Type I error rate. The stronger the relationship between students' scores for students within each school, the worse the impact on the Type I error rate.

There is a measure of the degree of dependence between individuals that is called the intra-class correlation (ICC). The more that characteristics of the context (say, school) in which an individual (student) finds himself have an effect on the outcome of interest, the stronger will be the ICC. In other words, the more related to the outcome are the experiences of individuals within each grouping, the stronger will be the ICC (Kreft and de Leeuw, 1998). For two-level datasets (in which individuals have only one level of grouping), the ICC can be interpreted as the proportion of the total variance in the outcome that occurs between the groups (as opposed to within the groups).

Snijders and Bosker (1999, p. 151) indicate that, "In most social science research, the intra-class correlation ranges between 0 and .4, and often narrower bounds can be identified." *Even an ICC that is slightly larger than zero can have a dramatic effect on Type I error rates,* as can be seen in Table 6.1, which is taken from Scariano and Davenport (1987). Note from the table that for an ICC of only .01, with three groups and 30 subjects per group, the actual alpha is inflated to .0985 for a one-way ANOVA. For a three-group, n = 30 scenario in which ICC=.10, the actual alpha is .4917.

Fortunately, researchers do not have to choose between the loss of information associated with aggregation of dependent data nor the inflated Type I error rates associated with disaggregated data. Thus, instead of choosing a level at which to conduct analyses of clustered or hierarchical data, researchers can instead use the technique called "multilevel modeling." This chapter will provide an introduction to some of the simpler multilevel models. Several excellent multilevel modeling texts are available (Raudenbush and Bryk,

2002; Hox, 2002; Snijders and Bosker, 1999; Kreft and de Leeuw, 1998) that will provide the interested reader additional details as well as discussion of more advanced topics in multilevel modeling.

Several terms are used to describe essentially the same family of multilevel models including: multilevel modeling, hierarchical linear modeling, (co)variance component models, multilevel linear models, random-effects or mixed-effects models and random coefficient regression models (Raudenbush and Bryk, 2002; Arnold, 1992). I will use "multilevel modeling" and "hierarchical linear modeling" in this introduction as they seem to provide the most comprehensible terms.

In this chapter, formulation of the multilevel model will first be introduced. This will be followed with an example of a two-level model. In this example, which involves students within classes, we will first consider what is called an unconditional model (no predictors at either level). Then we consider adding predictors at level 1 and then a predictor at level 2. After this example we consider evaluating the efficacy of treatments on some dependent variable, and compare the HLM6 analysis to an SPSS analysis of the same data. In conclusion, we offer some final comments on HLM.

15.3 Formulation of the Multilevel Model

Two algebraic formulations are possible for the hierarchical linear model (HLM). The set of equations for each level can be represented separately (while indexing the appropriate clusters), or alternatively, each level's equations can be combined to provide a single equation. The multiple levels' equations formulation (Raudenbush and Bryk, 1992; 2002) seems to be the easiest to comprehend for a neophyte HLM user in that it simplifies the variance component assignment and clearly distinguishes the levels. This formulation also is the one that is implemented in the multilevel software HLM (Raudenbush et al., 2000). Because the HLM software will be used to demonstrate estimation of HLM parameters in this chapter, the multiple levels formulation will be used.

15.4 Two-Level Model—General Formulation

Before presenting the general formulation of the two-level model, some terminology will first be explained. Raudenbush and Bryk (2002) distinguish between unconditional and conditional models. The unconditional model is one in which no predictors (at any of the levels) are included. A conditional model includes at least one predictor at any of the levels.

Multilevel modeling permits the estimation of fixed and random effects whereas ordinary least-squares (OLS) regression includes only fixed effects. For this reason, it is important to distinguish between fixed and random effects. If a researcher is interested in comparing two methods of counseling, for example, then he or she would not be interested in generalizing beyond those two methods. The inferences would be "fixed" or limited to the two methods under consideration. Thus, counseling method would be treated as a fixed factor. Similarly, if three diets (Atkins, South Beach, and Weight Watchers, for instance) were to be compared, then the diets were not randomly chosen from some population of diets, thus once again diets would be a fixed factor.

On the other hand, consider two situations in which a factor would be considered random. A researcher might be interested in comparing three specific teaching methods (fixed factor) used in nine different random schools in some metropolitan area. The researcher would wish to generalize inferences about the teaching methods' effects to the population of schools in this area. Thus, here, schools is a random factor and teaching method effects would be modeled as randomly varying across schools. As a second example, consider the design in which patients are clustered together in therapy groups. Although a researcher would be interested in limiting inferences to the specific counseling methods involved (fixed effect), she might want to generalize the inferences beyond the particular therapy groups involved. Thus, groups would be considered a random factor and counseling method effects modeled as randomly varying across groups. For further discussion of fixed and random effects, see Kreft and de Leeuw's discussion (1998).

This two-level example will involve investigating the relationship between students' scores on a mathematics achievement test in the 12th grade (*Math_12*) and a measure of the student's interest in mathematics (*IIM*). For students in a certain classroom, a simple one-level regression model could be tested:

$$Y_i = \beta_0 + \beta_1 X_i + r_i \tag{1}$$

where Y_i is student i's grade 12 Math score, X_i is student i's *IIM* score, β_1 is the slope coefficient representing the relationship between *Math_12* and *IIM*, and β_0 is the intercept representing the average *Math_12* score for students in the class's sample given a score of zero on X_i. The value of β_1 indicates the expected change in *Math_12* given a one unit increase in *IIM* score. The r_i represents the "residual" or deviation of student i's *Math_12* score from that predicted given the values of β_0, the student's X_i, and β_1. It is assumed that r_i is normally distributed with a mean of zero and a variance of σ^2, or $r_i \sim N(0,\sigma^2)$.

A brief note should be made about centering the values of a predictor. As mentioned above, the intercept, β_0, represents the value predicted for the outcome, Y_i, *given that* X_i *is zero*. It is important to ensure that a value of zero for X_i is meaningful. Interval-scaled variables are frequently scaled so that they are "centered" around their mean. To center the *IIM* scores, they would need to be transformed so that student i's value on X_i was the deviation of student i's *IIM* score from the sample mean of the *IIM* scores. If this centered predictor were used instead of the original raw *IIM* score predictor, then the intercept β_0 would be interpreted as the predicted *Math_12* score for a student with an average *IIM* score.

A regression equation just like Equation 1 might be constructed for students in a second classroom. The relationship between *Math_12* and *IIM*, however, might differ slightly for the second classroom. Similarly, the coefficients in Equation 1 might be slightly different for other classrooms also. The researcher might be interested in understanding the source of the differences in the classrooms' intercepts and slopes. For example, the researcher might want to investigate whether there might be some classroom characteristic that lessens or overcomes the relationship between a student's interest in mathematics (*IIM*) and his or her performance on the math test (*Math_12*). To investigate this question, the researcher might obtain a random sample of several classrooms to gather students' *Math_12* and *IIM* scores as well as measures of classroom descriptors. Now regression Equation 1 could be calculated for each classroom j such that:

$$Y_{ij} = \beta_{0j} + \beta_{1j} X_{ij} + r_{ij} \tag{2}$$

where the estimates for classroom j of the intercept, β_{0j}, and slope, β_{1j} might differ for each classroom. For each classroom's set of residuals, r_{ij}, it is assumed that their variances are homogeneous across classrooms, where $r_{ij} \sim N(0, \sigma^2)$.

The researcher would (hopefully) realize that, given a large enough sample of classrooms' data, multilevel modeling could be used for this analysis. Math scores of students within the same classroom are likely more similar to each other than to scores of students in other classrooms. This dependency needs to be modeled appropriately. This brings us to the multiple sets of equations formulation of the HLM.

If multilevel modeling were to be used in the current example, then students would be nested within classrooms. The higher level of grouping or clustering is associated with a higher value for the assigned HLM level. Thus, students will be modeled at level 1 and classrooms (within which students are "nested") at level 2. The level one (student level) equation has already been presented (in Equation 2). The classroom level (level two) equations are used to represent how the lower level's regression coefficients might vary across classrooms. *The regression coefficients, β_{0j} and β_{1j}, become response variables modeled as outcomes at the classroom level* (Raudenbush, 1984). Variation in classrooms' regression equations implies that the coefficients in these equations each might vary across classrooms. Variability in the intercept, β_{0j}, across classrooms would be represented as one of the level two equations by:

$$\beta_{0j} = \gamma_{00} + u_{0j} \tag{3}$$

where β_{0j} is the intercept for classroom j, γ_{00} *is the average intercept across classrooms* (or, in other words, the average *Math_12* score across classrooms, controlling for *IIM* score) and u_{0j} *is classroom j's deviation from γ_{00}*, where $u_{0j} \sim N(0, \tau_{00})$.

Variability in the relationship between *IIM* and *Math_12* (the slope coefficient) across classrooms is represented as a level two equation:

$$\beta_{1j} = \gamma_{10} + u_{1j} \tag{4}$$

where β_{1j} is the slope for classroom j, γ_{10} *is the average slope across classrooms* (or, in other words, the average measure of the relationship between *Math_12* and *IIM* scores across classrooms) and u_{1j} *is classroom j's deviation from γ_{10}*, where $u_{1j} \sim N(0, \tau_{11})$. It is commonly assumed that the intercept and slope (β_{0j} and β_{1j}) are bivariately normally distributed with covariance τ_{01} (Raudenbush and Bryk, 2002).

The two level-two equations (Equations 3 and 4) are usually more succinctly presented as:

$$\begin{cases} \beta_{0j} = \gamma_{00} + u_{0j} \\ \beta_{1j} = \gamma_{10} + u_{1j} \end{cases}. \tag{5}$$

In this two-level unconditional model (see Equations 2 and 5) there are three sources of random variability: the level one variability, r_{ij}, the level two (across classrooms) variability in the intercept, u_{0j}, and in the slope, u_{1j}. An estimate of the level one variability, σ^2, is provided. Estimates of the level two variance components, τ_{00} and τ_{11}, (describing the variability of u_{0j} and u_{1j}, respectively) can each be tested for statistical significance.

Testing the variability of the intercept across classrooms assesses whether the variability of classrooms' intercepts (as measured using the associated variance component, τ_{00}) differs from zero. If it is inferred that there is not a significant amount of variability in the intercept (or if it is hypothesized based on theory that the intercept should not vary across classrooms) then the random effects variability term, u_{0j}, can be taken out of Equation 3 (or Equation 5) and the intercept is then modeled as fixed.

If, on the other hand, it is inferred that there is a significant amount of variability in the intercept across classrooms, then variables describing classroom (level two) characteristics can be added to the model in Equation 3 (or equation for β_{0j} in Equation 5) to help explain that variability. (This will be demonstrated later in the chapter.) If the classroom characteristics are found to sufficiently explain the remaining variability in the intercept, then they can remain in the modified level two equation for the intercept and the random effect term can be taken out. With only level-two predictors in Equation 3, the intercept is considered to be modeled as "non-randomly varying" (Raudenbush and Bryk, 2002).

The variability in the slope coefficients can also be tested by inspecting the statistical significance of the slope's variance component, τ_{11}. If it is inferred that there is a significant amount of variability in the slopes (implying that the relationship between *Math_12* and *IIM* scores differs across classrooms), then a classroom predictor could be added to help explain the variability of β_{1j} (in Equation 4 or 5). The addition of a level-two predictor to the equation for the slope coefficient would be termed a "cross-level interaction," which is an interaction between variables describing different clustering levels (Hox, 2002). The variance component remaining (conditional upon including the level-two predictor) can then be tested again to see if it sufficiently explained the random variability in slopes. With the addition of a predictor that does influence the relationship between the level-one variable (here, *IIM*) and the outcome (*Math_12*), the remaining variability will be lowered, as will be the associated variance component, τ_{11}. The values of the level two variance components (for the intercept and slope coefficients) can be compared with their values in the unconditional (no predictors) model to assess the proportion of (classroom) level two variability explained by the predictors that were added to the model in Equation 5. This, as well as addition of level one and level-two predictors to the model, will be demonstrated further in the next section.

Having discussed the formulation of the two-level HLM, use of the HLM software (version 6) will now be introduced and then demonstrated using a worked example. This example will be presented to demonstrate the process of HLM model building involving addition of predictors to the two-levels of equations, as well as interpretation of the parameter estimates presented in the HLM output.

15.5 HLM6 Software

Raudenbush, Bryk, Cheong and Congdon's (2004) HLM software, version 6, for multi-level modeling provides a clear introduction for beginning multilevel modelers. In addition, it is possible for students to obtain a freeware copy of the program for simple multilevel analyses, most of which are covered in this chapter's introduction to HLM (www.ssicentral.com). This provides beginners with an easy way to evaluate for themselves whether they wish to purchase the entire program. The SS is an abbreviation for Scientific Software, which produces and distributes the HLM software. When you get to this site, click on HLM. You will get a dropdown menu, at which point click on free downloads.

The datasets being analyzed by HLM can be in any of the following formats: ASCII, SPSS, SAS portable, or SYSTAT. One of the complications of using HLM is that *separate* data files must be constructed for each level of clustering. For example, when investigating a two-level dataset, the user must construct a level one file as well as a level two file. These two files *must* be linked by a common ID on both files. (This will be *TeachId* in the example we are about to use). ***Data analysis via HLM involves four steps:***

1. Construction of the data files.
2. Construction of the multivariate data matrix (MDM) file, using the data files.
3. Execution of analyses based on the MDM file.
4. Evaluation of the fitted model(s) based on a residual file.

We will not deal with step 4, as this chapter is an introduction to HLM.

15.6 Two-Level Example—Student and Classroom Data

The first step in using HLM to estimate a multilevel model is to construct the relevant datasets. As mentioned, for a two-level analysis, two data files are needed: one for each level. The level two ID variable (*TeachId*) in the current example must appear in both files.

In this example, the researcher is interested in the relationship between scores on a 12th grade mathematics test (*Math_12*) and student and classroom characteristics. The researcher has information about students' gender and their individual scores on an interest in mathematics (*IIM*) inventory and on the outcome of interest (*Math_12*). Thus, *Math_12*, *IIM*, and *Gender* as well as the *TeachId* identifying the teacher/classroom for each student must appear in the level one dataset.

The researcher also has a measure of each classroom's "resources" (*Resource*) that assesses the supplies (relevant to mathematics instruction) accessible to a classroom of students. Thus, the level two dataset will contain *Resource* and *TeachId*. We will use SPSS data files.

15.6.1 Setting up the Datasets for HLM Analysis

The level one dataset contains the level two ID (*TeachId*) as well as the relevant student-level descriptors (*IIM* and *Gender*) and outcome (*Math_12*). Another minor complication encountered when using HLM is that the data should be sorted by level two ID and within level two ID, by student ID. A snapshot of the level one dataset appears in Figure 15.1.

As can be seen in Figure 15.1, the dataset is set up to mimic the clustering inherent in the data. Students are "nested" within classrooms that are identified using the variable *TeachId*. The first classroom (*TeachId* = 1) provides student-level information on three students (students 5, 7, and 9). The second classroom provides data for four students (14, 16, 19, and 20), and so on. The level two dataset appears in Figure 15.2.

In the level two dataset, the classroom information (here, the *TeachId* and the classroom's score on the *Resource* measure) are listed. Note that the *TeachId* values are ordered in both the level one and level two files as required by HLM software.

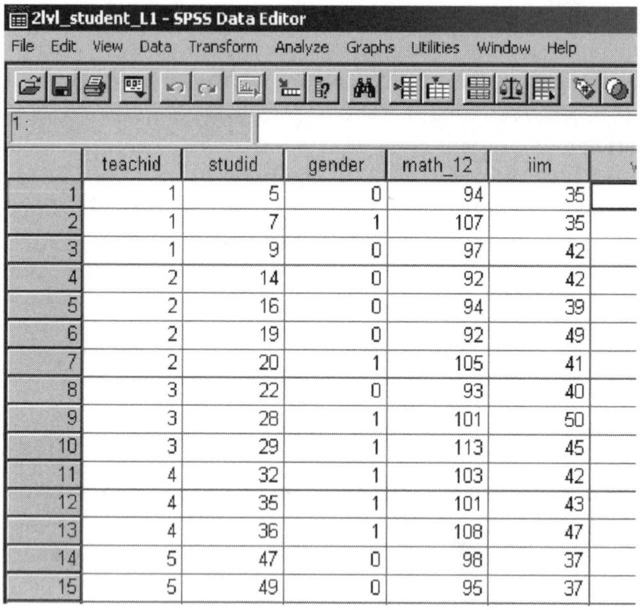

	teachid	studid	gender	math_12	iim
1	1	5	0	94	35
2	1	7	1	107	35
3	1	9	0	97	42
4	2	14	0	92	42
5	2	16	0	94	39
6	2	19	0	92	49
7	2	20	1	105	41
8	3	22	0	93	40
9	3	28	1	101	50
10	3	29	1	113	45
11	4	32	1	103	42
12	4	35	1	101	43
13	4	36	1	108	47
14	5	47	0	98	37
15	5	49	0	95	37

FIGURE 15.1
Two-level model – student level SPSS dataset.

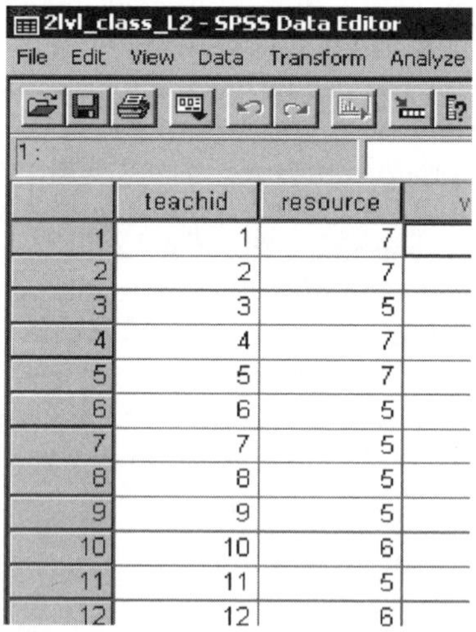

	teachid	resource
1	1	7
2	2	7
3	3	5
4	4	7
5	5	7
6	6	5
7	7	5
8	8	5
9	9	5
10	10	6
11	11	5
12	12	6

FIGURE 15.2
Two-level model – classroom level SPSS dataset.

15.6.2 Setting Up the MDM File for HLM Analysis

Before using HLM, the user needs to first construct what is called the "multivariate data matrix" or MDM file that sets up the datasets (regardless of their original format) into a format that can be used more efficiently when running the HLM program. (Note that in prior versions of HLM, an SSM file was constructed instead of an MDM file). Once the datasets are set up in SPSS (or other relevant statistical software programs) the following steps are taken to set up the MDM file.

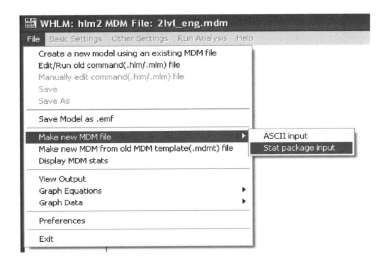

FIGURE 15.3
First HLM window for building MDM file.

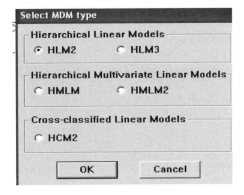

FIGURE 15.4
Second HLM window for building MDM file.

1. Once the HLM program is opened, click on FILE, scroll down to "Make new MDM file" and request STAT PACKAGE INPUT as shown in Figure 15.3.

2. You must then identify the kind of modeling to be used from the window displayed in Figure 15.4. Choose HLM2 for this two-level example and click on OK.

3. After clicking on HLM2, the "Make MDM – HLM2" HLM window appearing in Figure 15.5 will appear. Fill in a filename for the MDM file (under MDM File Name) being sure to include ".MDM" as the suffix. Given SPSS datasets are being analyzed, make sure to change INPUT FILE TYPE to SPSS/WINDOWS before attempting to find the relevant level one and level two data files. Because the first multilevel example involves students nested within classrooms, be sure to click on "persons within groups" instead of "measures within persons." Select the level one data file by clicking on BROWSE under LEVEL-1 SPECIFICATION and finding the relevant file (here, called 2lvl_student_L1.SAV). Note that the level one and level two SPSS files that are going to be used in the analysis should not be open in SPSS when the user is constructing the MDM file.

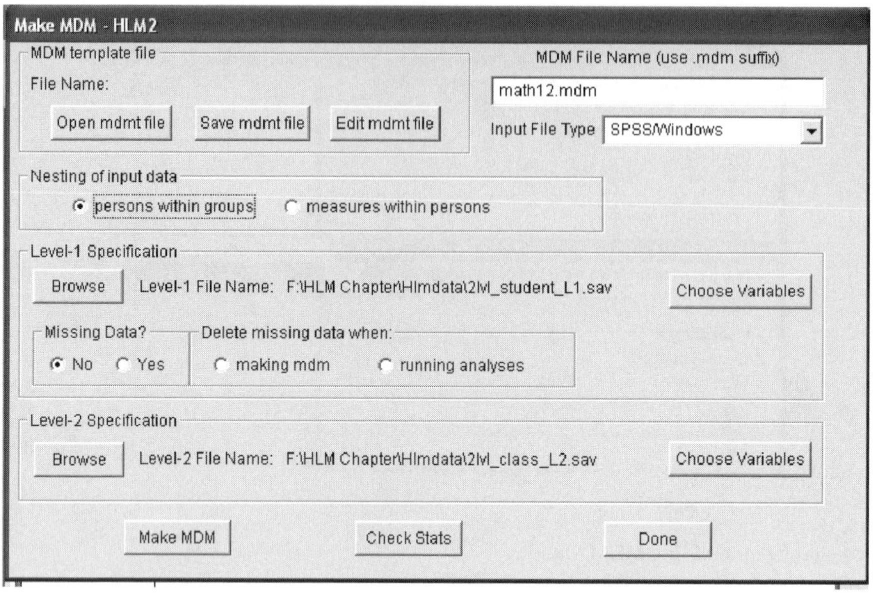

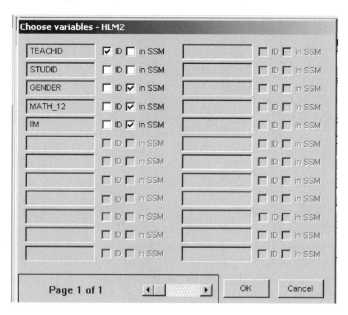

FIGURE 15.5
Third HLM window for building MDM file.

FIGURE 15.6
Setting up an MDM file – choosing variables at level one.

4. Click on CHOOSE VARIABLES and select the level two ID (*TeachId*) that links the level one and two files as well as the relevant level-one variables (*Gender, Math_12,* and *IIM* in the current example). Figure 15.6 displays this screen. In both Figures 15.6 and 15.7 it should read "in MDM" (since we using version 6 of HLM).

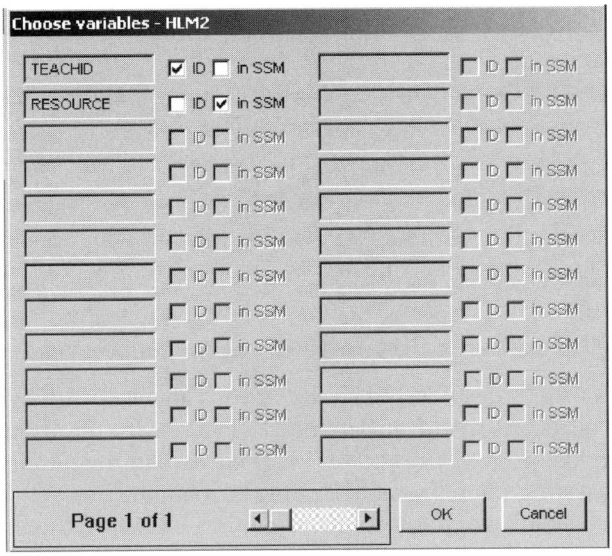

FIGURE 15.7
Setting up an MDM File – choosing variables at level two.

5. Follow the same procedure to identify the relevant level two file for use in the MDM by clicking on BROWSE and finding the level two .SAV file (here, the 2lvl_class_L2.SAV file). Again, click on CHOOSE VARIABLES and identify the level two ID (*TeachId*) and the level-two variables of interest (just *Resource* in the current example). The level two CHOOSE VARIABLE screen appears in Figures 15.6 and 15.7.

6. Next, you need to click on "Save mdmt file" (to save the MDM template file) and provide a name for the response (.MDMT) file.

7. Click on "Make MDM" to ensure that the data has been input correctly. A MS-DOS window will briefly appear (after clicking on MAKE MDM) ending in a count of the number of level two and level one units. If there seems to be a disparity between the group and within-group sample sizes, make certain that the original data files are sorted by the level two ID.

8. Before you can exit the MAKE MDM window, you must also click on CHECK STATS. Once this is done, you can click on DONE to be brought to the HLM window that allows you to build the model to be estimated.

15.6.3 The Two-Level Unconditional Model

The unconditional model (including no predictors) is the model typically estimated first when estimating multilevel models. Estimation of the unconditional model provides estimates of the partitioning of the variability at each level. In the current example, this means that the variability can be estimated between students and between classrooms. If there is not a substantial amount of variability between classrooms, then this additional level of clustering might not be needed.

At level one, in the unconditional model, the outcome (*Math_12*) for student i in classroom j is modeled only as a function of classroom j's intercept (i.e. average *Math_12* score) and the student's residual:

$$Math\_12_{ij} = \beta_{0j} + r_{ij}. \tag{6}$$

At level two, classroom j's intercept is modeled to be a function of the average intercept (*Math_12* score) across classrooms and a classroom residual:

$$\beta_{0j} = \gamma_{00} + u_{0j}. \tag{7}$$

HLM's presentation of these equations is very similar to Equations 6 and 7 although it does not include the relevant i and j subscripts.

15.6.3.1 Estimating Parameters of the Two-Level Unconditional Model

Once the MDM file is built, the HLM window that you can use to build your model appears with the newly constructed MDM automatically loaded. If you already have an MDM saved, then you can load it by clicking on FILE, then "Create a new model using an existing MDM" and requesting the relevant MDM file be loaded.

Once the MDM is loaded, a blank formula screen appears with the list of level-one variables appearing on the left-hand side of the screen. The steps necessary to build the unconditional two-level model are as follows:

1. Once the relevant MDM is loaded, the first thing a user must do is choose the relevant outcome variable (here, *Math_12*). Thus, click on *Math_12* and then OUTCOME VARIABLE as is shown in Figure 15.8.

   For a two-level model, HLM automatically presents the two-level "unconditional model" with no predictors at levels one nor two, as is shown in Figure 15.9.

   If you wish to run the model (without saving it) and examine the output, click on RUN ANALYSIS. When you click on RUN ANALYSIS, the program will respond that the model has not been saved; just click on RUN THE MODEL SHOWN (wait several seconds). Then click on FILE and scroll and click on VIEW OUTPUT. By doing this you can skip steps 2 through 5 below.

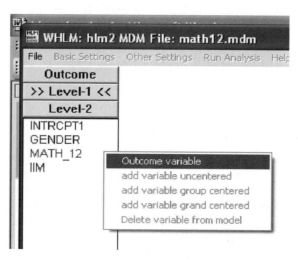

FIGURE 15.8
Selecting the outcome variable in HLM.

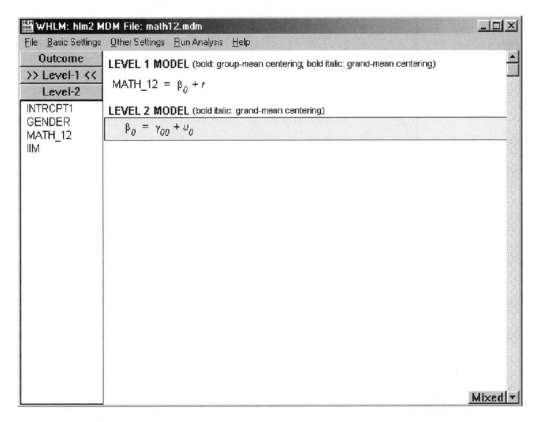

FIGURE 15.9
Unconditional model in HLM for two-level model.

2. Click on BASIC SETTINGS to change the output file name from the default HLM2.TXT to something meaningful (like TWO_LEV.OUT as demonstrated in Figure 15.10). It also helps to change the Title of the model from "no title" to something like "Unconditional two-level model," as this will appear on every page of the output. For details about the remaining options, the reader can refer to the HLM manual (Raudenbush, Bryk, Cheong, and Congdon, 2004). Click OK.

3. Save the model by clicking on FILE, then SAVE AS and typing in the model's filename.

4. Click on RUN ANALYSIS. Once the solution has converged, the MS-DOS window displaying the iterations (see below) will close and bring you back to the HLM model screen. (Based on HLM's defaults, if more than 100 iterations are needed, the user will be prompted whether the program should be allowed to iterate until convergence. For the current dataset, only six iterations were needed until the convergence criteria were met (Figure 15.11).

5. You can view the HLM output by clicking on FILE and then VIEW OUTPUT.

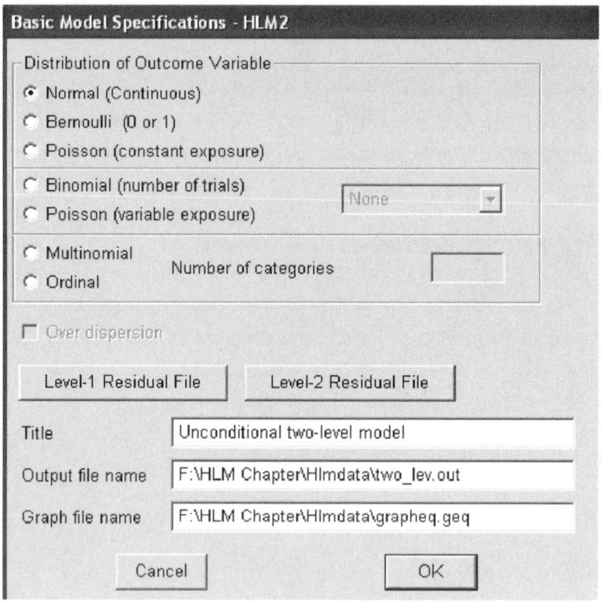

FIGURE 15.10
HLM basic model specification model.

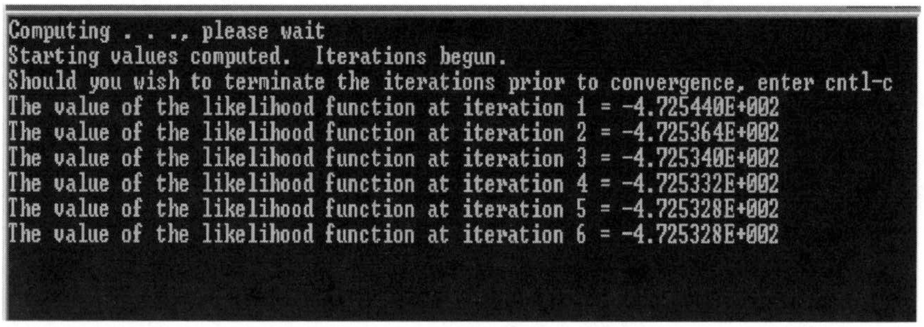

FIGURE 15.11
HLM DOS window presenting iterations while HLM is running.

15.7 HLM Software Output

The output containing the model's parameter estimates can be viewed if the user clicks on File ⇒ View Output. (If the user closes HLM, the output can also be viewed by opening any kind of editor and requesting the .OUT file specified when in the Basic Specifications window.) The output consists of several pages of output, not all of which will be presented here. The initial page lists the .MDM, .HLM, and output filenames. It also presents the equations that were estimated. The equations match the format of those presented in the original HLM window when the model was being built. This part of the output appears as follows:

```
Summary of the model specified (in equation format)
-----------------------------------------------------
Level-1 Model
       Y = B0 + R
Level-2 Model
       B0 = G00 + U0
```

The listing of the equations' coefficients is useful when the user needs to interpret the later output. Following the listing of the equations, the iterations and starting estimates for the various parameters are listed. After the information about the last iteration needed for the model's estimation, the message "Iterations stopped due to small change in likelihood function" appears and the results that follow include final parameter estimates.

The first parameter estimate that appears is the variance, σ^2, of students' *Math_12* scores within classrooms (assumed homogeneous across classrooms). The value for the current data set is 50.47. The only other level two variance component that is estimated (in this unconditional model) represents the variability of classrooms' intercepts, τ_{00}. The value of the τ_{00} estimate is 26.42 for the current example. Next, the reliability estimate of β_{0j} as an estimate of γ_{00} is provided and is .688 for the current data set. This indicates that the classrooms' intercept estimates tend to provide moderately reliable estimates of the overall intercept (see the HLM manual (Raudenbushet et al., 2000) and Raudenbush and Bryk's (2002) HLM text for more information about this form of reliability estimate).

In the output, there are two tables containing estimates of the relevant fixed effect(s). The second table lists the fixed effects estimates along with "robust standard errors." These should be used when summarizing fixed effects; however, if the standard errors in the two fixed effects' tables differ substantially, then the user might wish to re-consider the fit of some of the assumptions underlying the model being estimated. The table containing the fixed effect estimate with robust standard appears below:

```
Final estimation of fixed effects
 (with robust standard errors)
 ----------------------------------------------------------------
                                 Standard          Approx.
    Fixed Effect    Coefficient  Error   T-ratio   d.f.    P-value
 ----------------------------------------------------------------
For        INTRCPT1, B0
   INTRCPT2, G00     98.043234   1.112063  88.163    29    0.000
 ----------------------------------------------------------------
```

The only fixed effect estimated in the two-level unconditional model is the intercept, γ_{00} (see Equation 7). The estimate of the average *Math_12* value across schools is 98.04 with a standard error of 1.11. This coefficient differs significantly from zero ($t(29) = 88.163$, $p < .0001$).

The next part of the output presents the estimates of the variance components. We have two variance components that are estimated, the variability within classrooms, σ^2, and the variability between classrooms, τ_{00}. Values of these two components' estimates were presented earlier in the output (as mentioned above) but also appear in table summary as follows in the HLM output:

```
Final estimation of variance components:
-------------------------------------------------------------------------
Random Effect          Standard      Variance      df   Chi-square  P-value
                       Deviation     Component
-------------------------------------------------------------------------
INTRCPT1,    U0        5.14032       26.42291      29    96.72024    0.000
 level-1,    R         7.10441       50.47257
-------------------------------------------------------------------------
```

The variance component estimates match those mentioned earlier. The value of the τ_{00} estimate can be tested against a value of zero using a test statistic that is assumed to follow a χ^2 distribution (Raudenbush and Bryk, 2002). The results indicate that we can infer that there is a statistically significant amount of variability in *Math_12* scores between classrooms ($\chi^2(29) = 96.72$, $p < .0001$). This supports the two-level modeling of the clustering of students' *Math_12* scores within classrooms.

The estimates of the variance components can be combined to provide an additional descriptor of the possible nestedness of the data. The intraclass correlation provides a measure of the proportion of the variability in the outcomes that exists between units of one of the multilevel model's levels. Specifically, for the two-level model estimated here, the intraclass correlation provides a measure of the proportion of variability in *Math_12 between* classrooms. The formula for the intraclass correlation for a two-level model is:

$$\rho_{ICC} = \frac{\tau_{00}}{\tau_{00} + \sigma^2} \tag{8}$$

For the current data set, the intraclass correlation estimate is

$$\hat{\rho}_{ICC} = \frac{\hat{\tau}_{00}}{\hat{\tau}_{00} + \hat{\sigma}^2} = \frac{26.42}{26.42 + 50.47} = .34$$

which means that 34% of the variability in *Math_12* scores is estimated to lie between classrooms (and thus it can be inferred that about 66% lies *within* classrooms).

The last information appearing in the HLM output consists of the deviance statistic that can be used to compare the fit of a model to the data when comparing two models. (It should be noted that, to use the Deviance statistic to compare models, one model must be a simplified version of the other in that some of the parameters estimated in the more parameterized model are not estimated but are instead constrained to a certain value in the simplified model.) For the current unconditional model estimated, the deviance statistic's value is 945.07 with two covariance parameters estimated (σ^2 and τ_{00}).

Since a substantial amount of variability was found both within and among classrooms, student and classroom descriptors could be added to the model to explain some of this variability. We will start by adding two student predictors to the level one equation.

15.8 Adding Level-One Predictors to the HLM

The dataset contains two student descriptors including *Gender* and interest in mathematics (*IIM*) scores. The researcher was interested in first including *IIM* scores as a level-one predictor of *Math_12* scores. To add a level-one variable to a model using HLM software, the user must click on the relevant variable. When a variable is clicked on, HLM prompts for the kind of centering that is requested for the variable. The choices include: add variable *uncentered*, add variable *group centered*, and add variable *grand centered*.

Centering: Before continuing with the description of the formulation of the model using HLM software, brief mention should be made of centering. It should be remembered that even in a simple, *single-level* regression model ($Y_i = \beta_0 + \beta_1 X_i + e_i$) including a predictor, X_i, the intercept represents the average value of the outcome, Y_i, for person i with a zero on X_i. Users of single-level regression can "center" their predictors to ensure that the intercept is meaningful. This centering can be done by transforming subjects' scores on X_i so that X_i represents a person's deviation from the sample's mean on X_i. This would transform interpretation of the single-level regression equation's intercept to be the average value of Y_i for someone at the (sample) mean on X_i.

Alternatively, the simple regression might model the relationship between a dichotomous predictor variable (representing whether a subject was in the placebo [zero dosage] group or a treatment [10mg dosage] group) and some measure of, say, anxiety. The predictor could be dummy-coded such that a value of zero was assigned for those in the placebo group with a value of 1 for those in the treatment group. This would mean that the intercept would represent the predicted anxiety level for a person who was in the placebo condition.

The importance of assigning a meaningful reference point for a value of zero for the predictors in single-level regression extends to the inclusion of interactions between predictors in the single-level model. The reason for this is that the interpretation of a main effect can be affected by the inclusion of an interaction between predictors (resulting in the model: $Y_i = \beta_0 + \beta_1 X_i + \beta_2 Z_i + \beta_3 X_i {}^* Z_i + e_i$). Specifically, if an interaction is modeled between, say, predictor variables X and Z, then the coefficient for the main effect of X represents the *effect of X given Z is zero*. Thus, you want to ensure that a value of zero on Z is meaningful. Similarly, the main effect of Z would be interpreted (with the interaction of X and Z included in the model) as *the effect of Z given X is zero*.

The need for centering predictor variables extends beyond single-level regression equations to include multilevel modeling. In a two-level multilevel model, a choice of centering is available for any level-one predictor variables included in the level one equation. The level one equation depicted in Equation 2 ($Y_{ij} = \beta_{0j} + \beta_{1j} X_{ij} + r_{ij}$) represents a single level-one predictor, X_{ij}, added to the model to help explain variability in the outcome, Y_{ij}. As in a single-level regression equation, the intercept, β_{0j}, represents the predicted value of Y_{ij} for someone with $X_{ij} = 0$.

As in single-level regression, a score of zero on X_{ij} might be meaningful (as in the example in which membership in a placebo condition might be assigned a zero on X_{ij} as compared with a value of 1 assigned to those in a treatment condition). However, sometimes, a value of zero on the untransformed scale of X_{ij} might be unrealistic. Raudenbush and Bryk (2002) use an example in which X_{ij} is a subject's SAT score for which feasible values range only from 200 to 800. In scenarios in which the value of zero on untransformed X_{ij} is not meaningful, a researcher should center his or her predictor variable.

Given a two-level model, there are two primary options (beyond not centering at all) for centering the level-one predictor variable. One option involves centering the variable around the grand mean of the sample (as was described as an alternative for single-level regression), appropriately termed "grand-mean centering." This is accomplished by transforming the score on X_{ij} of subject i from group j (where, in the current example being demonstrated using HLM software, the grouping variable was "school") into the deviation of that score, X_{ij}, from the overall sample's mean score on X_{ij} (represented as $\bar{X}_{..}$). These transformed scores ($X_{ij} - \bar{X}_{..}$) are then used as the predictor of the outcome Y_{ij}

in Equation 2. This means that the intercept term in Equation 2 represents the predicted value on Y_{ij} for someone with a value of zero on the predictor: $(X_{ij} - \bar{X}_{..})$. A subject with a value of zero on the predictor has an X_{ij} value equal to the grand mean: $\bar{X}_{..}$. Thus, the intercept is the predicted value on Y_{ij} for someone at the grand mean on X_{ij}. This grand-mean centering results in the intercept's being interpretable as the mean on Y_{ij} for group j adjusted by a function of the deviation of the group's mean from the grand mean (Raudenbush and Bryk, 2002).

In multilevel modeling, another alternative is available for centering a level-one predictor variable. This alternative is termed "group-mean centering" and involves transforming the score, X_{ij}, of person i in group j into the deviation of that person's score from that (that person's) group j's mean on X_{ij}: $(X_{ij} - \bar{X}_{.j})$. This modifies interpretation of the intercept, β_{0j}, so that it becomes the predicted value on Y_{ij} for someone with zero for $(X_{ij} - \bar{X}_{.j})$, or someone with a score that is the equivalent of group j's mean on X_{ij}.

Several authors (including Kreft and de Leeuw, 1998; Raudenbush and Bryk, 2002) provide a detailed explanation for the correspondence between a model in which grand-mean centering is used and one in which variables are not centered. Essentially, when grand mean centering is used, a constant (the sample's mean on the relevant predictor) is subtracted from each case's value on the predictor. This means that the parameter estimates resulting from grand-mean centering can be linearly transformed to obtain the relevant uncentered variables' model's coefficients. This is not always the case when a variable has been group-mean centered. In group-mean centering, the mean of the case's group on the group-mean centered predictor is subtracted from the case's value on a predictor. Clearly, each group's mean will not be the same on the predictor and thus the same constant is not subtracted from each case's predictor value. The correspondence between a model with group-mean centered variables and models without centering or with grand-mean centering is not generally direct.

One should also be cautioned that, as in single-level modeling, choice of centering for predictors also impacts interpretation of main effects for variables when interactions that include that variable are modeled. This applies in multilevel modeling to same-level interactions between predictors as well as cross-level interactions in which, say, a level-two predictor might be used to explain the relationship between a level-one predictor and the outcome of interest.

Choice of grand-mean versus group-mean centering clearly impacts the interpretation of the intercept. However, as described in detail by Raudenbush and Bryk (2002), the choice of centering can also impact estimation of the level-two variances of the intercept and of the slope or coefficient of the predictor across groups (here, schools). This means that estimation of the variance in the u_{0j}, s and the u_{1j}, s (see Equation 5) will also be impacted by whether group-mean centering or grand-mean (or no centering) is used. As summarized by Raudenbush and Bryk (2002, p. 34):

> Be conscious of the choice of location for each level-1 predictor because it has implications for interpretation of β_{0j}, $\text{var}(\beta_{0j})$ and by implication, all of the covariances involving β_{0j}. In general, sensible choices of location depend on the purposes of the research. No single rule covers all cases. It is important, however, that the researcher carefully consider choices of location in light of those purposes; and it is vital to keep the location in mind while interpreting results.

Several authors provide more detailed discussion of choice of centering than can be presented here (Snijders and Bosker, 1999; Kreft and de Leeuw, 1998; Raudenbush and Bryk,

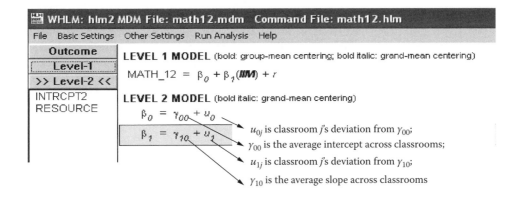

FIGURE 15.12
Adding a level-one predictor to a two-level model in HLM.

2002). The reader is strongly encouraged to refer to these texts to help understand centering in more detail.

In the example with which we demonstrate use of HLM software, we will use grand mean centering for the *IIM* variable. *IIM* is added as a grand-mean centered level-one variable by clicking on the variable and requesting "add variable grand centered." *In version 6 of HLM, the default is for a predictor's effect to be modeled as fixed. (In version 5 of HLM, the default was for the effect to be random.)* To model this effect as random, click on the level two equation for the coefficient of *IIM* and $\beta_1 = \Gamma_{10}$ will become $\beta_1 = \Gamma_{10} + u_1$ (see Figure 15.12). Again, the HLM model does not present the relevant *i* and *j* subscripts.

Note that the regression coefficients in level 1 are response (dependent) variables in level 2.

The output appears as before, although with additional parameters estimated, given that this second model includes an additional predictor. The fixed effect estimates will be presented and discussed first and then the random effects estimates. The user should be reminded that the first results that appear in HLM output are initial estimates. The user needs to look at the end of the output file to find the final estimates.

Only two fixed effects were modeled: the intercept, γ_{00}, and the slope, γ_{10}:

```
Final estimation of fixed effects
 (with robust standard errors)
-----------------------------------------------------------------------
                                    Standard              Approx.
     Fixed Effect      Coefficient  Error      T-ratio    d.f.    P-value
-----------------------------------------------------------------------
For       INTRCPT1, B0
     INTRCPT2, G00      98.768313   0.886268   111.443    29      0.000
For      IIM slope, B1
     INTRCPT2, G10       0.899531   0.172204     5.224    29      0.000
-----------------------------------------------------------------------
```

From the results above, both parameter estimates differ significantly from zero. The intercept, γ_{00}, estimate is 98.77 ($t(29) = 111.44$, $p < .0001$) and the slope, γ_{10}, estimate is .90 ($t(29) = 5.22$, $p < .0001$). This means that the average *Math_12* score, controlling for *IIM*, is predicted to be 98.77. Here, due to the grand-mean centering of *IIM*, the "controlling for *IIM*" can be interpreted as: "for a student with the mean score on *IIM*." The value of the slope coefficient estimate represents an estimate of the change in *Math_12* score predicted for a change of one in *IIM* score. Thus, these fixed effects coefficient estimates are interpreted very similarly to coefficients in OLS regression. Here, the higher a student's *IIM* score, the higher will be their predicted *Math_12* score.

The output describing the random effects estimates appear at the end of the output and are as follows:

```
Final estimation of variance components:
-----------------------------------------------------------------------------
Random Effect             Standard    Variance     df   Chi-square  P-value
                          Deviation   Component
-----------------------------------------------------------------------------
INTRCPT1,        U0       3.90385     15.24001     29     65.22134    0.000
    IIM slope,   U1       0.68000      0.46239     29     48.11048    0.014
level-1,         R        5.10085     26.01870
-----------------------------------------------------------------------------
```

The level-one variance explained by the addition of *IIM* to the model is seen in the reduction of the level-one variance estimate, σ^2, from a value of 50.47 in the unconditional model to a value of 26.02 in the current conditional model. In fact the proportion of the level-one variance explained with the addition of *IIM* to the model is: (50.47 − 26.02)/50.47 = .4844 or 48.44%. In terms of the variability in the outcome among classrooms, there is still a significant amount of variability remaining in the intercept ($\hat{\tau}_{00}$ = 15.24, $\chi^2(29)$ = 65.22, $p < .0001$). It cannot be assumed that the average *Math_12* score controlling for *IIM* can be assumed constant across classrooms. There is also a significant amount of variability in the *IIM* slope coefficient across classrooms ($\hat{\tau}_{11}$ = .46, $\chi^2(29)$ = 48.11, $p < .05$). Thus, it cannot be assumed that the relationship between *IIM* and *Math_12* can be assumed fixed across classrooms.

Additional random effects information appears in the output right after the information about the starting values and iterations required for convergence.

```
Tau
  INTRCPT1,B0      15.24001        0.43587
       IIM,B1       0.43587        0.46239

Tau (as correlations)
  INTRCPT1,B0   1.000   0.164
       IIM,B1   0.164   1.000
```

The first "Tau" (τ) matrix provides the estimates of the elements of the covariance matrix of level two random effects:

$$\begin{bmatrix} \tau_{00} & \tau_{01} \\ \tau_{01} & \tau_{11} \end{bmatrix}$$

where τ_{00} is the variance of the intercept residuals u_{0j}, τ_{11} is the variance of the slope residuals, u_{1j}, and τ_{01} is the covariance between the random effects, u_{0j} and u_{1j}. The second Tau matrix is the correlation matrix corresponding to the first Tau matrix. It seems that there is not a strong correlation (r = .164) between the intercepts and the slopes.

The last lines in the output indicate that the deviance of this second model is 880.09 associated with four covariance parameters that are estimated (including $\sigma^2, \tau_{00}, \tau_{11}, \tau_{01}$). The difference in the deviances between the unconditional model and the current conditional model is assumed to follow a (large-sample) χ^2 distribution with degrees of freedom (DF) equal to the difference in the number of random effects parameters that are estimated in the two "nested" models. The difference in the deviances: $945.07 - 880.10 = 64.97$ can thus be tested against a χ^2 statistic with 2 DF. The statistical significance of the deviance difference indicates that the fit of the simpler (unconditional) model is significantly worse and thus the simpler model should be rejected.

15.9 Adding a Second Level-One Predictor to the Level-One Equation

Because there still remains a substantial amount of variability in *Math_12* within classrooms, and since the researcher might hypothesize that there are gender differences in *Math_12* scores (controlling for *IIM*), a second level-one predictor (*Gender*) will be added to the level-one model. This is simply accomplished (in HLM software) by clicking on the relevant *Gender* variable. The variable *Gender* is coded with a zero for males and a 1 for females. The variable will be added as an uncentered predictor. Again, the default in HLM version 6 for adding a predictor is that it is to be modeled as a fixed effect. Click on the effect to change it so it is modeled as random and thus the level one equation to be estimated is:

$$Math\_12_{ij} = \beta_{0j} + \beta_{1j}IIM_{ij} + \beta_{2j}Gender_{ij} + r_{ij} \tag{9}$$

and the level two equation is:

$$\begin{cases} \beta_{0j} = \gamma_{00} + u_{0j} \\ \beta_{1j} = \gamma_{10} + u_{1j} \\ \beta_{2j} = \gamma_{20} + u_{2j} \end{cases} \tag{10}$$

This will appear in the HLM command window without *i* and *j* subscripts as can be seen in Figure 15.13.

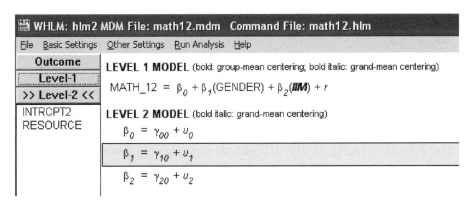

FIGURE 15.13
Adding a second level-one predictor to a two-level model in HLM.

The user can see that the centering used for *Gender* differs from that used for *IIM* in the different font style used in the HLM window for those variables in the model appearing in Figure 15.13. For uncentered variables, the variable name is not highlighted, for a group-mean centered variable, the variable appears in bold font and for a grand-mean centered variable, the variable's name is bolded and italicized.

The fixed effects results for the model contained in Equations 9 and 10 are as follows:

```
Final estimation of fixed effects
(with robust standard errors)
```

Fixed Effect	Coefficient	Standard Error	T-ratio	Approx. d.f.	P-value
For INTRCPT1, B0					
INTRCPT2, G00	92.717182	0.756761	122.518	29	0.000
For GENDER slope, B1					
INTRCPT2, G10	10.750966	0.900732	11.936	29	0.000
For IIM slope, B2					
INTRCPT2, G20	0.552540	0.102726	5.379	29	0.000

Now the intercept represents the average *Math_12* score for a boy with an *IIM* score equal to that of the sample's mean *IIM* score. The intercept is significantly greater than zero ($\hat{\gamma}_{00} = 92.72$, $t(29) = 122.52$, $p < .0001$). There is a significant *Gender* effect favoring girls over boys ($\hat{\gamma}_{10} = 10.75$, $t(29) = 11.94$, $p < .0001$). The magnitude of this gender effect indicates that girls are predicted to have scores over 10 points higher on the *Math_12* than do boys with the same *IIM* score. The coefficient for *IIM* is also significantly greater than zero ($\hat{\gamma}_{20} = 5.38$, $t(29) = 5.38$, $p < .0001$) indicating a strong positive relationship between students' interest in mathematics and their performance on the *Math_12*.

The table of random effects' estimates from the HLM output appears below:

```
Final estimation of variance components:
```

Random Effect	Standard Deviation	Variance Component	df	Chi-square	P-value
INTRCPT1, U0	2.24432	5.03699	18	12.50906	>.500
GENDER slope, U1	1.40596	1.97674	18	21.80177	0.240
IIM slope, U2	0.29608	0.08766	18	29.18635	0.046
level-1, R	4.21052	17.72844			

The estimate of the remaining level one variability is now 17.73, indicating that the addition of *Gender* has explained an additional 16.43% of the variability within classrooms (originally 50.47 in the unconditional model, down to 26.02 in the conditional model with *IIM* only as a predictor). Only 13.31% of the level one variability remains unexplained. The information contained in the table seems to indicate that there is not a significant amount of level two (among-classrooms) variability in the intercept or the *Gender* coefficient ($p > .05$). It should be emphasized that due to the small sample size within groups (i.e., the average number of children per classroom in this dataset is only 4.5) there is only low statistical power for estimation of the random effects (Hox, 2002).

The deviance is 794.63 with seven parameters estimated (three variances of random effects: u_{0j}, u_{1j}, u_{2j}, three covariances between the three random effects and σ^2). The difference in the deviances between this model and the one including only *IIM* is 85.47 which is still statistically significant ($\chi^2(3) = 85.47, p < .0001$), indicating that there would be a significant decrease in fit with *Gender* not included in the model.

Despite the lack of significance in the level-two variability and due to the likely lack of statistical power in the dataset for identifying remaining level-two variability (as well as for pedagogical purposes), addition of a level-two (classroom) predictor to the model will now be demonstrated.

15.10 Addition of a Level-Two Predictor to a Two-Level HLM

In the classroom dataset, there was a measure of each of the classroom's mathematics pedagogy resources (*Resource*). It was hypothesized that there was a positive relationship between the amount of such resources in a classroom and the class's performance on the *Math_12* controlling for gender differences and for students' interest in mathematics. This translates into a hypothesis that *Resource* would predict some of the variability in the intercept. The original level-one equation (see Equation 9) will remain unchanged. However, the set of level-two equations (Equation 10) needs to be modified to include *Resource* as a predictor of β_{0j}, such that:

$$\begin{cases} \beta_{0j} = \gamma_{00} + \gamma_{01}\,\mathrm{Re}source_j + u_{0j} \\ \beta_{1j} = \gamma_{10} + u_{1j} \\ \beta_{2j} = \gamma_{20} + u_{2j} \end{cases} \tag{11}$$

To accomplish this in HLM, the user must first click on the relevant level-two equation (the first of the three listed in Equation 11). In the current example, the user is interested in adding the level-two variable to the intercept equation (the one for β_{0j}) so the user should make sure that equation is highlighted. Then the user should click on the "Level 2" button in the upper left corner to call up the possible level-two variables. Only one variable, *Resource*, can be added. (It should be noted here that the default in HLM is to include an intercept in the model. This default can be overridden by clicking on the relevant Intercept variable. See the HLM manual for further details.) Once the user has clicked on *Resource*, the type of centering for the variable must be selected (from uncentered or grand-mean centered). Grand-mean centering will be selected so that the coefficient, γ_{01}, can be interpreted as describing a classroom with an average amount of resources. Once this is achieved, the HLM command screen appears as in Figure 15.14.

Once the output file has been specified in "Basic Specifications" and the command file saved, the analysis can be run. More iterations are needed than are specified as the default (100) as evidenced in the MS-DOS window that resulted (and is presented in Figure 15.15).

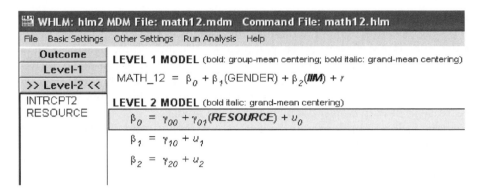

FIGURE 15.14
Adding a level-two predictor to a two-level model in HLM.

```
The value of the likelihood function at iteration 78 = -3.940063E+002
The value of the likelihood function at iteration 79 = -3.940061E+002
The value of the likelihood function at iteration 80 = -3.940059E+002
The value of the likelihood function at iteration 81 = -3.940058E+002
The value of the likelihood function at iteration 82 = -3.940056E+002
The value of the likelihood function at iteration 83 = -3.940054E+002
The value of the likelihood function at iteration 84 = -3.940053E+002
The value of the likelihood function at iteration 85 = -3.940051E+002
The value of the likelihood function at iteration 86 = -3.940049E+002
The value of the likelihood function at iteration 87 = -3.940048E+002
The value of the likelihood function at iteration 88 = -3.940046E+002
The value of the likelihood function at iteration 89 = -3.940045E+002
The value of the likelihood function at iteration 90 = -3.940043E+002
The value of the likelihood function at iteration 91 = -3.940041E+002
The value of the likelihood function at iteration 92 = -3.940040E+002
The value of the likelihood function at iteration 93 = -3.940038E+002
The value of the likelihood function at iteration 94 = -3.940037E+002
The value of the likelihood function at iteration 95 = -3.940035E+002
The value of the likelihood function at iteration 96 = -3.940034E+002
The value of the likelihood function at iteration 97 = -3.940032E+002
The value of the likelihood function at iteration 98 = -3.940031E+002
The value of the likelihood function at iteration 99 = -3.940029E+002

The maximum number of iterations has been reached, but the analysis has
not converged. Do you want to continue until convergence? _
```

FIGURE 15.15
MS-DOS window for a solution that was slow to converge.

The user is prompted at the bottom of the screen that the program will continue its iterations toward estimation of a final solution if the user so desires. Users should enter "Y" if they are willing to wait through additional iterations. It should be noted that the solution can be considered more stable with fewer iterations. In addition, the estimation of multiple random effects with possibly insufficient sample size can aggravate the location of a solution. Should users be prompted to use additional iterations, they might wish to continue with the solution but change the model to reestimate it by modeling one or several of the parameters as fixed instead of random.

When the model's estimation did converge after 1497 iterations, the additional fixed effect estimate, γ_{01}, appears in the output:

```
Final estimation of fixed effects
 (with robust standard errors)
-------------------------------------------------------------------------
                                  Standard             Approx.
    Fixed Effect      Coefficient  Error    T-ratio    d.f.     P-value
-------------------------------------------------------------------------
For       INTRCPT1, B0
   INTRCPT2, G00       92.716978   0.632195  146.659     28      0.000
   RESOURCE, G01        1.416373   0.605262    2.340      28      0.027
For   GENDER slope, B1
   INTRCPT2, G10       10.612002   0.852843   12.443      29      0.000
For       IIM slope, B2
   INTRCPT2, G20        0.598363   0.097142    6.160      29      0.000
-------------------------------------------------------------------------
```

The classroom *Resource* measure was found to be significantly positively related to *Math_12* controlling for gender and *IIM* ($\hat{\gamma}_{01}$ = 1.42, $t(28)$ = 2.34, $p < .05$). From the random effects' estimates output:

```
Final estimation of variance components:
-------------------------------------------------------------------------
Random Effect          Standard     Variance    df    Chi-square  P-value
                       Deviation    Component
-------------------------------------------------------------------------
INTRCPT1,      U0       1.54086      2.37425     17    11.53940    >.500
  GENDER slope, U1      0.78565      0.61724     18    21.40071     0.259
     IIM slope, U2      0.24638      0.06070     18    27.74502     0.066
  level-1,      R       4.22362     17.83898
-------------------------------------------------------------------------
```

Addition of *Resource* has reduced the level-two variability in the intercept from 5.04 (in the model that included *Gender* and *IIM*) to 2.37. The deviance of the current model in which seven covariance parameters were estimated was 787.94.

15.11 Evaluating the Efficacy of a Treatment

HLM can be used to evaluate whether two or more counseling (or, say teaching) methods have a differential effect on some outcome. This example is designed to investigate the impact of two counseling methods and whether they have a differential effect on empathy. It should be noted that in this example a smaller sample size is used than is typically recommended for HLM analyses. This is done to facilitate its presentation. Five groups of patients are treated with each counseling method. Each group has four patients. While groups are nested within counseling method, because the research question is about a comparison of the two counseling methods they do not constitute a clustering level. Thus, we have a two-level nested design, with patients (level one) nested within groups (level two) and counseling method used as a fixed level-two (group-level) variable. Counseling method will be used as a predictor to explain some of the variability between groups. We have two separate data files with group ID (*gp*) in both files. The level-one file contains group ID with data (scores on the empathy scale and the patient's ID number) for the four subjects in each of the ten groups. In addition, the level-one file includes a measure of the patient's contentment (*content*). The level-two file has the group ID variable along with the counseling method (*couns*) employed in the relevant group coded either as 0 or 1. The data files are given below:

	Level 1				Level 2	
PatId	Gp	Emp	Content		Gp	Couns
1	1	23	30		1	0
2	1	22	33		2	0
3	1	20	30		3	0
4	1	19	28		4	0
5	2	16	19		5	0
6	2	17	21		6	1
7	2	18	28		7	1
8	2	19	37		8	1
9	3	25	35		9	1
10	3	28	38		10	1
11	3	29	38			
12	3	31	37			
13	4	27	44			
14	4	23	30			
15	4	22	31			
16	4	21	25			
17	5	32	37			
18	5	31	46			
19	5	28	42			
20	5	26	39			
21	6	13	24			
22	6	12	19			
23	6	14	31			
24	6	15	25			
25	7	16	27			
26	7	17	34			
27	7	14	24			
28	7	12	22			
29	8	11	25			
30	8	10	17			
31	8	20	31			
32	8	15	30			
33	9	21	26			
34	9	18	28			
35	9	19	27			
36	9	23	33			
37	10	18	24			
38	10	17	33			
39	10	16	33			
40	10	23	29			

The MDM file is constructed and then the analysis conducted using HLM6. The model estimated includes counseling method as a fixed predictor. No level-one predictors are included in the model. The HLM results appear below:

```
Final estimation of fixed effects:
-----------------------------------------------------------------------
                                      Standard               Approx.
     Fixed Effect        Coefficient  Error      T-ratio     d.f.     P-value
-----------------------------------------------------------------------
For       INTRCPT1, B0
    INTRCPT2, G00        23.850000    1.825171   13.067      8        0.000
        COUNS, G01       -7.650000    2.581182   -2.964      8        0.019
-----------------------------------------------------------------------

The outcome variable is      EMP

Final estimation of fixed effects
(with robust standard errors)
-----------------------------------------------------------------------
                                      Standard               Approx.
     Fixed Effect        Coefficient  Error      T-ratio     d.f.     P-value
-----------------------------------------------------------------------
For       INTRCPT1, B0
    INTRCPT2, G00        23.850000    1.973069   12.088      8        0.000
        COUNS, G01       -7.650000    2.308679   -3.314      8        0.012
-----------------------------------------------------------------------
```

The robust standard errors are appropriate for datasets having a moderate to large number of level 2 units. These data do not meet this criterion.

```
Final estimation of variance components:
-----------------------------------------------------------------------
Random Effect           Standard     Variance     df    Chi-square  P-value
                        Deviation    Component
-----------------------------------------------------------------------
INTRCPT1,      U0       3.86868      14.96667      8    78.86560     0.000
 level-1,      R        2.59968       6.75833
-----------------------------------------------------------------------


Statistics for current covariance components model
----------------------------------------------------
Deviance                         = 204.746721
Number of estimated parameters = 2
```

As noted in the output, there is an insufficient number of level-two (group) units and thus the results with robust standard errors should not be used here. Note that the counseling method effect results [$t(8) = -2.964$, $p = .019$] indicate that the counseling method is statistically significant with the method coded using a zero having a stronger impact on empathy than the method coded with a 1. Note also that the degrees of freedom is 8, which corresponds to the degrees of freedom between groups for a regular ANOVA. In their text, Maxwell and Delaney (2004, p. 514) note that the proper error term for a nested design such as this is groups within methods. This is what would be used if SPSS had been used to analyze the data. Control lines and selected output from an SPSS analysis is given below:

SPSS Control Lines for Univariate Nested Design

```
DATA LIST FREE/COUNS GP SUB EMP.
BEGIN DATA.
0 1 1 23    0 1 2 22    0 1 3 20    0 1 4 19
0 2 1 16    0 2 2 17    0 2 3 18    0 2 4 19
0 3 1 25    0 3 2 28    0 3 3 29    0 3 4 31
0 4 1 27    0 4 2 23    0 4 3 22    0 4 4 21
0 5 1 32    0 5 2 31    0 5 3 28    0 5 4 26
1 6 1 13    1 6 2 12    1 6 3 14    1 6 4 15
1 7 1 16    1 7 2 17    1 7 3 14    1 7 4 12
1 8 1 11    1 8 2 10    1 8 3 20    1 8 4 15
1 9 1 21    1 9 2 18    1 9 3 19    1 9 4 23
1 10 1 18   1 10 2 17   1 10 3 16   1 10 4 23
END DATA
UNIANOVA EMP BY COUNS GP SUB/
RANDOM GP SUB/
DESIGN SUB(GP(COUNS)) GP(COUNS) COUNS /
PRINT=DESCRIPTIVES/.
```

Note that in the SPSS syntax, the first number indicates the counseling method (0 or 1), the second number the group the patient is in (1 through 10), and the third number indicates the subject number. Thus, the first set of four numbers represents that the subject is in the counseling method coded with a 0, is the first person in group 1 and has an empathy score of 23. The "RANDOM GP SUB/" line indicates that group and subject are being modeled as random factors. Last, the DESIGN command line indicates a nested design, with patients nested within groups that in turn are nested within counseling methods.

SPSS Printout for Three-Level Nested Design

Tests of Between-Subjects Effects

Dependent Variable: EMP

Source		Type III Sum of Squares	df	Mean Square	F	Sig.
Intercept	Hypothesis	16040.025	1	16040.025	240.751	.000
	Error	533.000	8	66.625(a)		
SUB(GP(COUNS))	Hypothesis	202.750	30	6.758	.	.
	Error	.000	0	.(b)		
GP(COUNS)	Hypothesis	533.000	8	66.625	9.858	.000
	Error	202.750	30	6.758(c)		
COUNS	Hypothesis	585.225	1	585.225	8.784	.018
	Error	533.000	8	66.625(a)		

(a) MS(GP(COUNS))
(b) MS(Error)
(c) MS(SUB(GP(COUNS)))

Note that the error term for the counseling method effect is groups within methods. Remember that there are five groups within each of the two counseling methods so that the degrees of freedom is 8. This can be seen on the SPSS output above where $F = 8.784$, $p = .018$ for the counseling effect (*couns*). This corresponds (with rounding error) to the square of the effect found with HLM for the *couns* variable: $(-2.964)^2 = 8.785$ indicating the correspondence between the SPSS and HLM analysis for this fixed effect. However, the error term for groups within counseling in SPSS is NOT correct because it is based on 30 degrees of freedom (for the error term). The degrees of freedom for error SHOULD be less than 30 because the observations within the groups are dependent. Here, one would prefer the results from the HLM6 analysis, which indicate significant group variability ($\chi^2 = 78.866$, $p < .05$). Note, finally, that for an analysis of three counseling methods, two dummy variables would be needed to identify group membership and both of these variables could be used as predictors at level two.

15.11.1 Adding a Level-One Predictor to the Empathy Model Data

In the model estimated for the *Empathy* data above where level one is formulated:

$$Emp_{ij} = \beta_{0j} + r_{ij}$$

and level two:

$$\beta_{0j} = \gamma_{00} + \gamma_{01}Tx_j + u_{0j},$$

the variability in the intercept across treatment groups (τ_{00}) even after controlling for treatment effects is seen to be significantly greater than zero [χ^2 (8) = 78.86560, $p < .05$]. A researcher might be interested in adding a level-one predictor to help explain some of this remaining variability in *Empathy* using the patient's level of *Contentment* with the level-one formulation's becoming:

$$Emp_{ij} = \beta_{0j} + \beta_{1j}Content_{ij} + r_{ij}$$

and at level two:

$$\begin{cases} \beta_{0j} = \gamma_{00} + \gamma_{01}Tx_j + u_{0j} \\ \beta_{1j} = \gamma_{10} + u_{1j} \end{cases}.$$

Addition of the level-one predictor (*Content*) modifies interpretation of the intercept, Γ_{00}, from the "predicted empathy score for patients in the group for which $Tx = 0$" to the "predicted empathy score for patients controlling for level of contentment (i.e. for whom $Content = 0$) in a treatment group for which $Tx = 0$." Note that we will grand-mean center *Content* so that a patient with $Content = 0$ is one at the mean on the contentment scale.

Estimating this model with HLM, we find the following fixed effect estimates:

```
Final estimation of fixed effects:
```

Fixed Effect	Coefficient	Standard Error	T-ratio	Approx. d.f.	P-value
For INTRCPT1, B0					
INTRCPT2, G00	22.584852	1.228768	18.380	8	0.000
TX, G01	-5.318897	1.719344	-3.094	8	0.016
For CON slope, B1					
INTRCPT2, G10	0.355810	0.073244	4.858	9	0.001

We see that the coefficient for *Content* is statistically significant ($\Gamma_{10} = 0.356$, $t(9) = 4.86$, $p < .05$). We can also see that a treatment effect is still found to favor the groups for whom $Tx = 0$ ($\Gamma_{01} = -5.319$, $t(8) = -3.094$, $p < .05$).

The random effects estimates were:

```
Final estimation of variance components:
```

Random Effect		Standard Deviation	Variance Component	df	Chi-square	P-value
INTRCPT1,	U0	2.44137	5.96028	8	29.46502	0.000
CON slope,	U1	0.04038	0.00163	9	9.39983	0.401
level-1,	R	2.22379	4.94526			

For this model in which *Content* is modeled to vary randomly across therapy groups we can thus see that a significant amount of variability remains in the intercept (even with *Content* added to the model). However, there is not a significant amount of variability between therapy groups in the relationship between patients' *Content* and their *Empathy* scores. Thus, our final model will include *Content* modeled as an effect that is fixed across therapy groups such that level two is modeled:

$$\begin{cases} \beta_{0j} = \gamma_{00} + \gamma_{01}Tx_j + u_{0j} \\ \beta_{1j} = \gamma_{10} \end{cases}$$

The fixed effects estimates were:

```
Final estimation of fixed effects:
```

Fixed Effect	Coefficient	Standard Error	T-ratio	Approx. d.f.	P-value
For INTRCPT1, B0					
INTRCPT2, G00	22.773094	1.249052	18.232	8	0.000
TX, G01	-5.496188	1.796275	-3.060	8	0.017
For CON slope, B1					
INTRCPT2, G10	0.341875	0.073204	4.670	37	0.000

These parameter estimates can be substituted into the level two formulation:

$$\begin{cases} \beta_{0j} = 22.77 - 5.50Tx_j + u_{0j} \\ \beta_{1j} = 0.34 \end{cases}$$

To facilitate interpretation of the results, it can help to obtain the single equation (by substituting the level two equations for β_{0j} and β_{1j} into the level-one equation to obtain:

$$Emp_{ij} = 22.77 - 5.50Tx_j + 0.34Content_{ij} + r_{ij} + u_{0j}$$

and then (as can be done with simple regression), values for the predictors can be substituted into this single equation. For example, substituting the relevant values into the single multilevel equation, the combinations of *Tx* and *Content* scores result in the predicted *Empathy* scores that appear in the following table:

	$Tx = 0$	$Tx = 1$
Content = 0	22.77	17.27
Content = 1	23.11	17.61
Content = 2	23.45	17.95

Thus, for example, the value for Γ_{00} represents the predicted *Emp* score when $Tx = 0$ and for someone at the mean on *Content* (i.e. for someone for whom *Content* = 0). The *Tx* coefficient represents the treatment's effect on *Emp* controlling for *Content* levels. In other words, for two participants with the same *Content* score, one of whom is in the $Tx = 0$ group while the other is in the $Tx = 1$ group, there will be a predicted difference of 5.5 points on the *Emp* scale (with the difference favoring the $Tx = 0$ member). In the table above, the difference for two people with *Content* = 0 is 22.77 − 17.27 = 5.5. Similarly, for two people with *Content* = 2 (2 points above the mean on *Content*), the predicted difference for those in $Tx = 0$ versus $Tx = 1$ is 23.45 − 17.95. Finally, the *Content* coefficient indicates that for two patients in the same *Tx* group, a difference of one on the *Content* scale is associated with an *Emp* score predicted to be .34 points higher. In other words, controlling for the treatment effect, the more contented a patient, the better his or her *Empathy* is anticipated to be. Thus, we see in the table that for two people in the $Tx = 0$ group, one with *Content* = 1 and the other with *Content* = 0, the difference in their predicted *Emp* scores is: 23.11 − 22.77 = 0.34. Similarly, for two people in $Tx = 1$, one with *Content* = 2, the other with *Content* = 1, the predicted difference in *Emp* is: 17.95 − 17.61.

15.12 Summary

It should be emphasized that this chapter has provided only a very brief introduction to multilevel modeling and the use of HLM software to estimate the model parameters. It should be also be noted that, despite the ease with which researchers can use software such as HLM to estimate their multilevel models, it behooves users to ensure that they understand the model being estimated, how to interpret the resulting parameter estimates and associated significance tests as well as the appropriateness of the assumptions made. While not demonstrated in this chapter, because this is an introductory treatment, a residual file can be easily created. As Raudenbush et al. note on p. 13 of the HLM5 manual and repeat on p. 15 of the HLM6 manual (2004):

> After fitting a hierarchical model, it is wise to check the tenability of the assumptions underlying the model:
>
> Are the distributional assumptions realistic?
> Are results likely to be affected by outliers or influential observations?
> Have important variables been omitted or nonlinear relationships been ignored?

HLM software can be used to provide the residuals for models estimated.

Aside from HLM, several other software programs can be used to estimate multilevel models including MLwiN (Goldstein et al., 1998), SAS Proc Mixed (Littell, Milliken, Stroup, & Wolfinger, 1996; see Singer, 1998 for a well-written introductory article describing use of PROC MIXED for multilevel modeling) and VARCL (Longford, 1988) among others. Even the latest versions of SPSS include some basic hierarchical modeling estimation routines. Kreft and de Leeuw (1998) provide some good descriptions of the available multilevel programs as well as website references for the interested user.

The list of multilevel textbooks provided earlier in the chapter can provide the reader with more detailed worked examples as well as fuller descriptions of the estimation used and the assumptions made when analyzing these multilevel models. In addition, the texts provide excellent resources to find out about more advanced multilevel modeling techniques including models with dichotomous or ordinal outcomes, models with multivariate outcomes, meta-analytic models, and models for use with cross-classified data structures.

The same caveats that apply to model-building using simple single-level regression analyses apply to model-building with multilevel models. Choosing a final model based on resulting estimates from a series of models can lead to selection of a model that is very sample-specific. As with any kind of model-fitting, if the analyst has a large enough sample, then the data can be randomly divided to provide a cross-validation sample to use to test the final model selected based on results from the other half of the sample (Hox, 2002).

It is hoped that researchers continue to become more familiar with the complexities of multilevel modeling and that they will be increasingly applied for the analysis of relevant data structures.

16

Structural Equation Modeling

Leandre R. Fabrigar
Queen's University

Duane T. Wegener
Purdue University

16.1 Introduction

In Chapter 11 the basic concepts underlying the theory and application of confirmatory factor analysis (CFA) were reviewed. In simple terms, structural equation modeling (SEM; also referred to as covariance structure modeling, latent variable modeling, or causal modeling) can be thought of as an extension of CFA that permits the specification and testing of a much broader range of factor analytic models. Recall that CFA involves specifying (a priori) models in which unobservable underlying factors are postulated to influence a set of observed variables. Thus, the researcher must specify the number of underlying factors that exist and which observed variables a particular factor will be permitted to influence. The researcher also must specify which factors will be permitted to correlate with one another. SEM extends this basic methodology to allow not only for correlations but also for directional relations among factors. That is, a researcher can specify models in which factors are postulated to be antecedents or consequences of other factors in the model.

This distinction between CFA and SEM models can best be illustrated by examining a path diagram depicting a typical SEM model (see Figure 16.1). This model is similar in many respects to the path diagrams of CFA models presented in Chapter 11 (e.g., see Figure 11.1). Each latent factor (represented as circles) is postulated to exert a directional influence (represented as single-headed arrows) on some subset of observed variables (represented as squares). Likewise, correlations (represented as double-headed arrows) are permitted among latent factors (as is the case for KSI 1 and KSI 2). However, this model differs from the models presented in Chapter 11 in that it postulates that the latent factors KSI 1 and KSI 2 exert directional influences on the latent factor ETA 1. The latent factor ETA 1 in turn exerts a directional influence on the latent factor ETA 2. Thus, the model depicted in Figure 16.1 represents not only the directional influence of latent factors on observed variables, but also both the nondirectional relations and directional influences among latent factors.

16.2 Introductory Concepts

Before beginning a detailed discussion of SEM, it is useful to introduce some basic concepts. In presenting these concepts, it is important to recognize that different SEM programs and mathematical frameworks use somewhat different terminology. We will follow

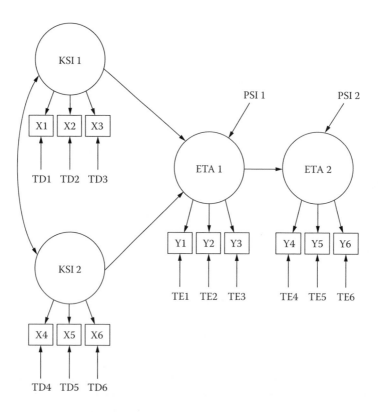

FIGURE 16.1
A hypothetical structural equation model path diagram.

the terminology used in the LISREL framework of SEM, although we will illustrate SEM analyses using both the LISREL and EQS programs.

16.2.1 Types of Variables

As in CFA, SEM distinguishes between two basic types of variables. A *measured variable* (also called a manifest variable) refers to a variable in the model that is directly measured. In contrast, a *latent variable* (similar to factors in CFA) is a hypothesized construct in the model that cannot be directly measured. In Figure 16.1, the model includes four latent variables and 12 measured variables. Latent variables can be further divided into two categories. *Exogenous* latent variables are not influenced by other latent variables in the model. These latent variables do not "receive" any directional arrows in the model (although they may send directional arrows to other latent variables and may be permitted to correlate with other exogenous latent variables). In the LISREL framework, exogenous latent variables are referred to as KSI (ξ) variables (see Figure 16.1). *Endogenous latent* variables do depend on other latent variables in the model (i.e., they receive one or more directional arrows). Endogenous latent variables are referred to as ETA (η) variables (see Figure 16.1). It is important to note that an endogenous latent variable can be both a consequence and an antecedent of other latent variables. For example, ETA 1 in Figure 16.1 is postulated to be a consequence of KSI 1 and KSI 2 and an antecedent of ETA 2. Measured variables are also divided into two categories. Measured variables postulated to be influenced by exogenous latent variables are referred to as X variables. Measured variables presumed to be influenced by endogenous latent variables are referred to as Y variables. In the present example, there are 6 X variables and 6 Y variables. When constructing the correlation matrix among measured variables for LISREL, it is customary to have all Y variables precede all X variables in the matrix.

16.2.2 Types of Error

Structural equation models represent two types of error. *Error in variables* reflects the lack of correspondence between a measured variable and the latent variable that is presumed to influence it. This lack of correspondence is assumed to be a result of both random error of measurement and systematic influences unique to that single measured variable (thus making it similar to unique variances in factor analysis). Error in variables is represented by deltas (δ) for X variables and epsilons (ϵ) or Y variables. *Error in equations* refers to the residual of one latent variable that is not explained by other latent variables in the model. Thus, it reflects the imperfection in predictions of latent variables by the other latent variables in the model. Errors in equations are represented by PSI terms (ψ) in the model. Because only endogenous latent variables are presumed to depend on other latent variables, PSI terms are associated only with endogenous latent variables.

16.2.3 Types of Association

SEM permits two types of associations between variables. Directional influences are represented as single-headed arrows. Directional influences are always assumed to exist between latent variables and measured variables. It is generally the case that latent variables are presumed to influence measured variables, although in some cases it may be conceptually sensible to postulate that the measured variables as a group make up or "cause" the latent variable. These causal indicator models specify directional influences of measured variables on one or more latent variables (see Bollen and Lennox, 1991; but see MacCallum and Browne, 1993). Directional influences are also presumed to exist between errors in variables and measured variables. Errors in variables are always assumed to influence measured variables because they reflect random and unique systematic influences on that measured variable. Errors in equations are also presumed to always influence endogenous latent variables, because these errors in equations are presumed to reflect the causal influence of variables not represented in the model.

Nondirectional relations are represented as double-headed arrows and imply an association among variables with no assumptions regarding causality. Nondirectional relations are most commonly specified among exogenous latent variables. However, they are also permitted in two other contexts. Although it is generally assumed that errors in variables are uncorrelated with one another, it is sometimes conceptually sensible to specify covariances among a set of error terms for X or Y variables. Likewise, errors in equations are usually presumed to be independent of each other. However, covariances can be specified. Such a specification is most commonly done when a researcher believes that two endogenous latent variables specified in the model are likely to be influenced by a common set of latent variables not represented in the model.

16.2.4 Measurement and Structural Components

The entire pattern of hypothesized relations among latent variables and between latent variables and measured variables is referred to as the *covariance structure model*. The model can be divided into two meaningful submodels. The *measurement model* reflects the pattern of hypothesized relations between latent variables and measured variables. The *structural model* consists of the hypothesized pattern of relations among the latent variables.

16.3 The Mathematical Representation of Structural Equation Models

The LISREL framework represents all information for the model in the form of eight matrices.* The meaning of the eight matrices will be discussed in the context of the model depicted in Figure 16.1 (for more detailed discussion, see Bollen, 1989).

16.3.1 Representing the Measurement Model

The measurement model consists of four matrices, two of which were already discussed in the context of CFA. Lambda X (LX or λx) represents the influence of the exogenous latent variables on the measured variables. Thus, the parameters in this matrix reflect the "factor loadings" of the X measured variables on the exogenous latent variables. For our example, the Lambda X matrix would appear as depicted in Table 16.1, where LX entries represent free parameters to be estimated from the data, 0 values represent parameters fixed at 0, and 1 values represent parameters fixed at 1. Notice that one factor loading for each latent variable has been fixed at 1. Because latent variables are unobservable constructs, they have no established scale of measurement. Thus, it is necessary for a researcher to set the scale for the model to be identified. In both exploratory and confirmatory factor analysis, this is traditionally done by assuming that the factors are in standardized form and thus the variances of the factors are fixed at 1. In some SEM programs (e.g., RAMONA), it is possible to do this to both exogenous and endogenous latent variables. However, in other programs, it is possible to do this only to exogenous latent variables. For this (and other reasons to be discussed later), the scale of measurement for latent variables is often set by designating one measured variable for each latent variable as a "reference variable" or "reference indicator." This is done by fixing the factor loading for the reference variable to 1 and leaving the variance of the latent variable as a free parameter to be estimated from the data. This has been done in the present example.

Theta delta (TD or $\Theta\delta$) is the covariance matrix of unique factors associated with measured variables influenced by the exogenous latent variables (i.e., X variables). Thus, the diagonal elements reflect the variances of unique factors, and the off-diagonal elements reflect the covariances among unique factors. For our example, TD entries represent free parameters to be estimated from the data and 0's represent parameters fixed at 0 (see Table 16.1). Although it is customary to assume that errors in variables are independent of one another (as is done in the present example), the model permits covariances. Such covariances would be reflected by free parameters in the off-diagonal elements.

---

* In this chapter, we discuss the mathematical framework originally proposed by Jöreskog (e.g., Jöreskog, 1970, 1978). This is the framework that serves as the basis for LISREL program. It is important to recognize that this is only one of several mathematical frameworks that have been proposed for representing structural equation models. Two other frameworks exist: The Bentler-Weeks model (Bentler & Weeks, 1980), which serves as the basis for the EQS program and the Reticular Action Model (RAM) (McCardle & McDonald, 1984), which serves as the basis for the RAMONA program. In general, any model that can be specified in one of these frameworks can also be specified in the other frameworks, although in some cases it is simpler to do so in one framework than the other.

TABLE 16.1

Matrix Representation for the Measurement Model

Lambda X (LX)

	KSI 1	KSI 2
X1	1	0
X2	LX_{21}	0
X3	LX_{31}	0
X4	0	1
X5	0	LX_{52}
X6	0	LX_{62}

Theta Delta (TD)

	X1	X2	X3	X4	X5	X6
X1	TD_{11}	0	0	0	0	0
X2	0	TD_{22}	0	0	0	0
X3	0	0	TD_{33}	0	0	0
X4	0	0	0	TD_{44}	0	0
X5	0	0	0	0	TD_{55}	0
X6	0	0	0	0	0	TD_{66}

Lambda Y (LY)

	ETA 1	ETA 2
Y1	1	0
Y2	LY_{21}	0
Y3	LY_{31}	0
Y4	0	1
Y5	0	LY_{52}
Y6	0	LY_{62}

Theta Epsilon (TE)

	Y1	Y2	Y3	Y4	Y5	Y6
Y1	TE_{11}	0	0	0	0	0
Y2	0	TE_{22}	0	0	0	0
Y3	0	0	TE_{33}	0	0	0
Y4	0	0	0	TE_{44}	0	0
Y5	0	0	0	0	TE_{55}	0
Y6	0	0	0	0	0	TE_{66}

Because LISREL models distinguish between exogenous and endogenous latent variables, SEM models have two matrices that make up the measurement model beyond that of traditional CFA models. Lambda Y (LY or λy) represents the influence of the endogenous latent variables on the measured variables. The parameters in this matrix reflect the "factor loadings" of the measured variables on the endogenous latent variables. Thus, LY is simply the endogenous latent variable version of LX. The LY matrix for our example is also shown in Table 16.1. LY entries represent free parameters to be estimated from the data, 0 values represent parameters fixed at 0, and 1 values represent parameters fixed at 1.

TABLE 16.2

Matrix Representation
for the Structural Model

Phi (PH)

	KSI 1	KSI 2
KSI 1	PH_{11}	
KSI 2	PH_{21}	PH_{22}

Gamma (GA)

	KSI 1	KSI 2
ETA 1	GA_{11}	GA_{12}
ETA 2	0	0

Beta (BE)

	ETA 1	ETA 2
ETA 1	0	0
ETA 2	BE_{21}	0

Psi (PS)

	ETA 1	ETA 2
ETA 1	PS_{11}	0
ETA 2	0	PS_{22}

Theta Epsilon (TE or $\Theta\epsilon$) represents the covariance matrix among unique factors associated with measured variables influenced by the endogenous latent variables. Thus, it is conceptually similar to the TD matrix. The TE entries represent free parameters to be estimated from the data and 0's represent parameters fixed at 0 (see Table 16.1). As with TD, it is customary, but not necessary, to assume TE's are independent of one another (i.e., no free parameters among the off-diagonal elements).

16.3.2 Representing the Structural Model

The structural model is represented in LISREL by four matrices, one of which was previously discussed in the context of CFA. As in CFA, Phi (PH or φ) is the matrix representing covariances among exogenous latent variables. The PH matrix for our example is shown in Table 16.2, where PH entries represent free parameters to be estimated from the data. Because the scale of measurement for latent variables has been set using a measured variable as a reference variable for each KSI, the diagonal of Phi has free parameters. That is, the variances for each of the exogenous variables will be estimated from the data. This is in contrast to the exploratory and confirmatory forms of factor analysis, where the diagonal of Phi is usually fixed to 1. The off-diagonal element of Phi represents the covariance between KSI 1 and KSI 2.

Because SEM models permit directional relations among latent variables, the structural portion of the model requires three matrices beyond the traditional CFA model. The first of these new matrices is the Gamma matrix (GA or Γ). This matrix represents directional relations between the exogenous latent variables and the endogenous latent variables. In GA, rows are endogenous latent variables (ETAs) and columns are exogenous latent variables (KSIs). Hence, column variables are assumed to influence row variables. The example GA entries in Table 16.2 represent free parameters to be estimated from the data and 0 entries are fixed parameters set to 0. This matrix states that KSI 1 and KSI 2 have a directional influence on ETA 1 but have no direct influence on ETA 2.

The Beta matrix (BE or β) reflects the directional relations among endogenous latent variables. In this matrix, direction is specified such that column variables influence row variables. The example BE matrix is also presented in Table 16.2 and shows that ETA 1 has a directional influence on ETA 2.

The final matrix in the structural model is Psi (PS or Ψ). This matrix represents the covariance matrix of errors in equations (see Table 16.2). PS_{11} reflects the variance in ETA 1 not accounted for by other latent variables in the model and PS_{22} reflects the variance in ETA 2 not explained by other latent variables in the model. The assumption made in the current example is that these errors in equations are independent of one another. However, the LISREL framework permits covariances to be represented by the off-diagonal elements.

16.3.3 System of Equations

You may recall from Chapter 11 that the goal of CFA was to understand the underlying structure of a set of observed variables (i.e., X variables). This relationship was represented using the following equation:

$$X = \lambda \xi + \delta$$

where λ represents the factor loadings, ξ represents scores on the latent variables, and δ the unique factors for the observed variables. Thus, a given person's score on a particular measured variable is assumed to be a function of the scores of that individual on the latent variables, the strength and direction of influence each latent variable exerts on that measured variable (i.e., the factor loadings), and the score on the unique factor associated with that measure.

You may also recall from the earlier discussion of CFA that because latent variables are unobservable constructs, we can never directly calculate a person's score on a latent variable. Hence, the goal of CFA was not to explain individual scores on measured variables, but instead to understand the structure of covariances (or correlations) among measured variables. As we saw in Chapter 11, modeling the structure of covariances did not require us to know the scores of individuals on latent variables. Instead, we needed to know only the factor loadings, the covariances among factors, and the unique variances. This was represented by the equation provided in Chapter 11:

$$\Sigma = \lambda \varphi \lambda' + \Theta_\delta$$

where Σ is the covariance matrix of measured variables, λ is the matrix of factor loadings on the latent variables, φ is the covariance matrix of latent variables, and Θ_δ is the covariance matrix of unique factors for measured variables.

The goal of SEM is similar to that of CFA. Once again, because latent variables cannot be directly observed, the objective in SEM is to account for the variances of and covariances among measured variables rather than individual scores on measured variables. The only difference is that now the task has been made more complex by the fact that we have two different types of measured variables whose underlying structure we wish to understand: X and Y variables. Thus, in addition to understanding the structure of covariances among X variables as in CFA, SEM also attempts to understand the structure of covariances among Y variables and between X and Y variables. This task requires the eight matrices we reviewed in the preceding section rather than the three matrices originally discussed for CFA models. Additionally, rather than the single CFA equation specified for representing the structure among measured variables, three equations make use of the different matrices to represent the model. One equation represents the variances of and covariances among X variables (the same equation as in CFA). A second equation represents the variances of and covariances among Y variables. The third equation reflects the covariances between Y and X variables. The precise nature of these equations is not essential for making use of SEM and thus we will not review them here (see Bollen, 1989). It is sufficient simply to realize that SEM models follow the same basic logic as CFA models but merely involve a more complex system of equations to account for the variances of and covariances among measured variables.

16.4 Model Specification

Methodologists have traditionally conceptualized SEM analyses as consisting of four basic steps: Model specification, model fitting, model evaluation, and model modification. As noted in Chapter 11, model specification is the use of the SEM mathematical framework to express one or more specific covariance structure models. This process requires the researcher to specify the number of endogenous and exogenous latent variables that will be included in the model and then indicate which parameters will be free (i.e., parameters with unknown values that will be estimated from the data), fixed (i.e., parameters set to a specific numerical value, usually 0 or 1), and constrained (i.e., parameters with unknown values that will be estimated from the data, but must hold a specified mathematical relation to one or more other parameters in the model). Model specification should be guided by substantive theories and past empirical findings in the domain of interest. Additionally, several important issues sometimes arise during the specification process.

16.5 Model Identification

One important issue that occasionally arises in CFA during model specification, but is perhaps more common in SEM, is the problem of model identification. A model is identified when it is possible to compute a unique solution for the model parameters. However, in some cases, a researcher might specify a model that is so complex that there is insufficient information to compute a unique solution. When this occurs, it is not possible to fit the model to the data. Unfortunately, determining if a model is identified is a difficult task. The only fail-safe method for doing so is to go through each structural equation in the model and algebraically prove that the model is identified. This process can be extremely complex with any but the simplest of models and thus often exceeds the mathematical skills of most researchers. However, some general considerations (several of which were previously discussed in Chapter 11) can help to manage model identification problems.

First, whenever specifying a model, two necessary (but not sufficient) conditions for model identification must always be satisfied:

1. The t rule: For a model to be identified, the number of free parameters in the model (sometimes called "t") must be less than or equal to the number of unique elements in the observed covariance (correlation) matrix. The number of unique elements in

the observed covariance matrix can be computed by using the formula: $p(p + 1)/2$ where p is the number of measured variables in the covariance or correlation matrix to be analyzed.

2. Establish a scale of measurement for the latent variables either by setting the variances of latent variables at 1 or by fixing the loading of one measured variable for each latent variable at 1. For all SEM programs, it is possible to fix an exogenous latent variable's variance to 1. For some programs, it is not possible to fix the variance of endogenous latent variables to 1, whereas for others it is possible to do so. All SEM programs permit loadings of measured variables on latent variables to be fixed to 1.

A second general point to keep in mind is that model parsimony, beyond its conceptual appeal, can also have practical benefits for avoiding identification problems. Thus, model parameters should be freed only if there is a clear substantive logic for doing so. In general, as long as the model specified is reasonably parsimonious (i.e., it has a substantial number of degrees of freedom), identification problems are relatively unlikely.

Beyond attempting to prevent identification problems from occurring in the first place, researchers should also undertake efforts to detect whether identification problems have arisen. SEM programs such as LISREL and EQS have automatic mathematical checks and empirical tests designed to detect identification problems (see Bollen, 1989; Jöreskog and Sörbom, 1996; Kenny, Kashy, and Bolger, 1998; Schumacker and Lomax, 2004). If these checks fail, the program will provide a warning to the researcher. Unfortunately, these program checks can make errors and thus should not be relied upon as definitive evidence for or against model identification.

Identification problems can also sometimes be detected by examining the output of an SEM analysis to look for classic "symptoms" of an under-identified model. One symptom is a model that fails to converge on a solution during the model fitting process or produces highly implausible parameter estimates (e.g., impossible values such as negative variances, estimates with signs opposite of what would be expected from substantive theory or past research, or estimates with extremely large standard errors). If any time parameter estimation problems of this sort occur, a researcher should carefully consider if this problem might be a result of model identification. However, it is important to recognize that neither the presence nor absence of such symptoms is definitive in its own right. As discussed later, there are several reasons that parameter estimation problems might be encountered, of which model identification is only one. It is also possible that a model that is not identified could converge on a solution and produce reasonable estimates.

Another symptom of models with identification problems is that they often produce very different solutions, depending on the start values that are provided to begin calculations. Thus, it can be quite useful to run SEM analyses several times using slightly different start values. If the model produces substantially different estimates, it is possible (although not certain) that the model has identification problems. On the other hand, if the model produces the same or extremely similar estimates with different start values, it is much less likely that the model has identification problems.

A final obvious question that occurs in the context of model identification is what to do if a model is found to be under-identified. The only real solution in such a situation is to simplify the model to a point where it is identified. That is, the researcher must fix one or more free parameters in order to make the model less complex.

16.5.1 Defining Latent Variable Scales of Measurement

As discussed in Chapter 11 and earlier in this chapter, latent variables are unobservable constructs that have no clear scale of measurement. Hence, it is necessary to define a scale of measurement for a latent variable in order to estimate its effects on measured variables and other latent variables. In factor analysis, the scale of measurement for latent variables has been traditionally defined by fixing the variances of latent variables to 1. Because latent variables are generally assumed to have means of 0, this essentially specifies the latent variables to be on a Z score metric. The second method of establishing a scale of measurement for latent variables is to specify a "reference variable" or "reference indicator" for each latent variable. This involves fixing the factor loading of one measured variable on each latent variable to 1. When this is done, a researcher is specifying that the latent variable will be assumed to have the same scale of measurement as the reference variable. For example, if the reference indicator is on a particular 1–7 scale, the latent variable is mapped to that same 1–7 scale.

The implications of using reference indicators to specify latent variable scales of measurement are sometimes misunderstood by researchers. Thus, several points should be kept in mind about this approach (see Bollen, 1989; Maruyama, 1998). First, this practice does not imply that the reference variable is a perfect measure of the latent variable. This would only be true if the corresponding unique variance in the $\Theta\delta$ or $\Theta\epsilon$ matrix was also fixed to 0. Additionally, the approach used to define the scale of measurement for latent variables does not alter the fit of the model or the number of parameters. Thus, fixing latent variable variances to 1 or choosing different reference variables will not alter the values of model fit indices. Finally, the specific reference indicator chosen will not alter the proportional relation of factor loadings to one another for different indicators of the same latent variable. The unstandardized values of the loadings may differ as a result of which variable is chosen as the reference variable because the latent variable may be on a different metric, but the proportional relations among loadings will not change. The variance in each measured variable accounted for by the latent variable will also not change as a function of which particular measured variable serves as the reference variable.

Although fixing latent variable variances to 1 is almost always used to establish latent variable scales of measurement in EFA and CFA, the reference variable approach is the more common procedure in the context of SEM. This is the case for two reasons. First, many SEM programs permit latent variable variances to be fixed to 1 only for exogenous latent variables and require use of a reference variable for endogenous latent variables. Second, setting latent variable variances to 1 can be problematic in some contexts (see Bollen, 1989; Maruyama, 1998; Williams and Thomson, 1986). For example, sometimes the parameter estimates of a SEM model may be directly compared across two or more groups of people. In such cases, it may be inappropriate to assume that latent variable variances are equivalent across groups. Fixing variances to 1 requires such an assumption. Similarly, in longitudinal data, it may be inappropriate to assume that the variance of a latent variable remains constant over time, as is implied by setting variances to 1.

16.5.2 Specifying Single Indicator Models

Another situation that sometimes arises in model specification is how to specify a model when only a single measured variable is available to represent a hypothesized latent variable. For example, if one of the exogenous variables in a model is an experimental manipulation with two levels, one does not have multiple measures to represent the manipulation.* In such a context, one cannot specify a latent variable per se because such variables represent variance that is common among a set of measured variables hypothesized to load on that latent variable. However, models can still be specified that include variables for which there is only a single indicator. In some programs (e.g., RAMONA), this can be done by directly representing the measured variable as an endogenous or exogenous variable in the structural portion of the model. In the case of LISREL, this is not an option. Instead, the model is specified as if there were a latent variable, but that variable has only the single measured variable loading on it. Typically, the factor loading for the measured variable is fixed to 1. In some cases, the unique variance of the measured variable is fixed to 0. This implies that the measured variable is a perfect indicator of the latent variable (an implicit assumption made in many common statistical methods such as regression). A second approach is to fix the unique variance of the measured variable to a non-zero value on the basis of an assumption regarding the reliability of the measured variable (perhaps from past data). As discussed by Schumacker and Lomax (2004), one can calculate a predicted unique variance as Unique Variance = (variance of measured variable) (1 – reliability).

Regardless of the approach taken to specifying single indicator models, it is important to keep in mind that such variables are not latent variables and therefore are susceptible to the same distortions that can arise with any directly observed score (e.g., the existence of random error). Thus, use of single indicators sacrifices many of the potential benefits of SEM and should be avoided when possible. Nonetheless, when only a single indicator is available to represent a construct, it is often preferable to represent the construct in the model (however imperfectly) rather than fail to take into account the construct's potential effects.

16.6 Specifying Alternative Models

Regardless of the precise model specified, another issue that should always be considered during the model specification process is the possibility of alternative models. Alternative models can take several forms. For instance, as in CFA, it is often the case that a researcher may wish to test specific hypotheses regarding parameter estimates in the model. This can be done by specifying and then fitting alternative models that place equality constraints on parameters. For example, consider the model depicted in Figure 16.1. A researcher might wish to examine which KSI variable exerts a greater influence on ETA 1. This could be done by placing an equality constraint on the two paths and then conducting a chi-square difference test with the original model. Thus, when specifying a model, the researcher should clearly delineate alternative models with equality constraints that test substantive hypotheses of interest.

Another type of alternative model that should be considered addresses models that make substantively different assumptions about the nature of associations among constructs in the domain of interest. Although it is certainly useful to demonstrate that an advocated model fits the data well and produces sensible parameter estimates, such a demonstration is more impressive in the context of comparisons with other theoretically

---

* One might represent a manipulated variable with one or more manipulation check measures, but this turns the experimental comparison into a correlational (internal) analysis that includes both variance due to the manipulation itself and variance within conditions of the experiment. There may be a variety of settings in which one wants to model the effects of the manipulation per se.

plausible models (Wegener and Fabrigar, 2000). Thus, at the model specification phase, a researcher should consider whether other theoretically plausible models exist that should also be specified. Such competing models may be suggested by different theoretical perspectives or existing data in the literature. These models may postulate different patterns of relations among latent variables or between latent variables and measured variables, but nonetheless be theoretically defensible. Indeed, in some cases, there may be no preferred model, but merely a set of equally plausible competing models to be tested (Browne and Cudeck, 1989, 1992).

One problem, first noted in Chapter 11, that is sometimes encountered when specifying alternative models is the issue of model equivalency. Two models are said to be equivalent when, despite postulating different patterns of relations, they produce identical implied covariance (correlation) matrices. Equivalent models are guaranteed to produce the same values for fit indices when fit to any data set. Thus, these models cannot be differentiated on the basis of fit. When specifying a model to be tested, a researcher should always attempt to ascertain what equivalent models exist for the specified model. If such a model does exist (and they often do, see MacCallum, Wegener, Uchino, and Fabrigar, 1993), the researcher must then consider what basis can be used to differentiate this model from the preferred model.

Unfortunately, there are no easy solutions for equivalent models. There is no definitive way to determine if equivalent models exist for a given model. Methodologists have formulated rules that can be used to generate equivalent models (e.g., Lee and Hershberger, 1990; Stelzl, 1986). However, these rules are designed to generate specific classes of equivalent models and thus are not exhaustive. Moreover, SEM programs do not include algorithms that implement these rules. Instead, a researcher must visually examine the proposed model and then attempt to identify the changes permitted by the rule.

Lee and Hershberger's (1990) "replacement rule" is probably the most general rule that has been proposed to generate equivalent models. Although the application of this rule is by no means simple, careful study of the replacement rule and practice using it with various examples is generally sufficient to provide a researcher with the necessary expertise to effectively use it in practice (see MacCallum et al., 1993). The replacement rule covers a wide range of changes that can be introduced to a model while still maintaining model equivalency. However, in practice, two special cases of the rule are particularly important to understand: "saturated preceding blocks" and "symmetric focal blocks." These two special cases accounted for nearly all of the equivalent models identified by MacCallum et al. (1993) in their analysis of past applications of SEM and they are the two special cases most likely to produce equivalent models with substantively different theoretical implications (e.g., the reversal of directional relations in the structural portion of the model). To help illustrate how these special cases of the rule can be applied in practice, we briefly consider them in the context of a hypothetical model.

The replacement rule is based on the premise that the structural portion of a model can be conceptualized as consisting of "blocks" of latent variables (i.e., subsets of latent variables). Blocks must include at least two latent variables, but in theory could be as large as the total number of latent variables in the model. In many models there are multiple combinations of latent variables that might be used to partition the model into blocks. In some cases, blocks can be independent of one another (i.e., they can consist of completely different latent variables). In other cases, smaller blocks can be subsumed within larger blocks (i.e., one block may be a subset of a larger block). Still other cases can involve partially overlapping blocks (i.e., situations in which some, but not all of the latent variables in the two blocks are shared).

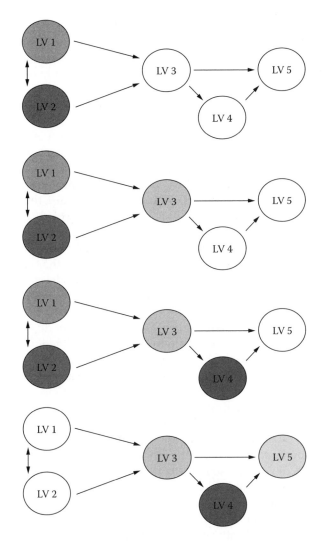

FIGURE 16.2
Path diagrams for hypothetical structural equation model and illustrations of criteria for saturated preceding blocks.

The replacement rule holds that certain changes can be made within a block if the block satisfies specific conditions. One special case of these conditions is when the block is a saturated preceding block. A saturated preceding block is any set of latent variables for which (a) all latent variables composing the block have a relation of some sort (i.e., a directional path, a nondirectional path, or correlated PSI terms) with all other variables making up the block, and (b) no variable in the block is dependent on latent variables from outside the block (i.e., none of the variables can receive arrows from variables outside the block).

To illustrate this concept, consider the hypothetical model depicted in Panel A of Figure 16.2. For ease of presentation, in this figure we have dropped the KSI/ETA distinction (latent variables are simply designated LV 1, LV 2, etc.) and we have omitted the measurement model. Let us first consider a block within this model consisting of LV 1 and LV 2 (i.e., the two shaded latent variables in Panel A). This two-variable block satisfies the conditions for a saturated preceding block. Specifically, all variables in the block have a relation specified with all other variables in the block (LV 1 and LV 2 are postulated to correlate with one another) and no variables in the block receive arrows from outside the block. Because these conditions are satisfied, the replacement rule holds that any relation among latent variables within the saturated preceding block can be changed to any other type of relation while still maintaining the equivalency of the model. For example, a model replacing the correlation between LV 1 and LV 2 with a directional relation from LV 1 to LV 2 would be mathematically equivalent to the model in Panel A of Figure 16.2. Likewise, a model with a directional path from LV 2 to LV 1 would also be equivalent to the original model.

Interestingly, the LV 1/LV 2 block is not the only saturated preceding block in the model. As depicted by the shaded latent variables in Panel B of Figure 16.2, the block highlighted in Panel A is part of a larger saturated preceding block consisting of LV 1, LV 2, and LV 3. Note that this set of latent variables is saturated (i.e., each variable has a relation with the other two variables in the block) and none of the variables receive directional arrows from outside the block. Thus, the replacement rule permits a change in the type of relation for any of the relations among these three variables. For example, a model reversing one or both of the relations of LV 3 with LV 1 and LV 2 would have the same fit as the original model. The reader should note that reversing a path between LV 3 and either LV 1 or LV 2 would make that variable endogenous rather than exogenous. Some, but not all, SEM programs allow for correlations (nondirectional paths) involving endogenous latent variables.

To further clarify the concept of saturated preceding blocks, it is also useful to consider blocks in the model that do not satisfy the criteria. For example, consider the block of shaded latent variables depicted in Panel C (i.e., LV 1, LV 2, LV 3, and LV 4). This set of variables is not a saturated preceding block. Although it satisfies the criterion that none of the variables receives arrows from outside the block, it is not saturated in that LV 4 has no relation with LV 1 and LV 2. Thus, changes to the relation between LV 3 and LV 4 would not produce an equivalent model. Likewise, the block of shaded variables depicted in Panel D (i.e., LV 3, LV 4, and LV 5) would also not constitute a saturated preceding block. Although the block is saturated, one variable in the block (LV 3) receives arrows from variables outside the block. Hence, changes such as a reversal of paths of LV 3 with LV 4 or LV 5 would not produce an equivalent model.

Another important aspect of saturated preceding blocks and model equivalency is that changes made in a saturated preceding block can sometimes produce new saturated preceding blocks that can themselves be changed while still maintaining model equivalency. This is illustrated in Figure 16.3. Consider the original hypothetical model illustrated in Panel A of Figure 16.3. As already noted, the shaded set of three latent variables in this model are a saturated preceding block. Thus, relations in this block can be changed to different types of relations to produce equivalent models. For example, the correlation between LV 1 and LV 2 can be replaced with a directional path from LV 1 to LV 2 as is depicted in Panel B. The model in Panel B is equivalent to the model in Panel A. Of course, the shaded block of variables in Panel B can be further changed to produce additional equivalent models. For instance, the two paths leading to LV 3 can be reversed to produce the equivalent model depicted in Panel C. Although substantively quite different, this model in Panel C is mathematically equivalent to the prior two models.

Another interesting feature of the model is illustrated in Panel C. The changes introduced to produce this model have actually created two partially overlapping saturated preceding blocks. The LV 1, LV 2 and LV 3 block remains a saturated preceding block. However, LV 3, LV 4, and LV 5 now also satisfy the conditions for a saturated preceding block (the block

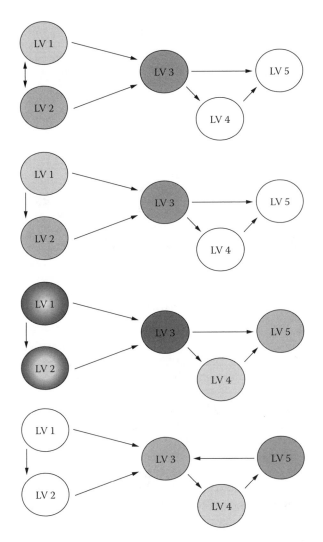

FIGURE 16.3
Path diagrams for hypothetical structural equation model and mathematically equivalent models generated from saturated preceding blocks.

no longer receives arrows from outside the block and relations exist among all variables in the block). Because of this fact, the rule now permits changes in the paths among these three variables. Panel D depicts one possible change that could be made to this block (i.e., the reversal of the path between LV 3 and LV 5). Interestingly, this change made in Panel D results in LV 1, LV 2, and LV 3 no longer satisfying the conditions for a saturated preceding block (i.e., the block now receives an arrow from LV 5, which is outside the block). For this reason, further changes to the paths among LV 1, LV 2, and LV 3 would not result in equivalent models if made for the model in Panel D.

A comparison of the model in Panel D with the original model in Panel A provides a striking contrast in conceptual assumptions regarding the nature of relations among the latent variables. Despite this fact, these two models are mathematically equivalent and will fit any data set equally well. Thus, this brief example of the concept of saturated preceding

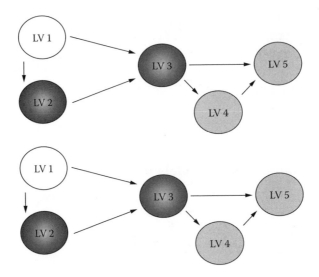

FIGURE 16.4
Path diagrams for hypothetical structural equation model and a mathematically equivalent model generated from symmetric focal blocks.

blocks serves to highlight that repeated use of the rule with a given model can lead a researcher to equivalent models that bear little resemblance to the original model and would not have been obviously equivalent upon first examination of the original model (see also MacCallum et al., 1993).

Although saturated preceding blocks are the most common and generally consequential special case of the replacement rule in practice, researchers sometimes also encounter symmetric focal blocks, which represent another special case of the replacement rule. A symmetric focal block is any two endogenous latent variable blocks where the two variables have a relation of some sort specified between them and the two variables are dependent on exactly the same set of latent variables (i.e., the variables making up the block receive directional arrows from the same set of latent variables). When a block satisfies these conditions, the replacement rule holds that reversal of the relation between the variables or replacement of a directional relation between the variables with correlated PSI terms will produce an equivalent model.

For example, consider the model depicted in Panel A of Figure 16.4. This model has two blocks (consisting of the shaded sets of latent variables) that satisfy the criteria for a symmetric focal block. Note that LV 2 and LV 3 (the darkly shaded variables) have a relation specified between them and receive directional arrows from the same set of latent variables (i.e., LV 1). Likewise, LV 4 and LV 5 (the lightly shaded variables) also have a relations specified between them and are dependent on the same set of latent variables in the model (LV 3). Thus, in both cases, the paths between these two-variable blocks can be reversed without altering the fit of the model. These changes have been made in Panel B of Figure 16.4.

As has been illustrated by the prior examples, the examination of a model for saturated preceding blocks and focal symmetric blocks can be extremely useful in identifying equivalent models. Of course, once the researcher has identified equivalent models, it is then necessary to consider how these equivalent models and the original model will later be differentiated from one another. In some cases, models may be differentiated on their conceptual plausibility. Not all equivalent models will make equal sense conceptually. In other cases, the researcher may be able to include design features (e.g., experimental manipulations) in the study that preclude some equivalent models as plausible representations. Finally, as will be discussed later, parameter estimates may sometimes provide a basis for preferring one model over the other (see MacCallum et al., 1993, for additional discussion).

16.7 Specifying Multi-Sample Models

A researcher may have hypotheses regarding how parameter estimates in a given model will differ across two or more groups of people. Such groups may represent people assigned to different experimental conditions or groups who differ on some individual difference (e.g., sex, ethnic group, or a personality trait). It is possible to test between-group differences in model parameters by specifying a multi-sample SEM analysis that simultaneously fits a proposed model to two or more samples and obtains an overall assessment of fit for the model across the samples. The researcher can then test hypotheses about differences in parameters across the groups by running models that constrain specific parameters to be equivalent across groups. P^2 difference tests can then be conducted to compare the constrained models with the unconstrained model.

Multi-sample analysis is not available in all SEM programs, but both LISREL and EQS have such capabilities. Detailed discussion of how such models are specified and the analytic strategies necessary to properly implement them go beyond the scope of the present chapter. However, it is important for readers to be aware that multi-sample models present some challenges that are not typically encountered when specifying single sample models (Bielby, 1986; Williams & Thomson, 1986; Sobel & Arminger, 1986). Many introductory texts on SEM provide overviews of the conceptual and practical issues involved in the specification and testing of multi-sample models (see Bollen, 1989; Maruyama, 1998; Shumacker & Lomax, 2004).

16.7.1 Specifying Nonlinear and Interaction Models

Cross-sample differences in a structural parameter represents group-based moderation of the structural influence of one variable on the other. This can make cross-group analyses very useful for testing effects that are otherwise difficult in SEM contexts. Of course, the grouping variable is not latent and is often categorical. This works well when an experimental manipulation creates the groups, but when an interval-level measured variable is the hypothesized moderator, one would ideally have a way to test the hypothesized moderation without abandoning SEM's advantages in terms of using latent variables that control for measurement error. Such a model requires the specification of an interaction among latent variables. A number of techniques have been designed to test latent variable interaction effects (as well as other nonlinear latent variable effects) in SEM (Kenny & Judd, 1984; Ping, 1996; see Bollen, 1989; Wegener & Fabrigar, 2000). These methods are relatively complex and detailed discussion of them is not possible within the context of the present chapter. However, it is important for readers to recognize that such models can be specified, although it may be impractical to do so when models involve complex interaction hypotheses (e.g., three-way interactions).

16.8 Specifying Models in LISREL

Up to this point, the discussion of the model specification process has covered general issues that arise during this stage of SEM analyses. However, to fully understand how model specification occurs, it is also useful to consider the process in the context of a more specific example. Thus, we turn our attention to demonstrating the specification of a structural equation model using LISREL.

16.8.1 Introduction to Model Specification Example

Figure 16.5 presents the path diagram representation of a previously published structural equation model (Sidanius, 1988) that will serve as our example for model specification as well as for subsequent topics in the chapter. This model was originally proposed to explain processes involved in the interface between personality and political ideology. It was used to model the correlations among a set of 13 measured variables.

The model postulates the existence of one exogenous latent variable: cognitive orientation. Cognitive orientation refers to an individual's need to understand politics. It is presumed to exert a positive impact on the endogenous latent variable of print media usage (i.e., the degree to which people use the print media to obtain information about politics). Additionally, cognitive orientation and print media usage are both postulated to have a positive influence on the endogenous latent variable of political sophistication (i.e., the amount and complexity of information that an individual has regarding politics). Political sophistication in turn is presumed to exert a positive influence on the endogenous latent variables of political deviance (i.e., the extent to which people deviate from political norms) and self-confidence (i.e., the degree to which people believe in their abilities and their likelihood of succeeding in life). Finally, self-confidence is assumed to exert a positive influence on political deviance and a negative effect on racism (i.e., the degree to which people express negative attitudes toward individuals of other races). One other notable feature of this model that can be seen in Figure 16.5 is that two of the hypothesized latent variables (print media usage and racism) have only a single measured variable representing them.

As we noted in our introduction to the mathematical framework underlying the LISREL approach to SEM, any proposed model can be mathematically represented using the eight matrices discussed earlier. This matrix representation provides an alternative form to the path diagram for expressing structural equation models. The matrix representation of the four matrices composing the measurement model for the present example is provided in Table 16.3. The matrix representation for the four matrices making up the structural model portion of the example are presented in Table 16.4.

Because LISREL, EQS, and other SEM programs generally do not require researchers to specify their models in matrix form, we will not discuss the matrix representation of our example in detail. Tables 16.3 and 16.4 are merely provided for comparative purposes so that interested readers can see another example of how the path diagram representation of a model is translated into its more formal mathematical representation. Instead, we will focus on the path diagram representation of the model and how this form of representation is specified in the LISREL and EQS programs.

16.8.2 Specifying Model Representations in LISREL

LISREL permits specification of models in one of two different syntax languages: LISREL and SIMPLIS. LISREL syntax was the original syntax language for LISREL and defines

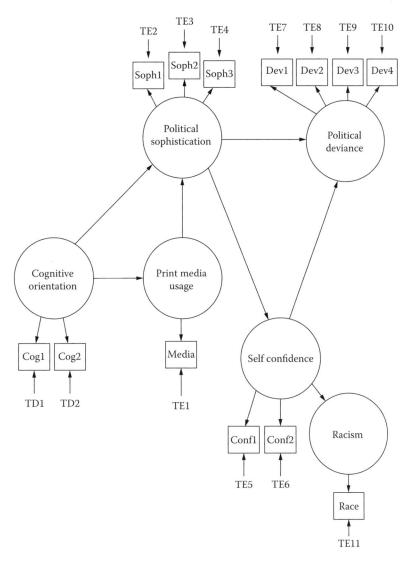

FIGURE 16.5
Path diagram for a structural equation model reported in Sidanius (1988).

models using the matrix representation of the model. SIMPLIS is a newer syntax language designed to provide a more intuitive and simple method for specifying SEM models in LISREL (although some advanced functions of the program cannot be implemented in this syntax language). This language generally derives its form of expression from the path diagram representational format rather than the matrix representational format.

SIMPLIS code for Sidanius (1988) is provided in Table 16.5. Line 1 of this code is referred to as the title line and can include any sort of alphanumeric text (other than text that begins with a SIMPLIS command). The next 17 lines of the program specify properties of the data set to be analyzed. Line 2 indicates that information regarding the measured variables will be provided next. Line 3 indicates the labels that will be used for the measured variables and, by virtue of the number of labels provided, the number of measured variables that will be analyzed. It should be noted that the order of these labels is not arbitrary. The order

TABLE 16.3

Matrix Representation for the Measurement Model of Sidanius (1988)

Lambda X (LX)

	Cognitive Orientation
Cog1	LX_{11}
Cog2	LX_{21}

Lambda Y (LY)

	Print Media	Political Sophistication	Self-Confidence	Political Deviance	Racism
Med	1	0	0	0	0
Soph1	0	1	0	0	0
Soph2	0	LY_{32}	0	0	0
Soph3	0	LY_{42}	0	0	0
Conf1	0	0	1	0	0
Conf2	0	0	LY_{63}	0	0
Dev1	0	0	0	1	0
Dev2	0	0	0	LY_{84}	0
Dev3	0	0	0	LY_{94}	0
Dev4	0	0	0	LY_{104}	0
Race	0	0	0	0	1

Theta Delta (TD)

	Cog1	Cog2
Cog1	TD_{11}	
Cog2	0	TD_{22}

Theta Epsilon (TE)

	Med	Soph1	Soph2	Soph3	Conf1	Conf2	Dev1	Dev2	Dev3	Dev4	Race
Med	0										
Soph1	0	TE_{22}									
Soph2	0	0	TE_{33}								
Soph3	0	0	0	TE_{44}							
Conf1	0	0	0	0	TE_{55}						
Conf2	0	0	0	0	0	TE_{66}					
Dev1	0	0	0	0	0	0	TE_{77}				
Dev2	0	0	0	0	0	0	0	TE_{88}			
Dev3	0	0	0	0	0	0	0	0	TE_{99}		
Dev4	0	0	0	0	0	0	0	0	0	TE_{1010}	
Race	0	0	0	0	0	0	0	0	0	0	0

TABLE 16.4

Matrix Representation for the Structural Model of Sidanius (1988)

Gamma (GA)

	Cognitive Orientation
Print Media	GA_{11}
Political Sophistication	GA_{21}
Self-Confidence	0
Political Deviance	0
Racism	0

Beta (BE)

	Print Media	Political Sophistication	Self-Confidence	Political Deviance	Racism
Print Media	0	0	0	0	0
Political Sophistication	BE_{21}	0	0	0	0
Self-Confidence	0	BE_{32}	0	0	0
Political Deviance	0	BE_{42}	BE_{43}	0	0
Racism	0	0	BE_{53}	0	0

Phi (PH)

	Cognitive Orientation
Cognitive Orientation	1

PSI (PS)

	Print Media	Political Sophistication	Self-Confidence	Political Deviance	Racism
Print Media	PS_{11}				
Political Sophistication	0	PS_{22}			
Self-Confidence	0	0	PS_{33}		
Political Deviance	0	0	0	PS_{44}	
Racism	0	0	0	0	PS_{55}

of the labels is assumed to match the order of the measured variables in the correlation or covariance matrix to be analyzed. LISREL also assumes that Y variables will be listed first in the matrix to be analyzed. If they are not, the ordering of variables specified in the model can be re-ordered from the original correlation matrix by placing a syntax line immediately following the actual correlation matrix with the syntax command "Reorder Variables:" The labels of the measured variables in their desired order should then be listed after the colon. This command can also be used to analyze only a subset of the measured variables within the matrix. This is done by simply listing only those measured

TABLE 16.5

SIMPLIS Code for Sidanius (1988)

(1)	COVARIANCE STRUCTURE MODEL EXAMPLE (SIDANIUS, 1988)
(2)	Observed Variables
(3)	MED SOPH1 SOPH2 SOPH3 CONF1 CONF2 DEV1 DEV2 DEV3 DEV4 RACE COG1 COG2
(4)	Correlation Matrix
(5)	1.000
(6)	.204 1.000
(7)	.077 .136 1.000
(8)	.215 .124 .139 1.000
(9)	.180 .123 .048 −.031 1.000
(10)	.142 −.068 −.026 .031 .424 1.000
(11)	.238 .052 .041 .202 .248 .123 1.000
(12)	.228 .159 .227 .153 .262 .141 .186 1.000
(13)	.125 .130 −.001 .124 .214 .124 .231 .284 1.000
(14)	.075 .254 .023 .184 −.002 −.021 .230 .175 .243 1.000
(15)	.043 .015 −.067 .064 −.157 −.135 −.166 −.113 −.043 −.129 1.000
(16)	.471 .174 .143 .135 .146 .080 .238 .290 .029 .048 −.079 1.000
(17)	.396 .181 .117 .180 .159 .149 .266 .276 .050 .131 −.198 .637 1.000
(18)	Sample Size = 168
(19)	Latent Variables MEDIA SOPHIST CONFID DEVIANCE RACISM COGORIEN
(20)	Relationships
(21)	MED = 1.00*MEDIA
(22)	SOPH1 = 1.00*SOPHIST
(23)	SOPH2 = SOPHIST
(24)	SOPH3 = SOPHIST
(25)	CONF1 = 1.00*CONFID
(26)	CONF2 = CONFID
(27)	DEV1 = 1.00*DEVIANCE
(28)	DEV2 = DEVIANCE
(29)	DEV3 = DEVIANCE
(30)	DEV4 = DEVIANCE
(31)	RACE = 1.00*RACISM
(32)	COG1 = COGORIEN
(33)	COG2 = COGORIEN
(34)	SOPHIST = MEDIA
(35)	CONFID = SOPHIST
(36)	DEVIANCE = SOPHIST CONFID
(37)	RACISM = CONFID
(38)	MEDIA = COGORIEN
(39)	SOPHIST = COGORIEN
(40)	Set the Variance of COGORIEN to 1.00
(41)	Set the Error Variance of MED to 0.00
(42)	Set the Error Variance of RACE to 0.00
(43)	Path Diagram
(44)	Print Residuals
(45)	LISREL Output: RS MI SC EF WP
(46)	Method of Estimation: Maximum Likelihood
(47)	End of Problem

variables to be analyzed on the reorder command. Omitted variables will be dropped from the subsequent analysis.

Line 4 indicates that the matrix to be analyzed will appear next and that this matrix will be a correlation matrix. Had the matrix to be analyzed been a covariance matrix, this line would have been replaced with "Covariance Matrix." Lines 5–17 provide the matrix of correlations among the measured variables. It should be noted that LISREL also permits a researcher to read a correlation matrix or covariance matrix from an external file rather than including it in the actual syntax file. Raw data can also be analyzed either as part of the syntax file or from an external file. Line 18 indicates the sample size upon which the correlation matrix is based.

Lines 19–42 specify the parameters of the model. More specifically, line 19 indicates the number of latent variables, by virtue of the number of labels provided, and the names of the latent variables that will be included in the model (in the order their measured variable indicators appear in the correlation matrix). Line 20 indicates that relations composing the model (i.e., the parameters of the model) will be specified in the lines to follow. Lines 21–33 specify the directional relations that make up the measurement model. As can be seen, the structure of the syntax for directional relations is such that dependent variables preceded independent variables in the statements. For example, line 21 indicates that the measured variable of "Med" is influenced by the latent variable of "Media." Likewise, in line 22, the measured variable of "Soph1" is postulated to be influenced by the latent variable of "Sophist." The inclusion of "1.00*" in lines 21 and 22 indicates that these paths will be fixed at 1. Note that line 23 has no such value specified. Thus, the path will be a free parameter to be estimated from the data.

Lines 34–39 specify the directional relations composing the structural model (i.e., directional relations among latent variables). The syntax structure of these lines is similar to that of the lines for the measurement model. Dependent variables precede independent variables. Thus, for example, line 34 indicates that the latent variable of "Sophist" is influenced by the latent variable of "Media."

Lines 40–42 specify nondirectional relations in the model. Because programs written in SIMPLIS default to assume the elements in the covariance matrix of exogenous variables (Phi) are free, it is necessary to specifically indicate when a value must be fixed. Line 40 sets the variance for the exogenous latent variable of "Cogorien" to be fixed at 1, in order to set the scale of measurement for this latent variable. Programs written in SIMPLIS also default to assume that the diagonal elements of theta delta and theta epsilon are free and off-diagonal elements are fixed at 0. Thus, if diagonal elements are to be fixed, this must be specifically stated in the program. Lines 41–42 indicate that the values of the unique variances associated with the measured variables of "Med" and "Race" will be fixed to 0. Recall that both of these measured variables are the sole indicators of their respective variables. Thus, these lines indicate that the model treats these measured variables as perfect indicators of latent variables. As noted earlier, this means that the "Media" and "Racism" latent variables are not really latent at all. They are represented in the model as if they are perfectly captured by the single measure (without error), as they would be treated in alternative analyses such as regression and path analysis. Therefore, the model's treatment of these latent variables does not take advantage of the ability of SEM to identify commonalities among a set of measured variables separate from random measurement error. In the present example, the default assumption that errors in measured variables are independent of one another is retained. However, if for example one had wanted to allow errors in measured variables to covary, this could have been done using the command "Set the Error Covariance between (name of measured variable) and (name of measured variable) Free."

Lines 43–45 specify additional features for the output of the analyses. Specifically, lines 43 and 44 specify that a path diagram should be generated and that the residuals associated with the model should be provided. Parameter estimates, standard errors, and t-values are provided in equation form in SIMPLIS output. However, as illustrated in line 45, the researcher can also specify that output should be given in LISREL format. When this is done, a number of additional options are available, such as modification indices and completely standardized solutions, that are not available in SIMPLIS output. It might be instructive for readers to run the program with and without Line 45 in order to see that the parameter estimates, standard errors, and t-values presented in equations in the SIMPLIS output (and labeled as LISREL estimates in both types of output) are the same as the parameter estimates, standard errors, and t-values presented in matrices in the LISREL format. Line 46 indicates that maximum likelihood estimation will be used and line 47 that the SIMPLIS program is completed.

16.9 Specifying Models in EQS

EQS code is, in a number of ways, similar to SIMPLIS code. The model is specified using a series of equations, rather than a set of matrices. EQS code for the Sidanius (1988) example is listed in Table 16.6. Lines 1–2 provide a title for the program. Lines 3–6 read in the data, specify the number of measured variables and number of cases, and list the type of analysis to take place. The method listed in line 6 is maximum likelihood, to analyze a correlation matrix that is read in using matrix form rather than raw data (the covariance matrix form of the data lists means of 0 and standard deviations of 1 for all variables, because the matrix is a correlation matrix rather than a covariance matrix). Lines 7–10 provide labels for the measured variables. In EQS, all measured variables are referred to using Vs (with numbers 1–13 corresponding to the location of the variable in the correlation or covariance matrix).

Lines 11–29 specify the measurement and structural paths in the model. In the equations, each latent variable is given an F label (for factor), and each error term is given an E label. Lines 12–24 list the measurement model, with the measured variable's being influenced by its respective latent variable (factor) and error term. In these equations, asterisks preceding the latent variables represent free parameters to be estimated, and 1's represent paths fixed at 1 to set the scale of measurement for the latent variables. Note that in this program, the scale of the Cognitive Orientation latent variable is set by fixing the path between the latent variable and measure COG1 (i.e., V12) to 1. In the LISREL programs, the scale of the exogenous latent variable was set by fixing its variance at 1. In lines 25–29, the structural relations among the latent variables are specified. Note that these latent variables are also influenced by disturbances (i.e., Ds) reflecting the residuals in the endogenous latent factors (a.k.a, "errors in equations").

Lines 30–49 specify variances in the exogenous latent variable (F6), the measured variables (V1–V13), and the residual variances (disturbances) in the endogenous latent variables. Again, asterisks represent free parameters to be estimated. The variance of F6 is free, because the scale was set by fixing the factor loading for COG1 (i.e., V12) at 1. E1 and E11 are set at 0, because MEDIA and RACE are single (therefore, treated as perfect) indicators of their respective latent variables.

Lines 50–53 specify features for the printed output of the analyses. These commands specify that all available fit indices should be printed and that the parameter estimates will be presented in equation form. The printed output includes a completely standardized solution along with unstandardized parameter estimates, standard errors, and t-values (i.e., tests of significance for the parameter estimates). Line 54 and 55 specify that the Lagrange Multiplier and Wald tests should be conducted, respectively. These tests are also included in the printed output. Line 56 ends the program.

TABLE 16.6

EQS Code for Sidanius (1988)

```
(1)   /TITLE
(2)   Sidanius (1988)
(3)   /SPECIFICATIONS
(4)   DATA='c:\eqs files\sidan88.ess';
(5)   VARIABLES=13; CASES=168;
(6)   METHOD=ML; ANALYSIS=CORRELATION; MATRIX=CORRELATION;
(7)   /LABELS
(8)   V1=MEDIA; V2=SOPH1; V3=SOPH2; V4=SOPH3; V5=CONF1;
(9)   V6=CONF2; V7=DEV1; V8=DEV2; V9=DEV3; V10=DEV4;
(10)  V11=RACE; V12=COG1; V13=COG2;
(11)  /EQUATIONS
(12)  V1 = 1F1 + E1;
(13)  V2 = 1F2 + E2;
(14)  V3 = *F2 + E3;
(15)  V4 = *F2 + E4;
(16)  V5 = 1F3 + E5;
(17)  V6 = *F3 + E6;
(18)  V7 = 1F4 + E7;
(19)  V8 = *F4 + E8;
(20)  V9 = *F4 + E9;
(21)  V10 = *F4 + E10;
(22)  V11 = 1F5 + E11;
(23)  V12 = 1F6 + E12;
(24)  V13 = *F6 + E13;
(25)  F1 = *F6 + D1;
(26)  F2 = *F1 + *F6 + D2;
(27)  F3 = *F2 + D3;
(28)  F4 = *F2 + *F3 + D4;
(29)  F5 = *F3 + D5;
(30)  /VARIANCES
(31)  F6 = *;
(32)  E1 = 0.00;
(33)  E2 = *;
(34)  E3 = *;
(35)  E4 = *;
(36)  E5 = *;
(37)  E6 = *;
(38)  E7 = *;
(39)  E8 = *;
(40)  E9 = *;
(41)  E10 = *;
(42)  E11 = 0.00;
(43)  E12 = *;
(44)  E13 = *;
(45)  D1 = *;
(46)  D2 = *;
(47)  D3 = *;
(48)  D4 = *;
(49)  D5 = *;
(50)  /PRINT
(51)  EIS;
(52)  FIT=ALL;
(53)  TABLE=EQUATION;
(54)  /LMTEST
(55)  /WTEST
(56)  /END
```

16.10 Model Fitting

Once a model (or models) has been specified, the next step in an SEM analysis is to fit this model to the data. The task of model fitting (also called parameter estimation) in SEM is similar to the same task for CFA. As noted in Chapter 11, given a particular CFA model and a set of parameter estimates for that model, it is possible to generate an implied covariance (or correlation) matrix. This matrix reflects the predicted pattern of covariances among the measured variables in the population that should occur if the model is a perfect representation of the data and the specific set of parameter estimates for the model are the true values in the population. This predicted covariance matrix can then be compared to the observed covariance matrix generated from the data to determine the discrepancy between the model and the data.

Simply put, the goal of model fitting is to find the specific set of parameter estimates for a given model that best account for the observed data. That is, model fitting procedures attempt to arrive at the set of parameter estimates that will produce the implied covariance matrix that comes closest to the observed covariance matrix to which the model is being fit. This basic goal is the same for both CFA and SEM, with the only difference being that CFA models involve obtaining parameter estimates for models with 3 matrices whereas SEM models require obtaining parameter estimates for all 8 matrices.

16.10.1 Model Fitting Procedures

A number of different model fitting procedures have been proposed. These share some features in common. Each procedure involves the goal of obtaining parameter estimates that best account for the data. Additionally, all model fitting procedures are iterative in nature. That is, for these procedures, it is not possible to directly calculate the estimates. Instead, model fitting procedures begin with an initial set of estimates, calculate the discrepancy between the model and the data given those estimates, and then adjust these estimates in an attempt to reduce the discrepancy between the model and the data. The process continues with a new set of estimates at each step (i.e., iteration) until the procedure cannot find a new set of estimates that appreciably improves upon the previous estimates. At this point, the procedure is said to have "converged" on a solution.

The fundamental distinction between different model fitting procedures is reflected in how the discrepancy between a model and data is mathematically defined. The specific mathematical function used to define discrepancy between a model and data is referred to as the "discrepancy function." Distinctions between model fitting procedures thus reflect attempts to minimize different discrepancy functions. Although a comprehensive review of model fitting procedures goes beyond the scope of this chapter (e.g., see Bollen, 1989; Joreskog and Sorbom, 1996), we will briefly discuss some of the better known procedures.

16.10.2 Maximum Likelihood Estimation

Maximum likelihood (ML) estimation is by far the most popular method of model fitting in SEM analyses. In simple terms, the discrepancy function for ML estimation defines discrepancy between the model and the data in terms of the likelihood that a model with a particular set of estimates could have produced the observed data. Thus, the conceptual goal of ML estimation is to arrive at the set of parameter estimates that, given the model, are maximally likely to have produced the data. Rather than maximizing the likelihood function, it has been found to be more computationally convenient to work with an alternative function that is inversely related to the likelihood function. Hence, the smaller this function, the greater the likelihood that the model with that set of estimates could have produced the data. This numerical value is referred to as the ML discrepancy function, F_{ML}. It is always equal to or greater than 0 and it will equal 0 if and only if the model fits the data perfectly. The ML discrepancy function is defined by the following equation:

$$F_{ML} = \log \left\| \sum \right\| + tr(S \sum {}^{-1}) - \log \|S\| - (p + q)$$

where Σ is the implied covariance matrix, S the observed covariance matrix from the data, p the number of X variables, q the number of Y variables, and tr the trace of the matrix (i.e., the sum of the diagonal elements).

As will be discussed in more detail in the model evaluation section, ML parameter estimation provides two primary types of information. First, it produces estimates of the free parameters as well as standard errors for these estimates. It is possible to compute confidence intervals for estimates as well as significance tests. Second, the ML discrepancy function permits the computation of a variety of indices of model fit. These indices attempt to quantify in different ways the discrepancy between the model and the data.

ML estimation makes two important assumptions regarding the data. First, ML assumes that the data are based on a random sample drawn from some defined population. Second, it assumes that the distribution of measured variables is multivariate normal in the population. There has been considerable attention devoted to the issue of how robust ML is to violations of assumptions of normality (e.g., Chou, Bentler, and Satorra, 1991; Curran, West, and Finch, 1996; Hu, Bentler, and Kano, 1992). To date, simulation studies have suggested that ML is more robust to such violations than originally thought. For example, West, Finch, and Curran (1995) found that ML functioned fairly well as long as measured variables were not severely non-normal (i.e., skew >2, kurtosis >7).

16.10.3 Other Model Fitting Procedures

Although ML is easily the most popular method for estimating model parameters, readers may sometimes encounter two other model fitting procedures in the SEM literature. Normal theory generalized least squares (GLS) estimation was developed with the intention of producing a parameter estimation method that had the same desirable properties of ML, but required less stringent distributional assumptions and was more computationally robust (Browne, 1982, 1984). Essentially, this method defines discrepancy between the model and the data as a function of the squared residuals between the elements of the observed covariance matrix and the implied covariance matrix. However, this procedure differentially weights elements in the residual matrix according to their variances and covariances with other elements.

Like ML, GLS produces parameter estimates and standard errors for estimates. It is also possible to compute fit indices comparable to those computed for ML. Unfortunately, there is comparatively little evidence that GLS is substantially more robust to violations of assumptions of multivariate normality than ML (e.g., Hu, Bentler, and Kano, 1992; West et al., 1995). Moreover, GLS does not seem to have any clear estimation advantages over ML, although it may be more robust computationally than ML in that it is less sensitive to poor starting values and will converge in some situations where ML does not. When the model fits well, GLS and ML produce similar model fit values and parameter estimates.

Asymptotically distribution free (ADF) estimation is a model fitting procedure developed to provide a parameter estimation method that does not require the assumption of multivariate normality (Browne, 1982, 1984). Like ML, ADF provides parameter estimates, standard errors of estimates, and model fit indices. Unfortunately, although ADF does not require multivariate normality, research has indicated that model fit and parameter estimates may be appropriate only when the procedure is used with extremely large sample sizes (Hu et al., 1992; Raykov and Widaman, 1995; West et al., 1995). Thus, ADF may not be a practical option in many situations.

16.10.4 Fitting Models to Correlation versus Covariance Matrices

One issue that sometimes arises in the context of SEM analyses is whether models should be fit to covariance matrices or correlation matrices of measured variables. Throughout the prior discussion of factor analysis in Chapter 11, it was generally assumed that the model was being fit to a correlation matrix. This is almost always the case in EFA and often true in CFA. However, in SEM, models are often fit to covariance matrices. Indeed, some have suggested that it is generally advisable to fit models to covariance matrices rather than correlation matrices (Tanaka, Panter, Winborne, and Huba, 1990).

There are several reasons for this recommendation. First, although standard SEM programs provide appropriate parameter estimates and model fit indices when fitting a model to a correlation matrix, many programs (e.g., LISREL) do not provide the correct standard errors for estimates when fit to correlation matrices (see Browne, 1982; Cudeck, 1989).* Second, use of correlation matrices is usually inappropriate when conducting multi-sample SEM analyses (Bielby, 1986; Cudeck, 1989; Williams and Thomson, 1986; Sobel and Arminger, 1986). Correlation matrices involve standardizing measured variables such that variances are 1. If variances actually differ across groups, misleading comparisons can result from such standardization. Similarly, in longitudinal data, it might be inappropriate to use correlation matrices because it implies that the variances of a given variable over time remain constant (i.e., the variances will always be 1).

16.10.5 Problems in Model Fitting

Several problems are occasionally encountered during parameter estimation in SEM and CFA. Some of these problems were briefly alluded to during our discussion of model identification. However, because these problems are not solely a result of model identification issues, it is useful to consider them within a broader context of the many factors that can contribute to problems in model fitting (see Anderson and Gerbing, 1984; Bollen, 1989; van Driel, 1978).

16.10.5.1 Failure to Begin Iteration

One potential problem is the inability of the program to begin iteration. To begin the iterative process of parameter estimation, SEM programs must compute an initial set of "start values" for the parameters. Most programs have algorithms for computing start values, but sometimes these algorithms generate poor values and the program is unable to begin iteration. In such cases, the user must specify a better set of start values. Virtually all SEM

---

* It is useful to note that there are alternative ways to parameterize models in LISREL that can be used to obtain appropriate standard errors for SEM analyses of correlation matrices (see Jöreskog, Sörbom, du Toit, and du Toit, 2000).

programs allow a researcher to provide specific start values for a model. There are no clear rules for generating start values, but often, past research, existing theory, and properties of the data will provide some guidance in this regard. For example, prior information about the reliability of measured variables can provide a basis for specifying start values for the unique variances associated with measured variables.

16.10.5.2 Nonconvergence

On occasions, SEM programs fail to converge on a solution. Often this occurs because the program has exceeded its maximum number of iterations. This problem can frequently be corrected by specifying a higher limit to the maximum iterations allowed. On other occasions, even large numbers of iterations will not be sufficient for convergence. Sometimes this problem is due to poor start values and can be corrected with better start values. On other occasions, this can reflect a misspecified model (i.e., a model that is a very poor representation of the data), lack of model identification, poor model identification, or problems in the data (e.g., the data severely violate assumptions of the model fitting procedure). Many of these causes are particularly problematic when sample sizes are very small.

16.10.5.3 Inadmissible Solutions (Improper or Boundary Solutions)

Sometimes parameters have logical bounds on their values but the program produces estimates that fall beyond these bounds. Some programs (e.g., RAMONA) constrain these estimates to remain within logical bounds, but report that the constraint was placed on the parameter. Other programs (e.g., LISREL) permit the estimates to go beyond these logical boundaries. If only one or two such estimates occur (especially in models with many parameters) and their violations are slight, this is cause for substantial caution but may not be a serious problem. If multiple problematic estimates are obtained or these values deviate substantially from theoretically possible values, then the results are likely misleading. Improper solutions can result from a variety of factors. For example, they often occur when samples sizes are small and the true population values are close to boundaries. Alternatively, they can occur when the model has been misspecified, the model is poorly identified, the model is not identified, or problems exist in the data (e.g., severely nonnormal data). Sometimes a model fitting procedure can produce parameter estimates that are conceptually possible, but the standard errors associated with these estimates are extremely large. This problem is usually indicative of a model that has been misspecified, is only poorly identified, or is not identified.

16.10.5.4 Local Minima

A final potential problem is that of a local minimum in the discrepancy function. Sometimes a program may iterate to a solution, but this solution is only the best fitting solution for a limited class of solutions rather than the single best fitting solution for the model. When this occurs, model fitting procedures may mistakenly terminate the iteration process. Typically, local minima are easy to diagnose because model fit is usually very poor or parameter estimates are extremely implausible. One way to check whether a solution is a local minimum is to fit the model using several different sets of start values. If the model converges on the same solution, it is extremely unlikely that this solution is caused by a local minimum. Local minima can result from misspecifications of the model or data that severely violate parameter estimation assumptions.

16.11 Model Evaluation and Modification

Once a model has been specified and fit to the data, the researcher evaluates the model's performance. This involves examining indices of the overall fit of the model as well as the specific parameter estimates for the model. It is important to recognize that both of these sources of information are valuable in assessing a model. Failure to consider both can lead to erroneous conclusions. In addition, when considering model fit, it is generally useful to examine fit of the hypothesized model when compared with alternative theoretical models. In so doing, the relative parsimony of the competing models should be considered. Regarding the specific parameter estimates, interpretability of the solution given existing theories is of the utmost importance.

16.11.1 Model Fit

As noted in the previous section, model fitting (i.e., parameter estimation) involves determining the values for the parameters that minimize the discrepancy between the covariance/correlation matrix implied by the model and that observed in the sample. Even these "best" parameter estimates are unlikely to reduce the discrepancy to 0. Indices of model fit, therefore, are used to express the amount of discrepancy between the matrix implied by the final model solution (i.e., the best parameter estimates) and the observed matrix. If no values can be found that lead to small discrepancies between model and data (i.e., the model fit is poor), then the model is regarded as an implausible representation of the structure underlying the data. If, however, parameter values can be found that produce small discrepancies between model and data, then the model is regarded as a plausible representation of the underlying structure.

As discussed in the chapter on EFA and CFA, a number of fit indices have been developed (for thorough reviews, see Bollen, 1989; Marsh, Balla, and McDonald, 1988; Mulaik, James, Van Alstine, Bennett, Lind, and Stilwell, 1989; and Tanaka, 1993). The present discussion is confined to some of the more widely used indices that reflect different conceptual approaches to assessing fit. A number of these indices were originally developed for the context of factor analysis (even exploratory factor analysis, see Fabrigar et al., 1999). However, these indices are equally applicable to more general structural equation models. Other more recently proposed indices have been developed primarily for structural equation modeling, but are equally appropriate for factor analysis using the same common factor model.

As with factor analysis, one of the most typical indices of model fit is the likelihood ratio (also called the P^2 goodness-of-fit test). The likelihood ratio serves as a *statistical test* of whether the discrepancy between the matrix implied by the model and the observed data is greater than 0. That is, the likelihood ratio is a test of exact fit (see Section 11.16). Although there are a number of possible reasons to question the utility of the likelihood ratio test, perhaps the most important are that the hypothesis of exact fit is never realistic and that the likelihood ratio is inherently sensitive to sample size (see MacCallum, 1990). For these reasons, methodologists generally regard the chi-square test of model fit as an index of limited utility. A variant of the chi-square test that is sometimes reported is the P^2/df index. That is, some methodologists have argued that a useful index of model fit is to compute the P^2 divided by its degrees of freedom (with smaller number suggesting better fit). The logic of this index is that it allows a researcher to assess the chi-square value in the context of model parsimony. Models with fewer parameters will have more degrees of freedom. Thus, given two models that produce the same chi-square, the model with fewer parameters will produce a better (i.e., smaller) P^2/df value. Such an index also allows a researcher to gauge the model using a less stringent standard than perfect fit. Specifically, the model need not perform perfectly but only perform well relative to its degrees of freedom. Although the idea underlying this variant of the P^2 makes some sense, there are significant limitations to this approach. First, there is no clear conceptual and empirical basis for guidelines provided for interpreting this index. Indeed, recommendations have varied dramatically. Second, adjusting for degrees of freedom does nothing to address the problem of sample size in P^2 tests. Thus, even a good fitting model could appear to perform poorly at very large sample sizes and a poor fitting model appear to perform well at small sample sizes.

Because of these issues, methodologists have long suggested that it may be more useful to provide *descriptive indices* of model fit (e.g., Tucker and Lewis, 1973). Rather than assess fit via a formal hypothesis test of perfect fit, these indices express model fit in terms of the magnitude of the discrepancy between the model and the data. Thus, the issue is not whether discrepancy between the model and the data exists (which it almost always does), but rather how large that discrepancy is. Descriptive indices are typically divided into the categories of *absolute* fit indices and *incremental* or *comparative* fit indices. Absolute fit indices attempt to quantify discrepancy between the model and the data without any reference to a comparison point, whereas incremental fit indices quantify the discrepancy between a proposed model and the data relative to some comparison model. In theory, incremental fit indices can be computed comparing any two models. However, as described in Section 11.16, incremental fit indices usually compare a hypothesized model to a null model (i.e., a model in which all measures are assumed to have variances but no relations with one another).

16.11.1.1 Absolute Fit Indices

Absolute fit indices described in Section 11.16 included the GFI, AGFI, and RMSEA. Root Mean Square Residual (RMR; Jöreskog and Sörbom, 1986) is also routinely reported by SEM programs. It is the square root of the mean squared residuals between the elements of the observed covariance matrix of measured variables and the elements of the predicted covariance matrix of measured variables. A value of 0 indicates perfect fit and larger numbers reflect poorer fit. Unfortunately, because RMR values are scale dependent, there are no clear guidelines for interpreting this index. Thus, the Standardized Root Mean Square Residual (SRMR; Jöreskog and Sörbom, 1981) is also widely reported by SEM programs. This index is the square root of the standardized mean squared residuals between the elements of the observed covariance matrix of measured variables and the elements of the predicted covariance matrix of measured variables. A value of 0 indicates perfect fit and larger numbers reflect poorer fit. Because SRMR values are based on standardized residuals, SRMR values are not dependent on the scaling of the measured variables. Hence, it is possible to specify guidelines for interpreting this index. Values of .08 or lower are generally regarded as indicative of good fit.

16.11.1.2 Incremental Fit Indices

The Tucker-Lewis Index (TLI; Tucker and Lewis, 1973) was originally developed for factor analytic models. It was the first descriptive fit index to be developed. In SEM settings, the index is often referred to as the nonnormed fit index (NNFI; Bentler and Bonnett, 1980; see Section 11.16). Like all incremental fit indices, the TLI/NNFI compares the performance of the proposed model relative to the null model. Larger values reflect better fit. The TLI/ NNFI is not constrained to fall between 0 and 1, though in practice it usually does. Another index with similar properties is the Incremental Fit Index (IFI) proposed by Bollen (1989). The other incremental fit index discussed in Section 11.16 was the NFI (Bentler and Bonnett, 1980). The NFI is constrained to fall between 0 and 1.

16.11.1.3 Summary Comments on Descriptive Fit Indices

Because so many indices have been proposed (more than a dozen), there is considerable confusion among researchers regarding exactly which indices to consider when evaluating a model. Some researchers think these indices provide very similar information and thus the selection of indices to report is an arbitrary decision. Others choose to focus on a single preferred index (e.g., the index that produces the best fit) and report only this value. Still others conclude that because no fit index is perfect, a researcher should report numerous indices (or perhaps all indices provided by the program). Unfortunately, none of these views is entirely sensible. Researchers should recognize that the various indices attempt to quantify fit using very different conceptual approaches. Thus, one cannot assume that these indices are interchangeable and that choosing among them is an arbitrary decision. It is true that there is no clear consensus regarding which fit index is the best. Even very good fit indices are not perfect, so it is unwise to base evaluation of fit on a single index. Indeed, because these indices define fit in different ways, it can be instructive to compare the performance of a model across these indices. However, indiscriminate use of numerous indices is also not advisable. Not all of the indices perform well. Inclusion of poorly performing indices has the potential to obscure rather than clarify the performance of the model. In the end, it seems most advisable for a researcher to rely on a small set of fit indices. These fit indices should be selected on the basis of their performance in detecting errors in model specification and in terms of their conceptual properties.

Various fit indices may react differently to different types of model misspecification. For example, a model might be misspecified because it fails to include free parameters that are nonzero in the population (i.e., model underparameterization). On the other hand, a model could include free parameters that are 0 in the population (i.e., overparameterization). In practice, because overparameterized models result in solutions that empirically demonstrate which parameters were unnecessary, underparameterization is the more serious problem. In simulations examining the sensitivities of various fit indices to model misspecifications involving underparameterization, Hu and Bentler (1998) found that the SRMR, TLI/NNFI, IFI, and RMSEA generally performed better than the GFI, AGFI, or NFI. Much more work of this type is required, however. Because simulations often reflect only certain properties of the data and a restricted set of models, different results could occur when studying different models or data with alternative characteristics (for related discussion in the area of EFA, see Fabrigar et al., 1999).

One conceptual property that often seems desirable is the sensitivity of a fit index to model parsimony. The AGFI, RMSEA, TLI/NNFI, and IFI all take model parsimony into account in some way (as does the P^2/df ratio). By taking into account the number of free parameters in the model, these indices will not necessarily improve simply by adding free parameters to the model. Similarly, given two models with equal discrepancy function values, parsimony-sensitive indices will tend to favor the more parsimonious model. However, the various indices do this in different ways, and little work has addressed the adequacy of the various means of "rewarding" parsimonious models in indices of fit.

Though not generally reported, one can compute confidence intervals for the absolute fit indices GFI, AGFI, and RMSEA using their monotonic relations with the likelihood ratio (P^2) test statistic (see Browne and Cudeck, 1993; Maiti and Mukherjee, 1990; Steiger, 1989). Perhaps because proponents of the RMSEA index have emphasized (and provided early development of) confidence intervals for the measure, the 90% confidence interval is routinely provided for the RMSEA (Steiger, 1990; see also Section 11.16). This is very useful, because confidence intervals provide information about the precision of the point estimate, which also makes the index useful for model comparisons (see later discussion of such comparisons). Because guidelines for RMSEA have been conceptualized in terms of gradations of fit, the guidelines seem somewhat more consistent with the original intent of descriptive indices as reflections of amount of discrepancy. The availability of confidence intervals around the point estimate of RMSEA also allows the researcher to assess the likelihood of the model's achieving these various gradations of fit. This lies in contrast to many other measures for which a single cut-off value has been held as a marker of "good fit." Unfortunately, confidence intervals are not available for the incremental (comparative) fit indices, nor are they available for the RMR or SRMR. The lack of known distributional properties (and, in some cases, lack of scale of the measure) makes it difficult to calibrate the indices in terms of amount of fit (or lack of fit). Also, for many of the traditional measures, standards of "good fit" may be changing. For example, although values of .90 or higher have been held as indicative of good fit for the GFI, AGFI, TLI/ NNFI, NFI, and IFI, Hu and Bentler (1995, 1999) suggested that values of .95 or higher may be a more appropriate guideline for many of these indices. This does not mean that a fit index with a value of .96 represents a fine model and a value of .91 a rotten model. Yet, when using RMSEA or other indices for which confidence intervals are available, the researcher can compare the overlap in confidence intervals around the point estimates for each model. When using indices not associated with confidence intervals (and also when using those that are associated with confidence intervals), distinguishing between models must include an examination of the meaningfulness of the parameter estimates, given existing theory.

When evaluating models, it seems advisable to consider RMSEA because of its many desirable properties. It also seems sensible to consider SRMR because of its ability to detect misspecified models and the fact that it reflects a different conceptual approach than RMSEA to assessing absolute fit. If incremental fit indices are desired, TLI/NNFI or IFI are reasonable candidates for consideration. One final point to make is that, in addition to considering model fit indices, it is always a good idea to examine the residual matrix. The residual matrix can provide an additional view of model performance by indicating not only how well the model is doing, but also where its errors seem to occur. Moreover, although model fit indices and the residual matrix will usually tend to lead to similar conclusions about the performance of the model (i.e., when model fit indices are indicative of good fit, residuals will be small), in rare contexts this is not the case. Specifically, Browne, MacCallum, Kim, Andersen, and Glaser (2002) have shown that many model fit indices can sometimes be poor even when the residuals are very small. This can occur when unique variances are very small. The precise mathematical reasons for this mismatch are not central to the current discussion, but one should always consider the residual matrix in addition to the model fit indices. In the case discussed by Browne et al. (2002), this disjoint between traditional models of fit and the residuals was also borne out in discrepancies between the fit indices that are directly based on the residuals (e.g., RMR) and those that are based on more than the residuals (e.g., GFI, AGFI, RMSEA).

16.11.2 Parameter Estimates

A common error in the application of SEM occurs when models are evaluated solely on the basis of fit. Examining the parameter estimates is equally important. A model that fits well but produces theoretically implausible parameter estimates should always be treated with suspicion. For example, the existence of multiple boundary or cross-boundary estimates (e.g., negative values for estimates of variances) can undermine the interpretability of the model, regardless of the model's overall fit. Alternatively, one model might include parameter estimates that fit well with existing theory and research about a given construct, but an alternative model might provide one or more estimates that would be difficult to reconcile with existing data or theory. This might provide sufficient reason to prefer the former to the latter model, especially if the unexpected values of the parameter(s) have not been replicated. Thus, when evaluating models, researchers should always examine the parameter estimates of the model. When doing so, the researcher should consider whether these estimates are theoretically plausible and consistent with past data. Odd parameter estimates are often indicative of a misspecified model. It is also a good idea to examine standard errors of estimates. Extremely large standard errors can suggest a misspecified model. When possible, examining the stability of the parameter estimates across samples can also be informative. Unstable parameter estimates are a cause for concern.

16.11.2.1 Model Comparisons

Some methodologists have voiced a preference for comparisons between alternative models as a means to provide additional support to a researcher's preferred model (e.g., Browne and Cudeck, 1992). Even when the fit of two models is similar or identical, the parameter estimates for each alternative model can provide a basis for preferring one model over the other. Specifically, the estimates for one model may be more compatible with the theoretical implications of that model than the set of estimates for the other model. For example, imagine two competing mediational models. In research conducted under the rubric of the Elaboration Likelihood Model of persuasion (Petty and Cacioppo, 1986), when amount of elaboration is high, independent variables such as Argument Quality are hypothesized to influence the Thoughts that come to mind while receiving a persuasive message, which, in turn, influence the Attitudes that people report following the message (see Figure 16.5). Because thought measures are often taken after the message rather than during the message (so measures of attitudes and thoughts are contiguous in either a thought-attitude or attitude-thought order), researchers have sometimes questioned whether attitudes precede or follow thoughts in the causal progression (see Petty, Wegener, Fabrigar, Priester, and Cacioppo, 1993, for discussion). One could easily imagine a comparison of SEM parameters with the two hypothesized models (i.e., thoughts mediating argument quality effects on attitudes, and attitudes mediating argument quality effects on thoughts). If the argument quality-to-thoughts and thoughts-to-attitude parameters are strong and significant in the first model, this would support the hypothesized mediational pattern. When attitudes are modeled as the mediator, it could be that argument quality would have stronger effects on attitudes than in the first model (because effects of thoughts are no longer controlled), that the direct effect of argument quality on thoughts remains substantial, and that the influence of attitudes on thoughts is relatively weak (for example values, see Figure 16.5). Because this simple model is saturated in both cases, the overall fit of the model would be mathematically equivalent (see earlier discussion). Yet, the pattern of parameter estimates would be more supportive of the thought-as-mediator model than the attitude-as-mediator model (because the direct effect of argument quality on thoughts remains substantial, whether influences of attitudes on thoughts are controlled and because the influence of attitudes on thoughts in the second model was substantially weaker than the influence of thoughts on attitudes in the first model). Of course, parameter estimates on their own will not always provide a clear basis for preferring one model over another. Because sometimes they do, however, researchers should routinely examine parameter estimates when evaluating models.

In many cases, one alternative model is "nested" within the other. Nesting occurs when one model includes all of the free parameters of the other and adds one or more additional free parameters. This often occurs when alternative factor structures are compared in CFA and also occurs when paths are added to structural models. For example, when a direct (A –> C) path is added to a full mediation model (i.e., A –> B –> C) to model "partial mediation" (Baron and Kenny, 1986), the original model (i.e., A –> B –> C) is nested within the model that adds the direct path. Nested models are compared in a couple of primary ways. The most typical method is to subtract the value of the P^2 (likelihood ratio) for the model with the fewest degrees of freedom from the P^2 for the model with the most degrees of freedom. This P^2 difference is also distributed as a P^2 with degrees of freedom equal to the difference in degrees of freedom between the two models. If the P^2 difference significantly differs from 0, this shows that the addition of free parameters in the model resulted in a significant increase in fit. As with other P^2 tests, the P^2 difference is more likely to be significant when sample sizes are large (given the same drop in the discrepancy function associated with addition of a set of free parameters).

As one might notice from this discussion, almost all tests of parameter estimates could be cast as comparisons of nested models. That is, a significance test of a single free parameter (e.g., the direct path from IV to DV added to the full mediation model) could be obtained by conducting a P^2 difference test between two models—one in which the path is fixed at 0 (left out of the model) and one in which the path is left free to vary (included in the model). Similarly, if one free parameter is hypothesized to have a more positive value than another, one could use a P^2 difference test between two models—one in which the two parameters are constrained to be equal and one in which they are free to vary. If allowing the parameters to vary results in a significant increase in fit, the values of the two free parameters differ from one another. When focused only on a specific parameter (or specified set of specific parameters) one might argue that increases in sample size give one greater confidence that observed differences between parameter estimates do exist and are not due to chance. Thus, one might argue that the sample size dependency of the P^2 difference test does not pose as much of a problem for specific tests of parameter significance or of differences between parameter values as it does for assessments of overall model fit.

Another way to compare models (whether nested or not) is to compare fit indices for the two models when those fit indices are associated with confidence intervals (e.g., RMSEA, GFI, AGFI). This procedure does not take advantage of the nested nature of the models and does not provide a significance test of the difference between models. However, the confidence intervals around point estimates often provide reasonable grounds for preferring one model over another. For example, if the confidence intervals for the two values do not overlap, or do so very little, this would provide some basis for arguing that the model with the smaller RMSEA (or larger GFI or AGFI) value is, in fact, the superior model. The confidence intervals around the point estimate will be influenced by sample size, but, in the case of RMSEA, the point estimate itself is uninfluenced by sample size. Therefore, decision criteria comparing two models can be equitably applied across sample size settings. In many cases, one would want to look at both the P^2 difference test and the difference in

RMSEA values for the models under consideration in order to ensure that differences in fit observed using the P^2 difference test are not due primarily to sample size. When the most plausible models are not nested, RMSEA point estimates and confidence intervals form the best rationale for empirical model comparisons (with minimal overlap in confidence intervals providing reasonable grounds for preferring one model over the other; see Browne and Cudeck, 1989, 1992, for additional discussion).

16.12 Model Parsimony

Even if two models have similar fit, a researcher might prefer the more parsimonious of the two models. This might especially be true when fit is based on measures that ignore parsimony, such as the NFI. Even if fit indices are sensitive to model parsimony (such as RMSEA or TLI), however, a researcher might argue that additional parameters are only strongly justified if they substantially improve fit. Simpler theories are often to be preferred unless the more complex theory can substantially improve understanding of the phenomenon or can substantially broaden the types of phenomena understood using that theoretical approach.

16.13 Model Modification

The final possible step in an SEM analysis is to modify the model if needed and justified. In many situations, a researcher might find that the model does not provide a satisfactory representation of the data. This could be because the model does not fit the data well or because the parameter estimates do not support the theoretical position that was guiding the research. In such cases, a researcher will often consider possible modifications to the model in an attempt to improve fit or to test other possible theoretical accounts. This usually involves freeing parameters in the model that were previously fixed (although in some cases a researcher might fix a free parameter).

Many computer packages include indices (e.g., the modification index, Lagrange Multiplier test, or Wald test) that reflect the change in fit if certain parameters are added or deleted from the model (see MacCallum, Roznowski, and Necowitz, 1992). In practice, authors often acknowledge that model parameters have been added to or deleted from a theoretical model based on these empirical indices (see Breckler, 1990; MacCallum et al., 1992; for discussion). However, researchers should approach purely empirical model modifications with caution (MacCallum, 1986, 1995). Although modifications based on the data at hand seem intuitively reasonable, the approach does not seem to work well in practice. One problem is that the modification indices do not take into account the theoretical plausibility of freeing a parameter, so blindly following these indices can lead to freeing parameters where there is little theoretical justification to do so. A second problem is that modification indices tend to capitalize on chance fluctuations in the data, and thus, in isolation, do not provided reliable (or, often, valid) suggestions for model changes. For instance, MacCallum (1986) simulated 160 data sets of sample sizes 100 and 300 in which the model was missing one or more parameters (from the true model used to generate the data). Modification indices identified only the true model for 22 of the 160 samples (all with N = 300). In addition, of the 22 successful modifications, only four were guided purely by the largest modification index, regardless of its theoretical meaning (or lack thereof). Eighteen of the successful modifications occurred only when knowledge of the true model (not typical of real research) did not allow misspecifications to be introduced by blindly following the largest modification indices. Likewise, empirically guided model modifications often result in models with poor two-sample cross-validation indices (Cudeck and Browne, 1983) unless sample size is quite large (e.g., N = 800 and above; MacCallum et al., 1992). MacCallum and colleagues even questioned the utility of showing that a modified model has a better two-sample cross-validation index than the original model. Instead, they recommended that, if researchers feel compelled to modify models using data-driven modification indices, that they should conduct specification searches on two samples. This would allow the researchers to assess the consistency of the modification indices and goodness of fit across samples. If the same modifications are indicated by the data for the two samples, MacCallum et al. suggested that researchers obtain two two-sample cross-validation indices (one treating the original sample as the calibration sample and the second sample as the cross-validation sample, and a second swapping the status of the samples). If these indices provide consistent results, support for the modifications would be strong. MacCallum et al. believed, however, that consistent results of data-driven modifications would primarily occur when sample sizes are large and when model misspecifications are systematic and the model is poor.

Some methodologists have questioned whether it is appropriate to modify a model at all. If modifications are guided purely by the size of modification indices, we would agree with this conservative stance. However, most methodologists think it is reasonable to modify a model if it is done in a sensible way. Model modification inherently means moving from a purely confirmatory approach to a quasi-confirmatory (at least partly exploratory) approach. This should be acknowledged by the researcher. If a final model includes modifications, it seems most defensible to also report the original model, note how it was modified, and state the justifications for such modifications. Researchers should make changes only when there are sound conceptual justifications. As noted by MacCallum et al. (1992), this advice is often given (e.g., Bollen, 1989; Jöreskog and Sörbom, 1988; MacCallum, 1986), but seemingly often ignored (e.g., with inclusion of *wastebasket* parameters meant primarily to improve model fit without adding substantive understanding of the phenomenon, Browne, 1982). Researchers might profit from planning in advance to test the most substantively meaningful alternatives (Cudeck and Browne, 1983; MacCallum et al., 1992). When model modifications are made, researchers should replicate or cross validate changes in the original model to ensure that improvements in fit are not a result of idiosyncratic characteristics of a particular data set. If they cannot do so, the researchers should at least acknowledge the instability of data-driven modifications.

16.14 LISREL Example of Model Evaluation

To help illustrate the process of model evaluation, it is useful to return to the Sidanius (1988) example used to illustrate model specification. The numerous fit statistics reported using the SIMPLIS syntax in LISREL appear in Table 16.7. Notable, given our earlier discussion, is that the likelihood ratio (shown as Minimum Fit Function Chi-Square) is relatively

TABLE 16.7

LISREL/SIMPLIS Goodness of Fit Statistics for Sidanius (1988)

Goodness of Fit Statistics

Degrees of Freedom = 60
Minimum Fit Function Chi-Square = 74.54 (P = 0.098)
Normal Theory Weighted Least Squares Chi-Square = 72.16 (P = 0.14)
Estimated Non-centrality Parameter (NCP) = 12.16
90 Percent Confidence Interval for NCP = (0.0 ; 37.70)

Minimum Fit Function Value = 0.45
Population Discrepancy Function Value (F0) = 0.073
90 Percent Confidence Interval for F0 = (0.0 ; 0.23)
Root Mean Square Error of Approximation (RMSEA) = 0.035
90 Percent Confidence Interval for RMSEA = (0.0 ; 0.061)
P-Value for Test of Close Fit (RMSEA < 0.05) = 0.80

Expected Cross-Validation Index (ECVI) = 0.80
90 Percent Confidence Interval for ECVI = (0.73 ; 0.96)
ECVI for Saturated Model = 1.09
ECVI for Independence Model = 2.29

Chi-Square for Independence Model with 78 Degrees of Freedom = 356.60
Independence AIC = 382.60
Model AIC = 134.16
Saturated AIC = 182.00
Independence CAIC = 436.21
Model CAIC = 262.00
Saturated CAIC = 557.28

Normed Fit Index (NFI) = 0.79
Non-Normed Fit Index (NNFI) = 0.93
Parsimony Normed Fit Index (PNFI) = 0.61
Comparative Fit Index (CFI) = 0.95
Incremental Fit Index (IFI) = 0.95
Relative Fit Index (RFI) = 0.73

Critical N (CN) = 199.02

Root Mean Square Residual (RMR) = 0.061
Standardized RMR = 0.061
Goodness of Fit Index (GFI) = 0.94
Adjusted Goodness of Fit Index (AGFI) = 0.91
Parsimony Goodness of Fit Index (PGFI) = 0.62

small and nonsignificant (p >.05). The RMSEA value shows good fit (RMSEA = .035), with almost all of the 90% confidence interval falling below a value of .05 (90%CI = 0.0; 0.061). The SRMR also shows good fit (SRMR = .061), as do the incremental fit indices we emphasized earlier, with the TLI/NNFI = .93 and the IFI = .95. There was no consistent pattern for the location of the largest residuals (the presence of which might suggest the presence of structural relations where none had been hypothesized). Most residuals were reasonably small, and the largest of the residuals were often for individual measured variables relating to another measured variable, when other indicators of the same latent construct showed small or directionally opposite residuals related to the same other variable.

TABLE 16.8

LISREL Parameter Estimates for Sidanius (1988)

Completely Standardized Solution

LAMBDA-Y

	MEDIA	SOPHIST	CONFID	DEVIANCE	RACISM
MEDIA	1.00	—	—	—	—
SOPH1	—	0.38	—	—	—
SOPH2	—	0.26	—	—	—
SOPH3	—	0.39	—	—	
CONF1	—	—	0.81	—	—
CONF2	—	—	0.52	—	—
DEV1	—	—	—	0.49	—
DEV2	—	—	—	0.57	—
DEV3	—	—	—	0.44	—
DEV4	—	—	—	0.34	—
RACE	—	—	—	—	1.00

LAMBDA-X

	COGORIEN
COG1	0.84
COG2	0.76

BETA

	MEDIA	SOPHIST	CONFID	DEVIANCE	RACISM
MEDIA	—	—	—	—	—
SOPHIST	0.25	—	—	—	—
CONFID	—	0.29	—	—	—
DEVIANCE	—	0.71	0.32	—	—
RACISM	—	—	−0.22	—	—

GAMMA

	COGORIEN
MEDIA	0.55
SOPHIST	0.45
CONFID	—
DEVIANCE	—
RACISM	—

The standardized parameter estimates of most substantive interest for the measurement and structural portions of the model are found in Tables 16.8 and 16.9, respectively. The standardized output comes from the LISREL output option available using the SIMPLIS language, and thus is presented in matrix form. Recall that unstandardized parameter

TABLE 16.9

EQS Fit Statistics for Sidanius (1988)

GOODNESS OF FIT SUMMARY FOR METHOD = ML

INDEPENDENCE MODEL CHI-SQUARE = 356.596 ON 80 DEGREES OF FREEDOM

INDEPENDENCE AIC = 196.596	INDEPENDENCE CAIC = –133.321
MODEL AIC = –45.375	MODEL CAIC = –292.813

CHI-SQUARE = 74.625 BASED ON 60 DEGREES OF FREEDOM
PROBABILITY VALUE FOR THE CHI-SQUARE STATISTIC IS .09688

THE NORMAL THEORY RLS CHI-SQUARE FOR THIS ML SOLUTION IS 72.165.

FIT INDICES
- - - - - - - - - - -

BENTLER-BONETT NORMED FIT INDEX	= .791
BENTLER-BONETT NON-NORMED FIT INDEX	= .930
COMPARATIVE FIT INDEX (CFI)	= .947
BOLLEN'S (IFI) FIT INDEX	= .951
MCDONALD'S (MFI) FIT INDEX	= .957
JORESKOG-SORBOM'S GFI FIT INDEX	= .938
JORESKOG-SORBOM'S AGFI FIT INDEX	= .905
ROOT MEAN-SQUARE RESIDUAL (RMR)	= .061
STANDARDIZED RMR	= .061
ROOT MEAN-SQUARE ERROR OF APPROXIMATION (RMSEA)	= .038
90% CONFIDENCE INTERVAL OF RMSEA	(.000, .064)

estimates, standard errors, and t-values are presented in equation form using the SIMPLIS output or in matrix form using the LISREL output. When the matrix format is used, the effects are of column variables on row variables. In Tables 16.8 and 16.9, all of the hypothesized paths are significant or nearly so (t values >1.74). The slight discrepancies between the obtained values and the significance tests reported by Sidanius (1988) might be attributable to rounding error or to our use of the published correlation matrix, rather than the original correlation or covariance matrix.

LISREL also provides other potentially helpful information (using either SIMPLIS or LISREL language) such as parameter estimates for the errors in variables (TD and TE) and the errors in equations (PS). LISREL and SIMPLIS output also reports squared multiple correlations for the measured variables (i.e., the proportion of variance in each measured variable accounted for by the latent variables) and the structural equations (i.e., the proportion of variance in endogenous latent variables accounted for by other variables in the model). For instance, in the present example, 74% of the variance in the deviance latent variable was accounted for, but only 5% of the variance in the racism variable.

16.15 EQS Example of Model Evaluation

The fit indices output by EQS include many of the same indices provided by LISREL (see Table 16.9). The obtained results appear to be the same, at least within rounding error of the LISREL results. The format of the parameter estimate output is similar in EQS to that of

TABLE 16.10

EQS Parameter Estimates for Sidanius (1988)

MAXIMUM LIKELIHOOD SOLUTION
(NORMAL DISTRIBUTION THEORY)

STANDARDIZED SOLUTION:		R-SQUARED
MEDIA = V1 = 1.000 F1 + .000 E1		1.000
SOPH1 = V2 = .377 F2 + .926 E2		.142
SOPH2 = V3 = .263*F2 + .965 E3		.069
SOPH3 = V4 = .390*F2 + .921 E4		.152
CONF1 = V5 = .809 F3 + .588 E5		.654
CONF2 = V6 = .518*F3 + .856 E6		.268
DEV1 = V7 = .487 F4 + .874 E7		.237
DEV2 = V8 = .570*F4 + .822 E8		.325
DEV3 = V9 = .441*F4 + .897 E9		.195
DEV4 = V10 = .344*F4 + .939 E10		.119
RACE = V11 = 1.000 F5 + .000 E11		1.000
COG1 = V12 = .836 F6 + .549 E12		.699
COG2 = V13 = .762*F6 + .647 E13		.581
F1 = F1 = .547*F6 + .837 D1		.299
F2 = F2 = .248*F1 + .445*F6 + .787 D2		.380
F3 = F3 = .289*F2 + .957 D3		.084
F4 = F4 = .712*F2 + .315*F3 + .514 D4		.735
F5 = F5 = −.221*F3 + .975 D5		.049

the SIMPLIS version of LISREL (see Table 16.10). The series of equations used to set up the model in EQS is produced with numeric parameter estimate values taking the place of the asterisks that represented free parameters in those equations (see Table 16.10).

As noted in Section 11.19, EQS uses the Lagrange Multiplier (LM) for the same purpose as LISREL's modification indices. Like the modification index, the LMs each represent the extent to which the model P^2 would decrease if the parameter were added to the model. The Wald test notes the extent to which the model P^2 would increase if the parameter were deleted from the model. In LISREL, consideration of path deletion would likely be based on observation of nonsignificant path parameters in the original solution.

16.16 Comparisons with Alternative Models in Model Evaluation

Sidanius (1988) compared the obtained solution with that for two alternative models. One alternative simply added a direct path from cognitive orientation to political deviance. Because the original model is nested within the alternative, a P^2 difference test was used and shown to produce a nonsignificant benefit of adding the cognitive orientation ÷ political deviance path, $P^2(1) = .06$. We could add that the RMSEA for the alternative model was .036. Adding the nonsignificant path decreased the fit very slightly when using the RMSEA index, though the 90% Confidence Interval still mostly corresponded to good fit by the model (90%CI = 0.0; .063). Though the overall fit provides little reason to prefer one model over the other (aside from the relative parsimony of the original model), the lack of significance of the path added in the alternative model suggests that the alternative model is no better than the original.

A more radical alternative model was also considered by Sidanius (1988). In this model, political deviance was hypothesized to be an exogenous variable predicting cognitive orientation and media usage. Cognitive orientation was still hypothesized to influence media usage, and both cognitive orientation and media usage were still hypothesized to predict political sophistication, which, in turn, predicted self confidence. Self confidence was still hypothesized to predict racism. The fit indices for this model presented a bit less clear picture than for the primary model. The P^2 value was a little higher than for the primary model [$P^2(60) = 94.71$, p<.003]. The RMSEA (= .054; 90%CI = .028, .077) and SRMR (= .075) both showed reasonably good fit, but the TLI/NNFI (= .84) and IFI (= .88) were somewhat lower than preferred. As one would expect given the fit indices, the standardized residuals also tended to be larger for this model compared with the first two models. Some large residuals corresponded with paths that had been in the previous models. For example, large residuals appeared for the relation between one measure of self confidence and three of the deviance measures (along with moderate residuals for the other self confidence item with the same three deviance items). This made sense given the significant influence of the self confidence latent variable on the deviance latent variable in the previous models. In addition, the solution produced nonsignificant parameter estimates for the impact of political deviance on media usage and for the impact of media usage on political sophistication. Sidanius (1988) took the lack of impact of political deviance on media usage as undermining this deviance-guides-use-of-media alternative. Thus, Sidanius' rejection of this second alternative model was based more on parameter estimates not fitting the theory than on the somewhat less acceptable fit of the overall model.

Though Sidanius (1988) noted that many additional alternative models might be considered, he did not note that many alternative models could have identical fit to the original model. Using the special cases of the replacement rule discussed earlier, MacCallum et al. (1993) generated 51 additional models that were mathematically equivalent to the original Sidanius (1988) model. At first, this may seem to be a surprisingly large number. However, one starts to see how this is possible when one considers that various portions of the model can each become saturated preceding blocks in which any of the paths can change direction or can become covariances (if between exogenous variables). For example, as can be seen by referring back to the original model depicted in Figure 16.5, the block of Cognitive Orientation, Political Sophistication, and Print Media form a saturated preceding block in that relations exist among all variables making up the block and none of the variables receives directional arrows from variables outside the block. Therefore, the relations among latent variables in this block can be changed to other types of relations without altering the fit of the model. For example, one equivalent model would suggest that high levels of political sophistication lead to greater use of print media rather than being created by media use. When this is specified, levels of political sophistication and cognitive orientation could simply be correlated, rather than cognitive orientation influencing political sophistication, or political sophistication could influence cognitive orientation, instead of the other way around (as in the original model). Figure 16.6 presents the paths for nine equivalent models considering changes only in the block of cognitive orientation, political sophistication, and print media.

As noted earlier, sometimes changes in a model permitted by the replacement rule can create new saturated preceding blocks in a model that permit further changes. The Sidanius (1988) model presents just such a case. When the original model (Panel A of Figure 16.7) is changed to make political sophistication influence cognitive orientation and print media, this makes the block of political sophistication, political deviance, and self confidence into another saturated preceding block (i.e., this saturated block no longer receives directional

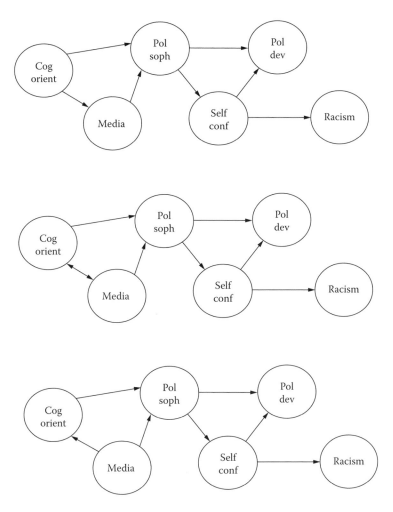

FIGURE 16.6
Example equivalent models for Sidanius (1988) generated using a saturated preceding block.

arrows from outside the block, see Panel B of Figure 16.7). And when self confidence is modeled as influencing both political sophistication and political deviance, then the self confidence-racism block is a saturated preceding block (because it too no longer receives arrows from outside the block, see Panel C of Figure 16.7). Thus, the present example illustrates how the number of equivalent models can rise quickly when changes in one part of the model are multiplied by changes that can be made simultaneously in other parts of the model.

Finally, it is important to note that saturated blocks are not the only places in which the nature of relations between latent variables can be changed without changing the fit of the model. As noted previously, the replacement rule also specifies that a directional path can be replaced by a path in the opposite direction (or by a covariance between latent variable residuals) when a block satisfies the criteria for a symmetric focal block (i.e., influences on the two variables are the same). Thus, in the Sidanius (1988) example, the direction of the path between cognitive orientation and print media usage can also be reversed (again multiplying the number of distinct alternative models created by changes within the political

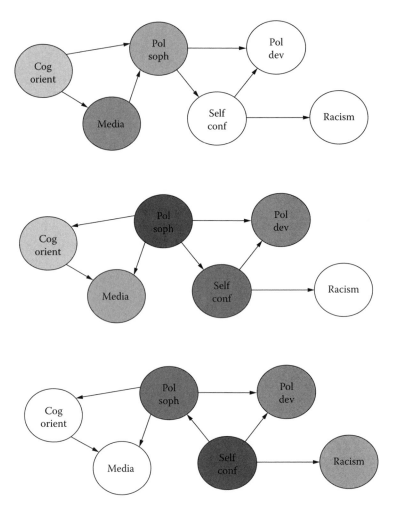

FIGURE 16.7
Example of new saturated preceding blocks for Sidanius (1988).

sophistication-political deviance-self confidence saturated preceding block). MacCallum et al. (1993) describe a number of alternatives for the Sidanius model that use this special case of the replacement rule.

For example, in one alternative model discussed by MacCallum et al., five of the seven structural paths are reversed in direction (see Figure 16.8 for the standardized parameter estimates for the structural paths and compare with the parameter estimates listed in Tables 16.8 and 16.10). Because a number of the changes to the original model seem consistent with past research and theory, this makes it difficult to support one version of the model over another (recall that the fit to the data is equal across versions). Whenever one considers mathematically equivalent (or nearly equivalent) models, the only bases for preferring one model over the other are the fit of the paths and parameter estimates to existing theory and any design features that make certain alternative models implausible (see MacCallum et al., 1993, for additional discussion). Therefore, it should come as no surprise that fit with theory is often a primary consideration that should be explicitly addressed when evaluating a hypothesized model in comparison with alternative models (see also Bollen, 1989; Section 11.17).

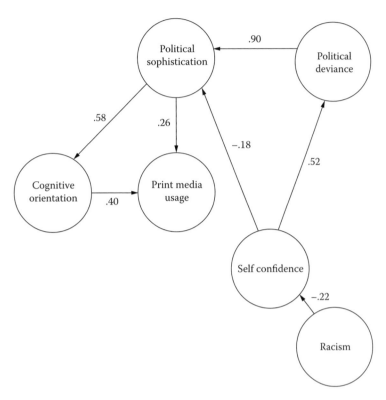

FIGURE 16.8
Equivalent model reversing five of seven paths from the original Sidanius (1988) model.

16.17 Summary

SEM is without question a very valuable analytic tool. Nonetheless, this method has its limitations. One challenge is that, because the method is relatively complex, it is often subject to misuse. Therefore, it is especially important that those using this approach not only know how to generate SEM analyses, but also understand the logic underlying this method. The chapter has provided only an introduction to the basics of this methodology. For more extensive treatments, the reader is directed to Bollen (1989), Hoyle (1995), and Maruyama (1998).

One relatively common misunderstanding related to SEM concerns the issue of causality. Some researchers and methodologists have made rather strong claims regarding the ability of SEM to confer a basis for reaching causal inferences. However, these claims have been overly optimistic. The ability to reach causal inferences is more a function of design features of the study than it is the type of statistical analysis (see also MacCallum et al., 1993; Wegener and Fabrigar, 2000). Although SEM has some advantages over more traditional statistical methods for establishing the conditions necessary to infer causality (see Bollen, 1989), SEM cannot compensate for the central role of design features in causal inference. Thus, when designing a study in which SEM is to be used, a researcher should consider design features that will confer a stronger basis for causal inferences (e.g., longitudinal designs, experimental manipulations of key variables, see Reis and Judd, 2000, for additional discussion).

Despite these limitations, SEM provides researchers with an extremely useful technique. Among the primary strengths of SEM are the ability to account for random and systematic measurement error, flexibility in dealing with many different types of hypotheses, and ability to simultaneously assess relations among many variables. These advantages should not be underestimated. Indeed, SEM has been called, with some justification, one of the most important advances in statistical methodology for the social sciences in the past 30 years (Bentler, 1980; Coovert, Penner, and MacCallum, 1990).

References

Abramson, J. (2004). *Overdosed America: The broken promise of American medicine*. New York: Harper Collins.

Agresti, A. (1984). *Analysis of ordinal categorical data*. New York: Wiley.

Agresti, A. (1990). *Categorical data analysis*. New York: Wiley.

Akaike, H. (1987). Factor analysis and the AIC. *Psychometrika, 52*, 317–332.

Ambrose, A. (1985). The development and experimental application of programmed materials for teaching clarinet performance skills in college woodwind techniques courses. Unpublished doctoral dissertation, University of Cincinnati, OH.

Amlung, S. R. (1996). A secondary data analysis of the Health Belief Model using structural equation modeling. Unpublished doctoral dissertation, University of Cincinnati, OH.

Anderson, D. A., & Carney, E. S. (1974). Ridge regression estimation procedures applied to canonical correlation analysis. Unpublished manuscript, Cornell University, Ithaca, NY.

Anderson, J. C., & Gerbing, D. W. (1984). The effect of sampling error on convergence, improper solutions, and goodness-of-fit indices for maximum likelihood confirmatory factor analysis. *Psychometrika, 49*, 155–173.

Anderson, N. H. (1963). Comparison of different populations: Resistance to extinction and transfer. *Psychological Bulletin, 70*, 162–179.

Anderson, T. W. (1958). *An introduction to multivariate statistical analysis*. New York: Wiley.

Anscombe, V. (1973). Graphs in statistical analysis. *American Statistician, 27*, 13–21.

Arbuckle, J. & Wothke, W. (1999). *AMOS 4.0 User's Guide*, Chicago, IL: SPSS Inc.

Arnold, C. L. (1992). An introduction to hierarchical linear models. *Measurement and evaluation in counseling and development, 25*, 58–90.

Bandalos, D. L. (1993). Factors influencing the cross-validation of confirmatory factor analysis models. *Multivariate Behavioral Research, 28*, 351–374.

Barcikowski, R. S. (1981). Statistical power with group mean as the unit of analysis. *Journal of Educational Statistics, 6*, 267–285.

Barcikowski, R. S. (1983). *Computer packages and research design, Vol. 3: SPSS and SPSSX*. Washington, DC: University Press of America.

Barcikowski, R. S., & Robey, R. R. (1984). Decisions in a single group repeated measures analysis: Statistical tests and three computer packages. *The American Statistician, 38*, 248–250.

Barcikowski, R., & Stevens, J. P. (1975). A Monte Carlo study of the stability of canonical correlations, canonical weights and canonical variate-variable correlations. *Multivariate Behavioral Research, 10*, 353–364.

Barnett, V., & Lewis, T. (1978). *Outliers in statistical data*. New York: Wiley.

Baron, R. M., & Kenny, D. A. (1986). The moderator-mediator distinction in social psychological research: Conceptual, strategic, and statistical considerations. *Journal of Personality and Social Psychology, 51*, 1173–1182.

Becker, B. (1987). Applying tests of combined significance in meta analysis. *Psychological Bulletin, 102*, 164–171.

Belsley, D. A., Kuh, E., & Welsch, R. (1980). *Regression diagnostics: Identifying influential data and sources of collinearity*. New York: Wiley.

Benedetti, J. K., & Brown, M. B. (1978). Strategies for the selection of log linear models. *Biometrics, 34*, 680–686.

Benson, J., & Bandalos, D. L. (1992). Second-order confirmatory factor analysts of the Reactions to Tests scale with cross-validation. *Multivariate Behavioral Research, 27*, 459–487.

Bentler, P. M. (1989). *EQS Structural equations program manual*. Los Angeles: BMDP Statistical Software.

Bentler, P. M. (1992a). *EQS: Structural equations program manual*. Los Angeles: BMDP Statistical Software.

Bentler, P. M., & Bonett, D. G. (1980). Significance tests and goodness of fit in the analysis of covariance structures. *Psychological Bulletin, 88,* 588–606.

Bentler, P. M., & Weeks, D. G. (1980). Linear structural equations with latent variables. *Psychometrika, 45,* 289–308.

Benton, S., Kraft, R., Groover, J., & Plake, B. (1984). Cognitive capacity differences among writers. *Journal of Educational Psychology, 76,* 820–834.

Bielby, W. T. (1986). Arbitrary metrics in multiple-indicator models of latent variables. *Sociological Methods and Research, 15,* 3–23.

Bird, K. D. (1975). Simultaneous contrast testing procedures for multivariate experiments. *Multivariate Behavior Research, 10,* 343–351.

Bishop, Y., Fienberg, S., & Holland, P. (1975). *Discrete multivariate analysis: Theory and practice.* Cambridge, MA: MIT Press.

Block, J. (1995). A contrarian view of the five-factor model approach to personality description. *Psychological Bulletin, 187–215.*

Bock, R. D. (1975). *Multivariate statistical methods in behavioral research.* New York: McGraw-Hill.

Bock, R. D., & Haggard, E. (1968). The use of multivariate analysis of variance in behavioral research. In D. K. Whitla (Ed.), *Handbook of measurement and assessment in behavioral sciences.* Reading, MA: Addison Wesley.

Boik, R. J. (1981). A priori tests in repeated measures design: Effects of nonsphericity. *Psychometrika, 46,* 241–255.

Bollen, K. A. (1989). *Structural equations with latent variables.* New York: Wiley.

Bollen, K. A., & Lennox, R. (1991). Conventional wisdom on measurement: A structural equation perspective. *Psychological Bulletin, 110,* 305–314.

Bollen, K. A., & Long, J. S. (1993). *Testing structural equation models.* Newbury Park, CA: Sage.

Bolton, B. (1971). A factor analytical study of communication skills and nonverbal abilities of deaf rehabilitation clients. *Multivariate Behavioral Research, 6,* 485–501.

Bonnett, D., & Bentler, P. (1983). Goodness of fit procedures for the evaluation and selection of log linear models. *Psychological Bulletin, 93,* 149–166.

Boomsma, A. (1982). The robustness of LISREL against small sample sizes in factor analysis models. In K. G. Jöreskog & H. Wold (Eds.), *Systems under indirect observation: Causality, structure, prediction* (pp. 149–173). Amsterdam: North-Holland.

Box, G. E. P. (1949). A general distribution theory for a class of likelihood criteria. *Biometrika, 36,* 317–346.

Box, G. E. P. (1954). Some theorems on quadratic forms applied in the study of analysis of variance problems: II. Effect of inequality of variance and of correlation between errors in the two-way classification. *Annals of Mathematical Statistics, 25,* 484–498.

Bradley, R., Caldwell, B., & Elardo, R. (1977). Home environment, social status and mental test performance. *Journal of Educational Psychology, 69,* 697–701.

Breckler, S. J. (1990). Applications of covariance structure modeling in psychology: Cause for concern? *Psychological Bulletin, 107,* 260–273.

Brown, M. B. (1976). Screening effects in multidimensional contingency tables. *Applied Statistics, 25,* 37–46.

Browne, M. W. (1968). A comparison of factor analytic techniques. *Psychometrika, 33,* 267–334.

Browne, M. W. (1982). Covariance structures. In D. M. Hawkins (Ed.), *Topics in multivariate analysis* (pp. 72–141). Cambridge, UK: Cambridge University Press.

Browne, M. W. (1984). Asymptotic distribution free methods in the analysis of covariance structures. *British Journal of Mathematical and Statistical Psychology, 37,* 62–83.

Browne, M. W. (1984). The decomposition of multitrait-multimethod matrices. *British Journal of Mathematical and Statistical Psychology, 37,* 1–21.

Browne, M. W. (1989). Relationships between an additive model and a multiplicative model for multitrait-multimethod matrices. In R. Coppi & S. Bolasco (Eds.), *Multiway data analysis* (pp. 507–520). North-Holland: Elsevier Science Publishers.

Browne, M. W., & Cudeck, R. (1989). Single sample cross-validation indices for covariance structures. *Multivariate Behavioral Research, 24,* 445–455.

Browne, M. W., & Cudeck, R. (1992). Alternative ways of assessing model fit. *Sociological Methods and Research, 21,* 230–258.

Browne, M. W., MacCallum, R. C., Kim, C., Andersen, B. L., & Glaser, R. (2002). When fit indices and residuals are incompatible. *Psychological Methods, 7,* 403–421.

Bryant, J. L., & Paulson, A. S. (1976). An extension of Tukey's method of multiple comparisons to experimental design with random concomitant variables. *Biometrika,* 631–638.

Bryk, A. S. (1992) Hierarchical linear models: Applications and data analysis methods (1st edition). Thousand Oaks, CA: Sage.

Bryk, A. D., & Weisberg, H. I. (1977). Use of the nonequivalent control group design when subjects are growing. *Psychological Bulletin, 85,* 950–962.

Burstein, L. (1980). The analysis of multilevel data in educational research and evaluation. *Review of Research in Education, 8,* 158–233.

Byrne, B. M. (1994). *Structural equation modeling with EQS and EQS/Windows: Basic concepts, applications, and programming.* Newbury Park, CA: Sage.

Carlson, J. E., & Timm, N. H. (1974). Analysis of non-orthogonal fixed effect designs. *Psychological Bulletin, 8,* 563–570.

Cattell, R. B. (1966). The meaning and strategic use of factor analysis. In R. B. Cattell (Ed.), *Handbook of multivariate experimental psychology* (pp. 174–243). Chicago: Rand McNally.

Cattell, R. B., & Jaspers, J. A. (1967). A general plasmode for factor analytic exercises and research. *Multivariate Behavior Research Monographs, 3,* 1–212.

Christensen, W., & Rencher, A. (1995). A comparison of Type I error rates and power levels for seven solutions to the multivariate Behrens-Fisher problem. Paper presented at the meeting of the American Statistical Association, Orlando, FL.

Chou, C., Bentler, P. M., & Satorra, A. (1991). Scaled test statistics and robust standard errors for non-normal data in covariance structure analysis: A Monte Carlo study. *British Journal of Mathematical and Statistical Psychology, 44,* 347–357.

Church, A., & Burke, P. (1994). Exploratory and confirmatory tests of the Big Five and Tellegen's three- and four-dimensional models. *Journal of Personality and Social Psychology, 66,* 93–114.

Cliff, N. (1983). Some cautions concerning the application of causal modeling methods. *Multivariate Behavioral Research, 18,* 115–126.

Cliff, N. (1987). *Analyzing multivariate data.* New York: Harcourt, Brace Jovanovich.

Cliff, N., & Hamburger, C. D. (1967). The study of sampling errors in factor analysis by means of artificial experiments. *Psychological Bulletin, 68,* 430–445.

Cliff, N., & Krus, D. J. (1976). Interpretation of canonical analysis: Rotated vs. unrotated solutions. *Psychometrika, 41,* 35–42.

Clifford, M. M. (1972). Effects of competition as a motivational technique in the classroom. *American Educational Research Journal, 9,* 123–134.

Cochran, W. G. (1957). Analysis of covariance: Its nature and uses. *Biometrics, 13,* 261–281.

Cohen, J. (1968). Multiple regression as a general data-analytic system. *Psychological Bulletin, 70,* 426–443.

Cohen, J. (1977). *Statistical power analysis for the behavioral sciences.* New York: Academic Press.

Cohen, J. (1990). Things I have learned (so far). *American Psychologist, 45,* 1304–1312.

Cohen, J., & Cohen, P. (1975). *Applied multiple regression/correlation analysis for the behavioral sciences.* Hillsdale, NJ: Lawrence Erlbaum.

Cohen, J., & Cohen, P. (1983). *Applied multiple regression/correlation analysis for the behavioral sciences.* Hillsdale, NJ: Lawrence Erlbaum.

Collier, R. O., Baker, F. B., Mandeville, C. K., & Hayes, T. F. (1967). Estimates of test size for several test procedures on conventional variance ratios in the repeated measures design. *Psychometrika, 32,* 339–353.

Conover, W. J., Johnson, M. E., & Johnson, M. M. (1981). Composite study of tests for homogeneity of variances with applications to the outer continental shelf bidding data. *Technometrics, 23,* 351–361.

Cook, R. D. (1977). Detection of influential observations in linear regression. *Technometrics, 19,* 15–18.

Cook, R. D., & Weisberg, S. (1982). *Residuals and influence in regression.* New York: Chapman & Hall.

Cooley, W. W., & Lohnes, P. R. (1971). *Multivariate data analysis.* New York: Wiley.

Coombs, W., Algina, J., & Oltman, D. (1996). Univariate and multivariate omnibus hypothesis tests selected to control Type I error rates when population variances are not necessarily equal. *Review of Educational Research, 66,* 137–179.

Coovert, M. D., Penner, L. A., & MacCallum, R. C. (1990). Covariance structure modeling in personality and social psychological research: An introduction. In C. Hendrick & M. S. Clark (Eds.), *Research methods in personality and social psychology* (pp. 185–216). Newbury Park, CA: Sage.

Cramer, E., & Nicewander, W. A. (1979). Some symmetric, invariant measures of multivariate association. *Psychometrika, 44,* 43–54.

Crocker, L., & Benson, J. (1976). Achievement, guessing and risk-taking behavior under norm referenced and criterion referenced testing conditions. *American Educational Research Journal, 13,* 207–215.

Cronbach, L. J. (1975). Beyond the two disciplines of scientific psychology. *The American Psychologist, 30,* 116–127.

Cronbach, L. & Snow, R. (1977). *Aptitudes and instructional methods: A handbook for research on interactions.* New York: Irvington Publishers.

Crowder, R. (1975). An investigation of the relationship between social I.Q. and vocational evaluation ratings with an adult trainable mental retardate work activity center population. Unpublished doctoral dissertation, University of Cincinnati, OH.

Crystal, G. (1988). The wacky, wacky world of CEO pay. *Fortune, 117,* 68–78.

Cudeck, R. (1989). Analysis of correlation matrices using covariance structure models. *Psychological Bulletin, 105,* 317–327.

Cudeck, R., & Browne, M. W. (1983). Cross-validation of covariance structures. *Multivariate Behavioral Research, 18,*147–167.

Curran, P. J., West, S. G., & Finch, J. F. (1996). The robustness of test statistics to nonnormality and specification error in confirmatory factor analysis. *Psychological Methods, 1,* 16–29.

Dalal, S. R., Fowlkes, E. B., & Hoadley, B. (1989). Risk analysis of the space shuttle: Pre-Challenger prediction of failure, *Journal of American Statistical Association, 74,* 945–957.

Daniels, R. L., & Stevens, J. P. (1976). The interaction between the internal-external locus of control and two methods of college instruction. *American Educational Research Journal, 13,* 103–113.

Darlington, R. B., Weinberg, S., & Walberg, H. (1973). Canonical variate analysis and related techniques. *Review of Educational Research, 43,* 433–454.

Davidson, M. L. (1972). Univariate versus multivariate tests in repeated measures experiments. *Psychological Bulletin, 77,* 446–452.

Draper, N. R., & Smith, H. (1981). *Applied regression analysis.* New York: Wiley.

Dizney, H., & Gromen, L. (1967). Predictive validity and differential achievement on three MLA Comparative Foreign Language tests. *Educational and Psychological Measurement, 27,* 1127–1130.

Dunnett, C. W. (1980). Pairwise multiple comparisons in the homogeneous variance, unequal sample size cases. *Journal of the American Statistical Association, 75,* 789–795.

Edwards, D. S. (1984). Analysis of faculty perceptions of deans' leadership behavior and organizational climate in baccalaureate schools of nursing. Unpublished doctoral dissertation, University of Cincinnati, OH.

Efron, B. (1979). Bootstrap methods: Another look at the jackknife. *The Annals of Statistics, 7* (1): 1–26.

Elashoff, J. D. (1969). Analysis of covariance: A delicate instrument. *American Educational Research Journal, 6,* 383–401.

Elashoff, J. D. (1981). Data for the panel session in software for repeated measures analysis of variance. Proceedings of the Statistical Computing Section of the American Statistical Association.

Everitt, B. S. (1979). A Monte Carlo investigation of the robustness of Hotelling's one and two sample T2 tests. *Journal of the American Statistical Association, 74,* 48–51.

Fabrigar, L. R., Wegener, D. T., MacCallum, R. C., & Strahan, E. J. (1999). Evaluating the use of factor analysis in psychological research. *Psychological Methods, 4,* 272–299.

Feshbach, S., Adelman, H., & Williamson, F. (1977). Prediction of reading and related academic problems. *Journal of Educational Psychology, 69,* 299–308.

Fienberg, S. (1980). *The analysis of cross classified categorical data.* Cambridge, MA: MIT Press.

Finn, J. (1974). *A general model for multivariate analysis.* New York: Holt, Rinehart & Winston.

Finn, J. (1978). *Multivariance: Univariate and multivariate analysis of variance, covariance and regression.* Chicago: National Educational Resources.

Fisher, R. A. (1936). The use of multiple measurement in taxonomic problems. *Annals of Eugenics, 7,* 179–188.

Frane, J. (1976). Some simple procedures for handling missing data in multivariate analysis. *Psychometrika, 41,* 409–415.

Freeman, D. (1987). *Applied categorical data analysis.* New York: Marcel Dekker.

Friedman, G., Lehrer, B., & Stevens, J. (1983). The effectiveness of self directed and lecture/discussion stress management approaches and the locus of control of teachers. *American Educational Research Journal, 20,* 563–580.

Gerbing, D. W., & Anderson, J. C. (1985). The effects of sampling error and model characteristics on parameter estimation for maximum likelihood confirmatory factor analysis. *Multivariate Behavioral Research, 20,* 255–271.

Glass, G. C., & Hopkins, K. (1984). *Statistical methods in education and psychology.* Englewood Cliffs, NJ: Prentice-Hall.

Glass, G. & Stanley, J. (1970). *Statistical methods in education and psychology.* Englewood Cliffs, NJ: Prentice-Hall.

Glass, G., Peckham, P., & Sanders, J. (1972). Consequences of failure to meet assumptions underlying the fixed effects analysis of variance and covariance. *Review of Educational Research, 42,* 237–288.

Glassnapp, D., & Poggio, J. (1985). *Essentials of statistical analysis for the behavioral sciences.* Columbus, OH: Charles Merrill.

Gnanadesikan, R. (1977), *Methods for statistical analysis of multivariate observations.* New York: Wiley.

Goldberg, L. (1990). An alternative "description of personality": Big Five factor structure. *Journal of Personality and Social Psychology, 59,* 1216–1229.

Golding, S., & Seidman, E. (1974). Analysis of multitrait-multimethod matrices: A two step principal components procedure. *Multivariate Behavioral Research 9,* 479–496.

Goldstein, H., Rasbash, J., Plewis, I., Draper, D., Browne, W., Yang, M., et al. (1998). *A user's guide to MLwiN.* Multilevel Models Project, University of London.

Goodman, L. (1970). The analysis of multidimensional contingency tables: Stepwise procedures and direct estimation methods for building models for multiple classifications. *Technometrics, 13,* 33–61.

Green, S. (1990). Power analysis in repeated measures analysis of variance with heterogeneity correlated trials. Paper presented at the annual meeting of the American Educational Research Association, Boston, MA.

Greenhouse, S. W., & Geisser, S. (1959). On methods in the analysis of profile data. *Psychometrika, 24,* 95–112.

Groves, R. M., Dillman, D. A., Eltinge, J. L., & Little, R.J. (2001). *Survey nonresponse.* New York: Wiley.

Guadagnoli, E., & Velicer, W. (1988). Relation of sample size to the stability of component patterns. *Psychological Bulletin, 103,* 265–275.

Guttman, L. (1941). Mathematical and tabulation techniques. Supplementary study B. In P. Horst (Ed.), *Prediction of personnel adjustment.* New York: Social Science Research Council.

Haase, R., Ellis, M., & Ladany, N. (1989). Multiple criteria for evaluating the magnitude of experimental effects. *Journal of Consulting Psychology, 36,* 511–516.

Haberman, S. J. (1973). The analysis of residuals in cross classified tables. *Biometrics, 29,* 205–220.

Hakstian, A. R., Roed, J. C., & Lind, J. C. (1979). Two sample T procedures and the assumption of homogeneous covariance matrices. *Psychological Bulletin, 86,* 1255–1263.

Hakstian, A. R., Rogers, W. D., & Cattell, R. B. (1982). The behavior of numbers factors rules with simulated data. *Multivariate Behavioral Research, 17,* 193–219.

Harman, H. (1983). *Modern factor analysis.* Chicago: University of Chicago Press.

Harris, R. J. (1976). The invalidity of partitioned U tests in canonical correlation and multivariate analysis of variance. *Multivariate Behavioral Research, 11,* 353–365.

Hawkins, D. M. (1976). The subset problem in multivariate analysis of variance. *Journal of the Royal Statistical Society, 38,* 132–139.

Hayduk, L. A. (1987). *Structural equation modeling with LISREL: Essentials and advances.* Baltimore, MD: Johns Hopkins University Press.

Hays, W. (1963). *Statistics for psychologists.* New York: Holt, Rinehart & Winston.

Hays, W. L. (1981), *Statistics* (3rd ed.). New York: Holt, Rinehart & Winston.

Hedges, L. (2007). Correcting a statistical test for clustering. *Journal of Educational and Behavioral Statistics, 32,* 151–179.

Herzberg, P. A. (1969). The parameters of cross validation. *Psychometrika* (Monograph supplement, No. 16).

Hoaglin, D., & Welsch, R. (1978). The hat matrix in regression and ANOVA. *American Statistician, 32,* 17–22.

Hoerl, A. E., & Kennard, W. (1970). Ridge regression: Biased estimation for non-orthogonal problems. *Technometrics, 12,* 55–67.

Hogg, R. V. (1979). Statistical robustness. One view of its use in application today. *American Statistician, 33,* 108–115.

Holland, J. L. (1966). *The psychology of vocational choice.* Waltham, MA: Blaisdell.

Holloway, L. N., & Dunn, O. J. (1967). The robustness of Hotelling's T2. *Journal of the American Statistical Association,* 124–136.

Hopkins, J. W., & Clay, P. P. F. (1963). Some empirical distributions of bivariate T2 and homoscedasticity criterion M under unequal variance and leptokurtosis. *Journal of the American Statistical Association, 58,* 1048–1053.

Hotelling, H. (1931). The generalization of Student's ratio. *Annals of Mathematical Statistics,* 360–378.

Hox, J. J. (2002). Multilevel analysis: Techniques and applications. Mahwah, NJ: Lawrence Erlbaum Associates.

Hoyle, R. (Ed.). (1995). *Structural equation modeling: Concepts, issues and applications.* Newbury Park, CA: Sage.

Hoyle, R. H., & Panter, A. T. (1995). Writing about structural equation models. In R. H. Hoyle (Ed.). *Structural equation modeling: Concepts, issues, and applications* (pp. 158–176). Thousand Oaks, CA: Sage.

Hu, L., & Bentler, P. M. (1995). Evaluating model fit. In R. H. Hoyle (Ed.), *Structural equation modeling: Concepts, issues, and applications* (pp. 76–97). Thousand Oaks, CA: Sage.

Hu, L., & Bentler, P. M. (1998). Fit indices in covariance structure modeling: Sensitivity to underparameterized model misspecification. *Psychological Methods, 3,* 424–453.

Hu, L., & Bentler, P. M. (1999). Cutoff criteria for fit indexes in covariance structure analysis: Conventional criteria versus new alternatives. *Structural Equation Modeling, 6,* 1–55.

Hu, L., Bentler, P. M., & Kano, Y. (1992). Can test statistics in covariance structure analysis be trusted? *Psychological Bulletin, 112,* 351–362.

Huber, P. (1977). *Robust statistical procedures* (No. 27, Regional conference series in applied mathematics). Philadelphia: SIAM.

Huberty, C. J. (1975). The stability of three indices of relative variable contribution in discriminant analysis. *Journal of Experimental Education,* 59–64.

Huberty, C. J. (1984). Issues in the use and interpretation of discriminant analysis. *Psychological Bulletin, 95,*156–171.

Huberty, C. J. (1989). Problems with stepwise methods—better alternatives. In B. Thompson (Ed.), *Advances in social science methodology* (Vol. 1, pp. 43–70). Stanford, CT; JAI.

Huberty, C. (1994). *Applied discriminant analysis.* New York: Wiley.

Huck, S., Cormier, W., & Bounds, W. (1974). *Reading statistics and research.* New York: Harper & Row.

Huck, S., & McLean, R. (1975). Using a repeated measures ANOVA to analyse the data from a pretest-posttest design: A potentially confusing task. *Psychological Bulletin, 82,* 511–518.

Huitema, B. (1980). *The analysis of covariance and alternatives.* New York: Wiley.

Hummel, T. J., & Sligo, J. (1971). Empirical comparison of univariate and multivariate analysis of variance procedures. *Psychological Bulletin, 76,* 49–57.

Hutchinson, S. R. (1994). The stability of post hoc model modifications in covariance structure models. Paper presented at the annual meeting of the American Educational Research Association, New Orleans, LA.

Huynh, H., & Feldt, L. S. (1970). Conditions under which mean square ratios in repeated measurement designs have exact F distributions. *Journal of the American Statistical Association, 65,* 1582–1589.

Huynh, H., & Feldt, L. (1976). Estimation of the Box collection for degrees of freedom from sample data in the randomized block and split plot designs. *Journal of Educational Statistics, 1,* 69–82.

Hykle, J., Stevens, J. P., & Markle, G. (1993). Examining the statistical validity of studies comparing cooperative learning versus individualistic learning. Paper presented at the annual meeting of the American Educational Research Association, Atlanta, GA.

Ito, K. (1962). A comparison of the powers of two MANOVA tests. *Biometrika, 49,* 455–462.

Iverson, G., & Gergen, M. (1997). *Statistics: A conceptual approach.* New York: Springer-Verlag.

Jacobson, N. S. (Ed.). (1988). Defining clinically significant change [Special issue]. *Behavioral Assessment, 10(2).*

James, L. R., Mulaik, S. A., & Brett, J. (1982). *Causal analysis: Models, assumptions, and data.* Beverly Hills, CA: Sage.

Jennings, E. (1988). Models for pretest-posttest data: Repeated measures ANOVA revisited. *Journal of Educational Statistics, 13,* 273–280.

Johnson, N., & Wichern, D. (1988). *Applied multivariate statistical analysis.* Englewood Cliffs, NJ: Prentice-Hall.

Johnson, N., & Wichern, D. (2002). *Applied multivariate statistical analysis*, 5th ed. Englewood Cliffs, NJ: Prentice-Hall, 124–137.

Jones, L. V., Lindzey, G., & Coggelshall, P. (Eds.). (1982). *An assessment of research-doctorate programs in the United States: Social and behavioral sciences.* Washington, DC: National Academy Press.

Jöreskog, K. G. (1967). Some contributions to maximum likelihood factor analysts. *Psychometrika, 32,* 443–482.

Jöreskog, K. G. (1969). A general approach to confirmatory maximum likelihood factor analysis. *Psychometrika, 34,* 183–202.

Jöreskog, K. G., (1993). Testing structural equation models. In K. A. Bollen & J. S. Long (Eds.), *Testing structural equation models* (pp. 294–313). Newbury Park, CA: Sage.

Jöreskog, K. G. (1970). A general method for analysis of covariance structures. *Biometrika, 57,* 239–251.

Jöreskog, K. G. (1978). Structural analysis of covariance and correlation matrices. *Psychometrika, 43,* 443–477.

Jöreskog, K. G., & Lawley, D. N. (1968). New methods in maximum likelihood factor analysis. *British Journal of Mathematical and Statistical Psychology, 21,* 85–96.

Jöreskog, K. G., & Sörbom, D. (1981). *LISREL V: Analysis of linear structural relationships by the method of maximum likelihood.* Chicago: National Educational Resources.

Jöreskog, K. G., & Sörbom, D. (1986). *LISREL VI: Analysis of linear structural relationships by maximum likelihood and least square methods.* Mooresville, IN: Scientific Software.

Jöreskog, K. G., & Sörbom, D. (1993). *LISREL 8 user's reference guide.* Chicago; Scientific Software.

Jöreskog, K. G., & Sörbom, D. (1996). *PRELIS 2: User's reference guide.* Chicago: Scientific Software.

Jöreskog, K. G., & Sörbom, D. (1996). *LISREL 8: User's Reference Guide.* Chicago: Scientific Software.

Jöreskog, K. G., Sörbom, D., du Toit, S., & du Toit, M. (2000). *LISREL 8: New Statistical Features.* Lincolnwood, IL: Scientific Software.

Kaiser, H. F. (I960). The application of electronic computers to factor analysis. *Educational and Psychological Measurement, 20,* 141–151.

Kazdin, A. (2003) *Research design in clinical psychology.* Boston, MA: Allyn & Bacon.

Kegeles, S. (1963). Some motives for seeking preventive dental care. *Journal of the American Dental Association*, *67*, 90–98.

Kennedy, J. (1983). *Analyzing qualitative data*. New York: Praeger.

Kenny, D. A., & Judd, C. M. (1984). Estimating the nonlinear and interactive effects of latent variables. *Psychological Bulletin, 96*, 201–210.

Kenny, D., & Judd, C. (1986). Consequences of violating the independent assumption in analysis of variance. *Psychological Bulletin, 99*, 422–431.

Kenny, D. A., Kashy, D. A., & Bolger, N. (1998). Data analysis in social psychology (pp. 233–265). In D. T. Gilbert, S.T. Fiske, & G. Lindzey (Eds.), *Handbook of social psychology* (4th edition, vol. 1). New York: McGraw-Hill.

Keppel, G. (1983). *Design and analysis: A researchers' handbook*. Englewood Cliffs, NJ: Prentice-Hall.

Kerlinger, F., & Pedhazur, E. (1973). *Multiple regression in behavioral research*. New York: Holt, Rinehart & Winston.

Keselman, H. J., Murray, R., & Rogan, J. (1976). Effect of very unequal group sizes on Tukey's multiple comparison test. *Educational and Psychological Measurement, 36*, 263–270.

Keselman, H. J., Rogan, J. C., Mendoza, J. L., & Breen, L. L. (1980). Testing the validity conditions of repeated measures F tests. *Psychological Bulletin, 87*, 479–481.

Kirk, R. E. (1982). *Experimental design: Procedures for the behavioral sciences*. Belmont, CA: Brooks-Cole.

Krasker, W. S. & Welsch R. E. (1979). Efficient bounded-influence regression estimation using alternative definitions of sensitivity, Technical Report #3, Center for Computational Research in Economics and Management Science, Massachusetts Institute of Technology, Cambridge, MA.

Kreft, I. & de Leeuw, J. (1998). *Introducing Multilevel Modeling*. Thousand Oaks, CA: Sage.

Kvet, E. (1982). Excusing elementary students from regular classroom activities for the study of instrumental music: The effect of sixth grade reading, language and mathematics achievement. Unpublished doctoral dissertation, University of Cincinnati, OH.

Lachenbruch, P. A. (1967). An almost unbiased method of obtaining confidence intervals for the probability of misclassification in discriminant analysis. *Biometrics, 23*, 639–645.

Lauter, J. (1978). Sample size requirements for the T^2 test of MANOVA (tables for one-way classification). *Biometrical Journal, 20*, 389–406.

Lawley, D. N. (1940). The estimation of factor loadings by the method of maximum likelihood. *Proceedings of the Royal Society of Edinburgh, 60*, 64.

Lee, S., & Hershberger, S. (1990). A simple rule for generating equivalent models in covariance structure modeling. *Multivariate Behavioral Research, 25*, 313–334.

Lehrer, B., & Schimoler, G. (1975). Cognitive skills underlying an inductive problem-solving strategy. *Journal of Experimental Education, 43*, 13–21.

Light, R., & Pillemer, D. (1984). *Summing up: The science of reviewing research*. Cambridge, MA: Harvard University Press.

Light, R., Singer, J., & Willett, J. (1990). *By design*. Cambridge, MA: Harvard University Press.

Lindeman, R. H., Merenda, P. F., & Gold, R. Z. (1980). *Introduction to bivariate and multivariate analysis*. Glenview, IL: Scott, Foresman.

Linn, R. L. (1968). A Monte Carlo approach to the number of factors problem. *Psychometrika, 33*, 37–71.

Littell, R. C., Milliken, G. A., Stroup, W. W., & Wolfinger, R. D. (1996). *SAS system for mixed models*. Cary, NC: SAS Institute, Inc.

Loehlin, J. C. (1992). *Latent variable models: An introduction to factor, path, and structural analysis* (2nd ed.). Hillsdale, NJ: Lawrence Erlbaum Associates.

Lohnes, P. R. (1961). Test space and discriminant space classification models and related significance tests. *Educational and Psychological Measurement, 21*, 559–574.

Lord, F. (1969). Statistical adjustments when comparing pre-existing groups. *Psychological Bulletin, 70*, 162–179.

Longford, N. T. (1988). Fisher scoring algorithm for variance component analysis of data with multilevel structure. In R. D. Bock (Ed.), *Multilevel analysis of educational data* (pp. 297–310). Orlando, FL: Academic Press.

Lord, R., & Novick, M. (1968). *Statistical theories of mental test scores.* Reading, MA: Addison-Wesley.

MacCallum, R. (1986). Specification searches in covariance structure modeling. *Psychological Bulletin, 100,* 107–120.

MacCallum, R. C. (1990). The need for alternative measures of fit in covariance structure modeling. *Multivariate Behavioral Research, 25,* 157–162.

MacCallum, R. C. (1995). Model specification: Procedures, strategies, and related issues. In R. H. Hoyle (Ed.), *Structural equation modeling: Concepts, issues, and applications* (pp. 16–36). Thousand Oaks, CA: Sage.

MacCallum, R. C., Kim, C., Malarkey, W. B., & Kiecolt-Glaser, J. K. (1997). Studying multivariate change using multilevel models and latent curve models. *Multivariate Behavioral Research, 32,* 215–253.

MacCallum, R. C., Roznowski, M., & Necowitz, L. B. (1992). Model modifications in covariance structure analysis: The problem of capitalization on chance. *Psychological Bulletin, 111,* 490–504.

MacCallum, R. C., & Browne, M. W. (1993). The use of causal indicators in covariance structure models: Some practical issues. *Psychological Bulletin, 114,* 533–541.

MacCallum, R. C., Wegener, D. T., Uchino, B. N., & Fabrigar, L. R. (1993). The problem of equivalent models in applications of covariance structure analysis. *Psychological Bulletin, 114,* 185–199.

Mahalanobis, P. C. (1936). On the generalized distance in statistics. *Proceedings of the National Institute of Science of India, 12,* 49–55.

Maiman, L., Becker, M., Kirscht, J., Haefner, D., & Drachmas, R. (1977). Scales for measuring Health Belief Model dimensions: A test of predictive value, internal consistency, and relationships among beliefs. *Health Education Monographs, 5,* 215–230.

Mallows, C. L. (1973), Some comments on Cp. *Technometrics, 15,* 661–676.

Marascuilo, L., & Busk, P. (1987). Loglinear models: A way to study main effects and interactions for multidimensional contingency tables with categorical data. *Journal of Counseling Psychology, 34,* 443–455.

Maradia, K. V. (1971). The effect of non-normality on some multivariate tests and robustness to non-normality in the linear model. *Biometrika, 58,* 105–121.

Marsh, H. W., Balla, J. R., & McDonald, R. P. (1988). Goodness-of-fit indexes in confirmatory factor analysis: The effect of sample size. *Psychological Bulletin, 103,* 391–410.

Marsh, H. W., & Grayson, D. (1995). Latent variable models for multitrait-multimethod data. In R. H. Hoyle (Ed.), *Structural equation modeling: Concepts, issues, and applications* (pp. 177–198). Thousand Oaks, CA: Sage.

Maruyama, G. M. (1998). *Basics of structural equation modeling.* Thousand Oaks, CA: Sage Publications.

Maxwell, S. E. (1980). Pairwise multiple comparisons in repeated measures designs. *Journal of Educational Statistics, 5,* 269–287.

Maxwell, S. E., & Delaney, H. D. (2004). *Designing experiments and analyzing data: A model comparison perspective* (2nd edition). Mahwah, NJ: Lawrence Erlbaum.

Maxwell, S., Delaney, H. D., & Manheimer, J. (1985). ANOVA of residuals and ANCOVA: Correcting an illusion by using model comparisons and graphs. *Journal of Educational Statistics, 95,* 136–147.

McCardle, J. J., & McDonald, R. P. (1984). Some algebraic properties of the Reticular Action Model for moment structures. *British Journal of Mathematical and Statistical Psychology, 37,* 234–251.

McLean, J. A. (1980). *Graduation and nongraduation rates of black and white freshmen entering two state universities in Virginia.* Unpublished doctoral dissertation, Ohio State University.

Mendoza, J. L., Markos, V. H., & Gonter, R. (1978). A new perspective on sequential testing procedures in canonical analysis: A Monte Carlo evaluation. *Multivariate Behavioral Research, 13,* 371–382.

Meredith, W. (1964). Canonical correlation with fallible data. *Psychometrika, 29,* 55–65.

Merenda, P., Novack, H., & Bonaventure, E. (1976). Multivariate analysis of the California Test of mental maturity, primary forms. *Psychological Reports, 38,* 487–493.

Milligan, G. (1980). Factors that affect type I and type II error rates in the analysis of multidimensional contingency tables. *Psychological Bulletin, 87,* 238–244.

Moore, D., & McCabe, G. (1989). *Introduction to the practice of statistics.* New York: Freeman.

Morris, J. D. (1982). Ridge regression and some alternative weighting techniques: A comment on Darlington. *Psychological Bulletin, 91*, 203–210.

Morrison, D. F. (1976). *Multivariate statistical methods.* New York: McGraw-Hill.

Morrison, D. F. (1983). *Applied linear statistical methods.* Englewood Cliffs, NJ: Prentice Hall.

Mosteller, F., & Tukey, J. W. (1977). *Data analysis and regression.* Reading, MA: Addison-Wesley.

Mulaik, S. A., James, L. R., Van Alstroe, J., Bennett, N., Lind, S., & Stilwell, C. D. (1989). Evaluation of goodness of fit indices for structural equation models. *Psychological Bulletin, 105*, 430–445.

Muthén, B. (1987). *LISCOMP: Analysis of linear structural equations with a comprehensive measurement model.* Mooresville, IN: Scientific Software, Inc.

Muthén, B. (1993). Goodness of fit with categorical and other nonnormal variables. In K. A. Bollen & J. S. Long (Eds.), *Testing structural equation models* (pp. 204–234). Newbury Park, CA: Sage.

Myers, J. L. (1979). *Fundamentals of experimental design.* Boston: Allyn & Bacon.

Myers, J., & Well, A. (2002). *Research design and statistical analysis*, 2nd ed. New York: Harper Collins.

Myers, J. L., Dicecco, J. V., and Lorch, R. F. (1981). Group dynamics and individual performances: Pseudogroup and Quasi-F analyses. *Journal of Personality and Social Psychology, 40,* (86–98).

Myers, R. (1990). *Classical and modern regression with applications* (2nd ed.). Boston, MA: Duxbury.

Neter, J., Wasserman, W., & Kutner, M. (1989). *Applied linear regression models.* Boston: Irwin.

Nold, E., & Freedman, S. (1977). An analysis of readers' responses to essays. *Research in the Teaching of English, 15,* 65–74.

Novince, L. (1977). The contribution of cognitive restructuring to the effectiveness of behavior rehearsal in modifying social inhibition in females. Unpublished doctoral dissertation, University of Cincinnati, OH.

Nunnally, J. (1978). *Psychometric theory.* New York: McGraw-Hill.

O'Brien, R., & Kaiser, M. (1985). MANOVA method for analyzing repeated measures designs: An extensive primer. *Psychological Bulletin,* 316–333.

O'Grady, K. (1982). Measures of explained variation: Cautions and limitations. *Psychological Bulletin, 92,* 766–777.

Olson, C. L. (1974). Comparative robustness of six tests in multivariate analysis of variance. *Journal of the American Statistical Association, 69,* 894–908.

Olson, C. L. (1976). On choosing a test statistic in MANOVA. *Psychological Bulletin, 83,* 579–586.

Overall, J. E., & Spiegel, D. K. (1969). Concerning least squares analysis of experimental data. *Psychological Bulletin, 72,* 311–322.

Park, C., & Dudycha, A. (1974). A cross validation approach to sample size determination for regression models. *Journal of the American Statistical Association, 69,* 214–218.

Pedhazur, E. (1982). *Multiple regression in behavioral research* (2nd ed.). New York: Holt, Rinehart & Winston.

Pedhazur, E., & Schmelkin, L. (1991). *Measurement, design, and analysis.* Hillsdale, NJ: Lawrence Erlbaum.

Petty, R. E., & Cacioppo, J. T. (1986). *Communication and persuasion: Central and peripheral routes to attitude change.* New York: Springer-Verlag.

Petty, R. E., Wegener, D. T., Fabrigar, L. R., Priester, J. R., & Cacioppo, J. T. (1993). Conceptual and methodological issues in the Elaboration Likelihood Model of persuasion: A reply to the Michigan State critics. *Communication Theory, 3,* 336–363.

Pillai, K., & Jayachandian, K. (1967). Power comparisons of tests of two multivariate hypotheses based on four criteria. *Biometrika, 54,* 195–210.

Ping, R. A. (1996). Latent variable interaction and quadratic effect estimation: A two-step technique using structural equation analysis. *Psychological Bulletin, 119,* 166–175.

Plackett, R. L. (1974). *The analysis of categorical data.* London: Griffin.

Plante, T., & Goldfarb, L. (1984). Concurrent validity for an activity vector analysis index of social adjustment. *Journal of Clinical Psychology, 40,* 1215–1218.

Pollack, M., Jackson, A., & Pate, R. (1980) Discriminant analysis of physiological differences between good and elite runners. *Research Quarterly, 51,* 521–532.

Pope, J., Lehrer, B., & Stevens, J. P. (1980). A multiphasic reading screening procedure. *Journal of Learning Disabilities, 13,* 98–102.

Porebski, O. R. (1966). Discriminatory and canonical analysis of technical college data. *British Journal of Mathematical and Statistical Psychology, 19*, 215–236.

Press, S. J., & Wilson, S. (1978). Choosing between logistic regression and discriminant analysis. *Journal of the American Statistical Association, 7*, 699–705.

Pruzek, R. M. (1971). Methods and problems in the analysis of multivariate data. *Review of Educational Research, 41*, 163–190.

Ramsey, F., & Schafer, D. (1997). *The statistical sleuth.* Belmont, CA: Duxbury.

Raudenbush, S. W. (1984). Applications of a hierarchical linear model in educational research. Unpublished doctoral dissertation, Harvard University.

Raudenbush, S., & Bryk, A. S. (2002). *Hierarchical linear models: applications and data analysis methods* (2nd edition). Thousand Oaks, CA: Sage.

Raudenbush, S., Bryk, A., Cheong, Y. F., & Congdon, R. (2004). *HLM 6: Hierarchical linear and nonlinear modeling.* Chicago: Scientific Software International.

Raykov, T., & Widaman, K. F. (1995). Issues in applied structural equation modeling research. *Structural Equation Modeling, 2*, 289–318.

Reichardt, C. (1979). The statistical analysis of data from nonequivalent group designs. In T. Cook & D. Campbell (Eds.), *Quasi-experimentation: Design and analysis issues for field settings.* Chicago: Rand McNally.

Reis, H. T., & Judd, C. M. (Eds.). (2000). *Handbook of research methods in social and personality psychology.* New York: Cambridge University Press.

Rencher, A. C., & Larson, S. F. (1980). Bias in Wilks' Λ in stepwise discriminant analysis. *Technometrics, 22*, 349–356.

Rogan, J. C., Keselman, H. J., & Mendoza, J. L. (1979). Analysis of repeated measurements. *British Journal of Mathematical and Statistical Psychology, 32*, 269–286.

Rogosa, D. (1977). Some results for the Johnson-Neyman technique. Unpublished doctoral dissertation, Stanford University, CA.

Rogosa, D. (1980). Comparing non-parallel regression lines. *Psychological Bulletin, 88,* 307–321.

Rosenstock, I. (1974). Historical origins of the health belief model. *Health Education Monographs, 2*, 1–8.

Rosenthal, R., & Rosnow, R. (1984). *Essentials of behavioral research.* New York: McGraw-Hill.

Rouanet, H., & Lepine, D. (1970). Comparisons between treatments in a repeated measures design: ANOVA and multivariate methods. *British Journal of Mathematical and Statistical Psychology, 23*, 147–163.

Roy, J., & Bargmann, R. E. (1958). Tests of multiple independence and the associated confidence bounds. *Annals of Mathematical Statistics, 29*, 491–503.

Roy, S. N., & Bose, R. C. (1953). Simultaneous confidence interval estimation. *Annals of Mathematical Statistics, 24*, 513–536.

Rummel, R. J. (1970). *Applied factor analysis.* Evanston, IL: Northwestern University Press.

Sarason, I. G. (1984). Stress, anxiety, and cognitive interference: Reactions to tests. *Journal of Personality and Social Psychology, 46*, 929–938.

SAS Institute Inc. (1999) SAS/STATS USER'S GUIDE, version 8, three volume set. Cary, NC.

Scandura, T. (1984). Multivariate analysis of covariance for a study of the effects of leadership training on work outcomes. Unpublished research paper, University of Cincinnati, OH.

Scariano, S., & Davenport, J. (1987). The effects of violations of the independence assumption in the one way ANOVA. *The American Statistician, 41*, 123–129.

Schutz, W. (1977). *Leaders of schools: FIRO theory applied to administrators.* La Jolla, CA: University Associates.

Shanahan, T. (1984). Nature of the reading-writing relation: An exploratory multivariate analysis. *Journal of Educational Psychology, 76*, 466–477.

Shadish, W. R., Cook, T. D., & Campbell, D. T. (2002). *Experimental and quasi-experimental designs for generalized causal inference.* Boston, MA: Houghton Mifflin.

Sharp, G. (1981). Acquisition of lecturing skills by university teaching assistants: Some effects of interest, topic relevance and viewing a model videotape. *American Educational Research Journal, 18*, 491–502.

Shavelson, R., Hubner, J., & Stanton, G. (1976). Self concept: Validation of construct interpretations. *Review of Educational Research, 46*, 407–441.

Shiffler, R. (1988). Maximum z scores and outliers. *American Statistician, 42*, 79–80.

Shin, S. H. (1971). Creativity, intelligence and achievement: A study of the relationship between creativity and intelligence, and their effects on achievement. Unpublished doctoral dissertation, University of Pittsburgh, PA.

Sidanius, J. (1988). Political sophistication and political deviance: A structural equation examination of context theory. *Journal of Personality and Social Psychology, 55*, 37–51.

Singer, J., & Willett, J. (1988). Opening up the black box of recipe statistics: Putting the data back into data analysis. Paper presented at the annual meeting of the American Educational Research Association, New Orleans, LA.

Singer, J. D. (1998). Using SAS PROC MIXED to fit multilevel models, hierarchical models, and individual growth models. *Journal of Educational and Behavioral Statistics, 23*, 323–355.

Singer, J. D., & Willett, J. B. (2003). *Applied longitudinal data analysis: Modeling change and event occurrence*. Oxford University Press.

Smart, J. C. (1976). Duties performed by department chairmen in Holland's model environments. *Journal of Educational Psychology, 68*, 194–204.

Smith, A. H. (1975). A multivariate study of factor analyzed predictors of death anxiety in college students. Unpublished doctoral dissertation, University of Cincinnati, OH.

Sobel, M. E., & Arminger, G. (1986). Platonic and operational true scores in covariance structure analysis. *Sociological Methods and Research, 15*, 44–58.

SPSS BASE 15.0 USER'S GUIDE. (2006). Chicago, IL.

Snijders, T. & Bosker, R. (1999). *Multilevel analysis*. Thousand Oaks, CA: Sage.

Steiger, J. H. (1979). Factor indeterminancy in the 1930s and the 1970s: Some interesting parallels. *Psychometrika, 44*, 157–167.

Steiger, J. H. (1990). Some additional thoughts on components, factors, and factor indeterminacy. *Multivariate Behavioral Research, 25*, 41–45.

Stein, C. (1960). Multiple regression. In I. Olkin (Ed.), *Contributions to probability and statistics, essays in honor of Harold Hotelling*. Stanford, CA: Stanford University Press.

Stelzl, I. (1986). Change a causal hypothesis without changing the fit: Some rules for generating equivalent path models. *Multivariate Behavioral Research, 9*, 251–266.

Stevens, J. P. (1972). Four methods of analyzing between variation for the k group MANOVA problem. *Multivariate Behavioral Research, 7*, 499–522.

Stevens, J. P. (1979). Comment on Olson: Choosing a test statistic in multivariate analysis of variance. *Psychological Bulletin, 86*, 355–360.

Stevens, J. P. (1980). Power of the multivariate analysis of variance tests. *Psychological Bulletin, 88*, 728–737.

Stevens, J. P. (1984). Cross validation in the loglinear model. Paper presented at the annual meeting of the American Educational Research Association, New Orleans, LA.

Stevens, J. P. (1984). Outliers and influential data points in regression analysis, *Psychological Bulletin, 95*, 334–344.

Stewart, D., & Love, W. (1968). A general canonical correlation index. *Psychological Bulletin, 70*, 160–163.

Stilbeck, W., Acousta, F., Yamamoto, J., & Evans, L. (1984). Self reported psychiatric symptoms among black, hispanic and white outpatients. *Journal of Clinical Psychology, 40*, 1184–1192.

Stoloff, P. H. (1967). An empirical evaluation of the effects of violating the assumption of homogeneity of covariance for the repeated measures design of the analysis of variance (Tech. Rep.). College Park, MD: University of Maryland.

Tanaka, J. S. (1993). Multifaceted conceptions of fit in structural equation models. In K. A. Bollen & J. S. Long (Eds.), *Testing structural equation models* (pp. 10–39). Newbury Park, CA: Sage.

Tanaka, J. S., Panter, A. T., Winborne, W. C., & Huba, G. J. (1990). Theory testing in personality and social psychology with structural equation models: A primer in 20 questions. In C. Hendrick & M. S. Clark (Eds.), *Research methods in personality and social psychology* (pp. 217–242). Newbury Park, CA: Sage Publications.

Tatsuoka, M. M. (1971). *Multivariate analysis: Techniques for educational and psychological research.* New York: Wiley.

Tatsuoka, M. M. (1973). Multivariate analysis in behavioral research. In F. Kerlinger (Ed.), *Review of research in education.* Itasca, IL: F. F. Peacock.

Tetenbaum, T. (1975). The role of student needs and teacher orientations in student ratings of teachers. *American Educational Research Journal, 12,* 417–433.

Thorndike, R., & Hagen, E. (1977). *Measurement and evaluation in psychology and education.* New York: Wiley.

Timm, N. H. (1975). *Multivariate analysis with applications in education and psychology.* Monterey, CA: Brooks-Cole.

Tucker, L. R., Koopman, R. E, & Linn, R. L. (1969). Evaluation of factor analytic research procedures by means of simulated correlation matrices. *Psychometrika, 34,* 421–459.

Tucker, L. R, & Lewis, C. (1973). A reliability coefficient for maximum likelihood factor analysis. *Psychometrika, 38,* 1–10.

van Driel, O. P. (1978). On various causes of improper solutions in maximum likelihood factor analysis. *Psychometrika, 43,* 225–243.

Wegener, D. T., & Fabrigar, L. R. (2000). Analysis and design for nonexperimental data: Addressing causal and noncausal hypotheses. In H. T. Reis & C. M. Judd (Eds.), *Handbook of research methods in social and personality psychology* (pp. 412–450). New York: Cambridge University Press.

Wegener, D. T., & Fabrigar, L. R. (2004). Constructing and evaluating quantitative measures for social psychological research: Conceptual challenges and methodological solutions. In C. Sansone, C. C. C. Morf, & A. T. Panter (Eds.), *The SAGE handbook of methods in social psychology* (pp. 145–172). New York: Sage.

Weinberg, S. L., & Darlington, R. B. (1976). Canonical analysis when the number of variables is large relative to sample size. *Journal of Educational Statistics, 1,* 313–332.

Weisberg, S. (1985). *Applied linear regression.* New York: Wiley.

West, S. G., Finch, J. F., & Curran, P. J. (1995). Structural equation models with nonnormal variables: Problems and remedies. In R. H. Hoyle (Ed.), *Structural equation modeling: Concepts, issues, and applications* (pp. 56–75). Thousand Oaks, CA: Sage.

Wherry, R. J. (1931). A new formula for predicting the shrinkage of the coefficient of multiple correlation. *Annals of Mathematical Statistics, 2,* 440–457.

Wickens, T. (1989). *Multiway contingency tables analysis for the social sciences.* Hillsdale, NJ: Lawrence Erlbaum.

Wilk, H. B., Shapiro, S. S., & Chen, H. J. (1965). A comparative study of various tests of normality. *Journal of the American Statistical Association, 63,* 1343–1372.

Wilkinson, L. (1979). Tests of significance in stepwise regression. *Psychological Bulletin, 86,* 168–174.

Williams, R., & Thomson, E. (1986). Normalization issues in latent variable modeling. *Sociological Methods and Research, 15,* 24–43.

Winer, B. J. (1971). *Statistical principles in experimental design* (2nd ed.). New York: McGraw-Hill.

Wothke, W. (1993). Nonpositive definite matrices in structural modeling. In K. A. Bollen & J. S. Long (Eds.), *Testing structural equation models.* Newbury Park, CA: Sage.

Zwick, R. (1985). Nonparametric one-way multivariate analysis of variance: A computational approach based on the Pillai-Bartlett trace. *Psychological Bulletin, 97,* 148–152.

Appendix A: Statistical Tables

CONTENTS

TABLE A.1

Percentile Points for χ^2 Distribution

					Probability									
df	.99	.98	.95	.90	.80	.70	.50	.30	.20	.10	.05	.02	.01	.001
1	.03157	.03628	.00393	.0158	.0642	.148	.455	1.074	1.642	2.706	3.841	5.412	6.635	10.827
2	.0201	.0404	.103	.211	.446	.713	1.386	2.408	3.219	4.605	5.991	7.824	9.210	13.815
3	.115	.185	.352	.584	1.005	1.424	2.366	3.665	4.642	6.251	7.815	9.837	11.345	16.268
4	.297	.429	.711	1.064	1.649	2.195	3.357	4.878	5.989	7.779	9.488	11.668	13.277	18.465
5	.554	.752	1.145	1.610	2.343	3.000	4.351	6.064	7.289	9.236	11.070	13.388	15.086	20.517
6	.872	1.134	1.635	2.204	3.070	3.828	5.348	7.231	8.558	10.645	12.592	15.033	16.812	22.457
7	1.239	1.564	2.167	2.833	3.822	4.671	6.346	8.383	9.803	12.017	14.067	16.622	18.475	24.322
8	1.646	2.032	2.733	3.490	4.594	5.527	7.344	9.524	11.030	13.362	15.507	18.168	20.090	26.125
9	2.088	2.532	3.325	4.168	5.380	6.393	8.343	10.656	12.242	14.684	16.919	19.679	21.666	27.877
10	2.558	3.059	3.940	4.865	6.179	7.267	9.342	11.781	13.442	15.987	18.307	21.161	23.209	29.588
11	3.053	3.609	4.575	5.578	6.989	8.148	10.341	12.899	14.631	17.275	19.675	22.618	24.725	31.264
12	3.571	4.178	5.226	6.304	7.807	9.034	11.340	14.011	15.812	18.549	21.026	24.054	26.217	32.909
13	4.107	4.765	5.892	7.042	8.634	9.926	12.340	15.119	16.985	19.812	22.362	25.472	27.688	34.528
14	4.660	5.368	6.571	7.790	9.467	10.821	13.339	16.222	18.151	21.064	23.685	26.873	29.141	36.123
15	5.229	5.985	7.261	8.547	10.307	11.721	14.339	17.322	19.311	22.307	24.996	28.259	30.578	37.697
16	5.812	6.614	7.962	9.312	11.152	12.624	15.338	18.418	20.465	23.542	26.296	29.633	32.000	39.252
17	6.408	7.255	8.672	10.085	12.002	13.531	16.338	19.511	21.615	24.769	27.587	30.995	33.409	40.790
18	7.015	7.906	9.390	10.865	12.857	14.440	17.338	20.601	22.760	25.989	28.869	32.346	34.805	42.312
19	7.633	8.567	10.117	11.651	13.716	15.352	18.338	21.689	23.900	27.204	30.144	33.687	36.191	43.820
20	8.260	9.237	10.851	12.443	14.578	16.266	19.337	22.775	25.038	28.412	31.410	35.020	37.566	45.315
21	8.897	9.915	11.591	13.240	15.445	17.182	20.337	23.858	26.171	29.615	32.671	36.343	38.932	46.797
22	9.542	10.600	12.338	14.041	16.314	18.101	21.337	24.939	27.301	30.813	33.924	37.659	40.289	48.268
23	10.196	11.293	13.091	14.848	17.187	19.021	22.337	26.018	28.429	32.007	35.172	38.968	41.638	49.728
24	10.856	11.992	13.848	15.659	18.062	19.943	23.337	27.096	29.553	33.196	36.415	40.270	42.980	51.179
25	11.524	12.697	14.611	16.473	18.940	20.867	24.337	28.172	30.675	34.382	37.652	41.566	44.314	52.620
26	12.198	13.409	15.379	17.292	19.820	21.792	25.336	29.246	31.795	35.563	38.885	42.856	45.642	54.052
27	12.879	14.125	16.151	18.114	20.703	22.719	26.336	30.319	32.912	36.741	40.113	44.140	46.963	55.476
28	13.565	14.847	16.928	18.939	21.588	23.647	27.336	31.391	34.027	37.916	41.337	45.419	48.278	56.893
29	14.256	15.574	17.708	19.768	22.475	24.577	28.336	32.461	35.139	39.087	42.557	46.693	49.588	58.302
30	14.953	16.306	18.493	20.599	23.364	25.508	29.336	33.530	36.250	40.256	43.773	47.962	50.892	59.703

Note: For larger values of df, the expression $\sqrt{2\chi^2} - \sqrt{2df - 1}$ may be used as a normal deviate with unit variance, remembering that the probability for χ^2 corresponds with that of a single tail of the normal curve.

Source: Reproduced from E. F. Lindquist, *Design and Analysis of Experiments in Psychology and Education*, Houghton Mifflin, Boston, 1953, p. 29, with permission.

TABLE A.2

Critical Values for *t*

	Level of Significance for One-Tailed Test					
	.10	.05	.025	.01	.005	.0005
	Level of Significance for Two-Tailed Test					
Df	.20	.10	.05	.02	.01	.001
1	3.078	6.314	12.706	31.821	63.657	636.619
2	1.886	2.920	4.303	6.965	9.925	31.598
3	1.638	2.353	3.182	4.541	5.841	12.941
4	1.533	2.132	2.776	3.747	4.604	8.610
5	1.476	2.015	2.571	3.365	4.032	6.859
6	1.440	1.943	2.447	3.143	3.707	5.959
7	1.415	1.895	2.365	2.998	3.449	5.405
8	1.397	1.860	2.306	2.896	3.355	5.041
9	1.383	1.833	2.262	2.821	3.250	4.781
10	1.372	1.812	2.228	2.764	3.169	4.587
11	1.363	1.796	2.201	2.718	3.106	4.437
12	1.356	1.782	2.179	2.681	3.055	4.318
13	1.350	1.771	2.160	2.650	3.012	4.221
14	1.345	1.761	2.145	2.624	2.977	4.140
15	1.341	1.753	2.131	2.602	2.947	4.073
16	1.337	1.746	2.120	2.583	2.921	4.015
17	1.333	1.740	2.110	2.567	2.898	3.965
18	1.330	1.734	2.101	2.552	2.878	3.922
19	1.328	1.729	2.093	2.539	2.861	3.883
20	1.325	1.725	2.086	2.528	2.845	3.850
21	1.323	1.721	2.080	2.518	2.831	3.819
22	1.321	1.717	2.074	2.508	2.819	3.792
23	1.319	1.714	2.069	2.500	2.807	3.767
24	1.318	1.711	2.064	2.492	2.797	3.745
25	1.316	1.708	2.060	2.485	2.787	3.725
26	1.315	1.706	2.056	2.479	2.779	3.707
27	1.314	1.703	2.052	2.473	2.771	3.690
28	1.313	1.701	2.048	2.467	2.763	3.674
29	1.311	1.699	2.045	2.462	2.756	3.659
30	1.310	1.697	2.042	2.457	2.750	3.646
40	1.303	1.684	2.021	2.423	2.704	3.551
60	1.296	1.671	2.000	2.390	2.660	3.460
120	1.289	1.658	1.980	2.358	2.617	3.373
∞	1.282	1.645	1.960	2.326	2.576	3.291

Source: Reproduced from E. F. Lindquist, *Design and Analysis of Experiments in Psychology and Education.* Boston: Houghton-Mifflin, 1953. With permission.

TABLE A.3

Critical Values for F

df Error	α	df for Numerator							
		1	2	3	4	5	6	8	12
1	.01	4052	4999	5403	5625	5764	5859	5981	6106
	.05	161.45	199.50	215.71	224.58	230.16	233.99	238.88	243.91
	.10	39.86	49.50	53.59	55.83	57.24	58.20	59.44	60.70
	.20	9.47	12.00	13.06	13.73	14.01	14.26	14.59	14.90
2	.01	98.49	99.00	99.17	99.25	99.30	99.33	99.36	99.42
	.05	18.51	19.00	19.16	19.25	19.30	19.3(3	19.37	19.41
	.10	8.53	9.00	9.16	9.24	9.29	9.33	9.37	9.41
	.20	3.56	4.00	4.16	4.24	4.28	4.32	4.36	4.40
3	.001	167.5	148.5	141.1	137.1	134.6	132.8	130.6	128.3
	.01	34.12	30.81	29.46	28.71	28.24	27.91	27.49	27.05
	.05	10.13	9.55	9.28	9.12	9.01	8.94	8.84	8.74
	.10	5.54	5.46	5.39	5.34	5.31	5.28	5.25	5.22
	.20	2.68	2.89	2.94	2.96	2.97	2.97	2.98	2.98
4	.001	74.14	61.25	56.18	53.44	51.71	50.53	49.00	47.41
	.01	21.20	18.00	16.69	15.98	15.52	15.21	14.80	14.37
	.05	7.71	6.94	6.59	6.39	6.26	6.16	6.04	5.91
	.10	4.54	4.32	4.19	4.11	4.05	4.01	3.95	3.90
	.20	2.35	2.47	2.48	2.48	2.48	2.47	2.47	2.46
5	.001	47.04	36.61	33.20	31.09	29.75	28.84	27.64	26.42
	.01	16.26	13.27	12.06	11.39	10.97	10.67	10.29	9.89
	.05	6.61	5.79	5.41	5.19	5.05	4.95	4.82	4.68
	.10	4.06	3.78	3.62	3.52	3.45	3.40	3.34	3.27
	.20	2.18	2.26	2.25	2.24	2.23	2.22	2.20	2.18
6	.001	35.51	27.00	23.70	21.90	20.81	20.03	19.03	17.99
	.01	13.74	10.92	9.78	9.15	8.75	8.47	8.10	7.72
	.05	5.99	5.14	4.76	4.53	4.39	4.28	4.15	4.00
	.10	3.78	3.46	3.29	3.18	3.11	3.05	2.98	2.90
	.20	2.07	2.13	2.11	2.09	2.08	2.06	2.04	2.02
7	.001	29.22	21.69	18.77	17.19	16.21	15.52	14.63	13.71
	.01	12.25	9.55	8.45	7.85	7.46	7.19	6.84	6.47
	.05	5.59	4.74	4.35	4.12	3.97	3.87	3.73	3.57
	.10	3.59	3.26	3.07	2.96	2.88	2.83	2.75	2.67
	.20	2.00	2.04	2.02	1.99	1.97	1.96	1.93	1.91
8	.001	25.42	18.49	15.83	14.39	13.49	12.86	12.04	11.19
	.01	11.26	8.65	7.59	7.01	6.63	6.37	6.03	5.67
	.05	5.32	4.46	4.07	3.84	3.69	3.58	3.44	3.28
	.10	3.46	3.11	2.92	2.81	2.73	2.67	2.59	2.50
	.20	1.95	1.98	1.95	1.92	1.90	1.88	1.86	1.83

TABLE A.3 (*Continued*)

Critical Values for *F*

df Error	α	df for Numerator							
		1	2	3	4	5	6	8	12
9	.001	22.86	16.39	13.90	12.56	11.71	11.13	10.37	9.57
	.01	10.56	8.02	6.99	6.42	6.06	5.80	5.47	5.11
	.05	5.12	4.26	3.86	3.63	3.48	3.37	3.23	3.07
	.10	3.36	3.01	2.81	2.69	2.61	2.55	2.47	2.38
	.20	1.91	1.94	1.90	1.87	1.85	1.83	1.80	1.76
10	.001	21.04	14.91	12.55	11.28	10.48	9.92	9.20	8.45
	.01	10.04	7.56	6.55	5.99	5.64	5.39	5.06	4.71
	.05	4.96	4.10	3.71	3.48	3.33	3.22	3.07	2.91
	.10	3.28	2.92	2.73	2.61	2.52	2.46	2.38	2.28
	.20	1.88	1.90	1.86	1.83	1.80	1.78	1.75	1.72
11	.001	19.69	13.81	11.56	10.35	9.58	9.05	8.35	7.63
	.01	9.65	7.20	6.22	5.67	5.32	5.07	4.74	4.40
	.05	4.84	3.98	3.59	3.36	3.20	3.09	2.95	2.79
	.10	3.23	2.86	2.66	2.54	2.45	2.39	2.30	2.21
	.20	1.86	1.87	1.83	1.80	1.77	1.75	1.72	1.68
12	.001	18.64	12.97	10.80	9.63	8.89	8.38	7.71	7.00
	.01	9.33	6.93	5.95	5.41	5.06	4.82	4.50	4.16
	.05	4.75	3.88	3.49	3.26	3.11	3.00	2.85	2.69
	.10	3.18	2.81	2.61	2.48	2.39	2.33	2.24	2.15
	.20	1.84	1.85	1.80	1.77	1.74	1.72	1.69	1.65
13	.001	17.81	12.31	10.21	9.07	8.35	7.86	7.21	6.52
	.01	9.07	6.70	5.74	5.20	4.86	4.62	4.30	3.96
	.05	4.67	3.80	3.41	3.18	3.02	2.92	2.77	2.60
	.10	3.14	2.76	2.56	2.43	2.35	2.28	2.20	2.10
	.20	1.82	1.83	1.78	1.75	1.72	1.69	1.66	1.62
14	.001	17.14	11.78	9.73	8.62	7.92	7.43	6.80	6.13
	.01	8.86	6.51	5.56	5.03	4.69	4.46	4.14	3.80
	.05	4.60	3.74	3.34	3.11	2.96	2.85	2.70	2.53
	.10	3.10	2.73	2.52	2.39	2.31	2.24	2.15	2.05
	.20	1.81	1.81	1.76	1.73	1.70	1.67	1.64	1.60
15	.001	16.59	11.34	9.34	8.25	7.57	7.09	6.47	5.81
	.01	8.68	6.36	5.42	4.89	4.56	4.32	4.00	3.67
	.05	4.54	3.68	3.29	3.06	2.90	2.79	2.64	2.48
	.10	3.07	2.70	2.49	2.36	2.27	2.21	2.12	2.02
	.20	1.80	1.79	1.75	1.71	1.68	1.66	1.62	1.58
16	.001	16.12	10.97	9.00	7.94	7.27	6.81	6.19	5.55
	.01	8.53	6.23	5.29	4.77	4.44	4.20	3.89	3.55
	.05	4.49	3.63	3.24	3.01	2.85	2.74	2.59	2.42
	.10	3.05	2.67	2.46	2.33	2.24	2.18	2.09	1.99
	.20	1.79	1.78	1.74	1.70	1.67	1.64	1.61	1.56

TABLE A.3 (*Continued*)

Critical Values for *F*

		df for Numerator							
df Error	α	1	2	3	4	5	6	8	12
17	.001	15.72	10.66	8.73	7.68	7.02	6.56	5.96	5.32
	.01	8.40	6.11	5.18	4.67	4.34	4.10	3.79	3.45
	.05	4.45	3.59	3.20	2.96	2.81	2.70	2.55	2.38
	.10	3.03	2.64	2.44	2.31	2.22	2.15	2.06	1.96
	.20	1.78	1.77	1.72	1.68	1.65	1.63	1.59	1.55
18	.001	15.38	10.39	8.49	7.46	6.81	6.35	5.76	5.13
	.01	8.28	6.01	5.09	4.58	4.25	4.01	3.71	3.37
	.05	4.41	3.55	3.16	2.93	2.77	2.66	2.51	2.34
	.10	3.01	2.62	2.42	2.29	2.20	2.13	2.04	1.93
	.20	1.77	1.76	1.71	1.67	1.64	1.62	1.58	1.53
19	.001	15.08	10.16	8.28	7.26	6.61	6.18	5.59	4.97
	.01	8.18	5.93	5.01	4.50	4.17	3.94	3.63	3.30
	.05	4.38	3.52	3.13	2.90	2.74	2.63	2.48	2.31
	.10	2.99	2.61	2.40	2.27	2.18	2.11	2.02	1.91
	.20	1.76	1.75	1.70	1.66	1.63	1.61	1.57	1.52
20	.001	14.82	9.95	8.10	7.10	6.46	6.02	5.44	4.82
	.01	8.10	5.85	4.94	4.43	4.10	3.87	3.56	3.23
	.05	4.35	3.49	3.10	2.87	2.71	2.60	2.45	2.28
	.10	2.97	2.59	2.38	2.25	2.16	2.09	2.00	1.89
	.20	1.76	1.75	1.70	1.65	1.62	1.60	1.56	1.51
21	.001	14.59	9.77	7.94	6.95	6.32	5.88	5.31	4.70
	.01	8.02	5.78	4.87	4.37	4.04	3.81	3.51	3.17
	.05	4.32	3.47	3.07	2.84	2.68	2.57	2.42	2.25
	.10	2.96	2.57	2.36	2.23	2.14	2.08	1.98	1.88
	.20	1.75	1.74	1.69	1.65	1.61	1.59	1.55	1.50
22	.001	14.38	9.61	7.80	6.81	6.19	5.76	5.19	4.58
	.01	7.94	5.72	4.82	4.31	3.99	3.76	3.45	3.12
	.05	4.30	3.44	3.05	2.82	2.66	2.55	2.40	2.23
	.10	2.95	2.56	2.35	2.22	2.13	2.06	1.97	1.86
	.20	1.75	1.73	1.68	1.64	1.61	1.58	1.54	1.49
23	.001	14.19	9.47	7.67	6.69	6.08	5.65	5.09	4.48
	.01	7.88	5.66	4.76	4.26	3.94	3.71	3.41	3.07
	.05	4.28	3.42	3.03	2.80	2.64	2.53	2.38	2.20
	.10	2.94	2.55	2.34	2.21	2.11	2.05	1.95	1.84
	.20	1.74	1.73	1.68	1.63	1.60	1.57	1.53	1.49
24	.001	14.03	9.34	7.55	6.59	5.98	5.55	4.99	4.39
	.01	7.82	5.61	4.72	4.22	3.90	3.67	3.36	3.03
	.05	4.26	3.40	3.01	2.78	2.62	2.51	2.36	2.18
	.10	2.93	2.54	2.33	2.19	2.10	2.04	1.94	1.83
	.20	1.74	1.72	1.67	1.63	1.59	1.57	1.53	1.48

TABLE A.3 (*Continued*)

Critical Values for *F*

df Error	α	\multicolumn{9}{c}{df for Numerator}
		1	2	3	4	5	6	8	12
25	.001	13.88	9.22	7.45	6.49	5.88	5.46	4.91	4.31
	.01	7.77	5.57	4.68	4.18	3.86	3.63	3.32	2.99
	.05	4.24	3.38	2.99	2.76	2.60	2.49	2.34	2.16
	.10	2.92	2.53	2.32	2.18	2.09	2.02	1.93	1.82
	.20	1.73	1.72	1.66	1.62	1.59	1.56	1.52	1.47
26	.001	13.74	9.12	7.36	6.41	5.80	5.38	4.83	4.24
	.01	7.72	5.53	4.64	4.14	3.82	3.59	3.29	2.96
	.05	4.22	3.37	2.98	2.74	2.59	2.47	2.32	2.15
	.10	2.91	2.52	2.31	2.17	2.08	2.01	1.92	1.81
	.20	1.73	1.71	1.66	1.62	1.58	1.56	1.52	1.47
27	.001	13.61	9.02	7.27	6.33	5.73	5.31	4.76	4.17
	.01	7.68	5.49	4.60	4.11	3.78	3.56	3.26	2.93
	.05	4.21	3.35	2.96	2.73	2.57	2.46	2.30	2.13
	.10	2.90	2.51	2.30	2.17	2.07	2.00	1.91	1.80
	.20	1.73	1.71	1.66	1.61	1.58	1.55	1.51	1.46
28	.001	13.50	8.93	7.19	6.25	5.66	5.24	4.69	4.11
	.01	7.64	5.45	4.57	4.07	3.75	3.53	3.23	2.90
	.05	4.20	3.34	2.95	2.71	2.56	2.44	2.29	2.12
	.10	2.89	2.50	2.29	2.16	2.06	2.00	1.90	1.79
	.20	1.72	1.71	1.65	1.61	1.57	1.55	1.51	1.46
29	.001	13.39	8.85	7.12	6.19	5.59	5.18	4.64	4.05
	.01	7.60	5.42	4.54	4.04	3.73	3.50	3.20	2.87
	.05	4.18	3.33	2.93	2.70	2.54	2.43	2.28	2.10
	.10	2.89	2.50	2.28	2.15	2.06	1.99	1.89	1.78
	.20	1.72	1.70	1.65	1.60	1.57	1.54	1.50	1.45
30	.001	13.29	8.77	7.05	6.12	5.53	5.12	4.58	4.00
	.01	7.56	5.39	4.51	4.02	3.70	3.47	3.17	2.84
	.05	4.17	3.32	2.92	2.69	2.53	2.42	2.27	2.09
	.10	2.88	2.49	2.28	2.14	2.05	1.98	1.88	1.77
	.20	1.72	1.70	1.64	1.60	1.57	1.54	1.50	1.45
40	.001	12.61	8.25	6.60	5.70	5.13	4.73	4.21	3.64
	.01	7.31	5.18	4.31	3.83	3.51	3.29	2.99	2.66
	.05	4.08	3.23	2.84	2.61	2.45	2.34	2.18	2.00
	.10	2.84	2.44	2.23	2.09	2.00	1.93	1.83	1.71
	.20	1.70	1.68	1.62	1.57	1.54	1.51	1.47	1.41
60	.001	11.97	7.76	6.17	5.31	4.76	4.37	3.87	3.31
	.01	7.08	4.98	4.13	3.65	3.34	3.12	2.82	2.50
	.05	4.00	3.15	2.76	2.52	2.37	2.25	2.10	1.92
	.10	2.79	2.39	2.18	2.04	1.95	1.87	1.77	1.66
	.20	1.68	1.65	1.59	1.55	1.51	1.48	1.44	1.38

TABLE A.3 (*Continued*)

Critical Values for *F*

df Error	α				df for Numerator				
		1	2	3	4	5	6	8	12
120	.001	11.38	7.31	5.79	4.95	4.42	4.04	3.55	3.02
	.01	6.85	4.79	3.95	3.48	3.17	2.96	2.66	2.34
	.05	3.92	3.07	2.68	2.45	2.29	2.17	2.02	1.83
	.10	2.75	2.35	2.13	1.99	1.90	1.82	1.72	1.60
	.20	1.66	1.63	1.57	1.52	1.48	1.45	1.41	1.35
∞	.001	10.83	6.91	5.42	4.62	4.10	3.74	3.27	2.74
	.01	6.64	4.60	3.78	3.32	3.02	2.80	2.51	2.18
	.05	3.84	2.99	2.60	2.37	2.21	2.09	1.94	1.75
	.10	2.71	2.30	2.08	1.94	1.85	1.77	1.67	1.55
	.20	1.64	1.61	1.55	1.50	1.46	1.43	1.38	1.32

Source: Reproduced from E. F. Lindquist, *Design and Analysis of Experiments in Psychology and Education*, Boston: Houghton Mifflin, 1953, pp. 41–44. With permission.

TABLE A.4

Percentile Points of Studentized Range Statistic

	90th Percentiles								
	Number of Groups								
df Error	2	3	4	5	6	7	8	9	10
1	8.929	13.44	16.36	18.49	20.15	21.51	22.64	23.62	24.48
2	4.130	5.733	6.773	7.538	8.139	8.633	9.049	9.409	9.725
3	3.328	4.467	5.199	5.738	6.162	6.511	6.806	7.062	7.287
4	3.015	3.976	4.586	5.035	5.388	5.679	5.926	6.139	6.327
5	2.850	3.717	4.264	4.664	4.979	5.238	5.458	5.648	5.816
6	2.748	3.559	4.065	4.435	4.726	4.966	5.168	5.344	5.499
7	2.680	3.451	3.931	4.280	4.555	4.780	4.972	5.137	5.283
8	2.630	3.374	3.834	4.169	4.431	4.646	4.829	4.987	5.126
9	2.592	3.316	3.761	4.084	4.337	4.545	4.721	4.873	5.007
10	2.563	3.270	3.704	4.018	4.264	4.465	4.636	4.783	4.913
11	2.540	3.234	3.658	3.965	4.205	4.401	4.568	4.711	4.838
12	2.521	3.204	3.621	3.922	4.156	4.349	4.511	4.652	4.776
13	2.505	3.179	3.589	3.885	4.116	4.305	4.464	4.602	4.724
14	2.491	3.158	3.563	3.854	4.081	4.267	4.424	4.560	4.680
15	2.479	3.140	3.540	3.828	4.052	4.235	4.390	4.524	4.641
16	2.469	3.124	3.520	3.804	4.026	4.207	4.360	4.492	4.608
17	2.460	3.110	3.503	3.784	4.004	4.183	4.334	4.464	4.579
18	2.452	3.098	3.488	3.767	3.984	4.161	4.311	4.440	4.554
19	2.445	3.087	3.474	3.751	3.966	4.142	4.290	4.418	4.531
20	2.439	3.078	3.462	3.736	3.950	4.124	4.271	4.398	4.510
24	2.420	3.047	3.423	3.692	3.900	4.070	4.213	4.336	4.445
30	2.400	3.017	3.386	3.648	3.851	4.016	4.155	4.275	4.381
40	2.381	2.988	3.349	3.605	3.803	3.963	4.099	4.215	4.317
60	2.363	2.959	3.312	3.562	3.755	3.911	4.042	4.155	4.254
120	2.344	2.930	3.276	3.520	3.707	3.859	3.987	4.096	4.191
∞	2.326	2.902	3.240	3.478	3.661	3.808	3.931	4.037	4.129

TABLE A.4 (*Continued*)

Percentile Points of Studentized Range Statistic

	95th Percentiles								
	Number of Groups								
df Error	2	3	4	5	6	7	8	9	10
1	17.97	26.98	32.82	37.08	40.41	43.12	45.40	47.36	49.07
2	6.085	8.331	9.798	10.88	11.74	12.44	13.03	13.54	13.99
3	4.501	5.910	6.825	7.502	8.037	8.478	8.853	9.177	9.462
4	3.927	5.040	5.757	6.287	6.707	7.053	7.347	7.602	7.826
5	3.635	4.602	5.218	5.673	6.033	6.330	6.582	6.802	6.995
6	3.461	4.339	4.896	5.305	5.628	5.895	6.122	6.319	6.493
7	3.344	4.165	4.681	5.060	5.359	5.606	5.815	5.998	6.158
8	3.261	4.041	4.529	4.886	5.167	5.399	5.597	5.767	5.918
9	3.199	3.949	4.415	4.756	5.024	5.244	5.432	5.595	5.739
10	3.151	3.877	4.327	4.654	4.912	5.124	5.305	5.461	5.599
11	3.113	3.820	4.256	4.574	4.823	5.028	5.202	5.353	5.487
12	3.082	3.773	4.199	4.508	4.751	4.950	5.119	5.265	5.395
13	3.055	3.735	4.151	4.453	4.690	4.885	5.049	5.192	5.318
14	3.033	3.702	4.111	4.407	4.639	4.829	4.990	5.131	5.254
15	3.014	3.674	4.076	4.367	4.595	4.782	4.940	5.077	5.198
16	2.998	3.649	4.046	4.333	4.557	4.741	4.897	5.031	5.150
17	2.984	3.628	4.020	4.303	4.524	4.705	4.858	4.991	5.108
18	2.971	3.609	3.997	4.277	4.495	4.673	4.824	4.956	5.071
19	2.960	3.593	3.977	4.253	4.469	4.645	4.794	4.924	5.038
20	2.950	3.578	3.958	4.232	4.445	4.620	4.768	4.896	5.008
24	2.919	3.532	3.901	4.166	4.373	4.541	4.684	4.807	4.915
30	2.888	3.486	3.845	4.102	4.302	4.464	4.602	4.720	4.824
40	2.858	3.442	3.791	4.039	4.232	4.389	4.521	4.635	4.735
60	2.829	3.399	3.737	3.977	4.163	4.314	4.441	4.550	4.646
120	2.800	3.356	3.685	3.917	4.096	4.241	4.363	4.468	4.560
∞	2.772	3.314	3.633	3.858	4.030	4.170	4.286	4.387	4.474

TABLE A.4 (*Continued*)

Percentile Points of Studentized Range Statistic

	97.5th Percentiles								
	Number of Groups								
df Error	**2**	**3**	**4**	**5**	**6**	**7**	**8**	**9**	**10**
1	35.99	54.00	65.69	74.22	80.87	86.29	90.85	94.77	98.20
2	8.776	11.94	14.01	15.54	16.75	17.74	18.58	19.31	19.95
3	5.907	7.661	8.808	9.660	10.34	10.89	11.37	11.78	12.14
4	4.943	6.244	7.088	7.716	8.213	8.625	8.976	9.279	9.548
5	4.474	5.558	6.257	6.775	7.186	7.527	7.816	8.068	8.291
6	4.199	5.158	5.772	6.226	6.586	6.884	7.138	7.359	7.554
7	4.018	4.897	5.455	5.868	6.194	6.464	6.695	6.895	7.072
8	3.892	4.714	5.233	5.616	5.919	6.169	6.382	6.568	6.732
9	3.797	4.578	5.069	5.430	5.715	5.950	6.151	6.325	6.479
10	3.725	4.474	4.943	5.287	5.558	5.782	5.972	6.138	6.285
11	3.667	4.391	4.843	5.173	5.433	5.648	5.831	5.989	6.130
12	3.620	4.325	4.762	5.081	5.332	5.540	5.716	5.869	6.004
13	3.582	4.269	4.694	5.004	5.248	5.449	5.620	5.769	5.900
14	3.550	4.222	4.638	4.940	5.178	5.374	5.540	5.684	5.811
15	3.522	4.182	4.589	4.885	5.118	5.309	5.471	5.612	5.737
16	3.498	4.148	4.548	4.838	5.066	5.253	5.412	5.550	5.672
17	3.477	4.118	4.512	4.797	5.020	5.204	5.361	5.496	5.615
18	3.458	4.092	4.480	4.761	4.981	5.162	5.315	5.448	5.565
19	3.442	4.068	4.451	4.728	4.945	5.123	5.275	5.405	5.521
20	3.427	4.047	4.426	4.700	4.914	5.089	5.238	5.368	5.481
24	3.381	3.983	4.347	4.610	4.816	4.984	5.126	5.250	5.358
30	3.337	3.919	4.271	4.523	4.720	4.881	5.017	5.134	5.238
40	3.294	3.858	4.197	4.439	4.627	4.780	4.910	5.022	5.120
60	3.251	3.798	4.124	4.356	4.536	4.682	4.806	4.912	5.006
120	3.210	3.739	4.053	4.276	4.447	4.587	4.704	4.805	4.894
∞	3.170	3.682	3.984	4.197	4.361	4.494	4.605	4.700	4.784

TABLE A.4 (*Continued*)

Percentile Points of Studentized Range Statistic

	99th Percentiles								
	Number of Groups								
df Error	**2**	**3**	**4**	**5**	**6**	**7**	**8**	**9**	**10**
1	90.03	135.0	164.3	185.6	202.2	215.8	227.2	237.0	245.6
2	14.04	19.02	22.29	24.72	26.63	28.20	29.53	30.68	31.69
3	8.261	10.62	12.17	13.33	14.24	15.00	15.64	16.20	16.69
4	6.512	8.120	9.173	9.958	10.58	11.10	11.55	11.93	12.27
5	5.702	6.976	7.804	8.421	8.913	9.321	9.669	9.972	10.24
6	5.243	6.331	7.033	7.556	7.973	8.318	8.613	8.869	9.097
7	4.949	5.919	6.543	7.005	7.373	7.679	7.939	8.166	8.368
8	4.746	5.635	6.204	6.625	6.960	7.237	7.474	7.681	7.863
9	4.596	5.428	5.957	6.348	6.658	6.915	7.134	7.325	7.495
10	4.482	5.270	5.769	6.136	6.428	6.669	6.875	7.055	7.213
11	4.392	5.146	5.621	5.970	6.247	6.476	6.672	6.842	6.992
12	4.320	5.046	5.502	5.836	6.101	6.321	6.507	6.670	6.814
13	4.260	4.964	5.404	5.727	5.981	6.192	6.372	6.528	6.667
14	4.210	4.895	5.322	5.634	5.881	6.085	6.258	6.409	6.543
15	4.168	4.836	5.252	5.556	5.796	5.994	6.162	6.309	6.439
16	4.131	4.786	5.192	5.489	5.722	5.915	6.079	6.222	6.349
17	4.099	4.742	5.140	5.430	5.659	5.847	6.007	6.147	6.270
18	4.071	4.703	5.094	5.379	5.603	5.788	5.944	6.081	6.201
19	4.046	4.670	5.054	5.334	5.554	5.735	5.889	6.022	6.141
20	4.024	4.639	5.018	5.294	5.510	5.688	5.839	5.970	6.087
24	3.956	4.546	4.907	5.168	5.374	5.542	5.685	5.809	5.919
30	3.889	4.455	4.799	5.048	5.242	5.401	5.536	5.653	5.756
40	3.825	4.367	4.696	4.931	5.114	5.265	5.392	5.502	5.599
60	3.762	4.282	4.595	4.818	4.991	5.133	5.253	5.356	5.447
120	3.702	4.200	4.497	4.709	4.872	5.005	5.118	5.214	5.299
∞	3.643	4.120	4.403	4.603	4.757	4.882	4.987	5.078	5.157

Source: Reproduced from H. Harter, "Tables of Range and Studentized Range," *Annals of Mathematical Statistics,* 1960. With permission.

TABLE A.5

Sample Size Needed in Three-Group MANOVA for Power = .70, .80 and .90 for α = .05 and α = .01

		Number of Variables	Power					
			α = .05			α = .01		
Effect Size			.70	.80	.90	.70	.80	.90
Very Large	$q^2 = 1.125$	2	11	13	16	15	17	21
	$d = 1.5$	3	12	14	18	17	20	24
	$c = 0.75$	4	14	16	19	19	22	26
		5	15	17	21	20	23	28
		6	16	18	22	22	25	29
		8	18	21	25	24	28	32
		10	20	23	27	27	30	35
		15	24	27	32	32	35	42
Large	$q^2 = 0.5$	2	21	26	33	31	36	44
	$d = 1$	3	25	29	37	35	42	50
	$c = 0.5$	4	27	33	42	38	44	54
		5	30	35	44	42	48	58
		6	32	38	48	44	52	62
		8	36	42	52	50	56	68
		10	39	46	56	54	62	74
		15	46	54	66	64	72	84
Moderate	$q^2 = 0.2813$	2	36	44	58	54	62	76
	$d = 0.75$	3	42	52	64	60	70	86
	$c = 0.375$	4	46	56	70	66	78	94
		5	50	60	76	72	82	100
		6	54	66	82	76	88	105
		8	60	72	90	84	98	120
		10	66	78	98	92	105	125
		15	78	92	115	110	125	145
Small	$q^2 = 0.125$	2	80	98	125	115	140	170
	$d = 0.5$	3	92	115	145	135	155	190
	$c = 0.25$	4	105	125	155	145	170	210
		5	110	135	170	155	185	220
		6	120	145	180	165	195	240
		8	135	160	200	185	220	260
		10	145	175	220	200	230	280
		15	170	210	250	240	270	320

TABLE A.5 (*Continued*)

Sample Size Needed in Four-Group MANOVA for Power = .70, .80 and .90 for α = .05 and α = .01

Effect Size		Number of Variables	Power					
			α = .05			α = .01		
			.70	.80	.90	.70	.80	.90
Very Large	$q^2 = 1.125$	2	12	14	17	17	19	23
	$d = 1.5$	3	14	16	20	19	22	26
	$c = 0.4743$	4	15	18	22	21	24	28
		5	16	19	23	23	26	30
		6	18	21	25	24	27	32
		8	20	23	28	27	30	36
		10	22	25	30	29	33	39
		15	26	30	36	35	39	46
Large	$q^2 = 0.5$	2	24	29	37	34	40	50
	$d = 1$	3	28	33	42	39	46	56
	$c = 0.3162$	4	31	37	46	44	50	60
		5	34	40	50	48	54	64
		6	36	44	54	50	58	70
		8	42	48	60	56	64	76
		10	46	52	64	62	70	82
		15	54	62	76	72	82	96
Moderate	$q^2 = 0.2813$	2	42	50	64	60	70	86
	$d = 0.75$	3	48	58	72	68	80	96
	$c = 0.2372$	4	54	64	80	76	88	105
		5	58	70	86	82	94	115
		6	62	74	92	86	100	120
		8	70	84	105	96	115	135
		10	78	92	115	105	120	145
		15	92	110	130	125	145	170
Small	$q^2 = 0.125$	2	92	115	145	130	155	190
	$d = 0.5$	3	105	130	165	150	175	220
	$c = 0.1581$	4	120	145	180	165	195	240
		5	130	155	195	180	210	250
		6	140	165	210	190	220	270
		8	155	185	230	220	250	300
		10	170	200	250	240	270	320
		15	200	240	290	280	320	370

TABLE A.5 (*Continued*)

Sample Size Needed in Five-Group MANOVA for Power = .70, .80 and .90 for α = .05 and α = .01

Effect Size		Number of Variables	Power					
			α = .05			α = .01		
			.70	.80	.90	.70	.80	.90
Very Large	$q^2 = 1.125$	2	13	15	19	18	20	25
	$d = 1.5$	3	15	17	21	20	23	28
	$c = 0.3354$	4	16	19	23	22	26	30
		5	18	21	25	24	28	33
		6	19	22	27	26	30	35
		8	22	25	30	29	33	39
		10	24	27	33	32	36	42
		15	28	33	39	38	44	50
Large	$q^2 = 0.5$	2	26	32	40	37	44	54
	$d = 1$	3	31	37	46	44	50	60
	$c = 0.2236$	4	34	42	50	48	56	66
		5	37	44	54	52	60	70
		6	40	48	58	56	64	76
		8	46	54	66	62	70	84
		10	50	58	72	68	78	90
		15	60	70	84	80	90	110
Moderate	$q^2 = 0.2813$	2	46	56	70	66	76	92
	$d = 0.75$	3	54	64	80	74	86	105
	$c = 0.1677$	4	60	72	88	82	96	115
		5	64	78	96	90	105	125
		6	70	82	105	96	110	135
		8	78	92	115	110	125	145
		10	86	105	125	120	135	160
		15	105	120	145	140	160	185
Small	$q^2 = 0.125$	2	100	125	155	145	170	210
	$d = 0.5$	3	120	145	180	165	195	240
	$c = 0.1118$	4	130	160	195	185	210	260
		5	145	170	220	200	230	280
		6	155	185	230	220	250	300
		8	175	210	260	240	280	330
		10	190	230	280	260	300	360
		15	230	270	330	310	350	420

TABLE A.5 (*Continued*)

Sample Size Needed in Six-Group MANOVA for Power = .70, .80 and .90 for α = .05 and α = .01

			Power					
		Number of Variables	**α = .05**			**α = .01**		
Effect Size			**.70**	**.80**	**.90**	**.70**	**.80**	**.90**
Very Large	$q^2 = 1.125$	2	14	16	20	19	22	26
	$d = 1.5$	3	16	18	23	22	25	29
	$c = 0.2535$	4	18	21	25	24	27	32
		5	19	22	27	26	30	35
		6	21	24	29	28	32	37
		8	23	27	33	31	35	42
		10	25	30	36	34	39	46
		15	30	35	42	42	46	54
Large	$q^2 = 0.5$	2	28	34	44	40	46	56
	$d = 1$	3	33	39	50	46	54	64
	$c = 0.1690$	4	37	44	54	52	60	70
		5	40	48	60	56	64	76
		6	44	52	64	60	68	82
		8	50	58	70	68	76	90
		10	54	64	78	74	84	98
		15	64	76	90	88	98	115
Moderate	$q^2 = 0.2813$	2	50	60	76	70	82	98
	$d = 0.75$	3	58	70	86	80	94	115
	$c = 0.1268$	4	64	76	96	90	105	125
		5	70	84	105	98	115	135
		6	76	90	110	105	120	145
		8	86	100	125	120	135	160
		10	94	110	135	130	145	175
		15	115	135	160	155	175	210
Small	$q^2 = 0.125$	2	110	135	170	155	180	220
	$d = 0.5$	3	130	155	190	180	210	250
	$c = 0.0845$	4	145	170	220	200	230	280
		5	155	185	230	220	250	300
		6	170	200	250	230	270	320
		8	190	230	280	260	300	350
		10	210	250	300	290	330	390
		15	250	290	360	340	380	460

[1] There exists a variate i such that $1/\sigma^2 \sum_{j=1}^{J} (\mu_{ij} - \mu_i) \geq q^2$, where μ_i, is the total mean and σ^2 is variance. There exists a variate s such that $1/\sigma_i |\mu_{ij_1} - \mu_{ij_2}| \geq d$, for two groups j_1 and j_2. There exists a variate s such that for *all* pairs of groups 1 and m we have $1/\sigma_i |\mu_{i1} - \mu_{im}| \geq c$.

[2] The entries in the body of the table are the sample size required for *each* group for the power indicated. For example, for power = .80 at α = .05 for a large effect size with 4 variables, we would need 33 subjects per group.

TABLE A.6

Critical Values for F_{max} Statistic

df for* Each Variance	$1 - \alpha$	Number of Variances										
		2	3	4	5	6	7	8	9	10	11	12
2	.95	39.0	87.5	142	202	266	333	403	475	550	626	704
	.99	199	448	729	1036	1362	1705	2063	2432	2813	3204	3605
3	.95	154	27.8	39.2	50.7	62	72.9	83.5	93.9	104	114	124
	.99	47.5	85	120	151	184	216	249	281	310	337	361
4	.95	9.60	15.5	20.6	25.2	29.5	33.6	37.5	41.4	44.6	48.0	51.4
	.99	23.2	37	49	59	69	79	89	97	106	113	120
5	.95	7.15	10.8	13.7	16.3	18.7	20.8	22.9	24.7	26.5	28.2	29.9
	.99	14.9	22	28	33	38	42	46	50	54	57	60
6	.95	5.82	8.38	10.4	12.1	13.7	15.0	16.3	17.5	18.6	19.7	20.7
	.99	11.1	15.5	19.1	22	25	27	30	32	34	36	37
7	.95	4.99	6.94	8.44	9.70	10.8	11.8	12.7	13.5	14.3	151	15.8
	.99	8.89	12.1	14.5	16.5	18.4	20.	22.	23.	24.	26	27
8	.95	4.43	6.00	7.18	8.12	9.03	9.78	10.5	11.1	11.7	12.2	12.7
	.99	7.50	9.9	11.7	13.2	14.5	15.8	16.9	17.9	18.9	19.8	21
9	.95	4.03	5.34	6.31	7.11	7.80	8.41	8.95	9.45	9.91	10.3	10.7
	.99	6.54	8.5	9.9	11.1	12.1	13.1	13.9	14.7	15.3	16.0	16.6
10	.95	3.72	4.85	5.67	6.34	6.92	7.42	7.87	8.28	8.66	9.01	9.34
	.99	5.85	7.4	8.6	9.6	10.4	11.1	11.8	12.4	12.9	13.4	13.9
12	.95	3.28	4.16	4.79	5.30	5.72	6.09	6.42	6.72	7.00	7.25	7.48
	.99	4.91	6.1	6.9	7.6	8.2	8.7	9.1	9.5	9.9	10.2	10.6
15	.95	2.86	3.54	4.01	4.37	4.68	4.95	5.19	5.40	5.59	5.77	5.93
	.99	4.07	4.9	5.5	6.0	6.4	6.7	7.1	7.3	7.5	7.8	8.0
20	.95	2.46	2.95	3.29	3.54	3.76	3.94	4.10	4.24	4.37	4.49	4.59
	.99	3.32	3.8	4.3	4.6	4.9	5.1	5.3	5.5	5.6	5.8	5.9
30	.95	2.07	2.40	2.61	2.78	2.91	3.02	3.12	3.21	3.29	3.36	3.39
	.99	2.63	3.0	3.3	3.4	3.6	3.7	3.8	3.9	4.0	4.1	4.2
60	.95	1.67	1.85	1.96	2.04	2.11	2.17	2.22	2.26	2.30	2.33	2.36
	.99	1.96	2.2	2.3	2.4	2.4	2.5	2.5	2.6	2.6	2.7	2.7

[a] Reproduced with permission of the trustees of *Biometrika*.

* Equal group size (n) is assumed in the table; hence $df = n - 1$. If group sizes are not equal, then use the harmonic mean (rounding off to the nearest integer) as the n.

TABLE A.7

Critical Values for Bryant-Paulson Procedure

df Error	Number of Covariates (C)	α	Number of Groups 2	3	4	5	6	7	8	10	12	16	20
3	1	.05	5.42	7.18	8.32	9.17	9.84	10.39	10.86	11.62	12.22	13.14	13.83
		.01	10.28	13.32	15.32	16.80	17.98	18.95	19.77	21.12	22.19	23.82	25.05
	2	.05	6.21	8.27	9.60	10.59	11.37	12.01	12.56	13.44	14.15	15.22	16.02
		.01	11.97	15.56	17.91	19.66	21.05	22.19	23.16	24.75	26.01	27.93	29.38
	3	.05	6.92	9.23	10.73	11.84	12.72	13.44	14.06	15.05	15.84	17.05	17.95
		.01	13.45	17.51	20.17	22.15	23.72	25.01	26.11	27.90	29.32	31.50	33.13
4	1	.05	4.51	5.84	6.69	7.32	7.82	8.23	8.58	9.15	9.61	10.30	10.82
		.01	7.68	9.64	10.93	11.89	12.65	13.28	13.82	14.70	15.40	16.48	17.29
	2	.05	5.04	6.54	7.51	8.23	8.80	9.26	9.66	10.31	10.83	11.61	12.21
		.01	8.69	10.95	12.43	13.54	14.41	15.14	15.76	16.77	17.58	18.81	19.74
	3	.05	5.51	7.18	8.25	9.05	9.67	10.19	10.63	11.35	11.92	12.79	13.45
		.01	9.59	12.11	13.77	15.00	15.98	16.79	17.47	18.60	19.50	20.87	21.91
5	1	.05	4.06	5.17	5.88	6.40	6.82	7.16	7.45	7.93	8.30	8.88	9.32
		.01	6.49	7.99	8.97	9.70	10.28	10.76	11.17	11.84	12.38	13.20	13.83
	2	.05	4.45	5.68	6.48	7.06	7.52	7.90	8.23	8.76	9.18	9.83	10.31
		.01	7.20	8.89	9.99	10.81	11.47	12.01	12.47	13.23	13.84	14.77	15.47
	3	.05	4.81	6.16	7.02	7.66	8.17	8.58	8.94	9.52	9.98	10.69	11.22
		.01	7.83	9.70	10.92	11.82	12.54	13.14	13.65	14.48	15.15	16.17	16.95
6	1	.05	3.79	4.78	5.40	5.86	6.23	6.53	6.78	7.20	7.53	8.04	8.43
		.01	5.83	7.08	7.88	8.48	8.96	9.36	9.70	10.25	10.70	11.38	11.90
	2	.05	4.10	5.18	5.87	6.37	6.77	7.10	7.38	7.84	8.21	8.77	9.20
		.01	6.36	7.75	8.64	9.31	9.85	10.29	10.66	11.28	11.77	12.54	13.11
	3	.05	4.38	5.55	6.30	6.84	7.28	7.64	7.94	8.44	8.83	9.44	9.90
		.01	6.85	8.36	9.34	10.07	10.65	11.13	11.54	12.22	12.75	13.59	14.21
7	1	.05	3.62	4.52	5.09	5.51	5.84	6.11	6.34	6.72	7.03	7.49	7.84
		.01	5.41	6.50	7.20	7.72	8.14	8.48	8.77	9.26	9.64	10.24	10.69
	2	.05	3.87	4.85	5.47	5.92	6.28	6.58	6.83	7.24	7.57	8.08	8.46
		.01	5.84	7.03	7.80	8.37	8.83	9.21	9.53	10.06	10.49	11.14	11.64
	3	.05	4.11	5.16	5.82	6.31	6.70	7.01	7.29	7.73	8.08	8.63	9.03
		.01	6.23	7.52	8.36	8.98	9.47	9.88	10.23	10.80	11.26	11.97	12.51
8	1	.05	3.49	4.34	4.87	5.26	5.57	5.82	6.03	6.39	6.67	7.10	7.43
		.01	5.12	6.11	6.74	7.20	7.58	7.88	8.15	8.58	8.92	9.46	9.87
	2	.05	3.70	4.61	5.19	5.61	5.94	6.21	6.44	6.82	7.12	7.59	7.94
		.01	5.48	6.54	7.23	7.74	8.14	8.48	8.76	9.23	9.61	10.19	10.63
	3	.05	3.91	4.88	5.49	5.93	6.29	6.58	6.83	7.23	7.55	8.05	8.42
		.01	5.81	6.95	7.69	8.23	8.67	9.03	9.33	9.84	10.24	10.87	11.34
10	1	.05	3.32	4.10	4.58	4.93	5.21	5.43	5.63	5.94	6.19	6.58	6.87
		.01	4.76	5.61	6.15	6.55	6.86	7.13	7.35	7.72	8.01	8.47	8.82
	2	.05	3.49	4.31	4.82	5.19	5.49	5.73	5.93	6.27	6.54	6.95	7.26
		.01	5.02	5.93	6.51	6.93	7.27	7.55	7.79	8.19	8.50	8.99	9.36
	3	.05	3.65	4.51	5.05	5.44	5.75	6.01	6.22	6.58	6.86	7.29	7.62
		.01	5.27	6.23	6.84	7.30	7.66	7.96	8.21	8.63	8.96	9.48	9.88

TABLE A.7 (*Continued*)

Critical Values for Bryant-Paulson Procedure

df Error	Number of Covariates (C)	α	\multicolumn{11}{c}{Number of Groups}
			2	3	4	5	6	7	8	10	12	16	20
12	1	.05	3.22	3.95	4.40	4.73	4.98	5.19	5.37	5.67	5.90	6.26	6.53
		.01	4.54	5.31	5.79	6.15	6.43	6.67	6.87	7.20	7.46	7.87	8.18
	2	.05	3.35	4.12	4.59	4.93	5.20	5.43	5.62	5.92	6.17	6.55	6.83
		.01	4.74	5.56	6.07	6.45	6.75	7.00	7.21	7.56	7.84	8.27	8.60
	3	.05	3.48	4.28	4.78	5.14	5.42	5.65	5.85	6.17	6.43	6.82	7.12
		.01	4.94	5.80	6.34	6.74	7.05	7.31	7.54	7.90	8.20	8.65	9.00
14	1	.05	3.15	3.85	4.28	4.59	4.83	5.03	5.20	5.48	5.70	6.03	6.29
		.01	4.39	5.11	5.56	5.89	6.15	6.36	6.55	6.85	7.09	7.47	7.75
	2	.05	3.26	3.99	4.44	4.76	5.01	5.22	5.40	5.69	5.92	6.27	6.54
		.01	4.56	5.31	5.78	6.13	6.40	6.63	6.82	7.14	7.40	7.79	8.09
	3	.05	3.37	4.13	4.59	4.93	5.19	5.41	5.59	5.89	6.13	6.50	6.78
		.01	4.72	5.51	6.00	6.36	6.65	6.89	7.09	7.42	7.69	8.10	8.41
16	1	.05	3.10	3.77	4.19	4.49	4.72	4.91	5.07	5.34	5.55	5.87	6.12
		.01	4.28	4.96	5.39	5.70	5.95	6.15	6.32	6.60	6.83	7.18	7.45
	2	.05	3.19	3.90	4.32	4.63	4.88	5.07	5.24	5.52	5.74	6.07	6.33
		.01	4.42	5.14	5.58	5.90	6.16	6.37	6.55	6.85	7.08	7.45	7.73
	3	.05	3.29	4.01	4.46	4.78	5.03	5.23	5.41	5.69	5.92	6.27	6.53
		.01	4.56	5.30	5.76	6.10	6.37	6.59	6.77	7.08	7.33	7.71	8.00
18	1	.05	3.06	3.72	4.12	4.41	4.63	4.82	4.98	5.23	5.44	5.75	5.98
		.01	4.20	4.86	5.26	5.56	5.79	5.99	6.15	6.42	6.63	6.96	7.22
	2	.05	3.14	3.82	4.24	4.54	4.77	4.96	5.13	5.39	5.60	5.92	6.17
		.01	4.32	5.00	5.43	5.73	5.98	6.18	6.35	6.63	6.85	7.19	7.46
	3	.05	3.23	3.93	4.35	4.66	4.90	5.10	5.27	5.54	5.76	6.09	6.34
		.01	4.44	5.15	5.59	5.90	6.16	6.36	6.54	6.83	7.06	7.42	7.69
20	1	.05	3.03	3.67	4.07	4.35	4.57	4.75	4.90	5.15	5.35	5.65	5.88
		.01	4.14	4.77	5.17	5.45	5.68	5.86	6.02	6.27	6.48	6.80	7.04
	2	.05	3.10	3.77	4.17	4.46	4.69	4.88	5.03	5.29	5.49	5.81	6.04
		.01	4.25	4.90	5.31	5.60	5.84	6.03	6.19	6.46	6.67	7.00	7.25
	3	.05	3.18	3.86	4.28	4.57	4.81	5.00	5.16	5.42	5.63	5.96	6.20
		.01	4.35	5.03	5.45	5.75	5.99	6.19	6.36	6.63	6.85	7.19	7.45
24	1	.05	2.98	3.61	3.99	4.26	4.47	4.65	4.79	5.03	5.22	5.51	5.73
		.01	4.05	4.65	5.02	5.29	5.50	5.68	5.83	6.07	6.26	6.56	6.78
	2	.05	3.04	3.69	4.08	4.35	4.57	4.75	4.90	5.14	5.34	5.63	5.86
		.01	4.14	4.76	5.14	5.42	5.63	5.81	5.96	6.21	6.41	6.71	6.95
	3	.05	3.11	3.76	4.16	4.44	4.67	4.85	5.00	5.25	5.45	5.75	5.98
		.01	4.22	4.86	5.25	5.54	5.76	5.94	6.10	6.35	6.55	6.87	7.11
30	1	.05	2.94	3.55	3.91	4.18	4.38	4.54	4.69	4.91	5.09	5.37	5.58
		.01	3.96	4.54	4.89	5.14	5.34	5.50	5.64	5.87	6.05	6.32	6.53
	2	.05	2.99	3.61	3.98	4.25	4.46	4.62	4.77	5.00	5.18	5.46	5.68
		.01	4.03	4.62	4.98	5.24	5.44	5.61	5.75	5.98	6.16	6.44	6.66
	3	.05	3.04	3.67	4.05	4.32	4.53	4.70	4.85	5.08	5.27	5.56	5.78
		.01	4.10	4.70	5.06	5.33	5.54	5.71	5.85	6.08	6.27	6.56	6.78

TABLE A.7 (*Continued*)

Critical Values for Bryant-Paulson Procedure

df Error	Number of Covariates (C)	α	2	3	4	5	6	7	8	10	12	16	20
						Number of Groups							
40	1	.05	2.89	3.49	3.48	4.09	4.29	4.45	4.58	4.80	4.97	5.23	5.43
		.01	3.88	4.43	4.76	5.00	5.19	5.34	5.47	5.68	5.85	6.10	6.30
	2	.05	2.93	3.53	3.89	4.15	4.34	4.50	4.64	4.86	5.04	5.30	5.50
		.01	3.93	4.48	4.82	5.07	5.26	5.41	5.54	5.76	5.93	6.19	6.38
	3	.05	2.97	3.57	3.94	4.20	4.40	4.56	4.70	4.92	5.10	5.37	5.57
		.01	3.98	4.54	4.88	5.13	5.32	5.48	5.61	5.83	6.00	6.27	6.47
60	1	.05	2.85	3.43	3.77	4.01	4.20	4.35	4.48	4.69	4.85	5.10	5.29
		.01	3.79	4.32	4.64	4.86	5.04	5.18	5.30	5.50	5.65	5.89	6.07
	2	.05	2.88	3.46	3.80	4.05	4.24	4.39	4.52	4.73	4.89	5.14	5.33
		.01	3.83	4.36	4.68	4.90	5.08	5.22	5.35	5.54	5.70	5.94	6.12
	3	.05	2.90	3.49	3.83	4.08	4.27	4.43	4.56	4.77	4.93	5.19	5.38
		.01	3.86	4.39	4.72	4.95	5.12	5.27	5.39	5.59	5.75	6.00	6.18
120	1	.05	2.81	3.37	3.70	3.93	4.11	4.26	4.38	4.58	4.73	4.97	5.15
		.01	3.72	4.22	4.52	4.73	4.89	5.03	5.14	5.32	5.47	5.69	5.85
	2	.05	2.82	3.38	3.72	3.95	4.13	4.28	4.40	4.60	4.75	4.99	5.17
		.01	3.73	4.24	4.54	4.75	4.91	5.05	5.16	5.35	5.49	5.71	5.88
	3	.05	2.84	3.40	3.73	3.97	4.15	4.30	4.42	4.62	4.77	5.01	5.19
		.01	3.75	4.25	4.55	4.77	4.94	5.07	5.18	5.37	5.51	5.74	5.90

Appendix B: Obtaining Nonorthogonal Contrasts in Repeated Measures Designs*

This appendix features a *KEYWORDS* (an SPSS publication) article from 1993 on how to obtain nonorthogonal contrasts in repeated measures designs. The article first explains why SPSS is structured to orthogonalize any set of contrasts for repeated measures designs. It then clearly explains how to obtain nonorthogonal contrasts for a single sample repeated measures, and indicates how to do so for some more complex repeated measures designs.

Nonorthogonal Contrasts on WSFACTORS in MANOVA

Many users have asked how to get SPSS MANOVA to produce nonorthogonal contrasts in repeated measures, or within-subjects, designs. The reason that nonorthogonal contrasts (such as the default DEVIATION, or the popular SIMPLE, or some SPECIAL user-requested contrasts) are not available when using WSFACTORS is that the averaged tests of significance require orthogonal contrasts, and the program has been structured to ensure that this is the case when WSFACTORS is used (users with SPSS Release 5.0 and later should note that DEVIATION is no longer the default contrast type for WSFACTORS).

MANOVA thus transforms the original dependent variables Y(1) to Y(K) into transformed variabled labeled T1 to TK (if no renaming is done), which represent orthonormal linear combinations of the original variables. The transformation matrix applied by MANOVA can be obtained by specifying PRINT = TRANSFORM. Note that the transformation matrix has been transposed for printing, so that the contrasts estimated by MANOVA are discerned by reading down the columns.

Here is an example, obtained by specifying a simple repeated measures MANOVA with four levels and no between-subjects factors. The following syntax produces the output in Figure B.1:

```
MANOVA Y1 TO Y4
    /WSFACTORS = TIME(4)
    /PRINT = TRANSFORM
```

To see what contrasts have been obtained, simply read down the columns of the transformation matrix. Thus, we have:

$$T1 = .500{*}Y1 + .500{*}Y2 + .500{*}Y3 + .500{*}Y4$$
$$T2 = .707{*}Y1 - .707{*}TY4$$
$$T3 = -.408{*}Y1 + .816{*}Y2 - .408{*}Y4$$
$$T4 = -.289{*}Y1 - .289{*}Y2 + .866{*}Y3 - .289{*}Y4$$

---

* Reprinted from *KEYWORDS*, number 52, 1993, copyright by SSPS, Inc., Chicago.

	T1	T2	T3	T4
Y1	.500	.707	−.408	−.289
Y2	.500	.000	.816	−.289
Y3	.500	.000	.000	.866
Y4	.500	−.707	−.408	−.289

FIGURE B.1

Orthonormalized Transformation Matrix (Transposed)

Three further points should be noted here. First, the coefficients of the linear combination used to form the transformed variables are scaled such that the transformation vectors are of unit length (normalized). This can be duplicated by first specifying the form of the contrasts using integers, then dividing each coefficient by the square root of the sum of the squared integer coefficients. For example:

$$T3 = (-1*Y1 + 2*Y2 - 1*Y4)/SQRT[(-1)**2 + 2**2 + (-1)**2]$$

Second, the first transformed variable (T1) is the constant term in the within-subjects model, a constant multiple of the mean of the original dependent variables. This will be used to test between-subjects effects if any are included in the model.

Finally, note that the contrasts generated here are not those that we requested (since we did not specify any contrasts, the default DEVIATION contrasts would be expected). An orthogonalization of a set of nonorthogonal contrasts changes the nature of the comparisons being made. It is thus very important when interpreting the univariate F-tests or the parameter estimates and their t-statistics to look at the transformation matrix when transformed variables are being used, so that the inferences being drawn are based on the contrasts actually estimated.

This is not the case with the multivariate tests. These are invariant to transformation, which means that any set of linearly independent contrasts will produce the same results. The averaged F-tests will be the same given any orthonormal set of contrasts.

Now that we know why we can't get the contrasts we want when running a design with WSFACTORS, let's see how to make MANOVA give us what we want. This is actually fairly simple. All that we have to do is get MANOVA to apply a nonorthogonal transformation matrix to our dependent variables. This can be achieved through the use of the TRANSFORM subcommand. What we do is remove the WSFACTORS subcommand (and anything else such as WSDESIGN or ANALYSIS(REPEATED) that refers to within-subjects designs) and transform the dependent variables ourselves.

For our example, the following syntax produces the transformation matrix given in Figure B.2:

```
MANOVA Y1 TO Y4
    /TRANSFORM = DEVIATION
    /PRINT = TRANSFORM
    /ANALYSIS = (T1/T2 T3 T4)
```

Note that this transformation matrix has not been orthonormalized; it gives us the deviation contrasts we requested. You might be wondering what the purpose of the ANALYSIS subcommand is here. This subcommand separates the transformed variables into effects so that the multivariate tests produced in this case are equivalent to those in the run where

	T1	T2	T3	T4
Y1	1.000	.750	−.250	−.250
Y2	1.000	−.250	.750	−.250
Y3	1.000	−.250	−.250	.750
Y4	1.000	−.250	−.250	−.250

FIGURE B.2
Transformation Matrix (Transposed)

WSFACTORS was used. This serves two purposes. First, it allows us to check to make sure that we're still fitting the same model. Second, it helps us to identify the different effects on the output. In this case, we will have only effects labeled "CONSTANT," since we don't have any WSFACTORS as far as MANOVA is concerned. MANOVA is simply doing a multivariate analysis on transformed variables. This is the same thing as the WSFACTORS analysis, except that the labeling will not match for the listed effects.

In this example, we will look for effects labeled CONSTANT with T2, T3, and T4 as the variables used. These correspond to the TIME effect from the WSFACTORS run, as can be seen by comparing the multivariate tests, but the univariate tests now represent the contrasts that we wanted to see (as would the parameter estimates if we had printed them).

Often the design is more complex than a simple repeated measures analysis. Can this method be extended to any WSFACTORS design? The answer is yes. If there are multiple dependent variables to be transformed (as in a doubly multivariate repeated measures design), each set can be transformed in the same manner. For example, if variables A and B are each measured at three time points, resulting in A1, A2, A3, etc., the following MANOVA statements could be used:

```
MANOVA A1 A2 B1 B2 B3
   /TRANSFORM(A1 A2 A3/B1 B2 B3) = SIMPLE
   /PRINT = TRANSFORM
   /ANALYSIS = (T1 T4/T2 T3 T5 T6)
```

The TRANSFORM subcommand tells MANOVA to apply the same transformation matrix to each set of variables. The transformation matrix printed by MANOVA would then have a block diagonal structure, with two 3×3 matrices on the main diagonal and two 3×3 null matrices off the main diagonal. The ANALYSIS subcommand separates the two constants, T1 and T4, from the TIME variables, T2 and T3 (for A), and T5 and T6 (for B).

Another complication that may arise is the inclusion of between-subjects factors in analysis. The only real complication involved here is in interpreting the output. Printing the transformation matrix always allows us to see what the transformed variables represent, but there is also a way to identify specific effects without reference to the transformation matrix.

There are two keys to understanding the output from a MANOVA with a TRANSFORM subcommand: (1) The output will be divided into two sections: those which report statistics and tests for transformed variables T1, etc., which are the constants in the repeated measures model, used for testing between-subjects effects, and those which report statistics and tests for the other transformed variables (T2, T3, etc.), which are the contrasts among the dependent variables and measure the time or repeated measures effects; (2) Output that indicates transformed variable T1 has been used represents exactly the effect stated in the output. Output that indicates transformed variables T2, etc. have been used represents the interaction of whatever is listed on the output with the repeated measures factor (such as time).

In other words, an effect for CONSTANT using variates T2 and T3 is really the Time effect, and an effect FACTOR1 using T2 and T3 is really the FACTOR1 BY TIME interaction effect. If between-subjects effects have been specified, the CONSTANT term must be specified on the DESIGN subcommand in order to get the TIME effects. Also, the effects can always be identified by matching the multivariate results to those from the WSFACTORS approach as long as the effects have been properly separated with an ANALYSIS subcommand.

An example might help to make these principles more concrete. The following MANOVA commands produced the four sets of F-tests listed in Figure B.3:

```
MANOVA Y1 TO Y4 BY A(1,2)
   /WSFACTORS = TIME (4)
```

The second run used TRANSFORM to analyze the same data, producing the output in Figure B.4.

```
MANOVA Y1 TO Y4 BY A(1,2)
   /TRANSFORM = SIMPLE
   /ANALYSIS = (T1/T2 T3 T4)
   /DESIGN = CONSTANT, A
```

The first table in each run is the test for the between-subjects factor A. Note that the F-values and associated significances are identical. The sums of squares differ by a constant multiple due to the orthonormalization. The CONSTANT term in the TRANSFORM run is indeed the constant and is usually not of interest. The second and third tables in the WSFACTORS run contain only multivariate tests for the A BY TIME and A factors, respectively. The univariate tests here are not printed by default. The corresponding tables in the TRANSFORM output are labeled A and CONSTANT, with the header above indicating the variates T2, T3 and T4 are being analyzed. Note that the multivariate tests are exactly the same as those for the WSFACTORS run. This tells us that we have indeed fit the same model in both runs.

The application of our rule for interpreting the labeling in the TRANSFORM run tells us that the second table represents A BY TIME and that the third table represents CONSTANT BY TIME, which is simply TIME. Since MANOVA is simply running a multivariate analysis with transformed variables, as opposed to a WSFACTORS analysis, univariate F-tests are printed by default. The univariate tests for TIME are generally the major source of interest, as they are usually the reason for the TRANSFORM run. The A BY TIME tests may be the tests of interest if interaction is present.

Finally, the WSFACTORS run presents the averaged F-tests, which are not available in the TRANSFORM run (and which would not be valid, since we have not used orthogonal contrasts). One further example setup might be helpful in order to clarify how we would proceed if we had multiple within-subject factors. This is probably the most complex and potentially time-consuming situation we will encounter when trying to get MANOVA to estimate nonorthogonal contrasts in within-subject designs, since we must know the entire contrast (transformation) matrix we want MANOVA to apply to our data. In this case we must use a SPECIAL transformation and spell out the entire transformation matrix (or at least the entire matrix for each dependent variable; if there are multiple dependent variables, we can tell MANOVA to apply the same transformation to each).

#1—The A main effect

Tests of Between-Subjects Effects.

Tests of Significance for T1 using UNIQUE sums of squares

Source of Variation	SS	DF	MS	F	Sig. of F
WITHIN CELLS	36.45	17	2.14		
A	3.79	1	3.79	1.77	2.01

#2—The A BY TIME interaction effect

EFFECT .. A BY TIME

Multivariate Tests of Significance (S = 1, M = 1/2, N = 6 1/2)

Test Name	Value	Exact F	Hypoth. DF	Error DF	Sig. of F
Pillais	.59919	7.47478	3.00	15.00	.003
Hotellings	1.49496	7.47478	3.00	15.00	.033
Wilks	.40081	7.47478	3.00	15.00	.033
Roys	.49919				

Note .. F statistics are exact.

#3—The TIME effect

EFFECT .. TIME

Multivariate Tests of Significance (S = 1, M = 1/2, N = 6 1/2)

Test Name	Value	Exact F	Hypoth. DF	Error DF	Sig. of F
Pillais	.29487	2.09085	3.00	15.00	.144
Hotellings	.41817	2.09085	3.00	15.00	.144
Wilks	.70513	2.09085	3.00	15.00	.144
Roys	.29487				

Note .. F statistics are exact.

#4—The averaged F-tests for TIME and A BY TIME

Tests involving 'TIME' Within-Subject Effect.

AVERAGED Tests of Significance for Y using UNIQUE sums of squares

Source of Variation	SS	DF	MS	F	Sig. of F
WITHIN CELLS	231.32	51	4.54		
TIME	25.97	3	8.66	1.91	.140
A BY TIME	30.55	3	10.18	2.25	.094

FIGURE B.3

Order of Variables for Analysis

Variates   Covariates

T1

#1—The A main effect

Tests of Significance for T1 using UNIQUE sums of squares

Source of variation	SS	DF	MS	F	Sig. of F
WITHIN CELLS	145.79	17	8.58		
CONSTANT	8360.21	1	8360.21	974.86	.000
A	15.16	1	15.16	1.77	.201

Order of Variables for Analysis

	Variates	Covariates
	T2	
	T3	
	T4	

#2—The A BY TIME interaction effect

Effect .. A

Multivariate Tests of Significance (S = 1, M = 1/2, N = 6 ½)

Test Name	Value	Exact F	Hypoth. DF	Error DF	Sig. of F
Pillais	.59919	7.47478	3.00	15.00	.003
Hotellings	1.49496	7.47478	3.00	15.00	.003
Wilks	.40081	7.47478	3.00	15.00	.003
Roys	.59919				

Note .. F statistics are exact.

EFFECT .. A

Univariate F-tests with (1,17) D.F.

Variable	Hypoth. SS	Error SS	Hypoth. MS	Error MS	F	Sig. of F
T2	18.73743	135.78889	18.73743	7.98758	2.34582	.144
T3	9.58129	227.15556	9.58129	13.36209	.71705	.409
T4	2.24795	108.48889	2.24795	6.38170	.35225	.561

#3—The TIME effect

EFFECT .. CONSTANT

Multivariate Tests of Significance (S =1, M =1/2, N= 6 1/2)

Test Name	Value	Exact F	Hypoth. DF	Error DF	Sig. of F
Pillais	.29487	2.09085	3.00	15.00	.144
Hotellings	.41817	2.09085	3.00	15.00	.144
Wilks	.70513	2.09085	3.00	15.00	.144
Roys	.29487				

Note .. F statistics are exact.

EFFECT .. CONSTANT

Univariate F-tests with (1,17) D.F.

Variable	Hypoth. SS	Error SS	Hypoth. MS	Error MS	F	Sig. of F
T2	23.15848	135.78889	23.15848	7.98758	2.89931	.107
T3	4.94971	227.15556	4.94971	13.36209	.37043	.551
T4	45.19532	108.48889	45.19532	6.38170	7.08202	.016

FIGURE B.3

Let's look at a situation where we have a 2 × 3 WSDESIGN and we want to do SIMPLE contrasts on each of our WSFACTORS. The standard syntax for the WSFACTORS run would be:

```
MANOVA V1 TO V6
  /WSFACTORS = A(2) B(3)
```

The syntax for the TRANSFORM run would be:

```
MANOVA V1 TO V6
  /TRANSFORM = SPECIAL (1    1    1    1    1    1
                        1    1    1   -1   -1   -1
                        1    0   -1    1    0   -1
                        0    1   -1    0    1   -1
                        1    0   -1   -1    0    1
                        0    1   -1    0   -1    1)
  /PRINT = TRANSFORM
  /ANALYSIS = (T1/T2/T3 T4/T5 T6)
```

Note that the final two rows of the contrast matrix are simply coefficient by coefficient multiples of rows two and three and two and four, respectively. Also, the ANALYSIS subcommand here separates the effects into four groups: the CONSTANT and A effects (each with one degree of freedom), and the B and A BY B interaction effect (with two degrees of freedom). Once again, this separation allows us to compare the TRANSFORM output with appropriate parts of the WSFACTORS output.

Though this use of SPECIAL transformations can be somewhat tedious if there are many WSFACTORS or some of these factors have many levels, it is also very general and will allow us to obtain the desired contrasts for designs of any size.

Answers

CHAPTER 1

1. The consequences of a type I error would be false optimism. For example, if the treatment is a diet and a type I error is made, you would be concluding that a diet is better than no diet, when in fact that is not the case. The consequences of a type II error would be false negativism. For example, if the treatment is a drug and a type II error is made, you would be concluding that the drug is no better than a placebo, when in fact, that is not the case.

3. (a) Two-way ANOVA with six dependent variables. How many tests were done? For each dependent variable there are three tests: two main effects and an interaction effect. Thus, the total number of tests done is $6(3) = 18$. The Bonferroni upper bound is $18(.05) = .90$. The tighter upper bound $= 1 - (.95)^{18} = .603$.

   (b) Three way ANOVA with four dependent variables. There are seven tests for each dependent variable: A, B, and C main effects, AB, AC, and BC interactions and the ABC interaction. Thus, a total of $4(7) = 28$ tests were done. The Bonferroni upper bound is $28(.05) = 1.4$. The tighter upper bound is $1 - (.95)^{28} = .762$.

5. (a) The differences on each variable may combine to isolate the subject in the space of the four variables.

   (b) It would be advisable to test at the .001 level since 150 tests are being done.

CHAPTER 2

1. (a) $\mathbf{A} + \mathbf{C} = \begin{bmatrix} 3 & 7 & 6 \\ 9 & 0 & 6 \end{bmatrix}$

   (b) $\mathbf{A} + \mathbf{B}$ not meaningful; must be of the same dimension to add.

   (c) $\mathbf{A}\,\mathbf{B} = \begin{bmatrix} 13 & 12 \\ 14 & 24 \end{bmatrix}$

   (d) $\mathbf{A}\,\mathbf{C}$ not meaningful; number of rows of $\mathbf{C}$ is not equal to number of columns of $\mathbf{A}$.

   (e) $\mathbf{u}'\mathbf{D}\,\mathbf{u} = 70$

   (f) $\mathbf{u}'\mathbf{v} = 23$

   (g) $(\mathbf{A} + \mathbf{C})' = \begin{bmatrix} 3 & 9 \\ 7 & 0 \\ 6 & 6 \end{bmatrix}$

(h) $3\mathbf{C} = \begin{bmatrix} 3 & 9 & 15 \\ 18 & 6 & 3 \end{bmatrix}$

(i) $|\mathbf{D}| = 20$

(j) $\mathbf{D}^{-1} = \dfrac{1}{20} \begin{bmatrix} 6 & -2 \\ -2 & 4 \end{bmatrix}$

(k) $|\mathbf{E}| = 1 \begin{vmatrix} 3 & 1 \\ 1 & 10 \end{vmatrix} - (-1) \begin{vmatrix} -1 & 1 \\ 2 & 10 \end{vmatrix} + 2 \begin{vmatrix} -1 & 3 \\ 2 & 1 \end{vmatrix} = 3$

by expanding along the first row.

The same answer (i.e., 3) should be obtained by expanding along any row or column.

(l) $\mathbf{E}^{-1} = ?$ Matrix of cofactors $= \begin{bmatrix} 29 & 12 & -7 \\ 12 & 6 & -3 \\ -7 & -3 & 2 \end{bmatrix} |\mathbf{E}| = 3$

Therefore, $\mathbf{E}^{-1} = \dfrac{1}{3} \begin{bmatrix} 29 & 12 & -7 \\ 12 & 6 & -3 \\ -7 & -3 & 2 \end{bmatrix}$

(m) $\mathbf{u}' \mathbf{D}^{-1} \mathbf{u} = 30/20$

(n) $\mathbf{BA} = \begin{bmatrix} 8 & 0 & 11 \\ 7 & 6 & 7 \\ 18 & 4 & 23 \end{bmatrix}$

(o) $\mathbf{X}'\mathbf{X} = \begin{bmatrix} 51 & 64 \\ 64 & 90 \end{bmatrix}$

3. $\mathbf{S}(\text{covariance matrix}) = \dfrac{1}{4} \begin{bmatrix} 26.8 & 24 & -14 \\ 24 & 24 & -14 \\ -14 & -14 & 52 \end{bmatrix}$

5. A could not be a covariance matrix, since the determinant is −113 and the determinant of a covariance matrix represents the generalized variance.

7. When the SPSS MATRIX program is run the following output is obtained:

```
           A
       6   2   4
       2   3   1
       4   1   5
```

DETA

32.00000000

AINV

.4375000000 −.1875000000 −.3125000000
−.1875000000 .4375000000 .0625000000
−.3125000000 .0625000000 .4375000000

CHAPTER 3

3. (a) If x_1 enters the equation first, it will account for $(.60)^2 \times 100$, or 36% of the variance on y.

(b) To determine how much variance on y predictor x_1 will account for if entered second we need to partial out x_2. Hence we compute the following semipartial correlation:

$$r_{y1.2(s)} = \frac{r_{y1} - r_{y2}r_{12}}{\sqrt{1 - r_{12}^2}}$$

$$= \frac{.60 - .50(.80)}{\sqrt{1 - (.8)^2}} = .33$$

$$r_{y1.2(s)}^2 = (.33)^2 = .1089$$

Thus, x_1 accounts for about 11% of the variance if entered second.

(c) Since x_1 and x_2 are strongly correlated (multicollinearity), when a predictor enters the equation influences greatly how much variance it will account for. Here when x_1 entered first it accounted for 36% of variance, while it accounted for only 11% when entered second.

5. (a) Show that the multiple correlation of .346 is not significant at the .05 level.

$$F = [(.346)^2/4]/[(1 - (.346)^2)/63] = .03/.014 = 2.14$$

The critical value at the .05 level is 2.52. Since 2.14 < 2.25, we fail to reject the null hypothesis.

(b) $F = \dfrac{[(.682)^2 - (.555)^2]/6}{[1 - (.682)^2]/(57 - 11)} = \dfrac{.026}{.012} = 2.17$

Since 2.17 is less than the critical value of 2.3, we conclude that the Home inventory variables do *not* significantly increase predictive power.

7. (a) We cannot have much faith in the reliability of the regression equations. It was indicated in the chapter that generally about 15 subjects per predictor are needed for a reliable equation. Here, in the second case, the N/k ratio is 114/16 = 7/1, far short of what is needed. In the first case, we have a double capitalization on chance, with preselection (picking the 6 out of 16) and then the capitalization due to the mathematical maximization property for multiple regression.

(b) Herzberg Formula

$$\hat{\rho}_c^2 = 1 - (113/97)(112/96)(115/114)(1 - .32)$$

$$\hat{\rho}_c^2 = 1 - .933 = .067$$

Thus, if the equation were cross validated on many other samples from the same population we could expect to account for only about 7% of the variance on social adjustment.

9. Control lines for SPSS:

```
TITLE 'EXERCISE 9 IN CHAPTER 3'.
DATA LIST FREE/X1 X2 X3 X4 X5 X6 X7 X8 X9 X10 X11 X12 X13 X14 X15.
BEGIN DATA.
1 3 2 5 6 3 4 21 34 35 24 21 15 18 65    2 5 6 7 3 4 8 25 34 39 25 23 17 19 61
3 1 4 8 7 6 7 23 37 39 25 24 12 13 67    5 4 8 9 0 6 5 21 31 32 28 27 12 14 69
2 1 4 8 7 6 3 26 31 24 28 23 15 16 86    2 1 3 5 6 7 8 24 25 35 58 67 13 11 45
END DATA.
COMPUTE FIRSTNEW = X7 + X8.
COMPUTE SECNEW = X2 + X5 + X10.
LIST.
REGRESSION VARIABLES = X1 X3 X4 X11 X12 X13 X14 FIRSTNEW SECNEW/
DEPENDENT = X4/
CASEWISE = ALL ZRESID LEVER COOK/
SCATTERPLOT (*RES, *PRE)/.
```

11. We simply need to refer to the Park and Dudycha table for four predictors, with $\alpha = .95$, and $\epsilon = .10$. Since the table does not provide for an estimate of $\rho^2 = .62$, we interpolate between the sample sizes needed for $\rho^2 = .50$ and $\rho^2 = .75$. Those sample sizes are 43 and 25. Since .62 is about halfway between .50 and .75, the sample size required is 34 subjects.

13. We should not be impressed, since the expected value for the squared multiple correlation (when there is NO relationship) = 28/31 = .903!

   The Stein estimate, using a median value of 17, is −.33. Therefore, the equation has no generalizability.

15. SPSS CONTROL LINES FOR MORTALITY DATA:

```
TITLE 'MORTALITY DATA – P 322 IN STATISTICAL SLEUTH'.
DATA LIST FREE/MORTAL PRECIP SCHOOL NONW NOX SO2.
BEGIN DATA.
DATA LINES
END DATA.
REGRESSION VARIABLES = MORTAL TO SO2/
CRITERIA = POUT(.30)/
DEPENDENT = MORTAL/
ENTER PRECIP SCHOOL NONW/STEPWISE/
CASEWISE = ALL PRED ZRESID LEVER COOK/
SCATTERPLOT(*RES, *PRE)/.
```

17. Just one comment here. Based on 15 years of experience with hundreds of students from various content areas, I have found that authors rarely talk about validating their equation.

CHAPTER 4

1. (a) This is a three-way univariate ANOVA, with sex, socioeconomic status, and teaching method as the factors and Lankton algebra test score as the dependent variable.

   (b) This is a multivariate study, a two-group MANOVA with reading speed and reading comprehension as the dependent variables.

   (c) This is a multiple regression study, with success on the job as the dependent variable and high school GPA and the personality variables as the predictors.

   (d) This is a factor analytic study, where the items are the variables being analyzed.

   (e) This is a multivariable study, and a complex repeated measures design (to be discussed in Chapter 13). There is one between or classification variable (social class) and one within variable (grade) and the subjects are measured on three dependent variables (reading comprehension, math ability, and science ability) at three points in time.

3. You should definitely not be impressed with these results. Since this is a three-way design (call the factors A, B, and C) there are seven statistical tests (seven effects — A, B, and C main effects, the AB, AC, and BC interactions and the three-way interaction ABC) being done for each of the five dependent variables, making a total of 35 statistical tests that were done at the .05 level. The chance of three or four of these being type I errors is quite high. Yes, we could have more confidence if the significant effects had been hypothesized a priori. Then there would have been an empirical (theoretical) basis for expecting the effects to be "real," which we would then be empirically confirming. Since there are five correlated dependent variables, a three-way multivariate analysis of variance would have been a better way statistically of analyzing the data.

7. Multiplying, we find .494(36) = 17.784. Using D squared = 2.16 and Table 4.7, we find power is approximately .90. The harmonic mean is 16.24.

9. Using Table 4.6 with D^2=.64 (as a good approximation):

Variables	n	.64
3	25	.74
5	25	.68

   Interpolating between the power values of .74 for three variables and .68 for five variables, we see that about 25 subjects per group will be needed for power = .70 for four variables.

11. The Pope data shows multivariate significance at the .05 level (using Wilks', we see on the printout p = .003). All three of the univariate tests are significant at the .05 level.

13. The reason the correlations are embedded in the covariance matrix is that, to get the covariance for each pair of variables, we need to multiply the correlation by the standard deviations.

CHAPTER 5

1. (a) The multivariate null hypothesis is that the population mean vectors for the groups are equal, i.e., $\mu_1 = \mu_2 = \mu_3$. We do reject the multivariate null hypothesis at the .05 level since $F = 3.34$ (corresponding to Wilks' λ), $p < .008$.

   (b) Groups 1 and 2 are significantly different at the .05 level on the set of three variables since $F = 3.9247$, $p < .0206$. Also, groups 2 and 3 are significantly different since $F = 7.6099$, $p < .001$.

   (c) Only variable Y2 is significant at the .01 level for groups 1 and 2, since the t for this variable is t(pooled) $= -3.42$, $p < .003$.

   Variables Y2 and Y3 are significant at the .01 level for groups 2 and 3, since t(pooled) for Y3 is 4.41, $p < .001$.

   (d) Variables Y2 and Y3 are still significantly different for groups 1 and 2 with the Tukey confidence intervals, since the intervals do not cover 0.

   Variables Y2 and Y3 are still significantly different for groups 2 and 3, but Y1 is not significantly different since its interval does cover 0.

3. We could not place a great deal of confidence in these results, since from the Bonferroni Inequality the probability of *at least one* spurious significant result could be as high as 12 (.05) = .60. Thus, most of these four significant results could be type I errors. The authors did not a priori hypothesize differences on the variables for which significance was found.

5. The multivariate test is significant at the .05 level. Using Wilks', we have F = 12.201, $p < .001$.

   The univariate F's are NOT significant at the .05 level (p values of .065 and .061). As pointed out in Chapter 4, there is no necessary relationship between multivariate significance and univariate significance.

7. The reader needs to relate this to the appendix in Chapter 6 on analyzing correlated data.

9. (a) The **W** and **B** matrices are as follows:

$$\mathbf{W} = \begin{matrix} 89 & 38 \\ 38 & 135 \end{matrix} \qquad \mathbf{B} = \begin{matrix} 13 & -25 \\ -25 & 48.75 \end{matrix}$$

   (b) Wilks' lambda = 10571/18573.5 = .569

   (c) The null hypothesis is that the three population mean vectors are equal.

CHAPTER 6

1. Dependence of the observations would be present whenever the subjects are in groups: classrooms, counseling or psychotherapy groups.

3. The homogeneity of covariance matrices assumption in this case implies that the POPULATION covariance matrices are equal. This in turn implies that the population variances are equal for all three variables in all four groups and that the three population covariances are equal in all four groups.

7. If $p = .20$ (a distinct possibility with some data), then corrected t = 1.57 + and adjusted degrees of freedom = 20.7.

CHAPTER 7

1. (a) The number of discriminant functions is $\min(k - 1, p) = \min(3 - 1, 3) = 2$

   (b) Only the first discriminant function is significant at the .05 level. The tests occur under

   DIMENSION REDUCTION ANALYSIS

ROOTS	F	SIG of F
1 to 2	3.34	.008
2 to 2	.184	.833

   (d) The vector of raw discriminant coefficients is

   $$\mathbf{a}_1 = \begin{pmatrix} .47698 \\ -.77237 \\ -.83084 \end{pmatrix}$$

   The **B** matrix, from the printout is:

   $$\begin{bmatrix} 4.67798 & 8.71215 & 7.42010 \\ 8.71215 & 16.85415 & 14.27574 \\ 7.42010 & 14.27574 & 12.10131 \end{bmatrix}$$

   Now, rounding off to three decimal places, we compute $\mathbf{a}'_1 \mathbf{B} \mathbf{a}_1$

   $$(.477, \ -.772, \ -.831) \begin{bmatrix} 4.678 & 8.712 & 7.420 \\ 8.712 & 16.854 & 14.276 \\ 7.420 & 14.276 & 12.101 \end{bmatrix} \begin{pmatrix} .477 \\ -.772 \\ -.831 \end{pmatrix}$$

   $$\mathbf{a}'_1 \mathbf{B} \mathbf{a}_1 = (-10.66, \ -20.719, \ -17.538) \begin{pmatrix} .477 \\ -.772 \\ -.831 \end{pmatrix} = 25.484$$

   Now, rounding off the **W** matrix to three decimal places, we have

   $$\mathbf{a}'_1 \mathbf{W} \mathbf{a}_1 = (.477, \ -.772, \ -.831) \begin{bmatrix} 24.684 & 10.607 & 17.339 \\ 10.607 & 18.111 & 14.690 \\ 17.399 & 14.690 & 17.864 \end{bmatrix} \begin{pmatrix} .477 \\ -.772 \\ -.831 \end{pmatrix}$$

   $$\mathbf{a}'_1 \mathbf{W} \mathbf{a}_1 = (-10.873, \ -21.13, \ -17.886) \begin{pmatrix} .477 \\ -.772 \\ -.831 \end{pmatrix} = 25.989$$

Now, the largest eigenvalue is given by $a_1' \mathbf{B} a_1 / a_1' \mathbf{W} a_1$

$$\phi_1 = 25.484/25.989 = .98057$$

and this agrees with the value on the printout within rounding error.

3. (a) Since there were three significant discriminant functions in the Smart study, the association is diffuse and the Pillai-Bartlett trace is most powerful (see 5.12).

   (b) In the Stevens study there was only one significant discrimnant function (concentrated association), and in this case Roy's largest root has been shown to be most powerful (again see 5.12).

CHAPTER 8

1. (b) Using Wilks' lambda in all cases, all three multivariate effects are significant at the .05 level: FACA, $p = .011$, FACB, $p = .001$, FACA*FACB, $p = .013$.

   (c) For the main effects, both dependent variables are significant at the .025 level. For the interaction effect only dependent variable 1 is significant at the .025 level ($p = .016$).

   (d) The result will be the SAME. For equal cell n, which we have here, all three methods yield the same results.

3. (b) Using Wilks' lambda NONE of the multivariate tests is significant at the .025 level. Since seven statistical tests have been done, the overall alpha level is $7(.025) = .175$

   (c) The Box test ($p = .988$) indicates this assumption is very tenable.

   (d) Since none of the multivariate tests is significant, significance for the univariate tests is moot.

CHAPTER 9

1. (a) Control lines for Scandura MANCOVA on SPSS MANOVA:

```
TITLE 'MANCOVA 2 GROUPS – 5 DEP VARS AND 3 COVARIATES'.
DATA LIST FREE/TRTMT2 HOPPOCKA LMXA ERSA QUANAFT
   QUALAFT MPS OLI DTT.
BEGIN DATA.
   DATA LINES
END DATA.
LIST.
MANOVA HOPPOCKA TO DTT BY TRTMT2(1,2)/
   ANALYSIS = HOPPOCKA LMXA ERSA QUALAFT WITH MPS OLI DTT/
   PRINT = PMEANS/
   DESIGN/
   ANALYSIS = HOPPOCKA LMXA ERSA QUANAFT QUALAFT/
   DESIGN = MPS + OLI + DTT,TRTMT2, MPS BY TRTMT2 + OLI BY TRTMT2 + DTT BY TRTMT2/.
```

(b) To determine whether covariance is appropriate two things need to be checked:

(i) Is there a significant relationship between the dependent variables and the set of covariates, or equivalently is there a significant regression of the dependent variables on the covariates?

(ii) Is the homogeneity of the regression hyperplanes satisfied?

Under EFFECT ... WITHIN CELLS REGRESSION are the multivariate tests for determining whether the two sets of variables are related. The multivariate F corresponding to Wilks' λ shows there is a significant relationship at the .05 level ($F = 1.88, p < .027$). The test for the homogeneity of the regression hyperplanes appears under EFFECT ... MPS BY TRTMT2 + OLI BY TRTMT2 + DTT BY TRTMT2. This test is not significant at the .05 level ($F = .956, p < .503$), meaning that the assumption *is* satisfied. Thus, from the above two results we see that covariance is appropriate.

(c) The multivariate test for determining the two adjusted population mean vectors are equal appears under EFFECT ... TRTMT2. The tests, which are equivalent (since there are only two groups), show significance at the .05 level ($F = 2.669, p < .029$).

(d) The univariate tests show that only QUANAFT is significant at the .01 level ($F = 11.186, p < .001$).

(e) The adjusted means for QUANAFT are .392 (for treatment group) and .323 (for control group), with the treatment group doing better.

3. Covariance will not be useful in this study. First, the error reduction will be minimal. Second, the linear adjustment of the posttest means is questionable with such a weak linear relationship.

5. What we would have found had we blocked on I.Q. and run a factorial design on achievement is a block by method interaction.

CHAPTER 11

1. (a) Denote the linear combination for two variables as

$$y = a_1 x_1 + a_2 x_2$$

$$\text{var}(y) = (a_1, a_2) \begin{bmatrix} s_1^2 & s_{12} \\ s_{12} & s_2^2 \end{bmatrix} \begin{pmatrix} a_1 \\ a_2 \end{pmatrix}$$

$$= a_1^2 s_1^2 + 2a_1 a_2 s_{12} + a_2^2 s_2^2$$

Denote the linear combination for three variables as

$$y_1 = a_1 x_1 + a_2 x_2 + a_3 x_3$$

$$\text{var}(y_1) = (a_1, a_2, a_3) \begin{bmatrix} s_1^2 & s_{12} & s_{13} \\ s_{12} & s_2^2 & s_{23} \\ s_{13} & s_{23} & s_3^2 \end{bmatrix} \begin{pmatrix} a_1 \\ a_2 \\ a_3 \end{pmatrix}$$

After all the matrix multiplication and combining of like terms the following is obtained:

$$\text{var}(y_1) = a_1^2 s_1^2 + a_2^2 s_2^2 + a_3^2 s_3^2 + 2a_1 a_2 s_{12} + 2a_1 a_3 s_{13} + 2a_2 a_3 s_{23}$$

(b) $\mathbf{S} = \begin{bmatrix} 451.4 & 271.2 & 168.7 \\ 271.2 & 171.7 & 103.3 \\ 168.7 & 103.3 & 66.7 \end{bmatrix}$ $\begin{matrix} y_1 = & .81x_1 & +.50x_2 & +.31x_3 \\ & \downarrow & \downarrow & \downarrow \\ & a_1 & a_2 & a_3 \end{matrix}$

s_{12} s_{13} s_{23}

Now, plugging into the above formula for variance:

$$\text{var}(y_1) = (.81)^2(451.4) + (.5)^2(171.7)$$

$$+ (.31)^2(66.7)$$

$$+ 2(.81)(.5)(271.2) + 2(81)(.31)(168.7)$$

$$+ 2(.5)(.31)(103.3)$$

$$\text{var}(y_1) = 296.16 + 42.925 + 6.41 + 84.72 + 219.67 + 32.023 = 681.9$$

3. In Case 1 it is not necessary to apply Bartlett's sphericity test since eight of the correlations are at least moderate (>. 40) in size. In Case 2, on the other hand, only one of the 15 correlations is moderate (.40), and almost all the others are very small. Thus, Bartlett's sphericity test is advisable here. Using the Lawley approximation, we have:

$$\chi^2 = \left\{ 110 - \frac{2(6)+5}{6} \right\}$$

$$[(.29)^2 + (.18)^2 + (.04)^2 + \cdots + (-.14)^2 + (.12)^2)]$$

$$\chi^2 = (107.1667)(.4467) = 47.87$$

The critical value at $\alpha = .01$ is 30.58 (df = 1/2 (6) (5) = 15). We reject and therefore conclude that the variables are correlated in the population.

5. (a) Variance accounted for by component 1: 57.43%

   Variance accounted for by component 2: 35.92%

   (b) Variance accounted for by varimax factor 1: 50.44%

   Variance accounted for by varimax factor 2: 42.96%

   (c) The variance accounted for by the varimax rotated factors is spread out more evenly than for the components.

(d) The total amount of variance accounted for by the two components (93.35%) is the same, within rounding error, as that accounted for by the two varimax rotated factors (93.4%).

7. (a) The first varimax factor is a manual communication construct, while the second varimax factor is an oral communication construct.

(b) The empirical clustering of the variables which load very high on varimax factor 1 (C_5, C_6, C_9 and C_{10}) is consistent with how the variables correlate in the original correlation matrix. The simple correlations for each pair of the above four variables ranges from .86 to .94.

9. (a) We can have confidence in the reliability of the first two rotated factors since there are more than four loadings > .60.

(b) Factor 1 is reliable since there are four loadings > .60. Factors 2 and 3 are reliable since the AVERAGE of the four highest loadings is > .60. Factor 4 may be reliable but there is NOT sufficient evidence to support it.

11. (b) The critical value for a two tailed test at the .01 level is about 2.6. All the t's are significant, ranging from 9.13 to 14.71.

(c) The chi square does not indicate a good fit.

(d) The value of RMSEA = .15 does not indicate a good fit. Browne and Cudeck indicate that an RMSEA < .05 indicates a good fit.

(e) One should definitely NOT consider adding an error covariance. There is a danger of capitalization on chance (see MacCallum, 1992).

CHAPTER 12

1. Four features that canonical correlation and principal components have in common:

(a) Both are mathematical maximization procedures.

(b) Both use uncorrelated linear combinations of the variables.

(c) Both provide for an additive partitioning; in components analysis an additive partitioning of the total variance, and in canonical correlation an additive partitioning of the between association.

(d) Correlations between the original variables and the linear combinations are used in both procedures for interpretation purposes.

3. (a) The association between the two sets of variables is weak, since 17 of the 26 simple correlations are less than .30.

(b) Only the largest canonical correlation is significant at the .05 level—from the printout:

Chi-Sq	df	prob
92.96	36	.0000
21.70	25	.6533

(c) The following are the loadings from the printout:

Creativity		Achievement	
Ideaflu	.227	Know	.669
Flexib	.412	Compre	.578
Assocflu	.629	Applic	.374
Exprflu	.796	Anal	.390
Orig	.686	Synth	.910
Elab	.703	Eval	.542

The canonical correlation basically links the ability to synthesis (the loading of .910 dominates the achievement loadings) to the last four creativity variables, which have loadings of the same order of magnitude.

(d) Since only the largest canonical correlation was significant, about 20 subjects per variable are needed for reliable results, i.e., about 20(12) = 240 subjects. So, the above results, based on an N of 116, must be treated somewhat tenuously.

(e) The redundancy index for the creativity variables given the achievement variables is obtained from the following values on the printout:

Av. Sq. Loading times Sqed Can Correl (1st Set)
.17787
.00906
.00931
.00222 .
.00063
.00019
.19928

This indicates that about 20% of the variance on the set of creativity variables is accounted for by the set of achievement variables.

(f) The squared canonical correlations are given on the printout, and yield the following value for the Cramer-Nicewander index:

$$\frac{.48148+.10569+.06623+.01286+.00468+.00917}{6}=.112$$

This indicates that the "variance" overlap between the sets of variables is only about 11%, and is more accurate than the redundancy index since that index ignores the correlations among the dependent variables. And there are several significant correlations among the creativity variables, eight in the weak to moderate range (.32 to 46) and one strong correlation (.71).

CHAPTER 13

1. The difference in the population means being equal is the same as saying the population means are equal. Thus the population means for 1 and 2, 2 and 3, and 3 and 4 are equal. By transitivity, we have that the population means for 1 and 3 are equal. Continuing in this way we show that all the population means are equal.

3. (a) The stress management approach was successful: Multivariate F = 8.98043, $p = .006$

   (b) Only the STATDIFF variable is contributing: $p = .005$

5. The covariance for (y1–y2) and y3–y4) is given by:

$$[(2 - .8)(-18 - (-16.4)) + ... + (-16 - (-16.4))]/4 = -34.4./4 = -8.6$$

   The covariance for (y2–y3) is given by:

$$[(12 - 10)(-18 - (-16.4) + ... + (14 - 10)(-16 - (-16.4)]/4 = -76/4 = -19$$

7. (a) Only the linear GENDER BY YEAR interaction is significant at the .05 level (t=–2.3). This means that the linear effect is different for the genders. Examination of the cell means for the genders shows why this effect happened. The gap between the genders increases with age from about 1.6 to about 3.7 at age 14.

   (b) Only the linear YEAR effect is significant at the .05 level.

9. (a) Assuming sphericity, it is significant at the .05 level ($p = .042$ from printout).

   (b) The adjusted univariate F is NOT significant at the .05 level ($p = .053$, using GG).

   (c) The multivariate test is not significant at the .05 level ($p = .127$ from printout).

11.
```
TITLE 'CH 13 – EXERCISE 11'.
DATA LIST FREE/AGE TIME CONTEXT SMHOME SMOFFICE SAHOME SAOFFICE.
BEGIN DATA.
1 1 1 10 8 9 13  1 1 2 11 12 14 15  12 1 3 4 2 5
2 1 1 11 3 6 7   2 1 2 13 4 5 8 2 2 1 21 12 13 16  2 2 2 3 5 6 7
3 1 1 12 13 23 13  3 1 2 11 12 14 15 32 1 21 20 9 8  3 2 2 5 6 7 8
END DATA.
LIST.
MANOVA SMHOME TO SAOFFICE BY AGE(1,3)/
 WSFACTOR = TIME(2), CONTEXT(2)/
 WSDESIGN/
 DESIGN/.
```

13. (a) The multivariate test is significant at the .05 level, since .024 < .05.

   (b) Both univariate tests are significant at the .05 level since each p value < .05.

15. The reader will find that relative power is rarely discussed, and the adjusted univariate test (which has been available for a long time) is very infrequently mentioned.

CHAPTER 14

1. The control lines for the backward selection are:

   ```
   TITLE 'LOG3WAY – EXERCISE1'.
   DATA LIST FREE/AGE HIST INSILIN FREQ.
   WEIGHT BY FREQ.
   BEGIN DATA.
   1 1 1 6    1 1 2  1    1 2 1 16    1 2 2  2
   2 1 1 6    2 1 2 36    2 2 1  8    2 2 2 48
   END DATA.
   HILOGLINEAR AGE(1,2) HIST(1,2) INSULIN(1,2)/
     METHOD = BACKWARD/
     DESIGN/.
   ```

   The model selected is [AGE*INSULIN,HIST].

3. (a) Control lines for the three-way run are given below:

   ```
   TITLE 'THREE WAY LOGLINEAR ON SURVEY DATA'.
   DATA LIST FREE/YEAR COLOR RESPONSE FREQ.
   WEIGHT BY FREQ.
   BEGIN DATA.
   1 1 1  81   1 1 2  23    1 1 3  4    1 2 1 325   1 2 2 253   1 2 1 5 4
   2 1 1 224   2 1 2 144    2 1 3 24   2 2 1 600   2 2 2 636   2 2 3 158
   END DATA.
   HILOGLINEAR YEAR (1,2) COLOR(1,2) RESPONSE(1,3)/
     METHOD = BACKWARD/
     DESIGN/.
   ```

   Model Selected: [YEAR*COLOR, YEAR*RESPONSE, COLOR*RESPONSE]

   (b) Since the model selected has all two-way interactions, it is not valid to collapse on any category. Thus, the contrasts need to be done on the cell frequencies.

5. (a) Control lines for the four-way run are given below:

   ```
   TITLE 'DEMO AND PARKER-4 WAY LOG LINEAR'.
   DATA LIST FREE/SEX GPA RACE ESTEEM FREQ.
   WEIGHT BY FREQ.
   BEGIN DATA.
   1 1 1 1 15   1 1 1 2  9    1 1 2 1 17    1 1 2 2 10
   1 2 1 1 26   1 2 1 2 17    1 2 2 1 22    1 2 2 2 26
   2 1 1 1 13   2 1 1 2 22    2 1 2 1 22    2 1 2 2 32
   2 2 1 1 24   2 2 1 2 23    2 2 2 1  3    2 2 2 2 17
   END DATA.
   HILOGLINEAR SEX(1,2) GPA(1,2) RACE(1,2) ESTEEM(1,2)/
     METHOD = BACKWARD/
     DESIGN/.
   ```

   The model selected is: [SEX*GPA*RACE, GPA*RACE*ESTEEM, SEX*ESTEEM]

   (b) Is it valid to collapse over race and GPA in interpreting the SEX*ESTEEM interaction? The answer is no. Although superficially it may seem okay, since there are no SEX*ESTEEM*RACE or SEX*ESTEEM*GPA interactions in the model, from Exercise 14.7 we also need either sex to be independent of both race and GPA (which it is not since we have the SEX*RACE*GPA interaction effect) or esteem to be independent of both race and GPA (which it is not, since we have GPA*RACE*ESTEEM in the model).

7. The collapsibility conditions to validly collapse AB over C and D are several. We need ABCD = 0, as well as ABC = ABD = 0. Note that if either ABC or ABD is not 0, then the association for AB is different for the levels of C or D, and it obviously would not make sense to combine over those levels. In addition, either A must be independent of both C and D, or B must be independent of both C and D. In symbols, all of this means that at least one of the following models holds:

[AB, BCD] or [AB, ACD]

See Agresti (1990, pp. 145–146).

9. (a) The odds ratio for each clinic is 1, implying that treatment efficacy and success are independent.

(b) When the data are lumped together, the odds ratio = 4, implying there is a relationship between treatment efficacy and success.

(c) As pointed out in the text, there is no relationship between marginal association and partial association.

Index